Professional Azure SQL Managed Database Administration – Third Edition

Efficiently manage and modernize data in
the cloud using Azure SQL

Ahmad Osama and Shashikant Shakya

Professional Azure SQL Managed Database Administration – Third Edition

Authors: Ahmad Osama and Shashikant Shakya

Technical Reviewers: John Martin and Aaditya Pokkunuri

Managing Editors: Aditya Datar and Mamta Yadav

Technical Editor: Neha Pande

Acquisitions Editor: Ben Renow-Clarke

Production Editor: Deepak Chavan

Editorial Board: Vishal Bodwani, Ben Renow-Clarke, Arijit Sarkar, Dominic Shakeshaft, and Lucy Wan

First Published: July 2018

Second Published: July 2019

Third Published: January 2021

Production Reference: 3220221

ISBN: 978-1-80107-652-4

Published by Packt Publishing Ltd.

Livery Place, 35 Livery Street

Birmingham B3 2PB, UK

Table of Contents

Chapter 3: Migration

87

Preface

About

This section briefly introduces the authors and reviewers, what this book covers, the technical skills you'll need to get started, and the hardware and software requirements needed to complete all of the activities and exercises.

About Professional Azure SQL Managed Database Administration, Third Edition

Despite being the cloud version of SQL Server, Azure SQL Database and Azure SQL Managed Instance stands out in various aspects when it comes to management, maintenance, and administration. Updated with the latest Azure features, *Professional Azure SQL Managed Database Administration* continues to be a comprehensive guide for becoming proficient in data management.

The book begins by introducing you to the Azure SQL managed databases (Azure SQL Database and Azure SQL Managed Instance), explaining their architecture, and how they differ from an on-premises SQL server. You will then learn how to perform common tasks, such as migrating, backing up, and restoring a SQL Server database to an Azure database.

As you progress, you will study how you can save costs and manage and scale multiple SQL databases using elastic pools. You will also implement a disaster recovery solution using standard and active geo-replication. Finally, you will explore the monitoring and tuning of databases, the key features of databases, and the phenomenon of app modernization.

By the end of this book, you will have mastered the key aspects of an Azure SQL database and Azure SQL managed instance, including migration, backup restorations, performance optimization, high availability, and disaster recovery.

About the authors

Ahmad Osama works for Pitney Bowes Pvt. Ltd. as a technical architect and is a former Microsoft Data Platform MVP. In his day job, he works on developing and maintaining high performant, on-premises and cloud SQL Server OLTP environments as well as deployment and automating tasks using PowerShell. When not working, Ahmad blogs at DataPlatformLabs and can be found glued to his Xbox.

Shashikant Shakya is a passionate technologist with decades of experience in the sphere of databases. He works for Microsoft as a senior support engineer. In his day job, he works on Azure SQL Database, Azure Database for MySQL, and PostgreSQL. Apart from his work, he is a regular speaker at the **SQLBangalore** community group.

About the reviewers

Aaditya Pokkunuri is an experienced senior database engineer with a history of working in the information technology and services industry. He has a total of 11 years' experience. He is skilled in performance tuning, MS SQL Database server administration, SSIS, SSRS, Power BI, and SQL development.

He possesses an in-depth knowledge of replication, clustering, SQL Server high availability options, and ITIL processes, as well as expertise in Windows administration tasks, Active Directory, and Microsoft Azure technologies.

He also has expertise in AWS Cloud and is an AWS solution architect associate. Aaditya is a strong information technology professional with a Bachelor of Technology degree focused on computer science and engineering from Sastra University, Tamil Nadu.

John Martin is an experienced data platform professional and Microsoft Data Platform MVP, having spent over a decade working with the Microsoft data and cloud platform technologies. In this time, John has learned how to get the most out of these platforms as well as the key pitfalls that should be avoided.

Learning objectives

- Understanding Azure SQL database configuration and pricing options
- Provisioning a new SQL database or migrating an existing on-premises SQL Server database to an Azure SQL database
- Backing up and restoring an Azure SQL database
- Securing and scaling an Azure SQL database
- Monitoring and tuning an Azure SQL database
- Implementing high availability and disaster recovery with an Azure SQL database
- Managing, maintaining, and securing managed instances

Audience

This book is designed to benefit database administrators, database developers, or application developers who are interested in developing new applications or migrating existing ones with Azure SQL Database.

Prior experience of working with an on-premises SQL server or Azure SQL database, along with a basic understanding of PowerShell scripts and C# code, is necessary to grasp the concepts covered in this book.

Approach

Professional Azure SQL Managed Database Administration is a perfect blend of deep theoretical knowledge and detailed descriptions of implementation techniques and numerous tips that are essential for making its readers ready for real-world challenges.

Hardware and software requirements

Hardware requirements

For the optimal learning experience, we recommend the following hardware configuration:

- Windows 10/Mac/Linux
- Processor: Pentium 4, 1.8 GHz or higher (or equivalent)
- Memory: 4 GB RAM
- Hard disk: 10 GB free space
- An internet connection

Software requirements

We also recommend that you have the following software configuration in advance:

- PowerShell 7: https://github.com/PowerShell/powershell/releases
- RML Utilities: https://www.microsoft.com/download/details.aspx?id=4511
- SQL Server Management Studio: https://docs.microsoft.com/sql/ssms/download-sql-server-management-studio-ssms?view=sql-server-ver15
- Power BI Desktop (optional): https://powerbi.microsoft.com/downloads/
- Azure Data Studio: https://docs.microsoft.com/sql/azure-data-studio/download-azure-data-studio?view=sql-server-ver15
- Azure Az PowerShell module: https://docs.microsoft.com/powershell/azure/new-azureps-module-az?view=azps-5.2.0

Conventions

Code words in the text, database names, folder names, filenames, and file extensions are shown as follows.

"The query gets the details for the `cpu_percent`, `physical_data_read_percent`, `log_write_percent`, `workers_percent`, and `sessions_percent` metrics."

Here's a sample block of code:

```
AzureMetrics

| where ResourceProvider=="MICROSOFT.SQL" | where ResourceId contains "/SERVERS/"

| where ResourceId contains "/DATABASES/" and MetricName in ('cpu_ percent', 'physical_data_read_percent', 'log_write_percent', 'workers_ percent', 'sessions_percent')
```

Downloading resources

The code bundle for this book is also hosted on GitHub at https://github.com/PacktPublishing/Professional-Azure-SQL-Database-Administration-Third-Edition. Here, you can find the YAML and other files used in this book, which are referred to as relevant instances.

We also have other code bundles from our rich catalog of books and videos available at https://github.com/PacktPublishing/. Check them out!

Acknowledgement

We are grateful to Microsoft and their team of SMEs for reviewing the book and providing suggestions that enhanced this edition. Acknowledging their contribution, we have listed down the names of the experts who contributed to this book.

Anna Hoffman | Shreya Verma | Borko Novakovic | Denzil Ribeiro
Venkata Raj Pochiraju | Morgan Oslake | Mladen Andzic | Andreas Wolter
Mirek Sztajno | Joachim Hammer | David Trigano | Srini Acharya
Uros Milanovic | Emily Lisa | Joe Sack | Mara-Florina Steiu | Davide Mauri

For successful completion of this edition of
Professional Azure SQL Managed Database Administration,
special thanks our authors, **Ahmad Osama** for his contribution on
Azure SQL Database and **Shashikant Shakya** for his contribution on
Azure SQL Managed Instance.

Introduction to Azure SQL managed databases

There are very few relational database systems as established and widely used as Microsoft's SQL Server. SQL Server on Microsoft Azure comes in three different flavors (commonly known as the **Azure SQL family**): SQL Server on **Azure Virtual Machines (VM)** (**infrastructure as a service**, or **IaaS**), Azure SQL Database (**platform as a service**, or **PaaS**), and Azure SQL Managed Instance (**PaaS**).

Each of these products has specific use cases, which makes it easy for us to move to Azure SQL whether we're starting up with a new application or migrating an existing workload to Azure.

The IaaS offering, SQL Server on Azure VM, is similar to an on-premises service where Microsoft manages the hardware, virtualization, and infrastructure, and **database administrators** (**DBAs**) manage every aspect of SQL Server.

The PaaS offerings, Azure SQL Database and Azure SQL Managed Instance, allow DBAs to focus more on monitoring, capacity planning, and tuning, while Microsoft takes care of areas such as backup, high availability, and more.

This chapter introduces the Azure SQL Database architecture, the Azure SQL Managed Instance connectivity architecture, and the differences between the SQL Database, SQL Managed Instance, and SQL Server (on-premises or using Azure VM) offerings.

In this chapter, we will be covering the following topics:

- Describing the architecture of SQL Database

- Identifying the differences between an on-premises SQL Server, SQL Database, and SQL Managed Instance

- The connectivity architecture of SQL Managed Instance

- Provisioning an Azure SQL Database and Azure SQL Managed Instance using the Azure portal and Windows PowerShell

Who manages what?

Figure 1.1 lists the tasks that you (the DBA) and Microsoft manage for Azure SQL PaaS:

You	Microsoft
Capacity planning	Hardware, datacenter, virtualization
Migration	Operating system
Monitoring	SQL installation, configuration, patches
Performance tuning	Backup and restore
Database-level configuration	High availability and disaster recovery
Database maintenance	Security
Fixing outages	Scaling
Database design	Auditing
Automation	
Cost optimization	

Figure 1.1: Who manages what?

> **Note**
>
> Fixing outages here refers to application outages that arise due to blockages, deadlocks, and broken releases, rather than infrastructure outages.

In an Azure SQL PaaS environment, the DBA works closely with application developers to understand the application and database design, help with the migration (when moving from on-premises to Azure), choose the right performance tier to start with, and then continuously monitor performance for cost optimization.

The DBA also has to work closely with DevOps and often get into DevOps' shoes to automate the release and deployment process and provision the database infrastructure.

This requires learning a new set of skills, such as familiarity with different Azure services, DevOps, and monitoring and management tools.

This chapter introduces the two Azure SQL PaaS offerings, SQL Database and SQL Managed Instance. We'll learn about the SQL Database and SQL Managed Instance architectures, provision SQL Database and SQL Managed Instance, and identify the key differences between SQL Database, SQL Managed Instance, and on-premises SQL Server.

Throughout this book, you will also learn more about the different aspects of managing and administrating SQL Database and SQL Managed Instance, such as provisioning, migration, backup, restore, security, monitoring, and performance.

> **Note**
>
> Azure SQL Database is also commonly referred to as SQL Azure or SQL Database instances.

The Azure SQL Database architecture

Azure SQL Database is a highly scalable, multi-tenant, and highly available **Platform-as-a-Service (PaaS)** or **Database-as-a-Service (DBaaS)** offering from Microsoft.

Azure SQL Database, first released on February 1, 2010, is a cloud database service that is based on Microsoft SQL Server.

It is compatible with most SQL Server database-level features and is optimized for **Software-as-a-Service (SaaS)** applications.

As organizations are adopting cloud computing and moving their applications into the cloud, Azure SQL Database offers everything that DBaaS can offer. Azure SQL Database is a DBaaS option for any organization with applications built on SQL Server databases.

SQL Database uses familiar Transact-SQL programming and a user interface that is well known and easy to adopt. As companies move their workloads to the cloud, it is important for SQL Server DBAs and developers to learn how to use Azure SQL Database for a smooth transition from SQL Server (on-premises or on Azure VM) to SQL Database.

> **Note**
>
> Microsoft takes care of the **operating system (OS)**, storage, networking, virtualization, servers, installation, upgrades, infrastructure management, and maintenance.

Azure SQL Database has the following deployment options:

- Single database
- Elastic pool

Azure SQL Database allows users to focus only on managing data and is divided into four layers that work together to provide users with relational database functionality, as shown in *Figure 1.2*:

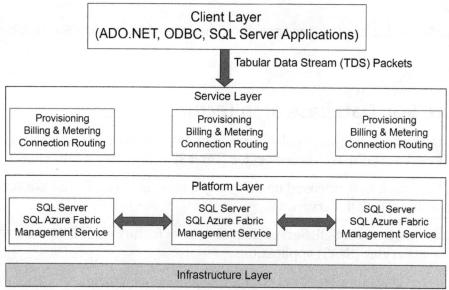

Figure 1.2: The four layers of Azure SQL Database

> **Note**
>
> If you were to compare SQL Database's architecture to the on-premises SQL Server architecture, other than the service layer, the architecture is pretty similar.

The Client Layer

The client layer acts as an interface for applications to access an SQL Database. It can be either on-premises or on Microsoft Azure. The **Tabular Data Stream** (**TDS**) is used to transfer data between an SQL Database and applications. SQL Server also uses TDS to communicate with applications. This allows applications such as .NET, ODBC, ADO. NET, Python, and Java applications to easily connect to Azure SQL Database without any additional requirements.

The Service Layer

The service layer acts as a gateway between the client and platform layers. It is responsible for provisioning an SQL Database, user authentication, SQL Database validation, enforcing security (including firewall rules and denial-of-service attacks), billing and metering for SQL Databases, and routing connections from the client layer to the physical server hosting the SQL Database in the platform layer.

The Platform Layer

The platform layer consists of physical servers hosting SQL Databases in datacenters. Each SQL database is stored on one physical server and is replicated across two different physical servers to provide high availability.

As shown in *Figure 1.2*, the platform layer has two other components: Azure Service Fabric and Management Service. **Azure Service Fabric** is responsible for load balancing, automatic failover, and the automatic replication of SQL Databases between physical servers. **Management Service** takes care of an individual server's health monitoring and patch updates.

The Infrastructure Layer

This layer is responsible for the administration of the physical hardware and the OS.

The Azure SQL Database request flow

Figure 1.3 shows the platform layer:

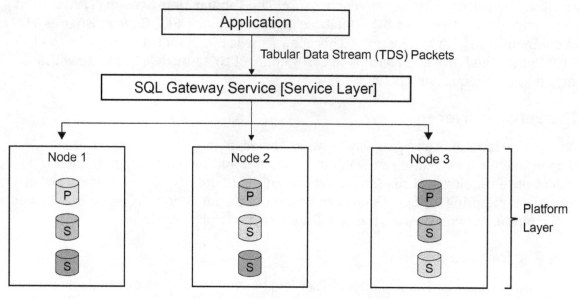

Figure 1.3: Platform layer – nodes

The application sends a TDS request (login, DML, or DDL queries) to the SQL Database. The TDS request is not directly sent to the platform layer. The request is first validated by the SQL Gateway Service at the service layer.

The **Gateway Service** validates the login and firewall rules and checks for denial-of-service attacks. It then dynamically determines the physical server on which the SQL Database is hosted and routes the request to that physical server in the platform layer. Dynamic routing allows the SQL Database to be moved across physical servers or SQL instances in the event of hardware failures.

> **Note**
>
> Here, a node is a physical server. A single database is replicated across three physical servers internally by Microsoft to help the system recover from physical server failures. The Azure SQL Server user connects to just a logical name.

Dynamic routing refers to routing the database request to the physical server that hosts an Azure SQL Database. This routing is done internally and is transparent to the user. If one physical server hosting the database fails, dynamic routing will route the requests to the next available physical server hosting the Azure SQL Database.

The internals of dynamic routing are out of the scope of this book.

As shown in *Figure* 1.3, the platform layer has three nodes: Node 1, Node 2, and Node 3. Each node has a primary replica of an SQL Database and two secondary replicas of two different SQL Databases from two different physical servers. The SQL Database can fail over to the secondary replicas if the primary replica fails. This ensures the high availability of the SQL Database.

Provisioning an Azure SQL Database

Provisioning an Azure SQL Database refers to creating a new and blank Azure SQL Database.

In this section, we'll create a new SQL Database in Azure using the Azure portal:

1. Open a browser and log in to the Azure portal using your Azure credentials: https://portal.azure.com.

2. In the left-hand navigation pane, select **Create a resource**:

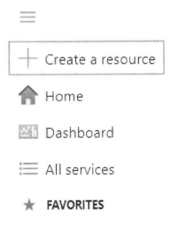

Figure 1.4: Azure pane

3. On the **New** page, under **Databases**, select **SQL Database**:

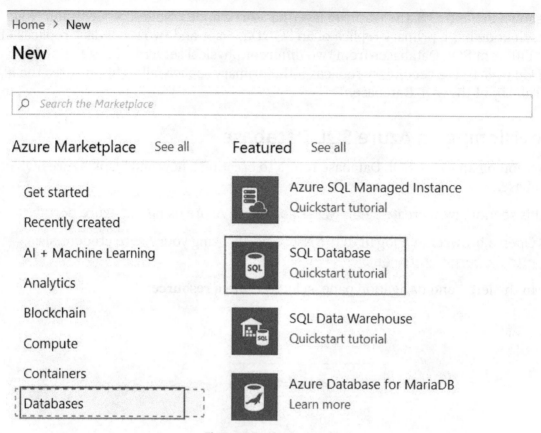

Figure 1.5: Azure panel

4. On the **SQL Database** page, under the **Project details** heading, provide the **Subscription** and **Resource group** details. Click the **Create new** link under the **Resource group** textbox. In the pop-up box, set the **Resource group** name as **toystore**.

> **Note**
>
> A resource group is a logical container that is used to group the Azure resources required to run an application.
>
> For example, the toystore retail web application uses different Azure resources, such as Azure SQL Database, Azure VMs, and Azure Storage. All of these resources can be grouped into a single resource group, say, **toystore**.

The SQL Database name should be unique across Microsoft Azure and should follow the following naming rules and conventions: https://docs.microsoft.com/azure/cloud-adoption-framework/ready/azure-best-practices/naming-and-tagging:

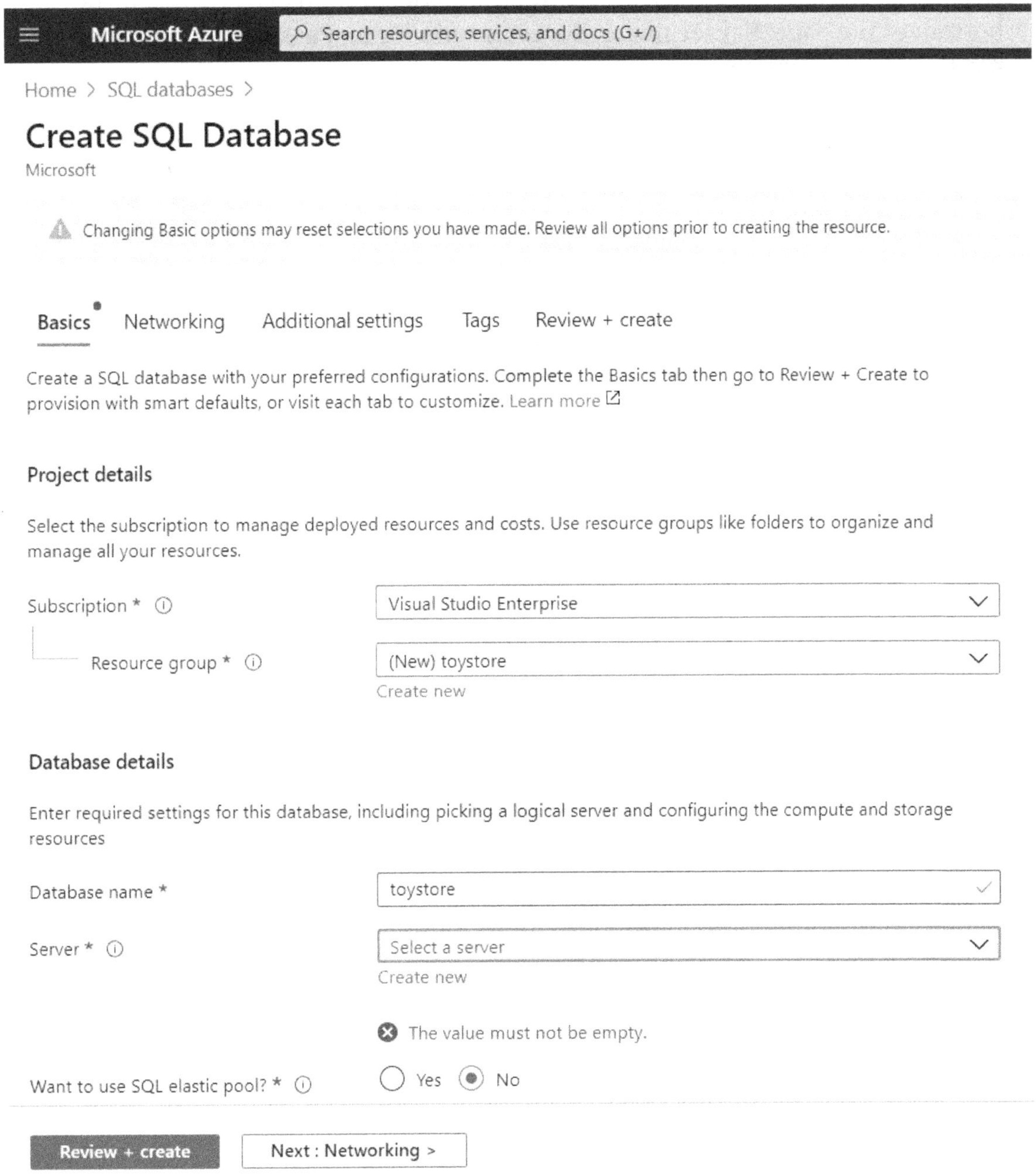

☰   **Microsoft Azure**   🔍 Search resources, services, and docs (G+/)

Home > SQL databases >

Create SQL Database

Microsoft

⚠ Changing Basic options may reset selections you have made. Review all options prior to creating the resource.

Basics   Networking   Additional settings   Tags   Review + create

Create a SQL database with your preferred configurations. Complete the Basics tab then go to Review + Create to provision with smart defaults, or visit each tab to customize. Learn more ☑

Project details

Select the subscription to manage deployed resources and costs. Use resource groups like folders to organize and manage all your resources.

Subscription * ⓘ	Visual Studio Enterprise ∨
Resource group * ⓘ	(New) toystore ∨
	Create new

Database details

Enter required settings for this database, including picking a logical server and configuring the compute and storage resources

Database name *	toystore ✓
Server * ⓘ	Select a server ∨
	Create new
	❌ The value must not be empty.
Want to use SQL elastic pool? * ⓘ	◯ Yes ⦿ No

Review + create   Next : Networking >

Figure 1.6: SQL Database panel

5. Under the **Database details** heading, enter the database name and server.

6. To create a new server, click on **Create new** under the **Server** textbox.

    On the **New server** page, provide the following details and click **Select** at the bottom of the page: **Server name**, **Server admin login**, **Password**, **Confirm password**, and **Location**.

    The server name should be unique across Microsoft Azure and should follow the following naming rules and conventions: https://docs.microsoft.com/azure/cloud-adoption-framework/ready/azure-best-practices/naming-and-tagging:

Figure 1.7: Server pane

7. Under the **Want to use SQL elastic pool?** option, select **No**.

8. In **Compute + storage**, click **Configure database** and then select **Standard**:

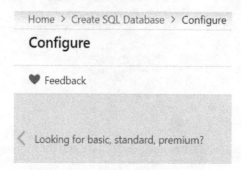

Figure 1.8: The Configure window

Note that you will have to click the **Looking for basic, standard, premium?** link for the standard option to be available:

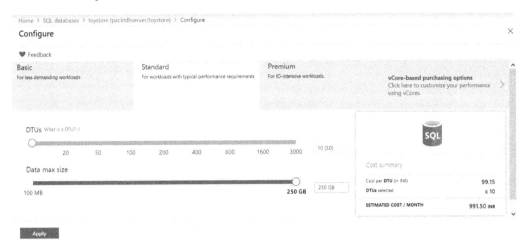

Figure 1.9: The Configure pane

9. Skip the options under **Networking** and **Additional** settings.

10. Click **Review + create** to continue:

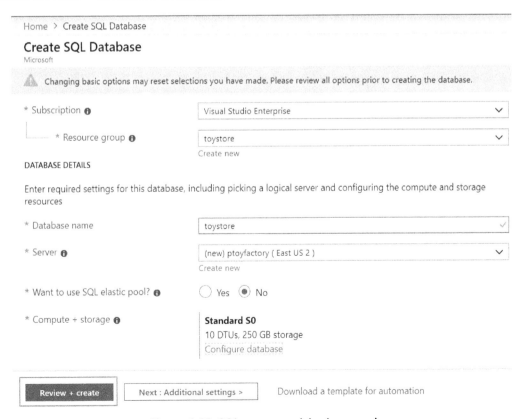

Figure 1.10: SQL pane provisioning panel

11. On the **TERMS** page, read through the terms and conditions and the configuration settings made so far:

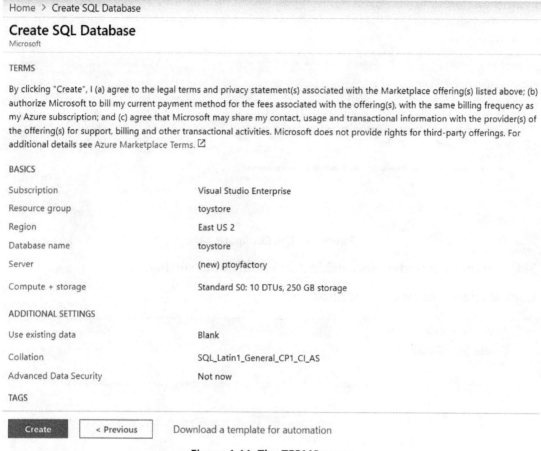

Figure 1.11: The TERMS page

12. Click **Create** to provision the SQL Database.

    Provisioning may take 2-5 minutes. Once the resources are provisioned, you'll get a notification, as shown in *Figure 1.12*:

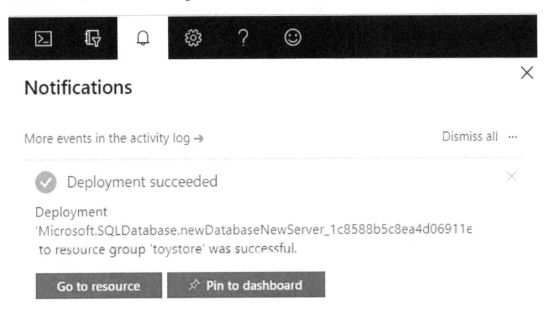

Figure 1.12: Notification after provision completion

13. You can click **Go to resource** to go to the newly created SQL Database.

You have now provisioned your first Azure SQL Database.

Connecting and querying the SQL Database from the Azure portal

In this section, we'll learn how to connect and query the SQL Database from the Azure portal:

1. From the **toystore** pane, select **Query editor (preview)**:

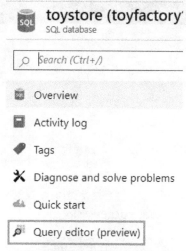

Figure 1.13: toystore pane

2. In the **Query editor (preview)** pane, select **Login**, and under **SQL server authentication**, provide the username and password:

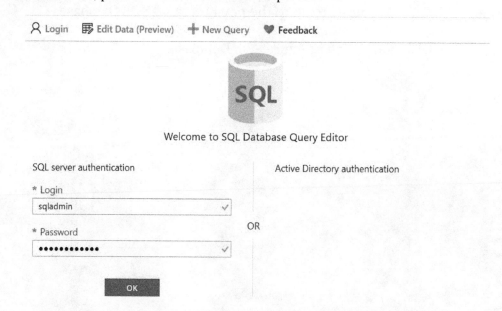

Figure 1.14: The Query Editor (preview) pane

Select **OK** to authenticate and return to the **Query editor (preview)** pane:

3. Open **C:\Code\Chapter01\sqlquery.sql** in Notepad. Copy and paste the query from Notepad into the **Query 1** window in the **Query editor** in the Azure portal.

The query creates a new table (**orders**), populates it with sample data, and returns the top 10 rows from the **orders** table:

```
-- create a new orders table CREATE TABLE orders
(
orderid INT IDENTITY(1, 1) PRIMARY KEY,
quantity INT, sales MONEY
);
--populate Orders table with sample data
;
WITH t1
AS (SELECT 1 AS a UNION ALL

SELECT 1),
t2
AS (SELECT 1 AS a FROM t1
CROSS JOIN t1 AS b),
t3
AS (SELECT 1 AS a FROM t2
CROSS JOIN t2 AS b),
t4
AS (SELECT 1 AS a FROM t3
CROSS JOIN t3 AS b),
t5
AS (SELECT 1 AS a FROM t4
CROSS JOIN t4 AS b),
nums
AS (SELECT Row_number()
OVER (
ORDER BY (SELECT NULL)) AS n
FROM t5)
INSERT INTO orders SELECT n,
n * 10
FROM nums;
GO
SELECT TOP 10 * from orders;
```

4. Select **Run** to execute the query. You should get the following output:

ORDERID	QUANTITY	SALES
1	1	10.0000
2	2	20.0000

Figure 1.15: Expected output

The query editor allows us to connect and query from the Azure portal; however, it's not as strong in features as clients such as SQL Server Management Studio and Azure Data Studio.

Connecting to and querying the SQL Database from SQL Server Management Studio

In this section, we'll connect to and query an Azure SQL Database from **SQL Server Management Studio (SSMS)**:

1. Open SSMS. In the **Connect to Server** dialog box, set the **Server type** as **Database Engine**, if not already selected.

2. Under **Server name**, provide the Azure SQL Server name. You can find the Azure SQL Server name in the **Overview** section of the **Azure SQL Database** pane in the Azure portal:

Figure 1.16: Overview pane of the toystore database

3. Select **SQL Server Authentication** as the authentication type.

4. Provide the login and password for Azure SQL Server and select **Connect**:

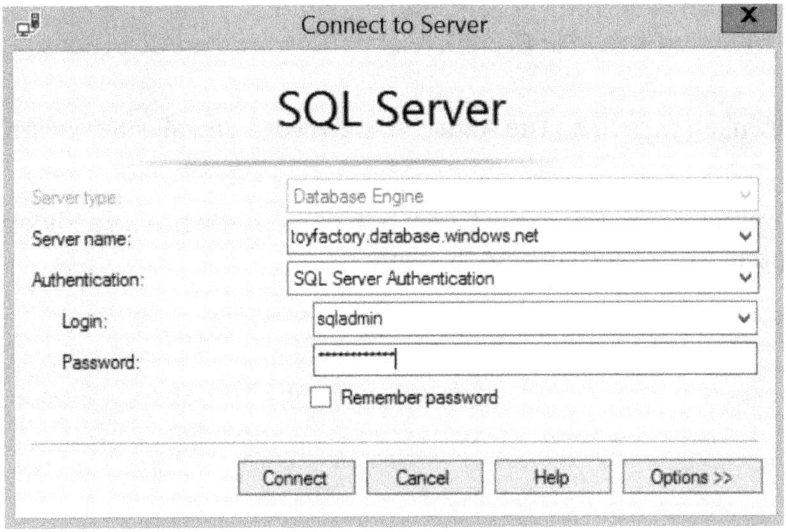

Figure 1.17: Login panel of SQL Server

You'll get an error saying `Your client IP address does not have access to the server`. To connect to Azure SQL Server, you must add the IP of the system you want to connect from under the firewall rule of Azure SQL Server. You can also provide a range of IP addresses to connect from:

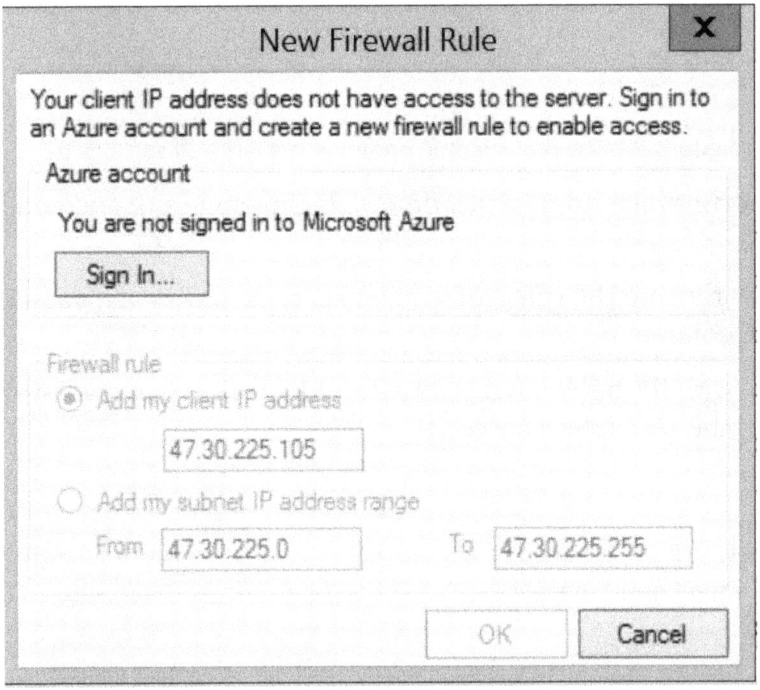

Figure 1.18: New Firewall Rule pane

> **Note**
>
> You can also sign in and add a client IP to the Azure SQL Server firewall by using the **Sign In** button shown in *Figure 1.18* and following the instructions.

To add your machine's IP to the Azure SQL Server firewall rule, switch to the Azure portal.

Open the **toystore** SQL Database **Overview** pane, if it's not already open. From the **Overview** pane, select **Set server firewall**:

Figure 1.19: Setting the server firewall in the Overview pane

5. In the **Firewall settings** pane, select **Add client IP**:

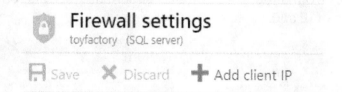

Figure 1.20: The Add client IP option in the Firewall settings pane

6. The Azure portal will automatically detect the machine's IP and add it to the firewall rule.

    If you wish to rename the rule, you can do so by providing a meaningful name in the **RULE NAME** column.

    All machines with IPs between **START IP** and **END IP** are allowed to access all of the databases on the **toyfactory** server:

> **Note**
>
> A virtual network can be used to add an SQL Database in Azure to a given network. A detailed explanation of virtual networks is out of the scope of this book.

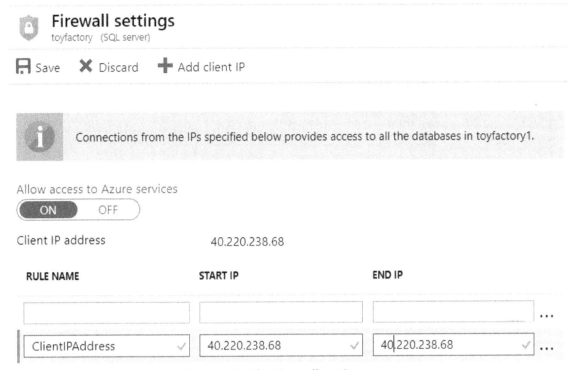

Figure 1.21: The Firewall settings pane

Click **Save** to save the firewall rule.

7. Switch back to SSMS and click **Connect**. You should now be able to connect to Azure SQL Server. Press F8 to open **Object Explorer**, if it's not already open:

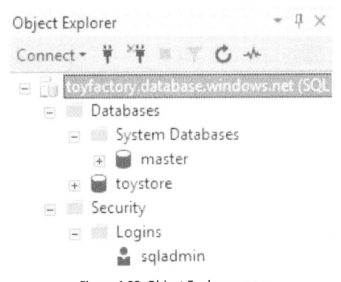

Figure 1.22: Object Explorer pane

8. You can view and modify the firewall settings using T-SQL in the master database. Press *Ctrl* + N to open a new query window. Make sure that the database is set to `master`.

> **Note**
>
> To open a new query window in the `master` database context, in **Object Explorer**, expand **Databases**, then expand **System Databases**. Right-click the `master` database and select `New Query`.

9. Enter the following query to view the existing firewall rules:

```
SELECT * FROM sys.firewall_rules
```

You should get the following output:

	id	name	start_ip_address	end_ip_address	create_date	modify_date
1	1	AllowAllWindowsAzureIps	0.0.0.0	0.0.0.0	2017-10-21 11:33:51.403	2017-10-21 11:33:51.403
2	3	ClientIPAddress_2017-10-22_03:58:23	47.30.225.105	47.30.225.105	2017-10-22 03:58:25.873	2017-10-22 03:58:25.873
3	2	Developer	47.30.12.132	47.30.12.132	2017-10-22 03:55:16.713	2017-10-22 03:55:16.713

Figure 1.23: Existing firewall rules

The `AllowAllWindowsAzureIps` firewall is the default firewall, which allows resources within Microsoft to access Azure SQL Server.

The rest are user-defined firewall rules. The firewall rules for you will be different from what is shown here.

You can use `sp_set_firewall_rule` to add a new firewall rule and `sp_delete_firewall_rule` to delete an existing firewall rule.

10. To query the **toystore** SQL Database, change the database context of the SSMS query window to **toystore**. You can do this by selecting the **toystore** database from the database dropdown in the menu:

Figure 1.24: Dropdown to select the toystore database

11. Copy and paste the following query into the query window:

```
SELECT COUNT(*) AS OrderCount FROM orders;
```

The query will return the total number of **orders** from the orders table. You should get the following output:

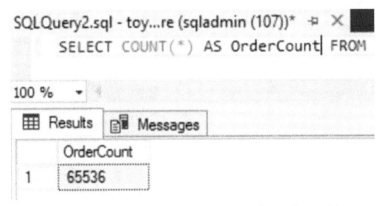

Figure 1.25: Total number of orders in the orders table

We can connect to and query Azure SQL Server from SSMS as we do for an on-premises SQL Server. However, SSMS doesn't have all of the features or options that are available in Azure SQL Database.

Deleting resources

To delete an Azure SQL Database, an Azure SQL Server instance, and Azure resource groups, perform the following steps:

> **Note**
>
> All resources must be deleted to successfully complete the activity at the end of this chapter.

1. Switch to the Azure portal and select **All resources** from the left-hand navigation pane.

2. From the **All resources** pane, select the checkbox next to the **toyfactory** Azure SQL Server instance and then select **Delete** from the top menu:

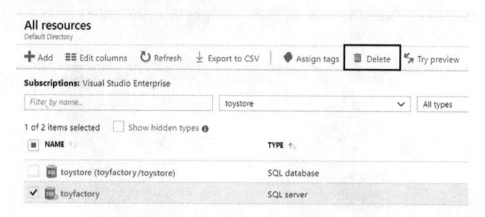

Figure 1.26: Deleting the toyfactory SQL Server

3. In the **Delete Resources** window, type **yes** in the confirmation box and click the **Delete** button to delete the Azure SQL Server instance and the Azure SQL Database:

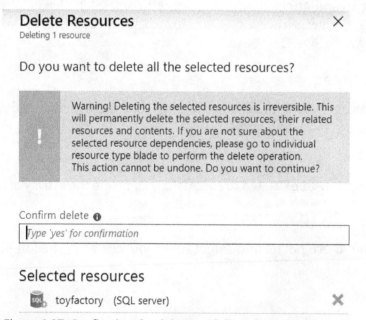

Figure 1.27: Confirming the deletion of the selected resources

Note

To only delete an Azure SQL Database, check the Azure SQL Database checkbox.

4. To delete the Azure resource group, select **Resource groups** from the left-hand navigation pane:

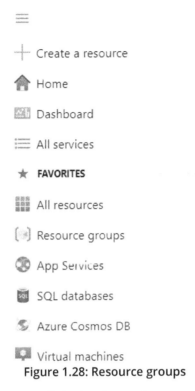

Figure 1.28: Resource groups

5. In the **Resource groups** pane, click the three dots next to the **toystore** resource group, and then select **Delete resource group** from the context menu:

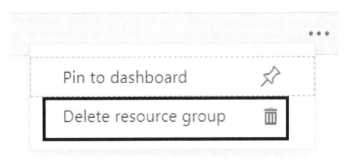

Figure 1.29: Delete resource group option

6. In the delete confirmation pane, type the resource under the **TYPE THE RESOURCE GROUP NAME** section, and then click **Delete**.

We can easily delete resources using the Azure portal. However, note that we may not be able to recover the deleted resource.

Introduction to Azure SQL Managed Instance

Azure SQL Managed Instance is a fully managed SQL Server instance offering announced in May 2017 and made generally available on October 1, 2018.

Azure SQL Managed Instance provides nearly 100% surface area compatibility with the latest SQL Server (Enterprise Edition) database engine, providing all the PaaS benefits available with Azure SQL Database, such as automatic patching and version updates, automatic backups, high availability, and so on.

Note that Azure SQL Managed Instance is its own product within the Azure SQL family, rather than being just a deployment option for Azure SQL Database, with near 100% compatibility with on-premises SQL Server instances.

Azure SQL Managed Instance supports most of the instance-scoped features of traditional SQL Server deployment, which were previously not available in Azure SQL Database, since Azure SQL Database is scoped at the database-level. Azure SQL Managed Instance, therefore, provides easy lift-and-shift migration from an on-premises environment to the cloud.

When you migrate to an Azure SQL Managed Instance on Azure, you don't only migrate databases, you can also migrate licenses too.

> **Note**
>
> You can save up to 82% on Azure SQL Managed Instance when migrating from SQL Server Enterprise or Standard edition with software assurance. For more details, please visit https://azure.microsoft.com/pricing/hybrid-benefit/ or contact Azure.

Some of the important features supported by Azure SQL Managed Instance that are not available in Azure SQL Database are as follows:

- Native backup and restore
- Global temporary tables
- Cross-database queries and transactions
- Linked servers
- CLR modules
- SQL agent
- Database mail

Here are some recently added features:

- Distributed transactions

- Instance pools

- Instance-level Azure Active Directory server principals (logins)

- Transactional replication

- Threat detection

- Long-term backup retention

- Machine learning services (R and Python)

These and other features of Azure SQL Managed Instance make it almost 100% compatible with SQL Server.

Connecting to Azure SQL Managed Instance

Azure SQL Managed Instance is a set of services hosted on one or more isolated virtual machines inside a virtual network subnet.

When we provision an Azure SQL Managed Instance, a virtual cluster is created. A virtual cluster can have one or more SQL Managed Instances.

Applications connect to databases via an endpoint, `<mi_name>.<dns_zone>.database. windows.net`, and should be inside a virtual network, a peered virtual network, or an on-premises network connected via VPN or Azure ExpressRoute.

Unlike Azure SQL Database, Azure SQL Managed Instance supports Azure **Virtual Network (VNet)**. An Azure VNet is a logical boundary or isolation that groups resources within a specified Azure region and enables secure communication between resources, the internet, and on-premises networks:

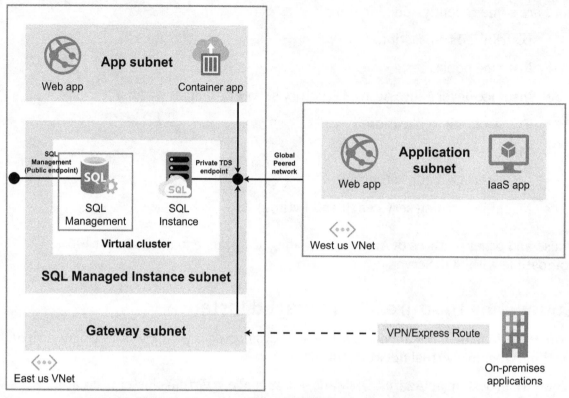

Figure 1.30: High-level connectivity architecture for SQL Managed Instances

Figure 1.30 shows a high-level connectivity architecture for SQL Managed Instances. Let's go through it:

- SQL Managed Instances are part of a virtual cluster and are in an SQL Managed Instance subnet in a virtual network in the **East US** region.

- Web and other applications in the same virtual network connect to the managed instance using a TDS private IP endpoint, for example, `sqlinstance.dnszone.database.windows.net`.

- Applications in the West US virtual network connect using the same endpoint; however, the two virtual networks are peered using global virtual network peering to allow connectivity between them. The same regional virtual network can be peered with SQL Managed Instance.

> **Note**
>
> Global virtual network peering support for SQL Managed Instance is new to SQL Managed Instance.

- On-premises applications connect using the same endpoint via VPN or an ExpressRoute gateway.

- To improve the overall experience and availability, Azure applies a network intent policy on virtual network infrastructure elements. The policy plays a major role in preventing network misconfiguration and ensures normal SQL Managed Instance operations.

Virtual cluster connectivity architecture

In the previous example, we saw connectivity to SQL Managed Instance from different networks. Here, we are going to learn about virtual cluster internal communication:

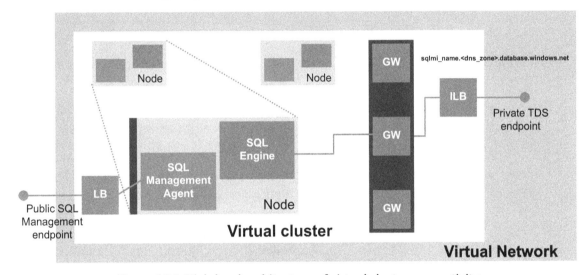

Figure 1.31: High-level architecture of virtual cluster connectivity

In *Figure* 1.31, applications/client connects to SQL Managed Instance using a **fully qualified domain name** (**FQDN**), `sqlmi_name.<dns_zone>.database.windows.net`. This hostname can only be resolved within a private network. The `dnz_zone` ID is automatically created when the virtual cluster is deployed. The private IP belongs to the **internal load balancer** (**ILB**) of SQL Managed Instance, and the load balancer forwards traffic to the SQL Managed **Instance gateway** (**GW**) service. Since multiple instances run inside the virtual cluster, the GW service redirects SQL traffic to the correct instance based on the instance name.

Management and deployment services connect to SQL Managed Instance using a **load balancer** (**LB**) that uses a public IP address. A built-in firewall only allows traffic from Microsoft IP addresses on specified management ports. All the communication inside the virtual cluster is encrypted using TLS protocols.

Network requirements

SQL Managed Instance needs to be deployed in a dedicated subnet in a virtual network. The subnet must have these characteristics:

- **Dedicated subnet**: The SQL Managed Instance subnet must be reserved only for managed instances. The subnet can't contain any other Azure services except SQL Managed Instance.

- **Sufficient IP addresses**: The SQL Managed Instance subnet must have at least 16 IP addresses and a minimum of 32 IP addresses for deployment. These IP addresses are reserved for virtual cluster resources and may vary depending on the hardware generation and SQL Managed Instance service tier. Visit https://docs.microsoft.com/azure/azure-sql/managed-instance/vnet-subnet-determine-size to determine the SQL Managed Instance subnet size.

- **Subnet delegation**: The SQL Managed Instance subnet needs to be delegated to the `Microsoft.Sql/managedInstances` resource provider.

- **Network security group (NSG)**: SQL Managed Instance requires port **1433** for TDS traffic and ports in the range **11000-11999** for redirection connection. An NSG must be associated with the SQL Managed Instance subnet.

- **A user-defined route (UDR) table**: A prerequisite is to create a route table that will allow SQL Managed Instance to communicate with the Azure Management Service.

These conditions are mandatory for SQL Managed Instance creation and management operations.

> **Note**
>
> A detailed explanation of the networking requirements can be found by visiting https://docs.microsoft.com/azure/azure-sql/database/connectivity-architecture.

Differences between SQL Database, SQL Managed Instance, and SQL Server

SQL Database and SQL Managed Instance are PaaS offerings from the Azure SQL family and therefore some of their features differ from the on-premises SQL Server. Some of the important features that differ are as follows:

Backup and restore

SQL Database

Conventional database backup and restore statements aren't supported on SQL Database. Backups are automatically scheduled and start within a few minutes of the database being provisioned. Backups are consistent, transaction-wise, which means that you can do a point-in-time restore.

There is no additional cost for backup storage until the amount stored goes beyond 100% of the database's size.

You can reduce the backup retention period to manage backup storage costs. You can also use the long-term retention period feature to store backups in a separate Azure blob container for a much lower cost for up to 10 years.

Apart from automatic backups, you can also export the Azure SQL Database **bacpac** or **dacpac** file to Azure Storage.

SQL Managed Instance

SQL Managed Instance automatically creates database backups that are kept for the duration of a specified retention period. Native **COPY_ONLY** backups on Azure blob containers are allowed on SQL Managed Instance.

Backup storage is free as an equal amount of storage is reserved for SQL Managed Instance, regardless of the backup retention period.

The long-term retention period for SQL Managed Instance is a limited preview feature currently (and will be in public preview soon) and is only available for **EA** and **CSP** subscriptions.

Recovery model

The default recovery model for SQL Database and SQL Managed Instance is **FULL**, and it can't be modified to any other recovery model as in on-premises recovery models.

The recovery model is set when the master database is created, meaning when an Azure SQL Server is provisioned, the recovery model can't be modified because the master database is read-only.

To view the recovery model of an Azure SQL Database, execute the following query:

```
SELECT name, recovery_model_desc FROM sys.databases;
```

> **Note**
>
> You can use either of the two methods discussed earlier in the chapter to run the query – the Azure portal or SSMS.

You should get the following output:

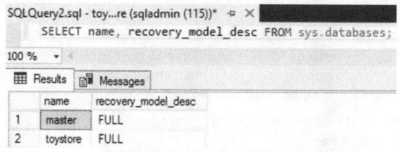

Figure 1.32: Recovery model of an SQL database

SQL Server Agent

SQL Database doesn't have SQL Server Agent, which is used to schedule jobs and send success/failure notifications. However, you can use the following workarounds:

- Create an SQL Agent job on an on-premises SQL server or on an Azure VM to connect and run on the SQL Database.

- Azure Automation allows users to schedule jobs in Microsoft Azure to automate manual tasks. This topic is covered in detail later in the book.

- Elastic Jobs is an Azure service that allows the scheduled execution of ad hoc tasks. This topic is covered in detail later in the book.

- Use PowerShell to automate a task and schedule PowerShell script execution with Windows Scheduler, on-premises, or Azure VM.

Azure SQL Managed Instance has SQL Server Agent and can be used to schedule jobs just like with on-premises SQL Server. However, some of the actions are not allowed, such as enabling and disabling SQL Server Agent, and the SQL Server Agent process is always in the running state.

For more information, please visit https://docs.microsoft.com/azure/azure-sql/ managed-instance/transact-sql-tsql-differences-sql-server#sql-server-agent.

Change Data Capture

Change Data Capture (CDC) allows you to capture data modifications to CDC-enabled databases and tables. The CDC feature is important in incremental load scenarios, such as incrementally inserting changed data to a data warehouse from an **online transaction processing (OLTP)** environment. CDC requires SQL Server Agent and therefore isn't available in SQL Database. However, you can use the temporal table, **SQL Server Integration Services (SSIS)**, or Azure Data Factory to implement CDC. CDC is supported in SQL Managed Instance.

Auditing

Audit logs are available for both SQL Database and SQL Managed Instance but with a few differences from on-premises SQL Server. In PaaS, file system-level access is not granted, hence audit logs need to be captured on Azure Blob Storage.

Mirroring

You can't enable mirroring between two SQL Databases, and the same goes for SQL Managed Instance databases. You can set up a readable secondary for an SQL Database and a failover group for SQL Managed Instance, which is better than mirroring.

Table partitioning

Table partitioning using a partition scheme and partition functions is allowed in SQL Database; however, because of the PaaS nature of the SQL Database, all partitions should be created on a primary filegroup. You won't get a performance improvement by having partitions on different disks (spindles); however, you will get a performance improvement with partition elimination.

In SQL Managed Instance, partitions can be created with different filegroups and files for each partition, meaning better performance by having multiple files per database.

Replication

Conventional replication techniques, such as snapshot, transactional, and merge replication, can't be done between two Azure SQL Databases. However, an SQL Database can be a subscriber to an on-premises or Azure VM SQL Server instance.

However, this too has limitations. It supports one-way transactional replication, not peer-to-peer or bi-directional replication; it supports only push subscription.

Note that you should have SQL Server 2012 or above when on-premises. Replication and distribution agents can't be configured on SQL Database.

SQL Managed Instance supports snapshot, transactional, and bi-directional transactional replication. Merge replication, peer-to-peer replication, and updatable subscriptions are not supported.

The publisher and distributor need to be configured on both SQL Managed Instance and on-premises SQL Server.

Multi-part names

Multi-part names and cross-database queries are supported on SQL Managed Instance.

For SQL Database, three-part names (**databasename.schemaname.tablename**) are only limited to **tempdb**, wherein you access a temp table as **tempdb.dbo.#temp**. For example, if there is a temporary table, say, **#temp1**, then you can run the following query to select all the values from **#temp1**:

```
SELECT * FROM tempdb.dbo.#temp1
```

You can't access the tables in different SQL Databases in Azure on the same Azure SQL Server using three-part names. Four-part names (**ServerName.DatabaseName.SchemaName.TableName**) aren't allowed at all.

You can use an elastic query to access tables from different databases from an Azure SQL Server. Elastic queries are covered in detail later in the book. You can access objects in different schemas in the same Azure SQL Database using two-part (**Schemaname.Tablename**) names.

To explore other T-SQL differences, visit https://docs.microsoft.com/azure/sql-database/sql-database-transact-sql-information.

SQL Server Browser

SQL Server Browser is a Windows service that provides instance and post information to incoming connection requests. This isn't required because SQL Database and SQL Managed Instance listen to port **1433** only.

FileStream

SQL Database and SQL Managed Instance don't support **FileStream** or **FileTable**, just because of the PaaS nature of the service. There is a workaround to use Azure Storage; however, that would require a re-working of the application and the database.

Common Language Runtime (SQL CLR)

SQL CLR is supported on SQL Managed Instance with a few differences. SQL CLR allows users to write programmable database objects such as stored procedures, functions, and triggers in managed code. This provides a significant performance improvement in some scenarios. This feature is not available in SQL Database.

Resource Governor

Resource Governor is supported on SQL Managed Instance. Resource Governor allows you to throttle/limit resources (CPU, memory, and I/O) for different SQL Server workloads. This feature is not available in SQL Database.

SQL Database comes with different service tiers, each suitable for different workloads. You should evaluate the performance tier your application workload will fit into and accordingly provision the database for that performance tier.

Global temporary tables

Local and global instance-scoped temporary tables are supported on SQL Managed Instance.

Global temporary tables are defined by **##** and are accessible across all sessions. These are not supported in SQL Database.

Local temporary tables are allowed. Global temporary tables created with **##** are accessible across all sessions for a particular database. For example, a global temporary table created in database **DB1** will be accessible to all sessions connecting to database **DB1** only.

Log shipping

Log shipping is the process of taking log backups on a primary server and copying and restoring them on a secondary server. Log shipping is commonly used as a high-availability or disaster-recovery solution, or to migrate a database from one SQL instance to another. SQL Database and SQL Managed Instance have built-in high availability and configurable business continuity features. Log shipping isn't supported by SQL Database and SQL Managed Instance.

SQL Trace and Profiler

SQL Profiler is supported on SQL Managed Instance. SQL Trace and Profiler can't be used to trace events on SQL Database. Currently, there isn't a direct alternative other than using **dynamic management views** (**DMVs**), monitoring using the Azure portal, and extended events.

Trace flags

Only a limited set of global traces is supported on SQL Managed Instance. Trace flags are special switches used to enable or disable a particular SQL Server functionality. These are not available in SQL Server.

System stored procedures

SQL Managed Instance supports nearly all system stored procedures. SQL Database doesn't support all the system stored procedures supported in an on-premises SQL Server. System stored procedures such as **sp_addmessage**, **sp_helpuser**, and **sp_configure** aren't supported. In a nutshell, procedures related to features unsupported in SQL Database aren't supported.

The USE statement

The **USE** statement is used to switch from one database context to another. This isn't supported in SQL Database, but SQL Managed Instance supports the **USE** statement.

Exercise: Provisioning an Azure SQL Managed Instance using the Azure portal

In this exercise, we'll provision and connect to an SQL Managed Instance. We'll also learn about virtual network support in SQL Managed Instance.

To provision an SQL Managed Instance, perform the following steps:

1. Log in to https://portal.azure.com using your Azure credentials.

2. Click on **+Create a resource**:

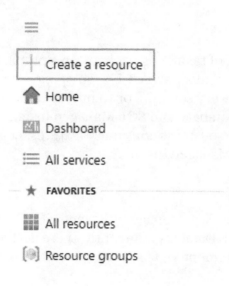

Figure 1.33: Creating a new resource

3. Search for **Azure SQL** in Azure Marketplace:

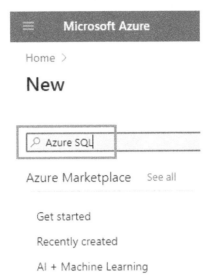

Figure 1.34: Searching for Azure SQL in Marketplace

4. Select the **Create** option; you can see more details by clicking on the **Show details** option:

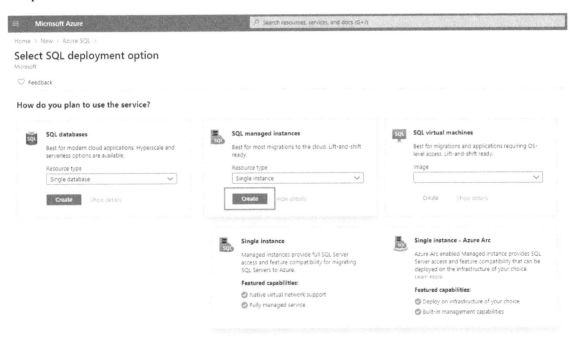

Figure 1.35: Selecting an SQL deployment option

5. In the **Basic** tab, provide the information shown in *Figure 1.36*:

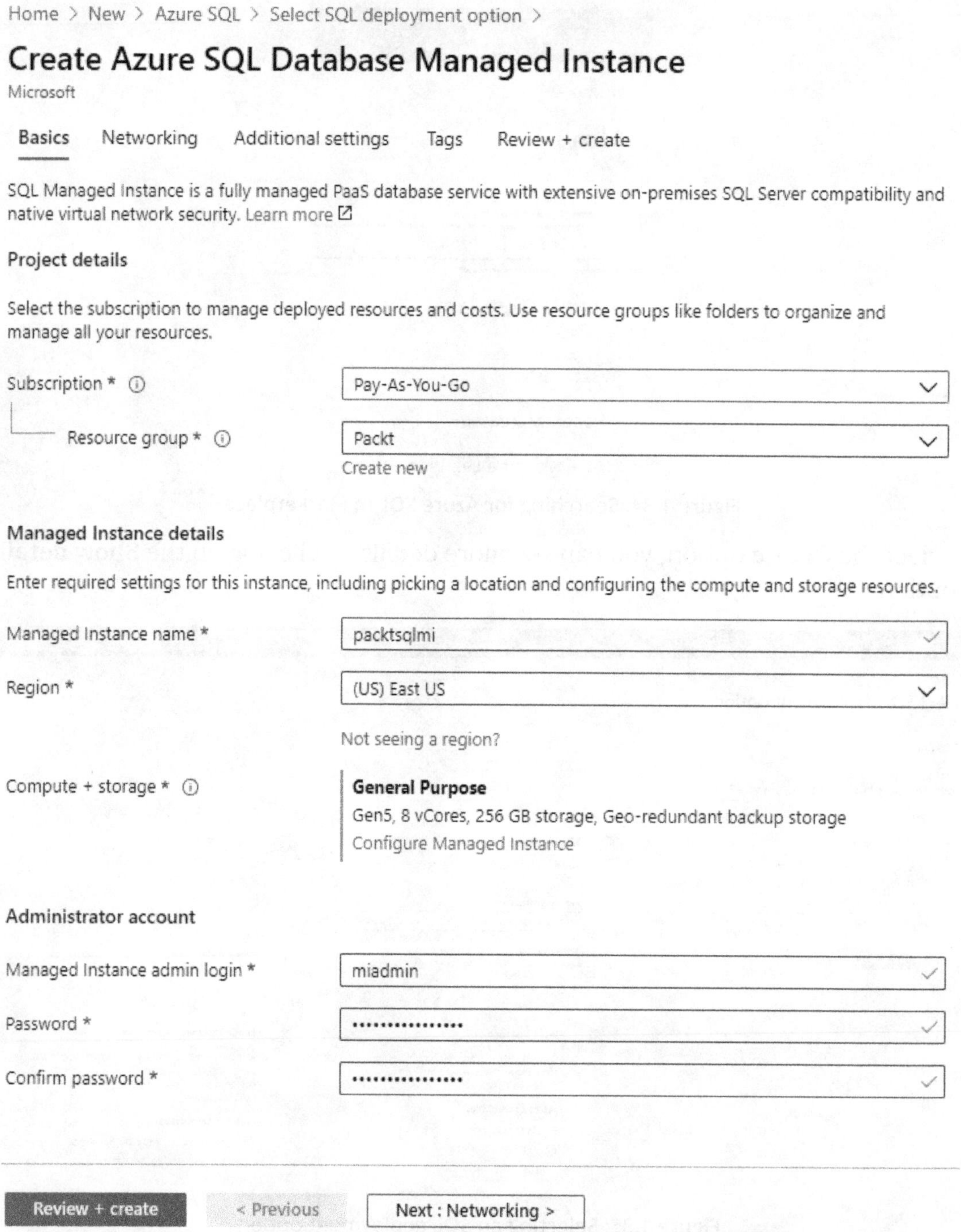

Home > New > Azure SQL > Select SQL deployment option >

Create Azure SQL Database Managed Instance

Microsoft

Basics   Networking   Additional settings   Tags   Review + create

SQL Managed Instance is a fully managed PaaS database service with extensive on-premises SQL Server compatibility and native virtual network security. Learn more ☑

Project details

Select the subscription to manage deployed resources and costs. Use resource groups like folders to organize and manage all your resources.

Subscription * ⓘ

> Pay-As-You-Go ⌄

Resource group * ⓘ

> Packt ⌄
> Create new

Managed Instance details

Enter required settings for this instance, including picking a location and configuring the compute and storage resources.

Managed Instance name *

> packtsqlmi ✓

Region *

> (US) East US ⌄

Not seeing a region?

Compute + storage * ⓘ

> **General Purpose**
> Gen5, 8 vCores, 256 GB storage, Geo-redundant backup storage
> Configure Managed Instance

Administrator account

Managed Instance admin login *

> miadmin ✓

Password *

> ••••••••••••••• ✓

Confirm password *

> ••••••••••••••• ✓

[Review + create]   [< Previous]   [Next : Networking >]

Figure 1.36: Information required to add the SQL Managed Instance

In the **Subscription** box, provide your Azure subscription type. SQL Managed Instances currently support the following subscription types: **Enterprise Agreement (EA)**, **Pay-As-You-Go**, **Cloud Service Provider (CSP)**, **Enterprise Dev/ Test**, **Pay-As-You-Go Dev/Test**, and subscriptions with monthly Azure credit for Visual Studio subscribers.

If you have a different subscription, you won't be able to create an SQL Managed Instance.

In the **Resource Group** box, choose to create a new or use an existing resource group for the SQL Managed Instance. A resource group is a logical container for all the resources in Azure.

The **Managed instance name** box is for the name of the managed instance you plan to create. It can be any valid name, in accordance with the naming rules at https:// docs.microsoft.com/azure/architecture/best-practices/naming-conventions.

For the **Region** box, select the desired Azure region for the SQL Managed Instance deployment. In general, apps and managed instances should be deployed in the same Azure region to avoid network latency.

The **Managed instance admin login** box is for any login name, as long as it fits the naming conventions at https://docs.microsoft.com/azure/architecture/best-practices/naming-conventions.

The password can be any password that follows these rules:

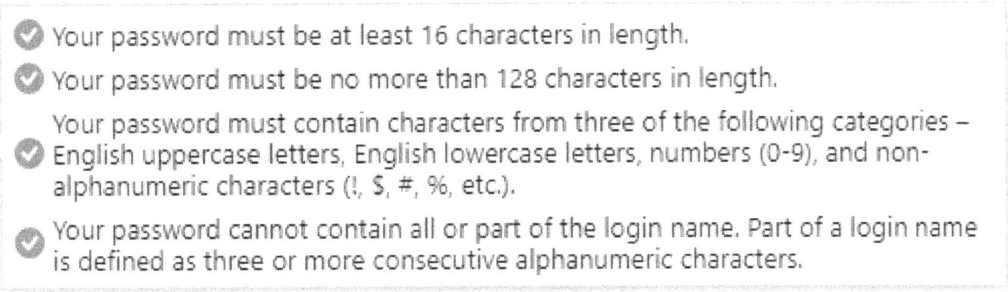

⊘ Your password must be at least 16 characters in length.

⊘ Your password must be no more than 128 characters in length.

⊘ Your password must contain characters from three of the following categories – English uppercase letters, English lowercase letters, numbers (0-9), and non-alphanumeric characters (!, $, #, %, etc.).

⊘ Your password cannot contain all or part of the login name. Part of a login name is defined as three or more consecutive alphanumeric characters.

Figure 1.37: Password requirements

6. Select **Configure Managed Instance** to choose compute and storage resources. Use sliders to choose the vCore and storage size.

Select **Azure Hybrid Benefits** if you already have SQL Server licenses with software assurance. In general, this can be used while migrating from an on-premises SQL Server to SQL Managed Instance.

Select the **Backup Storage** type; **Geo**, **Zone**, and **Locally-redundant** backup storage options are available. Choose this based on the desired recovery plan as it can't be changed after instance deployment. Read more about backup storage types at https://docs.microsoft.com/azure/azure-sql/database/automated-backups-overview?tabs=single-database.

When you are finished, select **Apply** to save changes:

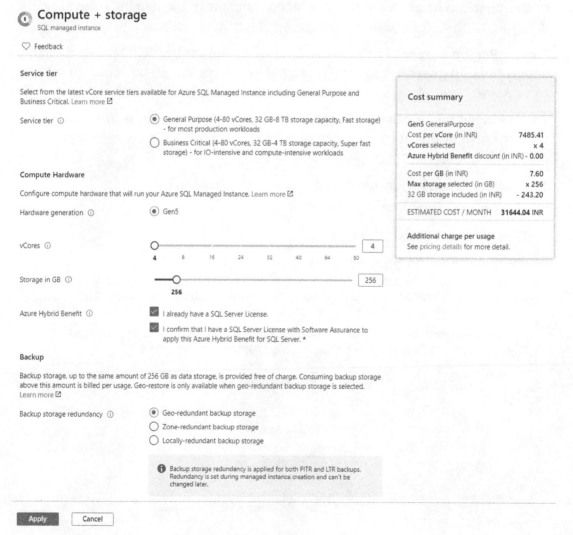

Figure 1.38: Compute + storage

7. After the instance resources configuration selection, move to the **Networking** tab to configure **Virtual network / subnet** for the SQL Managed Instance:

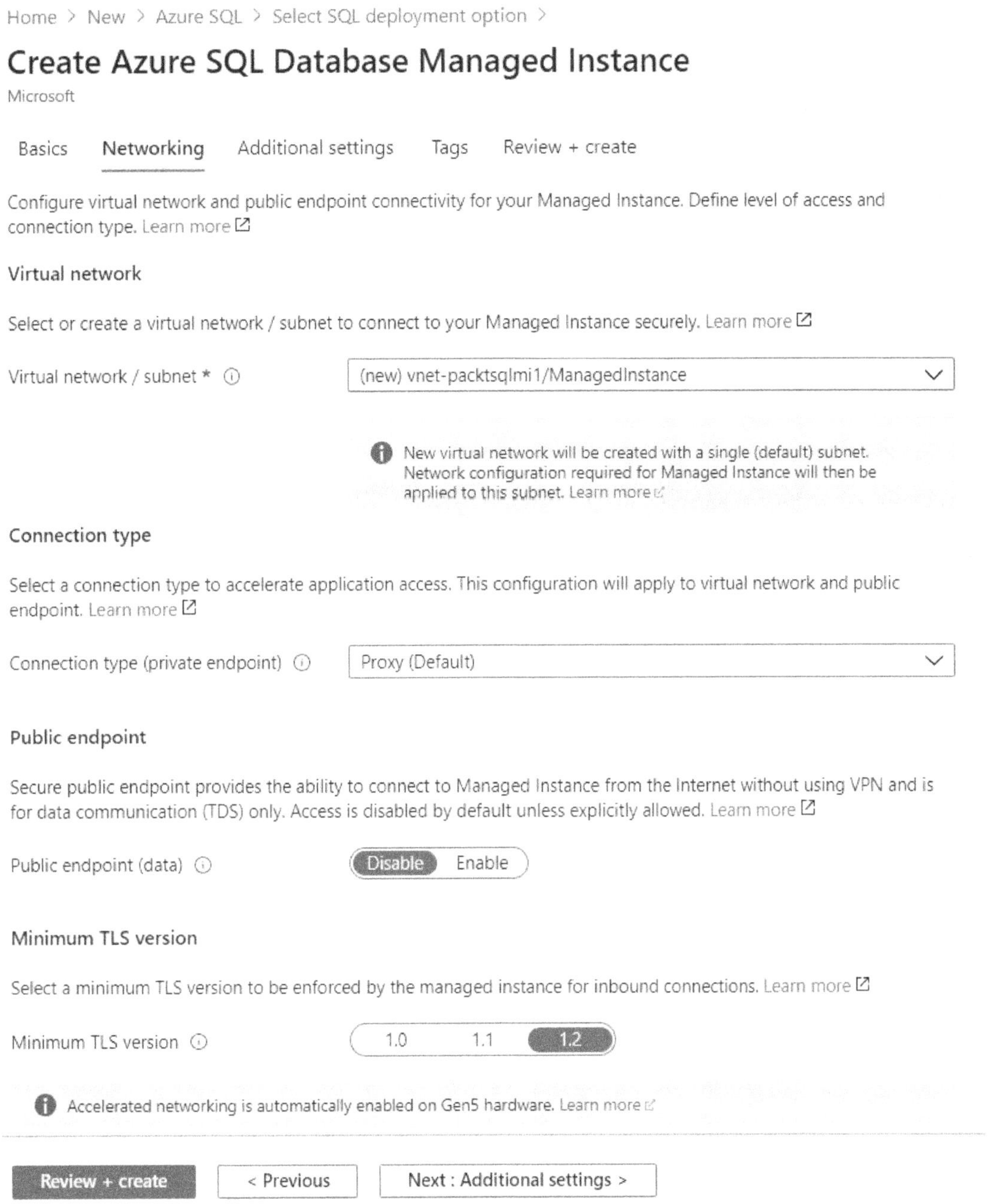

Home > New > Azure SQL > Select SQL deployment option >

Create Azure SQL Database Managed Instance
Microsoft

Basics   **Networking**   Additional settings   Tags   Review + create

Configure virtual network and public endpoint connectivity for your Managed Instance. Define level of access and connection type. Learn more ☑

Virtual network

Select or create a virtual network / subnet to connect to your Managed Instance securely. Learn more ☑

Virtual network / subnet * ⓘ | (new) vnet-packtsqlmi1/ManagedInstance   ⌄ |

ⓘ New virtual network will be created with a single (default) subnet. Network configuration required for Managed Instance will then be applied to this subnet. Learn more ☑

Connection type

Select a connection type to accelerate application access. This configuration will apply to virtual network and public endpoint. Learn more ☑

Connection type (private endpoint) ⓘ | Proxy (Default)   ⌄ |

Public endpoint

Secure public endpoint provides the ability to connect to Managed Instance from the Internet without using VPN and is for data communication (TDS) only. Access is disabled by default unless explicitly allowed. Learn more ☑

Public endpoint (data) ⓘ   (**Disable**   Enable)

Minimum TLS version

Select a minimum TLS version to be enforced by the managed instance for inbound connections. Learn more ☑

Minimum TLS version ⓘ   (1.0   1.1   **1.2**)

ⓘ Accelerated networking is automatically enabled on Gen5 hardware. Learn more ☑

[**Review + create**]   [< Previous]   [Next : Additional settings >]

Figure 1.39: Moving to the Network tab to set Virtual network / subnet

The **Virtual network / subnet** box is for setting the virtual network/subnet that the managed instance will be part of. If no network is provided, a new virtual network/subnet is created.

For the **Connection type** box, SQL Managed Instances support two connection types: `Redirect` and `Proxy`. `Redirect` is the recommended connection type because the client directly connects to the node hosting the database, and therefore it offers low latency and high throughput.

For the `Proxy` connection type, requests to the database are proxied through the SQL Database gateways.

Enable **Public endpoint** to allow SQL Managed Instance connectivity over the internet. By default, it's disabled until explicitly enabled.

Choose **Minimal TLS Version** to enforce a TLS version for the managed instance's inbound connection.

8. Fill out all the details in the **Additional settings** tab:

Create Azure SQL Database Managed Instance
Microsoft

Basics   Networking   **Additional settings**   Tags   Review + create

Customize additional configuration parameters including geo-replication, time zone, and collation.

Collation

Instance collation defines rules that sort and compare data, and cannot be changed after instance creation. The default instance collation is SQL_Latin1_CP1_CI_AS. Learn more ⧉

Collation * ⓘ

    SQL_Latin1_General_CP1_CI_AS

    Find a collation

Time zone

Time zone is defined at the instance level and it applies to all databases created in this Managed Instance. Time zone cannot be changed after the instance creation. Learn more ⧉

Time zone * ⓘ

    (UTC) Coordinated Universal Time   ⌄

Geo-Replication

Use this instance as a Failover Group secondary. Learn more ⧉

Use as failover secondary * ⓘ   No   Yes

Review + create   < Previous   Next : Tags >

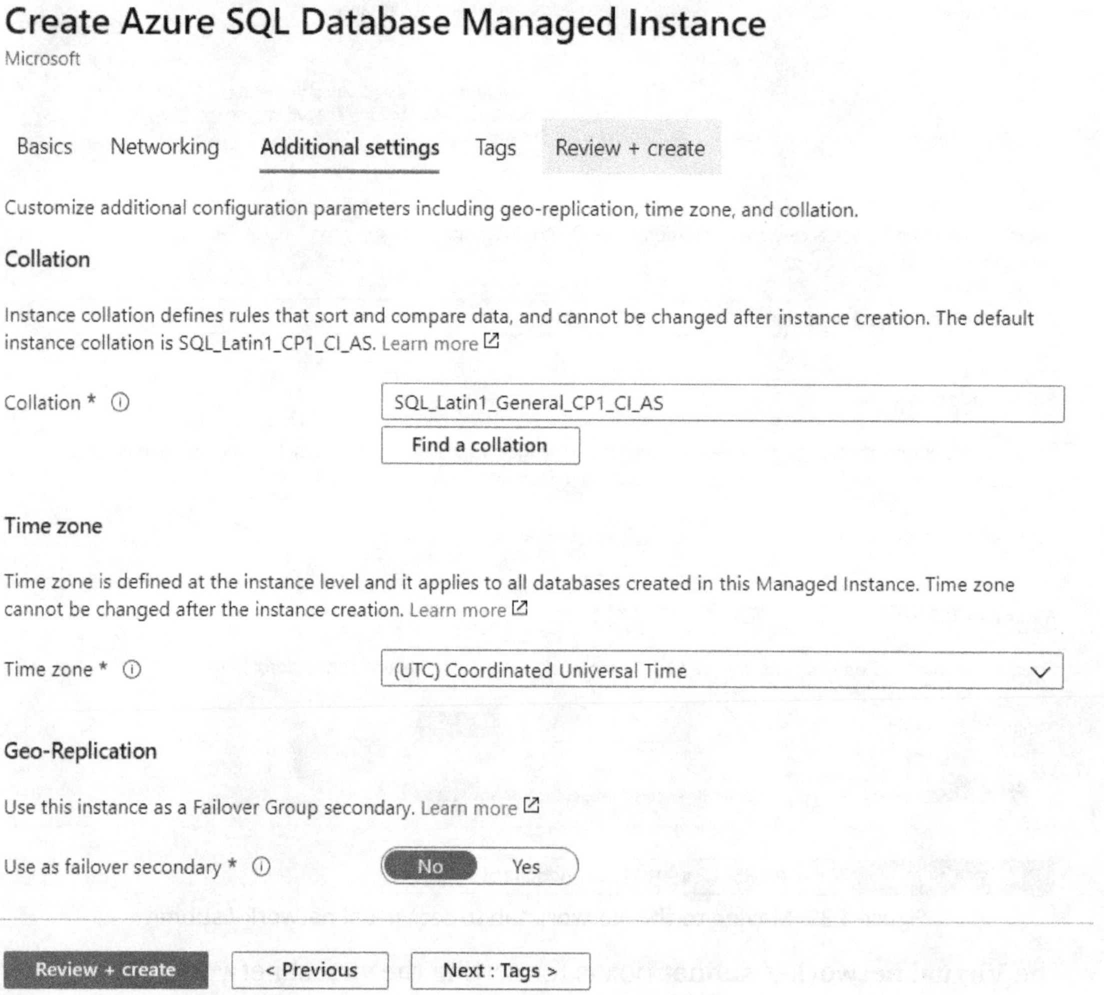

Figure 1.40: The Additional settings tab

Collation is the SQL Server collation that the managed instance will be in.

The **Time zone** box denotes the time zone of the managed instance. The preferred time zone is **UTC**; however, this will differ from business to business.

Select **Geo-Replication** to use this managed instance as a secondary instance in a failover group.

9. In the **Review + create** tab, review your selection before you create the managed instance:

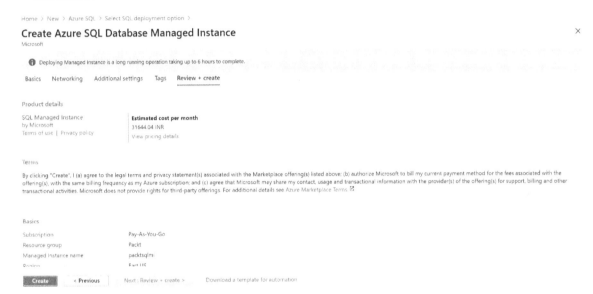

Figure 1.41: The Review + create tab

10. Click **Create** to validate and provision the SQL Managed Instance.

To monitor the progress, click the **Notifications** (bell) icon in the top-left corner:

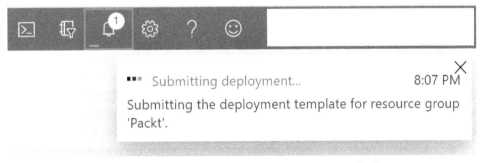

Figure 1.42: Notifications icon in the instance window

As we can see, the deployment is in progress:

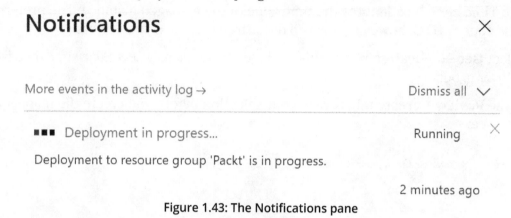

Figure 1.43: The Notifications pane

After the deployment is complete, a deployment complete notification will come up in the notification window:

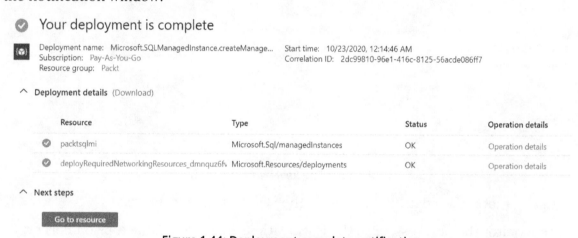

Figure 1.44: Deployment complete notification

Activity: Provisioning Azure SQL Server and SQL Database using PowerShell

This section discusses provisioning Azure SQL Server and SQL Database using PowerShell. To understand the process, let's take the example of Mike, who is the newest member of the data administration team at ToyStore Ltd., a company that manufactures toys for children. ToyStore has an e-commerce web portal that allows customers to purchase toys online. ToyStore has migrated the online e-commerce portal to Microsoft Azure and is therefore moving to Azure SQL Database from an on-premises SQL Server. Mike is asked to provision the Azure SQL Database and other required resources as his initial assignment. This can be achieved by following these steps:

> **Note**
>
> If you are short of time, you can refer to the `C:\Code\Chapter01\Provision-AzureSQLDatabase.ps1` file. You can run this file in the PowerShell console instead of typing the code as instructed in the following steps. Open a PowerShell console and enter the full path to execute the PowerShell script. You'll have to change the Azure resource group name, the Azure SQL Server, and the Azure SQL Database name in the script before executing it.

1. Save the Azure profile details into a file for future reference. Press *Windows* + *R* to open the **Run** command window.

2. In the **Run** command window, type `powershell` and then press *Enter*. This will open a new PowerShell console window:

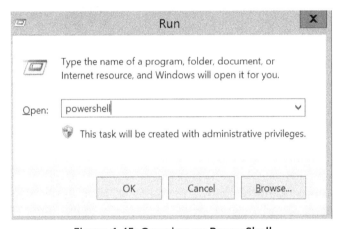

Figure 1.45: Opening up PowerShell

3. In the PowerShell console, run the following command:

```
Add-AzAccount
```

You'll have to enter your Azure credentials into the pop-up dialog box. After a successful login, the control will return to the **PowerShell** window.

4. Run the following command to save the profile details to a file:

```
Save-AzProfile -Path C:\Code\MyAzureProfile.json
```

The Azure subscription details will be saved in the **MyAzureProfile.json** file in **JSON** format. If you wish to explore the **JSON** file, you can open it in any editor to review its content:

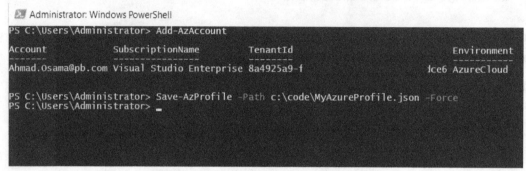

Figure 1.46: Saving the Azure credentials

> **Note**
>
> Saving the profile in a file allows you to use the file to log in to your Azure account from PowerShell instead of providing your credentials every time in the Azure authentication window.

Press *Windows* + R to open the **Run** command window. Type **PowerShell_ISE.exe** in the **Run** command window and press *Enter*. This will open a new PowerShell ISE editor window. This is where you'll write the PowerShell commands:

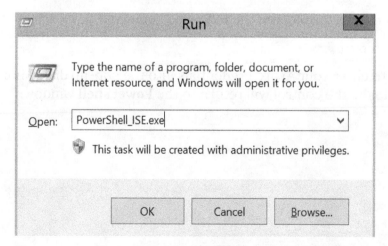

Figure 1.47: Run command window

5. In the PowerShell ISE, select **File** from the top menu, and then click **Save**. Alternatively, you can press *Ctrl* + S to save the file. In the **Save As** dialog box, browse to the C:\Code\Chapter01\ directory. In the **File name** textbox, type **Provision-AzureSQLDatabase.ps1**, and then click **Save** to save the file:

Figure 1.48: Saving the PowerShell ISE file

6. Copy and paste the following lines in the **Provision-AzureSQLDatabase.ps1** file one after another. The code explanation, wherever required, is given in the comments within the code snippet.

7. Copy and paste the following code to define the parameters:

```
param (
[parameter(Mandatory=$true)] [String] $ResourceGroup,
[parameter(Mandatory=$true)] [String] $Location,
[parameter(Mandatory=$true)] [String] $SQLServer,
[parameter(Mandatory=$true)] [String] $UserName,
[parameter(Mandatory=$true)] [String] $Password,

[parameter(Mandatory=$true)] [String] $SQLDatabase,
[parameter(Mandatory=$true)] [String] $Edition="Basic",
[parameter(Mandatory=$false)] [String] $AzureProfileFilePath
)
```

The preceding code defines the parameters required by the scripts:

ResourceGroup: The resource group that will host the logical Azure SQL Server and Azure SQL Database.

Location: The resource group location. The default is `East US 2`.

SQLServer: The logical Azure SQL Server name that will host the Azure SQL Database.

UserName: The Azure SQL Server admin username. The default username is `sqladmin`. Don't change the username; keep it as the default.

Password: The Azure SQL Server admin password. The default password is `Packt@pub2`. Don't change the password; keep it as the default.

SQLDatabase: The Azure SQL Database to create.

Edition: The Azure SQL Database edition. This is discussed in detail in *Chapter 3, Migration*.

AzureProfileFilePath: The full path of the file that contains your Azure profile details. You created this earlier in the activity.

8. Copy and paste the following code to log in to your Azure account from PowerShell:

```
Start-Transcript -Path .\log\ProvisionAzureSQLDatabase.txt -Append
if([string]::IsNullOrEmpty($AzureProfileFilePath))
{
$AzureProfileFilePath="..\..\MyAzureProfile.json"
}
if((Test-Path -Path $AzureProfileFilePath))
{
$profile = Import-AzContext-Path $AzureProfileFilePath
$SubscriptionID = $profile.Context.Subscription.SubscriptionId
}
else
{

Write-Host "File Not Found $AzureProfileFilePath"
-ForegroundColor Red
$profile = Login-AzAccount
$SubscriptionID = $profile.Context.Subscription.
SubscriptionId
}
Set-AzContext -SubscriptionId $SubscriptionID | Out-Null
```

The preceding code first checks for the profile details in the Azure profile file. If found, it retrieves the subscription ID of the profile; otherwise, it uses the **Login-AzAccount** command to pop up the **Azure login** dialog box. You have to provide your Azure credentials in the login dialog box. After a successful login, it retrieves and stores the subscription ID of the profile in the **$SubscriptionID** variable.

It then sets the current Azure subscription to yours for the PowerShell cmdlets to use in the current session.

9. Copy and paste the following code to create the resource group if it doesn't already exist:

```
# Check if resource group exists
# An error is returned and stored in the notexists variable if the
resource group exists
Get-AzResourceGroup -Name $ResourceGroup -Location $Location
-ErrorVariable notexists -ErrorAction SilentlyContinue

#Provision Azure Resource Group
if($notexists)
{

Write-Host "Provisioning Azure Resource Group $ResourceGroup"
-ForegroundColor Green
$_ResourceGroup = @{ Name = $ResourceGroup; Location = $Location;

}
New-AzResourceGroup @_ResourceGroup;
}
else
{

Write-Host $notexists -ForegroundColor Yellow
}
```

The **Get-AzResourceGroup** cmdlet fetches the given resource group. If the given resource group doesn't exist, an error is returned. The error returned is stored in the **notexists** variable.

The **New-AzResourceGroup** cmdlet provisions the new resource group if the **notexists** variable isn't empty.

10. Copy and paste the following code to create a new Azure SQL Server if one doesn't exist:

```
Get-AzSqlServer -ServerName $SQLServer -ResourceGroupName
$ResourceGroup -ErrorVariable notexists -ErrorAction SilentlyContinue
if($notexists)
{
Write-Host "Provisioning Azure SQL Server $SQLServer"
-ForegroundColor Green
$credentials = New-Object -TypeName System.Management.Automation.
PSCredential -ArgumentList $UserName, $(ConvertTo-SecureString
-String $Password -AsPlainText -Force)
$_SqlServer = @{
ResourceGroupName = $ResourceGroup; ServerName = $SQLServer; Location =
$Location; SqlAdministratorCredentials = $credentials; ServerVersion =
'12.0';
}

New-AzSqlServer @_SqlServer;
}
else
{
Write-Host $notexists -ForegroundColor Yellow
}
```

The **Get-AzSqlServer** cmdlet gets the given Azure SQL Server. If the given Azure SQL Server doesn't exist, an error is returned. The error returned is stored in the **notexists** variable.

The **New-AzSqlServer** cmdlet provisions the new Azure SQL Server if the **notexists** variable isn't empty.

11. Copy and paste the following code to create the Azure SQL Database if it doesn't already exist:

```
# Check if Azure SQL Database Exists
# An error is returned and stored in the notexists variable if the
resource group exists
Get-AzSqlDatabase -DatabaseName $SQLDatabase -ServerName
$SQLServer -ResourceGroupName $ResourceGroup -ErrorVariable notexits
-ErrorAction SilentlyContinue
if($notexists)
{
# Provision Azure SQL Database
```

```
Write-Host "Provisioning Azure SQL Database $SQLDatabase"
-ForegroundColor Green
$_SqlDatabase = @{
ResourceGroupName = $ResourceGroup; ServerName = $SQLServer; DatabaseName
= $SQLDatabase; Edition = $Edition;
};
New-AzSqlDatabase @_SqlDatabase;
}
else
{
Write-Host $notexists -ForegroundColor Yellow
}
```

Get-AzSqlDatabase gets the given Azure SQL Database. If the given Azure SQL Database doesn't exist, an error is returned. The error returned is stored in the **notexists** variable.

New-AzSqlDatabase provisions the new Azure SQL database if the **notexists** variable isn't empty.

12. Copy and paste the following code to add the system's public IP address to the Azure SQL Server firewall rule:

```
$startip = (Invoke-WebRequest http://myexternalip.com/ raw
--UseBasicParsing -ErrorVariable err -ErrorAction SilentlyContinue).
Content.trim()
$endip=$startip
Write-host "Creating firewall rule for $azuresqlservername with StartIP:
$startip and EndIP: $endip " -ForegroundColor Green
$NewFirewallRule = @{ ResourceGroupName = $ResourceGroup; ServerName =
$SQLServer; FirewallRuleName = 'PacktPub'; StartIpAddress = $startip;
EndIpAddress=$endip;
};
New-AzSqlServerFirewallRule @NewFirewallRule;
```

The preceding code first gets the public IP of the system (running this PowerShell script) by calling the http://myexternalip.com/raw website using the **Invoke-WebRequest** command. The link returns the public IP in text format, which is stored in the **$startip** variable.

The IP is then used to create the firewall rule by the name of **PacktPub** using the **New-AzSqlServerFirewallRule** cmdlet.

13. To run the PowerShell script, perform the following steps: Press *Windows* + *R* to open the **Run** command window. Type **PowerShell** and hit *Enter* to open a new PowerShell console window.

14. Change the directory to the folder that has the **shard-toystore.ps1** script. For example, if the script is in the **C:\Code\Chapter01** directory, then run the following command to switch to this directory:

```
cd C:\Code\Chapter01
```

15. In the following command, change the parameter values. Copy the command to the PowerShell console and hit *Enter*:

```
.\ProvisionAzureSQLDatabase.ps1 -ResourceGroup toystore -SQLServer
toyfactory -UserName sqladmin -Password Packt@pub2 -SQLDatabase toystore
-AzureProfileFilePath C:\Code\MyAzureProfile.json
```

The preceding command will create the **toystore** resource group, the **toyfactory** Azure SQL Server, and the **toystore** Azure SQL Database. It'll also create a firewall rule by the name of **PacktPub** with the machine's public IP address.

Exercise: Provisioning an Azure SQL Managed Instance

To provision a managed instance using a PowerShell script, perform the following steps:

1. Create a file called **ProvisionSQLMI.ps1** and add the following code:

```
<#
If you are using Pay-as-you-go subscription, do check the managed instance
cost
#>
param(
[string]$ResourceGroup="Packt-1",
[string]$Location="WestUS",
[string]$vNet="PackvNet-$(Get-Random)",
[string]$misubnet="PackSubnet-$(Get-Random)",
[string]$miname="Packt-$(Get-Random)",
[string]$miadmin="miadmin",
[string]$miadminpassword="CreateYourAdminPassword1",
[string]$miedition="General Purpose",
[string]$mivcores=4,
[string]$mistorage=32,
[string]$migeneration = "Gen5",
[string]$milicense="LicenseIncluded",
[string]$subscriptionid="6ee856b5-yy6d-4bc1-a901-byg5569842e1"
)
```

2. Add the following code for subnet delegation:

```
# Powershell module for subnet delegation
$AznetworkModels = "Microsoft.Azure.Commands.Network.Models"
$Azcollections = "System.Collections.Generic"
```

3. Add the following code to log in to the Azure account:

```
# login to azure

$Account = Connect-AzAccount

if([string]::IsNullOrEmpty($subscriptionid))
{
    $subscriptionid=$Account.Context.Subscription.Id
}
Set-AzContext $subscriptionid
```

4. Add the following code snippet to verify that the resource group exists:

```
# Check if resource group exists
# An error is returned and stored in notexists variable if resource group
exists
Get-AzResourceGroup -Name $ResourceGroup -Location $location
-ErrorVariable notexists -ErrorAction SilentlyContinue
```

5. Provision a resource group:

```
#Provision Azure Resource Group
if(![string]::IsNullOrEmpty($notexists))
{

Write-Host "Provisioning Azure Resource Group $ResourceGroup"
-ForegroundColor Green
$_ResourceGroup = @{
  Name = $ResourceGroup;
  Location = $Location;
  }
New-AzResourceGroup @_ResourceGroup;
}
else
{

Write-Host $notexists -ForegroundColor Yellow
}
```

6. Add the following code to add a virtual network, subnet, network security group, and route table:

```
Write-Host "Provisioning Azure Virtual Network $vNet" -ForegroundColor
Green
$obvnet = New-AzVirtualNetwork -Name $vNet -ResourceGroupName
$ResourceGroup -Location $Location -AddressPrefix "10.0.0.0/16"

Write-Host "Provisioning Managed instance subnet $misubnet"
-ForegroundColor Green

$obmisubnet = Add-AzVirtualNetworkSubnetConfig -Name $misubnet
-VirtualNetwork $obvnet -AddressPrefix "10.0.0.0/24"

$_nsg = "mi-nsg"
$_rt = "mi-rt"

Write-Host "Provisioning Network Security Group $_nsg" -ForegroundColor
Green
$nsg = New-AzNetworkSecurityGroup -Name $_nsg -ResourceGroupName
$ResourceGroup -Location $Location -Force

<#
Routing table is required for a managed instance to connect with Azure
Management Service.
#>
Write-Host "Provisioning Routing table $_rt" -ForegroundColor Green
$routetable = New-AzRouteTable -Name $_rt -ResourceGroupName
$ResourceGroup -Location $Location -Force
```

7. Assign a network security group to the managed instance subnet:

```
#Assign network security group to managed instance subnet
Set-AzVirtualNetworkSubnetConfig '
-VirtualNetwork $obvnet -Name $misubnet '
-AddressPrefix "10.0.0.0/24" -NetworkSecurityGroup $nsg '
-RouteTable $routetable | Set-AzVirtualNetwork

$obvnet = Get-AzVirtualNetwork -Name $vNet -ResourceGroupName
$ResourceGroup
$obmisubnet= $obvnet.Subnets[0]
```

8. Create a subnet delegation for **Microsoft.Sql/managedInstances**:

```
# Create a delegation
Write-Host "Create a subnet delegation" -ForegroundColor Green
$obmisubnet.Delegations = New-Object "$Azcollections.
List''1[$AznetworkModels.PSDelegation]"
$delegationName = "dlManagedInstance" + (Get-Random -Maximum 1000)
$delegation = New-AzDelegation -Name $delegationName -ServiceName
"Microsoft.Sql/managedInstances"
$obmisubnet.Delegations.Add($delegation)

Set-AzVirtualNetwork -VirtualNetwork $obvnet
$misubnetid = $obmisubnet.Id
$allowParameters = @{
    Access = 'Allow'
    Protocol = 'Tcp'
    Direction= 'Inbound'
    SourcePortRange = '*'
    SourceAddressPrefix = 'VirtualNetwork'
    DestinationAddressPrefix = '*'
}
$denyInParameters = @{
    Access = 'Deny'
    Protocol = '*'
    Direction = 'Inbound'
    SourcePortRange = '*'
    SourceAddressPrefix = '*'
    DestinationPortRange = '*'
    DestinationAddressPrefix = '*'
}
$denyOutParameters = @{
    Access = 'Deny'
    Protocol = '*'
    Direction = 'Outbound'
    SourcePortRange = '*'
    SourceAddressPrefix = '*'
    DestinationPortRange = '*'
    DestinationAddressPrefix = '*'
}
```

9. Configure the network rules in the network security group by adding the following code:

```
Write-Host "Configure network rules in network security group"
-ForegroundColor Green

Get-AzNetworkSecurityGroup '
        -ResourceGroupName $ResourceGroup '
        -Name $_nsg |
    Add-AzNetworkSecurityRuleConfig '
        @allowParameters '
        -Priority 1000 '
        -Name "allow_tds_inbound" '
        -DestinationPortRange 1433 |
    Add-AzNetworkSecurityRuleConfig '
        @allowParameters '
        -Priority 1100 '
        -Name "allow_redirect_inbound" '
        -DestinationPortRange 11000-11999 |
    Add-AzNetworkSecurityRuleConfig '
        @denyInParameters '
        -Priority 4096 '
        -Name "deny_all_inbound" |
    Add-AzNetworkSecurityRuleConfig '
        @denyOutParameters '
        -Priority 4096 '
        -Name "deny_all_outbound" |
    Set-AzNetworkSecurityGroup
```

10. Add the following code to create the credential:

```
# Creating credential
Write-Host "Creating credential" -ForegroundColor Green
  $creds = New-Object -TypeName System.Management.Automation.PSCredential
-ArgumentList $miadmin, (ConvertTo-SecureString -String $miadminpassword
-AsPlainText -Force)
```

11. Add the following code to provision an SQL Managed Instance:

```
# Provision managed instance
Write-Host "Provisioning SQL managed instance $miname" -ForegroundColor
Green
New-AzSqlInstance -Name $miname -ResourceGroupName $ResourceGroup
-Location $Location -SubnetId $misubnetid '
                        -AdministratorCredential $creds '
                        -StorageSizeInGB $mistorage -VCore $mivcores
-Edition $miedition '
                        -ComputeGeneration $migeneration -LicenseType
$milicense


<#
Clean-Up : Remove managed instance
Remove-AzSqlInstance -Name $miadmin -ResourceGroupName $ResourceGroup
-Force

#>
```

> **Note**
>
> The PowerShell script is self-explanatory. Review the comments in the script to
> understand what each command is used for.

12. Open a new PowerShell console window. Set the directory to the one containing the **ProvisionSQLMI.ps1** file.

13. Copy and paste the following command in the PowerShell window:

```
.\ProvisionSQLMI.ps1 -subscriptionid 6ee856b5-yy6d-4bc1-a901-byg5569842e1
-ResourceGroup Packt1 -Location westus2 -vNet mi-vnet -misubnet mi-subnet
-miname packtmi -miadmin miadmin -miadminpassword CreateYourAdminPassword1
-miedition "General Purpose" -mivcores 4 -mistorage 32 -migeneration Gen5
-milicense LicenseIncluded
```

You may change the parameter values if you wish to.

> **Note**
>
> If you have more than one subscription, specify the subscription ID in the preceding command for the parameter subscription ID.

This will create a new SQL managed instance with all the required network specifications.

> **Note**
>
> The first instance in an empty subnet takes 4 hours to finish 90% of the operations. To learn more about deployment durations for managed instances, please visit https://docs.microsoft.com/azure/azure-sql/managed-instance/management-operations-overview#duration.

14. Once you are done with the managed instance, execute the following command to delete it:

```
Remove-AzSqlInstance -Name $miadmin -ResourceGroupName $ResourceGroup
-Force
```

This command expects the managed instance name and the resource group to delete that managed instance.

In this exercise, we deployed Azure SQL Managed Instance using PowerShell. We deployed a new virtual network and added a network security group and a route table. We also added subnet delegation for management operations. This approach makes deployment much simpler and can be used to deploy multiple instances in a production environment.

Summary

This chapter was an introduction to the SQL PaaS offering from Microsoft. We learned about the Azure SQL architecture and the different layers that make up the Azure SQL infrastructure.

We also learned about the request flow through the different layers when a user connects to and queries an Azure SQL Database. We learned how to connect to and query a database from SQL Server Management Studio and the Azure portal.

We learned about the Azure SQL Managed Instance connectivity architecture and learned how to provision a managed instance using PowerShell.

Most importantly, the chapter covered the differences between Azure SQL Server, Azure SQL Database, and Azure SQL Managed Instance.

In the next chapter, we will discuss how to migrate data from an on-premises system to an Azure SQL Database and Azure SQL Managed Instance.

Service tiers

Azure provides multiple service (performance) tiers for Azure SQL Database and SQL Managed Instance. There are two purchasing options, the **Database Transaction Unit (DTU)** model and the vCore model. Each purchasing option has multiple service tiers. The purchasing option and service tier define the performance and cost of an SQL managed database. In this chapter, we'll look at the different purchasing options and service tiers and learn how to choose an appropriate starting performance tier when migrating to an SQL managed database.

We will learn about:

- DTUs and the vCore purchasing model

- Different service tier options for SQL Database and SQL Managed Instance

- Using **Data Migration Assistant (DMA)** to get service tier recommendations when migrating an on-premises SQL Server workload to SQL Database and SQL Managed Instance

Let's get started with understanding the DTU model.

The DTU model

In the DTU purchasing option, the amount of resources (CPUs, I/O, RAM, and storage) to be assigned to an SQL database in a particular service tier is calculated in DTUs.

DTUs guarantee that an SQL database will always have a certain amount of resources and a certain level of performance (offered under a particular DTU model) at any given point in time, independent of other SQL databases on the same SQL server or across Microsoft Azure.

The ratio for the aforementioned resources was calculated by Microsoft by running an **Online Transaction Processing (OLTP)** benchmark. One DTU roughly equates to 1 transaction/sec as per the benchmark.

The DTU purchasing model measures performance in DTUs instead of CPU and memory. Each DTU level and service tier provides predictable performance. The higher the DTU, the better the performance.

> **Note**
>
> The DTU purchasing model is not available with SQL Managed Instance.

In the DTU purchasing model, the compute and storage are bundled and priced together. For example, the 10 DTU standard service tier has a fixed storage capacity of 250 GB included within the DTU cost. Any additional storage is charged separately.

DTU service tiers

There are three service tiers available in the DTU-based purchasing option:

- **Basic service tier**: The Basic tier is the lowest tier available and applies to small, infrequently used applications, usually supporting one single active transaction at any given point in time.

The Basic tier has a size limit of 2 GB, a performance limit of 5 DTUs, and costs $5/month:

Basic service tier

Compute size	Basic
Max DTUs	5
Included storage (GB)	2
Max storage (GB)	2
Max in-memory OLTP storage (GB)	N/A
Max concurrent workers (requests)	30
Max concurrent sessions	300

Figure 2.1: Performance statistics for the Basic service tier

- **Standard service tier**: This is the most used service tier and is best for web applications or workgroups with low to medium I/O performance requirements. Unlike the Basic service tier, it has nine different performance levels: S0, S1, S2, S3, S4, S6, S7, S9, and S12. Each performance level offers the same size (250 GB); however, they differ in terms of DTUs and cost. S0, S1, S2, S3, S4, S6, S7, S9, and S12 offer 10, 20, 50, 100, 200, 400, 800, 1,600, and 3,000 DTUs and cost $15, $30, $75, $150, $300, $600, $1,200, $2400, and $4,500 per month, respectively:

Standard service tier

Compute size	S0	S1	S2	S3
Max DTUs	10	20	50	100
Included storage (GB)[1]	250	250	250	250
Max storage (GB)	250	250	250	1024
Max in-memory OLTP storage (GB)	N/A	N/A	N/A	N/A
Max concurrent workers (requests)	60	90	120	200
Max concurrent sessions	600	900	1200	2400

Figure 2.2: Performance statistics for the Standard service tier

Standard service tier (continued)

Compute size	S4	S6	S7	S9	S12
Max DTUs	200	400	800	1600	3000
Included storage (GB)[1]	250	250	250	250	250
Max storage (GB)	1024	1024	1024	1024	1024
Max in-memory OLTP storage (GB)	N/A	N/A	N/A	N/A	N/A
Max concurrent workers (requests)	400	800	1600	3200	6000
Max concurrent sessions	4800	9600	19200	30000	30000

Figure 2.3: Performance statistics for the Standard service tier (continued)

> **Note**
>
> The Basic and Standard S0, S1, and S2 tiers have less than one vCore (CPU). For CPU-intensive workloads, S3 or higher is recommended.

- **Premium service tier**: The Premium service tier is used for mission-critical, high-transaction-volume applications. It supports a large number of concurrent users and has high I/O performance compared to the Basic and Standard service tiers. It provides 25 IOPS per DTU.

It has six different performance levels: P1, P2, P4, P6, P11, and P15. Each performance level offers different sizes and DTUs. P1, P2, P4, P6, P11, and P15 are priced at $465, $930, $1,860, $3,720, $7,001, and $16,003 per month, respectively:

Premium service tier

Compute size	P1	P2	P4	P6	P11	P15
Max DTUs	125	250	500	1000	1750	4000
Included storage (GB)[1]	500	500	500	500	4096[2]	4096[2]
Max storage (GB)	1024	1024	1024	1024	4096[2]	4096[2]
Max in-memory OLTP storage (GB)	1	2	4	8	14	32
Max concurrent workers (requests)	200	400	800	1600	2800	6400
Max concurrent sessions	30000	30000	30000	30000	30000	30000

Figure 2.4: Performance statistics for the Premium service tier

> **Note**
> The prices listed here are for a single database and not for an elastic database pool.

The Premium service tier supports read scale-out and zone redundancy.

Read scale-out, when enabled, routes read queries to a read-only secondary replica. The read-only secondary is of the same compute and storage capacity as the primary replica.

An Availability Zone in an Azure region is an isolated datacenter building. There can be more than one Availability Zone in an Azure region. When opting for the Premium service tier, you can choose for SQL Database to be zone-redundant. This will ensure that a copy of the database is available in another zone within the same region to facilitate high availability.

The zone redundancy feature is available for databases up to 1 TB in size.

The vCore model

The vCore purchasing model decouples compute and storage. The compute is measured in terms of vCore. vCore characteristics such as physical/hyper-threading are defined by hardware generations.

Memory and I/O are defined per vCore and depend on the hardware generation and the service tier. vCore and storage are to be selected separately and are therefore priced separately. The vCore purchasing model also allows the use of existing SQL Server licenses at discounted rates for SQL managed databases under Azure Hybrid Benefit.

When configuring a vCore-based service tier, there are two license types available, `BasePrice` and `LicenseIncluded`.

`BasePrice` offers discounted rates for existing on-premises SQL Server licenses. You only pay for the underlying Azure infrastructure. This is the best option when migrating an on-premises database to SQL Database. `LicenseIncluded` includes the cost of the SQL Server license and Azure infrastructure.

For more details on Azure Hybrid Benefit, please visit https://docs.microsoft.com/ azure/azure-sql/azure-hybrid-benefit?tabs=azure-powershell.

vCore service tiers

There are three service tiers available with the vCore pricing model: General Purpose, Business Critical, and Hyperscale. The Hyperscale service tier is only available with SQL Database, whereas General Purpose and Business Critical are available with both SQL Database and Managed Instance.

The General Purpose service tier

The General Purpose service tier provides balanced compute and memory options and is suitable for most business workloads. It separates compute and storage, and the data and log files are stored in Azure Blob Storage whereas tempdb is stored in a local SSD.

Figure 2.5 shows the architecture model of a General Purpose service tier:

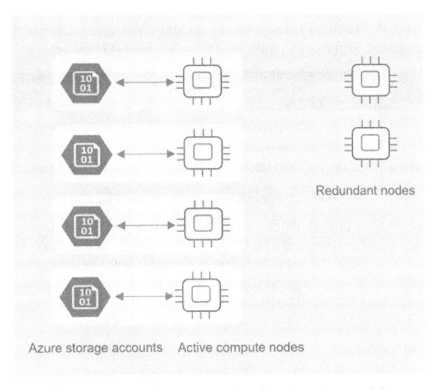

Figure 2.5: General Purpose service tier architecture model

In *Figure* 2.5, these four active compute nodes and two redundant compute nodes are just for illustration—the actual number of redundant nodes is determined by Azure Service Fabric to always deliver 99.99% availability. The active compute nodes have SQL Server installed. They contain transient data, such as the plan cache, buffer pool, and columnstore pool). The compute nodes write to data and log files stored in Blob Storage (premium performance type). The built-in availability and redundancy of Blob Storage make sure that no data loss happens in the event of an SQL Server or compute node crash. Blob Storage provides storage latency of between 5 and 10 milliseconds.

If any of the active compute nodes fail or are being patched, the node fails over to an available redundant node. The data and log files are attached to the new active node, thereby providing 99.99% availability. The failover behavior is similar to what we have in a failover cluster instance configuration.

Azure Premium Storage characteristics

In the SQL Managed Instance General Purpose service tier, every database file gets dedicated IOPS and throughput based on the database file size. Larger files get more IOPS and throughput. Refer to the following table for file I/O characteristics:

File size	>=0 and <=128 GiB	>128 and <= 512 GiB	>0.5 and <=1 TiB	>1 and <=2 TiB	>2 and <=4 TiB	>4 and <=8 TiB
IOPS per file	500	2,300	5,000	7,500	7,500	12,500
Throughput per file	100 MiB/s	150 MiB/s	200 MiB/s	250 MiB/s	250 MiB/s	480 MiB/s

Table 2.1: Premium storage characteristics

If you are noticing slow performance and high I/O latency in SQL Managed Instance, then increasing individual files might improve performance. In the General Purpose tier, you can only have 280 database files per instance. If you are hitting this limit, you might need to consider reducing the number of database files or moving to the Business Critical tier. Though all database files are placed on Azure Premium Storage, **tempdb** database files are stored on a local SSD for a faster response.

The following are some of the workload-related guidelines and best practices for SQL Managed Instance running on the General Purpose tier:

- **Short transactions**: Azure SQL Managed Instance runs on a cloud environment and there could be chances of transient network errors or failover, so you need to be prepared for that. It's best to always run short transactions as they will be quicker to recover.

- **Batch updates**: Always try to run updates in batches rather than running individual updates.

- **Table/index partitioning**: Use table partitioning for better I/O throughput and index partitioning to avoid long-running index maintenance. Partitioning may or may not benefit all workloads and therefore should be tested and then used.

- **Compression/columnstore**: In the General Purpose tier, there is latency between the compute and storage layer. Latency can be reduced by using a compression or columnstore.

The General Purpose service tier is suitable for generic workloads that require a 99.99% uptime SLA and storage latency between 5 and 10 milliseconds.

The Business Critical service tier

The Business Critical service tier has integrated compute and storage. *Figure 2.6* shows a Business Critical service tier architecture:

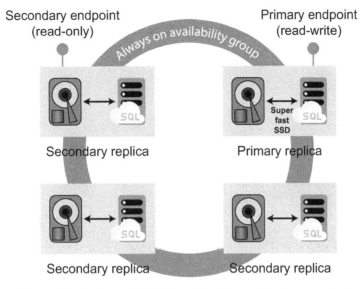

Figure 2.6: Business Critical service tier architecture model

It consists of four replicas in an Always On availability group. There is one primary replica and three secondary replicas. Each replica has local SSD storage to host data files, log files, and **tempdb**. This provides one to two milliseconds of storage latency.

There are two endpoints—the primary endpoint, which is used for read and write, and a secondary read-only endpoint. The read-only endpoint can be used to offload read-only queries to the secondary replica. The read-only endpoint is provided free of cost.

If the primary replica fails, one of the secondary replicas is promoted to the primary replica. Failover is faster than in the General Purpose service tier. When the primary replica recovers, it connects as a new secondary replica.

The Business Critical service tier with a zone-redundant configuration provides 99.995% uptime. It is suitable for workloads that require low I/O latency (one to two milliseconds) and highly available and highly resilient applications (faster failover).

The Hyperscale service tier

The Hyperscale service tier decouples the compute, storage, and log into microservices to provide a highly scalable and highly available service tier.

> **Note**
>
> The Hyperscale service tier isn't available in SQL Managed Instance.

A traditional database server, as shown in *Figure 2.7*, consists of compute (CPU and memory) and storage (data files and log files):

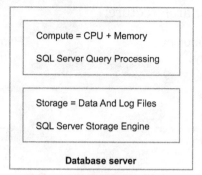

Figure 2.7: Database server architecture

An SQL Server engine is run by three main components: the query processor, the storage engine, and the SQL operating system:

- The query processor does query parsing, optimization, and execution.

- The storage engine serves the data required by the queries and manages the data and log files.

- The SQL operating system is an abstraction over the Windows/Linux operating system that is mainly responsible for task scheduling and memory management.

The Hyperscale service tier takes out the storage engine from the database server and splits it into independent scale-out sets of components, page servers, and a log service, as shown in *Figure 2.8*.

Comparing it with the traditional database server, observe that the data and log files are no longer part of the database server:

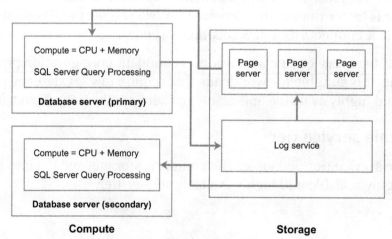

Figure 2.8: Architecture of the Hyperscale service tier

A detailed architecture diagram for the Hyperscale service tier is shown here:

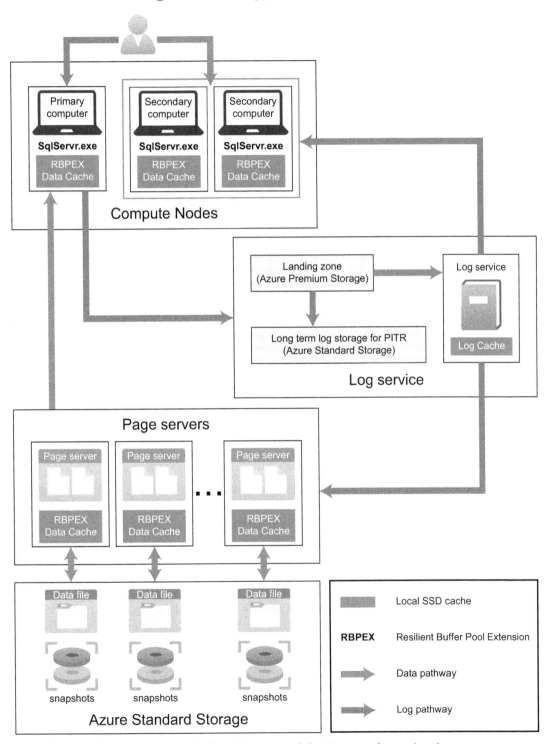

Figure 2.9: Detailed architecture of the Hyperscale service tier

The different Hyperscale service tier components are explained here:

- **Compute nodes**: A compute node is an SQL Server without the data files and the log files. Compute nodes are similar to the SQL Server query processor, responsible for query parsing, optimization, and execution. Users and applications connect and interact with the compute nodes.

  Each compute node has a local data cache, a non-covering data cache—the **Resilient Buffer Pool Extension** (**RBPEX**).

  > **Note**
  >
  > The RBPEX is an SQL Server feature that allows SSDs to be used as an extension of the buffer pool (server memory or RAM). With an RBPEX, data can be cached to extended buffers (SSDs), thereby decreasing physical disk reads and increasing I/O throughput.

  The primary compute node takes user and application transactions and writes them to the log service landing zone. If the data requested by a query isn't available in the primary node's buffer pool or its local **RBPEX cache**, it reads or requests the missing data from the page servers.

  The secondary compute nodes are used to offload reads from the primary compute node. The Hyperscale tier offers four secondary replicas for read scale-out, high availability, and disaster recovery. Each replica has the same vCore model as the primary replica and is charged separately. You connect to a secondary replica by specifying `ApplicationIntent` as `ReadOnly` in the connection string.

  Each secondary replica, similar to the case with the primary node, has a local cache (RBPEX). When a read request is received by a secondary replica, it first checks for the data in the buffer pool, then the local RBPEX cache, and then the page servers.

  When the primary compute node goes down, failover happens to a secondary node, and one of the secondary nodes promotes itself to a primary node and starts accepting read-write transactions. A replacement secondary node is provisioned and warms up.

  No action needs to be taken at the storage level as the compute nodes are separate from the storage. This is contrary to regular SQL Server architecture, where a database hosts the SQL Server engine and the storage, as explained earlier in this section. If the database server goes down, the storage (that is, the data files and the log files) also goes down.

- **Page server node**: The page server node is where the database data files are. Each page server node manages 1 TB of data and represents one data file. The data from each page server node is persisted on a standard storage account. This makes it possible to rebuild a page server from the data in a standard storage account in the event of a failure. Therefore, there's no loss of data.

  The page servers get the data modifications from the log service and apply them to the data files. Each page server node has its own local cache (RPBEX). The data is fully cached in the page server local cache to avoid any data requests being forwarded to the standard storage account. A database can have one or more pages of server nodes depending on its size. As the database grows in size, a new page server is automatically added if the existing page server is 80% full. The Hyperscale service tier, for now, supports databases up to 100 TB in size.

- **Log service node**: The log service node is the new transaction log and is again separated from the compute nodes. The log service node gets the log records from the primary node, in the landing zone, which is an Azure Premium Storage account. An Azure Premium Storage account has built-in high availability, which prevents the loss of any log records. It persists log records from the landing zone to a durable log cache.

  It also forwards log records to the secondary compute nodes and the page server nodes. It writes the log records to long-term log storage, which is an Azure Standard Storage account. The long-term log storage is used for point-in-time recovery. When the log records are written to long-term storage, they are deleted from the landing zone to free up space.

  The log records are kept in long-term log storage for the duration of the backup retention period that has been configured for the database. No transaction log backups are needed.

  There's no hot standby for a log service node because it's not required. The log records are persisted first in an Azure Premium Storage account, which has its own high-availability provision, and then in an Azure Standard Storage account.

The Hyperscale service tier, with this improved architecture, offers the following benefits:

- Nearly instantaneous backups. A backup is taken by taking a snapshot of the file in an Azure Standard Storage account. The snapshot process is fast and takes less than 10 minutes to back up a 50 TB database.

- Similar to database backups, database restores are also based on file snapshots and are a lot faster than in any other performance tier.

- Higher log throughput and faster transaction commits, regardless of data volumes:

  - The primary replica does not need to wait for an acknowledgment-of-transaction commit from the secondary replica. This is because the transaction log is managed by a log service.

  - Supports up to 100 TB database size.

  - Rapid read scale-out by creating read replicas.

  Note

  For details on resource limits for different service tiers, please visit https://docs. microsoft.com/azure/azure-sql/database/service-tiers-vcore?tabs=azure-portal.

The Hyperscale service tier is suitable for applications with large databases (over 4 TB in size and up to 100 TB), 1- to 10-millisecond storage latency, and instant backup and restore requirements, as well as for applications with a smaller database size requiring faster, and vertical and horizontal, compute scaling.

vCore hardware generations

Hardware generations apply only to the vCore purchasing option and define the compute and memory resources. There are three hardware generations for different types of workloads:

- **Gen5** offers up to 80 logical CPUs, based on Intel E5-2573 v4 (Broadwell) and 2.3 GHz processors, with 5.1 GB per core and fast eNVM SSD. Gen5 offers more compute scalability with 80 logical CPUs.

- **Fsv2-series** is for high-compute workloads and provides a faster CPU with a clock speed of 3.4 GHz to 3.7 GHz. The maximum memory is limited to 136 GB with 1.9 GB of memory per vCore.

- **M-series** is for high-memory workloads with a max memory of 3.7 TB and 29 GB of memory per vCore. M-series is available only in the Business Critical service tier.

For details on compute and memory specifications, please visit https://docs.microsoft. com/azure/azure-sql/database/service-tiers-vcore?tabs=azure-portal.

> **Note**
>
> SQL Managed Instance only supports Gen5 hardware generation at the time of writing this book.

An SQL workload can be categorized as a balanced, compute, or memory-optimized workload. Hardware generation makes it easier to map an on-premises workload to Azure SQL Database during migration. We can find out which category the on-premises workload belongs in and then choose the relevant hardware generation in Azure SQL.

Determining an appropriate performance tier

As an SQL Server DBA, when migrating to Azure SQL Database, you will need to have an initial estimate of DTUs so as to assign an appropriate service tier to Azure SQL Database. An appropriate service tier will ensure that you meet most of your application performance goals. Estimating a lower or a higher service tier will result in decreased performance or increased cost, respectively.

This section teaches you how to use DMA to make an appropriate initial estimate of the service tier. You can, at any time, change your service tier by monitoring SQL Database's performance once it's up and running.

DMA SKU recommendation

DMA is a free tool from Microsoft to facilitate migration from SQL Server (on-premises or IaaS) to SQL Database. It can assess the source database to list out the compatibility issues between SQL Server and SQL Database. Once you fix the compatibility issues, you can use it to migrate the schema and data to SQL Database.

It also helps with recommendations to select a starting service tier and SKU. To get recommendations, we first need to run a PowerShell script to collect the required performance counters. It's advised to run the script for at least two hours at different times and ensure we collect counters at peak business hours.

The activity requires DMA to be installed on your machine. You can download it here: https://www.microsoft.com/download/details.aspx?id=53595.

To get recommendations using DMA for the **toystore** database, perform the following steps:

1. Open ~/**Chapter02/DMA/RunWorkload.bat** in Notepad. You should see the following code:

    ```
    CD "C:\Program Files\Microsoft Corporation\RMLUtils"
    ostress -SXENA\sql2016 -E -dtoystore -Q"Execute usp_Workload" -n10
    -r100000 -q
    @echo off
    Pause
    ```

    Modify the **RMLUtils** directory location if required. Change the **ostress** parameter to point to the **toystore** database in your local environment.

    Save and close the file.

    Double-click on the file to run the workload.

2. Open ~/**Chapter02/DMA/RunSKURecommendation.bat**. You should see the following code:

    ```
    cd "C:\Program Files\Microsoft Data Migration Assistant\"
    powershell.exe -File .\SkuRecommendationDataCollectionScript.
    ps1 -ComputerName XENA -OutputFilePath "C:\Professional-Azure-
    SQL-Database-Administration-Third-Edition\Chapter02\DMA\Counter.
    csv" -CollectionTimeInSeconds 7200 -DbConnectionString "Server=XENA\
    SQL2016;Initial Catalog=master;Integrated Security=SSPI;"
    ```

    The preceding command runs the DMA **SkuRecommendationDataColletionScript.ps1** PowerShell script to collect the required counters. The script is available at the DMA installation location.

    Modify the parameter values to point the script to your SQL Server environment.

    Save and close the file.

    Double-click **RunSKURecommendation.batch** to run the **sku** counter collection script.

    The script will run for the time specified by the **CollectionTimeInSeconds** parameter and will write the counter values to the file specified by the **OutputFilePath** parameter.

To get more appropriate recommendations, it's advised you collect counters for at least two hours. You can also collect counters at different times of the day and generate recommendations to get the best results.

When the **sku** collection script completes successfully, a file named **counter.csv** is generated at the **~/chapter02/DMA** location.

3. Open **~/Chapter02/DMA/GetSKURecommendation.batch**. You should see the following code:

```
cd "C:\Program Files\Microsoft Data Migration Assistant"
.\DmaCmd.exe /Action=SkuRecommendation /
SkuRecommendationInputDataFilePath="C:\Professional-Azure-SQL-
Database-Administration-Third-Edition\Chapter02\DMA\Counter.
csv" /SkuRecommendationOutputResultsFilePath="C:\Professional-
Azure-SQL-Database-Administration-Third-Edition\Chapter02\DMA\
SKURecommedation.html" /SkuRecommendationPreventPriceRefresh=true /
SkuRecommendationTsvOutputResultsFilePath=C:\Professional-Azure-SQL-
Database-Administration-Third-Edition\Chapter02\DMA\SKURecommedation.tsv"
@echo off
Pause
```

The preceding command uses the DMA CLI command to generate recommendations. Provide the path to **counter.csv** in *step 2* to the **SKURecommendationInputDataFilePath** parameter.

Copy and save the results.

When run, the command will generate an **html** and **tsv** recommendation output file.

Double-click the **GetSKURecommendation.batch** file to generate the recommendations.

The recommendation script will generate **skurecommendation_SQL_DB** html and **tsv** files with recommendations for Azure SQL Database. It also generates similar files for SQL Managed Instance.

Figure 2.10 is a snapshot of the **skurecommendation_sql_db.html** file:

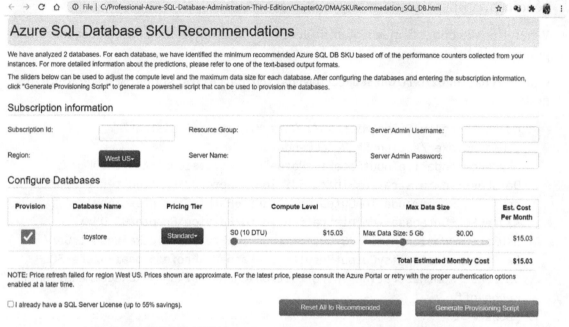

Figure 2.10: DMA SKU recommendations for SQL Managed Instance

Observe that it recommends using the General Purpose pricing tier with 8 vCores. You can select the pricing tier from the **Pricing Tier** drop-down menu.

4. The **tsv** file contains the reasons for considering or not considering a particular performance tier:

Figure 2.11: DMA SKU recommendation—tsv file

The DMA makes it easy to choose a starting service tier when migrating an existing on-premises SQL Server workload to an SQL managed database. Once we migrate the database to the selected service tier, we need to further test the application performance against the service tier and scale up or scale down as per the required performance.

Azure SQL Database compute tiers

There are two compute tiers, provisioned and serverless.

In the **provisioned compute tier**, the resources (vCores) are pre-allocated and can be changed by manually scaling to a different service tier as and when required. The provisioned compute tier cost is calculated per hour based on the number of vCores configured. The provisioned compute tier is suitable for scenarios with consistent and regular workloads.

In the **serverless compute** tier, compute resources for databases are automatically scaled based on workload demand and are billed based on the amount of compute used per second. The serverless compute tier also provides an option to automatically pause the database during inactive usage periods, when only storage is billed, and then automatically resume databases when activity returns. The serverless compute tier is price performance-optimized for single databases with intermittent, unpredictable usage patterns that can afford some delay in compute warm-up after low or idle usage periods.

Scaling up the Azure SQL Database service tier

In this section, we'll learn how to scale up the SQL Database service tier for better performance. Let's go back to our example of Mike, who observes that there is an increase in the load on the SQL database. To overcome this problem, he plans to change the service tier for the database so that it can handle the overload. This can be achieved via the following steps:

1. Open a new PowerShell console. In the PowerShell console, execute the following command to create a new SQL database from a **bacpac** file:

   ```
   C:\Code\Chapter02\ImportAzureSQLDB.ps1
   ```

2. Provide the SQL server name, SQL database name, SQL Server administrator user and password, **bacpac** file path, and **sqlpackage.exe** path, as shown in *Figure 2.12*:

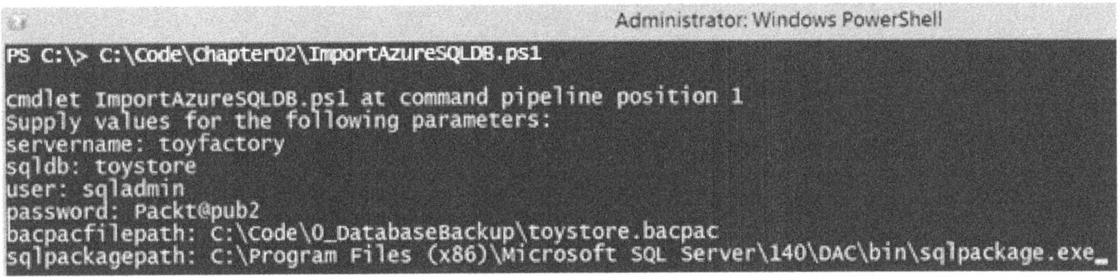

```
                                        Administrator: Windows PowerShell
PS C:\> C:\Code\Chapter02\ImportAzureSQLDB.ps1

cmdlet ImportAzureSQLDB.ps1 at command pipeline position 1
Supply values for the following parameters:
servername: toyfactory
sqldb: toystore
user: sqladmin
password: Packt@pub2
bacpacfilepath: C:\Code\0_DatabaseBackup\toystore.bacpac
sqlpackagepath: C:\Program Files (x86)\Microsoft SQL Server\140\DAC\bin\sqlpackage.exe_
```

Figure 2.12: The Windows PowerShell window

The script will use **sqlpackage.exe** to import the **bacpac** file as a new SQL database on the given SQL server. The database is created in the Basic service tier, as specified in the PowerShell script.

It may take 10 to 15 minutes to import the SQL database.

3. Open **C:\Code\Chapter02\ExecuteQuery.bat** in Notepad. It contains the following commands:

```
ostress -Sazuresqlservername.database.windows.net -Uuser
-Ppassword -dazuresqldatabase -Q"SELECT * FROM Warehouse.StockItems si
join Warehouse.StockItemholdings sh on si.StockItemId=sh.StockItemID join
Sales.OrderLines ol on ol.StockItemID = si.StockItemID" -n25 -r20 -1
```

4. Replace **azuresqlservername**, **user**, **password**, and **azuresqldatabase** with the appropriate values. For example, if you are running the preceding command against SQL Database with **toystore** hosted on the **toyfactory** SQL server with the username **sqladmin** and the password **Packt@pub2**, then the command will be as follows:

```
ostress -Stoyfactory.database.windows.net -Usqladmin -PPackt@pub2
-dtoystore -Q"SELECT * FROM Warehouse.StockItems si join Warehouse.
StockItemholdings sh on si.StockItemId=sh.StockItemID join Sales.
OrderLines ol on ol.StockItemID = si.StockItemID" -n25
-r20 -q
```

The command will run 25 (specified by the **-n25** parameter) concurrent sessions, and each session will execute the query (specified by the **-Q** parameter) 20 times.

5. Open the RML command prompt, enter the following command, and press *Enter*:

```
C:\Code\Chapter02\ExecuteQuery.bat
```

This will run the **OSTRESS** command. Wait for the command to finish executing. Record the execution time:

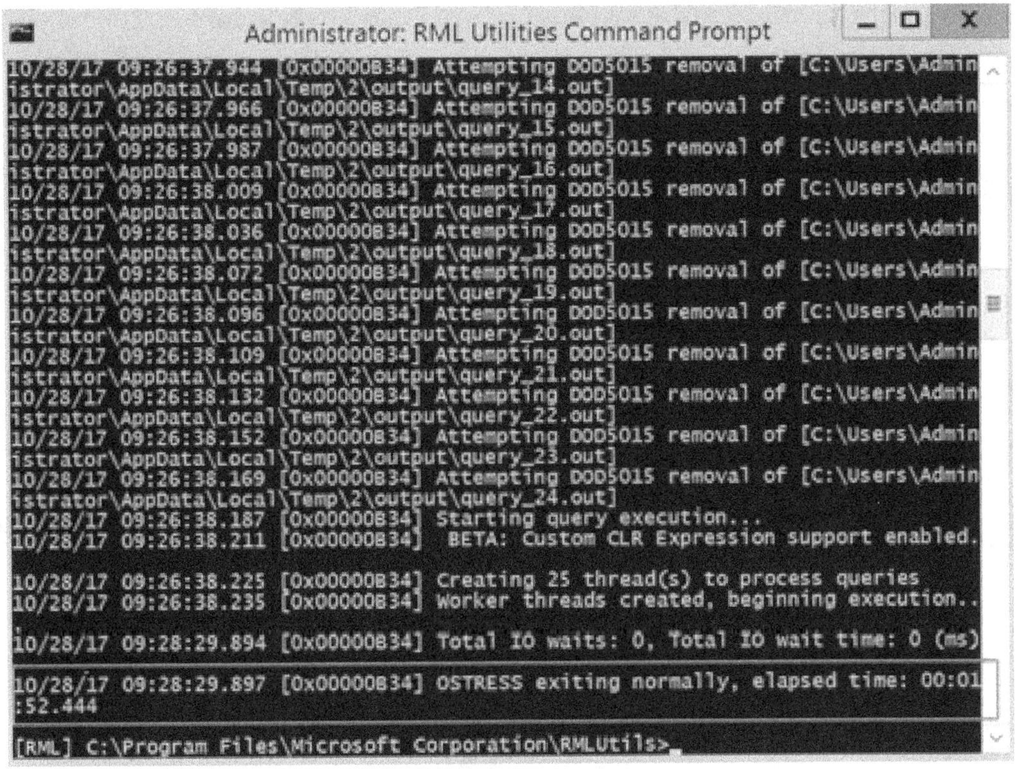

Figure 2.13: RML command prompt

As you can see, it took around 1 minute and 52 seconds to run 25 concurrent connections against the Basic service tier.

6. The next step is to scale up the service tier from **Basic** to **Standard S3**. In the PowerShell console, execute the following command:

```
C:\Code\Chapter02\ScaleUpAzureSQLDB.ps1
```

Provide the parameters as shown in *Figure 2.14*:

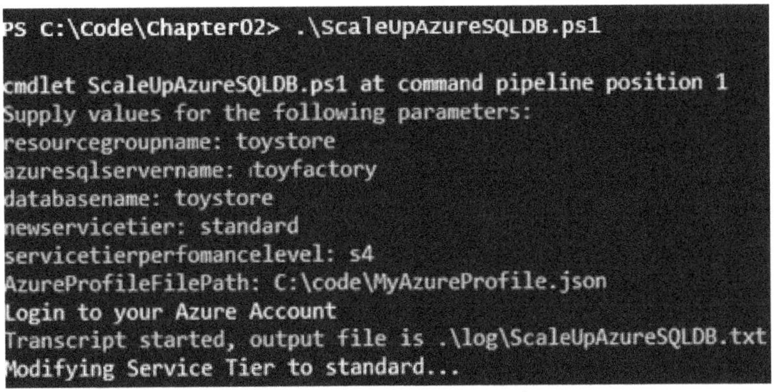

Figure 2.14: Scaling up the service tier

Observe that the database edition has been changed to **standard**.

7. Open a new RML command prompt and run the same **OSTRESS** command as in *step* 5. You should see a faster query execution time in the **Standard S3** tier than in the **Basic** tier.

Here's the output from the **ExecuteQuery.bat** command:

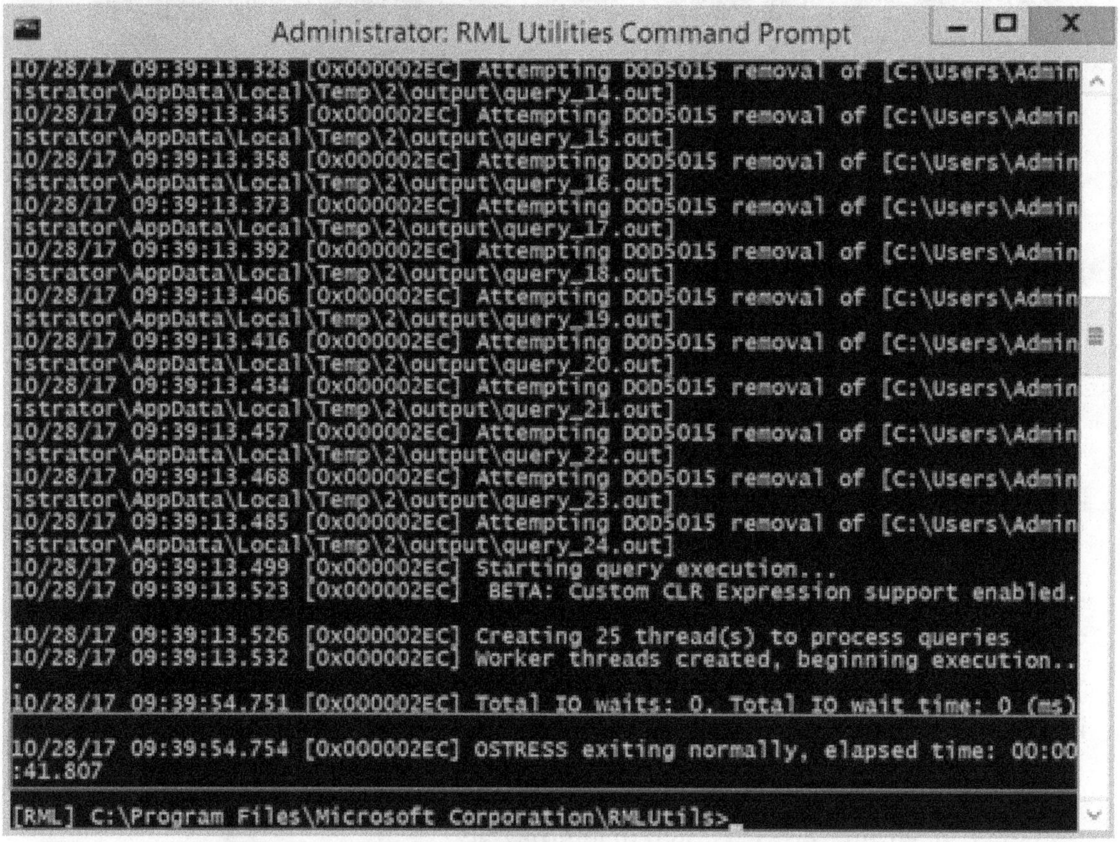

Figure 2.15: Output from the ExecuteQuery.bat command

It took around 42 seconds to run 25 concurrent connections against the **Standard S3** service tier. This is almost 60% faster than the Basic tier. You get the performance improvement just by scaling up the service tier, without any query or database optimization.

Changing a service tier

You can scale up or scale down SQL Database at any point in time. This gives the flexibility to save money by scaling down to a lower service tier in off-peak hours and scaling up to a higher service tier for better performance in peak hours.

You can change a service tier either manually or automatically. Service tier change is performed by creating a replica of the original database at the new service tier performance level. The time taken to change the service tier depends on the size as well as the service tier of the database before and after the change.

Once the replica is ready, the connections are switched over to the replica. This ensures that the original database is available for applications during the service tier change. This also causes all in-flight transactions to be rolled back during the brief period when the switch to the replica is made. The average switchover time is four seconds, and it may increase if there are a large number of in-flight transactions.

You may have to add retry logic in the application to manage connection disconnect issues when changing a service tier.

Exercise: Provisioning a Hyperscale SQL database using PowerShell

In this section, we'll provision a Hyperscale SQL database using PowerShell:

1. Open a new PowerShell console window and change the working directory to **C:\ Code\Chapter02**. Enter and execute the following PowerShell command:

    ```
    .\ProvisionAzureSQLDatabase.ps1 -ResourceGroup RGPackt -Location "East US
    2" -SQLServer sshsserver -SQLDatabase toystore -Edition Hyperscale
    ```

    The preceding command calls the **ProvisionAzureSQLDatabase.ps1** script to provision a new Hyperscale SQL database, **toystore**.

    > **Note**
    >
    > Change the **SQLServer** and **SQLDatabase** parameter values to avoid getting a **Server/Database already exists** error.

2. Once the script completes, log in to the Azure portal and click **All resources** in the left navigation pane.

3. Click **toystore** to open the details window:

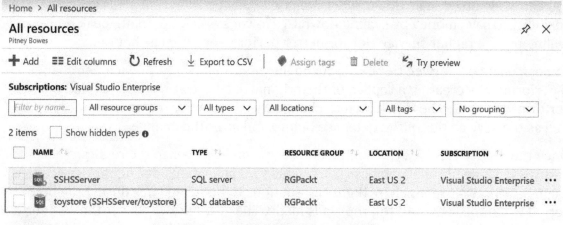

Figure 2.16: The All resources panel

The pricing tier is **Hyperscale, Gen4, 1 vCore**:

Figure 2.17: The Configure pane for the toystore SQL database

In this exercise, we provisioned an SQL database with the Hyperscale service tier. The Hyperscale service tier is costly and it's advised to delete the database if it's created as part of the exercise.

Choosing between vCore and DTU-based purchasing options

When choosing between vCore and DTU-based pricing tiers, consider the following:

Licensing

The vCore pricing model provides up to 30% cost savings by using existing on-premises SQL Server Standard or Enterprise licenses with software assurance. Therefore, if you are migrating an existing on-premises SQL Server infrastructure, consider opting for the vCore pricing model.

Flexibility

The DTU-based model bundles the compute, IOPs, and storage under DTUs and provides a pre-configured range of varying DTU amounts for different types of workloads. It's therefore best suited for when you need a simple pre-configured option.

The vCore model provides flexibility when selecting compute and storage options and is therefore best when you want more transparency and control over the compute and storage options.

Consider a scenario where you have a database with high compute requirements and low storage requirements; say, 125 DTUs with a database size of 200 GB. You'll have to opt for the Premium service tier and pay for the unused storage (300 GB):

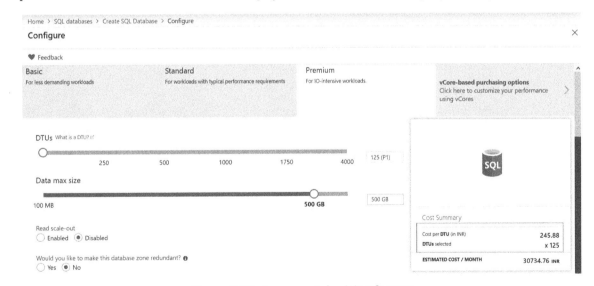

Figure 2.18: Azure portal pricing feature

Figure 2.18 is from the Azure portal and shows the pricing options for a Premium DTU-based tier. Observe that the pricing is calculated per DTU. The storage cost is inclusive of the DTUs. Therefore, in this instance, you will pay for all 500 GB of storage, even if it's not used.

In a vCore model, the compute and storage costs are calculated independently. Therefore, you only pay for the storage you use, which is 200 GB, and the vCores used:

> **Note**
>
> The Premium service tier includes 500 GB of free storage. An additional cost of approximately $0.16 is applied to additional storage (beyond 500 GB) up to 1 TB.

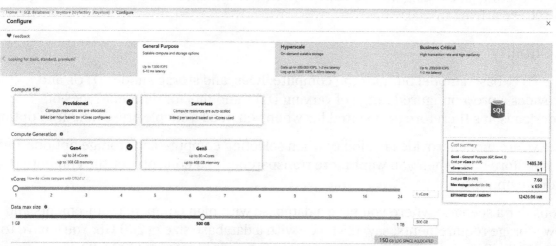

Figure 2.19: General Purpose vCore pricing model

Figure 2.19 is from the Azure portal and shows the pricing options for the General Purpose vCore pricing model. Observe that the pricing is calculated per vCore and per GB of storage used. Therefore, you pay for the storage you use. You can, however, scale the storage up or down at any time, as per your requirements.

Consider another scenario, where a team is just starting up with a product and is looking for an SQL database pricing tier; a Standard S2 or S3 tier with 50 to 100 DTUs and a maximum of 250 GB would be a good option to go for. As the product matures and the scalability requirements become clear, the team can scale up accordingly.

> **Note**
>
> Once you move to the Hyperscale service tier, you can't move to any other service tier.

You can scale between vCore-based and DTU-based service tiers. When scaling from DTU- to vCore-based pricing tiers, consider the following rule of thumb for choosing the correct compute size: **100 Standard tier DTUs = 1 vCore in the General Purpose tier** and **125 Premium tier DTUs = 1 vCore in the Business Critical tier**

Summary

Azure SQL Database and SQL Managed Instance have different purchasing options and service tiers to support varying workloads. SQL Database has two purchase options, DTU and vCore, while SQL Managed Instance is only available with the vCore model. The DTU purchasing option measures performance in DTUs. A DTU hides the complexity of measuring performance in terms of CPU and memory and provides a simple way of measuring performance. It's good for teams that don't have specialized DBAs and for new databases/applications where we don't have historical performance metrics for the database.

The vCore model is more similar to an on-premises SQL Server wherein we get to choose compute (vCore) and storage separately. It's best for teams with specialized DBAs and for migrating on-premises workloads to Azure (where we have historical performance metrics for the database).

We also looked at different service tiers for each purchasing model and underlaying architecture model differences and use cases.

We learned how to use DMA to get SKU recommendations when migrating an on-premises SQL workload to SQL Database or SQL Managed Instance.

In the next chapter, we'll learn about techniques and considerations to migrate an on-premises SQL Server database to Azure SQL managed database offerings.

3

Migration

Migrating existing on-premises SQL Server databases is an important task to be carried out by DBAs when moving applications to Azure. DBAs need to work closely with the application team to understand the requirements and prepare a migration path. A migration path can be used to migrate all of the application databases or to split the application into multiple individual microservices and migrate data relevant to the modules.

Irrespective of the migration path, you'll have to choose between Azure SQL Database and Azure SQL Managed Instance, along with an appropriate performance tier. You need to know about the tools and options to copy data and schema from on-premises to Azure.

In this chapter, you'll learn how to find and fix compatibility issues, determine an appropriate service tier, figure out a migration strategy and tool, and migrate to the cloud.

By the end of this chapter, you will be able to:

- Choose between Azure SQL Database and SQL Managed Instance
- Select a service tier for your migrated Azure SQL Database based on your needs
- **Database Transaction Units** (**DTUs**) and vCore purchasing models
- Identify and fix SQL Server to Azure SQL Database compatibility issues
- Migrate from an on-premises database to Azure SQL Database using different tools

Migration methodology

Migrating an on-premises SQL Server database is an important task and should be planned to perfection. An ideal migration methodology should be like the one shown in *Figure 3.1*:

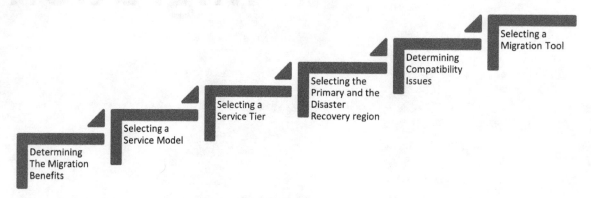

Figure 3.1: Migration methodology

We will discuss each of these steps now.

Determining the migration benefits

You should first identify and analyze the benefits of migrating an on-premises SQL database to Azure SQL Database. Migration involves a lot of time, effort, and cost, and it shouldn't be done just for the sake of having a cloud database.

Selecting a service model

The next step is to decide whether the database will be deployed individually, in an elastic pool, or as an SQL Managed Instance. This is important as the service model will affect the overall pricing, service tier, performance, and management of the database.

Selecting a service tier

The next step is to find an appropriate service tier and performance level for Azure SQL Database. This is important as it will directly affect the performance of an Azure SQL Database. A too-low service tier will result in bad performance, and a too-high service tier will result in unnecessary cost.

In *Chapter 2, Service tiers*, we learned about different service tiers available with Azure SQL Database. We also learned how to use Data Migration Assistant to get recommendations for an appropriate starting tier to use when migrating an on-premises workload to Azure SQL Database.

Selecting the primary region and disaster recovery region

The next step is to find the primary region and the disaster recovery region for your Azure SQL database. It's advisable to have the database in a region that will provide fast connectivity to your users.

Determining compatibility issues

The next step is to find out about any compatibility issues that may stop you from migrating to Azure SQL Database. In *Chapter 1, Introduction to Azure SQL managed databases*, we learned about the differences between SQL Server (on-premises and SQL Server on Azure Virtual Machines) and the features not supported in Azure SQL Database and SQL Managed Instance. It is important to find out the compatibility issues and re-write the application if required. For example, if your application has cross-database queries, which aren't supported in Azure SQL Database, you'll need to rewrite the application to use a workaround in order to move to Azure SQL Database, or choose SQL Managed Instance as the target, which supports cross-database queries.

Selecting a migration tool

Microsoft provides various tools to automate database migration. You can also write PowerShell or C# scripts to automate the database migration process. The best tool to choose largely depends on the database's size and the downtime SLA.

Before we perform any migration, however, we ought to consider whether we want to migrate to Azure SQL Database or SQL Managed Instance.

Choosing between Azure SQL Database and SQL Managed Instance

Azure SQL Database and SQL Managed Instance both offer the benefits of the **Platform-as-a-Service (PaaS)** model, in which the user doesn't manage the underlying hardware, software upgrades, and operating system configuration. The user therefore saves on the administrative cost of managing the platform.

These two deployments (SQL Database and SQL Managed Instance) provide additional services such as automated backups, Query Performance Insight (not available in SQL Managed Instance), Azure Defender for SQL, high availability, and disaster recovery. Each of the two deployments, therefore, provides a ready-to-use database for new or existing applications.

The two deployment options have common performance tiers, with Azure SQL Database now supporting the vCore pricing tiers.

With the two options each having similar sets of features, you should consider the following aspects when choosing between Azure SQL Database and Azure Managed Instance:

- Features
- Migration constraints
- Time to develop and market

Let's go over all of them now in detail.

Features

As mentioned in *Chapter 1, Introduction to Azure SQL managed databases*, in the *Introduction to Managed Instance* section, managed instances provide near 100% surface area compatibility and support almost all of the on-premises SQL Server features.

On the other hand, Azure SQL Database doesn't support some of the important on-premises features, such as **Common Language Runtime** (SQL **CLR**), global temporary tables, SQL Server Agent, cross-database queries, and log shipping (for a complete list, see the *Unsupported Features* section in *Chapter 1, Introduction to Azure SQL managed databases*).

Therefore, if you are looking to use any of the features not supported in Azure SQL Database, you should opt for SQL Managed Instance.

An especially important feature to consider is cross-database queries. If you have an application with two or more databases that performs cross-database queries, it's better to opt for SQL Managed Instance.

> **Note**
>
> For a list of features not supported by SQL Managed Instance, please visit https://docs.microsoft.com/azure/azure-sql/database/features-comparison.

Migration

An SQL Managed Instance provides speedy migration with little to no downtime, as it's almost 100% compatible with on-premises SQL Server features.

As you prepare to migrate and determine database compatibility issues, with SQL Managed Instance there will be zero or minimal migration constraints compared to those associated with Azure SQL Database.

Time to develop and market

Azure SQL Database provides fast database deployment for a team with limited database expertise and development and deployment time constraints. With DTU- or vCore-based pricing, a team can easily provision an Azure SQL Database and start the application development. As the application takes shape and the database and scalability requirements become clearer, the Azure SQL Database can easily be scaled to a higher DTU-based pricing tier or vCore pricing tier. Azure SQL Database's Serverless compute tier makes it easy to provision a test and development database without worrying about the cost. The Azure SQL Server database pauses automatically if there's no activity for the duration as specified by auto-pause delay. This makes Azure SQL Database serverless a good choice for a development database.

On the other hand, if a team migrates an existing application from an on-premises SQL Server, SQL Managed Instance provides fast and easy cloud migration with minimal application changes being required.

When opting for SQL Managed Instance for new applications, you need to choose the compute and storage resources in the vCore pricing tier. If a team doesn't have database expertise or clear compute and storage requirements, a DTU-based pricing model proves to be the best fit.

Tools for determining compatibility issues

Once you have chosen which deployment to use and determined the starting service tier, the next step is to migrate both schema and data from the on-premises SQL database to the Azure SQL Database. As we learned in *Chapter 1, Introduction to Azure SQL managed databases*, not all features are the same or supported on Azure SQL Server. Therefore, you will first have to do a compatibility test or assessment to find and fix the compatibility issues.

The following are the available tools for detecting compatibility issues. Although these tools can be used to migrate the database, in this section, we'll specifically talk about using them to assess compatibility.

Data Migration Assistant

Data Migration Assistant (DMA) is a standalone tool for detecting compatibility issues and migrating on-premises SQL Server databases to Azure SQL databases. It provides a wizard-like easy-to-use graphical user interface for compatibility assessment and migration. DMA detects and highlights compatibility issues. Once all compatibility issues are identified and fixed, you can migrate the database.

SQL Server Data Tools (SSDT) for Visual Studio

SSDT is the best tool for Azure SQL Database (V12) to find and fix incompatibility issues; it has the most recent compatibility rules. The compatibility issues can be fixed from SSDT itself, after which we can migrate the database.

SQL Server Management Studio (SSMS)

SSMS has two options to detect and migrate:

- **Export Data Tier Application**: This exports the data and schema in a `bacpac` file and, while doing so, lists out any of the incompatibilities found.

- **Deploy Database to Microsoft Azure SQL Database**: This deploys the database to Azure SQL Database, by first exporting the database in a `bacpac` file and then importing the `bacpac` file into Azure SQL Database. It lists incompatibilities when generating the `bacpac` file.

SQLPackage.exe

This is a command-line tool that helps to automate database development tasks such as importing, exporting, and extracting **bacpac** or **dacpac** files. Its actual use is to help automate database life cycle management; however, it can be used to detect and get a report of the incompatibilities found.

It is included in SSDT. You can download a different version of SSDT from here: https://docs.microsoft.com/sql/ssdt/download-sql-server-data-tools-ssdt?view=sql-server-2017.

Azure Database Migration Services

Azure **Database Migration Services**, or **DMS**, is a fully managed Azure service that enables seamless migrations from multiple data sources to Azure databases. We will be using Azure DMS in various activities throughout this chapter.

Here are some examples of migrations that DMS can do:

- Migrate an on-premises SQL Server to Azure SQL Database or SQL Managed Instance. Supports both online (zero downtime) and offline migrations

- Migrate Azure SQL Database to SQL Managed Instance

- Migrate an AWS SQL Server RDS instance to Azure SQL Database or SQL Managed Instance

- Migrate MySQL to Azure Database for MySQL

- Migrate PostgreSQL to Azure Database for PostgreSQL

- Migrate MongoDB to Azure Cosmos DB Mongo API

- Migrate an Oracle database to Azure Database for PostgreSQL

Choosing a migration tool and performing migration

Once you have found and fixed compatibility issues, the next step is to select a migration tool or method and perform the actual migration. There are different methods available for various scenarios. The selection largely depends on downtime, database size, and network speed/quality.

Here's a comparison of various migration methods to help you correctly choose a migration method:

Migration Method	Description	Downtime	Recommendations
SQL Server Management Studio - deploy database to Azure SQL Database	Wizard-based GUI for exporting an on-premises database to bacpac and importing the bacpac into Azure SQL Database. This only applies to Azure SQL Database.	Yes	Best to quickly deploy test/ development databases to Azure SQL Database.
SQLPackage. exe	Command-line utility for exporting an on-premises database to bacpac and importing the bacpac to Azure SQL Database. It can be used to migrate a database to Azure SQL Database and Managed Instance.	Yes	Uses parallel bcp when importing data into an Azure SQL Database. Suitable for production and development/test database migration.
Data Migration Assistant	Free wizard-based GUI tool from Microsoft. Detects and lists compatibility issues. Uses T-SQL scripts for schema migration and bcp to copy data. Option to choose database objects to migrate. It can be used to migrate a database to Azure SQL Database and Managed Instance.	Yes	Recommended for production, development, and test database migration.
Transactional replication	Azure SQL Database as a subscriber to an on-premises (SQL Server 2012 onward) SQL Server Publisher. Use the transaction replication filtering feature to migrate selective data. It can be used to migrate a database to Azure SQL Database and Managed Instance.	Near-zero downtime. In-process transactions may be affected when switching the application connection from on-premises to Azure SQL Database. However, this can be managed using retry logic in the application.	Recommended for zero-downtime production migration.
Azure Database Migration Service	Fully managed service to migrate schema and data. Incurs additional cost. Supports migration from heterogeneous databases. It can be used to migrate a database to Azure SQL Database and Managed Instance.	Near-zero downtime. In-process transactions may be affected when switching an application connection from on-premises to Azure SQL Database. However, this can be managed using retry logic in the application.	Recommended for zero-downtime production migration.

Table 3.1: Determining the migration method

Now for some activities that will show you how to perform migrations using a variety of the tools we have just discussed. In the following activities, we will:

- Migrate an on-premises SQL database to Azure SQL Database using DMA

- Migrate an SQL Server database on an Azure Virtual Machine to an Azure SQL database using Azure DMS

- Migrate an on-premises SQL Server database to Azure SQL Database using SSMS

- Migrate an SQL Server database to an Azure SQL database using transactional replication

- Migrate an on-premises SQL Server to SQL Managed Instance using the native backup and restore method (offline approach)

- Migrate an SQL Server on an Azure Virtual Machine to an SQL Managed Instance using Azure DMS (online approach)

Let's get started.

Activity: Migrating an on-premises SQL database to Azure SQL Database using DMA

This section describes how to migrate an SQL Server database, such as the **toystore** database, to an Azure SQL database using DMA:

1. Open **Data Migration Assistant** on your computer. From the left ribbon, click the + sign, as shown in F*igure 3.2*:

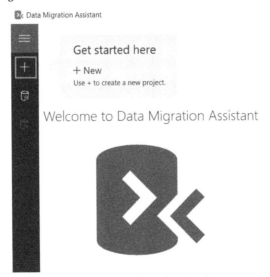

Figure 3.2: Data Migration Assistant

2. In the resulting window, you will need to set these fields:

    For **Project type**, select **Assessment**.

    For **Project name**, type toystore.

    For **Source server type**, select **SQL Server**.

    For **Target server type**, select **Azure SQL Database**.

    Click **Create** to create a new assessment project:

Figure 3.3: Creating a new Assessment project

3. In the resulting **Select report type** window, select the **Check database compatibility** and **Check feature parity** checkboxes. Click **Next** to continue:

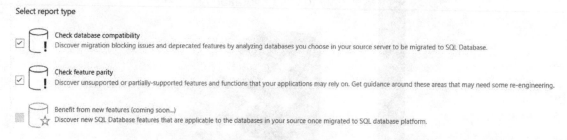

Figure 3.4: Checking feature parity

4. In the **Connect to a server** window, do the following:

   For **Server name**, provide the SQL server name.

   For **Authentication type**, select **Windows Authentication**. Click **Connect** to continue:

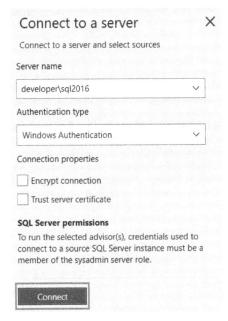

Figure 3.5: Connecting the server

5. In the **Add sources** window, select the database. You can also provide the extended events or the SQL Profile trace files for assessment. This is useful for assessing queries from the application using ORM tools (such as Entity Framework):

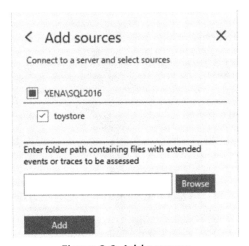

Figure 3.6: Add sources

Click **Add** to continue.

DMA connects to the database and fetches the compatibility and database size:

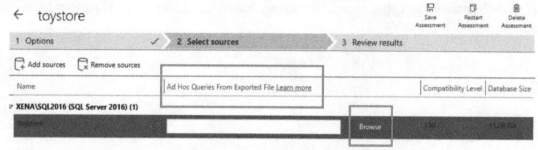

Figure 3.7: Running the assessment for the selected sources

> **Note**
>
> You can also assess queries from applications such as .NET. This is useful when the application uses ad hoc queries to query the database instead of stored procedures.

Click **Start Assessment** to find compatibility issues.

6. DMA will apply the compatibility rules to find and list the compatibility issues. It tells you the features that aren't supported in the **SQL Server feature parity** section:

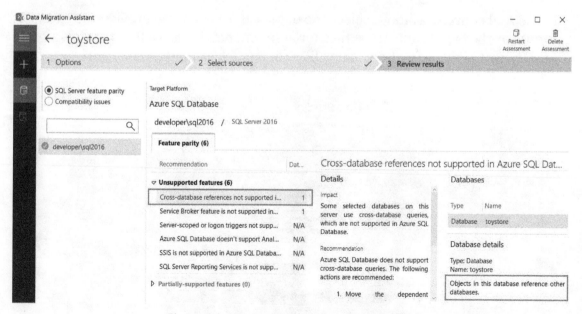

Figure 3.8: SQL Server feature parity section

According to DMA, you have one cross-database reference and one service broker instance, which aren't supported in Azure SQL Database.

7. Under **Options**, select the **Compatibility issues** radio button:

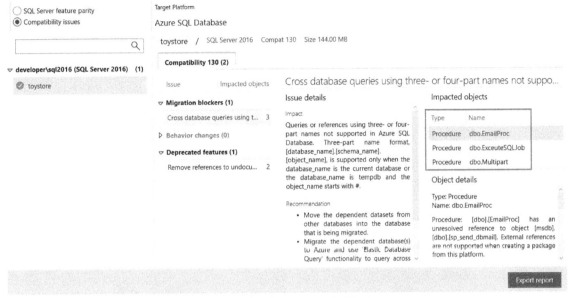

Figure 3.9: Selecting compatibility issues

DMA lists the stored procedures that failed the compatibility test. To fix the errors, open `C:\code\Chapter03\FixCompatibilityIssues.sql` in SSMS and execute it against the **toystore** database.

8. In the top-right corner, click **Restart Assessment**:

Restart
Assessment

Figure 3.10: Restart Assessment

DMA will re-assess and notify you that there are no compatibility issues:

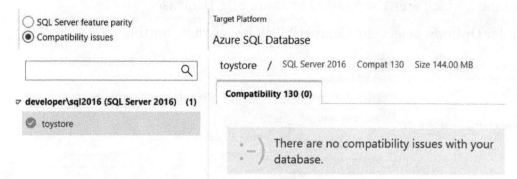

Figure 3.11: DMA ascertains that there are no compatibility issues

9. To migrate the database, in the left-hand navigation bar, click the **+** sign.

   In the resulting window, do the following:

   For **Project type**, select **Migration**.

   For **Project name**, type `toystoreMigration`.

   For **Source server type**, select **SQL Server**.

   For **Target server type**, select **Azure SQL Server**.

   For **Migration scope**, select **Schema** and **Data**.

   Click **Create** to create a new assessment project:

Figure 3.12: Creating a new assessment project

10. In the **Connect to source server** window, do the following:

    For **Server name**, provide the SQL Server name.

    For **Authentication type**, select **Windows Authentication**.

    Click **Connect** to continue:

Connect to source server

Server name

developer\sql2016   ∨

Authentication type

Windows Authentication   ∨

Connection properties

☐ Encrypt connection

☐ Trust server certificate

Source SQL Server permissions

Credentials used to connect to source SQL Server instance must have CONTROL SERVER permission.

Connect

Figure 3.13: Connecting to the source server

11. Select **toystore** from the list of available databases and click **Next**:

◉   toystore   130

Figure 3.14: Selecting the toystore database

12. In the **Connect to target server** window, do the following:

For **Server name**, provide the Azure SQL Server name.

For **Authentication type**, select **SQL Server Authentication**.

For **Username**, provide the Azure SQL Server admin user.

For **Password**, provide the password.

Clear the **Encrypt connection** checkbox.

Click **Connect** to continue:

Figure 3.15: Connect to the target server

13. In the resulting window, select the **toystore** database, and then click **Next** to continue:

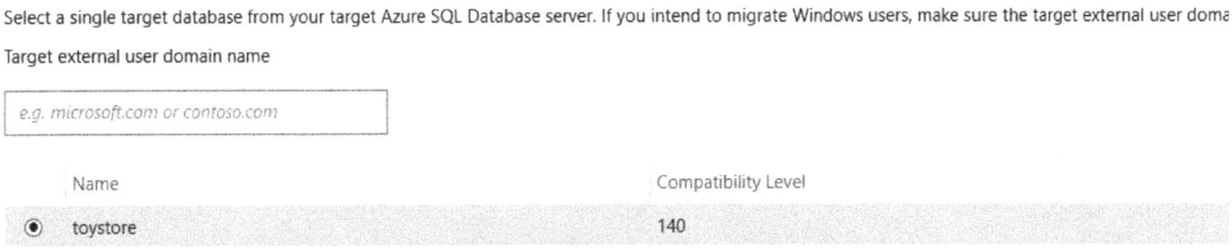

Select a single target database from your target Azure SQL Database server. If you intend to migrate Windows users, make sure the target external user doma

Target external user domain name

| e.g. microsoft.com or contoso.com |

Name	Compatibility Level
⦿ toystore	140

Figure 3.16: Selecting the toystore database

14. In the resulting **Select objects** window, you can select which objects to move to Azure SQL Database. Select all and click **Generate SQL Scripts** at the bottom of the window to continue:

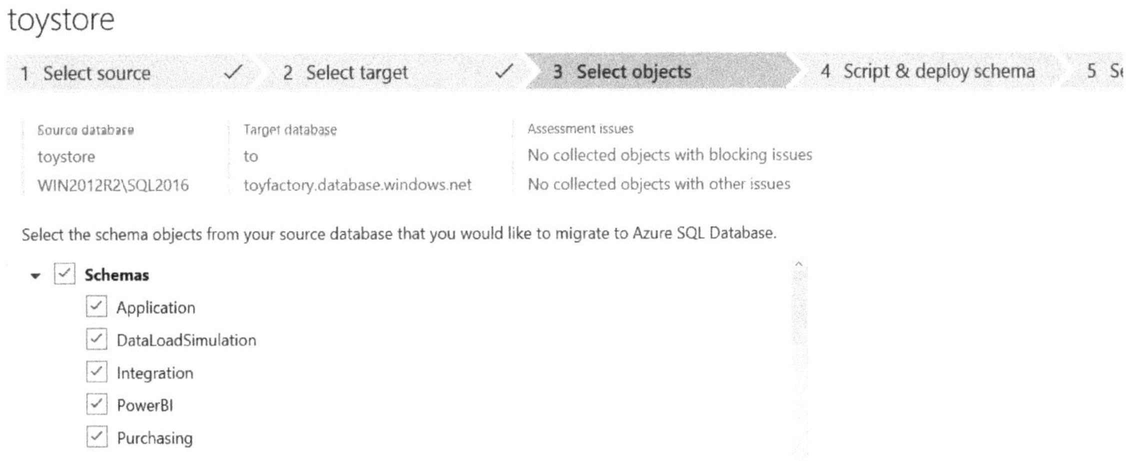

toystore

1 Select source	✓	2 Select target	✓	3 Select objects	4 Script & deploy schema	5 Se

Source database	Target database	Assessment issues
toystore	to	No collected objects with blocking issues
WIN2012R2\SQL2016	toyfactory.database.windows.net	No collected objects with other issues

Select the schema objects from your source database that you would like to migrate to Azure SQL Database.

- ▾ ☑ **Schemas**
  - ☑ Application
  - ☑ DataLoadSimulation
  - ☑ Integration
  - ☑ PowerBI
  - ☑ Purchasing

Figure 3.17: Generate the SQL scripts

DMA will generate a T-SQL script to deploy the database schema. If you wish to save the T-SQL script, you can do so by clicking on the **Save** option in the **Generated script** section:

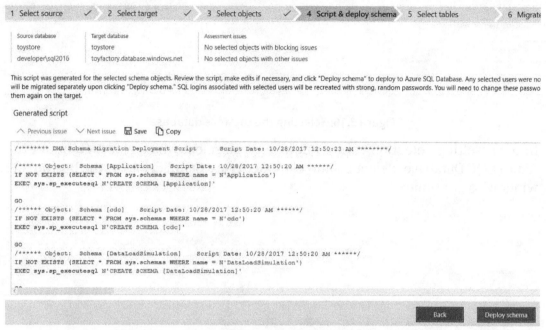

Figure 3.18: Generating a T-SQL script to deploy the database schema

15. In the **Script & Deploy schema** window, click the **Deploy schema** button to deploy the schema to the Azure server. DMA will execute the T-SQL script against the Azure SQL database to create the selected database objects.

Once schema migration is successful, click **Migrate data**:

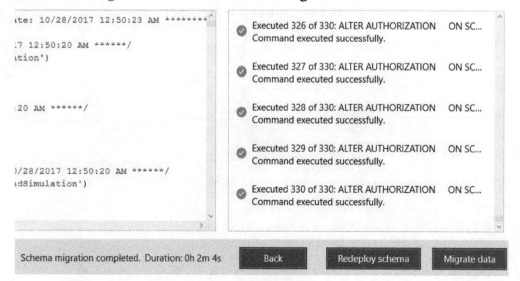

Figure 3.19: Creating database objects

16. In the resulting **Selected tables** window, you can choose what table data to migrate. Leave it as default, for this example, selecting all tables, and then click **Start data migration**:

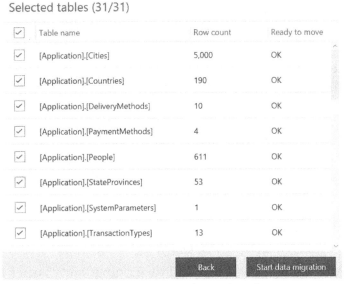

Selected tables (31/31)

	Table name	Row count	Ready to move
☑	[Application].[Cities]	5,000	OK
☑	[Application].[Countries]	190	OK
☑	[Application].[DeliveryMethods]	10	OK
☑	[Application].[PaymentMethods]	4	OK
☑	[Application].[People]	611	OK
☑	[Application].[StateProvinces]	53	OK
☑	[Application].[SystemParameters]	1	OK
☑	[Application].[TransactionTypes]	13	OK

Back   Start data migration

Figure 3.20: Starting data migration

This migrates data from the selected tables in parallel and therefore can be used for large to very large databases:

▽ Tables (31)

Status	Table name	Migration details
✔	[Application].[Cities]	Migration successful. Duration: 0 hrs 0 mins 14 secs
✔	[Application].[Countries]	Migration successful. Duration: 0 hrs 0 mins 14 secs
✔	[Application].[DeliveryMethods]	Migration successful. Duration: 0 hrs 0 mins 6 secs
✔	[Application].[PaymentMethods]	Migration successful. Duration: 0 hrs 0 mins 14 secs
✔	[Application].[People]	Migration successful. Duration: 0 hrs 0 mins 8 secs
✔	[Application].[StateProvinces]	Migration successful. Duration: 0 hrs 0 mins 8 secs
✔	[Application].[SystemParameters]	Migration successful. Duration: 0 hrs 0 mins 8 secs
✔	[Application].[TransactionTypes]	Migration successful. Duration: 0 hrs 0 mins 9 secs
✔	[Purchasing].[PurchaseOrderLines]	Migration successful. Duration: 0 hrs 0 mins 10 secs
✔	[Purchasing].[PurchaseOrders]	Migration successful. Duration: 0 hrs 0 mins 13 secs

Figure 3.21: Migrating the data from selected tables

In this activity, we learned how to use Data Migration Assistant to find compatibility issues and migrate an SQL Server database to an Azure SQL database.

Activity: Migrating an SQL Server database on an Azure virtual machine to an Azure SQL database using Azure DMS

In this activity, we'll use Azure **Database Migration Services** (**DMS**) to migrate a database from an SQL Server database on a virtual machine to an Azure SQL database.

> **Note**
>
> In the exercise, the source database is on an SQL server on an Azure Virtual Machine. To migrate an on-premises database, site-to-site connectivity is required via VPN or Azure ExpressRoute. To find out more about this, please visit the following sites: https://docs.microsoft.com/azure/expressroute/expressroute-introduction
>
> https://docs.microsoft.com/azure/vpn-gateway/vpn-gateway-about-vpngateways
>
> The rest of the steps for the migration are similar to those in the exercise.

Follow these steps to migrate an SQL Server database on Azure VM to Azure SQL Database:

1. Use Database Migration Assistant to find the compatibility issues in the source database and migrate the source schema to an Azure SQL Database. Before migrating the schema, make sure you have a blank Azure SQL database already provisioned.

    The steps to assess and migrate schema are given in *Activity: Migrating an on-premises SQL Database to Azure SQL Database using DMA.*

2. The next step is to register the `Microsoft.DataMigration` resource provider. To do this, type `Subscriptions` in the search box and then select **Subscriptions**:

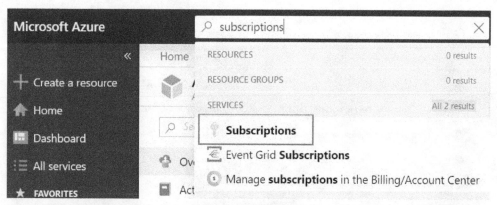

Figure 3.22: Registering the Microsoft.DataMigration resource provider

3. In the **Subscriptions** window, select the subscription in which you wish to create the Azure DMS instance:

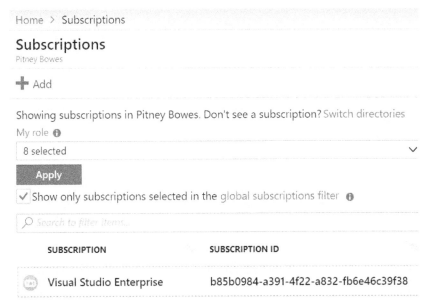

Figure 3.23: Subscriptions window

4. In the selected **Subscription** window, type **Resource Providers** in the search box:

Figure 3.24: Resource providers

5. Click **Resource providers** to open the **Resource providers** window. Click **Register** against **Microsoft.DataMigration** if it's not already registered:

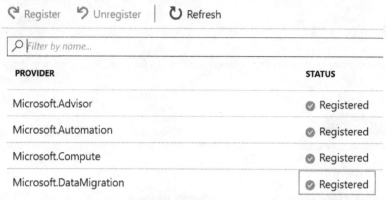

Figure 3.25: Registering Microsoft.DataMigration

6. Log in to the Azure portal and type `Azure Database Migration Services` in the search box:

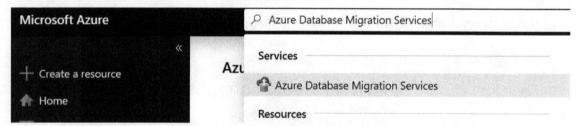

Figure 3.26: Searching for Azure Database Migration Services

Click the **Azure Database Migration Services** option link under **Services**. In the **Azure Database Migration Services** window, click **Add**.

7. In the **Create Migration Service** window's **Basics** tab, provide the **Subscription**, **Resource group**, **Migration service name**, **Location**, **Service mode**, and **Pricing tier** values as shown in F*igure* 3.27:

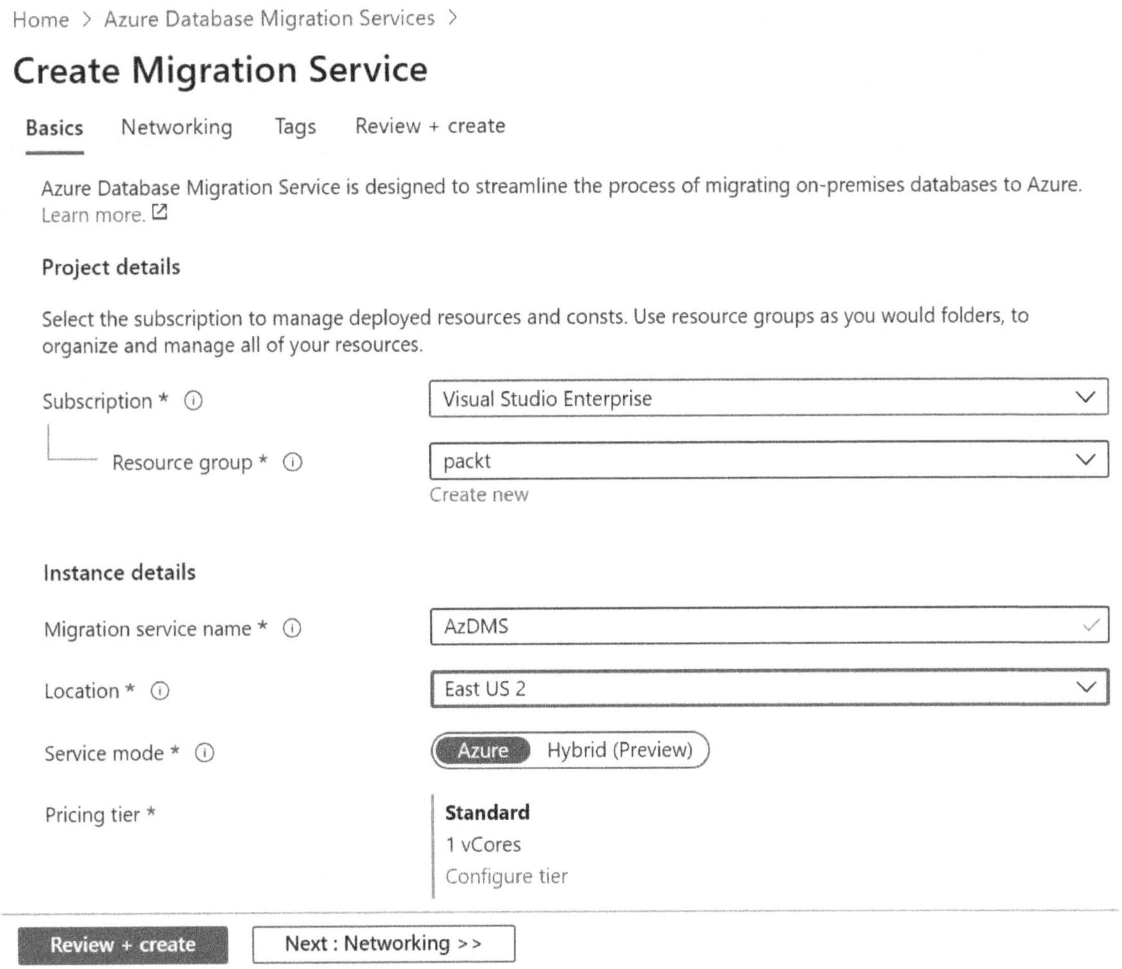

Home > Azure Database Migration Services >

Create Migration Service

Basics   Networking   Tags   Review + create

Azure Database Migration Service is designed to streamline the process of migrating on-premises databases to Azure. Learn more. ☑

Project details

Select the subscription to manage deployed resources and consts. Use resource groups as you would folders, to organize and manage all of your resources.

Subscription * ⓘ	Visual Studio Enterprise ⌄
Resource group * ⓘ	packt ⌄
	Create new

Instance details

Migration service name * ⓘ	AzDMS ✓
Location * ⓘ	East US 2 ⌄
Service mode * ⓘ	(**Azure** Hybrid (Preview))
Pricing tier *	**Standard** 1 vCores Configure tier

Review + create   Next : Networking >>

Figure 3.27: Create Migration Service—Basics tab

Other than the name, subscription, location, and resource group, DMS requires **Service mode** and **Pricing tier** information.

There are two service modes, **Azure** and **Hybrid** (in preview at the time of writing this book). In Azure mode, the Azure migration service instance (also known as the Azure worker) is hosted in Microsoft Azure; however, in Hybrid mode, the Azure migration instance (the Azure worker) is hosted on-premises. Hybrid DMS is also preferred when there's no site-to-site connectivity between Azure and on-premises.

DMS has two pricing tiers, **Standard** and **Premium**. The Standard tier is free and is for one-time or offline migrations. The Standard tier comes with 1, 2, or 4 vCores.

The Premium tier can be used for offline and online migrations. The Premium tier comes with 4 vCores:

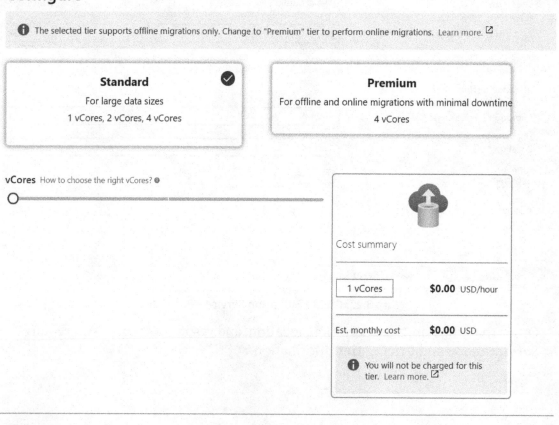

Figure 3.28: Pricing tiers

Click **Next: Networking** to move to the next step.

8. In the **Networking** tab, provide an existing virtual network or create a new virtual network. A virtual network allows DMS to connect to the target and source. For example, if your source is an on-premises SQL Server database, the DMS virtual network should be connected to the on-premises network either through a VPN or Azure ExpressRoute:

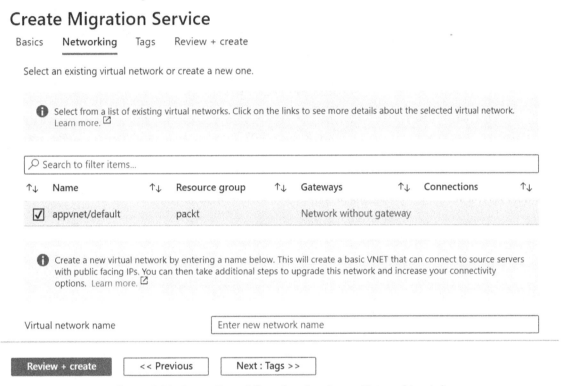

Figure 3.29: Azure Data Migration Services—Networking tab

Virtual networks in the selected location and resource group are listed as shown in *Figure 3.29*.

For the sake of the demonstration, the source is an SQL Server database on an Azure VM. The Azure VM and DMS are on the same virtual network in order to facilitate connectivity between them.

Click **Review + create** and then **Create** to provision the Azure Database Migration Service.

9. The next step is to create a new database migration project. To do that, open the **AzDMS** resource and click **New Migration Project**:

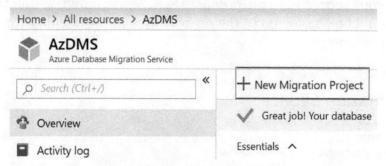

Figure 3.30: New Migration Project

In the **New Migration Project** window, fill in **Project name**, select **SQL Server** as the **Source server type**, and select **Azure SQL Database** as the **Target server type**.

Click **Create and run activity** to continue:

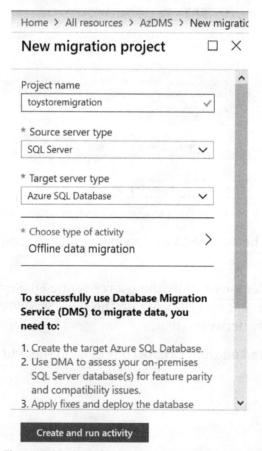

Figure 3.31: Creating a new migration project

10. In the next step, provide the source server details. The **Source SQL Server instance name** is the name or the IP of the source SQL server. The source server here is an Azure VM. The private IP of the virtual machine is therefore used to connect to it:

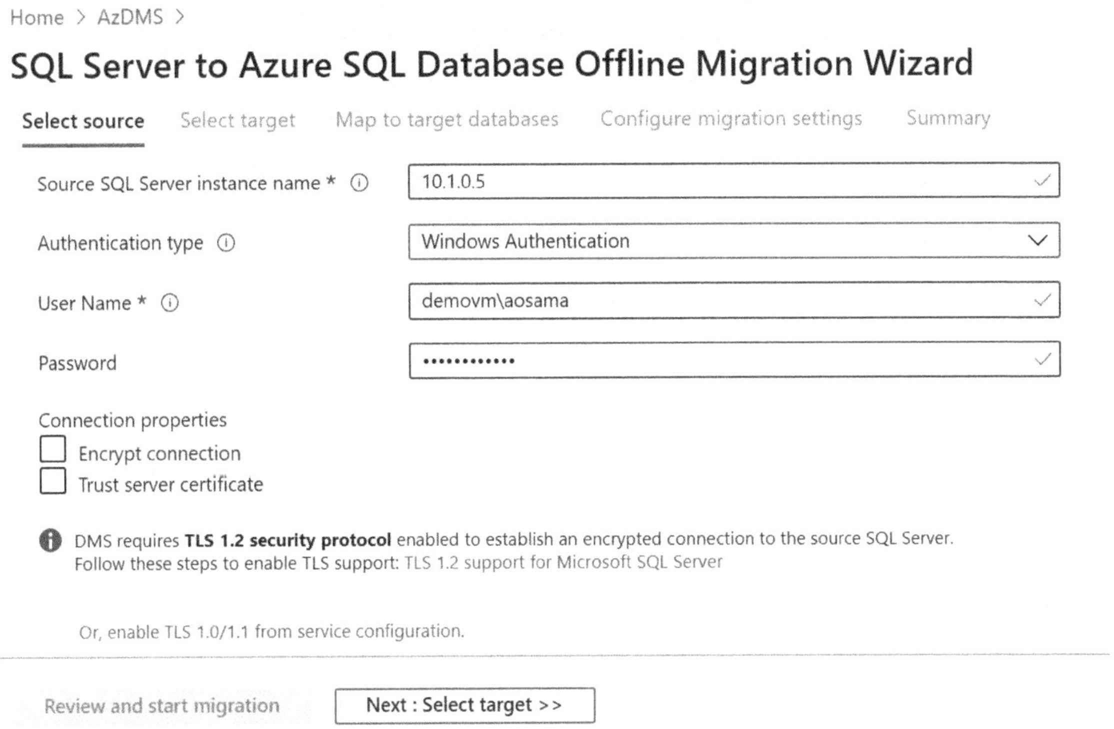

Home > AzDMS >

SQL Server to Azure SQL Database Offline Migration Wizard

Select source   Select target   Map to target databases   Configure migration settings   Summary

Source SQL Server instance name * ⓘ	10.1.0.5 ✓
Authentication type ⓘ	Windows Authentication ∨
User Name * ⓘ	demovm\aosama ✓
Password	•••••••••••• ✓

Connection properties
☐ Encrypt connection
☐ Trust server certificate

ⓘ DMS requires **TLS 1.2 security protocol** enabled to establish an encrypted connection to the source SQL Server. Follow these steps to enable TLS support: TLS 1.2 support for Microsoft SQL Server

Or, enable TLS 1.0/1.1 from service configuration.

Review and start migration   Next : Select target >>

Figure 3.32: Source server details

Click **Next: Select target** to go to the **Select target** tab.

The wizard will validate the connection information and will error out if it's unable to connect to the SQL Server on Azure VM. The wizard will go to the **Select target** tab after a successful validation.

11. In the **Select target** tab, provide the Azure SQL Server name and connection information:

Home > AzDMS >

SQL Server to Azure SQL Database Offline Migration Wizard

Select source　**Select target**　Map to target databases　Configure migration settings　Summary

Target server name * ⓘ `packtdbserver.database.windows.net` ✓

Authentication type ⓘ `SQL Authentication` ⌄

User Name * ⓘ `aosama` ✓

Password `•••••••••••` 👁 ✓

Connection properties
☑ Encrypt connection

Review and start migration　　<< Previous　　Next : Map to target databases >>

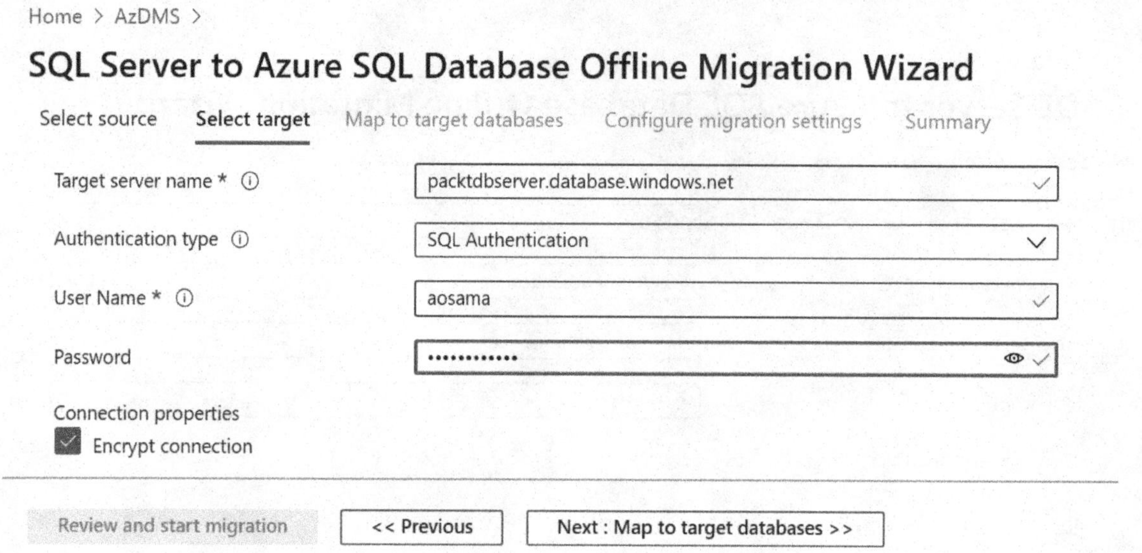

Figure 3.33: Migration Wizard—Select target tab

The Database Migration Service connects to Azure SQL Database using a private IP address. To make sure that the DMS can successfully connect to Azure SQL Database, enable a service endpoint or private endpoint as explained in *Chapter 6, Security*.

Click **Next: Map to target databases** to go to the next step. The wizard will validate the connection information and will error out if it's unable to connect to the database. Otherwise, it'll move to the next tab.

12. In **Map to target database**, select the source and target databases. Optionally, you can set source database read-only to facilitate faster migration. As we are performing offline migration, this can help to stop any data changes during the migration and therefore help complete the migration faster:

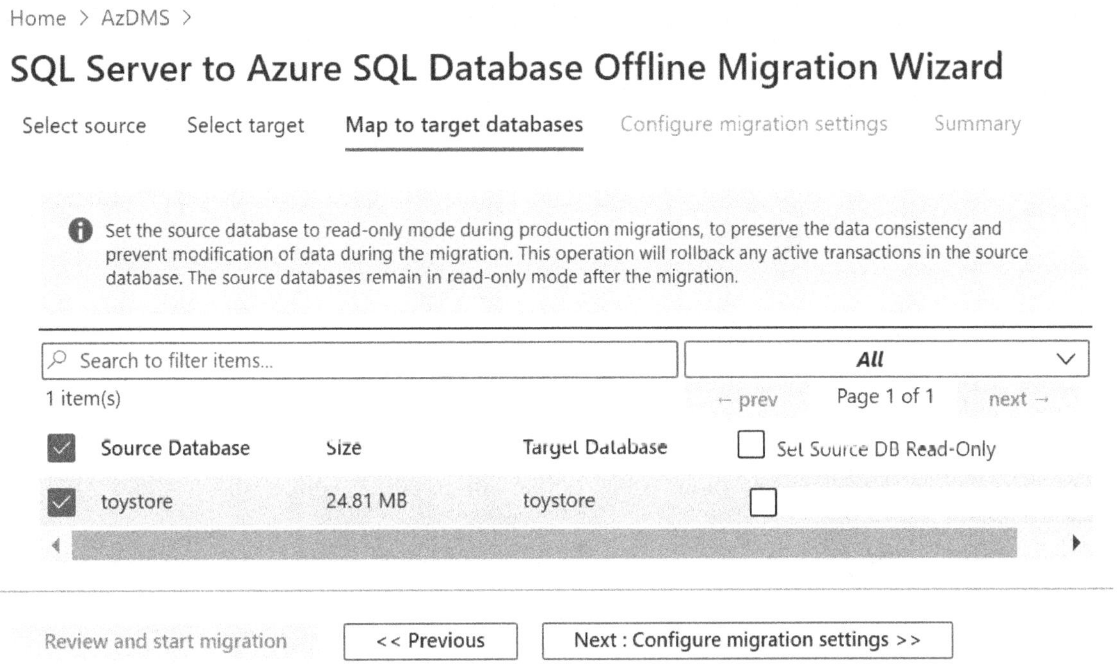

Home > AzDMS >

SQL Server to Azure SQL Database Offline Migration Wizard

Select source   Select target   **Map to target databases**   Configure migration settings   Summary

> ⓘ Set the source database to read-only mode during production migrations, to preserve the data consistency and prevent modification of data during the migration. This operation will rollback any active transactions in the source database. The source databases remain in read-only mode after the migration.

🔍 Search to filter items...			*All* ⌄

1 item(s)   ← prev   Page 1 of 1   next →

☑	Source Database	Size	Target Database	☐ Set Source DB Read-Only
☑	toystore	24.81 MB	toystore	☐

◀ ▶

Review and start migration   [<< Previous]   [Next : Configure migration settings >>]

Figure 3.34: Migration Wizard—Map to target database tab

Click the **Next: Configure migration settings** button to move to the next step.

13. **Configure migration settings** lists the tables from the source database. If a source table is not available in the target database, a **Target table does not exist** message is displayed against that table:

Figure 3.35: Migration wizard—Configure migration settings

Select the tables to migrate and then select **Next: Summary** to move to the next step.

In the **Summary** tab, provide the activity name, review the configuration, and then click the **Start migration** button.

A new page, **toystoremigrationactivity**, opens, displaying the migration status. You should get the following status when the migration completes:

Home > AzDMS >

toystoremigrationactivity

×

🗑 Delete migration   ◯ Stop migration   ◯ Refresh   ◌ Retry   ⬇ Download report

Source server
10.1.0.5

Target server
packtdbserver.database.windows.net

Source version
SQL Server 2019
15.0.4073.23

Target version
Azure SQL Database
12.0.2000.8

Databases
1

Name	Status	size	Migration details	Duration
toystore	Completed	15.94 MB	32 of 32 table(s) completed	00:00:25

Figure 3.36: Migration activity status

The migration wizard copied the data for 32 tables and took 25 seconds. The duration varies depending on the database size.

Once the data is migrated, you can point the application to the Azure SQL Database and run validation tests to make sure that the application is working as expected. After a successful functional validation, you can go live by pointing the application to connect to the Azure SQL Database.

Activity: Migrating an on-premises SQL Server database to Azure SQL Database using SSMS

Let's consider our example of Toystore Ltd. from the previous chapter. Mike has performed all the steps that he has to complete before he can migrate the SQL Server database to Azure. Now all he has to do is perform the migration using the tool of his choice. He selects SSMS. In this section, we'll see how to use SSMS to migrate a database to Azure:

1. Open SSMS. Press F8 to open **Object Explorer**. Connect to your SQL instance.

> **Note**
>
> A backup of toystore is available at `C:\Code\Chapter03\toystore.bak`.

2. In **Object Explorer**, right-click the `toystore` database and go to **Tasks | Deploy Database to Microsoft Azure SQL Database**:

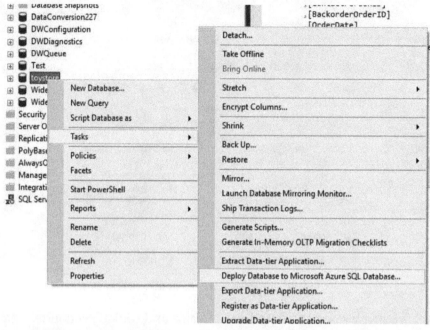

Figure 3.37: Deploying a database to Microsoft Azure SQL Database

3. In the **Deploy Database** wizard, click **Next** to continue:

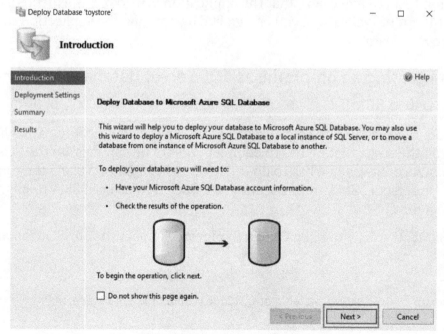

Figure 3.38: Deploy Database wizard

4. In the **Connect to Server** dialog box, provide your Azure SQL Server name, administrator login name, and password. Click **Connect** to connect to the Azure SQL server:

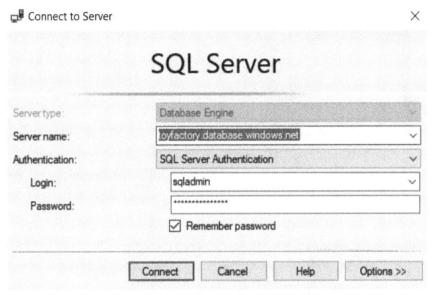

Figure 3.39: Connecting to the Azure SQL server

5. In the **Deployment Settings** window, under **New database name**, provide the name of the Azure SQL Database to which you wish to migrate your on-premises database. The Azure SQL Database edition and the **Service Objective** are automatically detected by SSMS.

6. Under **Other settings**, under **Temporary file name**, SSMS displays the path of the
    exported **bacpac** file. You can change it if you wish to, or you can leave it as the
    default. Click **Next** to continue:

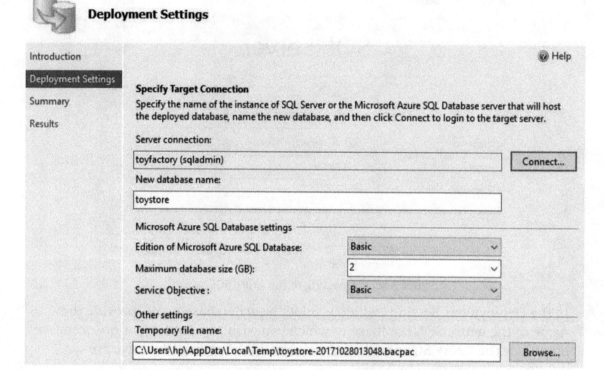

Figure 3.40: The Deployment Settings window

7. In the **Verify Specified Settings** window, review the **Source** and **Target** settings, and then click **Finish** to start the migration process:

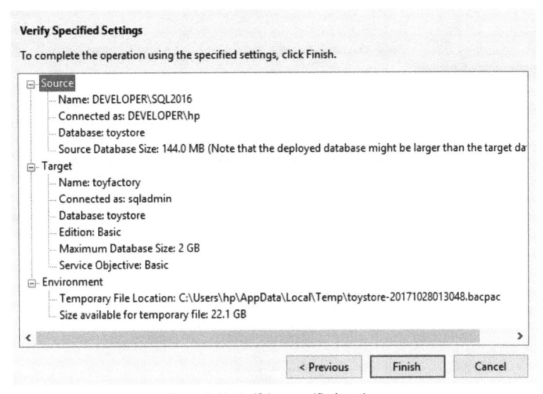

Figure 3.41: Verifying specified settings

SSMS checks for compatibility issues and the migration process terminates because there are compatibility issues. Click **Error**, next to **Exporting database**, to view the error's details:

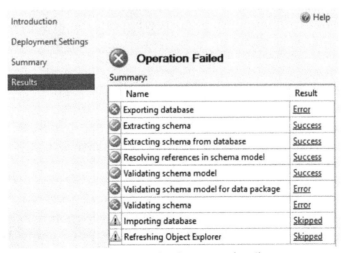

Figure 3.42: Viewing error details

Here is the output showing a detailed description of the error:

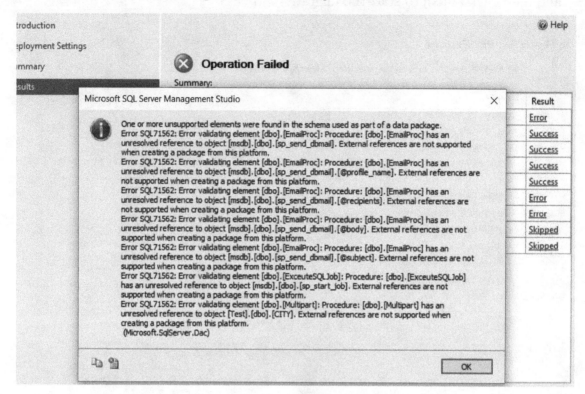

Figure 3.43: Description of the error

8. In the **Error Details** window, we can see that the migration was terminated because of unsupported objects found in the **bacpac** package. Click **OK** to close the **Error Details** window. The next step is to fix the errors.

9. Open **C:\code\Chapter03\FixCompatibilityIssues.sql** in SSMS. The script fixes the compatibility issues by commenting/correcting out the unsupported code within the stored procedures:

```
USE [toystore]
GO
ALTER proc [dbo].[BackUpDatabase] As
-- Backup command isn't supported on Azure SQL Database
--backup database toystore to disk = 'C:\toystore.bak'
--with init, stats=10
GO
```

```
ALTER proc [dbo].[EmailProc] As
-- Database mail isn't supported on Azure SQL Database
--EXEC msdb.dbo.sp_send_dbmail
--    @profile_name = 'toystore Administrator',
--    @recipients = 'yourfriend@toystore.com',
@body = 'The stored procedure finished successfully.',
--    @subject = 'Automated Success Message' ; select * from city
```

10. Press F5 to execute the script. Repeat *steps* 1-10 to successfully migrate the database:

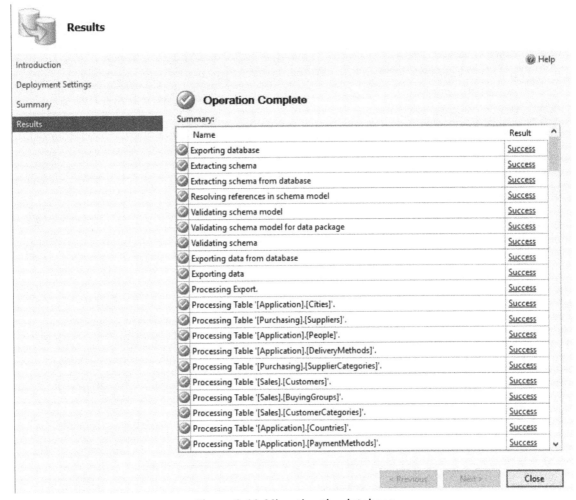

Figure 3.44: Migrating the database

11. To verify the migration, connect to Azure SQL Database using SSMS and run the following query:

```
SELECT TOP (1000) [OrderID]
,[CustomerID]
,[SalespersonPersonID]
,[PickedByPersonID]
,[ContactPersonID]
,[BackorderOrderID]
,[OrderDate]
,[ExpectedDeliveryDate]
,[CustomerPurchaseOrderNumber]
,[IsUndersupplyBackordered]
,[Comments]
,[DeliveryInstructions]
,[InternalComments]
,[PickingCompletedWhen]
,[LastEditedBy]
,[LastEditedWhen]
FROM [toystore].[Sales].[Orders]
```

Figure 3.45 shows the output of the preceding code:

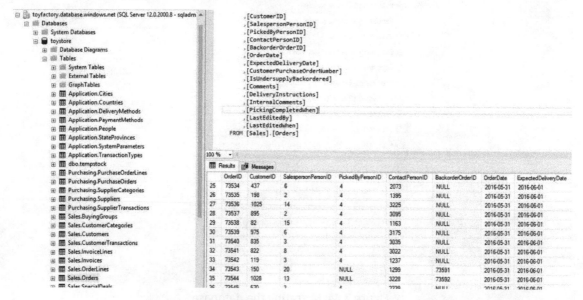

Figure 3.45: Verifying the migration

Congratulations! You have successfully migrated your SQL Server database to an Azure SQL database.

Activity: Migrating an SQL Server database to an Azure SQL database using transactional replication

In this section, we will make use of the toy manufacturing company introduced in an earlier chapter as an example to understand how to migrate an SQL Server database to an Azure SQL Database using transactional replication:

1. Open SSMS. Press F7 to open **Object Explorer**. In **Object Explorer**, click **Connect** to connect to your SQL server.

2. In **Object Explorer**, expand the **Replication** node, right-click **on Local Publications**, and click **on New Publication...**:

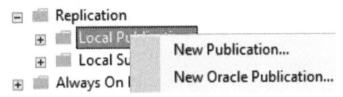

Figure 3.46: Creating a new publication

3. In the **New Publication Wizard** welcome screen, click **Next** to continue.

4. In the **Publication Database** window, select **toystore** as the database to be published. Click **Next** to continue:

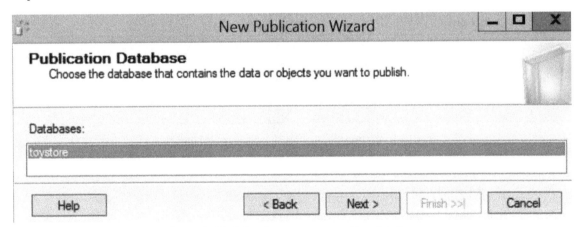

Figure 3.47: Selecting toystore as the database

5. In the **Publication Type** window, select **Transactional publication**. There are only two publication types allowed with Azure SQL Database as a subscriber. Click **Next** to continue:

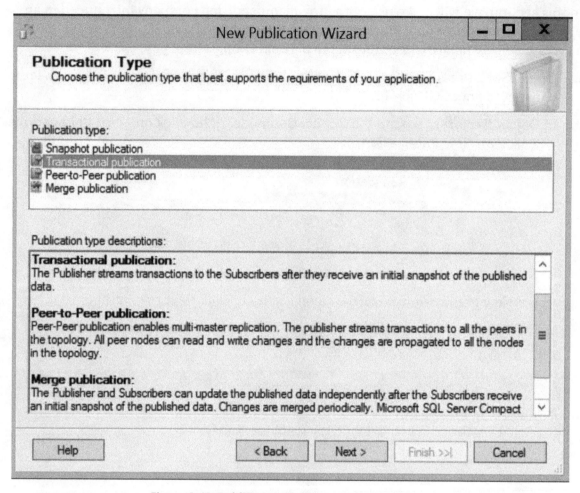

Figure 3.48: Publication and transactional window

6. In the **Articles** window, select all the objects to publish. Click **Next** to continue. If required, you can filter out objects that you don't want to migrate to an Azure SQL database here:

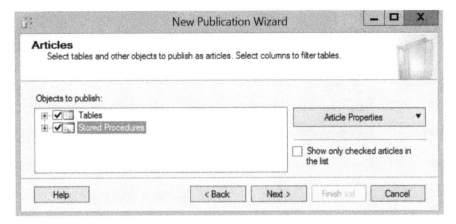

Figure 3.49: Selecting all the objects in the Articles page

7. The **Article Issues** window tells you that you should migrate all tables that are referenced by views, stored procedures, functions, and triggers. As we are migrating all the tables, we don't have anything to do here. Click **Next** to continue:

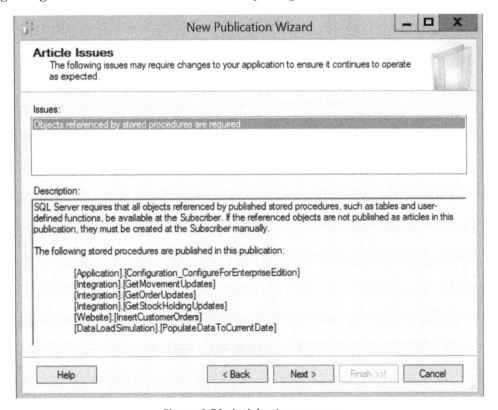

Figure 3.50: Articles Issues page

8. **Filter Table Rows** lets you filter unwanted rows that you don't want to publish. As you are publishing all rows, leave it as the default and click **Next** to continue:

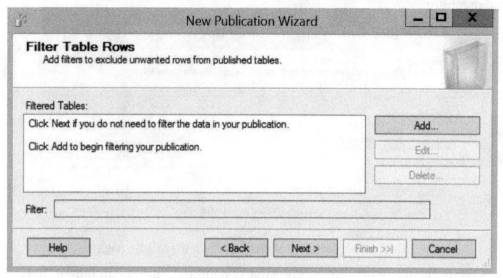

Figure 3.51: Filter Table Rows window

9. In the **Snapshot Agent** window, select the **Create a snapshot immediately and keep the snapshot available to initialize subscriptions** option. You can also schedule the **Snapshot Agent** to run at specific times:

Figure 3.52: Snapshot Agent window

10. In the **Agent Security** window, select the **Security Settings...** button:

Figure 3.53: Agent Security page

11. In the **Snapshot Agent Security** window, specify the account for the **Snapshot Agent** to run on. You can either give the domain account that has permission to access the SQL Server instance and the database, or you can have it run under the SQL Server agent service account, which isn't the recommended option.

Under the **Connect to the publisher** section, select **By impersonating the process account**. The process account must have read and write access to the publisher database:

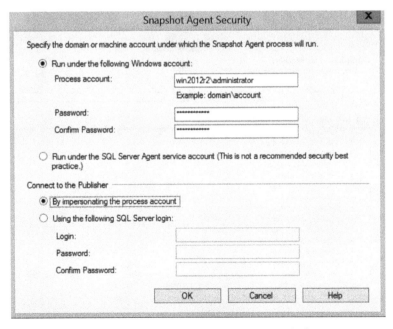

Figure 3.54: Snapshot Agent Security window

12. Click **OK** to continue. You'll be taken back to the **Agent Security** window. Check the **Use the security settings from the Snapshot Agent** box, under the **Log Reader Agent** text box. **Log Reader Agent** will run under the same account as the **Snapshot Agent**. You can choose different security settings for the **Log Reader Agent** if you wish to:

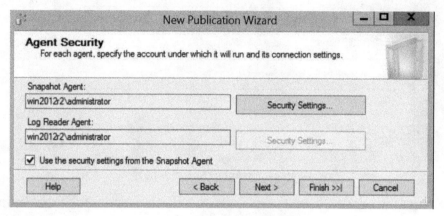

Figure 3.55: Agent Security window

Click **Finish** to continue.

13. In the **Complete the Wizard** window, under **Publication name**, provide a name for your publication. You can review the objects that are being published in this window.

Click **Finish** to create the publication:

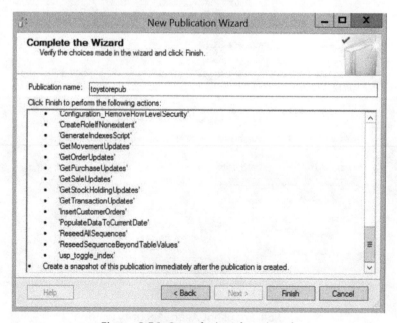

Figure 3.56: Completing the wizard

14. The **New Publication Wizard** will now create the publication. Add the selected articles to the publication and it will start the Snapshot Agent:

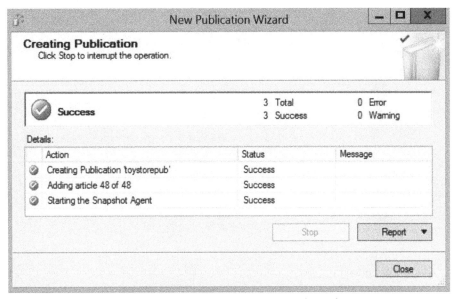

Figure 3.57: New Publication Wizard window

Click **Close** to close the **New Publication Wizard**.

In **Object Explorer**, expand the **Replication** node, and then expand **Local Publications**; the **toystorepub** publication has been added to the publication list:

Figure 3.58: Check that toystore has been added to the publication list

15. The next step is to create a subscription for the Azure SQL database. Open **Object Explorer**, expand the **Replication** node, and right-click the **Local Subscription** option. Select **New Subscriptions** to continue. Azure SQL Databases only support push subscriptions:

Figure 3.59: Creating a subscription for the Azure SQL Database

16. In **New Subscription Wizard**, select **Next** to continue:

Figure 3.60: New Subscription Wizard

17. In the **Publication** window, select the publication for which you wish to create the subscription. The **toystorepub** publication is listed under the **toystore** database. If it's the only publication, it'll be selected by default. Click **Next** to continue:

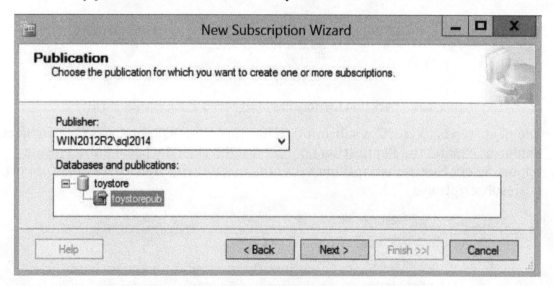

Figure 3.61: Selecting the toystore publication

18. In the **Distribution Agent Location** window, select **Run all agents at the Distributor**, which in our case is the **push subscription**. Pull subscriptions aren't allowed with Azure SQL Database as a subscriber. Click **Next** to continue:

Figure 3.62: Distribution Agent Location

19. In the **Subscribers** window, click the **Add Subscriber** button at the bottom of the window and select **Add SQL Server Subscriber**:

Figure 3.63: Creating a subscription for the Azure SQL database

In the **Connect to Server** dialog box, provide the Azure SQL Server name and SQL authentication login credentials to connect to the Azure SQL server. Click **Connect** to continue:

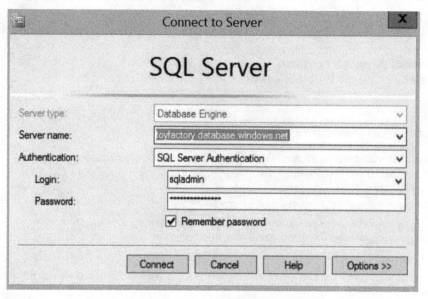

Figure 3.64: Connecting to the server

The **Subscribers** window will now list the Azure SQL server in the **Subscriber** column and the `toystore` database in the **Subscription Database** column. Select the Azure SQL server if it's not already selected and click **Next** to continue.

20. In the **Distribution Agent Security** window, click ... (for the options menu) to set the security option:

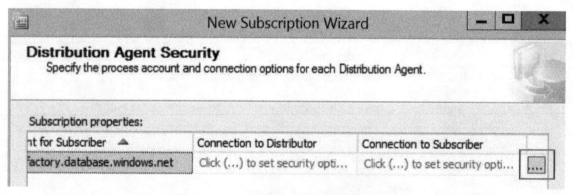

Figure 3.65: Distribution Agent Security

The distribution agent can run under the context of the domain account or the SQL Server Agent Service account (not recommended) for the agent. Provide a domain account that has appropriate access to the distribution server, which in our case is the same as the publication server.

In the **Connect to the Distributor** section, select the default option (by impersonating the process account). You can also use an SQL Server login if you wish to.

In the **Connect to the Subscriber** section, provide the Azure SQL server, SQL Server login, and password.

Click **OK** to go back to the **Distribution Agent Security** window. It'll now show the selected security options:

Figure 3.66: Connecting to the server

Click **Next** to continue.

21. In the **Synchronization Schedule** window, in the **Agent Schedule** section, select **Run Continuously** and click **Next** to continue:

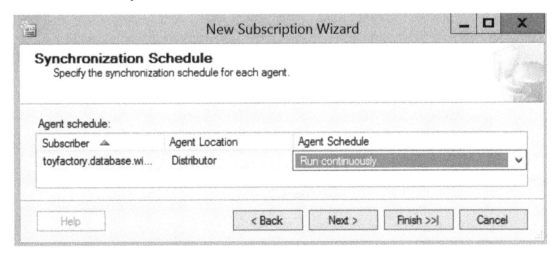

Figure 3.67: Synchronization schedule

22. In the **Initialize Subscriptions** window, under the **Initialize When** option, select **Immediately**, and then click **Next** to continue:

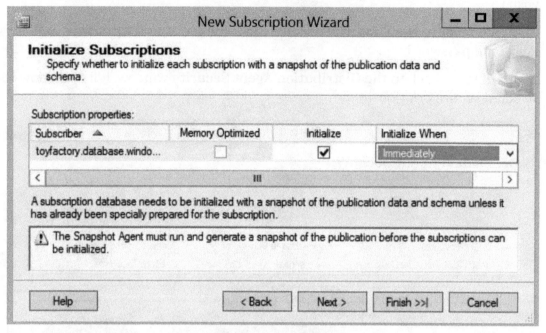

Figure 3.68: Initializing subscriptions

23. In the **Wizard Actions** window, select the **Create the subscription(s)** option and click **Next** to continue:

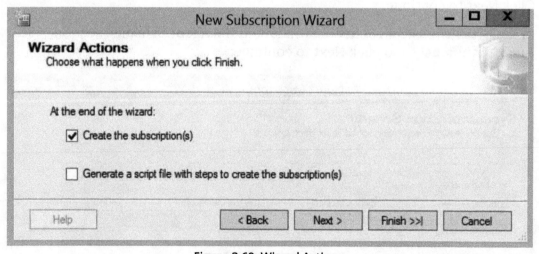

Figure 3.69: Wizard Actions

24. In the **Complete the Wizard** window, review the subscription settings and click **Finish** to create the subscription. The wizard will create the subscription and will initiate the Snapshot Agent to apply the initial snapshot on the subscriber.

Once the initial snapshot is applied, all of the transactions on the publisher will be sent to the subscriber.

Click **Close** to end the wizard.

To verify the replication, in **Object Explorer**, right-click the **Replication** node and select **Launch Replication Monitor**:

Figure 3.70: Launch Replication Monitor

In the replication monitor, expand the **My Publishers** node, then expand the SQL Server instance name node. The **toystorepub** publication will be listed there. Select the **toystorepub** publication to check the synchronization health:

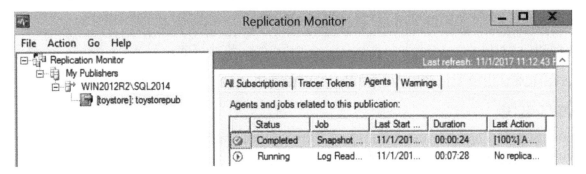

Figure 3.71: Replication Monitor

It may take time to generate and apply the initial snapshot depending on the database's size.

To further verify that the objects are migrated to Azure SQL Database, switch to SSMS and open **Object Explorer** if it's not already open.

Connect to your Azure SQL Database and expand the **Tables** node. Observe that all of the tables are listed under the **Tables** node:

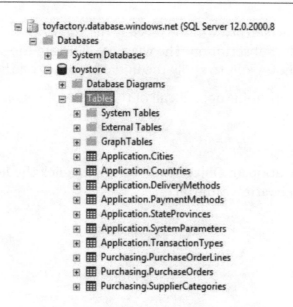

Figure 3.72: Observing the Tables node

In this activity, we configured transactional replication from an SQL Server (on-premises or SQL on Azure VM) to Azure SQL Database. Once configured, the schema and data modifications were copied to Azure SQL Database in near real time. We can test our application against the Azure SQL Database and modify the application to point to the Azure SQL Database after a successful application validation.

Activity: Migrating an on-premises SQL Server to Azure SQL Managed Instance using the native backup and restore method (offline approach)

Azure SQL Managed Instance supports the restore from URL option, a key capability that makes this offline migration easier.

The following is a high-level backup and restore process diagram:

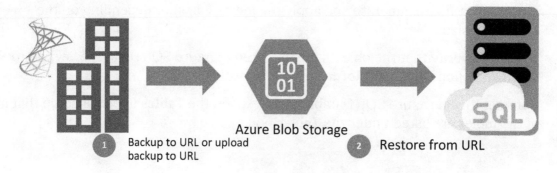

Figure 3.73: Native backup and restore process

Prior to SQL Server 2012 SP1 CU2, there was no option to take a backup directly from a URL, so you needed to upload the backup directly to Azure Blob Storage.

Please refer to *Table 3.2* to understand your backup options:

Step	SQL Server version	Backup/Restore method
Create a backup to Azure Storage	Prior to SQL Server 2012 SP1 CU2	Upload a .bak file directly to Azure Storage
	SQL Server 2012 SP1 CU2–2016	Direct backup using the deprecated WITH CREDENTIAL syntax
	SQL Server 2016 and above	Direct backup using the WITH SAS token
Restore from Azure Blob Storage to an SQL Managed Instance	Latest version of SQL Server	RESTORE FROM URL with an SAS token

Table 3.2: Backup options

In this activity, for our SQL Server, we are going to perform a backup to URL followed by a restore from URL. Here, we are using the open-source Azure Data Studio tool from Microsoft in order to connect our SQL Server and SQL Managed Instance:

1. Open the **SQLServer_backup_notebook.ipynb** notebook from the source code in **Azure Data Studio** and attach to the on-premises SQL Server connection:

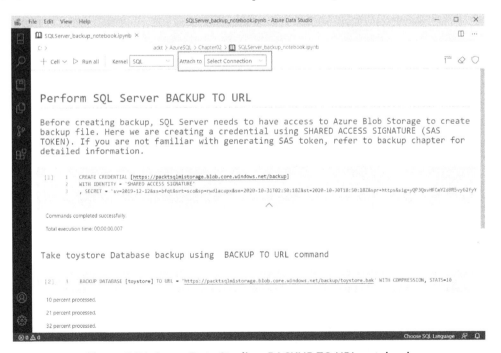

Figure 3.74: Azure Data Studio—BACKUP TO URL notebook

2. Run the first SQL statement, **CREATE CREDENTIAL**:

```
CREATE CREDENTIAL [https://packtsqlmistorage.blob.core.windows.net/backup]
WITH IDENTITY = 'SHARED ACCESS SIGNATURE'
, SECRET = 'sv=2019-12-12&ss=bfqt&srt=sco&sp=rwdlacupx&se=2020-10-
31T02:50:18Z&st=2020-10-30T18:50:18Z&spr=https&sig=yQP3QsvHFCmYZd8R5vy62f
yYWQLNjNFyo9BF9IGniOY%3D'
```

3. Initiate a **BACKUP TO URL** command:

```
BACKUP DATABASE [toystore] TO URL = 'https://packtsqlmistorage.blob.core.
windows.net/backup/toystore.bak' WITH COMPRESSION, STATS=10
```

4. Open the **SQLMI_restore_notebook.ipynb** notebook from source code and connect to Azure SQL Managed Instance to run statements:

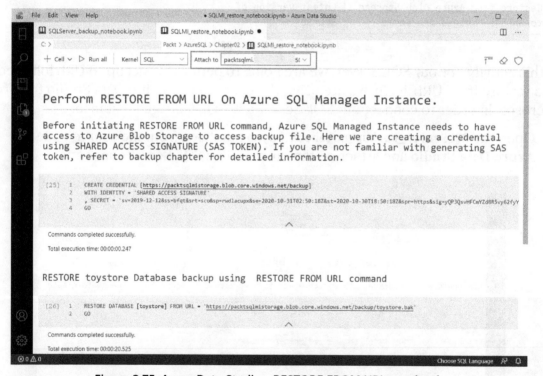

Figure 3.75: Azure Data Studio—RESTORE FROM URL notebook

5. Create a credential to grant access on Azure Blob Storage to Azure SQL Managed Instance:

```
CREATE CREDENTIAL [https://packtsqlmistorage.blob.core.windows.net/backup]
WITH IDENTITY = 'SHARED ACCESS SIGNATURE'
, SECRET = 'sv=2019-12-12&ss=bfqt&srt=sco&sp=rwdlacupx&se=2020-10-
31T02:50:18Z&st=2020-10-30T18:50:18Z&spr=https&sig=yQP3QsvHFCmYZd8R5vy62f
yYWQLNjNFyo9BF9IGniOY%3D'
```

6. Execute the **RESTORE FROM URL** command:

```
RESTORE DATABASE [toystore] FROM URL = 'https://packtsqlmistorage.blob.
core.windows.net/backup/toystore.bak'
GO
```

7. Verify the restored database:

```
SELECT NAME, CREATE_DATE, STATE_DESC FROM SYS.DATABASES WHERE
NAME='toystore'
GO
```

In this activity, we have learned how to migrate an SQL Server database to SQL Managed Instance using the native **BACKUP TO URL** and **RESTORE FROM URL** commands and the Azure Data Studio notebook. You can execute these commands using any of your preferred tools.

Activity: Migrating an SQL Server on an Azure Virtual Machine to SQL Managed Instance using Azure DMS (online approach)

The backup and restore method is an offline, manual approach for migrating an SQL Server instance to an Azure SQL Managed Instance and it is useful for applications that can afford downtime. However, there are times when you will need to migrate databases that are critical to business and can't afford longer downtime or times when you have a very large database and a backup and restore approach is not feasible.

The Azure Database Migration service is helpful for migrating an SQL Server instance to Azure SQL Managed Instance with nearly zero downtime. Azure DMS offers offline and online automatic approaches to migrating an on-premises SQL Server instance to the cloud.

With the offline approach, downtime starts with the start of migration activity, but with the online approach, activity downtime is only limited to the time taken by cutover at the end of the migration. Azure DMS offers Standard and Premium service tiers, and only the Premium service tier can be used for online migration. The Standard service tier offers offline migration and it's free to use. The Premium service tier with 4 vCores is free for 6 months (180 days). You are only allowed two DMS instances per subscription. Azure DMS supports SQL Server 2005 to 2019 as sources while migrating from an on-premises SQL Server.

If you have network constraints and can't have site-to-site connectivity between your on-premises network and Azure, then a DMS hybrid instance can be useful. Visit this link for more information on DMS hybrid instances:

https://docs.microsoft.com/azure/dms/quickstart-create-data-migration-service-hybrid-portal

> **Note**
>
> The creation and deployment of a DMS instance is beyond the scope of this book. Please refer to the following link to find a list of pre-requisites for Azure DMS:
>
> https://docs.microsoft.com/azure/dms/tutorial-sql-server-managed-instance-online#prerequisites

In this activity, we will learn about the online migration approach for migrating our **toystore** database from an Azure Virtual Machine to SQL Managed Instance with an easy Azure portal experience:

1. Go to the Azure portal at https://portal.azure.com and search for **Azure Database Migration Services**:

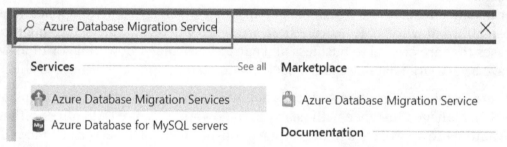

Figure 3.76: Azure portal search for DMS

2. Click on the deployed Azure DMS service instance:

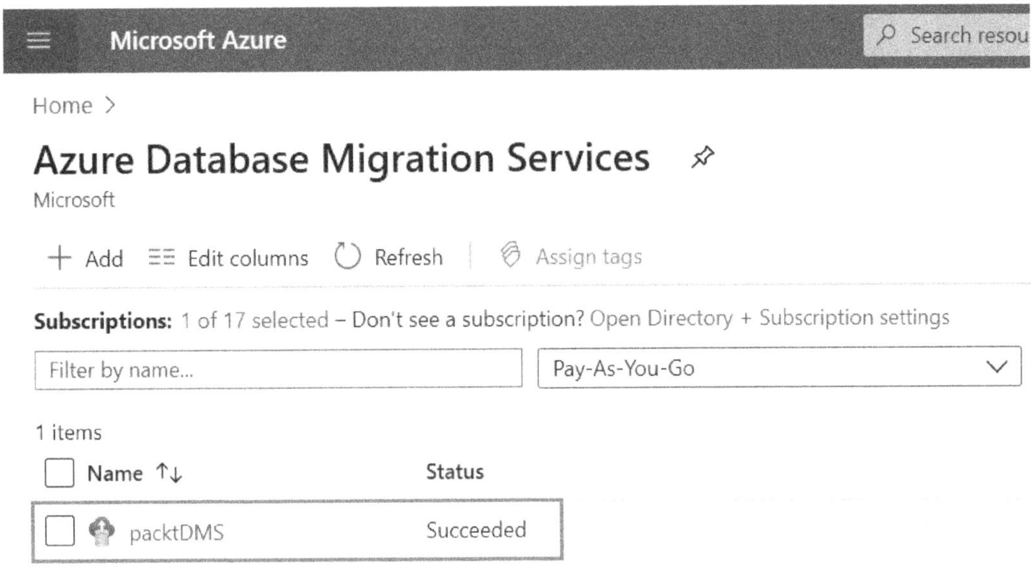

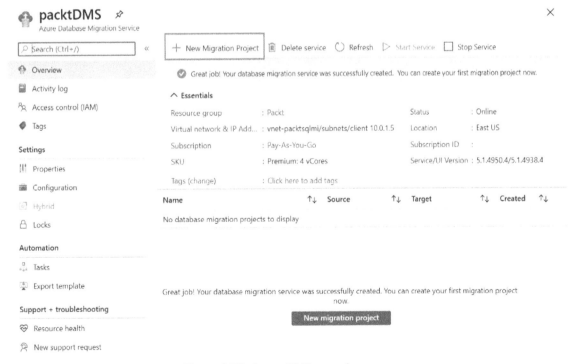

Figure 3.77: Azure DMS page

3. Click **New Migration Project** in the Azure DMS **Overview** tab:

Figure 3.78: Azure DMS overview page

4. Create a **New Migration Project** specifying the source as SQL Server and target as **Azure SQL Database Managed Instance** with an **Online data migration** activity. Click on **Create and run activity**:

Home > Azure Database Migration Services > packtDMS >

New migration project

Project name

toystore-to-sqlmi ✓

Source server type *

SQL Server ∨

Target server type *

Azure SQL Database Managed Instance ∨

*Choose type of activity >

Online data migration

To successfully use Database Migration Service (DMS) to migrate data, you need to:

1. Create the target Azure SQL Database Managed Instance.
2. Use DMA to assess your on-premises SQL Server database(s) for feature parity and compatibility issues.
3. Apply the fixes to target Azure Database Managed Instance as recommended by DMA after the migration.
4. Please implement the pre-requirements and review the known issues provided at the link before configuring the online migration.

Install Database Migration Assistant ⧉

Create and run activity

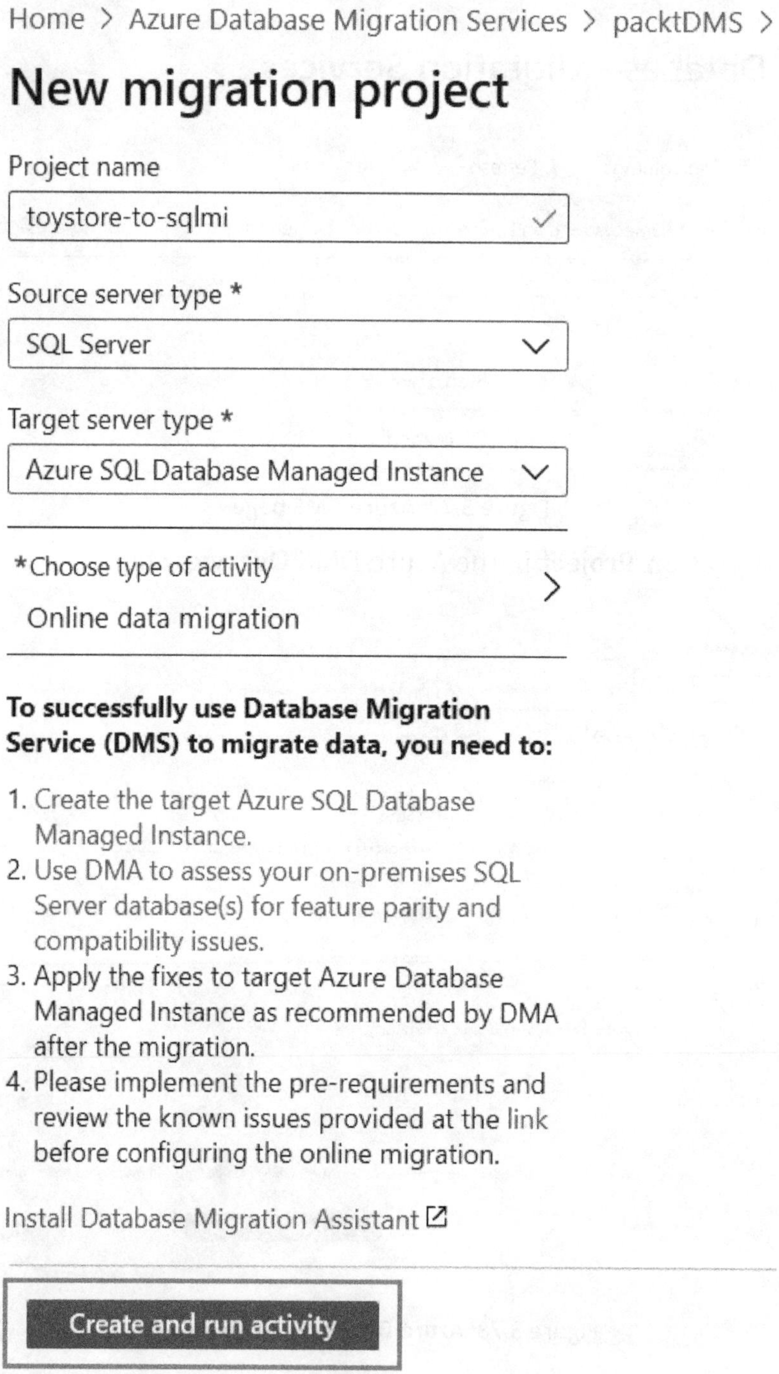

Figure 3.79: Azure DMS new migration project

5. Create a **New Online Activity** using the **toystore-to-sqlmi** migration project:

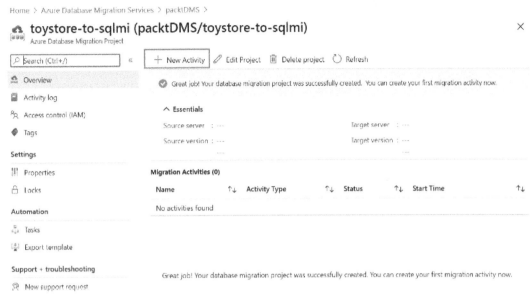

Figure 3.80: Migration project overview tab

6. Select the source server. Here we are connecting to the Azure SQL Server virtual machine using Windows authentication in the same subnet where Azure DMS is deployed:

Home > Azure Database Migration Services > packtDMS > toystore-to-sqlmi (packtDMS/toystore-to-sqlmi) >

SQL Server to Azure SQL Managed Instance Online Migration Wizard

Select source   Select target   Select databases   Configure migration settings   Summary

Source SQL Server instance name * ⓘ	packtsqlserver ✓
Authentication type ⓘ	Windows Authentication ⌄
User Name * ⓘ	packtsqlserver\sqladmin ✓
Password	•••••••••••••• ✓

Connection properties
☐ Encrypt connection
☐ Trust server certificate

ⓘ DMS requires **TLS 1.2 security protocol** enabled to establish an encrypted connection to the source SQL Server. Follow these steps to enable TLS support: TLS 1.2 support for Microsoft SQL Server

Or, enable TLS 1.0/1.1 from service configuration.

Review and start migration   [Next : Select target >>]

Figure 3.81: Migration activity source details

7. Select the target Azure SQL Managed Instance. An application ID with a contributor role on subscription and **Key** is needed for Azure DMS online migration. To learn more about this, please visit https://docs.microsoft.com/azure/active-directory/develop/howto-create-service-principal-portal:

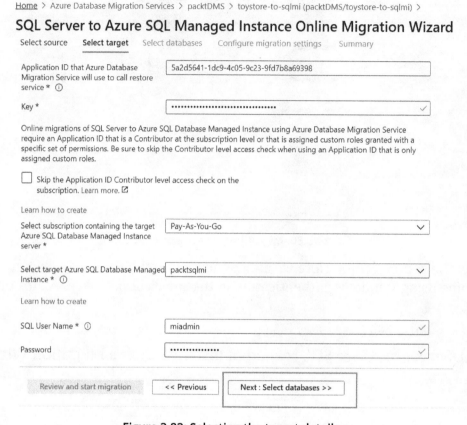

Figure 3.82: Selecting the target details

8. Select a database for migration:

Home > Azure Database Migration Services > packtDMS > toystore-to-sqlmi (packtDMS/toystore-to-sqlmi) >

SQL Server to Azure SQL Managed Instance Online Migration Wizard

Select source   Select target   **Select databases**   Configure migration settings   Summary

Source server name
packtsqlserver

Search to filter items...

☐ Source databases (1)

☑ toystore

Review and start migration   << Previous   Next : Configure migration settings >>

Figure 3.83: Selecting a database for migration

9. Set **Network share location** as the source for Azure DMS to read the backup, and **Storage account** that the Azure DMS service will use to upload the backup from the network location:

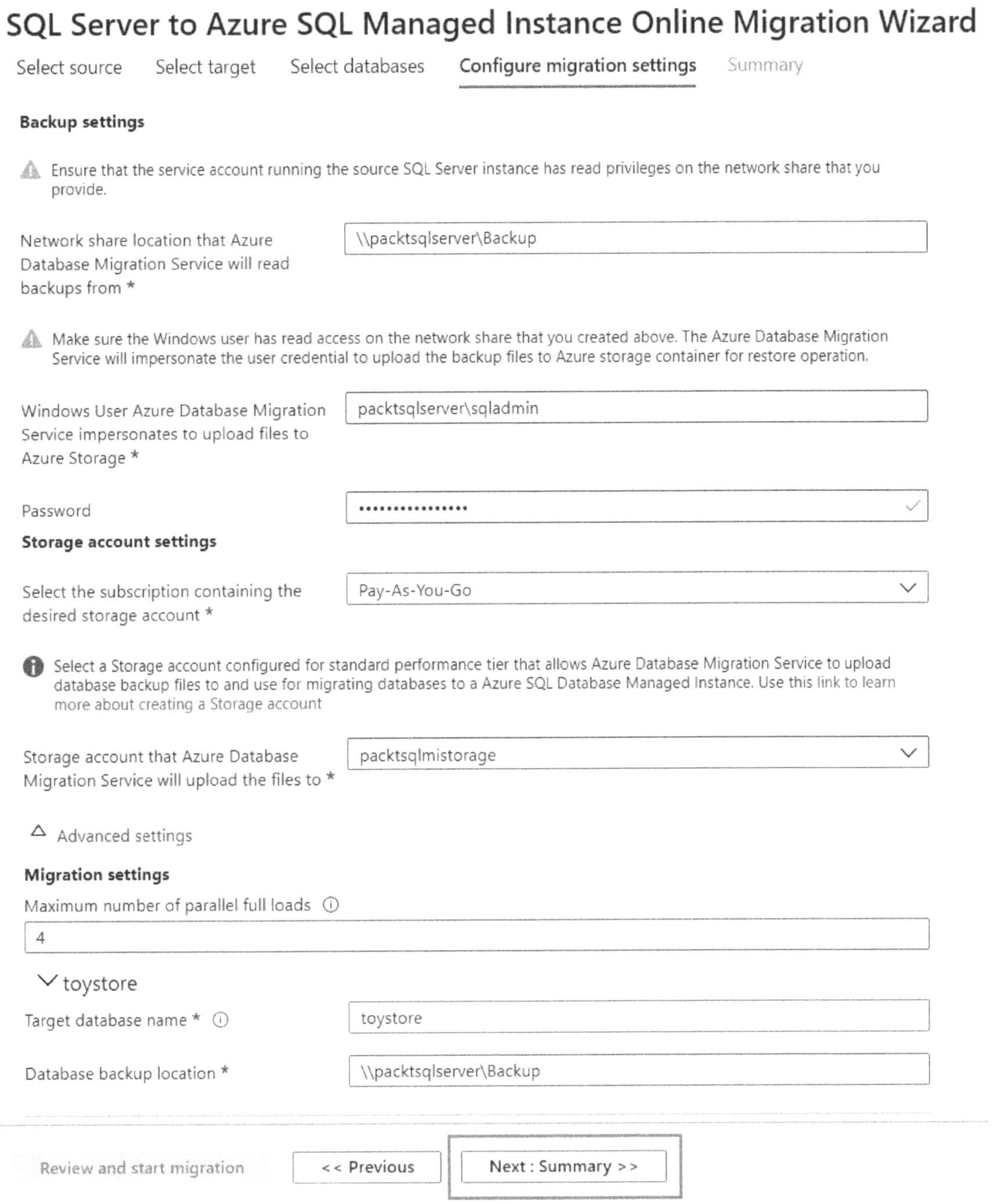

SQL Server to Azure SQL Managed Instance Online Migration Wizard

Select source   Select target   Select databases   **Configure migration settings**   Summary

Backup settings

⚠ Ensure that the service account running the source SQL Server instance has read privileges on the network share that you provide.

Network share location that Azure Database Migration Service will read backups from *

`\\packtsqlserver\Backup`

⚠ Make sure the Windows user has read access on the network share that you created above. The Azure Database Migration Service will impersonate the user credential to upload the backup files to Azure storage container for restore operation.

Windows User Azure Database Migration Service impersonates to upload files to Azure Storage *

`packtsqlserver\sqladmin`

Password

`•••••••••••••••` ✓

Storage account settings

Select the subscription containing the desired storage account *

`Pay-As-You-Go` ⌄

ℹ Select a Storage account configured for standard performance tier that allows Azure Database Migration Service to upload database backup files to and use for migrating databases to a Azure SQL Database Managed Instance. Use this link to learn more about creating a Storage account

Storage account that Azure Database Migration Service will upload the files to *

`packtsqlmistorage` ⌄

△ Advanced settings

Migration settings

Maximum number of parallel full loads ⓘ

`4`

⌄ toystore

Target database name * ⓘ

`toystore`

Database backup location *

`\\packtsqlserver\Backup`

Review and start migration   `<< Previous`   `Next : Summary >>`

Figure 3.84: Configuring a backup share path

10. Enter the activity name and click **Start migration**:

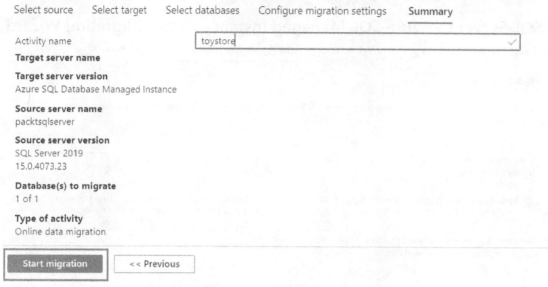

SQL Server to Azure SQL Managed Instance Online Migration Wizard

Select source   Select target   Select databases   Configure migration settings   **Summary**

Activity name   toystore

Target server name

Target server version
Azure SQL Database Managed Instance

Source server name
packtsqlserver

Source server version
SQL Server 2019
15.0.4073.23

Database(s) to migrate
1 of 1

Type of activity
Online data migration

Start migration   << Previous

Figure 3.85: Summary page for the activity

11. The activity is now created, and you will be auto-redirected to the migration activity page after the completion of the activity creation wizard, or you can navigate to Azure DMS and select the migration project and then select the newly added activity. Here you can monitor the **Activity status** and see more details about the sync by clicking on the database name.

Azure DMS uses log shipping in the back-end to transfer database backups from the network share to Azure Blob Storage. You need to take care of generating database backups. This can be done by scheduling an SQL Server Agent backup job on on-premises SQL Server, which will create database backups with a **CHECKSUM** option for the network share path. Azure DMS will read backups from the shared location and upload them to the storage account and start restoring in sequence:

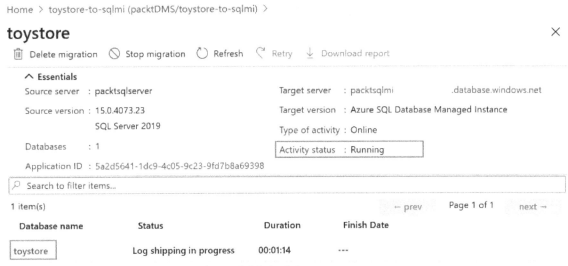

Figure 3.86: Activity status page

12. Check the restoration progress by clicking on the database name. As per the status in the preceding figure, log shipping is in progress. Log shipping takes a transaction log backup of the on-premises SQL Server and restores the transaction log backup to the SQL Managed Instance database. We can further check the transaction log backup restored by log shipping by getting the log shipping status:

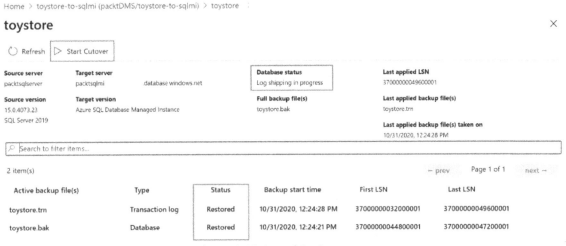

Figure 3.87: Log shipping status

13. At the same time, if you connect to the Azure SQL Managed Instance, you will see that the **toystore** database is in a restoring state:

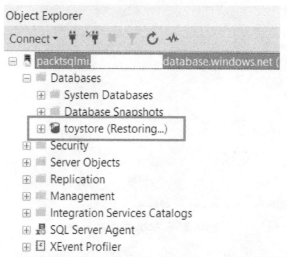

Figure 3.88: SSMS toystore restoring status

Performing a cutover

Stop the application workload, take the last log backup, and wait for it to apply to the managed instance. Once the last log backup is applied to the SQL Managed Instance, in parallel, you can work on changing your application connection strings point to SQL Managed Instance. Click on the **Start Cutover** button to change the **toystore** database from restoring to online on SQL Managed Instance:

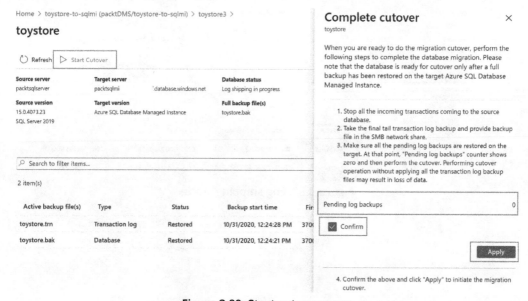

Figure 3.89: Start cutover page

14. Once you click on **Apply**, Azure DMS will take another few minutes to complete the cutover and change the database status from restoring to online on SQL Managed Instance:

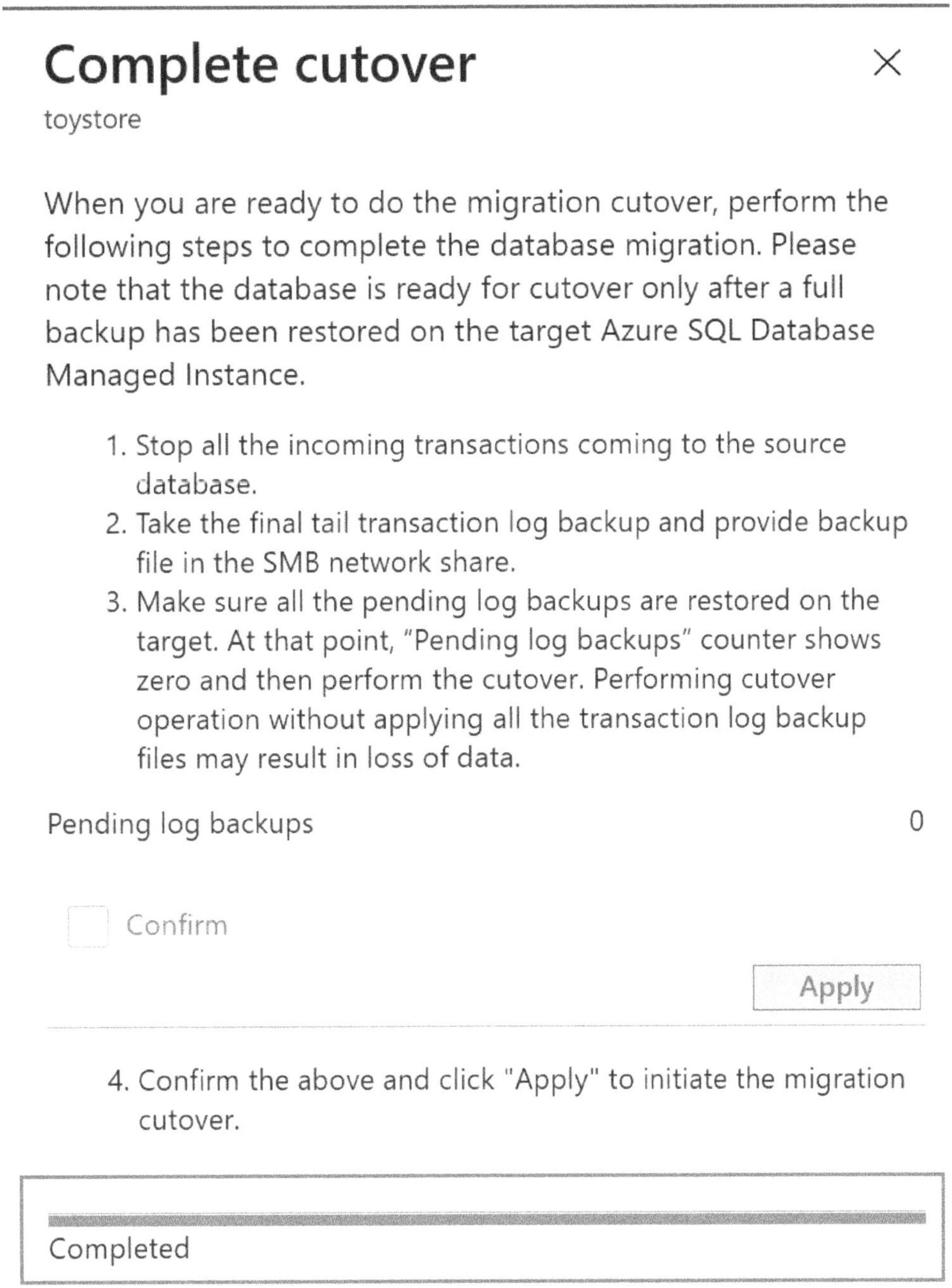

Complete cutover

toystore

When you are ready to do the migration cutover, perform the following steps to complete the database migration. Please note that the database is ready for cutover only after a full backup has been restored on the target Azure SQL Database Managed Instance.

1. Stop all the incoming transactions coming to the source database.
2. Take the final tail transaction log backup and provide backup file in the SMB network share.
3. Make sure all the pending log backups are restored on the target. At that point, "Pending log backups" counter shows zero and then perform the cutover. Performing cutover operation without applying all the transaction log backup files may result in loss of data.

Pending log backups   0

☐ Confirm

Apply

4. Confirm the above and click "Apply" to initiate the migration cutover.

Completed

Figure 3.90: Complete cutover page

15. At the same time, if you check the database status using SSMS, it will be online on SQL Managed Instance:

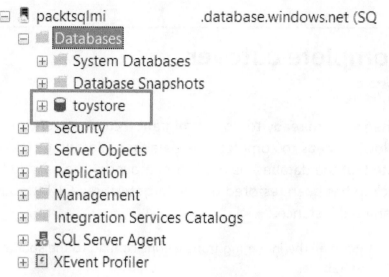

Figure 3.91: Database status showing the database is online

16. After cutover, the Azure DMS migration activity will show the status as completed:

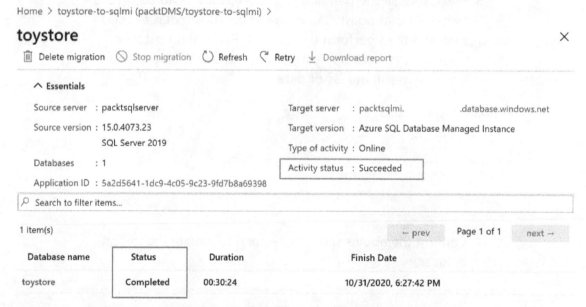

Figure 3.92: Azure DMS activity completion

In this activity, we have seen how to migrate an SQL Server instance to an SQL Managed Instance using Azure DMS. We learned how to create an online activity and how log shipping works behind the scenes. We also learned how to perform a cutover to end the migration activity.

Summary

Migrating to an Azure SQL Database or SQL Managed Instance is an important task and should be planned to perfection. This chapter talked about the migration strategy that you should follow when migrating from an on-premises database to an Azure SQL Database or SQL Managed Instance. A good database migration strategy includes the following steps: determining the migration benefits, selecting the right destination by choosing the correct pricing model and service tier, choosing primary and disaster recovery regions to deploy resources to, determining compatibility issues, and selecting a migration tool based on the migration approach.

In this chapter, we talked about assessment tools. We saw various ways to perform online/offline database migration to Azure SQL Database and SQL Managed Instance. We also covered different migration tools to migrate the data and the schema from an on-premises SQL Server database to an Azure SQL Database and SQL Managed Instance.

In the next chapter, we will learn how to perform manual and automatic backups for Azure SQL Databases and Managed Instances.

4
Backups

Database backups are among the most important tasks a database administrator must perform. A good database backup strategy can help recovery from system outages, unwanted deletions or updates, database corruption issues, and other related issues.

This chapter will help you back up an Azure SQL Database and an Azure SQL Managed Instance. You'll learn about automated and manual backups, explore automated backup features, and perform the manual backup of an Azure SQL Managed Instance.

This chapter explores different backup and restore options, such as automated backups, transactional consistent backups, and manual backups. We will be covering the following topics:

- Automatic backups
- Optimizing backup storage cost
- Configuring long-term backup retention for Azure SQL Database and Azure SQL Managed Instance
- Exporting an Azure SQL database using the Azure portal
- Exporting an Azure SQL database using PowerShell
- Performing a manual `COPY_ONLY` backup for Azure SQL Managed Instance

Automatic backups

Microsoft provides automated backups for Azure SQL Database and Azure SQL Managed Instance databases. Automatic backups consist of full, differential, and log backups. The first automatic full backup is performed immediately after the database is provisioned. Differential backups are scheduled to occur every 12-24 hours, and transaction log backups are scheduled for every 5-10 minutes. The frequency of transaction log backups is based on the compute size and the amount of database activity. A full backup is scheduled for once a week:

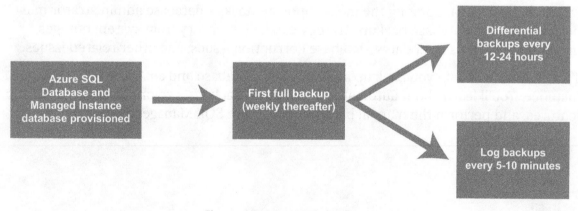

Figure 4.1: Automatic backups

> **Note**
> Differential and transaction log backups can run in parallel.

Backup storage

Azure SQL Database and SQL Managed Instance keep database backups in geo-redundant storage blobs by default, which are replicated to a paired region. This helps to recover the database in a different region if there is a regional outage in the primary region. You can choose between **locally-redundant**, **zone-redundant**, and **geo-redundant** backup storage redundancy for Azure SQL Database and Azure SQL Managed Instance. For Azure SQL Database, backup storage redundancy can be configured at the time of database creation and can also be updated for an existing database. For Azure SQL Managed Instance, this option is only available at the time of instance creation.

Backup storage redundancy impacts backup costs in the following way:

- Locally redundant storage price = x

- Zone-redundant storage price = 1.25x

- Geo-redundant storage price = 2x

Backup retention period

The backup retention period for all new, restored, and copied databases is, by default, 7 days for Azure SQL Database and Azure SQL Managed Instance. The point-in-time retention period for Azure SQL Database and Azure SQL Managed Instance can be changed to between 1 and 35 days. For Azure SQL Managed Instance, it is possible to set the **Point-in-time restore** (**PITR**) backup retention period once a database has been deleted to the 0-35 day range. You can extend the retention period through the LTR feature, which stores the backup in Azure Blob Storage for as long as 10 years. At the time of writing this book, **Long-term backup retention** (**LTR**) for Azure SQL Managed Instance is in preview and only available for limited subscription types.

> **Note**
>
> If you delete Azure SQL Database or Managed Instance, all the databases on Azure SQL Database or Managed Instance are also deleted and cannot be recovered.
>
> However, if you have configured LTR for an Azure SQL Database or Azure SQL Managed Instance database, those backups can be restored on a different Azure SQL Database or managed instance in the same subscription.

Optimize backup storage costs for Azure SQL Database and Azure SQL Managed Instance

Backup storage costs depend on the provisioned database pricing tier and type. For the DTU model, the Azure SQL Database backup storage cost is included in the pricing tier. With the vCore model, Microsoft gives you free backup storage, which is equal to the size of your maximum provisioned database storage or reserved maximum storage for Azure SQL Managed Instance. For example, if you have a 100 GB standard Azure SQL database, you get 100 GB of free backup storage, and the same applies to the reserved total space for Azure SQL Managed Instance. You can control the free backup storage size by limiting the retention period of backups.

For single databases, this equation is used to calculate the total billable backup storage usage:

Total billable backup storage size = (size of full backups + size of differential backups + size of log backups) – maximum data storage

For pooled databases, the total billable backup storage size is aggregated at the pool level and is calculated as follows:

Total billable backup storage size = (total size of all full backups + total size of all differential backups + total size of all log backups) – maximum pool data storage

For Azure SQL Managed Instance, the total billable backup storage size is aggregated at the instance level and is calculated as follows:

Total billable backup storage size = (total size of full backups + total size of differential backups + total size of log backups) – maximum instance data storage

To reduce the billing charges for excess usage of the backup storage space beyond the free backup storage space provided, you can control backup consumption using these general approaches:

- Choosing the right backup storage type
- Optimizing the database backup retention period
- Maximizing your free backup storage space
- Configuring LTR backups
- Using Azure Policy

Let's go over each of these in detail.

Choose the right backup storage type

Azure SQL Database and Azure SQL Managed Instance give the flexibility to choose between different backup storage redundancy options. Choose less expensive options, if applicable, to reduce the overall backup cost:

Backup storage type	Option	Cost versus protection	Notes
Geo-redundant storage	Default option	**The most expensive:** Allows a geo-restore of backups in another region, even if your primary region is down. **Provides maximum protection** of **3 backup copies** in your **primary** and **1 additional** backup copy in a secondary region.	Best suited to applications relying on geo-restore as their disaster recovery solution and for globally scaled applications requiring the most protection.
Zone-redundant storage	Available	**Less expensive:** Provides **redundancy protection** of **3 backup copies across** availability zones in your primary region. Geo-restore is not available with this option.	It can be used for data-residency compliance in cases of strict restrictions on data exiting the primary region.
Locally redundant storage	Available	**The cheapest option:** Provides a **single backup copy** in your primary region. Geo-restore is not available with this option.	It can be used for data-residency compliance in cases of strict restrictions on data exiting a single datacenter.

Table 4.1: Choosing the right backup storage type

Optimize the database backup retention period

You can change the default 7-day retention period to short-term retention of 1-35 days for all the active databases on Azure SQL Database and Azure SQL Managed Instance. You can also set deleted database retention to anything within the 0-35-day range, but only on Azure SQL Managed Instance.

Change backup retention for Azure SQL Database using the Azure portal

Using the Azure portal, navigate to the **Manage Backups** blade and click on **Configure retention**. The Azure portal only supports selecting the values provided in the drop-down menu. However, you can change the retention to any value between 1 and 35 days using the REST API or PowerShell, as shown in *Figure 4.2*:

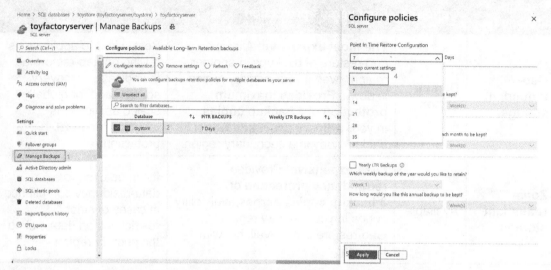

Figure 4.2: Changing backup retention for Azure SQL Database

Change backup retention for Azure SQL Managed Instance active databases using the Azure portal

Using the Azure portal, navigate to the **Managed database** page and click on **Configure backup retention**. You can select between 1 and 35 days, as shown in *Figure 4.3*:

Figure 4.3: Changing backup retention for Azure SQL Managed Instance

Using PowerShell commands to change PITR retention for deleted databases on Azure SQL Managed Instance

The Azure portal does not allow modifying backup retention for deleted databases on Azure SQL Managed Instance—it's only available using a PowerShell module. Keeping track of deleted databases' backup retention is important and can help save backup storage costs if you use it correctly.

Following are the steps to change backup retention for a deleted database on Azure SQL Managed Instance:

1. Open Azure Cloud Shell from the Azure portal:

Figure 4.4: Cloud Shell

2. Run the following set of commands to set variables:

```
#setting up variable as per our environment
$MisubId = "6ee856b5-yy6d-4bc1-xxxx-byg5569842e1"
$instance = "packtsqlmi"
$resourceGroup = "Packt"
$database = "toystore"
$days =0
```

3. Log in to your Azure account using the following command:

```
#Login to Azure Account
Connect-AzAccount
Select-AzSubscription -SubscriptionId $MisubId
```

4. Run the following command to get PITR retention for a deleted database:

```
# GET PITR backup retention for an individual deleted database
Get-AzSqlDeletedInstanceDatabaseBackup -ResourceGroupName
$resourceGroup -InstanceName $instance -DatabaseName $database |
Get-AzSqlInstanceDatabaseBackupShortTermRetentionPolicy
```

Figure 4.5 shows the retention period:

```
ResourceGroupName : Packt
InstanceName      : packtsqlmi
DatabaseName      : toystore
DeletionDate      : 10/24/2020 9:43:36 PM
RetentionDays     : 7
```

Figure 4.5: Get deleted database retention

5. Run the following commands to set backup retention to 0 days for a deleted database:

> **Note**
>
> Valid backup retention must be between 0 (no retention) and 35 days. A valid retention rate can only be lower than the length of the retention period when the database was active, or the remaining backup days of a deleted database.

```
# SET new PITR backup retention on an individual deleted database
Get-AzSqlDeletedInstanceDatabaseBackup -ResourceGroupName
$resourceGroup -InstanceName $instance -DatabaseName $database |
Set-AzSqlInstanceDatabaseBackupShortTermRetentionPolicy -RetentionDays
$days
```

Figure 4.6 shows that the retention has been set to 0 days:

```
ResourceGroupName : Packt
InstanceName      : packtsqlmi
DatabaseName      : toystore
DeletionDate      : 10/24/2020 9:43:36 PM
RetentionDays     : 0
```

Figure 4.6: Set deleted database retention

> **Note**
>
> Once you decrease backup retention for a deleted database on Azure SQL Managed Instance, it is no longer possible to increase it.

In this activity, we have used Cloud Shell to run **Az.sql** module commands to set backup retention for a deleted database on Azure SQL Managed Instance. Deleted database backups can cause higher backup storage billing, hence it is necessary to keep track of deleted database backup retention.

Maximize your free backup storage space

You can increase the maximum storage size and reserved instance size on Azure SQL Database and Azure SQL Managed Instance to reduce overall backup storage costs.

The following are quick steps to increase the maximum storage size for Azure SQL Database and Azure SQL Managed Instance.

Increase the maximum storage size for Azure SQL Database using the Azure portal

Go to Azure SQL Server and select a database for increasing the maximum storage. Use the **Configure** blade to increase the maximum storage size, as shown in *Figure* 4.7:

Figure 4.7: Increasing the max storage for Azure SQL Database

Increase the max storage size for Azure SQL Managed Instance using the Azure portal

Go to Azure SQL Managed Instance and select the **Compute + storage** blade to increase the max storage capacity, as shown in *Figure 4.8*:

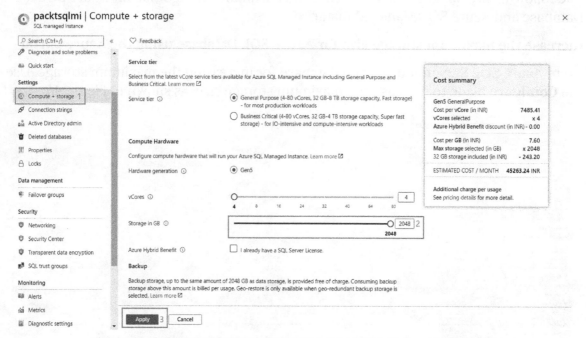

Figure 4.8: Increasing the max storage for Azure SQL Managed Instance

Configure LTR backups

Choose less expensive LTR backups over PITR retention for databases that are not restored frequently for Azure SQL Database and Azure SQL Managed Instance. LTR backups are in limited preview for Azure SQL Managed Instance. This topic is covered in detail later in this chapter.

Use Azure Policy

Use Azure Policy to block the deployment of Azure SQL Database and Azure SQL Managed Instance with default geo-redundant backup storage.

Visit the following link for the built-in definition of Azure Policy for Azure SQL Database and Azure SQL Managed Instance: https://docs.microsoft.com/azure/azure-sql/database/policy-reference.

> **Note**
>
> Azure policies are not enforced for T-SQL database creation. When you create a database using the T-SQL command, use the **LOCAL** or **ZONE** keywords for the **BACKUP_STORAGE_REDUNDANCY** parameter in the **CREATE DATABASE** statement.

Configure long-term backup retention for Azure SQL Database and Azure SQL Managed Instance

Consider the **toystore** SQL database created in *Chapter 3, Migration*. Mike has now been tasked with securing and backing up the data at ToyStore Ltd. In this section, we'll learn how to create and configure LTR for the **toystore** database:

1. Log in to the Azure portal and find and open the Azure SQL Server resource that the **toystore** SQL database is part of.

2. In the SQL Server detail window, find and select **Manage Backups** and then select the **toystore** database:

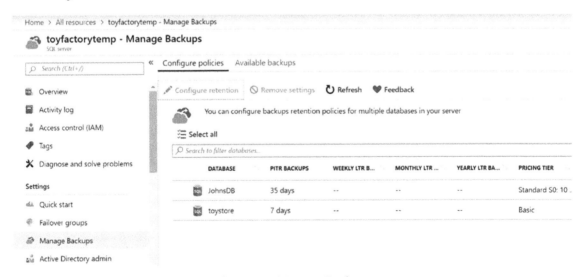

Figure 4.9: Manage Backups

3. Select the **Configure retention** option in the top menu:

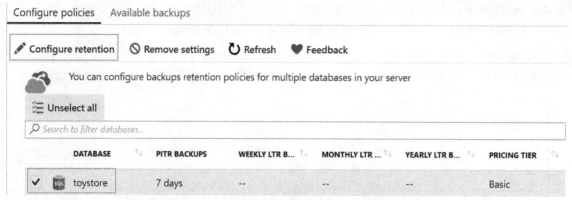

Figure 4.10: Select the database on which to configure LTR

4. In the **Configure policies** window, you can specify the retention period for the weekly, monthly, and yearly backups:

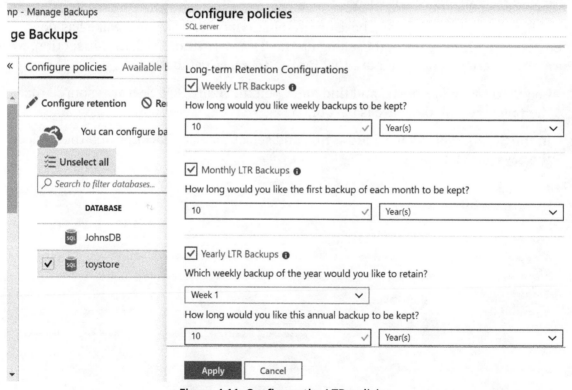

Figure 4.11: Configure the LTR policies

The configuration in *Figure 4.11* states the following:

- **Weekly LTR Backups**: Every backup will be retained for 10 years.
- **Monthly LTR Backups**: The first backup of each month will be retained for 10
- years.
- **Yearly LTR Backups**: The **Week 1** backup is retained for 10 years.

5. Click **Apply** to save the LTR configuration.

> **Note**
>
> Azure SQL Database long-term backups are copied and saved to Azure Blob Storage. It may take up to 7 days for the long-term backups to be available and visible for restore.

Long-term retention configuration on Azure SQL Managed Instance

LTR has recently been introduced for Azure SQL Managed Instance, but this feature is currently in preview and only available for limited **EA** and **CSP** subscriptions. LTR allows you to automatically retain database backups in separate Azure Blob Storage containers for up to 10 years. There is currently no Azure portal support for this feature, and it's only configurable using PowerShell.

Activity: Configure LTR Backups for Azure SQL Managed Instance using PowerShell

Let's get back to our example of ToyStore Ltd. Mike has been tasked with ensuring that a LTR policy is configured for the newly deployed **toystore** database on Azure SQL Managed Instance. Since this feature is new and only available using PowerShell, let's see various commands to manage LTR on Azure SQL Managed Instance.

In this activity, Mike first decides to create an LTR policy for 6 weeks of full backup retention. Then he will be changing it to 12 weeks and will retain the **Week 16** backup for 5 years using LTR. Later, he needs to ensure that the newly configured LTR policy and backup retention is properly configured. At last, he will make sure that restoring from LTR backups is working.

Perform the following steps to complete the activity:

1. Let's start with creating an LTR policy.

   Create an LTR policy, setting up variables as per our environment and subscription:

   ```
   # Get the SQL Managed Instance for your subscription
   $MisubId = "6ee856b5-yy6d-4bc1-xxx-byg5569842e1"
   $SQLinstanceName = "packtsqlmi"
   $ResourceGroup = "Packt"
   $InstancedbName = "toystore"
   $TargetInstancedbName = "toystore_restore"
   ```

2. Connect to your Azure account and get SQL Managed Instance details:

   ```
   #Login to Azure Account

   Connect-AzAccount
   Select-AzSubscription -SubscriptionId $MisubId

   $instance = Get-AzSqlInstance -Name $SQLinstanceName -ResourceGroupName
   $ResourceGroup
   ```

3. Create an LTR policy for keeping every weekly full backup to 6 weeks retention using the following PowerShell code:

   ```
   # create LTR policy with WeeklyRetention = 6 weeks. MonthlyRetention and
   YearlyRetention = 0 by default.

   Set-AzSqlInstanceDatabaseBackupLongTermRetentionPolicy -InstanceName
   $SQLinstanceName '
      -DatabaseName $InstancedbName -ResourceGroupName $ResourceGroup
   -WeeklyRetention P6W


   ResourceGroupName     : Packt
   ManagedInstanceName   : packtsqlmi
   DatabaseName          : toystore
   WeeklyRetention       : P6W
   MonthlyRetention      : PT0S
   YearlyRetention       : PT0S
   WeekOfYear            : 0
   Location              :
   ```

4. Now let's modify this policy, changing weekly backup retention from 6 to 12 weeks. Now each weekly full backup will be kept for 12 weeks. We are also setting up yearly retention for 5 years for a backup that was taken in the 16th week of the year:

```
# create LTR policy with WeeklyRetention = 6 weeks, YearlyRetention = 5
years and WeekOfYear = 16 (week of April 15). MonthlyRetention = 0 by
default.
Set-AzSqlInstanceDatabaseBackupLongTermRetentionPolicy -InstanceName
$SQLinstanceName '
    -DatabaseName $InstancedbName -ResourceGroupName $ResourceGroup
-WeeklyRetention P6W -YearlyRetention P5Y -WeekOfYear 16


ResourceGroupName    : Packt
ManagedInstanceName  : packtsqlmi
DatabaseName         : toystore
WeeklyRetention      : P6W
MonthlyRetention     : PT0S
YearlyRetention      : P5Y
WeekOfYear           : 16
Location             :
```

5. Now that the LTR policy is configured, let's run a command to view it:

```
<#View LTR Policies
# Gets the current version of LTR policy for a database#>

Get-AzSqlInstanceDatabaseBackupLongTermRetentionPolicy -InstanceName
$SQLinstanceName '
    -DatabaseName $InstancedbName -ResourceGroupName $ResourceGroup


ResourceGroupName    : Packt
ManagedInstanceName  : packtsqlmi
DatabaseName         : toystore
WeeklyRetention      : P6W
MonthlyRetention     : PT0S
YearlyRetention      : P5Y
WeekOfYear           : 16
Location             :
```

6. View the LTR backups.

Let's run a command to list the backups. These backups will not be visible for newly created policies; it may take up to 7 days before the first LTR backup shows up on the list:

```
#View LTR backups
# Get the list of LTR backups from the Azure region under the given
managed instance

Get-AzSqlInstanceDatabaseLongTermRetentionBackup -Location $instance.
Location -InstanceName $SQLinstanceName

ResourceId              : /subscriptions/6ee856b5-XXXX-4bc1-XXXX-
byg5569842e1/resourceGroups/Packt/providers/Microsoft.Sql/locations/
eastus/longTermRetentionManaged
                          Instances/packtsqlmi/longTermRetentionDatabases/
toystore/longTermRetentionManagedInstanceBackups/1de6d240-d800-4f7f-913b-
67133b445d3f;1324759
                          23660000000
BackupExpirationTime : 1/11/2021 2:46:06 PM
BackupName              : 1de6d240-d800-4f7f-913b-
67133b445d3f;132475923660000000
BackupTime              : 10/19/2020 2:46:06 PM
DatabaseName            : toystore
DatabaseDeletionTime :
Location                : eastus
ManagedInstanceName   : packtsqlmi
InstanceCreateTime    : 3/30/2020 10:56:54 AM
ResourceGroupName      : Packt
```

7. Delete an LTR backup.

Let's try to delete an LTR backup. Once the following command is submitted, it will ask for confirmation to remove the database backup:

```
#Delete LTR Backups
# remove the earliest backup

$ltrBackups = Get-AzSqlInstanceDatabaseLongTermRetentionBackup -Location
$instance.Location -InstanceName $SQLinstanceName -DatabaseName
$InstancedbName -OnlyLatestPerDatabase
$ltrBackup = $ltrBackups[0]
Remove-AzSqlInstanceDatabaseLongTermRetentionBackup -ResourceId
$ltrBackup.ResourceId

Are you sure you want to remove the Long Term Retention backup '1de6d240-
d800-4f7f-913b-67133b445d3f;132475923660000000' on database 'toystore' on
instance
'packtsqlmi' in location 'eastus'?
Permanantly removing the Long Term Retention backup '1de6d240-d800-4f7f-
913b-67133b445d3f;132475923660000000' on database 'toystore' on instance
'packtsqlmi' in
location 'eastus'?
[Y] Yes  [N] No  [S] Suspend  [?] Help (default is "Y"): Y
```

8. Perform a restore from LTR backups on the same instance.

Now let's see commands to perform a restore from LTR backup:

```
<##Restore from latest LTR backups#>
#Get latest LTR Backup

$ltrBackups = Get-AzSqlInstanceDatabaseLongTermRetentionBackup -Location
$instance.Location -InstanceName $SQLinstanceName -DatabaseName
$InstancedbName -OnlyLatestPerDatabase

#Initiate Restore

Restore-AzSqlInstanceDatabase -FromLongTermRetentionBackup -ResourceId
$ltrBackup.ResourceId '
    -TargetInstanceName $SQLinstanceName -TargetResourceGroupName
$ResourceGroup -TargetInstanceDatabaseName $TargetInstancedbName
```

9. Remove LTR policy.

    Run a PowerShell command to remove the LTR policy of a database:

    ```
    #Remove LTR Policy

    Set-AzSqlInstanceDatabaseBackupLongTermRetentionPolicy -InstanceName
    $SQLinstanceName -DatabaseName $InstancedbName -ResourceGroupName
    $ResourceGroup -RemovePolicy

    ResourceGroupName   : Packt
    ManagedInstanceName : packtsqlmi
    DatabaseName        : toystore
    WeeklyRetention     : PT0S
    MonthlyRetention    : PT0S
    YearlyRetention     : PT0S
    WeekOfYear          : 0
    Location            :
    ```

> **Note**
>
> Any modification to an LTR policy applies to future backups. If weekly backup
> retention (W), monthly backup retention (M), or yearly backup retention (Y) is
> changed, the new retention setting will only apply to new backups. The retention of
> existing backups will not be modified.

In this activity, we have used multiple PowerShell commands to manage LTR policies and backups on Azure SQL Managed Instance. We learned about creating, removing, listing, and updating existing LTR policies. We have also seen commands for managing LTR backups, such as listing backups for an individual database or instance level and deleting backups that are not required.

Manual Backups for Azure SQL Database

Conventional database backup statements don't work in Azure SQL Database. A manual backup consists of exporting the database as a **DACPAC** (schema) or **BACPAC** (schema + data) and **bcp (bulk copy program utility)** out the data into **CSV** files.

Manual backups can be performed in the following ways:

- Exporting a **BACPAC** to your Azure storage account using the Azure portal
- Exporting a **BACPAC** to your Azure storage account using PowerShell
- Exporting a **BACPAC** using SQL **Server Management Studio (SSMS)**
- Exporting a **BACPAC** or a **DACPAC** to an on-premises system using **sqlpackage.exe**

DACPAC and BACPAC

DACPAC stands for **Data-Tier Application Package** and contains the database schema in **.xml** format. A **BACPAC** is a **DACPAC** with data.

DAC is a database life cycle management tool that simplifies the development, deployment, and management of data tier elements supporting an application.

A **BACPAC** is generally used to move a database from one server to another or for migrating a database, as shown in *Chapter 3, Migration*.

> **Note**
>
> To find out more about DACPACs and BACPACs, visit https://docs.microsoft.com/sql/relational-databases/data-tier-applications/data-tier-applications?view=sql-server-2017.

A BACPAC's or a DACPAC's contents can be viewed by changing the file extension to **.zip** and extracting the **ZIP** folder.

Navigate to the **C:\Code\Chapter04** folder (or to the folder to which you exported the BACPAC in the previous section) and change the extension of the **toystore.bacpac** file to **.zip**.

Extract the **toystore.zip** file to the **toystore** folder:

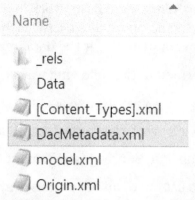

Figure 4.12: Details of the toystore ZIP file

Observe that it has the following files:

- **model.xml**: This contains the database objects in .**xml** format.

- **Origin.xml**: This contains the count of each database object, database size, export start date, and other statistics about the BACPAC and the database.

- **DacMetadata.xml**: This contains the DAC version and the database name.

- **Data**: This folder contains a subfolder for each of the tables in the database. These subfolders contain the table data in BCP format:

sson03 ▸ toystore ▸ Data ▸ Application.Cities	
Name	Date
TableData-000-00000.BCP	11/9/
TableData-001-00000.BCP	11/9/
TableData-002-00000.BCP	11/9/
TableData-003-00000.BCP	11/9/
TableData-004-00000.BCP	11/9/
TableData-005-00000.BCP	11/9/
TableData-006-00000.BCP	11/9/
TableData-007-00000.BCP	11/9/
TableData-008-00000.BCP	11/9/

Figure 4.13: Table data in BCP format

To take a manual backup using SSMS, follow the upcoming steps.

Backing up an Azure SQL Database Using SQL Server Management Studio (SSMS)

> **Note**
>
> We can also export the database in **BACPAC** format using the **Export** option on the Azure SQL Database page in the Azure portal.

In this section, we will back up the Azure SQL **toystore** database using SSMS:

1. Open SSMS and press F8 to open Object Explorer if it's not already open.

2. From **Object Explorer**, connect to Azure SQL Server. Once done, this is what you will see:

Figure 4.14: The toystore database in the Object Explorer pane

3. Right-click the **toystore** database, select **Tasks**, then select **Export Data-tier Application**. In the **Export Data-tier Application** introduction window, click **Next** to continue.

Upgrade Data-tier Application is used to upgrade an existing database to a new DAC version. For example, upgrading the database schema of the production environment to that of a staging environment is commonly used in continuous integration and deployment scenarios:

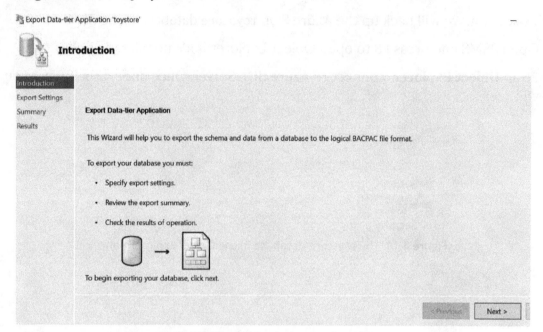

Figure 4.15: The Export Data-tier Application window

> **Note**
>
> The **Register Data-tier Application** and **Upgrade Data-tier Application** options aren't relevant to this chapter and are used for database deployment. To find out more about them, follow these links:
>
> **Register Data-tier Application**: https://docs.microsoft.com/sql/relational-databases/data-tier-applications/register-a-database-as-a-dac.
>
> **Upgrade Data-tier Application**: https://docs.microsoft.com/sql/relational-databases/data-tier-applications/upgrade-a-data-tier-application.

4. In the **Export Settings** window, on the **Settings** tab, select **Save to local disk** and provide a local path to save the BACPAC file. Alternatively, you can also save the BACPAC file on Azure Storage. Saving a BACPAC file on Azure Storage can be useful when the intent of the export is to move the export (restore the database) as an Azure SQL Database. You need an existing storage account to export the file to Azure Storage.

    Click **Next** to continue:

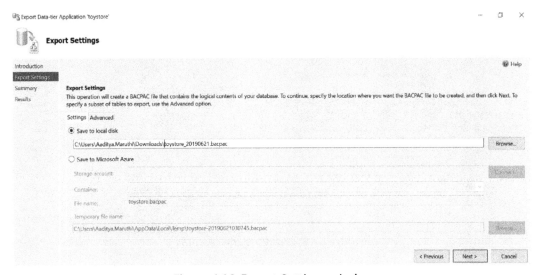

Figure 4.16: Export Settings window

5. In the **Summary** window, verify the **Source** and **Target** settings and click **Finish** to continue:

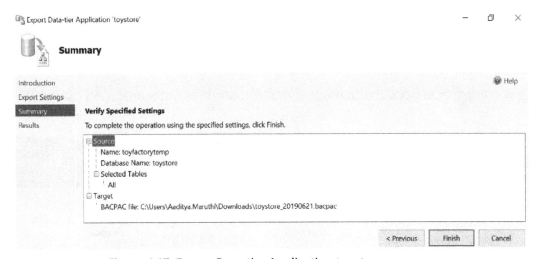

Figure 4.17: Export Data-tier Application toystore summary

6. SSMS first extracts the schema and then the data into a **BACPAC** package:

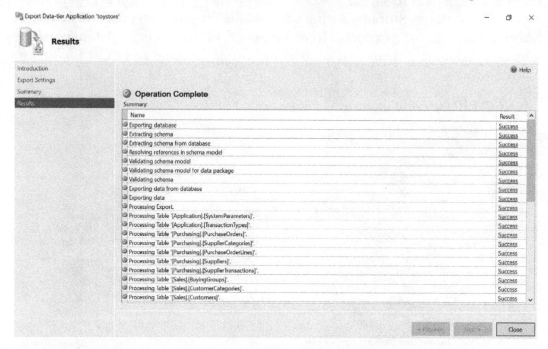

Figure 4.18: Checking the results

7. Click **Close** to close the wizard.

The **BACPAC** isn't transactionally consistent data. The BACPAC exports the table individually, and data may change in the time between the first and last table export. A workaround for this is to create a transactionally consistent database copy and then export it as a BACPAC.

Manual versus Automated Backups

Here is a comparison between manual and automated backups based on usability factors:

Backup Type	Designed for Disaster Recovery	Point-In-Time Restore	Operational Overhead	Transactionally Consistent	Additional Cost	On-Premises Restore
Manual (Export)	No	No	Yes, Export needs to be manually	No (Create a database copy and export it for a Transactionally Consistent backup)	Storage & additional DB cost	Yes
Built-In Automated Backups	Yes	Yes	No	Yes	No	No

Table 4.2: Features of manual versus built-in automated backups

Activity: Perform Manual Backups Using PowerShell

Let's get back to our example of ToyStore Ltd. Mike has been tasked with ensuring that all the data of ToyStore Ltd. is backed up for crises such as system outages, unwanted deletions or updates, database corruption issues, and other related issues. In order to automate this process, he wants to make use of PowerShell scripts. In this activity, we'll learn how to back up an Azure SQL Database using PowerShell scripts:

> **Note**
>
> You need an Azure storage account to carry out the activity. If you don't have an existing storage account, you can create one by running the following command:

```
New-AzStorageAccount -ResourceGroupName myresourcegroup '

-Name mystorageaccountname '

-SkuName Standard_LRS '

-Location 'East US' '

-Kind StorageV2 '

-AccessTier Hot
```

It's advised to create the storage account at the same location as the Azure SQL Database. This minimizes the network delay while copying the data to and from the storage account:

1. Press *Windows* + R to open the **Run** dialog box. In the **Run** dialog box, type **powershell ise** to open a new PowerShell editor window.

2. In the PowerShell ISE, click **File** in the top menu and then select **New** to create a new PowerShell script file:

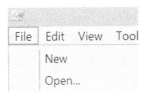

Figure 4.19: Creating a new PowerShell script file

> **Note**
>
> If you are running short of time, modify and run the **BackupAzureSQLDBToAzureStorage.ps1** PowerShell script, which is kept at **C:\ Code\Chapter04**.

3. In the new PowerShell script file, copy the code as instructed in the following steps.

4. Define the PowerShell script parameters. The parameters are self-explanatory:

```
param(
[string]$storageaccountname,
[string]$resourcegroupname,
[string]$sqlserver,
[string]$container,
[string]$database,
[string]$sqluser,
[string]$sqlpassword
)
```

5. Copy the following code. This will open a login window for a user to enter Azure credentials:

```
#Login to Azure account
Login-AzAccount
```

6. Copy the following code to validate the parameters. The PowerShell script will terminate with an error message if the user doesn't provide an Azure storage account name (**$storageaccountname**) or a valid Azure resource group:

```
#($resourcegroupname), and Azure Storage container ($container):

if([string]::IsNullOrEmpty($storageaccountname) -eq $true)
{
    Write-Host "Provide a valid Storage Account Name"
-ForegroundColor Red
    return
}
if([string]::IsNullOrEmpty($resourcegroupname) -eq $true)
{
    Write-Host "Provide a valid resource group" -ForegroundColor Red
    return
}
if([string]::IsNullOrEmpty($container) -eq $true)
{
    Write-Host "Provide a valid Storage Container Name"
-ForegroundColor Red
    return
}
```

7. Copy the following code to initialize the **BACPAC** filename. The **BACPAC** file is created as the database name plus the current timestamp:

```
# create bacpac file name

$bacpacFilename = $database + "_"+(Get-Date). ToString("ddMMyyyymm") +
".bacpac"
```

8. Copy the following code to get the storage account key and set the default storage account for the PowerShell script. The **BACPAC** file will be created in a container in the default Azure storage account. The storage account key is later used in the **export** cmdlet:

```
# set the current storage account

$storageaccountkey = Get-AzStorageAccountKey
-ResourceGroupName $resourcegroupname -Name $storageaccountname

# set the default storage account
Set-AzCurrentStorageAccount -StorageAccountName
$storageaccountname -ResourceGroupName $resourcegroupname | Out-Null
```

9. Copy the following code to set the storage URL. A storage URL defines the full path of the **BACPAC** file on the Azure storage account:

```
# set the bacpac location

$bloblocation = "https://$storageaccountname.blob.core.windows.
net/$container/$bacpacFilename"
```

10. Copy the following code to create a credential object. This allows you to pass the password in an encrypted format when calling the **export** cmdlet:

```
#set the credential

$securesqlpassword = ConvertTo-SecureString -String $sqlpassword
-AsPlainText -Force
$credentials = New-Object -TypeName System.Management.Automation.
PSCredential -ArgumentList $sqluser, $securesqlpassword
```

11. Copy the following code to export the **BACPAC** file to the given storage location. The **New-AzSqlDatabaseExport** cmdlet takes the specified parameters and exports a **BACPAC** file to the storage account:

```
Write-Host "Exporting $database to $bloblocation" -ForegroundColor Green

$export = New-AzSqlDatabaseExport -ResourceGroupName
$resourcegroupname -ServerName $sqlserver.Split('.')[0] -DatabaseName
$database -StorageUri $bloblocation -AdministratorLogin $credentials.
UserName -AdministratorLoginPassword $credentials.Password -StorageKeyType
StorageAccessKey -StorageKey $storageaccountkey.Value[0].Tostring()
```

> **Note**
>
> For the command to work, the **Allow Azure services and resources to access this server** option in the Azure SQL Server firewall should be enabled.

12. Copy the following code to check and output the export progress:

```
While(1 -eq 1)
    {
            $exportstatus = Get-AzSqlDatabaseImportExportStatus
-OperationStatusLink $export.OperationStatusLink
            if($exportstatus.Status -eq "Succeeded")
            {
                Write-Host $exportstatus.StatusMessage -ForegroundColor
Green
                return
            }
            If($exportstatus.Status -eq "InProgress")
            {
                Write-Host $exportstatus.StatusMessage -ForegroundColor
Green
                Start-Sleep -Seconds 5
            }
    }
```

Save the file as **ManualExport.ps1** to **C:\Code\Chapter04**, or to a location of your choice.

13. Open a PowerShell console and change the default directory to **C:\Code\Chapter04**, or to the directory where you have saved the PowerShell script.

    Type the following code and press *Enter* to start the export. You may have to change the parameter values as per your Azure environment:

    ```
    .\ManualExport.ps1 -storageaccountname "toyfactorystorage" -
    resourcegroupname "toystore" -container "backups" - sqlserver toyfactory
    -database "toystore" -sqluser "sqladmin" -sqlpassword "Packt@pub2"
    ```

14. The PowerShell script will ask you to log in to your Azure account through a login pop-up window. Once you log in, the export will start. You should get a similar output to this:

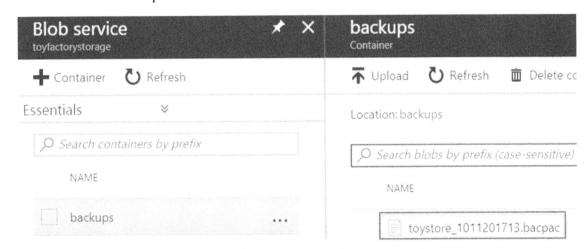

Figure 4.20: Export in progress

15. To verify the export, log in to the Azure portal with your credentials.

16. Open the storage account provided in the preceding script. You should see the **BACPAC** file in the specified container:

Figure 4.21: The backup bacpac file of the toystore database

Manual export can be required when moving databases in between developer, QA, or staging environments. PowerShell makes it easy to manually export databases.

Perform native COPY_ONLY backup on Azure SQL Managed Instance

A **COPY_ONLY** backup is a SQL Server backup that is independent of the conventional SQL Server backups. Usually, taking ad hoc full backups can break the point-in-time restore chain of an SQL Server database. But there could be scenarios in which you are required to take database backups (like moving the latest snapshot of a database to a development SQL Server instance). That's where you can use the **COPY_ONLY** backup option while taking a backup.

Azure SQL Managed Instance has automatic backups that are stored on Azure storage, fully encrypted and keeping you compliant. These backups can be used to perform a point-in-time restore, cross-instance restore, or geo-restore.

Microsoft's recommendation is to rely on these built-in automatic backups. Azure SQL Managed Instance also supports native SQL Server **COPY_ONLY** backups that are useful in scenarios such as keeping backups for longer periods on Azure Blob Storage.

All newly created databases on Azure SQL Database and Azure SQL Managed Instance are encrypted by default with service-managed **transparent data encryption (TDE)**. You cannot initiate a manual **COPY_ONLY** backup for TDE protected databases that use service-managed encryption in Azure SQL Managed Instance.

Following is the message you will see when you try to run a **BACKUP DATABASE** command with the **COPY_ONLY** option for a service-managed TDE protected database:

```
--Backup database to URL

 BACKUP DATABASE toystore

 TO URL = 'https://packtsqlmistorage.blob.core.windows.net/backup/toystore.
bak'

WITH COPY_ONLY


 Msg 41922, Level 16, State 1, Line 8

 The backup operation for a database with service-managed transparent data
 encryption is not supported on SQL Database Managed Instance.

 Msg 3013, Level 16, State 1, Line 8

 BACKUP DATABASE is terminating abnormally.
```

This functionality is designed to keep the data protected. For a seamless **COPY_ONLY** backup experience, you can configure customer-managed transparent data encryption for Azure SQL Managed Instance. For more information on CMK encryption, please visit this link: https://docs.microsoft.com/azure/azure-sql/database/transparent-data-encryption-byok-overview.

Perform a manual COPY_ONLY backup using T-SQL commands

Azure SQL Managed Instance allows **COPY_ONLY** backups but you are not allowed access to the underlying storage layer of the Azure SQL Managed Instance host due to the nature of the PaaS application. We need to use the **BACKUP TO URL** command to perform a backup. Before taking a backup, Azure SQL Managed Instance needs to have access to Blob Storage to create a backup file.

In this activity we will be going through all these steps:

1. First, let's create the credentials to access Azure Blob Storage. We need a **shared access signature (SAS)** before creating the credentials and access to the storage account firewall.

    Generate a SAS token using the Azure portal. To generate a SAS token, go to the storage account settings and select the **Shared access signature** blade. Select **Services** and specify the start and expiry token dates, then click on **Generate SAS and connection string** button:

Figure 4.22: Generate a SAS token using the portal

Once the token is generated, you will see it listed in the boxes below the **Generate SAS and connection string** button, as shown here:

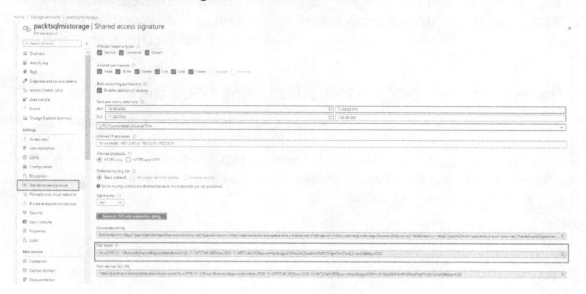

Figure 4.23: Copy the SAS token

2. For additional security, add the Azure SQL Managed Instance subnet to the storage account firewall for private access:

Figure 4.24: Storage account firewall

3. Now that we have a SAS token, run **CREATE CREDENTIAL** to allow Azure SQL Managed Instance access to Blob Storage. Remove the **?** symbol from SAS key before using it:

```
--Create credential to access blob storage.
CREATE CREDENTIAL [https://packtsqlmistorage.blob.core.windows.net/backup]
WITH IDENTITY='SHARED ACCESS SIGNATURE'
, SECRET = 'sv=2019-12-12&ss=bfqt&srt=c&sp=rwdlacupx&se=2020-10-
31T06:52:48Z&st=2020-10-01T22:52:48Z&spr=https&sig=7IXxTFEiCJOEAFMeE52HQu
MOZOVwXJgaP3%2FZLxrA8fg%3D';
```

4. Run the **Backup** command.

   Execute the following backup statement to take a **COPY_ONLY** backup for a small database. Here, we are taking a backup with a checksum and the **COPY_ONLY** option. Using a checksum is best practice. **CHECKSUM** ensures that the backup operation verifies each page for checksum and torn page, if enabled and available, and generates a checksum for the entire backup. Using backup checksums may affect the workload and backup throughput:

```
--Backup database to URL
 BACKUP DATABASE toystore
 TO URL = 'https://packtsqlmistorage.blob.core.windows.net/backup/
toystore.bak'
WITH COPY_ONLY,CHECKSUM
```

5. If your database is large enough and the backup file size is >200 GB, then you need to split your database backup into multiple files. You can also use a compression option to reduce the backup size. 200 GB is the maximum file size for block blob storage:

```
--Stripping backups if backup size is >200GB
BACKUP DATABASE toystore
 TO URL = 'https://packtsqlmistorage.blob.core.windows.net/backup/
toystore-4-1.bak',
 URL = 'https://packtsqlmistorage.blob.core.windows.net/backup/
toystore-4-2.bak',
 URL = 'https://packtsqlmistorage.blob.core.windows.net/backup/
toystore-4-3.bak',
 URL = 'https://packtsqlmistorage.blob.core.windows.net/backup/
toystore-4-4.bak'    WITH COPY_ONLY,COMPRESSION,FORMAT
```

6. Specify **MAXTRANSFERSIZE** as **4194304** to use larger block sizes, specifically 4 MB blocks:

```
--Backup database with MAXTRANSFERSIZE
BACKUP DATABASE toystore
TO URL = 'https://packtsqlmistorage.blob.core.windows.net/backup/
toystore-4-1.bak',
URL = 'https://packtsqlmistorage.blob.core.windows.net/backup/
toystore-4-2.bak',
URL = 'https://packtsqlmistorage.blob.core.windows.net/backup/
toystore-4-3.bak',
URL = 'https://packtsqlmistorage.blob.core.windows.net/backup/
toystore-4-4.bak'
WITH COPY_ONLY, MAXTRANSFERSIZE = 4194304,COMPRESSION,FORMAT
```

> **Note**
>
> To learn more about backing up VLDB to Azure Blob Storage, please visit this link: https://docs.microsoft.com/archive/blogs/sqlcat/backing-up-a-vldb-to-azure-blob-storage.

In this activity, we have used the native backup command to initiate a **COPY_ONLY** backup to Azure Blob Storage. We have also learned how to generate a SAS key using the Azure portal and best practices for taking backups for large databases. These backups can be useful for moving a database copy to an on-premises SQL server or a different Azure SQL Managed Instance in another region or on another subscription.

Summary

Azure SQL Database backups are different from on-premises database backups. The regular backup database command isn't supported in Azure SQL Database. In this chapter, we have learned about the automatic backups that are unique to Azure SQL Database and Azure SQL Managed Instance and that aren't available in an on-premises database.

We also learned about automatic backup frequency and backup storage, as well as multiple options for optimizing backup storage costs for Azure SQL Database and Azure SQL Managed Instance.

We also learned how to configure LTR backups for Azure SQL Database and Azure SQL Managed Instance, and discussed how to take manual backups of an Azure SQL database using SSMS and PowerShell, and native manual **COPY_ONLY** backups using T-SQL for Azure SQL Managed Instance.

In the next chapter, we will look at the restore options available for Azure SQL Database and Azure SQL Managed Instance.

5

Restoration

In the previous chapter, we talked about performing database backups for Azure SQL Database and Azure SQL Managed Instance. Similar to a database backup, a restore is another housekeeping activity that a DBA performs, whether to move or copy a database from one server to another or to recover from an outage or an accidental update/delete operation. In this chapter, we'll look at different ways to restore an Azure SQL Database and an SQL Managed Instance database.

Azure SQL Database and SQL Managed Instance have the following restore options:

- Point-in-time restore
- Restore from long-term backup
- Restore a deleted database
- Geo-restore a database
- Import a **BACPAC** – only for Azure SQL Database

Figure 5.1 shows the types of backup available with Azure SQL Database, the different restore options, and the ways to restore a database:

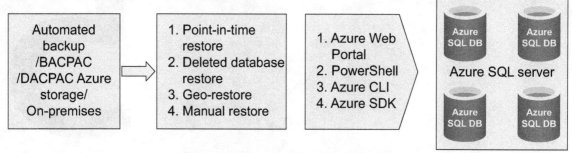

Figure 5.1: Types of database restore

A restore can be performed using the Azure portal, PowerShell, the Azure CLI, or the Azure SDK. This chapter teaches you the differences between the restore types and how to perform a restore. It also explores different restore options, such as point-in-time restores, restoring a deleted database, and geo-restoring a database. You'll also learn how to automate the restore task using PowerShell.

By the end of this chapter, you will be able to:

- Use point-in-time restore to recover from unexpected data modifications
- Restore a deleted database using the Azure portal
- Use geo-restore on a database
- Restore a database from a long-term retention backup
- Restore an Azure SQL Database by importing **BACPAC**

So, let's begin by deep-diving into the various restore options mentioned here.

Restore types

This section discusses the different types of restore available in Azure SQL Database and SQL Managed Instance.

Point-in-time restore

Point-in-time restore (**PITR**) isn't new in the world of SQL Server. On-premises SQL servers allow you to restore a database to a particular point in time by specifying the point-in-time option when restoring the database using the **restore** command.

Azure SQL Database and SQL Managed Instance backups are managed by the automatic backups feature of the PaaS offering. Point-in-time restores can only be performed using the Azure portal, PowerShell, the Azure CLI, or the Azure SDK. PITR uses the automatic **Full**, **Differential**, and **Log** backups.

For all new, restored, and copied databases on Azure SQL Database and SQL Managed Instance, the default retention period is 7 days. The retention period can be adjusted for existing or deleted databases (the latter is only available on SQL Managed Instance):

- For active databases on Azure SQL Database and SQL Managed Instance, you can change backup retention to any period between 1–35 days.

- Azure SQL Database Hyperscale only supports 7 days of backup retention; it cannot be adjusted.

- For deleted databases, you can change the backup retention period to any period between 0 and 35 days (only available on SQL Managed Instance).

To learn how to change the default retention period, please refer to the *Backup retention period* section of *Chapter 4, Backups*.

An Azure SQL Database can only be restored on the same Azure SQL Server as the original database with a different name, but on SQL Managed Instance, you can perform a restore on the same database or a restore on a different instance in the same region and subscription. If you are restoring a database using PITR to recover from a corruption issue and wish to use the restored database as the production database, you have to rename the database accordingly, after the restore completes.

PITR is useful for recovering from unexpected data modifications, corrupted databases, or for getting a database state from a previous state for application testing or debugging an issue.

> **Note**
>
> PITR always creates a new database, so you must drop an existing database or rename it later to keep the same database name.
>
> Cross-instance database restores are only allowed within the same region and subscription. Cross-region and cross-subscription PITR are not yet supported.

Performing a PITR on an Azure SQL Database using the Azure portal

To perform a PITR on an Azure SQL Database using the Azure portal, perform the following steps:

1. Open **SQL Server Management Studio (SSMS)** and connect to the Azure SQL server hosting the Azure SQL database you wish to perform a PITR on.

2. Open the **C:\Code\Chapter05\InsertNewColor.sql** file in SSMS. Make sure that the database's context is set to the **toystore** database.

3. Press F5 or click **Execute** in the top menu to run the query. The query adds a new row in the **Warehouse.Color** table with **ColorID=37**:

```
-- Insert a new color
INSERT INTO [Warehouse].[Colors]
SELECT
        37 AS ColorID
      ,'Dark Yellow' AS ColorName
      ,1 AS LastEditedBy
      ,GETUTCDATE() AS ValidFrom
      ,'9999-12-31 23:59:59.9999999' As Validto
GO
-- Verify the insert
SELECT [ColorID]
      ,[ColorName]
      ,[LastEditedBy]
      ,[ValidFrom]
      ,[ValidTo]
  FROM [Warehouse].[Colors]
  WHERE ColorID=37
```

You should get an output similar to *Figure* 5.2:

	ColorID	ColorName	LastEditedBy	ValidFrom	ValidTo
1	37	Dark Yellow	1	2017-11-12 12:45:52.2166667	9999-12-31 23:59:59.9999999

Figure 5.2: A new row added in the Warehouse.Color table

4. Log in to the Azure portal with your Azure credentials. From the left-hand navigation pane, select **All Resources** and click on the Azure SQL database you wish to perform a PITR on:

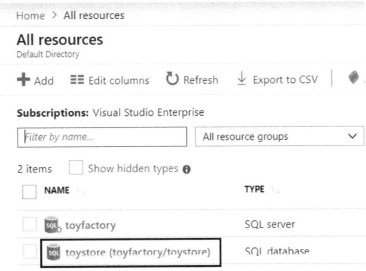

Figure 5.3: Selecting an Azure SQL database to perform a PITR

5. From the **toystore** SQL database overview section, click **Restore**:

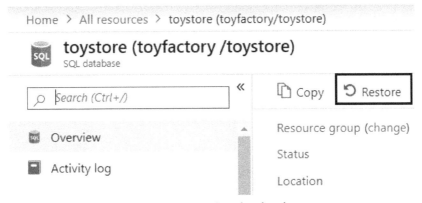

Figure 5.4: Restoring the database

6. You will now see the **Restore** pane:

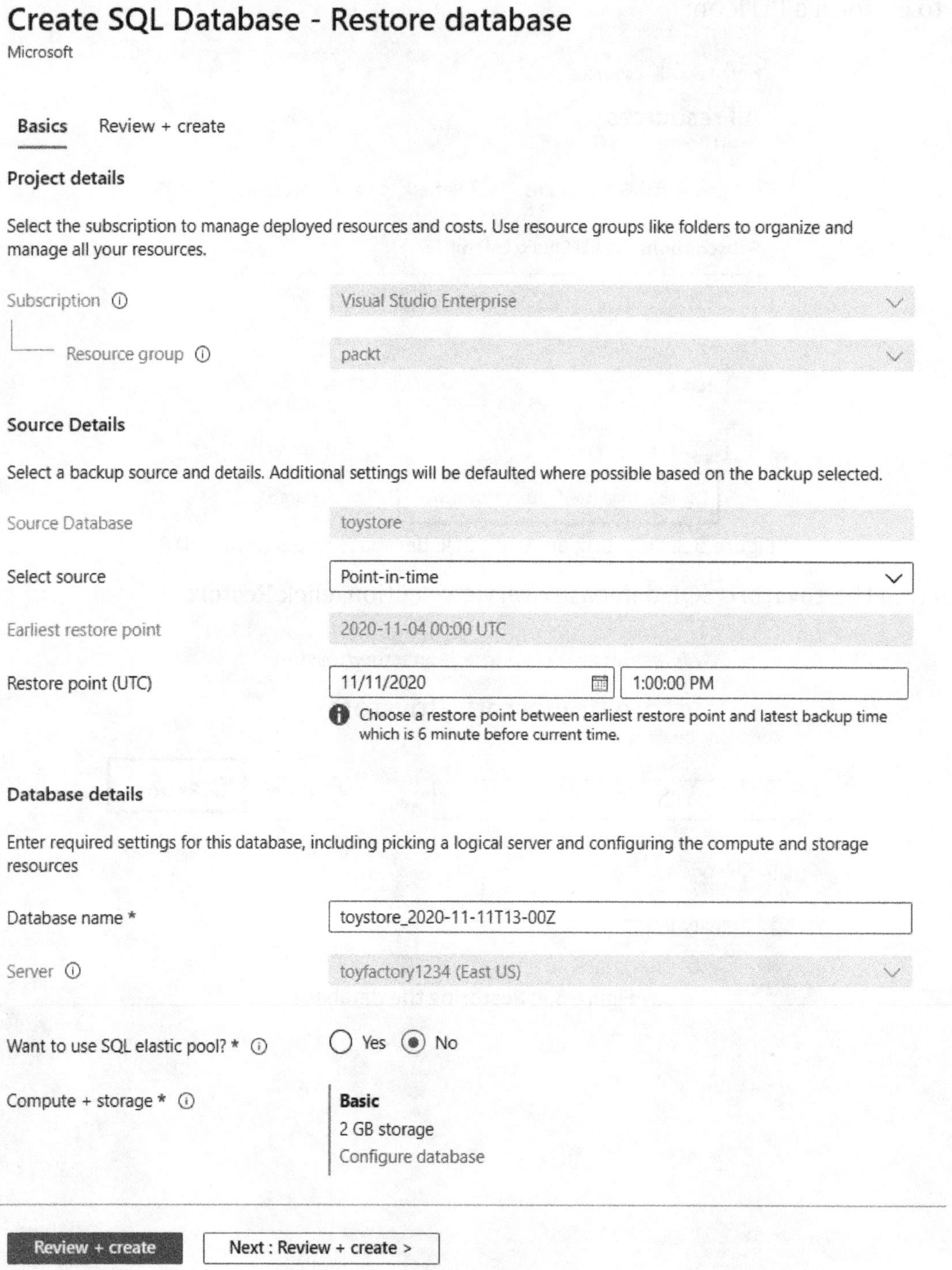

Create SQL Database - Restore database

Microsoft

Basics   Review + create

Project details

Select the subscription to manage deployed resources and costs. Use resource groups like folders to organize and manage all your resources.

Subscription ⓘ

> Visual Studio Enterprise ⌄

└──── Resource group ⓘ

> packt ⌄

Source Details

Select a backup source and details. Additional settings will be defaulted where possible based on the backup selected.

Source Database

> toystore

Select source

> Point-in-time ⌄

Earliest restore point

> 2020-11-04 00:00 UTC

Restore point (UTC)

> 11/11/2020   📅 | 1:00:00 PM

ⓘ Choose a restore point between earliest restore point and latest backup time which is 6 minute before current time.

Database details

Enter required settings for this database, including picking a logical server and configuring the compute and storage resources

Database name *

> toystore_2020-11-11T13-00Z

Server ⓘ

> toyfactory1234 (East US) ⌄

Want to use SQL elastic pool? * ⓘ   ◯ Yes ⦿ No

Compute + storage * ⓘ

> **Basic**
> 2 GB storage
> Configure database

[Review + create]   [Next : Review + create >]

Figure 5.5: PITR restore

Observe the oldest restore point available—this might be different in your case.

Under **Restore point**, specify the date when you want to perform the PITR. Observe that the **Database Name** value changes as you change the restore time.

The database name is `toystore_PITRDate`. For example, if we were restoring the database to 11 November 2020, 1:00 PM, then the database name would be `toystore_2020-11-11T13-00Z`.

You can change the database name if you want to. However, having the point in time in the database name is a good way of remembering the reason why and the time to which the database is being restored.

Observe that the **Azure SQL Server (Target server)** option is disabled. Therefore, the PITR can be only done on the same server as the original database.

Click **Review + Create** and then **Create** to start the database restore. The restore time depends on the size of the database being restored.

Wait for the restore to finish. You can look at the **Notifications** section on the Azure portal to see the progress of the restore:

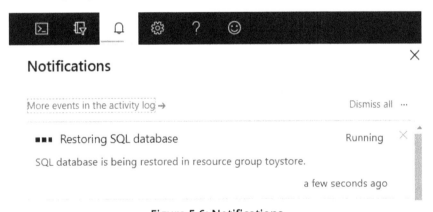

Figure 5.6: Notifications

7. Once the restore is complete, open the **All Resources** pane and verify that the database is listed there:

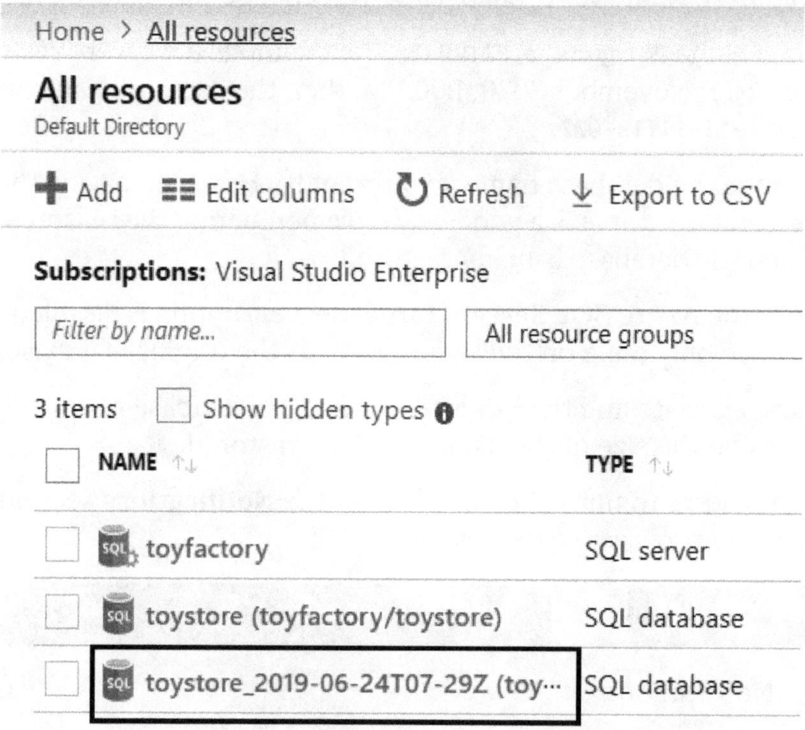

Figure 5.7: Verifying the completed restore

8. Since the database has been restored and has the same data and schema as it had on 11 November 2020, this database shouldn't contain `ColorID 37`, which we added in *step* 3.

   Switch to SSMS and open `C:\Code\Chapter05\InsertNewColor.sql`, if it's not already open.

   Change the database context to `toystore_2020-11-11T13-00Z`. This will be different in your case.

9. Select and execute the following query in SSMS:

```
-- Verify the insert
SELECT [ColorID]
      ,[ColorName]
      ,[LastEditedBy]
      ,[ValidFrom]
      ,[ValidTo]
  FROM [Warehouse].[Colors]
 WHERE ColorID=37
```

You should get an output similar to *Figure* 5.8:

```
-- Verify the insert
SELECT [ColorID]
      ,[ColorName]
      ,[LastEditedBy]
      ,[ValidFrom]
      ,[ValidTo]
   FROM [Warehouse].[Colors]
   WHERE ColorID=37
%  ▾
Results    Messages
   ColorID   ColorName   LastEditedBy   ValidFrom   ValidTo
```

Figure 5.8: Output of the SELECT query

Observe that none of the rows contain `ColorID 37` in the `Warehouse.Colors` table.

The **point-in-time (PITR)** restore can easily be done for an Azure SQL Database and provides a way to recover from an accidental delete/update or an outage. Now let's look at how to do the same thing for an Azure SQL Managed Instance.

Performing a PITR for an SQL Managed Instance using the Azure portal

To initiate a PITR using the Azure portal for SQL Managed Instance, please follow these steps:

1. Sign in to the Azure portal at https://portal.azure.com.

2. Go to SQL Managed Instance and select the database you wish to restore.

3. Click on the **Restore** option on the database page:

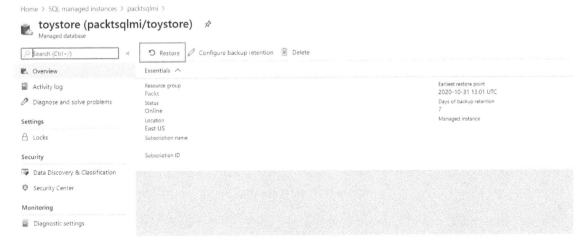

Figure 5.9: Selecting the Restore option from the database page

4. On the **Restore** page, enter a new database name, choose a restore point, and click on the **OK** button to initiate the restoration:

Home > SQL managed instances > packtsqlmi > toystore (packtsqlmi/toystore) >

Restore

toystore

> Backed up database is restored to a new database. To initiate the restore, type in a database name to which backed up database will be restored, and choose a restore point in time from the available backups.

Target server

packtsqlmi

Database name * ⓘ

toystore_restore ✓

Restore point (UTC) ⓘ

| 11/01/2020 📅 | 7:26:00 AM |

Earliest restore point
2020-10-31 13:02 UTC

Current time
2020-11-03 07:33 UTC

OK

Figure 5.10: Restore details

5. Check the deployment status and click on **Go to resource** to see the newly restored database:

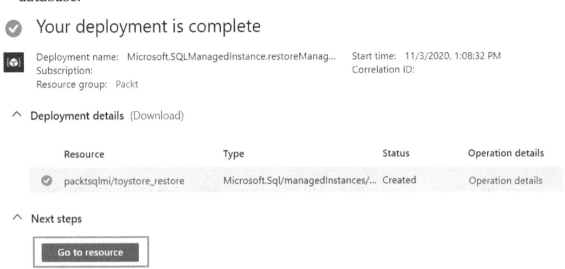

Figure 5.11: PITR deployment completion

As mentioned in the introduction, it is possible to perform all the different types of restoration we cover in this chapter (except for importing a BACPAC) with both Azure SQL Database and SQL Managed Instance. We have demonstrated how to do a PITR for both of them just now using the Azure portal, but for brevity, we won't always cover the restore process for both in the following sections.

Long-term database restore

A **Long-term database restore (LTDR)** allows you to restore a database configured for long-term retention backups. The backups are kept in Azure Blob Storage for a longer period of time.

An LTDR uses the same technique as a PITR to restore a database; however, here you can restore a database from the last 10 years.

> **Note**
>
> LTDR is currently in public preview for Azure SQL Managed Instance and is only available for limited subscription types, such as the EA and CSP subscriptions.

Performing an LTDR on an Azure SQL Database using the Azure portal

To perform a restore from long-term retention backup on an Azure SQL Database using the Azure portal, do the following:

1. Log in to the Azure portal with your Azure credentials. From the left-hand navigation pane, select **All Resources** and click on the Azure SQL Database you wish to perform an LTDR on:

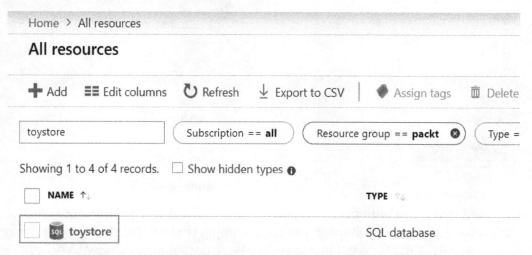

Figure 5.12: Selecting the Azure SQL database to perform an LTDR

2. From the **toystore** SQL database overview section, click **Restore**:

Figure 5.13: Restoring the database

3. In the **Restore** pane, from the **Select source** drop-down menu, select **Long-term backup retention**:

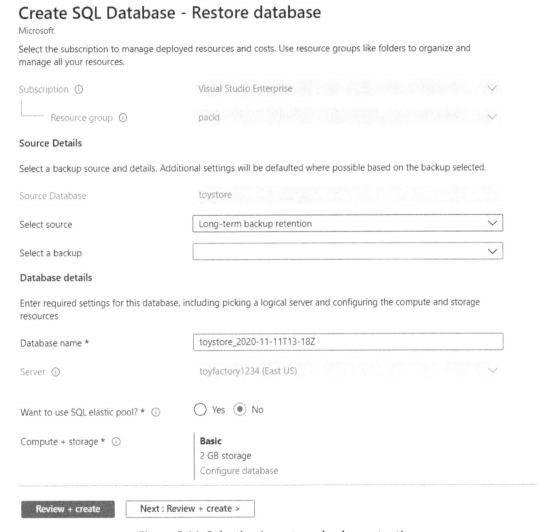

Create SQL Database - Restore database

Microsoft

Select the subscription to manage deployed resources and costs. Use resource groups like folders to organize and manage all your resources.

Subscription ⓘ   Visual Studio Enterprise   ⌄

     └─── Resource group ⓘ   packt   ⌄

Source Details

Select a backup source and details. Additional settings will be defaulted where possible based on the backup selected.

Source Database   toystore

Select source | Long-term backup retention   ⌄ |

Select a backup | ⌄ |

Database details

Enter required settings for this database, including picking a logical server and configuring the compute and storage resources

Database name * | toystore_2020-11-11T13-18Z |

Server ⓘ   toyfactory1234 (East US)   ⌄

Want to use SQL elastic pool? * ⓘ   ◯ Yes   ◉ No

Compute + storage * ⓘ   **Basic**
      2 GB storage
      Configure database

[Review + create]   [Next : Review + create >]

Figure 5.14: Selecting Long-term backup retention

Click **Select a backup** under the **Long-term backup retention** setting.

This setting will list all the backups from the vault. Choose a backup date from the resulting pane and click **Select**.

Observe that the **Target server** option is locked and can't be set to any server other than the original database server.

Change the database name to `toystore_2019-06-20T16-31Z`. Click **OK** to start the restoration process.

Click **Review + Create** and then **Create** to start the restore process

4. The restore time depends on the size of the database being restored. Wait for the restore to finish. You can look at the **Notifications** section on the Azure portal to see the progress of the restore:

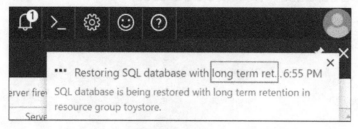

Figure 5.15: Checking restore notifications

Observe that the notification says that long-term retention is in progress.

5. Once the restore is complete, open the **All Resources** pane and verify that the database is listed there:

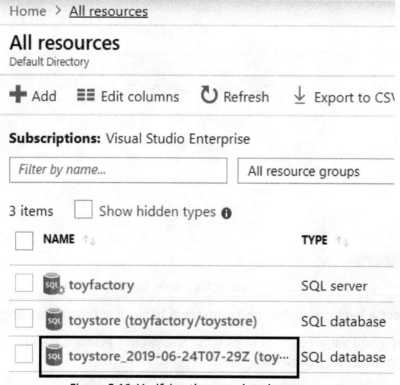

Figure 5.16: Verifying the completed restore

To verify the restore, follow *steps 8-9* under the *Point-in-time restore* section. The database shouldn't have a **ColorID 37** row in the **Warehouse.Colors** table.

Now let's do the same thing for SQL Managed Instance but using PowerShell commands.

Performing an LTDR for SQL Managed Instance using PowerShell

A long-term database restore allows us to restore a database from a long-term backup. This is particularly useful for reconciliation or for when data analysis needs to be performed on data that's older than a year or so.

In the preview period, there is no Azure portal support to perform a restore operation from LTDR backups on SQL Managed Instance. Here, we will instead see quick steps to perform a restore of a managed database from LTDR backups using PowerShell cmdlets.

Please follow these steps to complete this activity:

1. Open Cloud Shell from the Azure portal:

Figure 5.17: Cloud Shell

2. Run the following set of commands to set the variables:

```
# Set the environment variables
$subId = "0000000-xxxx-000000-xxxx-000xxx00"
$instanceName = "packtsqlmi"
$resourceGroup = "packt"
$sourceDbName = "toystore"
$targetDbname = 'toystore_restore'
```

3. Log in to your Azure account using following command:

```
# Login to Azure account and select subscription
Connect-AzAccount
Select-AzSubscription -SubscriptionId $subId
```

4. Run the following command to get SQL Managed Instance details:

```
# Get the instance details
$instance = Get-AzSqlInstance -Name $instanceName -ResourceGroupName $resourceGroup
```

5. Run the following command to get the latest LTDR backup for the **toystore** database:

    ```
    # get the latest LTR backup for a specific database from the Azure region
    under the given managed instance
    $ltrBackup = Get-AzSqlInstanceDatabaseLongTermRetentionBackup -Location
    $instance.Location -InstanceName $instanceName -DatabaseName $sourceDbName
    -OnlyLatestPerDatabase
    ```

6. Run the following command to initiate a restore operation from the LTDR backup:

    ```
    # restore a the LTR backup
    Restore-AzSqlInstanceDatabase -FromLongTermRetentionBackup
    -ResourceId $ltrBackup.ResourceId -TargetInstanceName $instanceName
    -TargetResourceGroupName $resourceGroup -TargetInstanceDatabaseName
    $targetDbname
    ```

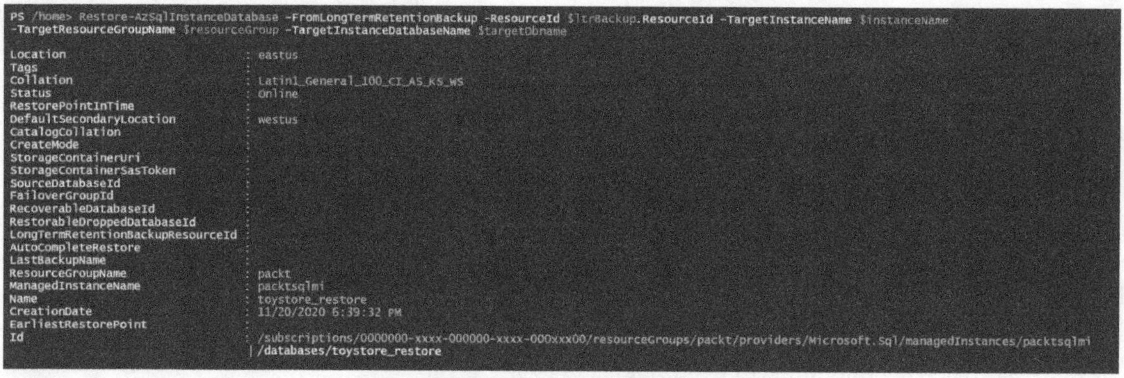

Figure 5.18: LTDR PowerShell output

In this activity, we have learned to perform a restore operation from LTDR backups on SQL Managed Instance using PowerShell commands.

Restoring deleted databases

Azure allows you to restore a deleted database to the time it was deleted, or to any time within the retention period. You can select the deleted database you wish to restore from the pool of deleted databases. You are able to restore a deleted database because the automatic backups are saved for a given retention period that depends on the service tier.

Restoring a deleted database on Azure SQL Database using the Azure portal

Let's restore a deleted database using the Azure portal:

1. Log in to the Azure portal using your Azure credentials. Open **All resources** from the left-hand navigation pane.

2. From the **All resources** pane, open the Azure SQL server that hosts the deleted database you wish to restore.

3. In the Azure SQL Server pane, from the **Settings** section, select **Deleted databases**:

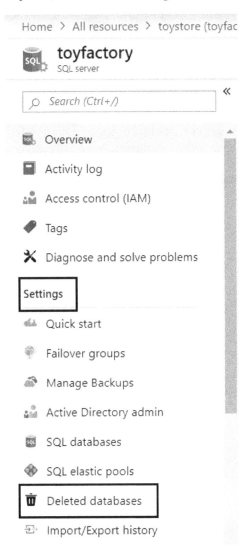

Figure 5.19: Navigating to deleted databases

4. The **Deleted databases** pane lists the databases and their deletion times. Select the **toystore** database for any deletion date you want to restore it to (if, for instance, you'd deleted and restored the database more than once in the past):

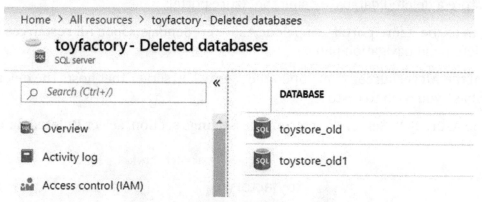

Home > All resources > toyfactory - Deleted databases

toyfactory - Deleted databases
SQL server

Search (Ctrl+/)

DATABASE

Overview   toystore_old

Activity log   toystore_old1

Access control (IAM)

Figure 5.20: List of deleted databases

5. In the **Restore** pane, provide the database name.

Observe that the **Target server** option is locked. Therefore, the deleted database can only be restored to the same server as that of the original database.

Observe that the **Restore point** option is set to the deletion date that you opted to restore the database to.

Click **OK** to restore the database:

Home > All resources > toyfactory- Deleted databases > Restore

Restore
toystore_old

* Database name

toystore_old_2019-06-24T07 -35Z

Target server

toyfactory

Restore point (UTC)

2019-06-24 07:35 UTC

Figure 5.21: Providing a database name for the restore

Monitor the database's restoration progress in the **Notification** pane, as mentioned in the previous section.

6. Once the database is restored, navigate to the **All resources** section from the left-hand navigation pane. Observe that the database is now listed here:

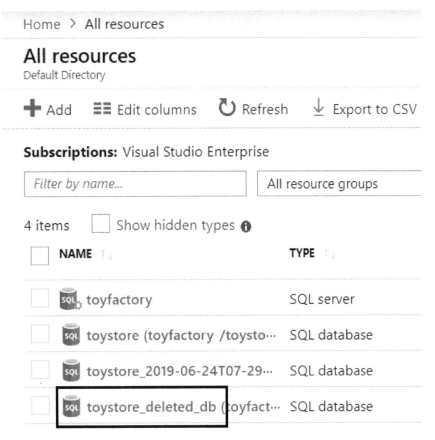

Figure 5.22: Verifying the restored database

You can use *steps 8-9* of the *Point-in-time restore* section to verify the restored database. The database shouldn't have a `ColorID 37` row in the `Warehouse.Colors` table.

Restoring a deleted database on SQL Managed Instance using the Azure portal

To recover a deleted database using the Azure portal, please follow these steps:

1. Navigate to SQL Managed Instance and select the **Deleted Databases** pane in the Azure portal.

2. Select the deleted database.

3. Enter the database name and select a timestamp.

4. Click on **OK** to initiate the restore:

Figure 5.23: Restoring a deleted SQL Managed Instance database using the Azure portal

5. Monitor the notification bell icon to see progress:

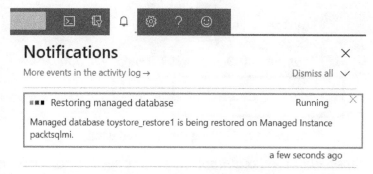

Figure 5.24: The restore operation is in progress

6. After the restore operation is complete, you will see a successful restore notification:

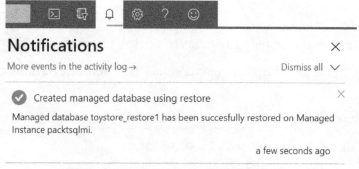

Figure 5.25: Successful restore notification

Restoring deleted databases allows us to recover from the accidental deletion of a database and can be easily done using the Azure portal, as shown in these demonstrations.

Geo-restoring databases

A geo-restore allows you to restore a database from a geo-redundant backup to any available Azure SQL servers and SQL Managed Instance, irrespective of the region.

The automatic backups of Azure SQL Database and SQL Managed Instance are geo-redundant by default, and are copied to a paired Azure region as and when they are taken. There is a maximum delay of one hour when copying a database to a paired geographical location. Therefore, in the case of a disaster, there can be up to an hour of data loss:

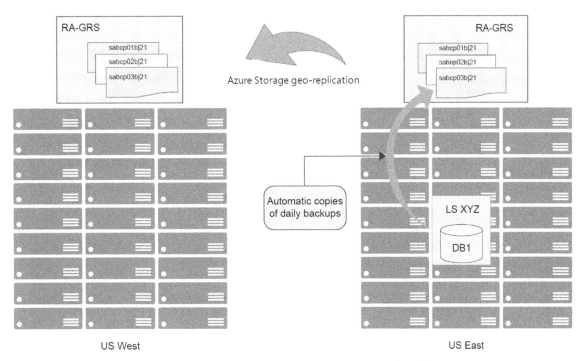

Figure 5.26: Geo-replication to a different geographical location

Geo-restore can be used to recover a database if an entire region is unavailable because of a disaster:

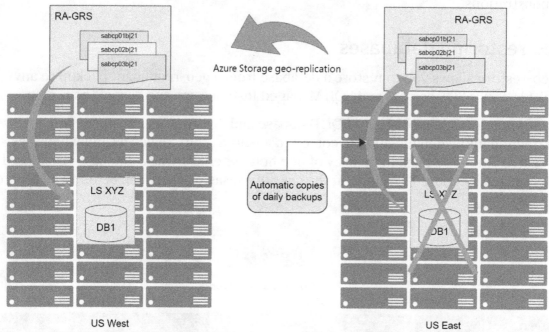

Figure 5.27: Use of geo-restore in the case of unavailability of an entire region

The most recent full and differential backups are used to perform a geo-restore.

Geo-restore doesn't support PITR. It is the most basic disaster recovery solution with the longest recovery time, which can be up to 12 hours. This may be a reasonable recovery solution for dev/test environments or applications that can take some downtime. For mission-critical applications that need to be up and running at all times, active geo-replication is highly recommended.

Performing a geo-restore on an SQL Database using the Azure portal

Let's perform a geo-restore of the **toystore** database on a new server in another region using the Azure portal:

1. Log in to the Azure portal using your Azure credentials. In the top search box, type **SQL servers** and then select **SQL servers** from the search options:

Figure 5.28: Selecting SQL servers

On the **SQL servers** page, click **Add** from the top menu to create a new SQL server.

2. On the **Create SQL Database Server** page, provide the subscription, resource group, server name, location, and the server administrator's username and password as shown in *Figure 5.29*:

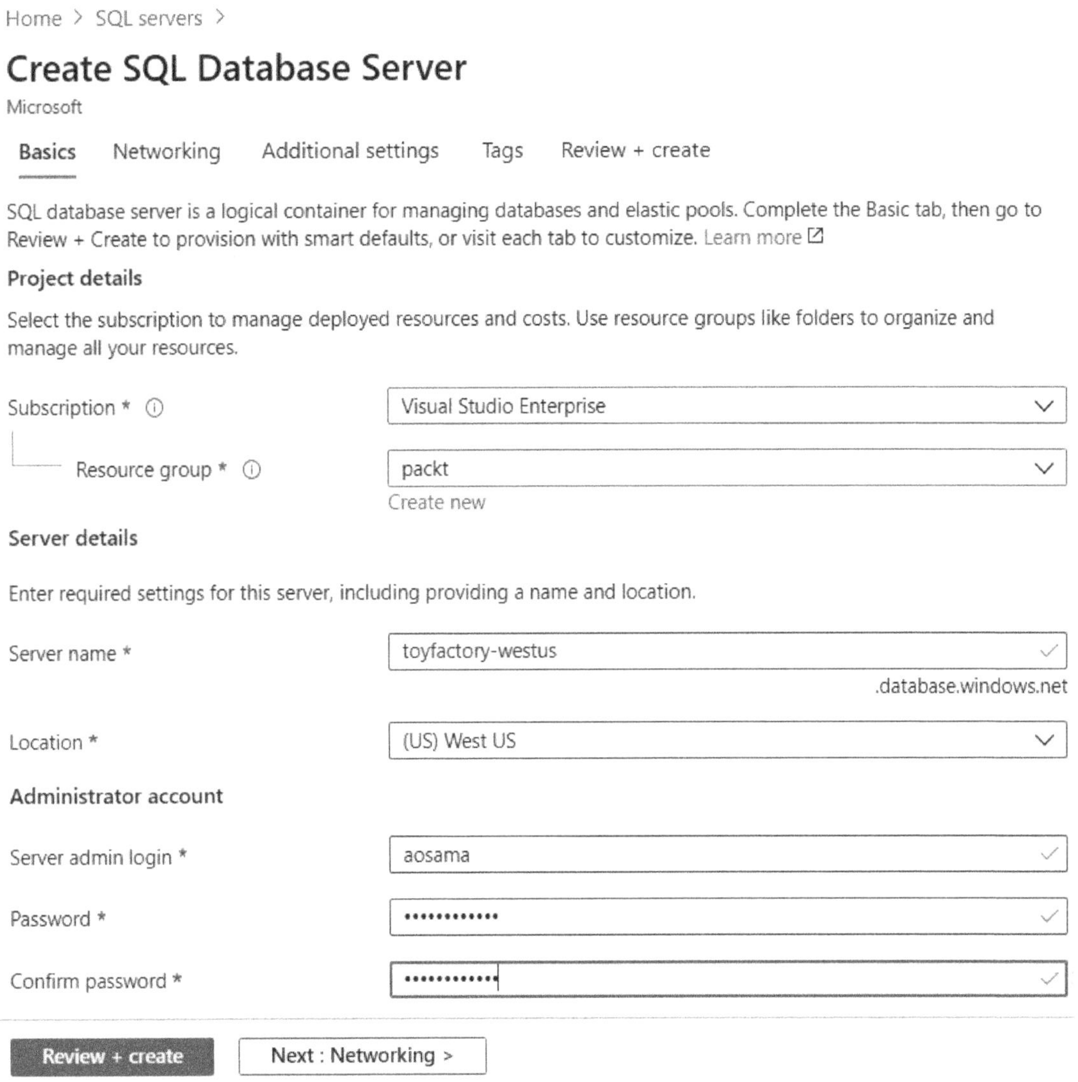

Home > SQL servers >

Create SQL Database Server

Microsoft

Basics   Networking   Additional settings   Tags   Review + create

SQL database server is a logical container for managing databases and elastic pools. Complete the Basic tab, then go to Review + Create to provision with smart defaults, or visit each tab to customize. Learn more ☑

Project details

Select the subscription to manage deployed resources and costs. Use resource groups like folders to organize and manage all your resources.

Subscription * ⓘ | Visual Studio Enterprise   ⌄ |

└─── Resource group * ⓘ | packt   ⌄ |
                           Create new

Server details

Enter required settings for this server, including providing a name and location.

Server name * | toyfactory-westus   ✓ |
                                                    .database.windows.net

Location * | (US) West US   ⌄ |

Administrator account

Server admin login * | aosama   ✓ |

Password * | ••••••••••••   ✓ |

Confirm password * | ••••••••••••   ✓ |

[Review + create]   [Next : Networking >]

Figure 5.29: Creating a new SQL server for geo-restore

The new server location should be different from that of the existing database.

Click **Review + create** and then **Create** to provision the new SQL server.

Wait for the SQL server to be created.

3. Open the new SQL server's page and select **Create database**:

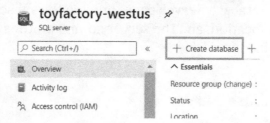

Figure 5.30: Creating a database using the new SQL server

4. On the **Create SQL Database** page, under the **Basic** tab, provide the database name and change the **Compute + Storage** setting to **Basic** (this is to save costs for the demonstration. In a production environment, this setting should be the same as that of the primary database):

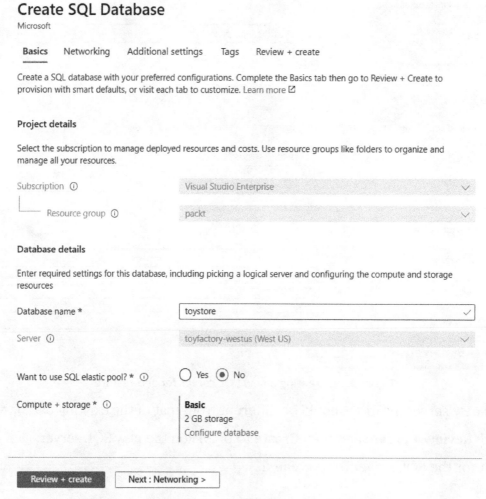

Figure 5.31: Creating an SQL database—Basics tab

5. Select the **Additional settings** tab. In the **Data source** section, select **Backup** as the **Use existing data** option. The **Select a backup** dropdown lists all of the available SQL database backups. Select the `toystore` database:

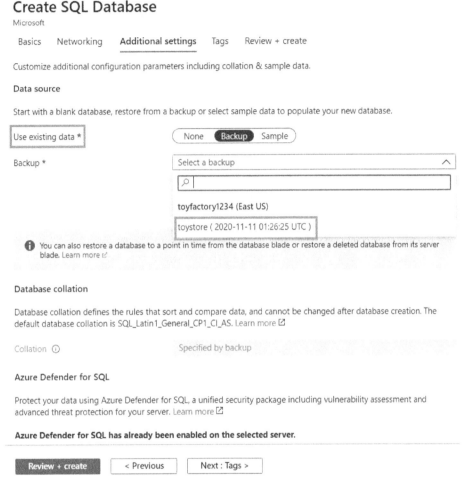

Figure 5.32: Restoring a database from an existing backup

Observe that the `toystore` database is in the `toyfactory1234` SQL server in East US. The new database we are restoring is in West US.

Click **Review + create** and then **Create** to restore the database.

A geo-restore helps us to restore SQL Databases across regions in order to recover from regional failures. However, to geo-restore an SQL Database, the backup storage redundancy of the source Azure SQL Database (or Managed Instance database) should be set to geo-redundant. The default backup storage redundancy is geo-redundant and can be changed using the `Set-AzSQLDatabase` PowerShell cmdlet by specifying the value (**Local**, **Zone**, or **Geo**) for the `BackupStorageRedundancy` option.

Performing a geo-restore on an SQL Managed Instance using the Azure portal

Geo-restore allows you to recover a database to a different region, and this can be used as a disaster recovery solution, but the recovery time depends on the database's size. Geo-backups are only available when SQL Managed Instance is configured with geo-redundant backup storage.

Let's quickly go through the steps for performing a geo-restore for SQL Managed Instance using the Azure portal:

1. Go to the Azure portal and navigate to the SQL Managed Instance **Overview** tab, where you need to initiate a geo-restore.

2. Select **New database**.

3. Type the desired database name.

4. Under **Use existing data**, select **Backup**.

5. Select a backup from the list of available geo-restore backups.

6. Click **OK** to initiate the restore operation:

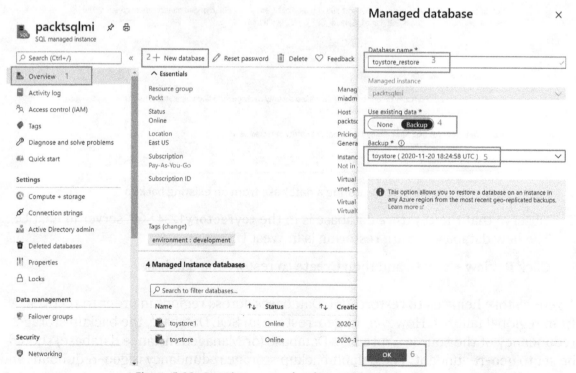

Figure 5.33: Creating a new database with geo-backup

7. Monitor the notification bell icon for a success notification:

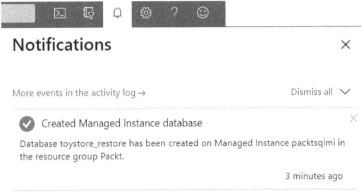

Figure 5.34: Successful geo-restore notification

This will create a new **toystore_restore** database from a geo-backup of **toystore** database hosted on SQL Managed Instance. This concludes the activity here.

The restore options we've talked about so far—point-in-time, delete, and geo-restore—were from managed backups. We didn't have access to the database backups, but we did get an option to restore the database. However, there are scenarios where we need to restore a database from a manual export (**BACPAC**). Let's see how we can import a database using an existing **BACPAC** file.

Importing a database (Azure SQL Database only)

You can import a database into an Azure SQL server from a **BACPAC** or **DACPAC** file kept in Azure Storage. The import operation will create a new Azure SQL database from the **BACPAC** file.

The **BACPAC** file can be imported to any of the available Azure SQL servers in any given region. This can be useful for quickly creating new test environments.

The import can be done through the Azure portal, PowerShell, the Azure CLI, or the Azure SDK. Let's learn how to import a database from a **BACPAC** file kept in Azure Storage. Open the Azure portal, go to https://portal.azure.com, and log in with your Azure credentials:

1. From the left-hand navigation pane, open the **All resources** section. Select the Azure SQL server you wish to import the database to.

2. In the Azure SQL Server **Overview** pane, select **Import database**:

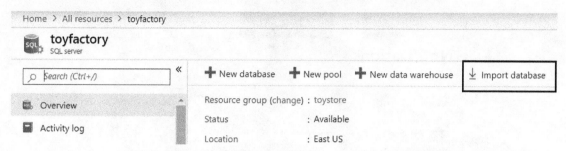

Figure 5.35: Selecting the Import database option

3. In the **Import database** pane, under **Subscription**, select your Azure subscription:

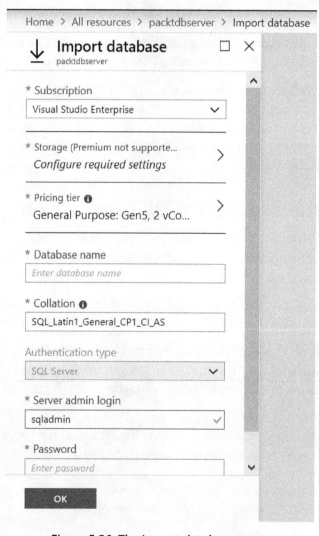

Figure 5.36: The Import database pane

Select **Storage**. In the **Storage accounts** pane, select the storage account where your file is located:

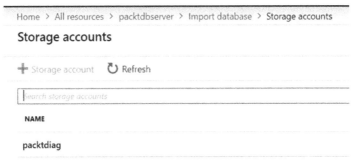

Figure 5.37: Selecting the container

Select the container, and then select the **BACPAC** file you wish to import by clicking on **Select**:

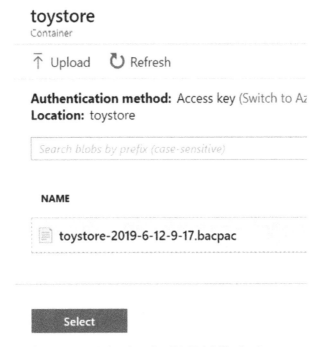

Figure 5.38: Selecting the BACPAC file for import

Under the **Pricing tier** option, choose your pricing tier.

Under the **Database Name** option, provide the database name.

Leave the **Collation** option as default.

Provide the username and password for the Azure SQL server.

4. Select **OK** to import the database:

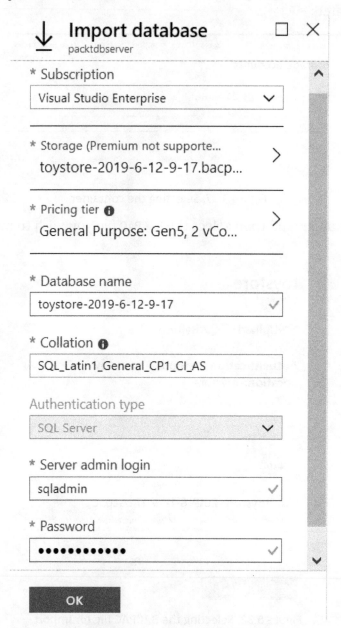

Figure 5.39: Importing the database

Importing a database using the `Import` option from a `BACPAC` file is useful when moving a database from on-premises to Azure SQL, or from one Azure SQL server to another.

We'll now move to the activities and learn how to perform different restores using PowerShell.

Activity: Performing a PITR for an Azure SQL Database with PowerShell

Consider the following scenario: Mike is a new DBA, so his trainer is aware that there might be some misses at his end. Therefore, his trainer wants to configure PITR on the databases that Mike is working on. In this section, we will perform a PITR using PowerShell by following these steps:

1. Press *Windows key* + R to open the **Run** dialog box. In the **Run** dialog box, type `powershell ise` to open a new PowerShell editor window.

2. In PowerShell, click **File** from the top menu and then select **New** to create a new PowerShell script file:

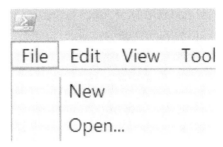

Figure 5.40: Creating a new PowerShell script

3. In the new PowerShell script file, copy and paste in the code from the following step.

4. Define the PowerShell script parameters. The parameters are self-explanatory:

```
param(
            [Parameter(Mandatory=$true)]
            [string]$sqlserver,
            [Parameter(Mandatory=$true)]
            [string]$database,
            [Parameter(Mandatory=$true)]
            [string]$sqluser,
            [Parameter(Mandatory=$true)]
            [string]$sqlpassword,
            [Parameter(Mandatory=$true)]
            [string]$resourcegroupname,
            [string]$newdatabasename
       )
```

5. Copy the following code to let the users log in to their Azure subscription by providing Azure credentials in a login window:

```
#Login to Azure account
Login-AzAccount
Select-AzSubscription -SubscriptionId $subscriptionId
```

6. Copy the following code to output the earliest restore point available and let the users provide a point in time to restore the database to:

```
While (1)
        {
            #Retrieve the distinct restore points from which a SQL
Database can be restored
            $restoredetails = Get-AzSqlDatabaseRestorePoints
-ServerName $sqlserver -DatabaseName $database -ResourceGroupName
$resourcegroupname
            #get the earliest restore date
        $erd=$restoredetails.EarliestRestoreDate.ToString();
            #ask for the point in time the database is to be restored
        $restoretime = Read-Host "The earliest restore time is $erd.'n
Enter a restore time between Earliest restore time and current time."
            #convert the input to datatime data type
        $restoretime = $restoretime -as [DateTime]
            #if restore time isn't a valid data, prompt for a valid
date
        if(!$restoretime)
            {
                Write-Host "Enter a valid date" -ForegroundColor Red
            }else
            {
            #end the while loop if restore date is a valid date
                break;
            }
        }
    }
```

You can read through the comments to understand what the code does.

7. Copy the following code to set the new database name if it hasn't already been provided by the user, and perform the PITR:

```
#set the new database name
        if([string]::IsNullOrEmpty($newdatabasename))
        {
            $newdatabasename = $database + (Get-Date).
ToString("MMddyyyymm")
        }

        # get the original database object
        $db = Get-AzSqlDatabase -DatabaseName $database -ServerName
$sqlserver -ResourceGroupName $resourcegroupname
            Write-Host "Restoring Database $database as of
$newdatabasename to the time $restoretime"

        #restore the database to point in time
        $restore = Restore-AzSqlDatabase -FromPointInTimeBackup
-PointInTime $restoretime -ResourceId $db.ResourceId -ServerName $db.
ServerName -TargetDatabaseName $newdatabasename -Edition $db.Edition
-ServiceObjectiveName $db.CurrentServiceObjectiveName -ResourceGroupName
$db.ResourceGroupName


        # restore deleted database

        if($rerror -ne $null)
        {
            Write-Host $rerror -ForegroundColor red;
        }
        if($restore -ne $null)
        {
            Write-Host "Database $newdatabasename restored
Successfully";
        }
```

You can read through the comments to understand what the code does.

8. Save the file as **PITRAzureSQLDB.ps1** to **C:\Code\Chapter05** or a location of your choice.

9. Open a PowerShell console and change the default directory to **C:\Code\Chapter05** or the directory where you have saved the PowerShell script.

10. Copy the following code and press *Enter* to start the export. You may have to change the parameter values to match your Azure environment:

```
.\PITRAzureSQLDB.ps1 -sqlserver toyfactory -database toystore
-sqluser sqladmin -sqlpassword Packt@pub2 -resourcegroupname toystore
-newdatabasename toystorepitr
```

The preceding command will restore the **toystore** database to a specified point in time on the **toyfactory** SQL server in the **toystore** resource group. The database will be restored as **toystorepitr**.

Once the script finishes, you should get an output similar to *Figure 5.41*:

```
PS C:\Code\Chapter05> .\PITRAzureSQLDB.ps1 -sqlserver toyfactory -database toystore -sqluser sqlad

Environment          : AzureCloud
Account              :
TenantId             :
SubscriptionId       :
CurrentStorageAccount :

The earliest restore time is 11/8/2017 7:20:19 AM.
 Enter a restore time between Earlist restore time and current time.: 11/10/2017 2:00:00 AM
Restoring Database toystore as of toystorepitr to the time 11/10/2017 02:00:00
Database toystorepitr restored Successfully
```

Figure 5.41: A successful PITR on the toystorepitr database

You can also verify whether or not the available restore is visible in the Azure portal.

Activity: Performing a geo-restore of an Azure SQL Database with PowerShell

Let's once again consider our example of ToyStore Ltd. Mike is aware that, although on the cloud, his data is still physically stored on servers. Hence, there is a possibility of data loss due to natural disasters. In these instances, he would have to perform a geo-restore operation. This section makes use of PowerShell to perform a geo-restore:

1. Press *Windows key* + R to open the **Run** dialog box. In the **Run** dialog box, type **powershell ise** to open a new PowerShell editor window.

2. In PowerShell, click **File** from the top menu, and then select **New** to create a new PowerShell script file:

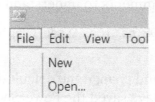

Figure 5.42: Creating a new PowerShell script

3. In the new PowerShell script file, copy the code as instructed in the following steps.

    Define the PowerShell script parameters. The parameters are self-explanatory:

    ```
    param(
                    [Parameter(Mandatory=$true)]
                    [string]$sqlserver,
                    [Parameter(Mandatory=$true)]
                    [string]$database,
                    [Parameter(Mandatory=$true)]
                    [string]$sqluser,
                    [Parameter(Mandatory=$true)]
                    [string]$sqlpassword,
                    [Parameter(Mandatory=$true)]
                    [string]$resourcegroupname,
                    [string]$newdatabasename
    )
    ```

    Copy the following code to open a login dialog box to log in to Azure:

    ```
    #Login to Azure subscription
    Login-AzAccount
    Select-AzSubscription -SubscriptionId $subscriptionId
    ```

    Copy the following code to get the details of the database that is to be geo-restored in a PowerShell object and display the details on the console:

    ```
    # get the geo database backup to restore

    $geodb = Get-AzSqlDatabaseGeoBackup -ServerName
    $sqlserver -DatabaseName $database -ResourceGroupName
    $resourcegroupname

    #Display Geo-Database properties
    $geodb | Out-Host
    ```

    Copy the following code to retrieve the name of the database that is to be restored:

    ```
    #get the database name from the geodb object
    $geodtabasename = $geodb.DatabaseName.ToString()
    ```

    Copy the following code to set the new database name if it hasn't already been provided by the user:

    ```
    #set the new database name
    if([string]::IsNullOrEmpty($newdatabasename))
    {
    ```

```
            $newdatabasename = $database + (Get-Date).ToString("MMddyyyymm")
    }
```

Copy the following code to perform the geo-restore:

```
Write-Host "Restoring database $geodtabasename from geo backup"
-ForegroundColor Green

# perform the geo restore
$restore = Restore-AzSqlDatabase -FromGeoBackup
-ResourceId $geodb.ResourceID -ServerName $sqlserver
-TargetDatabaseName $newdatabasename -Edition $geodb.Edition
-ResourceGroupName $resourcegroupname -ServiceObjectiveName
$serviceobjectivename

if($rerror -ne $null)
{
Write-Host $rerror -ForegroundColor red;
}

if($restore -ne $null)
{
$restoredb = $restore.DatabaseName.ToString()
Write-Host "Database $database restored from Geo Backup as database
$restoredb" -ForegroundColor Green
}
```

The new database has the same edition and performance level as the original database. You can change this by specifying different values in the **Restore-AzSqlDatabase cmdlet**.

4. Save the file as **GeoRestoreAzureSQLDB.ps1** to **C:\Code\Chapter05** or a location of your choice.

5. Open a PowerShell console and change the default directory to **C:\Code\Chapter05** or to the directory where you have saved the PowerShell script.

6. Copy the following code and press *Enter* to start the export. You may have to change the parameter values as per your Azure environment:

```
.\GeoRestoreAzureSQLDB.ps1 -sqlserver toyfactory -database toystore
-sqluser sqladmin -sqlpassword Packt@pub2
-resourcegroupname toystore -newdatabasename toystoregeorestore
```

The preceding command will restore the **toystore** database to a specified point in time on the **toyfactory** SQL server in the **toystore** resource group. The database will be restored as **toystoregeorestore**.

Once the script finishes, you should get an output similar to what is shown in *Figure 5.43*:

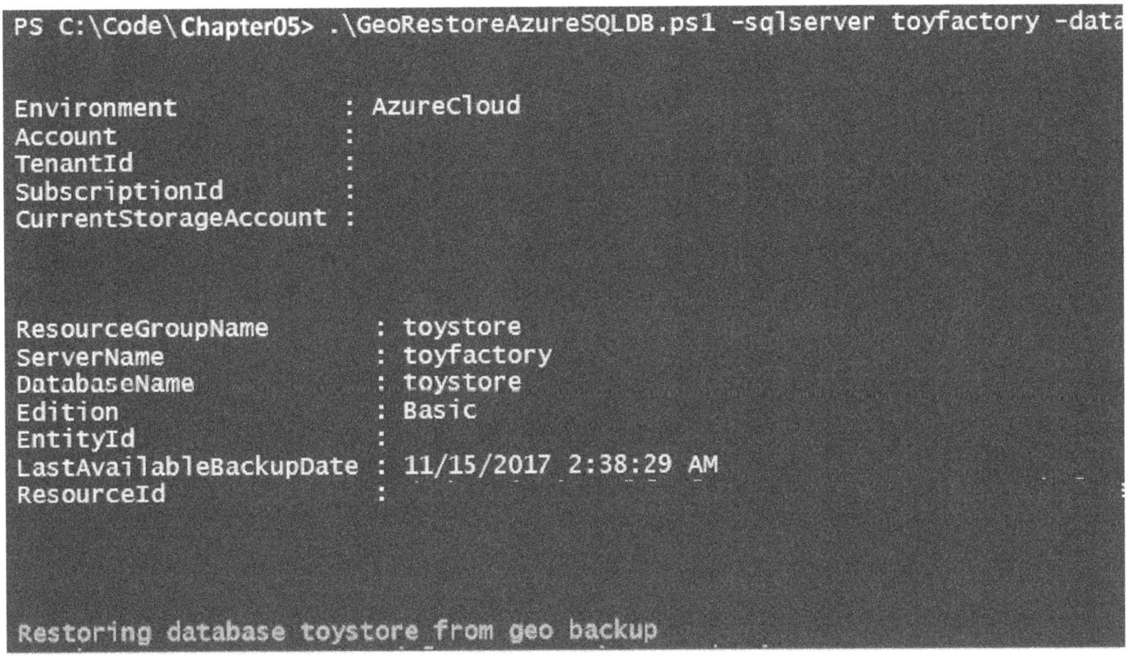

```
PS C:\Code\Chapter05> .\GeoRestoreAzureSQLDB.ps1 -sqlserver toyfactory -data


Environment          : AzureCloud
Account              :
TenantId             :
SubscriptionId       :
CurrentStorageAccount :


ResourceGroupName    : toystore
ServerName           : toyfactory
DatabaseName         : toystore
Edition              : Basic
EntityId             :
LastAvailableBackupDate : 11/15/2017 2:38:29 AM
ResourceId           :


Restoring database toystore_from geo backup
```

Figure 5.43: Successful completion of geo-restore

Your **toystore** database has been successfully restored.

Activity: Performing Point-In-Time restore for SQL Managed Instance with PowerShell

In this two-part activity, we will be performing a point-in-time restore of a database in SQL Managed Instance using PowerShell and then a cross-instance restore of a database (from one SQL Managed Instance to another SQL Managed Instance).

Part 1: Restoring a database to a point in time using PowerShell on one managed instance

To perform a point-in-time restore operation on the same SQL Managed Instance using PowerShell commands, please follow these steps:

1. Press *Windows key* + R to open the **Run** dialog box. In the **Run** dialog box, type **powershell ise** to open a new PowerShell editor window.

2. In PowerShell, click **File** from the top menu and then select **New** to create a new PowerShell script file:

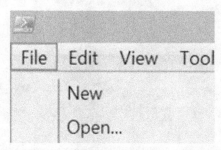

Figure 5.44: Creating a new PowerShell script

3. In the new PowerShell script file, copy in the code from the following step.

4. Define the PowerShell script parameters. The parameters are self-explanatory:

```
param(
[Parameter(Mandatory=$true)]
[string]$resourcegroupname,
[Parameter(Mandatory=$true)]
[string]$subscriptionId,
[Parameter(Mandatory=$true)]
[string]$managedInstanceName,
[Parameter(Mandatory=$true)]
[string]$databaseName,
[Parameter(Mandatory=$true)]
[string]$newdatabasename
)
```

5. Copy the following code to let the users log in to their Azure subscription by providing Azure credentials in a login window:

```
# Login to Azure subscription
Login-AzAccount
Select-AzSubscription -SubscriptionId $subscriptionId
```

6. Copy the following code to output the earliest restore point available and let the users provide a point in time to restore the database to:

```
# list the earliest restore point
# Ask user for the point in time the database is to be restored

While (1)
{
            #Retrieve the distinct restore points from which a Database
can be restored
$restoredetails = Get-AzSqlInstanceDatabase -InstanceName
$managedInstanceName -Name $databaseName -ResourceGroupName
$resourcegroupname

#get the earliest restore point
        $erd=$restoredetails.EarliestRestorePoint.ToString();

#ask for the point in time the database is to be restored
                $restoretime = Read-Host "The earliest restore time is
$erd.'n Enter a restore time between Earlist restore time and current
time."

#convert the input to datetime date type
                $restoretime = $restoretime -as [DateTime]

#if restore time isn't a valid data, prompt for a valid date
                if(!$restoretime)
            {
                Write-Host "Enter a valid date" -ForegroundColor Red
            }else
            {
                #end the while loop if restore date is a valid date
                break;
            }
}
```

You can read through the comments to understand what the code does.

7. Copy the following code to set the new database name if it hasn't already been provided by the user, and perform the PITR:

```
#set the new database name
        if([string]::IsNullOrEmpty($newdatabasename))
        {
            $newdatabasename = $databaseName + (Get-Date).
ToString("MMddyyyymm")
        }

Write-Host "Restoring Database $databaseName as of $newdatabasename to
the time $restoretime"

    #restore the database to point in time
$restore = Restore-AzSqlInstanceDatabase -FromPointInTimeBackup
-ResourceGroupName $resourcegroupname -InstanceName $managedInstanceName
-Name $databaseName -PointInTime $restoretime -TargetInstanceDatabaseName
$newdatabasename

if($rerror -ne $null)
    {
        Write-Host $rerror -ForegroundColor red;
    }
    if($restore -ne $null)
    {
Write-Host "Database $newdatabasename restored Successfully"
-ForegroundColor Green;
    }
```

You can read through the comments to understand what the code does.

8. Save the file as **SQLMI_PITROnSameInstance.ps1** to **C:\Code\Chapter05**, or a location of your choice.

9. Open a PowerShell console and change the default directory to **C:\Code\Chapter05** or to the directory where you have saved the PowerShell script.

10. Copy the following code and press *Enter* to start the export. You may have to change the parameter values to match your Azure environment:

```
.\SQLMI_PITROnSameInstance.ps1 -resourcegroupname Packt -subscriptionId
6ee856b5-yy6d-4bc1-a901-by00000002e1 -managedInstanceName packtsqlmi
-databaseName toystore -newdatabasename toystorepitr
```

The preceding command will restore the **toystore** database to a specified point in time on the **packtsqlmi** Azure SQL Managed Instance in the **Packt** resource group. The database will be restored as **toystorepit**r.

Once the script finishes, you should get a similar output to *Figure 5.45*:

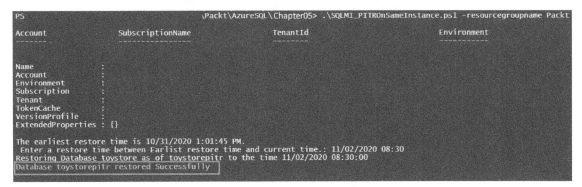

Figure 5.45: A successful PITR of the toystorepitr database

You can also verify this using the Azure portal:

Figure 5.46: A newly added toystorepitr database

Part 2: Performing a cross-instance point-in-time restore from an existing database

Cross-instance PITRs are useful for scenarios such as moving/migrating a database from one instance to another. You could alternatively use the **COPY_ONLY** backup/restore method, but this is a much easier approach than backup/restore.

Cross-instance PITR is limited to the same Azure region and subscription. You cannot initiate cross-instance PITR and perform it on another instance located in a different subscription or region. If you have a cross-region or subscription instance, then you can use the **Copy** method to copy a database.

> **Note**
> Cross-instance PITR is only supported using the PowerShell method.

Follow these steps to perform a cross-instance PITR:

1. Press *Windows key* + R to open the **Run** dialog box. In the **Run** dialog box, type **powershell ise** to open a new PowerShell editor window.

2. In PowerShell ISE, click **File** from the top menu and then select **New** to create a new PowerShell script file:

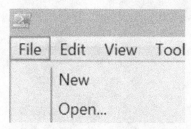

Figure 5.47: Creating a new PowerShell script

3. In the new PowerShell script file, copy the code from the following step.

4. Define the PowerShell script parameters. The parameters are self-explanatory:

```
param(
        [Parameter(Mandatory=$true)]
        [string]$resourcegroupname,
        [Parameter(Mandatory=$true)]
        [string]$subscriptionId,
        [Parameter(Mandatory=$true)]
        [string]$managedInstanceName,
        [Parameter(Mandatory=$true)]
        [string]$databaseName,
        [Parameter(Mandatory=$true)]
        [string]$targetResourceGroupName,
        [Parameter(Mandatory=$true)]
        [string]$targetManagedInstanceName,
        [Parameter(Mandatory=$true)]
        [string]$targetDatabaseName
)
```

5. Copy the following code to let the users log in to their Azure subscription by providing Azure credentials in a login window:

```
# Login to Azure subscription
Login-AzAccount
Select-AzSubscription -SubscriptionId $subscriptionId
```

6. Copy the following code to output the earliest restore point available and let the users provide a point in time to restore the database to:

```
# list the earliest restore point
# Ask user for the point in time the database is to be restored


While (1)
        {
            #Retrieve the distinct restore points from which a Database
can be restored
                $restoredetails = Get-AzSqlInstanceDatabase -InstanceName
$managedInstanceName -Name $databaseName -ResourceGroupName
$resourcegroupname
                #get the earliest restore point
            $erd=$restoredetails.EarliestRestorePoint.ToString();
            #ask for the point in time the database is to be restored
            $restoretime = Read-Host "The earliest restore time is $erd.'n
Enter a restore time between Earlist restore time and current time."
            #convert the input to datatime data type
            $restoretime = $restoretime -as [DateTime]
            #if restore time isn't a valid data, prompt for a valid
date
        if(!$restoretime)
            {
                Write-Host "Enter a valid date" -ForegroundColor Red
            }else
            {
            #end the while loop if restore date is a valid date
                break;
            }
        }
```

You can read through the comments to understand what the code does.

7. Copy the following code to set the new database name if it hasn't already been provided by the user, and perform the PITR:

```
#set the new database name
    if([string]::IsNullOrEmpty($targetDatabaseName))
        {
            $targetDatabaseName = $databaseName + (Get-Date).
ToString("MMddyyyymm")
        }


        Write-Host "Restoring Database $databaseName as
$targetDatabaseName on $targetManagedInstanceName to the time
$restoretime"

        #restore the database to point in time
        $restore = Restore-AzSqlInstanceDatabase -FromPointInTimeBackup
-ResourceGroupName $resourcegroupname -InstanceName $managedInstanceName
-Name $databaseName -PointInTime $restoretime -TargetInstanceDatabaseName
$targetDatabaseName -TargetResourceGroupName $targetResourceGroupName
-TargetInstanceName $targetManagedInstanceName
if($rerror -ne $null)
{
Write-Host $rerror -ForegroundColor red;
}
if($restore -ne $null)
{
Write-Host "Database $targetDatabaseName restored Successfully on SQL
Managed Instance $targetManagedInstanceName" -ForegroundColor Green;
}
```

You can read through the comments to understand what the code does.

8. Save the file as **SQLMI_PITROnCrossInstance.ps1** to **C:\Code\Chapter05** or a location of your choice.

9. Open a PowerShell console and change the default directory to **C:\Code\Chapter05** or the directory where you have saved the PowerShell script.

10. Copy the following code and press *Enter* to start the export. You may have to change the parameter values to match your Azure environment:

```
.\SQLMI_PITROnCrossInstance.ps1 -resourcegroupname Packt -subscriptionId
6ee856b5-yy6d-4bc1-a901-by0000000e1 -managedInstanceName
packtsqlmi -databaseName toystore -targetDatabaseName toystorepitr
-targetResourceGroupName Packt -targetManagedInstanceName packtsqlmi1
```

The preceding command will restore the **toystore** database to a specified point in time on the **packtsqlmi1** Azure SQL Managed Instance in the **Packt** resource group. The database will be restored as **toystorepitr**.

Once the script finishes, you should get a similar output to *Figure* 5.48:

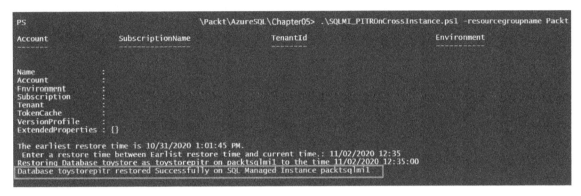

Figure 5.48: A successful cross-instance PITR of the toystorepitr database

You can also verify this using the Azure portal:

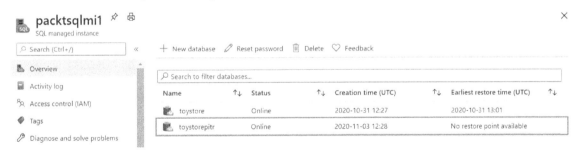

Figure 5.49: A newly added toystorepitr database

In this activity, we have learned about restoring an existing database of SQL Managed Instance to a previous point in time on the same instance using PowerShell. We also performed a cross-instance restore using PowerShell commands. Now let's look at how to do a geo-restore on SQL Managed Instance.

Activity: Geo-restoring a database hosted on SQL Managed Instance using the Az PowerShell module

Geo-restoring allows you to recover a database to a different region. This can be used as a database recovery solution, but the recovery time depends on the database size. Geo-backups are only available when SQL Managed Instance is configured with geo-redundant backup storage.

Let's quickly go through how to perform a geo-restore using PowerShell.

This activity is similar to the previous point-in-time restore we did using the `Az PowerShell` module, so all the steps are not covered here. We are only covering changes in the script.

`SQLMI_GeoRestore.ps1` is available in the source code and most of the code is similar to the point-in-time restore activity.

In our geo-restore PowerShell script, we are using the same `Restore-AzSqlInstanceDatabase` command, but instead of using `the -FromPointInTimeBackup` parameter, we are using the `-FromGeoBackup parameter`.

The following is a code snippet from the PowerShell script:

```
$restore = Restore-AzSqlInstanceDatabase -FromGeoBackup -ResourceGroupName
$resourcegroupname -InstanceName $managedInstanceName -Name $databaseName
-TargetInstanceDatabaseName $targetDatabaseName -TargetResourceGroupName
$targetResourceGroupName -TargetInstanceName $targetManagedInstanceName
```

In the next activity, we will learn to perform restore of a deleted database on Azure SQL Managed Instance using PowerShell module.

Activity: Restoring a deleted database on SQL Managed Instance using PowerShell

Restoring a deleted database on a managed instance can be done using the Azure portal, as we saw in the demonstrations earlier, and PowerShell. Cross-instance restoration for deleted databases can only be done using PowerShell.

Like active database point-in-time restore, cross-instance restore for deleted databases is only available in the same region and same subscription.

To restore deleted databases using PowerShell, you can use the following PowerShell scripts; these scripts are similar to the point-in-time restore and geo-restore scripts.

- `SQLMI_DeletedDatabaseOnSameInstancePITR.ps1`

- `SQLMI_DeletedDatabaseOnCrossInstancePITR.ps1`

This concludes the chapter. As we have seen, Azure SQL Managed Instance supports restoration for all possible scenarios. Use these PaaS capabilities to easily restore your managed databases to the same instance or across instances in the same region and subscription.

Summary

Restoring an Azure SQL database and Azure SQL Managed Instance is different from restoring an on-premises SQL Server database. In this chapter, you learned about the following restore options:

- Point-in-time restore

- Restoring a deleted database

- Geo-restoring a database

- Restoring a database from a long-term backup

- Importing a **BACPAC** file

Each of these options can be leveraged in different scenarios. For example, a PITR will help you recover from a corrupt database or accidental deletion in Azure SQL Database and SQL Managed Instance, whereas importing a **BACPAC** file in Azure SQL Database helps you set up a development environment with the same schema and data across development, testing, and integration.

In the next chapter, we will look at the security mechanisms available to secure an Azure SQL database and SQL Managed Instance.

6
Security

Security is a major concern for organizations when migrating to the cloud, making them hesitant to actually do so. The major security concerns with the cloud include ones about physical server security, data security at rest and in motion, and data infiltration. Microsoft provides strong security protection at the physical, logical, and data layers of Azure services. Microsoft datacenters are among the most secure datacenters in the world.

Azure SQL Database and SQL Managed Instance provide multiple layers of security to control access to databases using SQL Server or **Active Directory** (**AD**) authentication as well as firewall rules, which limit access to data through role-based permissions and row-level security.

SQL Database and SQL Managed Instance provide proactive security using Advanced Threat Protection, granular access control, and strong authentication. In addition to this, dynamic data masking and row-level security can be used to secure data.

Transparent data encryption for encrypting data at rest is also provided, as well as Always Encrypted to encrypt data at rest or in motion.

This chapter covers all of these security mechanisms and how to implement them to secure a SQL database or managed instance.

By the end of this chapter, you will be able to:

- Configure firewall settings for SQL Server and SQL Database.
- Configure service endpoints and private endpoints for SQL Server.
- Enforce a minimal TLS version for SQL Managed Instance.
- Configure and secure public endpoints for SQL Managed Instance.
- Implement audits and threat detection.
- Implement audits and track unwanted backup events for SQL Managed Instance.
- Implement encryption.
- Implement dynamic data masking and row-level security.
- Implement AD authentication for a SQL database.

Network security

SQL Database limits access to databases through firewall rules, which are authentication techniques that require users to log in to a database with a valid username and password. Firewall rules are not valid for SQL Managed Instance, so you need to configure **network security group (NSG)** inbound and outbound security rules. SQL Database and SQL Managed Instance further control access to underlying data through role-based permissions and row-level security. We'll now look at different access control methods in detail.

Firewall rules

SQL Database uses firewall rules to limit access to authorized IPs and block access to unauthorized IPs. This is the first level of access control provided by SQL Database. Firewall rules can be created at the server level and the database level.

When a SQL database is provisioned, it's inaccessible to everyone. To make it accessible, you first need to add a server-level firewall rule. A firewall allows an IP or a range of IP addresses to connect to a SQL database. You can then create database firewall rules to enable certain clients to access individual secure databases.

Connection requests to a SQL database are first validated against the firewall rules and the computers with the IPs specified in the firewall rules are allowed to connect to the database:

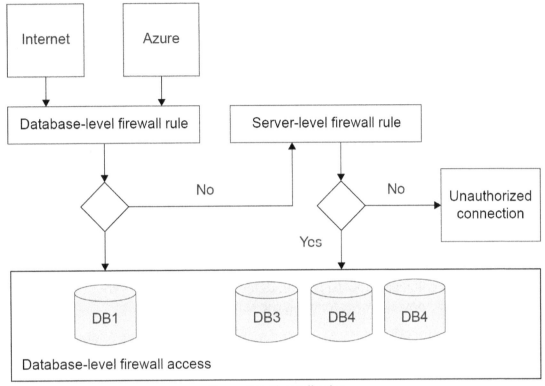

Figure 6.1: Firewall rules

If a computer attempts to connect to an Azure SQL database over the internet, then:

The computer's IP address is validated against the database-level firewall rules. If the IP address is in the IP range specified in the database firewall rules, the connection is made.

If the computer's IP address doesn't fall within the database-level firewall rules, then server-level firewall rules are checked. If the computer's IP address is in the server-level firewall rules, the connection is made.

If the computer's IP address doesn't fall within the database-level or server-level firewall rules, the connection is terminated with an error.

> **Note**
>
> To create a server-level firewall rule, you should be a subscription owner or subscription contributor. The subscription used here is a Microsoft Azure subscription, which you get when you sign up for a Microsoft Azure account.

To allow Azure applications to connect to a SQL database, you need to add the IP `0.0.0.0` as the start and end IP address to the server-level firewall rules.

The following table highlights the differences between server-level and database-level firewall rules:

Server-level firewall rule	Database-level firewall rule
Allows clients to access all SQL databases in given logical SQL Server.	Allows clients to access particular SQL databases within the logical SQL Server.
Rules are stored in the master database.	Rules are stored within individual SQL databases.
Can be configured using the Azure portal, PowerShell, and T-SQL.	Can only be configured using T-SQL after configuring the first server-level firewall rule.

Table 6.1: Firewall rule comparison

Next, let's find out more about how to manage server-level firewall rules.

Managing server-level firewall rules using the Azure portal

In this section, you will learn how to create, delete, and update server-level firewall rules from the Azure portal, by performing the following steps:

1. Log in to the Azure portal (https://portal.azure.com) using your Azure credentials.

2. Find and open the `toyfactorytemp` Azure SQL server to manage the firewall for it.

3. From the Azure SQL server **Overview** page, select the **Set server firewall** option:

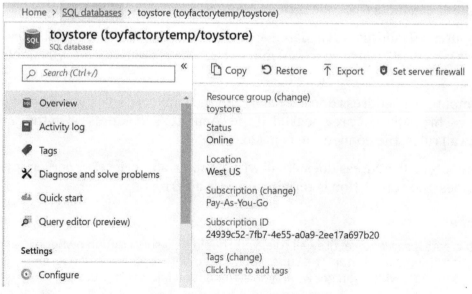

Figure 6.2: Setting the firewall

4. On the **Firewall settings** page, notice that no firewall rules have been configured:

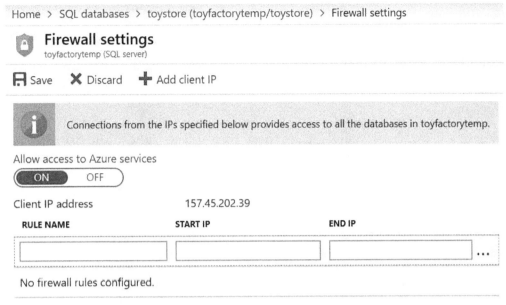

Figure 6.3: The Firewall settings page

Also, notice that it automatically detects and displays the public IP address of the computer from which the portal has been opened.

5. To add the client IP address, select **Add client IP** from the top menu:

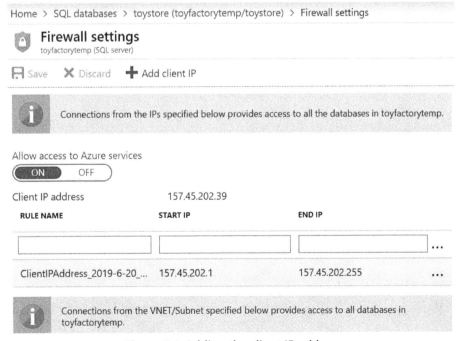

Figure 6.4: Adding the client IP address

A firewall rule with the same start and end IP as the client IP address is added. You can change the rule name if you wish to. Click **Save** in the top menu to save the firewall rule.

You can provide access to all systems within a specified IP range by specifying the start and end IP accordingly.

6. You can update a firewall rule by clicking anywhere on the firewall rule row you wish to update.

7. To delete a firewall rule, click on the three dots to the right of the firewall rule row and select **Delete**. Click **Save** to save the changes:

RULE NAME	START IP	END IP	
			...
ClientIPAddress_2019-6-20_...	157.45.202.1	157.45.202.255	Delete

Figure 6.5: Deleting a firewall

If you don't wish to delete a firewall rule and have accidentally clicked **Delete** instead of clicking **Save** in the top menu, click **Discard** to undo the changes.

8. To make an Azure SQL database accessible to Azure applications, toggle **Allow access to Azure services** to **ON** and click **Save** to save the configuration:

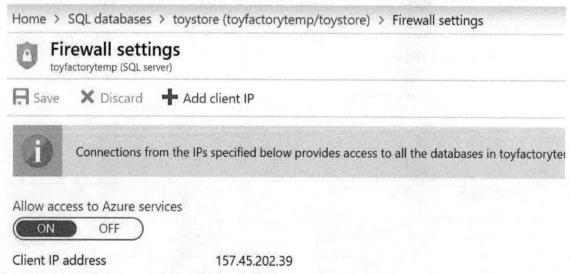

Figure 6.6: Firewall settings page

That's it for the Azure portal—now we'll learn how to do the same thing using Transact-SQL.

Managing server-level firewall rules using Transact-SQL

You can also make use of Transact-SQL instead of the Azure portal to manage server-level firewall rules. In this section, you will learn how to create, delete, and update server-level firewall rules using Transact-SQL:

1. Open **SQL Server Management Studio (SSMS)** and connect to your Azure SQL server. You should be able to connect now, since you have added a server-level firewall rule.

2. In the master database context, run the following query to list all of the existing server-level firewall rules:

    ```
    Select * from sys.firewall_rules
    ```

    The IP address will be different in your case. You should get an output like the one shown in *Figure 6.7*:

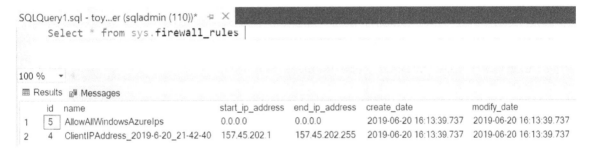

Figure 6.7: Listing the server-level firewall rules

3. Execute the following command to add a new server-level firewall rule:

    ```
    Execute sp_set_firewall_rule @name = N'Work',
    @start_ip_address = '115.118.1.0',
    @end_ip_address = '115.118.16.255'
    ```

Notice the **N** before **'Work'** in the preceding query. The query will fail if you don't add **N**. This is because the firewall rule is of the **NVARCHAR** data type, and **N** specifies that the string following it is a **Unicode** or **NVARCHAR** data type.

A new firewall rule, **Work**, is used when the start IP, **115.118.0.0**, and the end IP, **115.118.16.255**, are added to the firewall.

4. Execute the following command to verify whether or not the rule has been added:

```
Select * from sys.firewall_rules
```

You should get an output like the one shown in *Figure* 6.8:

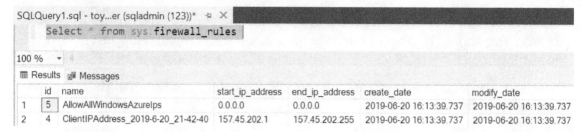

Figure 6.8: Verifying the added firewall

5. Firewall rule names are unique. If you wish to update a firewall rule, call the **sp_set_firewall_rule** procedure with the rule name you wish to update, as well as the updated IP addresses.

The following query updates the **Work** firewall rule with new IP addresses:

```
Execute sp_set_firewall_rule @name = N'Work',
@start_ip_address = '115.118.10.0',
@end_ip_address = '115.118.16.255'
```

6. Execute the following command to verify that the rule has been added:

```
Select * from sys.firewall_rules
```

You should get an output like the one shown in *Figure* 6.9:

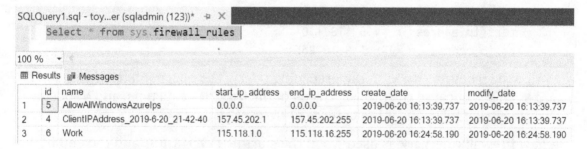

Figure 6.9: Verifying the added rule

Notice that the IP address for the **Work** firewall rule has been updated.

7. To delete a firewall rule, run the following query:

```
Execute sp_delete_firewall_rule @name= N'Work'
```

8. Execute the following command to verify that the rule has been deleted:

```
Select * from sys.firewall_rules
```

You should get an output like the one shown in *Figure 6.10*:

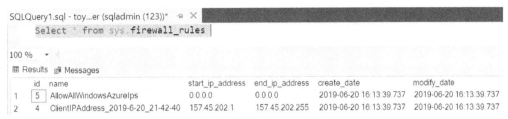

Figure 6.10: Verifying the firewall rule has been deleted

The **Work** firewall rule has been deleted from the firewall.

Managing database-level firewall rules using Transact-SQL

Like server-level firewall rules, database-level firewall rules can also be managed with Transact-SQL. In this section, you will learn how to create, delete, and update a database-level firewall rule with Transact-SQL:

1. Execute the following query to list the current database-level firewall rules:

> **Note**
>
> You can do this within the master database context or any user SQL database context.

```
SELECT * FROM sys.database_firewall_rules
```

Figure 6.11: Listing the current firewall rules

Notice that no database-level firewall rules exist.

2. Execute the following query to create a new database-level firewall rule:

```
Exec sp_set_database_firewall_rule @name=N'MasterDB',
@start_ip_address='115.118.10.0',
@end_ip_address='115.118.16.255'
```

3. Execute the following command to verify that the rule has been added:

```
Select * from sys.database_firewall_rules
```

You should get an output like the one shown in *Figure 6.12*:

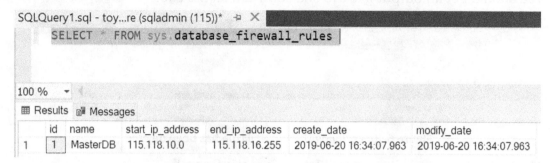

Figure 6.12: Verifying the added firewall rule

A new database-level firewall rule, **MasterDB**, has been added to the firewall.

4. To update a firewall rule, call the **sp_set_database_firewall_rule** procedure with the firewall rule you wish to update and the new start and end IP addresses. Execute the following query to update the **MasterDB** firewall rule created in the previous step:

```
Exec sp_set_database_firewall_rule @name=N'MasterDB',
@start_ip_address='115.118.1.0',
@end_ip_address='115.118.16.255'
```

5. Execute the following command to verify that the rule has been updated:

```
Select * from sys.database_firewall_rules
```

You should get an output like the one shown in *Figure 6.13*:

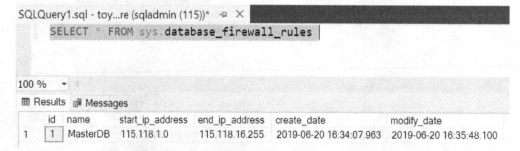

Figure 6.13: Verifying the updated firewall rule

Notice that the firewall rule has been updated.

6. To delete an existing database-level firewall rule, execute the following query:

```
Exec sp_delete_database_firewall_rule @name=N'MasterDB'
```

Execute the following command to verify whether or not the rule has been deleted:

```
Select * from sys.database_firewall_rules
```

You should get an output like the one shown in *Figure 6.14*:

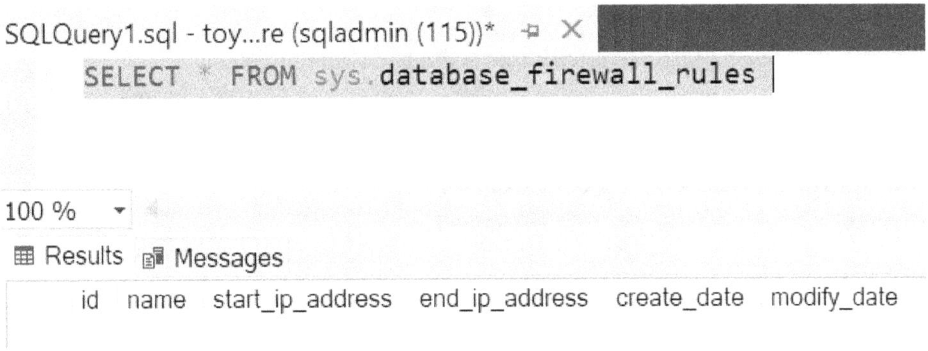

Figure 6.14: Deleting the firewall rule

The database-level firewall rule has been successfully deleted.

> **Note**
>
> Login details and server-level firewall rules are cached in each SQL database. The cache is periodically refreshed; however, you can run **DBCC FLUSHAUTHCACHE** to manually flush the authentication cache. This statement does not apply to the logical master database, because the master database contains the physical storage for the information about logins and firewall rules. The user executing the statement and other currently connected users remain connected.

As seen, we can allow listed IPs or a range of IPs in firewall rules to access a SQL database. However, this requires additional management for managing the allowed IPs. Service endpoints allow us to allow virtual networks instead of IPs. All virtual machines within a virtual machine or peered virtual machine can access a SQL database. Let's see how this is done in the next section.

Service endpoints

Service endpoints allow us to allow an Azure virtual network so as to allow connections from all **virtual machines (VMs)** in the given virtual network. With this, we don't need to allow IPs or IP ranges for VMs or Azure services in the virtual network.

The communication between a VM and a SQL database takes place over an Azure backbone network; however, instead of a VM's public IP, the Azure SQL database sees its private IP address. This makes management easy by not listing each and every allowed IP/IP range.

Configuring service endpoints for SQL Database

In this section, we'll allow a virtual network so as to allow connection from VMs or services within the virtual network to a SQL database. To do this, follow these steps:

> **Note:**
>
> You need an existing virtual network and VM to follow along.

1. In the Azure portal, navigate to SQL Server (**toyfactory**). In the **SQL Server** pane, find and open **Firewall and virtual networks**.

   Allow the VM public IP address in the SQL Server firewall and save the configuration:

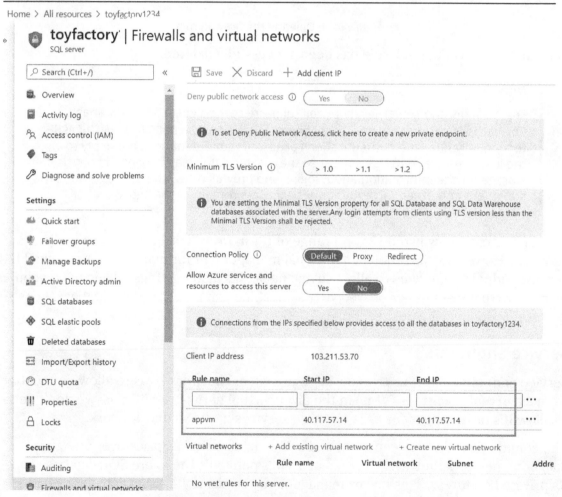

Figure 6.15: Allowing the VM public IP in the SQL Server firewall

The IP in our case is **40.117.57.15**. It'll be different for your VM.

2. Connect to SQL Database from the VM and execute the following query:

```
SELECT
    DB_NAME() AS [Database],
    client_net_address
FROM sys.dm_exec_connections
WHERE session_id=@@SPID
```

Figure 6.16: Verifying the VM IP

Observe that the connection is from the public IP address of the VM.

We'll now configure the service endpoint and allow the VM virtual network and then verify the IP in SQL Database.

3. We'll first enable the service endpoint for the VM subnet. To do that, open the virtual network in the Azure portal:

> **Note:**
>
> In this case, the virtual network is **packtvnet** and the subnet is **appnet**. You'll have a different virtual network and subnet name.

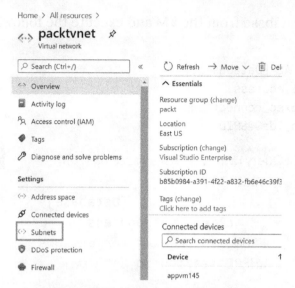

Figure 6.17: Virtual network pane

On the virtual network page, select **Subnets**. In the **Subnets** pane, click the subnet for which we want to enable the service endpoint. In the subnet pane, under the **SERVICE ENDPOINTS** heading, search and select `Microsoft.Sql`:

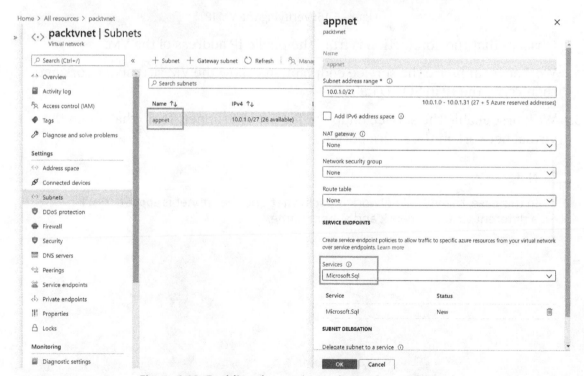

Figure 6.18: Enabling the service endpoint for a subnet

Click **OK** to save the configuration.

4. Switch to SQL Server and go to the **Firewall and Virtual Network** pane. In the **Virtual networks** section, click **Add existing virtual network**. In the **Create/ Update** pane, provide the virtual network rule name, subscription, virtual network, and the subnet for which we enabled the service endpoint in *step 3*:

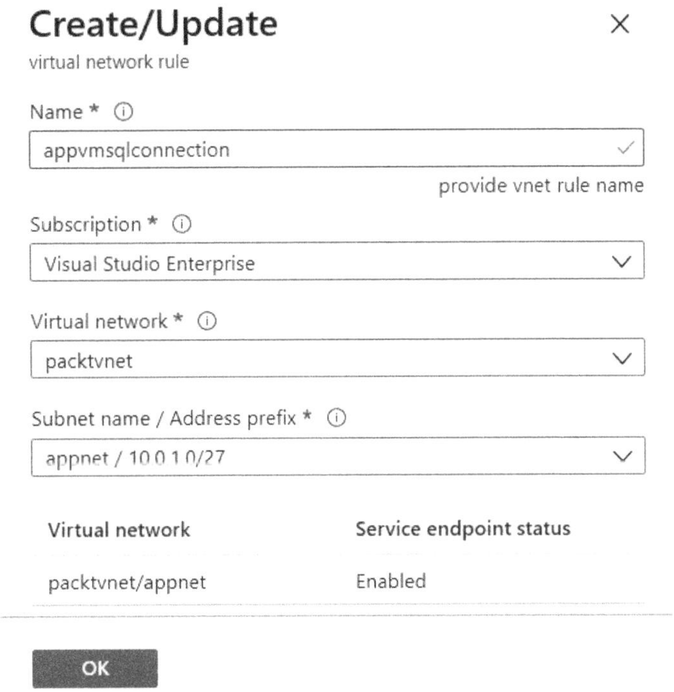

Create/Update   ✕
virtual network rule

Name * ⓘ

appvmsqlconnection	✓

provide vnet rule name

Subscription * ⓘ

Visual Studio Enterprise	⌄

Virtual network * ⓘ

packtvnet	⌄

Subnet name / Address prefix * ⓘ

appnet / 10.0.1.0/27	⌄

Virtual network	Service endpoint status
packtvnet/appnet	Enabled

OK

Figure 6.19: Allowing the virtual network

Click **OK** to save the configuration. It usually takes a minute for the configuration to be modified:

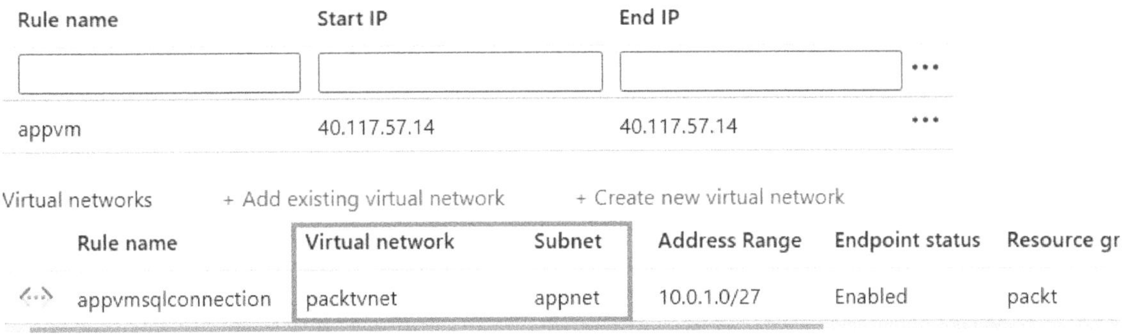

Rule name	Start IP	End IP	
			•••
appvm	40.117.57.14	40.117.57.14	•••

Virtual networks   + Add existing virtual network   + Create new virtual network

	Rule name	Virtual network	Subnet	Address Range	Endpoint status	Resource gr
⟨··⟩	appvmsqlconnection	packtvnet	appnet	10.0.1.0/27	Enabled	packt

Figure 6.20: Virtual network rule added to SQL Database

5. Let's switch to the VM and run the query in *step 2* to verify the IP address:

```
SELECT
    DB_NAME() AS [Database],
    client_net_address
FROM sys.dm_exec_connections
WHERE session_id=@@SPID
```

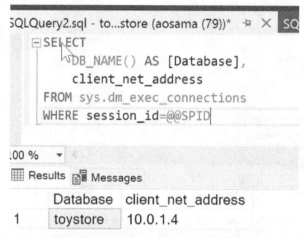

Figure 6.21: Verifying the VM IP address

Observe that after the service endpoint configuration, the VM connects to the Azure SQL database through the private IP address instead of the public IP address.

Any VM in the configured subnet can connect to SQL Database without having to allow the public IP address.

Service endpoints allow us to allow virtual networks, and connections to SQL Database are made using the VM private IP instead of a public IP. However, connections are still made to the SQL Database public endpoint. Let's understand how we can further secure SQL Database by using a private endpoint.

Private endpoint

When we provision an Azure VM, public and private IPs are assigned to it. To connect to a SQL server from an Azure VM, we can allow the public IP in the SQL Server firewall. This method has a drawback of having to manage IPs and IP ranges for every Azure VM that requires connectivity to SQL Server, and it's less secure as the connection is made over a public IP address.

If our security policy doesn't allow a public IP to be assigned to an Azure VM, we can enable **Allow Azure services and resources to access this server** on the **Firewall settings** page. This method opens up access to any Azure service in the subscription and so is not recommended.

Additionally, we can add network security group rules on Azure VM so as to only allow outbound connections to SQL Server in a specific region. This can be done by adding an outbound rule to the `Microsoft.Sql` service tag to the network security group as shown here:

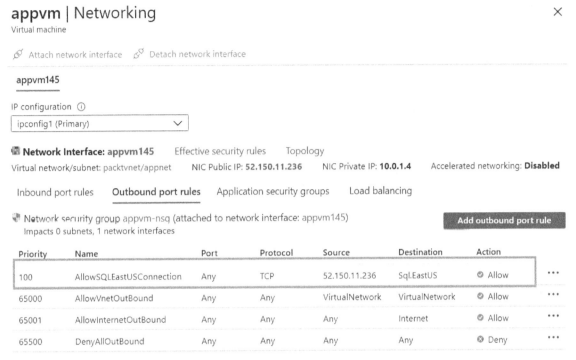

appvm | Networking
Virtual machine

Attach network interface   Detach network interface

appvm145

IP configuration ⓘ
ipconfig1 (Primary)

Network Interface: appvm145   Effective security rules   Topology
Virtual network/subnet: packtvnet/appnet   NIC Public IP: **52.150.11.236**   NIC Private IP: **10.0.1.4**   Accelerated networking: **Disabled**

Inbound port rules   **Outbound port rules**   Application security groups   Load balancing

Network security group appvm-nsg (attached to network interface: appvm145)   **Add outbound port rule**
Impacts 0 subnets, 1 network interfaces

Priority	Name	Port	Protocol	Source	Destination	Action	
100	AllowSQLEastUSConnection	Any	TCP	52.150.11.236	Sql.EastUS	⊘ Allow	...
65000	AllowVnetOutBound	Any	Any	VirtualNetwork	VirtualNetwork	⊘ Allow	...
65001	AllowInternetOutBound	Any	Any	Any	Internet	⊘ Allow	...
65500	DenyAllOutBound	Any	Any	Any	Any	⊗ Deny	...

Figure 6.22: Restricting access to SQL Server from an Azure VM

In the preceding figure, the `AllowSQLEastUSConnection` rule makes sure that the Azure VM with the public IP **52.150.11.236** can only make outbound connections on port **1433** and **11000-11999** to any Azure SQL database in the **East US** region.

> **Note:**
>
> The preceding method is a restriction on the Azure VM side and it doesn't change any configuration on the SQL Server side. We still need to allow the Azure VM public IP for SQL Server.

Service endpoints allow us to allow a virtual network in SQL Database, which in turn allows us to connect to SQL Database from an Azure VM private IP instead of a public IP, as explained previously. However, we still need the `AllowSQLEastUSConnection` rule so as to limit access to SQL databases in **East US**. The source for the rule changes to an Azure VM private IP instead of a public one, as mentioned earlier.

In order to allow connections to only a particular SQL database, we need to change the destination in the **AllowSQLEastUSConnection** rule to a particular IP. This is what a private endpoint does. A private endpoint assigns a private IP to a SQL database from a virtual network. The connection from the Azure VM to SQL Database now takes place over a private IP; we can say it never leaves the virtual network.

If we do **nslookup** on a SQL Server endpoint, we'll get the following output:

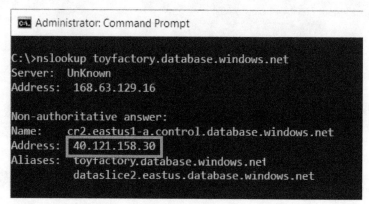

Figure 6.23: SQL Server—nslookup

As seen in the preceding figure, the connections to SQL Server are made to the public IP **40.121.158.30**.

We'll now configure the private endpoint and again check the output of **nslookup**.

To configure a private endpoint from the Azure portal, follow these steps:

1. In the Azure portal, find and open the **toyfactory** SQL server page. Search and open **Private endpoint connections** under the **Security** section. On the **Private endpoint connections** page, click **Private endpoint**:

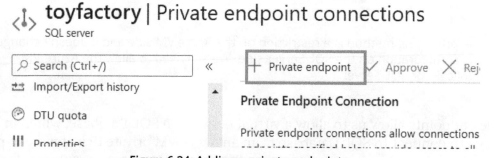

Figure 6.24: Adding a private endpoint

2. On the **Create a private endpoint** page, under the **Basics** tab, provide details for **Subscription**, **Resource group**, instance **Name**, and **Region**. The private endpoint should be in the same region as the virtual network:

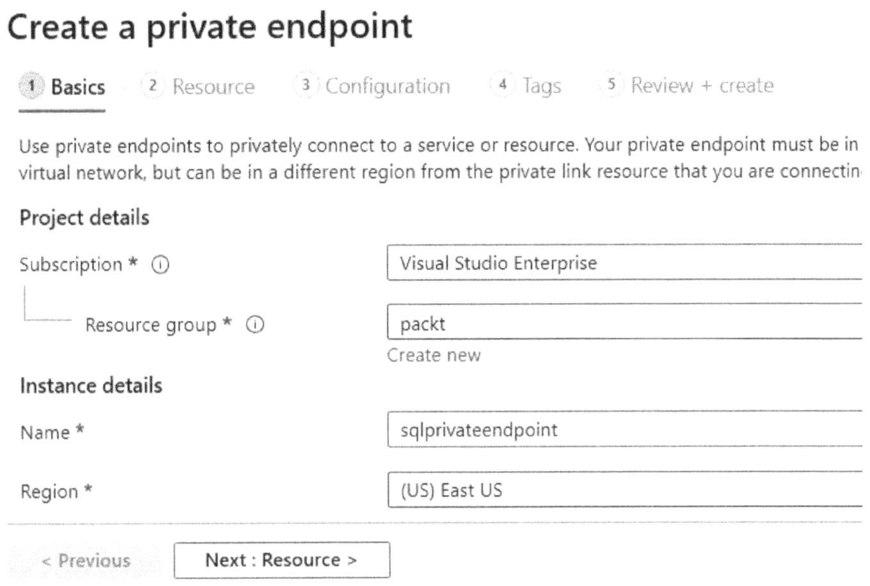

Create a private endpoint

1 **Basics**   2 Resource   3 Configuration   4 Tags   5 Review + create

Use private endpoints to privately connect to a service or resource. Your private endpoint must be in
virtual network, but can be in a different region from the private link resource that you are connectin

Project details

Subscription * ⓘ

> Visual Studio Enterprise

     Resource group * ⓘ

> packt

> Create new

Instance details

Name *

> sqlprivateendpoint

Region *

> (US) East US

< Previous   Next : Resource >

Figure 6.25: Private endpoint—Basics tab

Click **Next: Resource >** to continue.

3. In the **Resource** tab, set **Connection method** as **Connect to an Azure resource in my directory**.

   Select your subscription, set the resource type as `Microsoft.Sql/servers`, and enter `toyfactory` as follows:

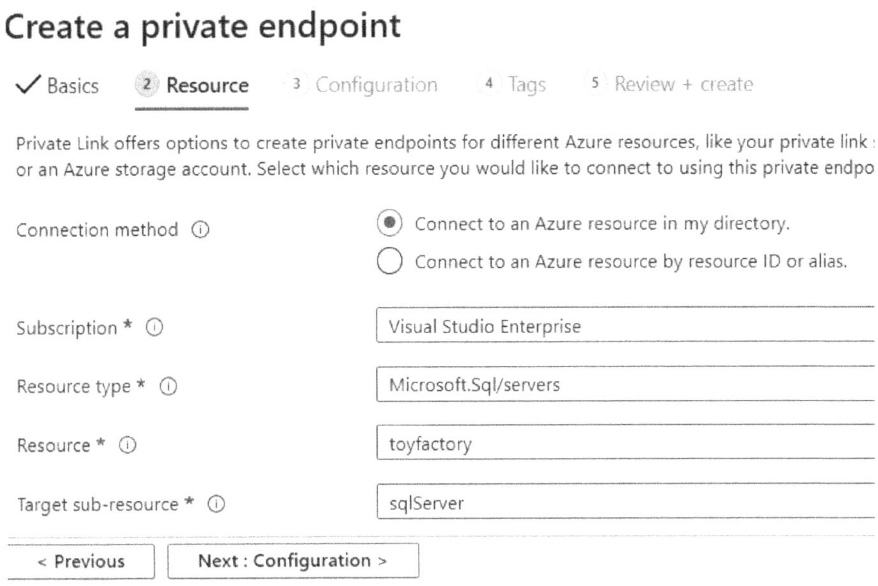

Create a private endpoint

✓ Basics   2 **Resource**   3 Configuration   4 Tags   5 Review + create

Private Link offers options to create private endpoints for different Azure resources, like your private link
or an Azure storage account. Select which resource you would like to connect to using this private endpo

Connection method ⓘ

- ⦿ Connect to an Azure resource in my directory.
- ◯ Connect to an Azure resource by resource ID or alias.

Subscription * ⓘ

> Visual Studio Enterprise

Resource type * ⓘ

> Microsoft.Sql/servers

Resource * ⓘ

> toyfactory

Target sub-resource * ⓘ

> sqlServer

< Previous   Next : Configuration >

Figure 6.26: Private endpoint—Resource tab

4. In the **Configuration** tab, provide the virtual network for the private endpoint and the subnet. This is usually the subnet of the Azure VM you would like to connect to SQL Database.

The private DNS integration creates a private DNS zone, `privatelink.database.windows.net`, to make sure that the connection is always made on a private endpoint. Think of it as a mapping between the SQL Database public endpoint and the private endpoint.

Select **Yes** for **Integrate with private DNS zone** if not already selected:

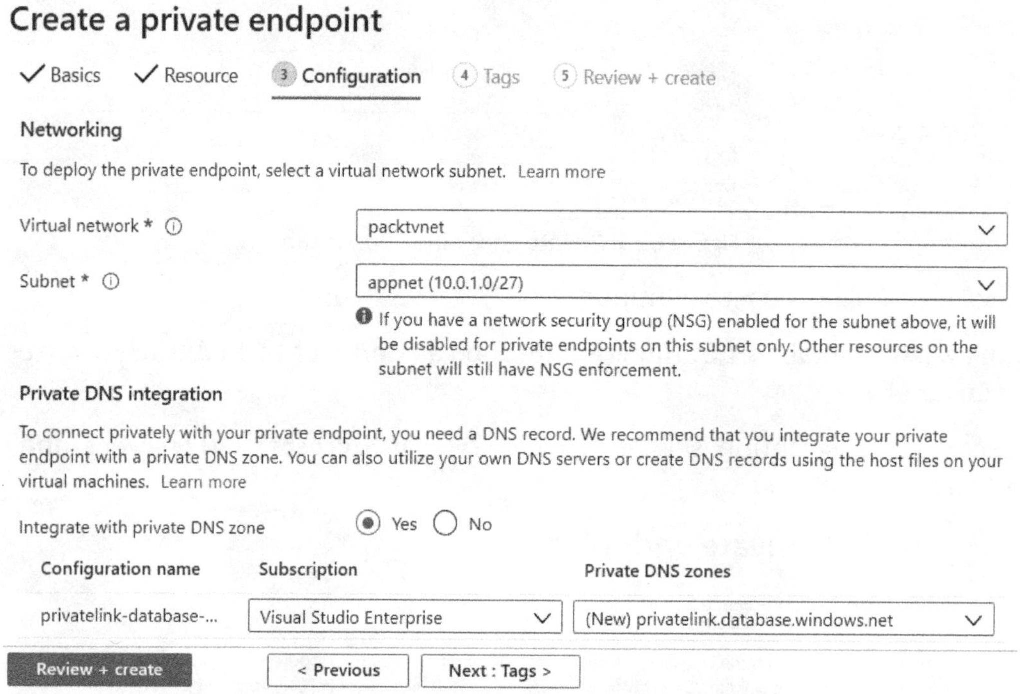

Create a private endpoint

✓ Basics ✓ Resource ③ **Configuration** ④ Tags ⑤ Review + create

Networking

To deploy the private endpoint, select a virtual network subnet. Learn more

Virtual network * ⓘ | packtvnet   ∨ |

Subnet * ⓘ | appnet (10.0.1.0/27)   ∨ |

ⓘ If you have a network security group (NSG) enabled for the subnet above, it will be disabled for private endpoints on this subnet only. Other resources on the subnet will still have NSG enforcement.

Private DNS integration

To connect privately with your private endpoint, you need a DNS record. We recommend that you integrate your private endpoint with a private DNS zone. You can also utilize your own DNS servers or create DNS records using the host files on your virtual machines. Learn more

Integrate with private DNS zone   ● Yes ○ No

Configuration name	Subscription	Private DNS zones
privatelink-database-...	Visual Studio Enterprise ∨	(New) privatelink.database.windows.net ∨

[Review + create]   [< Previous]   [Next : Tags >]

Figure 6.27: Private endpoint—Configuration tab

Click **Review + create** and then click **Create** to provision the private endpoint.

5. Navigate to the SQL Server **Private Endpoint Connection** page. You should see the new private endpoint, `sqlprivateendpoint`:

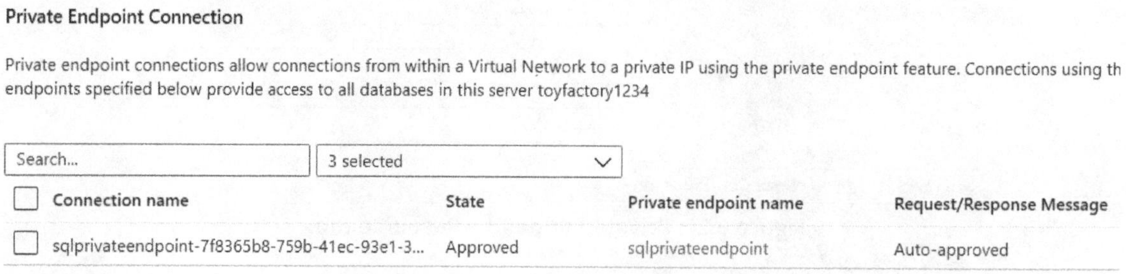

Private Endpoint Connection

Private endpoint connections allow connections from within a Virtual Network to a private IP using the private endpoint feature. Connections using th endpoints specified below provide access to all databases in this server toyfactory1234

Search...	3 selected ∨

☐ Connection name	State	Private endpoint name	Request/Response Message
☐ sqlprivateendpoint-7f8365b8-759b-41ec-93e1-3...	Approved	sqlprivateendpoint	Auto-approved

Figure 6.28: Viewing the private endpoint

Click the private endpoint name to view its configuration:

Figure 6.29: Viewing the endpoint configuration

Observe that the FQDN, **toyfactory.database.windows.net**, has a private IP, **10.0.1.5**, assigned to it.

Executing **nslookup** on **toyfactory.database.windows.net** now returns the private IP instead of the public IP:

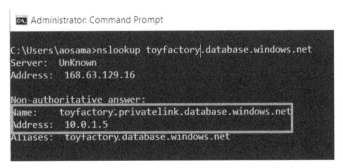

Figure 6.30: nslookup with the private endpoint

6. Navigate to the SQL Server **Firewalls and virtual networks** page. Select **Yes** for **Deny public network access** and click **Save**:

Figure 6.31: Denying public network access

SQL Server is not exposed to the public internet and this provides enhanced security. Services or Azure VMs in other virtual networks can access SQL Server through virtual network peering. On-premises services or VMs can access SQL Database through an express route or VPN connecting to the VPN gateway.

There are three ways we can restrict access to connect to a SQL database: the firewall, virtual networks (service endpoints), and private endpoints.

Let's now look at the authentication types available with SQL Database.

Authentication

Authentication refers to how a user identifies themselves when connecting to a database. There are two types of authentication mechanisms: SQL Server authentication and Azure AD authentication.

SQL authentication

This is similar to what we have in on-premises SQL servers; that is, it requires a username and password. When provisioning a SQL database, you have to provide a server admin login with a username and password. The server admin user has admin access to the SQL server and it's mapped to the **dbo** user in each user database and therefore has **dbowner** access on all databases in a particular SQL server.

There can be only one server admin account in a SQL database.

Azure AD authentication

Azure AD authentication allows users to connect to a SQL database and managed instance by using the identities stored in Azure AD.

Azure AD

When you create an Azure account, it creates a default directory for your account. This is where you can add users and give them permissions to access different Azure services as needed. To learn more about Azure AD, refer to the following link: https://docs.microsoft.com/azure/active-directory/fundamentals/active-directory-whatis.

You can add custom domains to the default directory, or you can create directories from here.

You can also integrate your on-premises Windows AD with Azure AD using Azure AD Connect.

To learn more about Azure AD Connect, refer to the following link: https://aadguide.azurewebsites.net/dirsync/aadconnect/.

There are three different ways to authenticate: **Active Directory - Universal with MFA support**, **Active Directory - Password**, and **Active Directory - Integrated**, as shown in *Figure 6.32*:

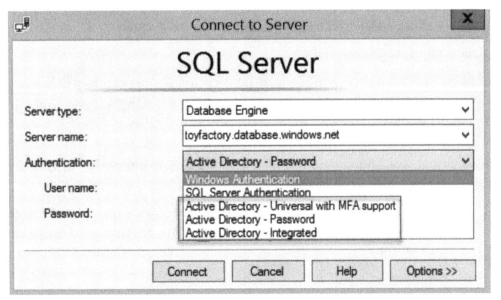

Figure 6.32: Authentication options

Active Directory - Password

This is the easiest way to get started with Azure AD authentication. It works with Azure AD managed domains and federated domains.

A user authenticating to a SQL database has to provide an Azure AD identity and password for successful authentication:

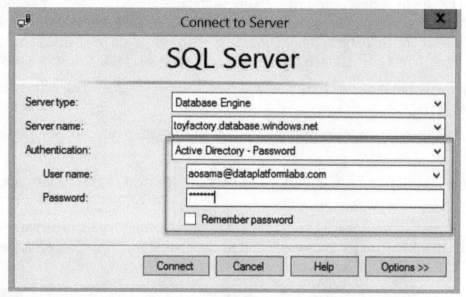

Figure 6.33: Active Directory - Password option

Active Directory - Integrated

This is similar to conventional Windows authentication in on-premises SQL servers. To authenticate using this method, a user has to provide the domain account that has access to a SQL database. The user doesn't have to provide the password—it's validated against Azure AD.

To get this method working, the on-premises AD should be integrated into Azure AD. This can be done using the free tool Azure AD Connect.

When using SSMS to authenticate using the **Active Directory - Integrated** method, it automatically takes the username as the logged-in username, similar to on-premises Windows authentication:

Figure 6.34: Active Directory - Integrated option

Active Directory - Universal with MFA support

MFA stands for multi-factor authentication. MFA allows you to provide a code received by a call, SMS, or by any other means. MFA requires conditional access with an Azure AD Premium P1 or P2 license.

To learn more about Azure MFA, refer to the following link: https://docs.microsoft. com/azure/active-directory/fundamentals/concept-fundamentals-mfa-get-started.

This further secures the authentication process, as the code received is only accessible by the person who has initiated the authentication process:

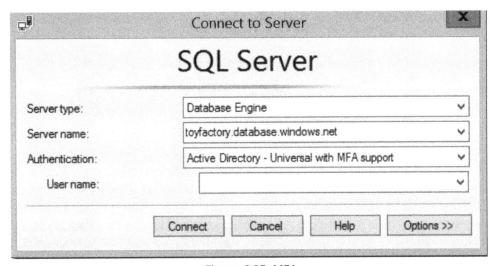

Figure 6.35: MFA

MFA requires you to provide a username, which is pre-populated after you configure MFA.

> **Note**
>
> Azure AD authentication isn't supported when connecting to a SQL database from a SQL server on an Azure VM; you should use a domain AD account.

Using Active Directory - Password to authenticate to a SQL database

This section covers how to authenticate to a SQL database using **Active Directory - Password**. Let's consider the toy manufacturing company introduced previously. Mike needs to ensure that, if any of his networking workplaces expect access to a database, he gives them access by utilizing **Active Directory - Password** to authenticate to a SQL database. He can achieve this by following these steps:

1. Log in to the Azure portal (https://portal.azure.com). From the left-hand navigation pane, find and open Azure AD.

2. From the **Overview** pane, find and click **New user** (in the **Quick tasks** section):

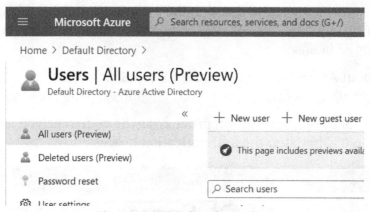

Figure 6.36: Quick tasks section

3. In the **Users** pane, provide a name and a username (the email is the username in this case). The email should belong to an existing verified domain in Azure AD.

> **Note**
>
> You can use the default domain when providing a user email. For example, if your Microsoft account email ID is **ahmad.osama1984@gmail.com**, then the default directory would be **ahmadosama1984.onmicrosoft.com**. Therefore, you can provide the username **chris@ahmadosama1984.onmicrosoft.com**. You can also create a guest user with a different email address. A notification is sent out to each user to accept the invitation.

4. You can find your default domain in the top-right corner of the Azure portal:

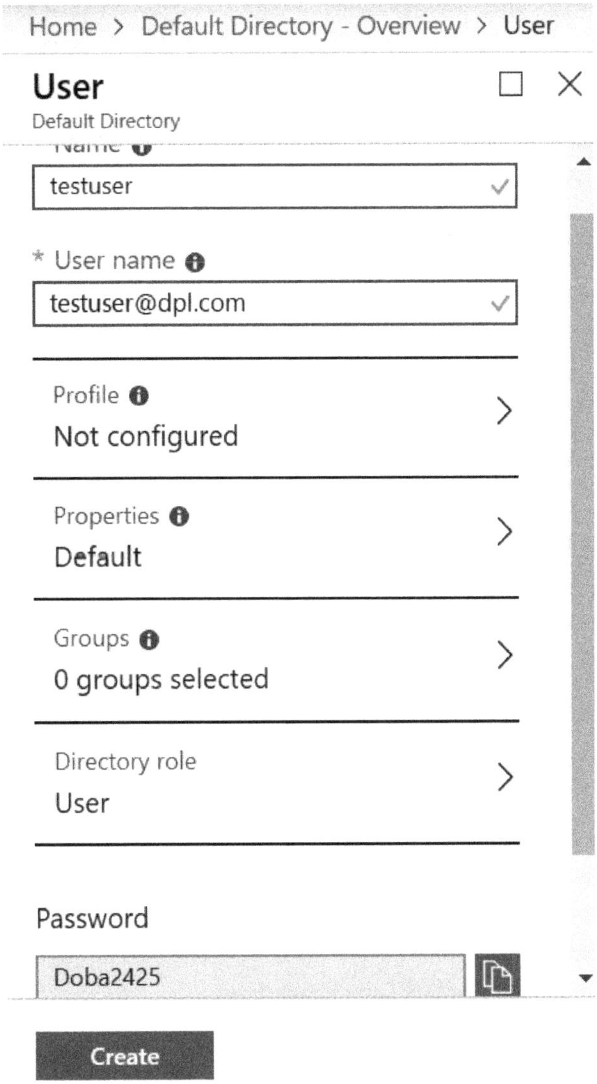

Figure 6.37: Creating a user

Check the **Show Password** checkbox and copy the password. You are not allowed to change the password.

Leave all the other options as the default values and click **Create** to create the user.

> **Note**
>
> Log out of the Azure portal and log in again using the new user credentials. You'll be asked to change the password. Once your password is changed, log out and log in with your Azure admin credentials.

5. Once you have created a user, the next step is to make the user a SQL Server AD admin. In the Azure portal, find and click the **toyfactorytemp** SQL server. In **toyfactorytemp**, find and select the **Active Directory admin** option in the **Settings** section:

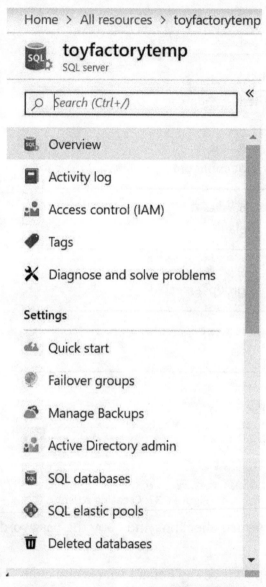

Figure 6.38: The toyfactorytemp SQL server

6.   In the **Active Directory admin** pane, select **Set admin** from the top menu:

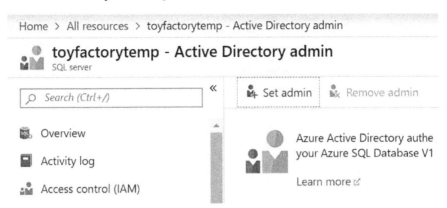

Figure 6.39: Active Directory admin pane

7.   In the **Add admin** pane, type the username in the **Select** field and select the user you created in *step 3* as the AD admin:

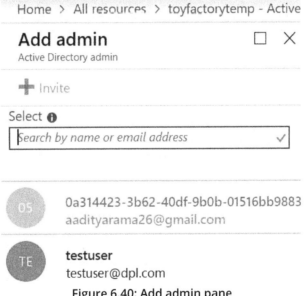

Figure 6.40: Add admin pane

You'll be taken back to the **Add admin** pane. Click **Save** to set the selected user as the AD admin:

Figure 6.41: Active Directory admin pane

8. You now have an AD admin defined for the `toyfactorytemp` SQL server. The AD admin has **dbowner** access to all of the databases on the `toyfactory` server.

   In the next step, you'll connect to the `toyfactory` server with the AD admin account using SSMS.

9. Open SSMS, and in the **Connect to Server** dialog box:

   Under **Server Type**, select `Database Engine`.

   Under **Server name**, enter the `toyfactorytemp` server name.

   Under **Authentication**, select **Active Directory - Password**.

   Under **Username**, enter the username (email) of the user created in *step 3*.

   Under **Password**, enter the user's password. Click **Connect**.

   If you get the following error, you will have to change the password by logging in to the Azure portal as this user:

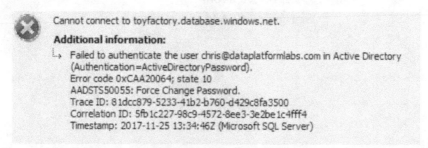

Figure 6.42: Connection error

You'll be asked to update the password on the login screen. Change the password and then try to connect to the SQL server from SSMS.

Notice that Object Explorer displays the username as **testuser@dpl.com**:

Figure 6.43: Object Explorer

Figure 6.43 indicates that the authentication was successful using AD authentication.

SQL Database authentication structure

SQL Database and SQL Managed Instance will always have two different administrators if Azure AD authentication is used: the original SQL Server administrator (SQL authentication) and the Azure AD admin. The Azure AD administrator login can be a **System-Managed Identity (SMI)**, **User-Managed Identity (UMI)**, an Azure application, a user, or a group. All users in the Azure AD admin group will have administrative access to a SQL server:

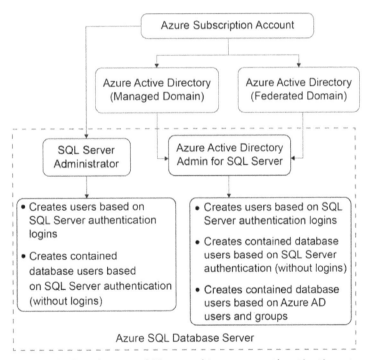

Figure 6.44: SQL Database and Managed Instance authentication structure

> **Note**
>
> An Azure administrator can either be a single user or a group. Only one Azure AD admin is allowed.

SQL Database and SQL Managed Instance authentication considerations

You must consider the following factors for SQL Database and SQL Managed Instance authentication:

- Create a dedicated Azure AD group as the SQL Server administrator instead of creating an individual user administrator.

- You can configure either an Azure AD group or a user as a SQL Server admin.

- You can create Azure AD logins in the master database in SQL Managed Instance. Currently, it's not supported for SQL Database.

- **bcp.exe** can't connect to a SQL database using Azure AD authentication, as it uses an old ODBC driver.

- SQLCMD versions **13.1** and above support Azure AD authentication.

- To use Azure AD authentication with SSMS, you need to have .NET Framework **4.6** or above installed on your system.

> **Note**
>
> For the automated creation of Azure AD objects, an Azure application should be considered instead of regular Azure AD users. For more information, please visit https://techcommunity.microsoft.com/t5/azure-sql-database/support-for-azure-ad-user-creation-on-behalf-of-azure-nad/ba-p/1491121.

Authentication allows us to connect to a SQL database using the authentication types discussed previously. We can further control access to database objects (such as tables and stored procedures) with proper authorization. Let's take a look at different server-level and database-level roles available with SQL Database.

Authorization

Authorization refers to any sort of access control mechanism. In the context of SQL Server, it starts at the server scope or database scope for contained users. For example, a user may have access to read one set of tables and to read-write another set of tables.

The authorization is done by adding the user to the relevant server-level or database-level roles.

Roles have a set of permissions applied to them; for example, the **db_datareader** database-level role allows users to read tables from a database.

Let's look at server-level administrative roles available with SQL Database.

Server-level administrative roles

There are two server-level administrative roles that reside in the master database: **dbcreators** and **loginmanagers** for SQL Database. Server roles are not supported for Azure AD admin or Azure AD users at the time of writing this book.

dbcreators

Members of database creators (**dbmanager**) are allowed to create new SQL databases. To create a new user with the database creator role:

1. Log in to SSMS with either an Azure AD admin or SQL Server admin.

2. Create a new login in the **master** database using the following query:

    ```
    CREATE LOGIN John WITH PASSWORD = 'Very$Stro9gPa$$w0rd';
    ```

3. Create a new user in the **master** database mapped to the **John** login using the following query:

    ```
    CREATE USER John FROM LOGIN John
    ```

4. Add the user **John** to the **dbmanager** role using the following query:

    ```
    ALTER ROLE dbmanager ADD MEMBER John;
    ```

5. Open a new query window in SSMS and log in as **John**.

6. Execute the following query to create a new SQL database:

    ```
    CREATE DATABASE JohnsDB
    ```

    John will have **db_owner** access to all the databases he creates.

loginmanagers

Members of this role can create new logins in the master database. To create a new user with the **loginmanager** role, follow the preceding steps to create a user and add them to the **loginmanager** role instead.

Non-administrative users

Non-administrative users don't have access to the master database and have limited access to the required databases and objects.

An example of a non-administrative user is an application user. An application user is one that is used by an application to connect to a database and perform **data manipulation language** (**DML**) operations.

A non-administrative user can either be an Azure AD user or a SQL Server authentication user.

Non-administrative users can be created by using the following two methods.

Creating a login

In this method, we first create a login in the master database. Then, we create users in each database to which the user requires access. When connecting to the database, we provide the username and the login password. Given here is the SQL query to create users using this method:

```
--Create login in the master database.
CREATE LOGIN Mike
    WITH PASSWORD = 'secure@Pass1234'
--Create the user in the user database using the login
CREATE USER Mike
FOR LOGIN Mike
WITH DEFAULT_SCHEMA = dbo
GO
-- Add user to the database reader fixed database role
EXEC sp_addrolemember N'db_datareader', N'Mike'
GO
```

The preceding code first creates a **Mike** login in the master database. It then creates a **Mike** user in the user database and adds the user to the **db_datareader** fixed database role. This role allows users to read data from all the database tables.

The following built-in database roles exist in a SQL database or managed instance: **db_accessadmin**, **db_backupoperator**, **db_datareader**, **db_ddladmin**, **db_denydatareader**, **db_denydatawriter**, **db_owner**, **db_securityadmin**, and public. You can also create custom database roles.

Similarly, we can add **Mike** to any other database within the server. Observe that the user password is the same for all the databases.

This method is good to use when a user needs access to more than one database in the server as we can use one password to connect to the databases the user has access to. However, this is tedious in geo-replication as the login is to be created in the secondary server so as to access the secondary server.

Contained database users

In this method, the user is created within the user database instead of the master database. The authentication information is therefore stored in the user database. Given here is the SQL query to create a contained database user:

```
--run in user database

CREATE USER [containeduser]

WITH PASSWORD = 'secure@Pass1234' ,

DEFAULT_SCHEMA = dbo;

-- add user to role(s) in db

ALTER ROLE db_datareader ADD MEMBER [containeduser];
```

The preceding script creates a user **containeduser** with a password (instead of a login, as in the previous **Creating a login** method).

The user is added to the **db_datareader** role, giving the user read access to database tables.

Let's see how we can add a contained database user for Azure AD authentication.

Creating contained database users for Azure AD authentication

In this section, you will learn how to create contained database users for Azure AD authentication for firms such as ToyStore Ltd., where there are many roles that require access to the database:

1. Open SSMS. From the top menu, select **File**, select **New**, and then select **Database Engine Query** to open a new query window:

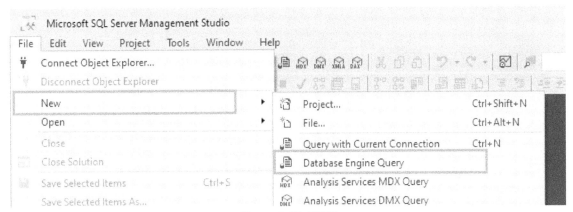

Figure 6.45: SSMS

2. Connect to Azure SQL Server with **Active Directory - Password** authentication.

3. Execute the following query to create a contained database user (SQL authentication) and add it to the **db_owner** role:

    ```
    --Create a contained database user (SQL Authentication) CREATE USER Mike
    WITH PASSWORD='John@pwd'
    GO
    -- Make Mike toystore database owner ALTER ROLE db_owner ADD MEMBER Mike
    ```

4. Execute the following query to create a contained database user (Azure AD authentication) and add it to the **db_datareader** role:

    ```
    --Create a contained database user (Azure AD Authentication)
    CREATE USER [John@dpl.com] FROM EXTERNAL PROVIDER
    -- Give read access to John on all tables
    ALTER ROLE db_datareader ADD Member [John@dpl.com]
    ```

    > **Note**
    >
    > You need to create an Azure AD user before you add them to the SQL database.
    > You can use the steps in the previous section to create a new Azure AD user.

5. Press F8 to open Object Explorer. In Object Explorer, connect to your SQL server if you're not already connected.

    Expand the **Databases** node. In the **Databases** node, expand the **toystore** database node. In the **toystore** database, expand the **Security** node and then expand the **Users** node.

    You should see the user **John@dpl.com** listed in the **Users** section:

⊟ 📷 toyfactorytemp.database.windows.net (SQL Server 12.0.2000.8
   ⊟ Databases
      ⊞ System Databases
      ⊞ 🗄 JohnsDB
      ⊟ 🗄 toystore
         ⊞ Database Diagrams
         ⊞ Tables
         ⊞ Views
         ⊞ External Resources
         ⊞ Synonyms
         ⊞ Programmability
         ⊞ Query Store
         ⊞ Extended Events
         ⊞ Storage
         ⊟ Security
            ⊟ Users
               🔒 dbo
               🔒 guest
               🔒 INFORMATION_SCHEMA
               🔒 John@dpl.com

Figure 6.46: Users section

Notice that **John@dpl.com** is not mapped to a server login. This is because he is a contained database user.

6. Press *Ctrl + N* to open a new query window. Click the change connection icon in the top menu, next to the database drop-down list:

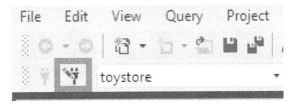

Figure 6.47: The change connection icon

7. In the **Connect to Server** dialog box:

    Under **Server name**, provide the SQL server name.

    Under **Authentication**, select **Active Directory - Password**.

    Enter the username as **john@dpl.com**.

    Enter the password for the aforementioned user.

    Click **Connect**:

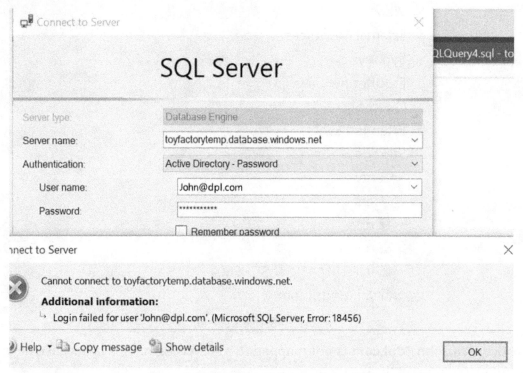

Figure 6.48: Connect to Server dialog box

You will get an error like the one shown in *Figure 6.48*. This is because SSMS tries to connect to the default database, which, in this case, is the master database. The master database doesn't contain the **john@dpl.com** user and so the connection fails.

8. Click **OK** in the error dialog box. In the **Connect to Database Engine** dialog box, select **Options** from the lower-left corner of the dialog box window.

   Under **Options**, select the **Connection Properties** tab, and in the **Connect to database** setting, set the database to **toystore**.

   Click **Connect** to continue:

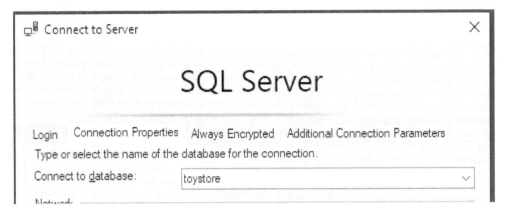

Figure 6.49: Setting the database to toystore

   You should now be able to connect to the **toystore** database.

You can add users to different roles and test out the security. For example, you can add a user in the **db_dbwriter** role and then log in using the user and verify that they're only able to write to tables and can't do any other database operations, such as creating tables, databases, and so on.

Groups and roles

Additionally, you can group users with similar sets of permissions in an Azure AD group or a SQL database role. You can then assign the permissions to the group and add users to it. Users with similar access requirements are added to the group.

Row-level security

Authorization controls whether or not a user can read or write one or more tables. SQL permissions are limited to the column level and cannot be applied to the row level. **row-level security (RLS)** controls permissions at the row level by controlling what data in a table the user has access to:

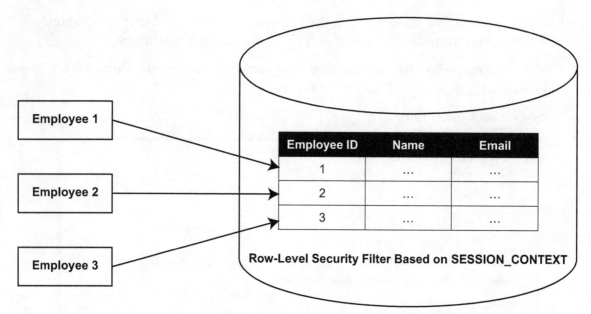

Figure 6.50: Row-level security

Let's say you have a Customers table in a database and you want users to access only those rows in a table that belong to them; for example, in a company, employees are restricted to viewing only their end customers' data. Employee 1 should only have access to rows with customer ID 1, and employee 2 should only access rows with customer ID 2, and so on and so forth.

RLS allows you to enable this at the database level and not the application level. This is a programmatic feature and would not help if users have direct access to the database. Prior to RLS, such security was only possible by implementing access logic at the application level.

RLS is implemented by writing the row access logic or the security predicate in an inline table-valued function and then creating a security policy on top of the security predicate.

The security predicate defines the criteria to determine whether or not a user has read or write access to a given set of rows in a particular table.

RLS supports two types of security predicates:

- Filter predicates: Filter predicates apply to **SELECT**, **UPDATE**, and **DELETE**, and silently filter out unqualified rows.

- Block predicates: Block predicates apply to **AFTER INSERT**, **AFTER UPDATE**, **BEFORE UPDATE**, and **BEFORE DELETE**, and block unqualified rows being written to the table.

Dynamic data masking

Dynamic data masking or DDM works on top of RLS and further restricts the exposure of sensitive data by masking it to non-privileged users:

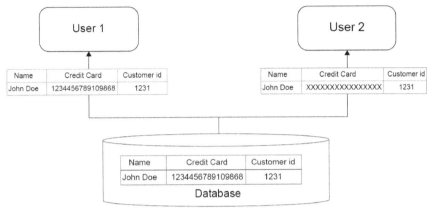

Figure 6.51: DDM

For example, say users John and Chris can read and write data that belongs to Customers. RLS ensures that they can only read and write data for customer 1 in the customer table. However, DDM will ensure that John can see the Social Security number of the customer and Chris can't, as he's not authorized to. Chris will see masked data in the Social Security number column, though he will be able to see data in the rest of the columns.

DDM is implemented by defining masks and applying them to columns as and when required. There aren't any changes required at the application level or the query level, as the masks are applied at the column level.

DDM can be used for full, partial, or random masking. For example, call-support workers need the last four characters of a user's password to identify them. This can be done by masking all characters except the last four.

DDM has the following four types of masks to obfuscate data:

- **Default:** Implements full masking depending on the data type of the column being masked.

- **Email:** Partial masking, which masks all characters except the first letter and the .com suffix of an email address. For example, `john1984@dataplatformlabs.com` would be masked as `jxxx@xxxx.com`.

- **Random:** Masks a column with a numeric data type with a random value within a specified range.

- **Custom String:** Partial masking, which masks all characters with a custom string, excluding the first and last letters.

DDM has the following limitations:

- Encrypted columns, filestreams, column sets, and sparse columns that are part of a column set can't be masked.

- Computed columns can't be masked; however, if a computed column depends on a masked column, the computed column will return masked values.

- A masked column can't be used as a full-text index key.

- A mask can't be applied to a column with dependencies. For example, if an index depends on a column, it can only be masked by dropping the index, applying the mask, and then creating the index.

- Unprivileged users with read access to a database can use inference or brute-force techniques to guess the underlying data and infer actual values.

DDM is helpful in masking sensitive information to non-privileged users, thereby making sure that information such as credit card details and social security numbers is protected and can be accessed only by users with correct permissions.

Data Discovery & Classification

The Data Discovery & Classification feature (in preview) can be used to discover, classify, label, and protect sensitive data in a SQL database. Data Discovery & Classification can help you achieve data privacy and regulatory compliance requirements, control and secure databases with highly sensitive data such as credit card numbers and confidential financial or other business information, and monitor and alert you to unusual access to sensitive data.

Data Discovery & Classification consists of the following:

Discovery and recommendations

The classification engine scans and identifies the column with a sensitive name in a SQL database. It also provides possible resolutions and ways to apply the resolutions.

Labeling

This allows the tagging of columns with sensitive data using the new classification metadata attributes available in the SQL engine.

There are two attributes used to classify the sensitivity of data—a label, which specifies the level of the data sensitivity in a given column, and information types, which provide additional details on the type of data stored in the column.

The classification details are available on a dashboard on the Azure portal and can also be downloaded for offline analysis.

Exercise: Configuring Data Discovery & Classification for SQL Database

To configure Data Discovery & Classification, follow these steps:

1. Navigate to the **SQL Database** page and then select the **Data Discovery & Classification** option from the **Security** section:

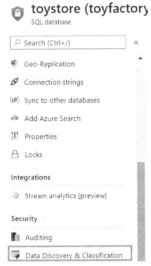

Figure 6.52: Selecting Data Discovery & Classification

2. **Data Discovery & Classification** provides auto-recommendations based on the tables in the database. We can also manually classify columns:

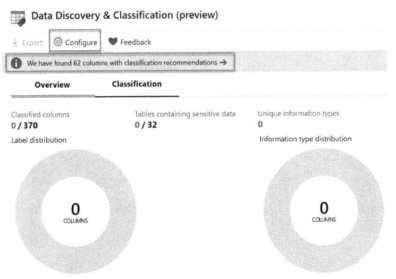

Figure 6.53: Data Discovery & Classification overview

Notice that there are **62** columns with classification recommendations; however, none of the columns are classified yet.

3. Click the **Configure** option to manage the sensitivity labels. A label defines the level of data sensitivity:

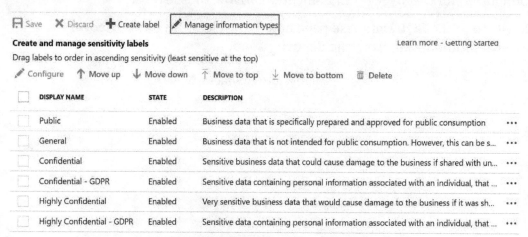

Figure 6.54: Managing information types

You can add, delete, and prioritize labels by moving them up or down the hierarchy. You can also import/export the information protection file to offline usage/management.

4. Click **Manage information types** in *Figure* 6.54 to add or delete information types:

➕ Create information type

Create and manage information types
Drag information types to order in ascending discovering ranking

✏ Configure   ↑ Move up   ↓ Move down   ↑ Move to top   ↓ Move to bottom   🗑 Delete

INFORMATION TYPE	STATE	ASSOCIATED LABEL	TYPE	
Networking	Enabled	Confidential	Built-in	•••
Contact Info	Enabled	Confidential	Built-in	•••
Credentials	Enabled	Confidential	Built-in	•••
Name	Enabled	Confidential - GDPR	Built-in	•••
National ID	Enabled	Confidential - GDPR	Built-in	•••
SSN	Enabled	Confidential - GDPR	Built-in	•••
Credit Card	Enabled	Confidential	Built-in	•••
Banking	Enabled	Confidential	Built-in	•••

Figure 6.55: Deleting information types

An information type details the type of data in a column; for example, the **Contact Info** information type is for the name, phone number, and address details of a person or business.

Each information type is associated with a label. This can be changed as per the business standard. For example, if **Contact Info** is allowed to be shared for a particular business, the label can be changed to **Public** from **Confidential**.

5. Let's now return to the **Data Discovery & Classification** page and look at the recommendations. To do this, click the **We have found 62 columns with classification recommendations** link:

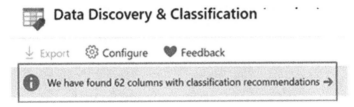

Figure 6.56: Classification recommendations

All of the classifications are listed under the **Classification** tab on the **Data Discovery & Classification** page.

You can filter the recommendations based on schema, table, column, information type, and label.

6. Let's look at the recommendations for the `Application.People` table:

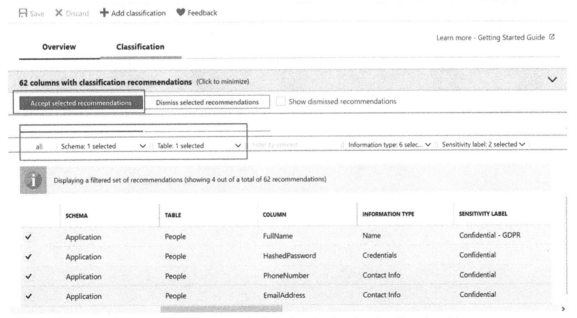

Figure 6.57: Recommendations for the Application.People table

Notice that the information type and sensitivity labels are correctly applied to the four columns.

7. Click **Accept selected recommendations** to apply the data classification:

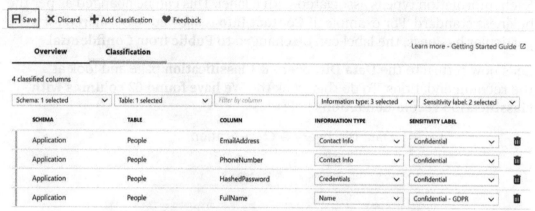

Figure 6.58: Applying data classification

8. Click **Save** and then select the **Overview** tab:

Figure 6.59: Overview tab

The **Overview** tab now shows a summary of the label and information type distribution and lists the data classifications.

Any access to the classified columns is captured in the audit logs when SQL database auditing is on. An example of an audit report is shown in the next section, *Auditing*.

Auditing

Auditing tracks and records database events to an audit log and can help you to:

- Maintain regulatory compliance.

- Understand database activity.

- Catch discrepancies or anomalies indicating security violations.

Auditing allows you to:

- Define what database actions are to be audited.

- Find unusual activities or trends by using preconfigured reports and dashboards.

- Understand and analyze the audit log.

Auditing can be configured on SQL Database and SQL Managed Instance at both the server level and database level, but on SQL Managed Instance, it can be configured using Transact-SQL. If auditing is configured at the server level, it will automatically apply to all the databases in the server. Auditing configured at the database level will only apply to a particular database.

It's recommended to audit the server instead of auditing individual databases.

Exercise: Configuring SQL Database auditing

To configure SQL database auditing using the Azure portal, follow these steps:

1. Open the **toystore** database overview page and search for **Auditing** in the search box:

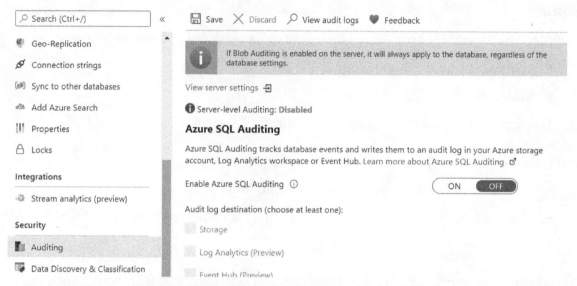

Figure 6.60: The toystore database auditing auditing

Click **Auditing** to open the **toystore Auditing** page.

2. On the **Auditing** page, click the **Auditing** toggle button to switch on auditing.

    There are three options to save the audit log: **Storage**, **Log Analytics (Preview)**, and **Event Hub (Preview)**.

    The storage account allows you to save the audit logs; however, it provides no native ways to perform analytics on saved logs.

    Log Analytics saves the log data in the Log Analytics workspace and uses Azure Monitor to provide analysis and actions on the logged data.

    Azure Event Hubs is a big data streaming and event ingestion service. Audit logs are streamed to an event hub as events. Events from an event hub can be used to perform real-time analysis and can be saved into another database (CSV, Cosmos DB, or another SQL database) for further analytics.

3. Check the **Storage** and **Log Analytics** options and configure them as follows.

    Configuring storage: To configure storage, click **Storage settings**. You can either select an existing storage account or create a new storage account:

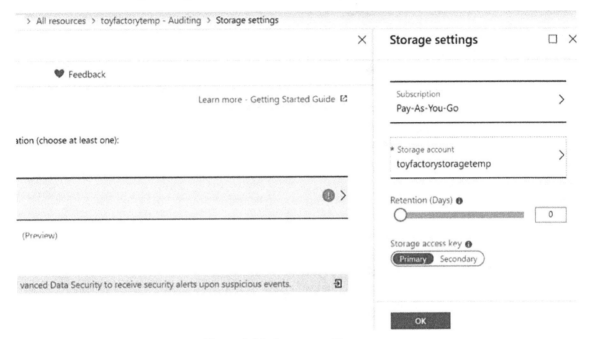

Figure 6.61: Storage settings page

To create a new storage account, click **Create new** and fill out the details as shown in *Figure 6.61*.

> **Note**
>
> You can opt for premium storage for faster performance if required. Standard blob storage is preferred for demo purposes.

Click the **OK** button to create and link the storage account to SQL database auditing.

4. Configuring log analytics: To configure log analytics, click **Log Analytics**. You can use an existing Log Analytics workspace or create a new one:

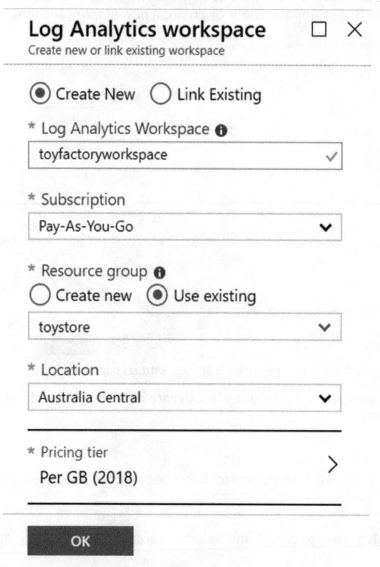

Figure 6.62: Log Analytics workspace page

To create a new workspace, click on the **Create New** option and fill out the details as shown in *Figure 6.62*.

There's only one pricing tier, **Per GB (2018)**, currently available with Log Analytics. Click **OK** to create and link the Log Analytics account with SQL database auditing.

After the storage account and Log Analytics workspace have been configured, click **Save** to save the configuration:

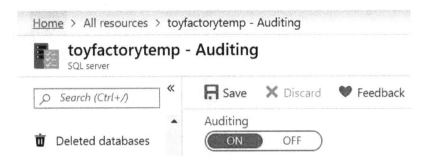

Figure 6.63: Creating a new workspace

This completes the auditing configuration. To view the audit logs, click on **View audit logs** in **toystoretemp - Auditing**:

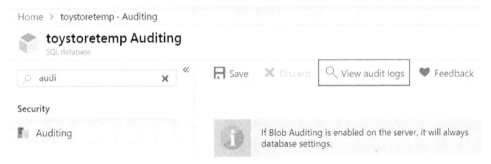

Figure 6.64: Viewing audit logs

5. Let's execute queries against the **toystore** database and monitor the audit logs.

> **Note**
>
> To execute a query, you can connect to the **toystore** database from SSMS or you can use the query editor provided in the Azure portal.

To execute the query from SSMS, make sure the IP address of your machine has been added to the SQL database firewall rule. For more on how to connect and execute a query against an SQL database, refer to *Chapter 1, Introduction to Azure SQL managed databases*:

```
SELECT
EmailAddress, PhoneNumber
FROM Application.People WHERE Fullname LIKE '%Edg%' GO
SELECT
*
FROM Purchasing.Suppliers
WHERE BankAccountName LIKE '%a%'
```

Here's what you should get when running queries from SSMS:

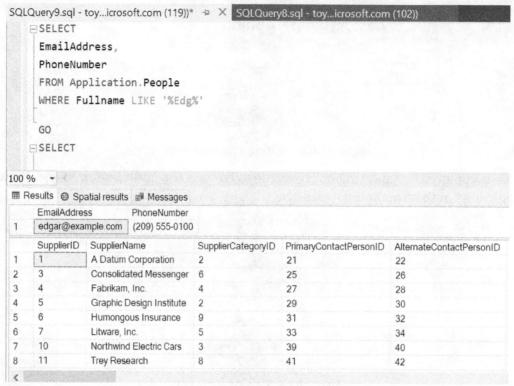

Figure 6.65: Running queries from SSMS

6. Let's switch to the Azure portal and open the **toystore - Auditing** page. On the **toystore - Auditing** page, click on **View audit logs**.

    The **Audit records** page lists the stored audit logs. Click **Run in Query Editor** to query the log files using a Transact-SQL query:

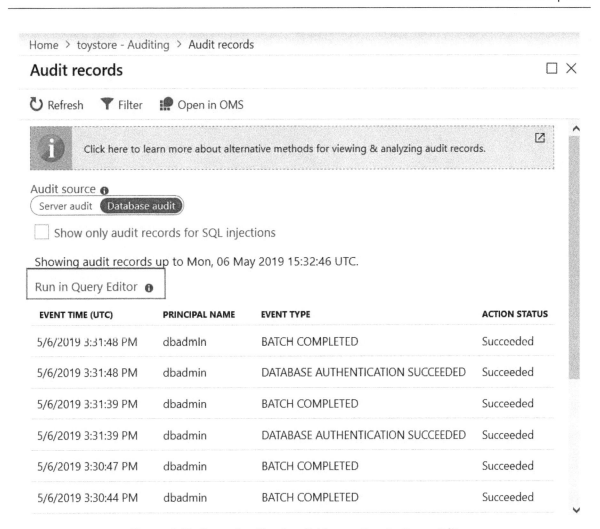

Figure 6.66: Query log files by clicking on Run in Query Editor

7. Log in to the query editor using SQL authentication, as shown in *Figure 6.67*:

Figure 6.67: The Login page of the query editor

A new query window opens up with the audit query. Replace the audit query with the following one:

```
SELECT TOP 100 event_time, server_instance_name, database_name, server_
principal_name, client_ip, statement, succeeded, action_id, class_type,
additional_information
FROM sys.fn_get_audit_file('https://toyfactorystoragetemp.blob.core.
windows.net/sqldbauditlogs/toyfactorytemp/toystore/SqlDbAuditing_Audit_
NoRetention/2019-06-20/18_57_50_932_0.xel', default, default)
WHERE (event_time <= '2019-06-20T19:03:22.910Z')
/* additional WHERE clause conditions/filters can be added here */ ORDER
BY event_time DESC
```

> **Note**
>
> You can execute the preceding query either in the query editor on the Azure portal or in SSMS.

The query uses the **sys.fn_get_audit_file** function to read the audit log file stored in Azure Storage. You'll have to replace the path of the audit log file with the one you got in the query editor in the previous step.

Here's the output from the query:

	event_time	server_instance_name	database_name	server_principal_name	client_ip	statement	succeeded
1	2019-06-20 19:00:49.0000673	toyfactorytemp	toystore	sqladmin	104.211.99.80	SELECT s.NAME AS SchemaName, t.NAME AS TableName...	1
2	2019-06-20 19:00:48.7500592	toyfactorytemp	toystore	sqladmin	104.211.99.80		1
3	2019-06-20 19:00:10.1868818	toyfactorytemp	toystore	sqladmin	104.211.99.80	;WITH CTE AS (SELECT TOP 100 event_time, ...	1
4	2019-06-20 19:00:09.9388275	toyfactorytemp	toystore	sqladmin	104.211.99.80		1
5	2019-06-20 18:59:15.1701815	toyfactorytemp	toystore	sqladmin	104.211.99.80	select 1	1
6	2019-06-20 18:59:14.9514039	toyfactorytemp	toystore	sqladmin	104.211.99.80		1
7	2019-06-20 18:58:35.1363895	toyfactorytemp	toystore		104.211.99.80		0
8	2019-06-20 18:57:50.9633526	toyfactorytemp		NT AUTHORITY\SYSTEM	Internal		1

Figure 6.68: Output of the previous query

Notice that the output has the label and the information type we assigned when configuring Data Discovery & Classification.

This information can be used to find out how often confidential information is accessed.

Exercise: Configuring auditing for SQL Managed Instance

To configure auditing for SQL Managed Instance, please follow these steps:

1. Go to the Azure portal using https://portal.azure.com.

2. Create a blob container for storing audit logs.

    Go to the storage account where you would like to store audit logs.

    Select the **Containers** option from the **Overview** tab:

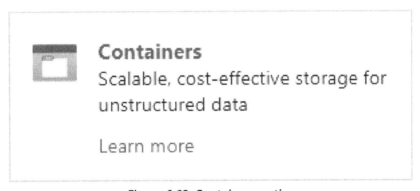

Figure 6.69: Containers option

Click on the **Container** option on the top menu:

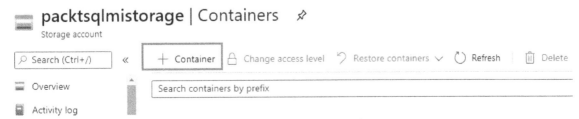

Figure 6.70: Container option

Input a container name, set the public access level to **Private**, and click on the **Create** button:

Figure 6.71: Creating a new container

Now the container is set up, so let's configure the target for auditing. This can be done using Transact-SQL or the SSMS GUI.

3. Set up a blob container for audit logs using the Transact-SQL command line.

    In the storage account, go to the newly created container and click on **Properties** to copy the container URL:

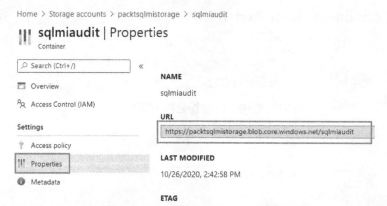

Figure 6.72: Container properties

Now, let's generate a SAS token to grant the managed instance access to the storage account.

Go to the same storage account setting and click on **Shared access signature** to generate the SAS key. Configure it as shown in *Figure 6.73*. Select the blob service, grant permissions, and choose the start and expiry dates. Click on **Generate SAS and connection string** to generate the SAS token.

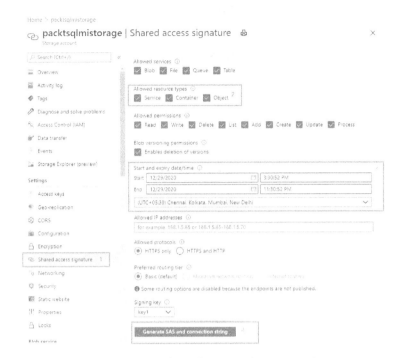

Figure 6.73: Shared access signature tab

Copy the SAS token to proceed further:

Figure 6.74: SAS token string

Note

Remove the question mark symbol **(?)** from the beginning of the token.

Connect to the managed instance using SSMS and run the following Transact-SQL command to create the credential:

```
CREATE CREDENTIAL [https://packtsqlmistorage.blob.core.windows.net/
sqlmiaudit]
WITH IDENTITY='SHARED ACCESS SIGNATURE',
SECRET = '<SAS TOEKN>'
GO
```

Once the credential is created, run the following command to create a new server audit.

```
CREATE SERVER AUDIT [auditlog]
TO URL ( PATH ='https://packtsqlmistorage.blob.core.windows.net/
sqlmiaudit' , RETENTION_DAYS =  30)
GO
```

4. Set up a blob container for the audit logs using SSMS.

Connect to the managed instance using the SSMS UI.

Expand the root node of Object Explorer.

Expand the **Security** node, right-click on the **Audits** node, and click on **New Audit...**

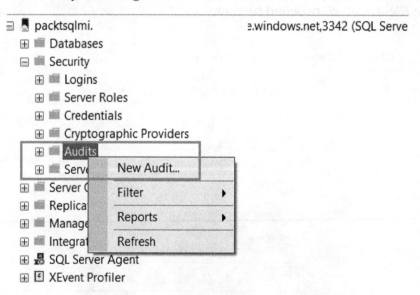

Figure 6.75: Creating a new audit using SSMS

In the **General** tab, select **URL** for **Audit destination** and click on **Browse**:

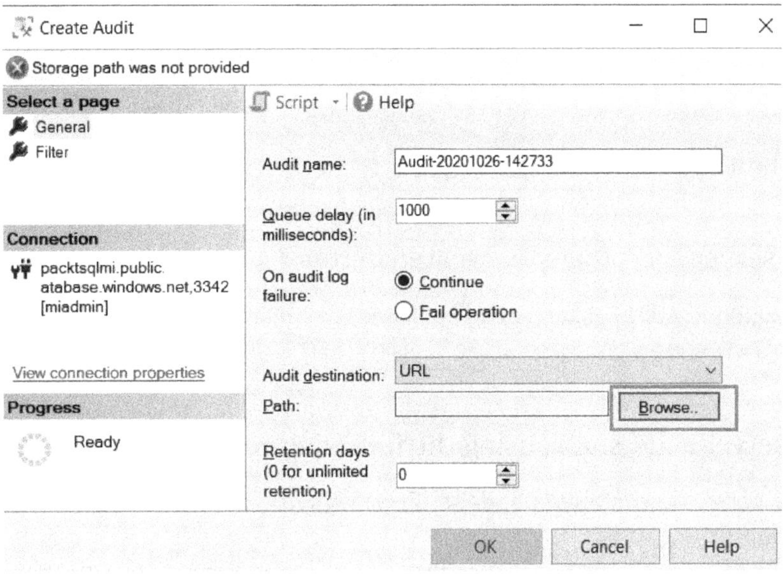

Figure 6.76: Create Audit- General tab

Log in to your Azure account using the **Sign In...** button:

Figure: 6.77: Browse window

Select your storage account and blob container from here and once you're finished, click **OK**. Make sure that your client has access to the storage account; if not, add your client IP to the storage account firewall:

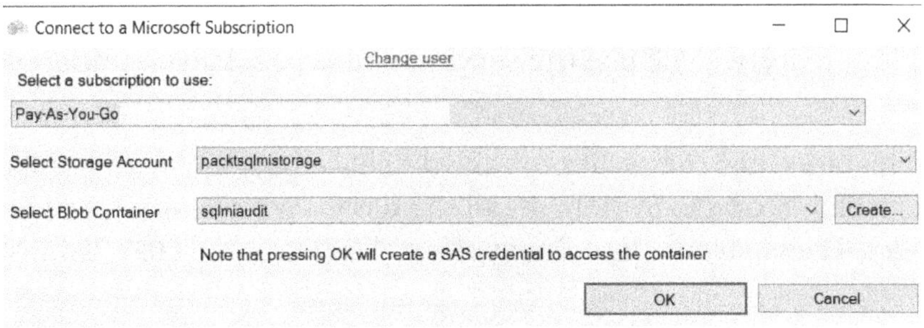

Figure: 6.78: Sign-in page

Finally, click **OK** to create the audit page.

5. Now that we have configured a blob container as the target for audit logs, let's create and enable a server audit or database audit specification like SQL Server:

Server audit specification: https://docs.microsoft.com/sql/t-sql/statements/create-server-audit-specification-transact-sql?view=sql-server-ver15.

Database audit specification: https://docs.microsoft.com/sql/t-sql/statements/create-database-audit-specification-transact-sql?view=sql-server-ver15.

6. Enable the server audit that you created in *step 4*:

```
ALTER SERVER AUDIT [auditlog]
WITH (STATE=ON);
GO
```

7. Verify the server audit status using the following command:

```
select name,status,status_desc from sys.dm_server_audit_status where
name='Audit-SQLMI';
```

You should get the following output:

Figure 6.79: Server audit status

In this activity, we have seen the steps to create a server audit for a managed instance using an Azure Blob Storage container. We have also learned how to enable and verify the server audit status using Transact-SQL commands.

Activity: Audit COPY_ONLY backup events on SQL Managed Instance using audit logs

In the previous activity, we saw the steps to enable a server audit for SQL Managed Instance. In this activity, we will use the server audit to track user-initiated COPY_ONLY database backups.

SQL Managed Instance has the ability to take database backups with the COPY_ONLY option on Azure Blob Storage. By default, all the databases are protected using a service-managed **Transparent Data Encryption (TDE)** key and COPY_ONLY backups are not allowed.

But there could be scenarios where a user who has higher access on an instance can disable service-managed TDE and take a COPY_ONLY backup of a database. You can track these events using audit logs.

Steps to configure an audit for backup and restore events

We have already seen how to configure a storage container for audit logs in a previous demo. Here we will create a server audit specification to track backup events.

You can skip the following steps if you have already configured a container for audit logs in the previous demo:

1. Create credentials to grant the managed instance access to the storage container:

    ```
    CREATE CREDENTIAL [https://packtsqlmistorage.blob.core.windows.net/
    sqlmiaudit]
    WITH IDENTITY='SHARED ACCESS SIGNATURE',
    SECRET = '<SAS TOEKN>'
    GO
    ```

2. Create an audit specification for **BACKUP_RESTORE_GROUP** and **AUDIT_CHANGE_GROUP**:

    ```
    -- Create server audit
    CREATE SERVER AUDIT [BackupRestoreAudit]
    TO URL (PATH = 'https://packtsqlmistorage.blob.core.windows.net/
    sqlmiaudit',RETENTION_DAYS = 30);
    GO

    -- Define events to audit
    CREATE SERVER AUDIT SPECIFICATION BackupRestoreAuditSpec
    FOR SERVER AUDIT [BackupRestoreAudit]
    ADD (BACKUP_RESTORE_GROUP),
    ADD (AUDIT_CHANGE_GROUP)
    WITH (STATE=ON);

    --Enable audit
    ALTER SERVER AUDIT [BackupRestoreAudit]
    WITH (STATE=ON);
    ```

3. This audit event will start capturing backup/restore information and it will also log events for audit configuration changes.

4. You can access these logs from the Transact-SQL command line.

    To view audit logs using Transact-SQL, first get the audit file path:

    ```
    --Get audit file path
    select name, audit_file_path
    from sys.dm_server_audit_status
    where name = 'BackupRestoreAudit' and audit_file_path is not null
    ```

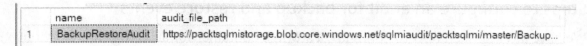

Run the following Transact-SQL query to view audit logs:

```
--Check backup logs from audit file
SELECT event_time, succeeded, statement, server_instance_name,
server_principal_name, client_ip, application_name, duration_milliseconds
FROM sys.fn_get_audit_file
('https://packtsqlmistorage.blob.core.windows.net/sqlmiaudit/packtsqlmi/
master/BackupRestoreAudit/2020-10-26/10_56_51_753_0.xel', default,
default);
```

	event_time	succeeded	statement	server_instance_name	server_principal_name	client_ip	application_name	duration_millisecor
1	2020-10-26 10:56:51.8159766	1		packtsqlmi	miadmin		Microsoft SQL Server Management Studio - Query	0
2	2020-10-26 11:21:50.9310303	1	ALTER SERVER AUDIT [auditlog] WITH (STATE = OFF)	packtsqlmi	miadmin		Microsoft SQL Server Management Studio	0
3	2020-10-26 11:21:51.1965765	1	DROP SERVER AUDIT [auditlog]	packtsqlmi	miadmin		Microsoft SQL Server Management Studio	0
4	2020-10-26 11:21:55.4000044	1	BACKUP DATABASE toystore TO URL = 'https://packts...	packtsqlmi	miadmin		Microsoft SQL Server Management Studio - Query	0

Figure 6.81: Audit logs output using Transact-SQL

5.   View the audit logs using the SSMS GUI.

Connect to SQL Managed Instance using SSMS.

Expand **Security and Audit** to see the configured audit name. Right-click and select the **View Audit Logs** option:

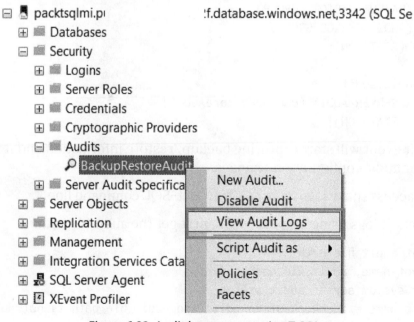

Figure 6.82: Audit logs output using T-SQL

You should get the following screen:

Figure 6.83: Log file viewer displaying the audit logs

6. Clean up the server audit.

    If you have configured this for testing purposes, then the following commands will clean up this audit configuration:

```
--Clean up
-- Drop server audit specification
ALTER SERVER AUDIT SPECIFICATION BackupRestoreAuditSpec
WITH (STATE=OFF);
DROP SERVER AUDIT SPECIFICATION BackupRestoreAuditSpec

-- Drop server audit
ALTER SERVER AUDIT [BackupRestoreAudit]
WITH (STATE=OFF);
DROP SERVER AUDIT [BackupRestoreAudit]

--Verify cleanup, empty results means server audit is stopped.

select name,status,status_desc from sys.dm_server_audit_status
where name='BackupRestoreAudit';
```

In this activity, we have seen steps to configure a server audit specification for backup and restore operations. This can help to track unwanted backups triggered by users who have privileges to disable service-managed transparent database encryption.

Transparent Data Encryption

Transparent Data Encryption (TDE) encrypts the user data at rest and therefore protects the database from offline malicious activity. TDE is enabled by default in newly deployed SQL databases and managed instances. TDE encrypts/decrypts the database, transaction log, and database backups in real time without any change in the application.

TDE works by encrypting each page before writing it to disk and decrypting each page when reading it from the disk. The encryption is done using a symmetric key known as a **database encryption key** (DEK). The DEK is protected by a TDE protector, which is either a service-managed certificate or a customer-managed asymmetric key stored in a key vault.

For more details on TDE, refer to https://docs.microsoft.com/azure/azure-sql/database/transparent-data-encryption-tde-overview.

Azure Defender for SQL

Azure Defender for SQL groups together the advanced SQL security capabilities, vulnerability assessment and Advanced Threat Protection. Azure Defender for SQL is priced at ~$15/per server/month and has a one-month free trial.

To enable Azure Defender for SQL from the Azure portal, navigate to the SQL Server page and then select **Security Center** from the **Security** section.

Enable Azure Defender for SQL by clicking on the toggle button. Provide an Azure storage account for the vulnerability assessment and an email address to send alerts. You can choose to run periodic recurring vulnerability scans by enabling the **Periodic recurring scans** option:

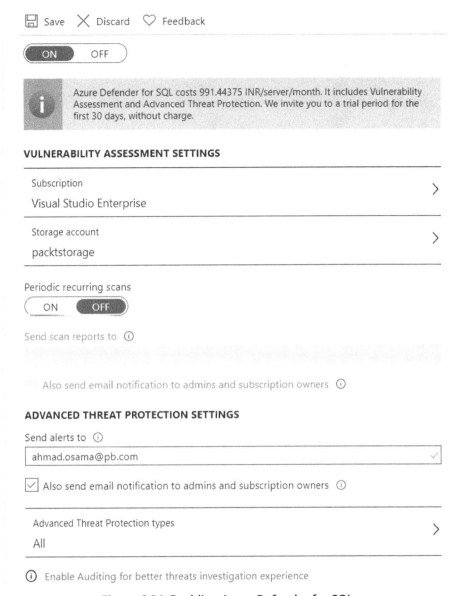

Figure 6.84: Enabling Azure Defender for SQL

We can enable the **Auditing** feature for better threat investigation. We can choose to enable specific, or all, **ADVANCED THREAT PROTECTION** features.

The two security features under Azure Defender for SQL are as follows:

- **Vulnerability assessment**: A vulnerability assessment, as the name suggests, checks a SQL database for any possible security vulnerabilities, database misconfigurations, extra permissions, unsecured data, firewall rules, and server-level permissions. A vulnerability assessment can help to meet data compliance and data privacy requirements.

- **Advanced Threat Protection**: Threat detection detects and alerts users about potential threats and suspicious activity. Alerts are integrated with Azure Security Center, which provides details about and possible solutions to alerts. Advanced Threat Protection alerts against the following threats:

- **SQL injection**: An alert is triggered when a SQL injection attack happens or if there's bad code that could result in a SQL injection attack.

- **Access from an unusual location**: An alert is triggered when a user logs in to a SQL database from a location that is different than the user's usual location.

- **Access from an unusual Azure datacenter**: An alert is triggered when someone logs into a SQL database from a datacenter other than the usual or the regular datacenter used to log in.

- **Access from an unfamiliar principal**: An alert is triggered when someone logs into a SQL database using an unfamiliar or unusual SQL login.

- **Access from a potentially harmful application**: An alert is triggered when a connection is made from a potentially harmful application; for example, common attack tools.

- **Brute-force SQL credentials**: An alert is triggered when there's an abnormally high number of failed logins attempted with different credentials.

- **Data exfiltration**: Data exfiltration is when an authorized user, say, a database administrator, can extract and move data from a SQL database to another location.

Securing data traffic

SQL Database and SQL Managed instance data traffic is always encrypted if the client driver supports SSL/TLS encryption. Data between a managed instance, a SQL database, and an Azure VM or any Azure service never leaves the Azure backbone network. All the communication within Azure happens using this Azure backbone. For on-premises connections, Microsoft recommends setting up Azure ExpressRoute, which helps to avoid sending data over the internet. For public endpoint access, Microsoft peering configuration is required for an ExpressRoute circuit for public communication.

Let's look at how to enforce a minimum **Transport Layer Security (TLS)** version for SQL Database or SQL Managed Instance.

Enforcing a minimal TLS version for SQL Database and SQL Managed Instance

A minimum TLS version allows users to control the version of TLS used by SQL Database and SQL Managed Instance.

Currently, SQL Database and SQL Managed Instance support TLS 1.0, 1.1, and 1.2. When you enforce a minimum TLS version, only higher and equal versions of TLS connection can communicate with a managed instance. For instance, if you have enforced a minimum TLS version of 1.1, then it means only connections with TLS versions 1.1 and 1.2 can communicate with SQL Database and SQL Managed Instance, and TLS 1.0 is rejected.

Microsoft recommends using TLS version 1.2, since it has all the fixes for previously reported vulnerabilities.

Activity: Setting a minimum TLS version using the Azure portal and PowerShell for SQL Managed Instance

The process of setting up a minimal TLS version for SQL Database and SQL Managed Instance using the Azure portal is almost the same. In this activity, we are using the SQL Managed Instance **Networking** tab to enforce a minimum TLS version for SQL Managed Instance, but the same can be done for SQL Database using the **Firewalls and Virtual Networks** tab.

Using the Azure portal

A minimum TLS version can be easily set using the Azure portal, but we should test application compatibility before enabling it in production:

1. Log in to the Azure portal: https://portal.azure.com.

2. Navigate to **SQL Managed Instance** and under **Security**, click on **Networking**:

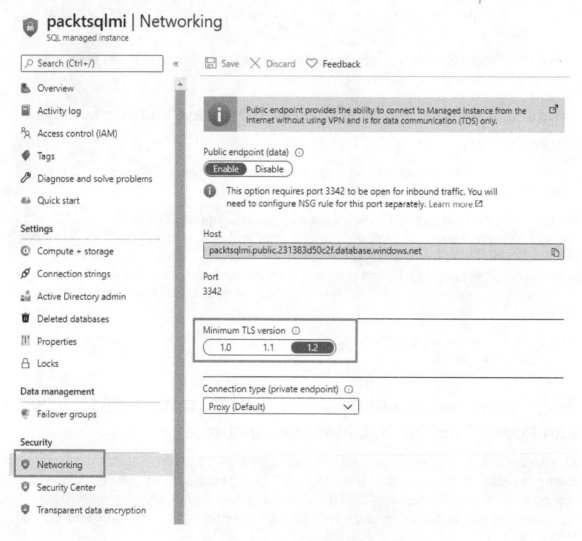

Figure 6.85: Networking tab

3. Select a minimum TLS version and click on **Save** to apply.

Using PowerShell

Use can use these PowerShell commands to set the minimum TLS version:

```
#setting up variable as per our environment

$MisubId = "6ee856b5-yy6d-4bc1-xxxx-byg5569842e1"

$InstanceName = "packtsqlmi"

$ResourceGroup = "Packt"


#Login to Azure Account

Connect-AzAccount


# Use your subscription ID in place of subscription-id below

Select-AzSubscription -SubscriptionId $MisubId


#Get the Minimal TLS Version property

(Get-AzSqlInstance -Name $InstanceName -ResourceGroupName $ResourceGroup).
MinimalTlsVersion
```

Figure 6.86: Using PowerShell to set the minimum TLS version

```
# Update Minimal TLS Version Property

Set-AzSqlInstance -Name $InstanceName -ResourceGroupName $ResourceGroup
-MinimalTlsVersion "1.2"
```

```
PS />
PS /> # Update Minimal TLS Version Property
PS /> Set-AzSqlInstance -Name $InstanceName -ResourceGroupName $ResourceGroup -MinimalTlsVersion "1.2"

Are you sure you want to set the Azure Sql Database Managed Instance 'packtsqlmi'?
Setting Azure Sql Database Managed Instance 'packtsqlmi'.
[Y] Yes  [N] No  [S] Suspend  [?] Help (default is "Y"): Y

Id                        :
Location                  : eastus
ResourceGroupName         : Packt
ManagedInstanceName       : packtsqlmi
Tags                      : {[environment, development]}
Identity                  : Microsoft.Azure.Management.Sql.Models.ResourceIdentity
Sku                       : Microsoft.Azure.Management.Internal.Resources.Models.Sku
FullyQualifiedDomainName  : packtsqlmi.                    base.windows.net
AdministratorLogin        : miadmin
AdministratorPassword     :
SubnetId                  : /subscriptions/
LicenseType               : LicenseIncluded
VCores                    : 4
StorageSizeInGB           : 32
Collation                 : SQL_Latin1_General_CP1_CI_AS
PublicDataEndpointEnabled : True
ProxyOverride             : Proxy
TimezoneId                : UTC
DnsZonePartner            :
DnsZone                   :
InstancePoolName          :
MinimalTlsVersion         : 1.2
BackupStorageRedundancy   : Geo
```

Figure 6.87: Using PowerShell to set the minimum TLS version

In this activity, we have seen the steps needed to enforce the minimum TLS version of SQL Managed Instance using both the Azure portal and PowerShell. The TLS protocol ensures an end-to-end secure communication channel and it is highly recommended to use TLS 1.2 or higher.

Configuring and securing public endpoints in SQL Managed Instance

A managed instance can be deployed to an Azure virtual network for the secure access of data within a private network. A public endpoint on a managed instance allows access to data from outside the virtual network. Using a public endpoint, you can access a managed instance from an on-premises network, a multi-tenant Azure service such as a web app, or Power BI.

In this activity, you will learn how to:

- Configure/manage a public endpoint on a managed instance using the Azure portal.

- Configure/manage a public endpoint on a managed instance using PowerShell.

- Secure public endpoint connections.

Let's look at the following steps to configure a public endpoint on SQL Managed Instance using the Azure portal and PowerShell cmdlets.

This is a two-step process, where you need to enable the public endpoint access and allow public endpoint TCP port **3342** in the managed instance NSG inbound rule. TCP port **3342** is the default for public endpoints, just like **1433** is for private endpoints, and it cannot be changed.

Enabling a public endpoint for a managed instance using the Azure portal

1. Go to the Azure portal at https://portal.azure.com/.

2. Search for `managed instances` using the search bar and select the managed instance that you want to configure the public endpoint on.

3. Under **Security**, select the **Networking** pane.

4. In the **Networking** pane, select **Enable** for the **Public endpoint (data)** option and then click the **Save** icon to update the configuration:

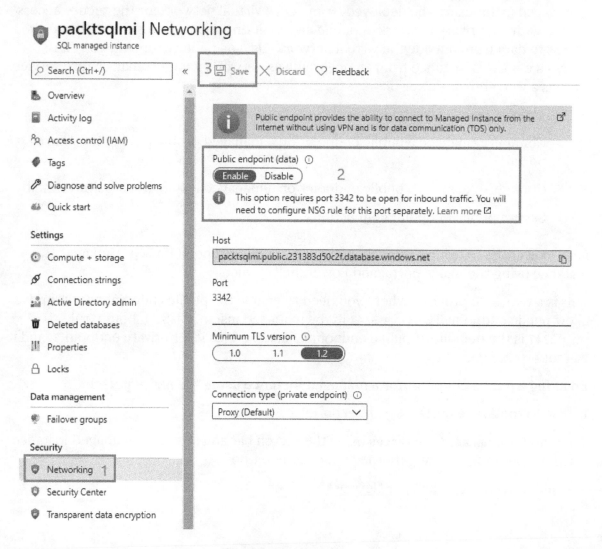

Figure 6.88: Networking tab

Enabling a public endpoint for a managed instance using PowerShell

You can run the following PowerShell commands to enable a public endpoint. Replace your environment variable before running these commands:

```
#setting up variable as per our environment
$MisubId = "6ee856b5-yy6d-4bc1-xxxx-byg5569842e1"

$instance = "packtsqlmi"

$resourceGroup = "Packt"


#Login to Azure Account
Connect-AzAccount


# Use your subscription ID in place of subscription-id below
Select-AzSubscription -SubscriptionId $MisubId


# Get the instance information using resource group and instance name.
$mi = Get-AzSqlInstance -ResourceGroupName $resourceGroup -Name $instance


# Set public endpoint access to true.
$mi = $mi | Set-AzSqlInstance -PublicDataEndpointEnabled $true -force


#Disable public endpoint access
$mi = $mi | Set-AzSqlInstance -PublicDataEndpointEnabled $false -force
```

Allowing public endpoint data traffic on a managed instance network security group

Here we are adding an inbound NSG rule for the managed instance to allow traffic on port **3342**. This is a network component change and is usually done by a network admin:

1. Navigate to the SQL Managed Instance **Overview** tab and click on the **Virtual network / subnet** hyperlink; this will take you to the virtual network **Overview** page:

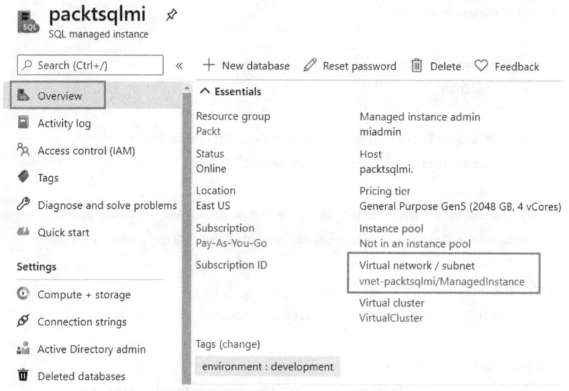

Figure 6.89: SQL Managed Instance - Overview tab

2. Select **Subnets** under **Settings** and make a note of the managed instance NSG name:

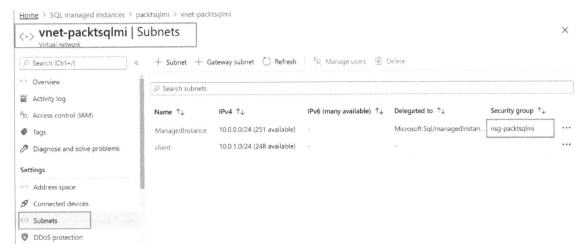

Figure 6.90: Subnets page for the virtual network

3. You can search for the nsg name using the main search bar or navigate to the resource group to find this network security group:

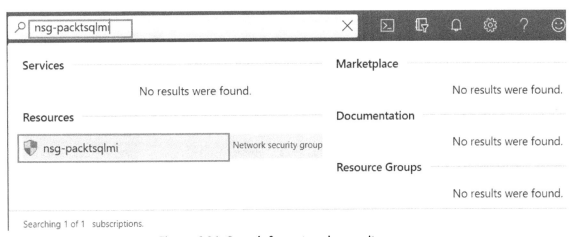

Figure 6.91: Search for network security group

4. Select the **Inbound security rules** tab under **Settings** and add an inbound rule for port **3342**, which should have higher priority than `deny_all_inbound rule`:

Figure 6.92: Inbound security rules tab

After adding the rule, it will be visible as shown here:

Priority	Name	Port	Protocol	Source	Destination	Action	
100	Microsoft.Sql-managedInstances_UseOnly_mi-sqlmg...	9000,9003,1438,1440,1452	TCP	SqlManagement	10.0.0.0/24	✓ Allow	•••
101	Microsoft.Sql-managedInstances_UseOnly_mi-corpsa...	9000,9003,1440	TCP	CorpNetSaw	10.0.0.0/24	✓ Allow	•••
102	Microsoft.Sql-managedInstances_UseOnly_mi-corpp...	9000,9003	TCP	CorpNetPublic	10.0.0.0/24	✓ Allow	•••
103	Microsoft.Sql-managedInstances_UseOnly_mi-health...	Any	Any	AzureLoadBalancer	10.0.0.0/24	✓ Allow	•••
104	Microsoft.Sql-managedInstances_UseOnly_mi-intern...	Any	Any	10.0.0.0/24	10.0.0.0/24	✓ Allow	•••
1000	allow_tds_inbound	1433	TCP	VirtualNetwork	10.0.0.0/24	✓ Allow	•••
1001	allow_public_endpoint	3342	TCP	Any	Any	✓ Allow	•••
1100	allow_redirect_inbound	11000-11999	TCP	VirtualNetwork	10.0.0.0/24	✓ Allow	•••
1200	allow_geodr_inbound	5022,5024	TCP	VirtualNetwork	10.0.0.0/24	✓ Allow	•••
4096	deny_all_inbound	Any	Any	Any	Any	⊘ Deny	•••
65000	AllowVnetInBound	Any	Any	VirtualNetwork	VirtualNetwork	✓ Allow	•••
65001	AllowAzureLoadBalancerInBound	Any	Any	AzureLoadBalancer	Any	✓ Allow	•••
65500	DenyAllInBound	Any	Any	Any	Any	⊘ Deny	•••

Figure 6.93: Newly added rule for the public endpoint

5. Now you can connect to the managed instance using SSMS from an on-premises network without having a VPN connection.

    Note that the public endpoint hostname comes in the `<mi_name>.public.<dns_zone>.database.windows.net` format and that the port used for the connection is **3342**:

Figure 6.94: SSMS connection string for the public endpoint

In this activity, we have seen steps to enable public endpoint access to SQL Managed Instance using the Azure portal and PowerShell cmdlets. We have also learned how to add inbound rules for a public endpoint in an SQL Managed Instance subnet network security group.

Securing SQL Managed Instance public endpoints

Up to now, we have learned how to configure a public endpoint on a managed instance; now we are going to learn about how to make it secure for data access.

Here are some quick insights about where to use a public endpoint connection.

SQL Managed Instance provides a private endpoint to allow connectivity within a virtual network. This default option provides maximum isolation and security. However, there could be use cases where you need public endpoint connections:

*   You need to integrate the managed instance with a multi-tenant-only **Platform as a service (PaaS)** offering.

*   You might require higher throughput for data exchange.

*   There may be network restrictions from company policies that prohibit having a PaaS offering inside a corporate network.

In the following sections, we will look at ways to secure public endpoint connections.

Locking traffic flow down using NSG or firewall rules

SQL Managed Instance has a dedicated private endpoint IP address and port that you can use to configure NSG outbound rules for a client within an Azure network and firewall rules for on-premises applications.

Also, you can lock down inbound traffic by configuring a correct set of inbound security rules in the managed instance NSG in a similar way to what we did in the previous activity.

The following is a traffic flow diagram within Azure and the on-premises network using public endpoint access:

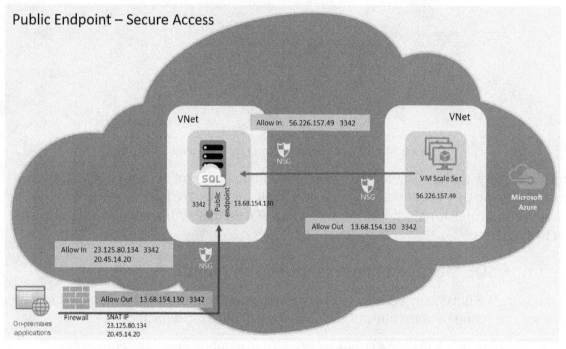

Figure 6.95: Securing public endpoint using NSG/firewall rules

In the next section, we will implement RLS for the **toystore** database.

Activity: Implementing RLS

In this section, we will look at how to implement RLS using our example of ToyStore Ltd. Mike has been asked to implement RLS so that every customer is able to view and edit only their records. The **CustomerAdmin** user, however, should be allowed to view and edit all customer records. Follow these steps to complete the activity:

1. Execute the following query to create the **dpl.Customers** table and populate it with sample records:

    ```
    CREATE TABLE Customers (
    CustomerID int identity, Name sysname, CreditCardNumber varchar(100),
    Phone varchar(100), Email varchar(100)
    )
    Go
    INSERT INTO Customers VALUES('Mike',0987654312345678,9876543210,'mike@
    outlook.com'), ('Mike',0987654356784567,9876549870,'mike1@outlook.
    com'), ('Mike',0984567431234567,9876567210,'mike2@outlook.com'), (' john@
    dpl.com ',0987654312345678,9876246210,'john@outlook.com'),
    ('john@dpl.com ',0987654123784567,9876656870,' john2@outlook.com'),
    ('john@dpl.com ',09856787431234567,9876467210, 'john3@outlook.com'),
    ('CustomerAdmin',0987654312235578,9873456210,'john@outlook. com'),
    ('CustomerAdmin',0984564123784567,9872436870,'mike2@outlook. com'),
    ('CustomerAdmin',0945677874312367,9872427210,'chris3@outlook. com')
    ```

2. Execute the following query to create a new user, **CustomerAdmin**:

    ```
    CREATE USER CustomerAdmin WITHOUT LOGIN
    CREATE USER Mike WITHOUT LOGIN
    CREATE USER John@aadityarama26gmail.com.onmicrosoft.com WITHOUT LOGIN
    ```

3. Execute the following query to grant read access to **Mike**, **John**, and **CustomerAdmin** on the **dpl.Customers** table:

    ```
    GRANT SELECT ON dpl.CustomersTO Mike
    GO
    GRANT SELECT ON dpl.CustomersTO [john@dpl.com]
    GO
    GRANT SELECT ON dpl.CustomersTO CustomerAdmin
    ```

4. Create a security predicate to filter out the rows based on the logged-in username:

    ```
    CREATE SCHEMA Security;
    GO
    CREATE FUNCTION Security.fn_securitypredicate(@Customer AS sysname)
    RETURNS TABLE WITH SCHEMABINDING AS
    RETURN
     SELECT 1 AS predicateresult
       WHERE @Customer = USER_NAME() OR
       USER_NAME() = 'CustomerAdmin';
    ```

    The preceding query first creates a schema, **Security**. It then creates an inline table-valued function, **fn_securitypredicate**, which will return **1** (**true**) when the logged-in username is equal to the **@Customer** parameter or when the logged-in user is **CustomerAdmin**.

    > **Note**
    >
    > The credit card numbers mentioned in plain text in the database are purely for demonstration purposes. Such information should be encrypted at all times.

5. Create a security policy for the preceding security predicate:

    ```
    CREATE SECURITY POLICY CustomerFilter
    ADD FILTER PREDICATE Security.fn_securitypredicate(Name)
    ON dbo.Customers,
    ADD BLOCK PREDICATE Security.fn_securitypredicate(Name) ON dpl.Customers
    AFTER INSERT WITH (STATE = ON);
    ```

    The preceding query adds the filter predicate created in *step* 4 to the security policy and sets the status to **ON**.

    The policy also implements an **AFTER INSERT** block predicate. Afterward, the **INSERT** predicate will stop inserts that don't comply with the security policy and will show an error message for them.

    The inline table-valued functions will take the customer name (the **Name** column) as the parameter and will return **true** if the passed parameter value is equal to the value returned by the **USER_NAME()** function.

6. Let's test the policy by executing the following query to switch the user context to **Mike** and return all the data from the **dpl.Customers** table:

```
EXECUTE AS USER='Mike'
GO
SELECT USER_NAME()
GO
SELECT * FROM dbo.Customers
```

You should get the following output:

Figure 6.96: Output of the preceding code

The query returns the records where the customer name is Mike. This is because the query is executed in the context of **Mike**.

7. Execute the following query to update John's record from Mike's security context:

```
EXECUTE AS USER='Mike' GO SELECT USER_NAME()
GO
-- CustomerID 11 belongs to John
UPDATE dpl.Customers SET Email='MikeBlue@outlook.com' WHERE CustomerID=11
GO


-- Switch User context to John
EXECUTE AS USER='john@dpl.com '

GO
SELECT USER_NAME()

GO
-- Verify if email is updated or not

SELECT * FROM dpl.Customers WHERE CustomerID=11
```

Mike can't update **CustomerID 11** as it belongs to John. You won't get an error; however, the value won't be updated.

You should get the following output:

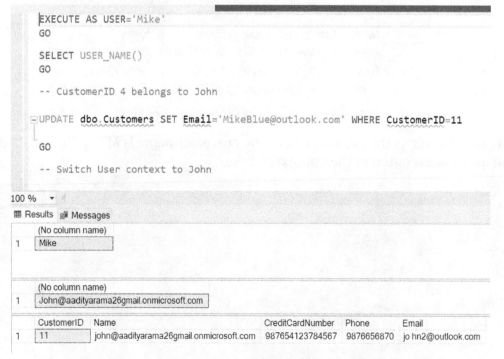

Figure 6.97: Updating John's record from Mike's security context

8. Execute the following query under Mike's security context to insert a record with a customer name of **john@dpl.com**:

```
EXECUTE AS USER='Mike'
GO
SELECT USER_NAME()
GO
INSERT INTO dpl.Customers VALUES('john@dpl.com'
,9876543445345678,65412396852,'Mike@dataplatformlabs.com')
```

The **AFTER INSERT BLOCK** predicate will block the insert, as defined by the security policy, and will show the following error:

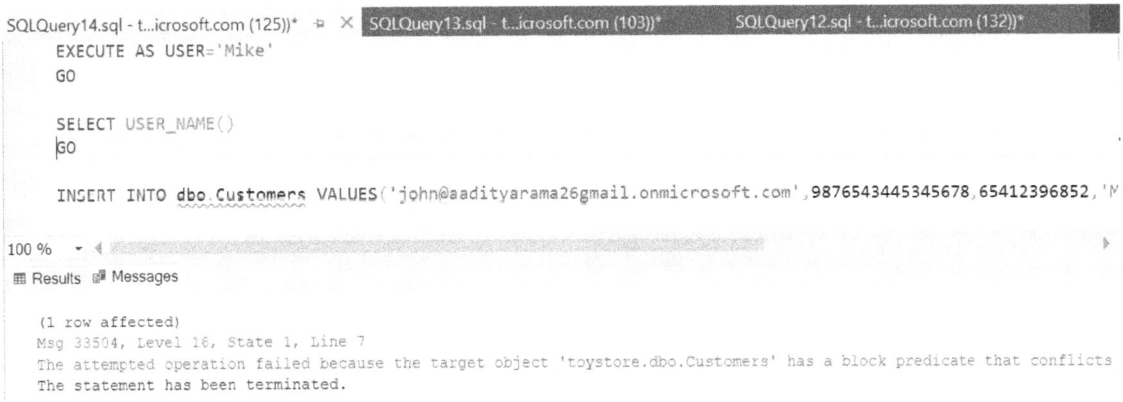

Figure 6.98: Inserting a record in Mike's security context

9. Execute the following query in the **CustomerAdmin** security context to return all of the rows from the **dpl.Customers** table:

```
REVERT;
GO
EXECUTE AS USER='CustomerAdmin'
GO
SELECT USER_NAME()
GO
SELECT * FROM dbo.Customers
```

You'll get all of the rows defined in the security predicate:

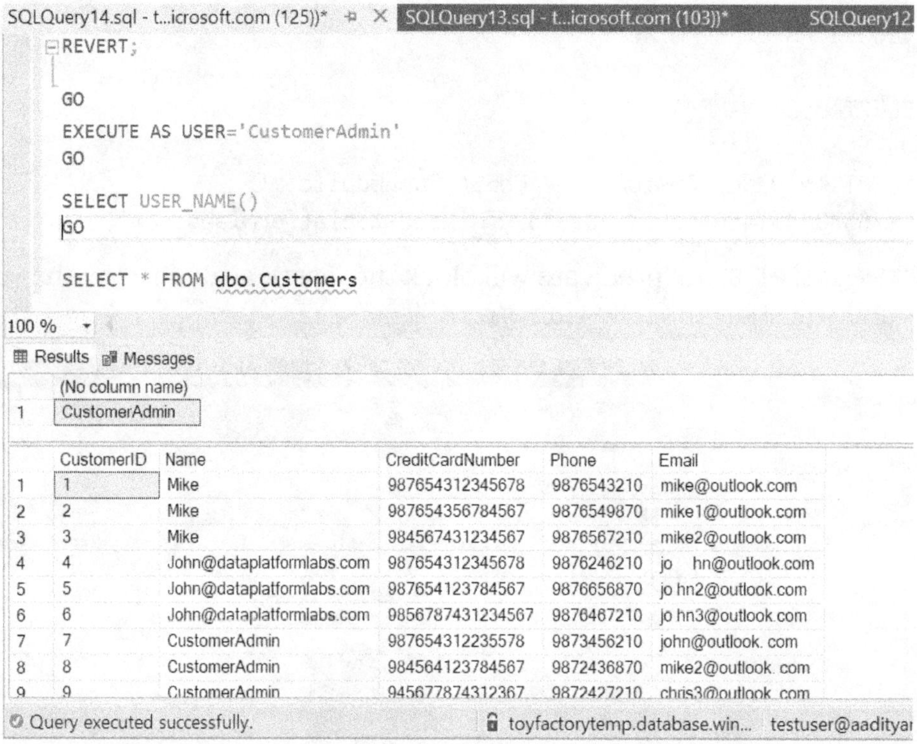

Figure 6.99: Adding a query in the security context to return rows from the dpl.Customers table

10. Execute the following query to switch off the security policy:

```
ALTER SECURITY POLICY CustomerFilter WITH (STATE = OFF);
```

In the activity, we learned how to configure RLS to make sure that a user only has access to their own data and isn't able to view or modify another user's data.

Activity: Implementing DDM

With RLS implemented in the previous activity, Mike has ensured that the customer can only view their own data; however, to take data security to the next level, he wants to mask some of the sensitive data that is shared by the customer. In order to do this, he has to implement DDM. In this activity, we'll implement DDM to mask the credit card number, phone number, and email ID of a customer:

1. Execute the following query to create a new user and grant select access to the user on the **dpl.Customers** table:

```
CREATE USER TestUser WITHOUT LOGIN; GO
GRANT SELECT ON dpl.Customers TO TestUser
```

2. Execute the following query to mask the **CreditCardNumber**, **Phone**, and **Email** columns using different masking functions:

```
ALTER TABLE dpl.Customers ALTER COLUMN Phone VARCHAR(100) MASKED WITH
(FUNCTION = 'default()')
GO
ALTER TABLE dpl.Customers ALTER COLUMN Email VARCHAR(100) MASKED WITH
(FUNCTION = 'email()')
GO
ALTER TABLE dpl.Customers ALTER COLUMN CreditCardNumber VARCHAR(100)
MASKED WITH (FUNCTION = 'partial(0,"XXX-XX-",4)')
```

The preceding query masks the phone number using the default masking function, the email with the email masking function, and **CreditCardNumber** with the partial masking function, which masks all characters excluding the last four.

3. Execute the following query in the context of **TestUser** to return all of the rows from the **dpl.Customers** table:

```
EXECUTE AS USER='TestUser'
GO
SELECT * FROM dbo.Customers;
```

Notice that the phone number, email, and credit card number columns are masked:

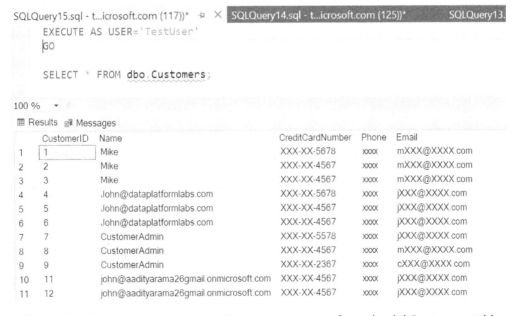

Figure 6.100: Execute a query in TestUser to return rows from the dpl.Customers table

4. Execute the following query to list the masked columns and the functions for the Customers table:

```
REVERT;
GO
SELECT mc.name, t.name as table_name,mc.masking_function FROM sys.masked_
columns AS mc
JOIN sys.tables AS t
ON mc.[object_id] = t.[object_id]
WHERE is_masked = 1 and t.name='Customers'
```

The **sys.masked_columns** table stores the masked columns metadata. The **is_masked** column tells you whether a column is masked or not.

You should get the following output:

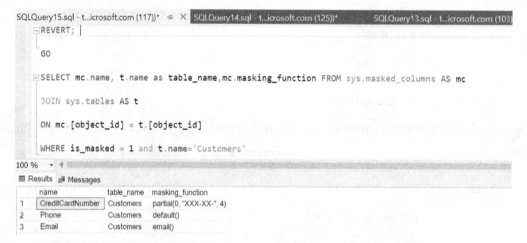

Figure 6.101: List of masked columns and functions for the Customers table

5. Execute the following query to allow **TestUser** to see the masked data:

```
GRANT UNMASK TO TestUser;
GO
EXECUTE AS USER='TestUser'
GO
SELECT * FROM dbo.Customers;
GO
```

The **UNMASK** permission allows **TestUser** to see the masked data.

You should get the following output:

Figure 6.102: Allowing TestUser to see the masked data

6. To mask the data again, run the following query:

```
REVERT;
REVOKE UNMASK TO TestUSER
```

The preceding query will mask the data again and the users will see the output as shown in *step* 3.

Activity: Implementing Azure Defender for SQL to detect SQL injection and brute-force attacks

Earlier in the chapter, we learned that Advanced Threat Protection automatically detects and alerts you about security issues such as SQL injection, brute-force attacks, and anonymous access.

In this two-part activity, we'll simulate SQL injection and a brute-force attack and study the email alerts raised by Advanced Threat Protection:

1. To configure email alerts for Advanced Threat Protection, open the Azure portal and then open the SQL server you want to configure alerts for.

   Under the **Security** section, select **Security Center**. Provide the email address that will receive the notifications, under the **ADVANCED THREAT PROTECTION SETTINGS** heading, as shown here:

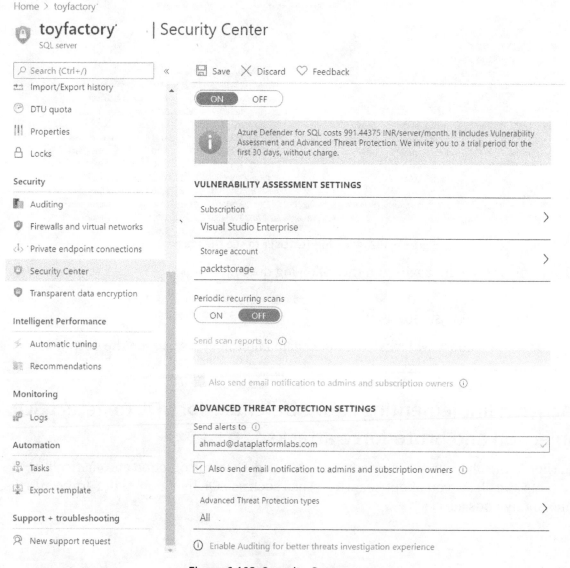

Figure 6.103: Security Center page

2. Click **Save** to save the settings.

Part 1: Simulating SQL injection

To simulate an SQL injection attack, perform the following steps:

1. Connect to the **toystore** database in SSMS and execute the following query:

```
CREATE TABLE users (userid INT, username VARCHAR(100),usersecret
VARCHAR(100))
GO
INSERT INTO users VALUES(1,'Ahmad','MyPassword'),(2,'John','Doe')
```

2. Navigate to **C:\Code\Chapter06\AdvancedThreatProtection\SQLInjection** and open the **SQLInjection.exe.config** file:

```
<?xml version="1.0" encoding="utf-8" ?>
<configuration>
<startup>
<supportedRuntime version="v4.0" sku=".
NETFramework,Version=v4.5.2" />
</startup>
<appSettings>
<add key="server" value="packtdbserver"/>
<add key="user" value="dbadmin"/>
<add key="database" value="toystore"/>
<add key="password" value="Awesome@1234"/>
</appSettings>
</configuration>
```

Under **appSettings**, replace the values for **server** (SQL server), **user** (SQL user), **database** (SQL database), and **password** (SQL user password) with yours and save the file.

3. Double-click **SQLInjection.exe** in the **C:\Code\Chapter06\AdvancedThreatProtection\ SQLInjection** folder to run it:

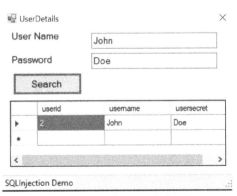

Figure 6.104: Running SQLInjection.exe

SQLInjection.exe is a simple Windows form application. It accepts a username and password as input and if the input matches the username and password in the database, the result is shown in the grid.

Enter the details as shown in *Figure 6.104* and then click the **Search** button. The result is shown in the grid.

Let's now try hacking the database using SQL injection.

4. Enter the following in the **User Name** text box and click the **Search** button:

```
' OR 1=1 union all select 1,name,name from sys.objects --'
```

Figure 6.105: Searching for the username in the text box

Notice that we are able to hack in and get a list of all the objects in the database.

5. Let's now insert a new user in the **users** table. Enter the following in the **User Name** text box and click the **Search** button:

```
' OR 1=1 insert into users values(100,'hacked','hacked') --'
```

The preceding query inserts a new row in the **users** table:

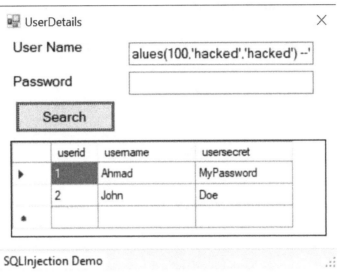

Figure 6.106: Adding a new row in the users table

Though we get the list of users, the **insert** query worked. Let's search for the **hacked** user that we inserted:

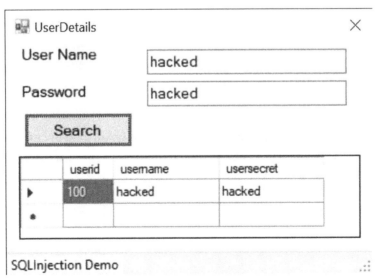

Figure 6.107: Searching for the inserted user

The **hacked** user was successfully inserted into the **users** table.

Part 2: Simulating and detecting brute-force attacks

In a brute-force attack, an attacker tries to connect with SQL Server by providing random values for a password, hoping that one of the random passwords will work and a connection to SQL Server will be made.

In this section, we'll simulate a brute-force attack by connecting to SQL Server using a random password. We'll then look at the Azure portal to see whether the attack was successfully identified or not, as well as seeing whether the SQL injection from the first part of the activity was detected.

To simulate a brute-force attack, follow these steps:

1. Navigate to **C:\Code\Chapter06\AdvancedThreatProtection\BruteForceAttack** and open **BruteForceAttack.exe.config** in Notepad:

    ```xml
    <?xml version="1.0" encoding="utf-8" ?>
    <configuration>
    <startup>
    <supportedRuntime version="v4.0" sku=".
    NETFramework,Version=v4.5.2" />
    </startup>

    <appSettings>
    <add key="Server" value="packtdbserver"/>
    <add key="database" value="toystore"/>

    </appSettings>
    </configuration>
    ```

    Under **appSettings**, change **Server** to the name of your SQL server and change **database** to your SQL database's name.

    Save the file.

2. In the **C:\Code\Chapter06\AdvancedThreatProtection\BruteForceAttack** folder, double-click **BruteForceAttack.exe** to start the attack. **BruteForceAttack.exe** is a Windows console application. It attempts to connect to the SQL server with a random username and password.

You should get the following output:

Figure 6.108: Executing BruteForceAttack.exe

Notice the username and password in each call. The connection attempt is made using a different username and password.

Double-click four or five times to run at least five instances of the **BruteForceAttack** application.

3. Let's now check the Azure portal for alerts, if any, about the SQL injection and brute-force attack simulations.

4. Log in to the Azure portal and open the **toystore** SQL database page. Search for and open the **Advanced Data Security** page:

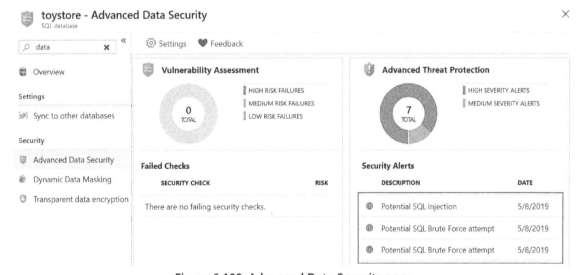

Figure 6.109: Advanced Data Security page

5. Notice that Advanced Threat Protection lists the security alerts for the SQL injection and brute-force attempts. Click on the **Potential SQL Injection** alert:

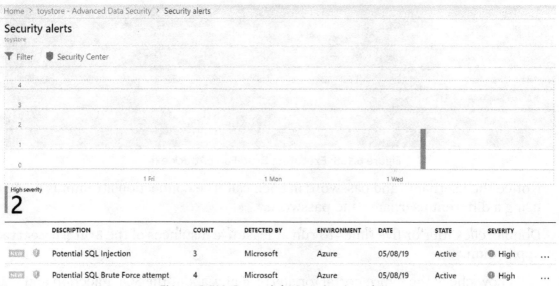

Figure 6.110: Potential SQL Injection alert

There are three SQL injection and four brute-force attempt alerts from Advanced Threat Protection.

6. Click on **Potential SQL Injection** to get their details:

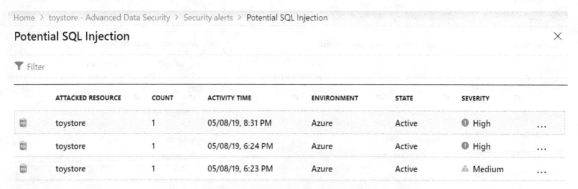

Figure 6.111: Potential SQL Injection details

The alert page gives details of the attached resource, count, time, environment, and severity.

7. Click on one of the **High** severity alerts to get its details:

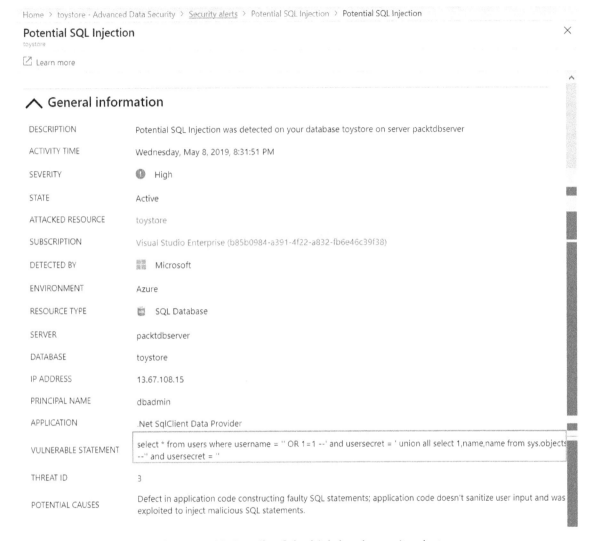

Home > toystore - Advanced Data Security > Security alerts > Potential SQL Injection > Potential SQL Injection

Potential SQL Injection   ✕
toystore

☐ Learn more

⋀ General information

DESCRIPTION	Potential SQL Injection was detected on your database toystore on server packtdbserver
ACTIVITY TIME	Wednesday, May 8, 2019, 8:31:51 PM
SEVERITY	🛈 High
STATE	Active
ATTACKED RESOURCE	toystore
SUBSCRIPTION	Visual Studio Enterprise (b85b0984-a391-4f22-a832-fb6e46c39f38)
DETECTED BY	▦ Microsoft
ENVIRONMENT	Azure
RESOURCE TYPE	🛢 SQL Database
SERVER	packtdbserver
DATABASE	toystore
IP ADDRESS	13.67.108.15
PRINCIPAL NAME	dbadmin
APPLICATION	.Net SqlClient Data Provider
VULNERABLE STATEMENT	select * from users where username = '' OR 1=1 --' and usersecret = ' union all select 1,name,name from sys.objects --'' and usersecret = ''
THREAT ID	3
POTENTIAL CAUSES	Defect in application code constructing faulty SQL statements; application code doesn't sanitize user input and was exploited to inject malicious SQL statements.

Figure 6.112: Details of the high-level security alert

The alert details are quite comprehensive and even display the query used as part of the SQL injection attack.

As a database administrator, you can pass on the details to the development team and have them fix the query.

8. Close the SQL injection alert page. To find details on the brute-force attempt alert, click on the **Potential SQL Brute Force attempt** alert on the **toystore - Advanced Data Security > Security alerts** page:

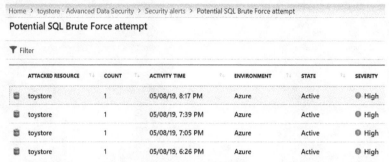

Figure 6.113: Potential SQL Brute Force attempt alerts

There are four high-severity brute force attempt alerts. Click on any one of them to get its details:

Figure 6.114: Details of brute-force alerts

Notice that the details page has the client IP address used for the brute-force attempt. To resolve the issue, make sure the mentioned IP address is blocked at the server firewall level.

Summary

Security is one of the deciding factors for an organization when opting to put their data in the cloud.

To connect to a SQL database and a managed instance, the machine's IP address or the client IP address should exist in the firewall settings or NSG rules. If not, the connection request will be denied.

Access to SQL Database can be restricted to one or more virtual networks using service endpoints. Private endpoints for SQL Database further strengthen security by assigning a private IP address to a SQL database from the customer's virtual network.

SQL Managed Instance can be deployed in a virtual network and offers strong security isolation, but SQL Database and SQL Managed Instance support similar secure connection options. SQL Managed Instance also gives an option to opt for a public endpoint connection, which can be secured by using NSG and firewall rules.

SQL Database and SQL Managed Instance allow SQL and Azure AD authentication. An organization can sync their domain with Azure, thereby allowing users to connect from Azure AD accounts instead of SQL logins. Organizations can also create Azure AD groups and give access to a group instead of giving access to individual Azure AD user accounts. In addition to this, you can use RLS and DDM to further secure data by allowing users to only see the data they need to do their work. SQL Database and SQL Managed Instance also provide proactive monitoring to detect threats such as SQL injection as and when they happen.

In the next chapter, we will learn about scaling out a SQL database or a managed instance based on the needs of the application.

Scalability

You can easily scale up or scale down an SQL database or managed instance, either automatically or manually. There are two types of scaling: **vertical** and **horizontal**.

Vertical scaling refers to switching to a higher or lower service tier or vertically partitioning data, which is done to store different schemas on different databases.

Horizontal scaling refers to dividing data from a single table into different individual databases.

This chapter will teach you how to autoscale SQL databases and shard a database. The chapter also talks about how to run cross-database queries.

By the end of this chapter, you will be able to:

- Perform vertical and horizontal scaling.

- Create and maintain SQL database shards.

- Run cross-database elastic queries.

- Scale a managed instance.

This chapter covers how to vertically and horizontally scale your system to optimize the performance of your application.

Vertical scaling

Vertical scaling refers to increasing or decreasing the resources of an SQL database or managed instance. The resources here refer to DTUs for DTU-based purchasing models and vCores for vCore-based purchasing models.

Vertical scaling can be of two types: scale-up or scale-down service tiers, or vertical partitions.

Scale-up or scale-down service tiers

Scaling up a service tier refers to switching to a higher service tier; for example, switching from General Purpose to Business Critical or switching from General Purpose **GP_Gen5_2** to General Purpose **GP_Gen5_4**.

Scaling down a service tier refers to switching to a lower service tier; for example, switching from General Purpose **GP_Gen5_4** to General Purpose **GP_Gen5_2**, or switching from Business Critical to General Purpose.

Scaling up a service tier allows you to maintain or improve database performance during peak business hours and scaling down a service tier allows you to save costs during off-peak business hours.

Service tiers can be changed on the fly with near-zero downtime. When a service tier change request is sent to Azure SQL Database, it first creates a copy of the database in the requested service tier and switches to the database in the new service tier once the copy is ready.

> **Note**
>
> Although there's no downtime in modifying service tiers, the in-process or in-flight transactions are cancelled when the switch from the old to the new service tier is done. This can be easily handled by adding retry logic in the application.

You are charged for the new service tier once the service tier is changed, and not from the time the service tier change request is received.

The SQL Database service tier can be changed from the Azure portal, using a T-SQL script, Azure PowerShell, or by putting the database in an elastic database pool. Except for the Azure portal, these methods allow you to automatically change the service tier.

> **Note**
>
> An elastic database pool is a group or pool of more than one Azure SQL database with varying usage. This is covered in detail in *Chapter 8, Elastic and instance pools*.

One of the most common vertical scaling use cases is to automatically scale up or scale down a service tier based on the CPU usage:

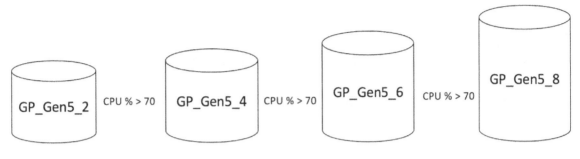

GP_Gen5_2
GP – General Purpose pricing tier
Gen5 – Generation 5 hardware
2 – Number of vCores

Figure 7.1: Scaling vCores in the General Purpose service tier

For example, you can put a script in place that will automatically scale to a higher vCore if the CPU usage increases past a specified threshold, such as switching to **GP_Gen5_4** if the CPU usage is greater than 70% (of the **GP_Gen5_2** service objective), and scale to a lower service tier if the CPU usage percentage is lower than the specified threshold, such as switching to the **GP_Gen5_2** if the CPU usage is less than 30% (of the **GP_Gen5_4** service objective).

Another use case is to schedule scaling up and scaling down based on peak and off-peak business hours. For example, if a business expects higher traffic between 1:00 PM and 3:00 PM, it could scale up to the Business Critical service tier during that time and scale down to the General Purpose service tier for the rest of the day.

Using T-SQL to change the SQL Database service tier

Let's consider a scenario where Mike faces higher traffic than usual between 1:00 PM and 3:00 PM on the **toystore** database; he can use T-SQL to change the service tier as follows:

> **Note**
>
> Refer to **C:\Code\Chapter07\ChangeDBServiceTier-TSQL.sql** for the queries provided in the section.

1. Open **SQL Server Management Studio (SSMS)** on your local machine and connect to the **toystore** SQL database.

   > **Note**
   >
   > You can refer to *Chapter 1, Introduction to Azure SQL managed databases*, for detailed steps to connect to SQL Database from SSMS.

2. Copy and paste the following query to get the current service tier of the **toystore** database:

   ```
   -- Get the current database service tier
   -- Run this in the toystore or your database context (and not master
   database context)

   SELECT * FROM sys.database_service_objectives
   ```

   You should get the following output from this query:

   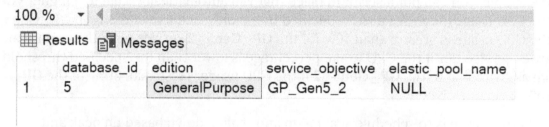

   Figure 7.2: Current service tier of the toystore database

The **sys.database_service_objectives** DMV returns the current SQL Database edition and the service objective or the performance level.

> **Note**
>
> You need the **dbowner** permission on the **toystore** database to run the query if you are not using the SQL Server administrator user.

3. Copy and paste the following code snippet in a new query window in SSMS to modify the **toystore** service objective from **GP_Gen5_2** to **GP_Gen5_4**. This will increase the number of vCores from two to four for the **toystore** database:

```
-- Query 1: Modify the service tier to GP_Gen5_4
ALTER DATABASE ToyStore MODIFY (Edition='GeneralPurpose', Service_
objective='GP_Gen5_4')
GO
-- Query 2: Verify the status of the change
While NOT EXISTS(SELECT 1 FROM sys.database_service_objectives where
service_objective='GP_Gen5_4')
BEGIN
wait for delay '00:00:01'
END
SELECT
      *
FROM sys.database_service_objectives
```

> **Note**
>
> T-SQL is not supported to vertically scale a managed instance. The other ways to do it are via the Azure portal, PowerShell, and the Azure CLI.

The preceding T-SQL snippet consists of two queries:

- **Query 1**: This runs an **ALTER DATABASE** command to change the SQL Database service objective to **GP_Gen5_4**.

- **Query 2**: This is to verify the status of the **MODIFY** command.

Select **Query 1** and **Query 2** and press F5 to execute them. You should get the following output:

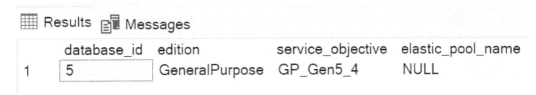

	database_id	edition	service_objective	elastic_pool_name
1	5	GeneralPurpose	GP_Gen5_4	NULL

Figure 7.3: Output of the queries

We can easily scale up or scale down by modifying an SQL Database service tier. The preceding queries consider scaling up the General Purpose service tier; however, we can similarly scale the DTU service tier (by specifying the DTU-based service tier as the service objective). We can also switch between the DTU and vCore purchasing modes by specifying the required service objective in the **ALTER DATABASE** command.

Vertical partitioning

In vertical partitioning, data is partitioned in such a way that different sets of tables reside in different individual databases:

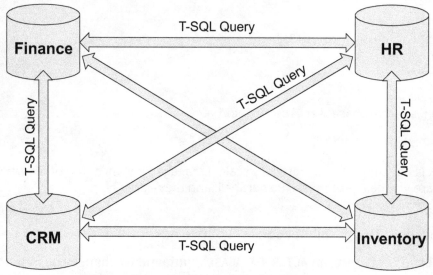

Figure 7.4: Vertical partitioning

For example, if there are four different schemas in a database, say, Finance, HR, CRM, and Inventory, then each one of them is stored in one independent database, as shown in *Figure 7.4*.

Vertical partitioning requires cross-database queries in order to generate reports, which require data from different tables in different databases.

SQL Database doesn't currently support three- or four-part object names, such as **databaseName.SchemaName.TableName** (excluding **tempdb**). Therefore, cross-database queries are made using elastic database queries. We'll learn how to implement elastic database queries in the *Activity: Using elastic database queries* section. For now, let's get started on learning how to create an alert.

Activity: Creating alerts

In this section, you'll learn how to create an SQL database alert. Consider the following scenario, involving **ToyStore Ltd**. Mike has an SQL database on the Basic service tier and has been asked to configure autoscaling to change the service objective to **GP_ Gen5_4** when the CPU percentage metric is greater than 70%. For this purpose, he needs to first create an SQL database alert that is triggered when the CPU percentage is greater than 70%. Let's see how this can be done.

Creating an Azure Automation account and configuring a runbook

Azure Automation is an Azure service that allows you to automate Azure management tasks through runbooks.

A runbook is a job that accepts PowerShell or Python code and executes it as and when scheduled, or when invoked from an external program through a webhook:

1. Open the Azure portal, https://portal.azure.com, and log in with your Azure credentials.

2. In the left-hand navigation menu, select **All services**. In the **More services** pane's search box, type `Automation`. Select the **Automation Accounts** option that appears as a search result:

Figure 7.5: Searching for Automation Accounts

3. In the **Automation Accounts** pane, click **Create Automation Accounts**:

No Automation Accounts to display

Try changing your filters if you don't see what you're looking for.

Create Automation Accounts

Figure 7.6: Automation Accounts pane

4. In the **Add Automation Account** pane, provide the following values:

  - Set the name of the automation account as **toystorejobs**.

  - Select your Azure subscription type.

  - Set **Resource group** as **toystore**.

  - Set **Location** as **East US 2**.

  - Set **Create Azure Run As account** to **Yes** (the default value).

5. Click **Create** to provision the automation account:

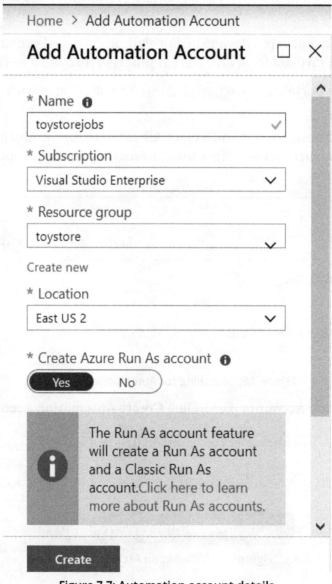

Figure 7.7: Automation account details

6. Navigate to the **Overview** pane of the newly created `toystorejobs` **Automation Account**. Locate and select **Runbooks** in the **Process Automation** section:

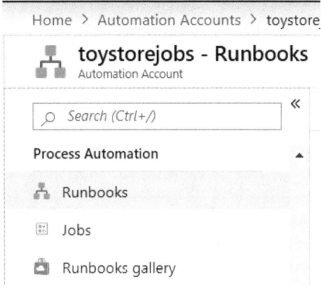

Figure 7.8: Runbooks pane under Process Automation

7. In the **Runbooks** pane, select **Import a runbook** from the top menu:

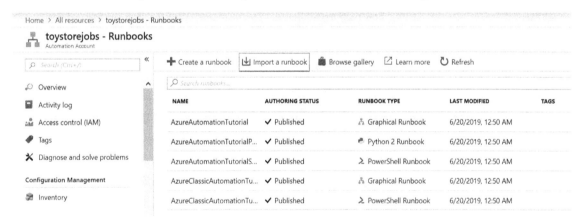

Figure 7.9: The Runbooks pane displaying the available runbooks and different options to manage runbooks

8. In the **Import a runbook** pane, under **Runbook file**, navigate to `C:\Code\Chapter07\`
    `VerticalScaling` and select the `Set-AzureSqldatabaseEdition.ps1` file. Provide a
    description (this is optional). Click **Create** to import the PowerShell runbook:

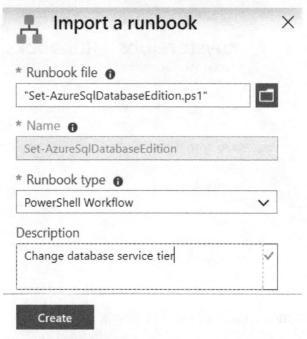

Figure 7.10: Importing a runbook

Once the runbook is imported, the **Edit PowerShell Workflow Runbook** pane will
be opened for the `Set-AzureSqlDatabaseEdition` runbook:

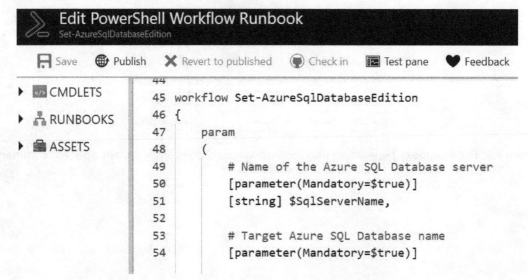

Figure 7.11: The Edit PowerShell Workflow Runbook page

This pane has the option to further modify the workflow if required. The PowerShell script is wrapped in a `workflow` tag specifying that it's a PowerShell Runbook workflow. The left-hand side of the window has three options:

- **CMDLETS** has all the PowerShell commands you can use to write a PowerShell runbook workflow.

- **RUNBOOKS** lists all existing PowerShell runbooks.

- **ASSETS** are the variables, connections, credentials, and certificates that are required by a runbook to run.

The PowerShell script is self-explanatory. It takes five parameters:

- `SqlServerName`: This is the logical server that hosts the SQL database.

- `databaseName`: This is the SQL database name whose service tier is to be modified.

- `Edition`: This is the desired SQL Database edition. The SQL database will be on this edition after script execution.

- `PerfLevel`: This is the desired service objective (S0, S1, and so on).

- `Credential`: This is the name of the runbook credential asset that contains the username and password to connect to the SQL database.

The PowerShell script connects to the given SQL database and uses the `Set-AzureSqldatabase` command to change the database edition.

Once you are familiar with the script, select **Publish** in the top menu to publish the runbook.

9. The next step is to create the credential asset to be used by the script to connect to the SQL database. Close the **Set-AzureSqldatabaseEdition** runbook pane. Navigate to the **toystorejobs - Runbooks** pane and find and select **Credentials** in the **Shared Resources** section:

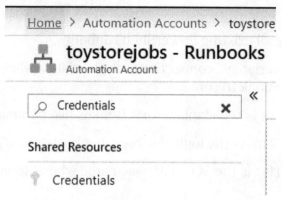

Figure 7.12: The Shared Resources section in the Runbooks pane

Select **Add a credential** from the top menu:

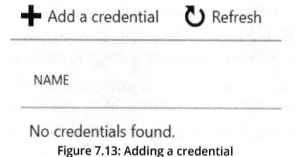

Figure 7.13: Adding a credential

10. In the **New Credential** pane, provide the following:

    - The credential name in the **Name** section

    - A description in the **Description** section—this is optional

    - Your SQL Server username

    - Your SQL Server password

11. Click **Create** to create the credential:

New Credential ✕

* Name
toystoreSqlDBCreds ✓

Description
toystore database credentials ✓

* User name
sqladmin ✓

* Password
•••••••••• ✓

* Confirm password
•••••••••• ✓

Create

Figure 7.14: Creating a new credential

Credentials are shared assets and can be used in multiple runbooks.

12. The next step is to create the webhook for this runbook. On the **toystorejobs - Runbooks** page, select the **Set-AzureSqlDatabaseEdition** runbook:

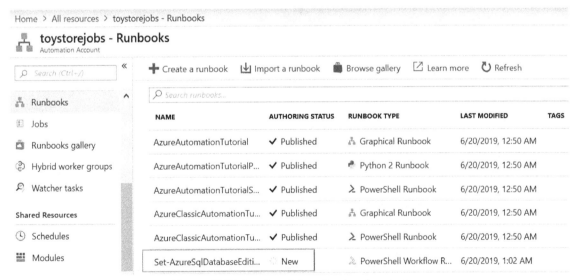

Home > All resources > toystorejobs - Runbooks

toystorejobs - Runbooks
Automation Account

Search (Ctrl+/)

➕ Create a runbook   📥 Import a runbook   📦 Browse gallery   ⎆ Learn more   ↻ Refresh

Search runbooks...

Runbooks

Jobs

Runbooks gallery

Hybrid worker groups

Watcher tasks

Shared Resources

Schedules

Modules

NAME	AUTHORING STATUS	RUNBOOK TYPE	LAST MODIFIED	TAGS
AzureAutomationTutorial	✔ Published	Graphical Runbook	6/20/2019, 12:50 AM	
AzureAutomationTutorialP...	✔ Published	Python 2 Runbook	6/20/2019, 12:50 AM	
AzureAutomationTutorialS...	✔ Published	PowerShell Runbook	6/20/2019, 12:50 AM	
AzureClassicAutomationTu...	✔ Published	Graphical Runbook	6/20/2019, 12:50 AM	
AzureClassicAutomationTu...	✔ Published	PowerShell Runbook	6/20/2019, 12:50 AM	
Set-AzureSqlDatabaseEditi...	New	PowerShell Workflow R...	6/20/2019, 1:02 AM	

Figure 7.15: toystorejobs - Runbooks page

Click on the **Set-AzureSqlDatabaseEdition** runbook to open it.

13. On the **Set-AzureSqlDatabaseEdition** runbook page, click **Add webhook**. This will open the **Add Webhook** page:

Figure 7.16: Adding a webhook

14. In the **Add Webhook** pane, select **Create new webhook**:

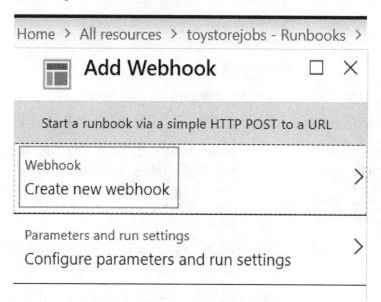

Figure 7.17: Creating a new webhook

In the **Create a new webhook** pane, enter the webhook name. The **Enabled** toggle is set to **Yes** by default—leave it as it is. The **Expires** data is set to one year—leave it as it is. Copy the webhook URL by clicking on the copy icon next to the **URL** text box.

> **Note**
>
> It's important to copy and paste the URL before you click OK as the URL is inaccessible once the webhook has been created.

Click **OK** to create the webhook:

Figure 7.18: Adding details

The webhook will be created. The next step is to provide the PowerShell runbook parameters to the webhook. These parameters will be used to run the `Set-AzureSqldatabaseEdition` PowerShell runbook.

> **Note**
>
> The parameters mentioned here are the ones defined in the PowerShell script discussed in *Step 7*.

15. In the **Add Webhook** pane, select **Configure parameters and run settings**. In the **Parameters** pane, provide values for **SQLSERVERNAME**, **DATABASENAME**, **EDITION**, **PERFLEVEL**, and **CREDENTIAL**. The credential used here is the one created in *Step 9*:

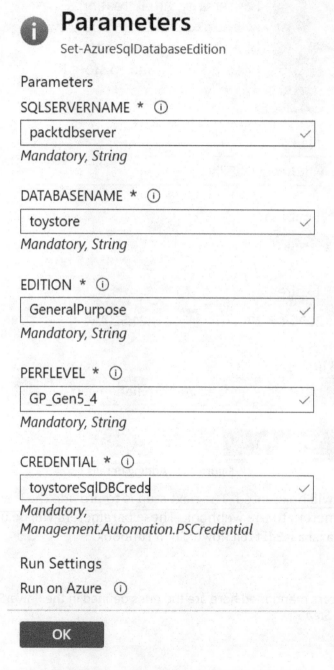

Figure 7.19: Adding parameters in the Add Webhook pane

16. Click **OK** to continue. In the **Add Webhook** pane, select **Create** to create the webhook and set the parameter values:

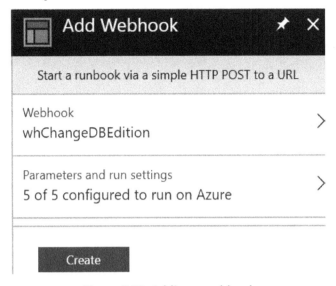

Figure 7.20: Adding a webhook

Now you have created and configured a PowerShell runbook, which runs a PowerShell command when triggered by a webhook.

Creating an SQL database alert

The next step is to create an SQL database alert that is triggered when the CPU percentage is greater than 70%. The alert, when triggered, will call the webhook we just created:

1. On the Azure portal, navigate to the **toystore** SQL database. In the **Overview** pane, find and click on **Alerts**, then select **New alert rule**:

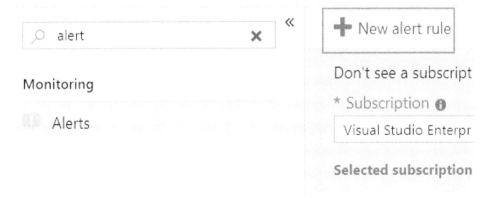

Figure 7.21: Adding a new alert rule

This opens the **Create alert rule** page. The **Create alert rule** page has three sections: **Scope**, **Condition**, and **Actions**. **RESOURCE** is the Azure resource on which the rule is to be created. This is automatically set to the **toystore** database. **Condition** is the alert condition that defines the metrics on which the alert is to be configured and the trigger logic. **Actions** defines the actions to be taken when an alert is triggered:

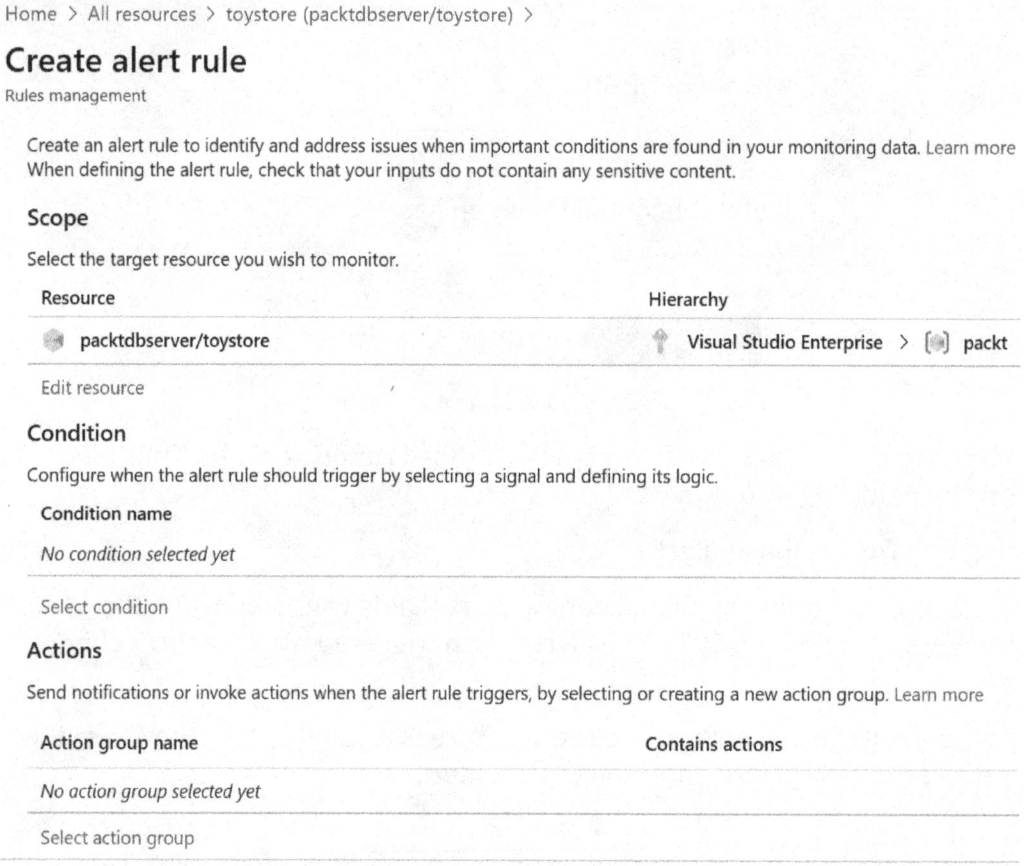

Home > All resources > toystore (packtdbserver/toystore) >

Create alert rule
Rules management

Create an alert rule to identify and address issues when important conditions are found in your monitoring data. Learn more
When defining the alert rule, check that your inputs do not contain any sensitive content.

Scope

Select the target resource you wish to monitor.

Resource	Hierarchy	
packtdbserver/toystore	Visual Studio Enterprise > [ ] packt	

Edit resource

Condition

Configure when the alert rule should trigger by selecting a signal and defining its logic.

Condition name

No condition selected yet

Select condition

Actions

Send notifications or invoke actions when the alert rule triggers, by selecting or creating a new action group. Learn more

Action group name	Contains actions
No action group selected yet	

Select action group

Figure 7.22: The Create alert rule page

2. Click **Select condition** under the **Condition** heading to add an alert condition. There can be more than one alert condition. On the **Configure signal logic** page, select **CPU percentage**:

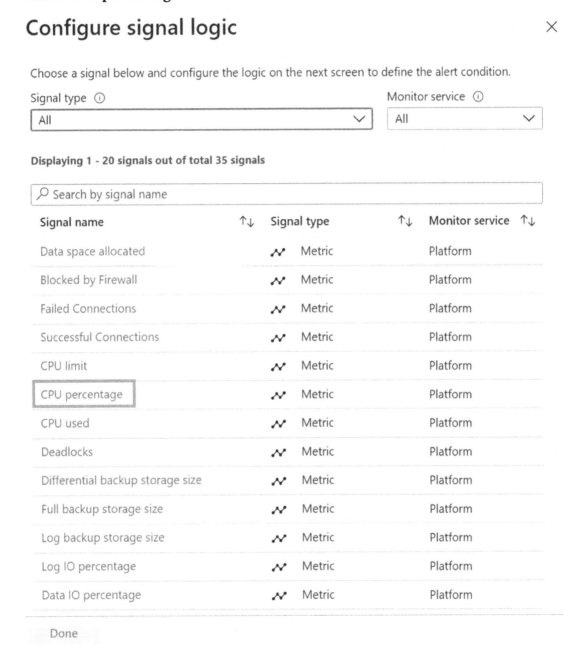

Figure 7.23: The Configure signal logic page

This opens the page to configure the alert's logic. Scroll down to locate the **Alert logic** section.

3. Select the **Static** threshold, set **Operator** to **Greater than**, set **Aggregation type** to **Maximum**, and set **Threshold value** to **70**. Leave the rest of the values as the defaults:

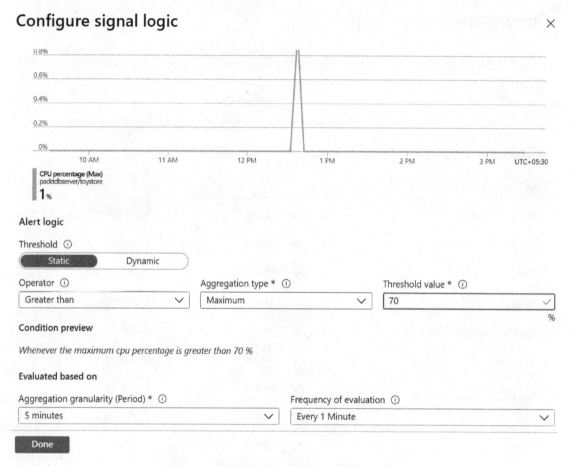

Figure 7.24: Selecting the Threshold value

Click **Done** to save the configuration. The next step is to define the action.

4. On the **Create alert rule** page, click the **Select action group** button under **Actions**:

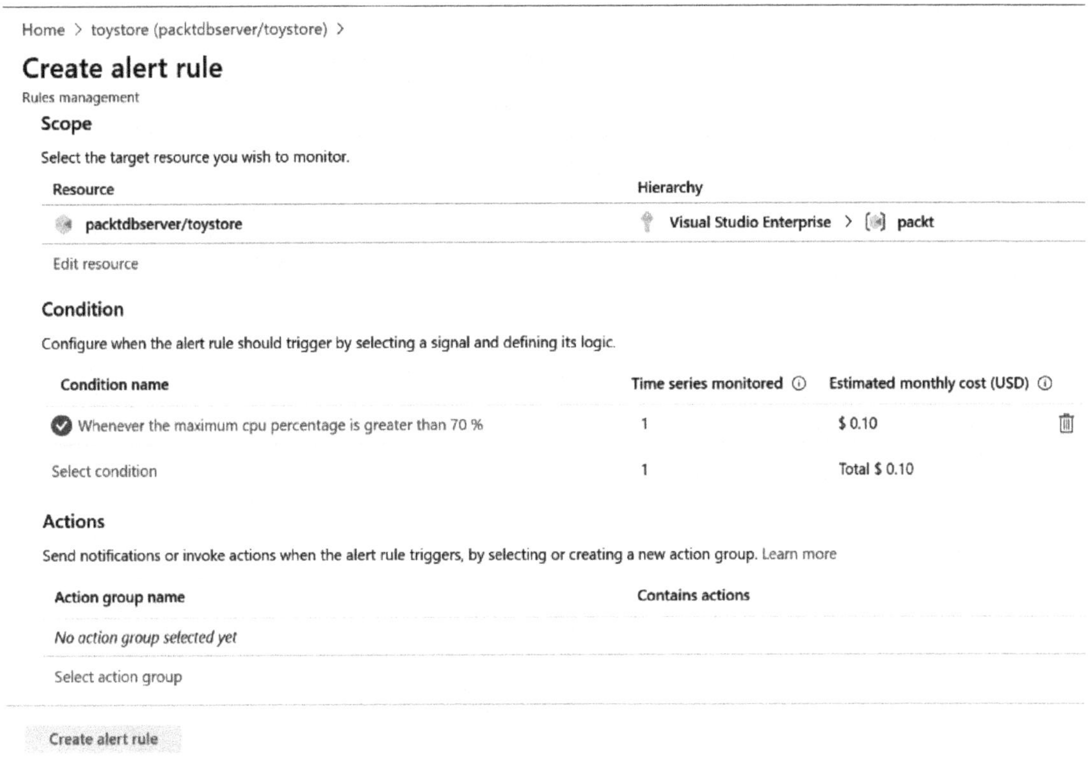

Home > toystore (packtdbserver/toystore) >

Create alert rule
Rules management

Scope

Select the target resource you wish to monitor.

Resource	Hierarchy
packtdbserver/toystore	Visual Studio Enterprise > packt

Edit resource

Condition

Configure when the alert rule should trigger by selecting a signal and defining its logic.

Condition name	Time series monitored ⓘ	Estimated monthly cost (USD) ⓘ	
✔ Whenever the maximum cpu percentage is greater than 70 %	1	$ 0.10	🗑
Select condition	1	Total $ 0.10	

Actions

Send notifications or invoke actions when the alert rule triggers, by selecting or creating a new action group. Learn more

Action group name	Contains actions
No action group selected yet	
Select action group	

Create alert rule

Figure 7.25: Selecting an action group

5. On the **Select an action group to attach to this alert rule** page, select **Create action group**:

Select an action group to attach to this alert rule
The action group selected will attach to this alert rule

➕ Create action group

Subscription ⓘ

Visual Studio Enterprise

🔍 Search to filter items...

Action group name	↑↓	Resource group	↑↓	Contain actions
No results				

Select

Figure 7.26: Creating an action rule

6. On the **Create action group** page, under the **Basics** tab, provide details for **Subscription**, **Resource group**, **Action group name**, and **Display name**:

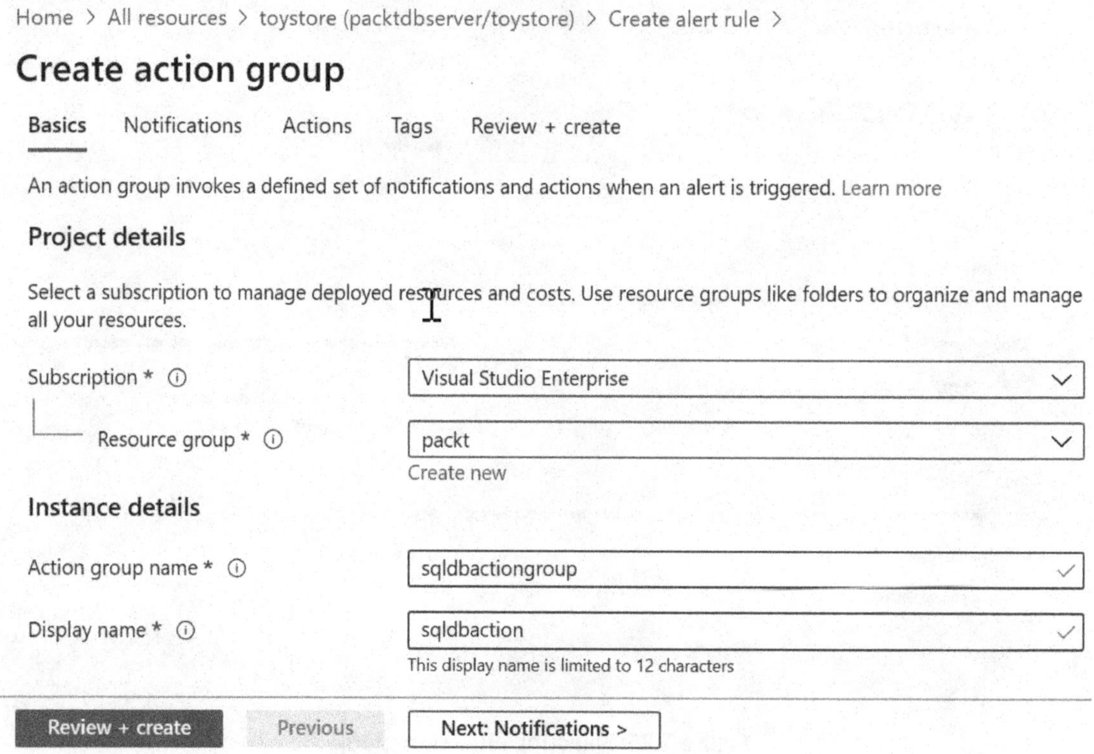

Home > All resources > toystore (packtdbserver/toystore) > Create alert rule >

Create action group

Basics   Notifications   Actions   Tags   Review + create

An action group invokes a defined set of notifications and actions when an alert is triggered. Learn more

Project details

Select a subscription to manage deployed resources and costs. Use resource groups like folders to organize and manage all your resources.

Subscription * ⓘ

| Visual Studio Enterprise | ⌄ |

⌐ Resource group * ⓘ

| packt | ⌄ |

Create new

Instance details

Action group name * ⓘ

| sqldbactiongroup | ✓ |

Display name * ⓘ

| sqldbaction | ✓ |

This display name is limited to 12 characters

Review + create   Previous   **Next: Notifications >**

Figure 7.27: Create action group—Basics tab

Click the **Actions** tab at the top to configure the action.

> **Note**
>
> You can additionally configure email notifications in the **Notifications** tab to send an email notification when the alert is triggered.

7. In the **Actions** tab, set **Name** as `ScaleSqlAction` and select **Webhook** from the **Action type** drop-down menu. Provide the webhook URI in the **Webhook** popup:

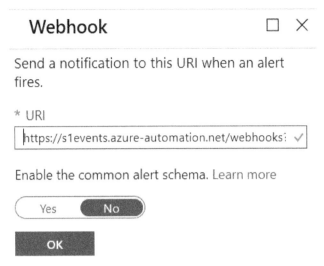

Figure 7.28: Webhook page

Click **OK** to save the webhook URI. The **Create action group** page should be similar to what is shown in *Figure 7.29*:

Home > All resources > toystore (packtdbserver/toystore) > Create alert rule >

Create action group

Basics   Notifications   **Actions**   Tags   Review + create

Actions

Configure the method in which actions are performed when the action group triggers. Select action types, fill out associated details, and add a unique description. This step is optional.

Action type ⓘ	Name ⓘ	Selected ⓘ
Webhook ∨	ScaleSqlAction ∨	URI ⓘ 🖉 🗑
∨		

Review + create   Previous   Next: Tags >

Figure 7.29: Create action group—Actions tab

Click **Review + create** and then **Create** to configure the alert action.

8. You'll then be taken to the **Create alert rule** page. Scroll to the **Alert Details** section. Set the alert rule name to **High CPU Alert** and set the severity to **sev 1**. Click **Create alert rule** to create the rule.

This completes the autoscale setup. The next step is to run the workload and see autoscaling in action.

Running and reviewing the workload

In this section, we'll run the workload and see how autoscaling works:

1. Open a new PowerShell window and change the directory to **~\Chapter07\ VerticalScaling**. Execute the following PowerShell command to start the workload:

```
.\Start-Workload.ps1 -sqlserver toyfactory -database toystore -sqluser
sqladmin -sqlpassword Packt@Pub2 -ostresspath "C:\Program Files\Microsoft
Corporation\RMLUtils\ostress.exe" -workloadsql .\workload.sql
```

The script parameters are as follows:

- **Sqlserver**: The logical server name

- **database**: The SQL database name for which you created an alert earlier in this activity

- **Sqluser**: The SQL Server admin username

- **Sqlpassword**: The SQL Server admin password

> **Note**
>
> The script parameter values may be different in your case.

```
cmdlet Start-Workload.ps1 at command pipeline position 1
Supply values for the following parameters:
sqlserver: toyfactory
database: toystore
sqluser: sqladmin
sqlpassword: Packt@pub2
-Stoyfactory.database.windows.net -Usqladmin -PPackt@pub2 -dtoystore -iC:\Code\Chapter07\workload.sql -n25 -r30 -q

Handles  NPM(K)    PM(K)     WS(K) VM(M)   CPU(s)      Id ProcessName
-------  ------    -----     ----- -----   ------      -- -----------
     14       2     4516       976    12     0.16    3932 ostress
```

Figure 7.30: Starting the workload

The scripts start an instance of the **ostress** utility. The **ostress** utility runs **25** threads in parallel, executing the **workload.sql** file **30** times in each thread.

2. While the workload is running, monitor the CPU percentage on the **toystore** overview page in the Azure portal:

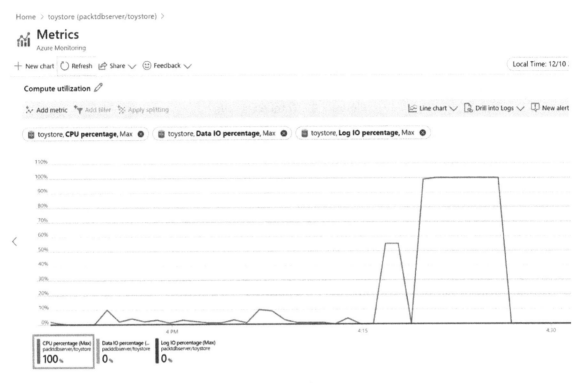

Figure 7.31: Monitoring the CPU percentage

3. To monitor the alert status, navigate to the **Alerts** section of the **toystore** database. We can see that one alert has been triggered:

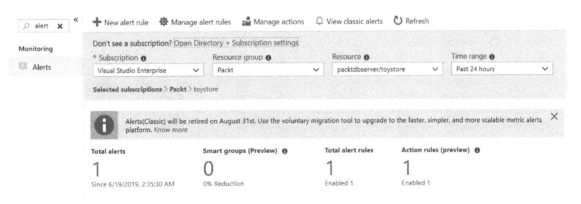

Figure 7.32: Triggered alerts in the Alerts section

4. Click on the **Total alerts** tile:

Figure 7.33: Total alerts tile

We can see that **High DTU Alert** has been triggered.

> **Note**
>
> It's advisable to open the **toystore** database's overview pane in one browser tab and the **Set-AzureSqldatabaseEdition** runbook pane in another tab for easy monitoring.

Once the alert is active, navigate to the **Set-AzureSqldatabaseEdition** runbook pane on the Azure portal. Select **Jobs** in the **Resources** section. You should see the job status as shown here:

↻ Refresh

RUNBOOK	JOB CREATED	STATUS	RAN ON	LAST STATUS UPDATE
Set-AzureSqlDatabaseEdit...	6/20/2019, 3:25:50 AM	✓ Completed	Azure	6/20/2019, 3:26:29 AM
Set-AzureSqlDatabaseEdit...	6/20/2019, 3:25:50 AM	✓ Completed	Azure	6/20/2019, 3:26:29 AM
Set-AzureSqlDatabaseEdit...	6/20/2019, 3:25:23 AM	✓ Completed	Azure	6/20/2019, 3:25:33 AM
Set-AzureSqlDatabaseEdit...	6/20/2019, 2:42:45 AM	✓ Completed	Azure	6/20/2019, 2:42:57 AM
Set-AzureSqlDatabaseEdit...	6/20/2019, 2:42:45 AM	✓ Completed	Azure	6/20/2019, 2:42:56 AM
Set-AzureSqlDatabaseEdit...	6/20/2019, 2:33:42 AM	✓ Completed	Azure	6/20/2019, 2:34:03 AM
Set-AzureSqlDatabaseEdit...	6/20/2019, 2:33:42 AM	✓ Completed	Azure	6/20/2019, 2:33:53 AM

Figure 7.34: Job statuses in the runbook pane

Click **Completed** to check the job status:

Home > All resources > toystorejobs - Runbooks > Set-AzureSqlDatabaseEditio

Set-AzureSqlDatabaseEdition 6/20/2019, 3:25 AM
Job

▶ Resume   ■ Stop   ❚❚ Suspend   ↻ Refresh

Id   : c11200df-27dc-4b4c-8511-aa9bb45fe884

Status : Completed

Ran on : Azure

Ran As : User

Input   Output   Errors   Warnings   All Logs   Exception

Figure 7.35: Checking job status details

You can verify the parameters passed to the job by clicking on **Input** and review the output from the PowerShell script by clicking on **Output**. The status indicates that the job has run successfully, and the database service tier has been updated.

Switch to the **toystore** database's **Overview** page and notice that the database service objective is now **GP_Gen5_4**.

This completes the activity.

Vertical scaling increases or decreases the performance of an SQL database as and when required. This directly affects the SQL database cost. As we scale up, we increase the cost and as we scale down, we decrease the cost. We can therefore save on costs by scaling down to a lower service tier in off-peak hours.

> **Note**
>
> The SQL Database serverless service tier provides autoscaling. However, it's only available with the vCore purchasing model and for the Gen5 hardware generation.

Horizontal scaling increases performance by dividing data into multiple SQL databases. Let's take a look at what it is and how it's done.

Horizontal scaling

Horizontal scaling, or sharding, refers to partitioning the data from one single big table in a database across multiple independent databases based on a sharding or partitioning key. For example, a customer table is partitioned across multiple independent databases on `CustomerID`. Each independent database stores data for one or more customers.

> **Note**
>
> Sharding is only available in SQL Database and it's not available for SQL Managed Instance.

Horizontal scaling can be helpful in the following situations:

- The data is too big to fit into one single database.

- The data is to be distributed to different locations for improved performance or for compliance. For example, European customers will get improved performance if their data is in a European datacenter rather than an Asian datacenter.

- Isolating tenants or customers to a database of their own for better management and performance. If all of the customer data is in a single database and there is blocking in the database because of a transaction made for a customer, say, X, then all of the other customer queries will have to wait for the blocking to get resolved, causing a bad performance experience for the rest of the customers.

- A single database requires a Business Critical service tier to manage one big table. Dividing customer data across multiple independent General Purpose service tier databases will reduce the cost.

- All (or most) of the queries are made to the database filter on the sharding key.

Sharding is supported natively in SQL Database, so we don't have to implement the sharding mechanism from scratch. However, we do need to create and manage shards. This can be done easily using **elastic database tools**. *Figure 7.36* represents a generic sharded environment:

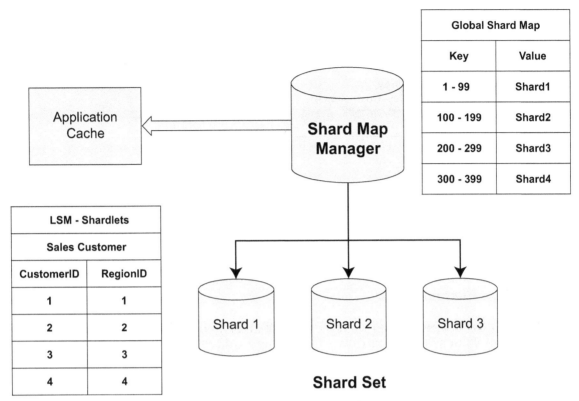

Figure 7.36: Horizontal partitioning

The customer table is horizontally partitioned across three shards: **Shard 1**, **Shard 2**, and **Shard 3**. Let's examine each of these components in detail:

- **Shard**: A shard is an individual database that stores a subset of rows of a sharded table. **Shard 1**, **Shard 2**, and **Shard 3** are the shards, each storing different rows of the customer table as defined by the mappings.

- **Shard set**: A group of shards that contains data for one single partitioned table is called a shard set. **Shard 1**, **Shard 2**, and **Shard 3** together are called a shard set.

- **Sharding key**: A sharding key is the column name based on which the data is partitioned between the shards. In our example, `CustomerID` is the sharding key. Each shard stores data for a different customer ID. You can also define a composite sharding key.

- **Shard map manager**: A special database that stores global mapping information about all available shards in a shard set. The application uses the mapping information to connect to the correct shard based on the sharding key.

- **Shard maps**: Shard maps define the data distribution between different shards based on the sharding key. There are two types of shard map:

- **List shard map**: This is a key-value pair with a one-to-one mapping between the sharding key and the shard. The key is the sharding key and the value is the shard (SQL database):

Key (Sharding Key–CustomerID)	Value (Shard/database)
1	Shard 1
2	Shard 2
3	Shard 3
4	Shard 1

Table 7.1: Key-value pairs between key and shard

This list shard map defines that **Shard 1** will store the data for **CustomerID 1** and **CustomerID 4**, **Shard 2** will store the data for **CustomerID 2**, and **Shard 3** will store the data for **CustomerID 3**.

- **Range shard map**: This is a key-value pair where the key (a sharding key) is a range of values defined as (low value to high value):

Key range (Sharding Key–CustomerID)	Value (Shard/database)
1–99	Shard 1
100–199	Shard 2
200–299	Shard 3
300–399	Shard 1

Table 7.2: Range shard map

This range shard map defines that **Shard 1** will store the data for customer IDs 1–99 and 300–399, **Shard 2** will store the data for customer IDs 100–199, and **Shard 3** will store the data for customer IDs 200–299.

- **Global Shard Maps (GSMs)**: GSMs are stored in a shard map manager database and record all the shard maps globally. This information is stored and managed by special tables and stored procedures created automatically under the _ ShardManagement schema in the shard map manager database.

- **Local Shard Maps (LSMs)**: Also referred to as shardlets, these are the shard maps that track the local shard data within individual shards. The LSMs or shardlets are stored in individual shards and not in the shard map manager database. This information is stored and managed by special tables and stored procedures created automatically under the **_ShardManagement** schema.

- **Reference tables**: These are tables that aren't sharded and are available in all shards. These can also be stored in another database, say, a reference database, instead of storing the same data in individual shards; for example, a table with a list of countries or cities that contains master data common to all shards.

- **Application cache**: Applications accessing the shard map manager cache the mappings in a local in-memory application cache. Applications use the cached mappings to route requests to the correct shards, instead of accessing the shard map manager for every request.

Let's now look into the shard map manager in detail.

Shard map manager

As discussed earlier, the shard map manager is a special database that maintains the global mapping information of a shard set. The mappings are maintained in tables that are automatically created under the **_ShardManagement** schema:

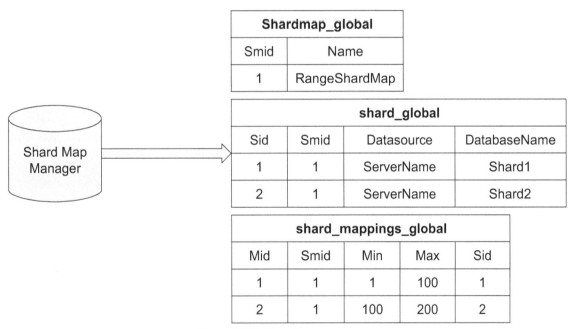

Figure 7.37: Shard map manager

The global shard maps are maintained in three tables, as shown in *Figure 7.37*:

- **Shardmap_global**: This table stores the type of shard map, which could be **ListShardMap** or **RangeShardMap**. In our example, we have **RangeShardMap**.

- **shard_global**: This table maps the shards (SQL databases) to the shard maps defined in the **Shardmaps_global** table. In our example, **RangeShardMap** has two shards, **Shard 1** and **Shard 2**. The table also stores the server name the shard belongs to. This information is used when connecting to the shards.

- **shard_mappings_global**: This is the global shard map that stores the sharding key to shard mapping. In our example, customer IDs 1–99 are mapped to **Shard 1** and 100–199 are mapped to **Shard 2**.

The information in the shard map manager is used by the client application to redirect requests to the correct SQL database based on the sharding key.

Let's now look at how the requests are directed to the correct shard using data-dependent routing.

Data-dependent routing

Data-dependent routing refers to routing a query to the correct database (shard) based on the sharding key specified in the query. This is the fundamental way of querying a sharded environment. The application doesn't maintain connection strings to the different shards. The application doesn't even implement the logic of selecting the shards based on the sharding key. This is done natively by using the functions provided in the elastic database client library.

The application defines a single connection using the **OpenConnectionForKey** method defined in the elastic database client library. The syntax for **OpenConnectionForKey** is given in the following snippet:

```
public SqlConnection OpenConnectionForKey<TKey>( TKey key,
string connectionString, ConnectionOptions options
)
```

It accepts three parameters, which are as follows:

- **TKey**: This is the sharding key used to determine which shard (or SQL database in a shard set) the query is to be made on.

- **connectionString**: The connection string only contains the SQL Server credentials. The database and the server name are taken from the shard map manager system tables, based on the sharding key.

- **ConnectionOptions**: A connection option can be either **none** or **validate**. When it's set to **validate**, it queries the LSM or shardlet to validate that the shard key exists in the databases specified in the cached maps (in the application). This is important in an environment where shard maps change frequently. If the validation fails, then the shard map manager queries the global shard maps for the correct values and updates the application cache.

If the parameters specified are correct, **OpenConnectionForKey** returns a database connection that can be used to query the correct shard.

When implementing sharding, there are two data models: single-tenant and multi-tenant. Let's look into these in detail.

Sharding data models

Sharding data models refer to how the tenants are placed in a sharded environment. There are two distinct models for placing tenants: database per tenant (single-tenant model) and a shared database–sharded (multi-tenant model):

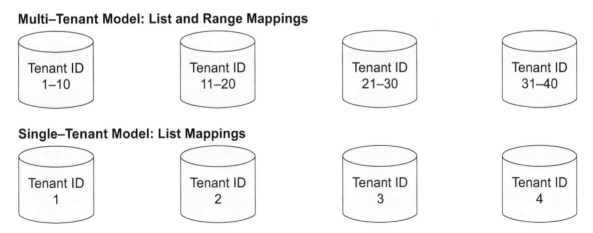

Figure 7.38: Multi-tenant and single-tenant data models

Single-tenant (database per tenant)

As the name suggests, each tenant gets its own database. The tenant-specific data is limited to the tenant's database and isolated from other tenants and their data.

Shared database–sharded

As the name suggests, a single shard or database is shared among multiple tenants. The tenants can either be mapped to shards or databases by using either range or list mappings, as discussed earlier.

Choosing between the two models depends on the following factors:

- **Isolation**: The single-tenant, or database-per-tenant, model offers a higher degree of isolation than the shared database–sharded model.

- **Maintenance**: The single-tenant model will have as many databases as the tenants, which could be customers or employees. For example, 100 customers would mean 100 databases in the single-tenancy model, but in the shared database–sharded model, you can have 5 databases with 20 tenants each. Maintaining 5 databases would be easier than maintaining 100 databases.

- **Cost**: The cost depends on the amount of resource sharing between tenants. The more resource sharing there is (resource here refers to a shard, an SQL database), the lower the cost. The single-tenant model is good if all tenants have predictable workloads. This allows you to select an appropriate service tier for each tenant or shard. However, if the workload isn't predictable, which is often the case, databases can be either oversized or undersized. On the other hand, the shared database–sharded model, with a higher degree of resource sharing, offers a more cost-effective solution.

- **DevOps**: DevOps refers to the deployment of new changes to databases to resolve issues or when new features are added to an application. With the single-tenant model, it costs more to deploy and maintain an application, as each change has to be applied to all of the single-tenant databases. For example, if an application adds a new feature that allows customers to generate sales reports, and there are 100 customers, then this change has to be deployed on 100 databases. However, it'll take less time and cost to roll out the same feature in the shared database–sharded model because of the smaller number of databases.

- **Business model**: An application's business model is an important factor when choosing between the two multi-tenant models. If the application's per-tenant revenue is small, then the shared database–sharded model makes sense. A shared database model will offer less isolation, but it'll have lower deployment and resource costs. On the other hand, if the per-tenant revenue is high, then it'll make sense to use the single-tenant model.

Now let's have a go at creating shards for the **toystore** database.

Activity: Creating shards

In this activity, we'll discuss how to shard our **toystore** database. Consider the following scenario: you have been asked to implement sharding to improve the application performance of the **toystore** database. For this purpose, you can shard the **Sales. Customers** and **Sales.Orders** tables into two shards, **toystore_Shard_1_100** (with values of **customerid** from 1–99) and **toystore_Shard_200** (with values from 100–199). The following steps describe how this can be done:

> **Note**
>
> The **Application.Countries** table will be the reference, or the common table present in all shards. You can, however, extend the scripts used in this activity to shard other tables.

1. Download the elastic database tool scripts.

2. Provision the **toystore_SMM** shard map manager database.

3. Rename the **toystore** database **toystore_Shard_1_100**.

4. Provision the **toystore_Shard_200** SQL database.

5. Promote **toystore_SMM** to the shard map manager. This will create the shard management tables and procedures in the **toystore_SMM** database.

6. Create the range shard map in the shard map manager database.

7. Add shards to the shard map.

8. Add the sharded table and reference table schema to the shard map manager database.

9. Verify the sharding by reviewing the shard map manager tables.

Let's start with downloading elastic database tool scripts.

Downloading the elastic database tool scripts

The elastic database tool scripts are a set of PowerShell modules and scripts provided by Microsoft to easily create and manage SQL database shards. They use the functions exposed by the elastic database client library to provide helper PowerShell cmdlets to easily create and manage shards.

> **Note**
>
> The elastic database tool scripts are available at `C:\Code\Chapter07\Elastic DB tool scripts`. You can download the latest version from here: https://gallery.technet.microsoft.com/scriptcenter/Azure-SQL-DB-Elastic-731883db

Navigate to `C:\Code\Chapter07\Elastic DB tool scripts\ShardManagement` and open the `ShardManagement.psm1` script. `ShardManagement.psm1` contains functions such as `New-ShardMapManager`, `Get- ShardMapManager`, `New-RangeShardMap`, and `Add-Shard`. Each function has a synopsis section, which briefly describes the function's purpose.

> **Note**
>
> We won't use all of the functions listed in `ShardManagement.psm1`. However, you are free to explore them once you have completed the activity. When you first import the `ShardManagement` module, it checks for the elastic database client libraries' DLLs (in the folder from where the PowerShell script is executed) and downloads and registers them if not found.

Let's move on to the next step to save the Azure profile details to a file.

Saving the Azure profile details to a file

Saving your Azure profile details to a file enables you to log in to your Azure account from PowerShell using the saved profile information. Otherwise, you would have to provide your Azure credentials in the **Authentication** dialog box every time you wanted to run an Azure command from PowerShell.

To save Azure profile details to a file, follow these steps:

> **Note**
>
> This isn't part of sharding; however, it'll save you time by not having to type your Azure credentials into PowerShell every time you run an Azure command in PowerShell.

1. Press *Windows* + R to open the **Run** command window. In the **Run** command window, type `powershell` and hit *Enter*. This will open a new PowerShell console window:

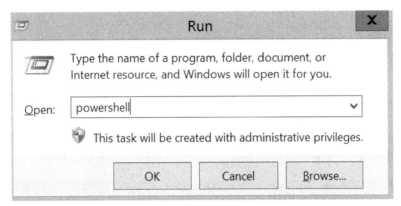

Figure 7.39: Opening a PowerShell console window

2. In the PowerShell console, execute the following command:

```
Add-AzAccount
```

You'll have to enter your Azure credentials in the pop-up dialog box. After a successful login, control will return to the PowerShell window.

Run the following command to save the profile details to a file:

```
Save-AzProfile -Path C:\code\MyAzureProfile.json
```

3. The Azure subscription details will be saved in the **MyAzureProfile.json** file in JSON format. If you wish to explore the **profile.json** file, you can open it in any editor to review its contents.

> **Note**
>
> The **C:\Code** path is where all of the book's code is kept.
>
> The PowerShell scripts later in the book use relative paths. If you have extracted the code to some other directory, say, **E:\Code**, then save the **profile.json** file in **E:\Code** to avoid invalid path errors.
>
> Also, the SQL Server PowerShell module can be installed from here: https://docs. microsoft.com/sql/powershell/download-sql-server-ps-module?view=sql-server-ver15&viewFallbackFrom=sql-serverver15

Sharding the `toystore` database

We'll now learn how to write PowerShell commands using the elastic database tool scripts to shard the existing **toystore** database:

> **Note**
>
> If you are short of time, you can execute the **C:\Code\Chapter07\Sharding\ Sharding.ps1** file, providing appropriate parameters.

1. Press the *Windows* key + R to open the **Run** command window. Type **PowerShell_ ISE.exe** in the **Run** command window and hit *Enter*. This will open a new PowerShell ISE editor window. This is where you'll write the PowerShell commands:

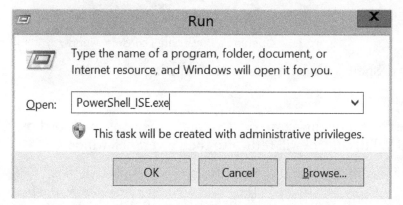

Figure 7.40: Opening the PowerShell ISE editor window

In the PowerShell ISE, select **File** from the top menu and click **Save**. Alternatively, you can press *Ctrl* + S to save the file. In the **Save As** dialog box, browse to the **C:\ Code\Chapter07\Sharding** directory. In the **File name** text box, type **Shard-toystore. ps1** and click on **Save** to save the file:

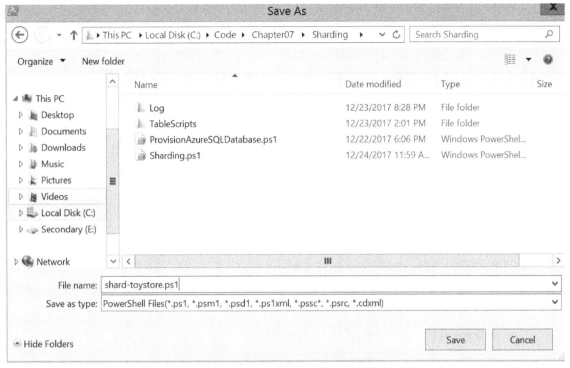

Figure 7.41: Saving the PowerShell file

2. Copy and paste all code into the **shard-toystore.ps1** file to implement sharding. The code explanation, wherever required, is given in the following code snippet and in the comments within the code snippet.

3. Copy and paste the following code to define the script parameters:

```
param (
[parameter(Mandatory=$true)] [String] $ResourceGroup,
[parameter(Mandatory=$true)] [String] $SqlServer,
[parameter(Mandatory=$true)] [String] $UserName,
[parameter(Mandatory=$true)] [String] $Password,
[parameter(Mandatory=$true)] [String] $ShardMapManagerdatabase,
[parameter(Mandatory=$true)] [String] $databaseToShard,
[parameter(Mandatory=$false)] [String] $AzureProfileFilePath
,
[parameter(Mandatory=$true)]
[String] $Basedirectory="C:\Professional-Azure-SQL-Database-
Administration-Third-Edition",
[parameter(Mandatory=$true)]
[String] $Elasticdbtoolscriptpath="C:\Professional-Azure-SQL-Database-
Administration-Third-Edition\Chapter06\Elastic DB tool scripts"
)
```

The script accepts nine parameters:

- **ResourceGroup**: This is the Azure resource group that contains the SQL server and the database. This should be the same as the one you provided when creating the **toystore** database in *Chapter 1, Introduction to Azure SQL managed databases*.

- **SqlServer**: This is the logical server name that hosts the **toystore** database.

- **UserName** and **Password**: This is the SQL Server admin username and password.

- **ShardMapManagerdatabase**: This is the name of the shard map manager database. Prefix **_SMM** to the **toystore** database name to name the shard map manager database.

- **databaseToShard**: The database you wish to shard—**toystore** in our case.

- **AzureProfileFilePath**: The path of the JSON file that contains your Azure profile details. If it's not yet created, follow the steps in the *Saving the Azure profile details to a file* section to create one.

- **Basedirectory**: The path of the base directory that contains the chapters.

- **Elasticdbtoolscriptpath**: The path of the elastic database tool script folder downloaded in the *Downloading the elastic database tool scripts* section.

4. Copy and paste the following code to set the Azure context to your Azure profile:

```
# log the execution of the script
Start-Transcript -Path ".\Log\Shard-toystore.txt" -Append
...
...
}


#Login to Azure Account
if((Test-Path -Path $AzureProfileFilePath))
{
$profile = Select-AzProfile -Path $AzureProfileFilePath
$SubscriptionID = $profile.Context.Subscription.SubscriptionId
...
Provide your Azure Credentials in the login dialog box
$profile = Login-AzAccount
$SubscriptionID = $profile.Context.Subscription.
SubscriptionId
...
...
#Set the Azure Context
```

```
Set-AzContext -SubscriptionId $SubscriptionID | Out-Null
```

This script does the following things:

- Logs the script execution in the **Sharding.txt** file in the **C:\Code\Chapter07\ Sharding\Log** folder.

- Sets the **AzureProfileFilePath** parameter to the Azure profile JSON file if the path isn't provided as the parameter.

- Logs in to the Azure account using the Azure profile JSON file. If the JSON path provided isn't valid, then it uses the **Login-AzAccount** command. In this case, you will have to provide your Azure subscription username and password in the pop-up window.

- Sets the default Azure profile to your profile using **Set- AzContext cmdlet**. This tells PowerShell to create and manage objects in your Azure profile.

Press *Ctrl* + *S* to save your work before moving on.

5. Copy and paste the following code to import the **shardmanagement** module. This will allow us to use the functions in **shardmanagement.psm1** in our PowerShell script:

```
# Import the ShardManagement module
$ShardManagementPath = $Elasticdbtoolscriptpath + "\ShardManagement\
ShardManagement.psm1"
Import-Module $ShardManagementPath
```

6. Copy and paste the following script to set the **SQLServerFQDN** variable:

```
$SQLServerFQDN = "$SqlServer.database.windows.net"
```

The **SQLServerFQDN** variable has a fully qualified logical Azure SQL server name.

This is required later in the script.

7. Copy and paste the following code to provision a new SQL database to act as the shard map manager:

```
# Provision a new Azure SQL database
# call ProvisionAzureSQLdatabase.ps1 created in Chapter 1 to create a new
Azure SQL database to act as Shard Map Manager

$path = $Basedirectory + "\Chapter01"
$command = $path + "\Provision-AzureSQLDatabase.ps1 -ResourceGroup
$ResourceGroup -SQLServer $SqlServer -UserName $UserName -Password
$Password -SQLDatabase $ShardMapManagerDatabase -Edition GeneralPurpose
-AzureProfileFilePath $AzureProfileFilePath"
Invoke-Expression -Command $command
```

The **command** variable specifies the **Provision-AzureSQLdatabase.ps1** file and the required parameters. You can check *Chapter 1, Introduction to Azure SQL managed databases*, to find out how to run the **Provision-AzureSQLdatabase.ps1** PowerShell script.

The **Invoke-Expression** cmdlet runs the command specified in the **command** variable.

8. Copy and paste the following code to set up the individual shards:

```
# Setup the shards
# Rename existing toystore database to toystore_shard1
$Shard1 = $databaseToShard + "_Shard_1_100"
$Shard2 = $databaseToShard + "_Shard_200"

#Rename the existing database as _shard1
Set-AzSqlDatabase -ServerName $SqlServer -ResourceGroupName $ResourceGroup
-DatabaseName $DatabaseToShard -NewName $shard1

# create shard2 Azure SQL Database
$command1 = "$path\Provision-AzureSQLDatabase.ps1 -ResourceGroup
$ResourceGroup -SQLServer $SqlServer -UserName $UserName
-Password $Password -SQLDatabase $shard2 -Edition GeneralPurpose
-AzureProfileFilePath $AzureProfileFilePath"
Invoke-Expression -Command $command1

# Create tables to be sharded in Shard2
$scriptpath = $Basedirectory + "\Chapter06\Sharding\TableScripts\"
$files = Get-ChildItem -Path $scriptpath
ForEach($file in $files)
{
Write-Host "Creating table $file in $shard2" -ForegroundColor Green
Invoke-Sqlcmd -ServerInstance $SQLServerFQDN -Username
$UserName -Password $Password -database $shard2 -InputFile $file. FullName
| out-null
}
```

The preceding code does the following things:

- Declares two variables, **Shard1** and **Shard2**. If the value of the **databaseToShard** variable is **toystore**, then **Shard1 = toystore_ Shard_1_100** and **Shard2 = toystore_ Shard_200**.

- Renames the existing **toystore** database to **Shard1**; that is, **toystore_ Shard_1_100**. The **Set-AzureSqldatabase** cmdlet is used to rename the database.

- Provisions the **Shard2** database, **toystore_Shard_200**. It uses **ProvisionAzureSQLdatabase.ps1** as described previously to provision a new database.

- Creates the required tables, **Sales.Customer**, **Sales.Orders**, and **Application. Countries**, in the newly provisioned **shard2** database.

- The create scripts for the tables are kept in **C:\Code\Chapter07\Sharding\ TableScripts**.

- The **Get-ChildItem** cmdlet gets all of the files present in the **TableScripts** directory.

- The **Invoke-Sqlcmd** cmdlet executes the scripts file on the **Shard2** database.

9. Copy and paste the following code to register the database created in the previous step as the shard map manager:

```
# Register the database created previously as the Shard Map Manager

Write-host "Configuring database $ShardMapManagerdatabase as Shard Map
Manager" -ForegroundColor Green
$ShardMapManager = New-ShardMapManager -UserName $UserName
-Password $Password -SqlServerName $SQLServerFQDN
-SqldatabaseName $ShardMapManagerdatabase    -ReplaceExisting $true
```

This code uses the **New-ShardMapManager** cmdlet from the **ShardManagement. psm1** module to register the newly created database (specified by the **$ShardMapManagerdatabase** parameter) in the previous steps as the shard map manager.

This creates the database objects required for shard management in the shard map manager database under the **ShardManagement** schema.

10. Copy and paste the following code to create a new shard map in the shard map manager database:

```
# Create Shard Map for Range Mapping
$ShardMapName = "toystorerangemap"
$ShardMap = New-RangeShardMap -KeyType $([int]) -ShardMapManager
$ShardMapManager -RangeShardMapName $ShardMapName
```

This code uses the **New-RangeShardMap** function from the **ShardManagement** module to create a new range shard map in the shard map manager database.

The **keytype** parameter defines the data type of the **sharding** key. In our case, the **sharding** key is **customerid**, which is of the integer data type.

ShardMapManager is the shard map manager object assigned to the **$ShardMapManager** variable in the preceding code snippet. This tells the function to create the shard map in this particular shard map manager.

The **RangeShardMapName** variable is the name of the shard map, **toystorerangemap**.

11. Copy and paste the following code to add the shards to the shard map created previously:

```
# Add shards (databases) to shard maps
Write-host "Adding $Shard1 and $Shard2 to the Shard Map
$ShardMapName" -ForegroundColor Green
$Shards = "$Shard1","$shard2" foreach ($Shard in $Shards)
{
Add-Shard -ShardMap $ShardMap -SqlServerName $SQLServerFQDN
-SqldatabaseName $Shard
}
```

This code uses the **Add-Shard** function from the **ShardManagement** module and adds the individual shards, **Shard1 (toystore_Shard_1_100)** and **Shard2 (toystore_ Shard_200)**, to the **toystorerangemap** object created previously.

ShardMap is the shard map object assigned to the **$ShardMap** variable in the previous steps. This tells the function the shard map to which the shards are to be added.

SqlServerName and **SqldatabaseName** are the logical server name and the database name of the shards to be added to the shard map.

This step will create the local shard management objects in the individual shards under the **ShardManagement** database.

12. Copy and paste the following code to add the low and high range key mappings on **Shard1** (`toystore_Shard_1_100`):

```
# Add Range Key Mapping on the first Shard
# Mapping is only required on the first shard; currently it has all the
data.

$LowKey = 0
$HighKey = 200
Write-host "Add range keys to $Shard1 (Shard1)" -ForegroundColor

Green
Add-RangeMapping -KeyType $([int]) -RangeShardMap $ShardMap
-RangeLow $LowKey -RangeHigh $HighKey -SqlServerName
$SQLServerFQDN -SqldatabaseName $Shard1
```

This code uses the **Add-RangeMapping** function from the **ShardManagement** module to specify the key range for the first shard only. It takes the following parameters:

- **Keytype**: The data type of the sharding key column. It is an integer in our case.

- **RangeShardMap**: The range shard map object. This is assigned to the **$ShardMap** variable created previously.

- **RangeLow**: The lower boundary of the range mapping, which is **0** in our case.

- **RangeHigh**: The higher boundary of the range mapping, which is 200 in our case.

- **SqlServerName**: The logical server name that hosts the shards.

- **SqldatabaseName**: The name of the shard.

Mappings are added only to the first shard because it has all of the customer records (200 customers) at the moment.

In the next activity, you'll split the records between the shards using the split-merge utility.

13. Copy and paste the following code to add the sharded and reference table schemas to the shard map manager database:

```
# Add Schema Mappings to the $shardMap
# This is where you define the sharded and the reference tables Write-
host "Adding schema mappings to the Shard Map Manager database"
-ForegroundColor Green
$ShardingKey = "Customerid"
$ShardedTableName = "Customers","Orders"
$ReferenceTableName = "Countries"
...

...
# Get the schema info collection for the shard map manager
$SchemaInfoCollection = $ShardMapManager GetSchemaInfoCollection()

# Add the SchemaInfo for this Shard Map to the Schema Info Collection if
($($SchemaInfoCollection | Where Key -eq $ShardMapName) -eq $null)
{
$SchemaInfoCollection.Add($ShardMapName, $SchemaInfo)
}
else
{
$SchemaInfoCollection.Replace($ShardMapName, $SchemaInfo)
}

Write-host "$databaseToShard is now Sharded." -ForegroundColor Green
```

This code adds the schema information of the sharded and reference tables to the shard map manager database. The schema information includes the schema name, table name, and key column. This is done by initializing a schema info object of the **Microsoft.Azure.Sqldatabase.ElasticScale.ShardManagement.Schema.SchemaInfo** type, and then adding the table details to this object using the **Add** function. The **Schemainfo.Add** function takes three arguments: schema name, table name, and key column name. The **SchemaInfoCollection** variable gets the shard map manager schema info collection object. The schema is then added to the shard map manager by a **SchemaInfoCollection.Add** function call that takes two arguments: the shard map to add the schema details to and the schema details as defined in the schema info object.

14. This completes the script. Press *Ctrl* + S to save the script. Before you run the script, make sure you have configured the file paths correctly wherever required.

    If you don't have a **toystore** database ready, you can restore it using the **bacpac** file provided with the code files, `C:\Code\0_databaseBackup\toystore.bacpac`.

This completes the **Shard-toystore.ps1** script. Let's now run the **Shard-toystore.ps1** script to shard the **toystore** database.

Executing the PowerShell script

To execute the **shard-toystore.ps1** script, follow these steps:

1. Press the *Windows* key + R to open the **Run** command window. Type **PowerShell** and hit *Enter* to open a new PowerShell console window.

2. Change the directory to the folder that has the **shard-toystore.ps1** script. For example, if the script is in the `C:\Code\Chapter07\Sharding` directory, then run the following command to switch to this directory:

    ```
    cd C:\Code\Chapter07\Sharding
    ```

3. In the following command, change the parameter values as per your environment. You can also copy the command from the `C:\Code\Chapter07\Executions.txt` file:

    ```
    .\shard-toystore.ps1 –ResourceGroup toystore –SqlServer toyfactory
    –UserName sqladmin –Password Packt@pub2
    –ShardMapManagerdatabase toystore_SMM –databaseToShard toystore
    –AzureProfileFilePath C:\Code\MyAzureProfile.json
    ```

    > **Note**
    >
    > You may get the following warning during script execution. Ignore such warnings:
    >
    > ```
    > WARNING: Could not obtain SQL Server Service information. An attempt
    > to connect to WMI on 'Microsoft.WindowsAzure.Commands. Sqldatabase.
    > dll' failed with the following error: The RPC server is unavailable.
    > (Exception from HRESULT: 0x800706BA)
    > ```

    Refer to the *Sharding the toystore database* section for parameter details.

Once you have changed the parameter values, hit *Enter* to run the command. This command will do the following:

- Create a `Shard-toystore.txt` file in the `Log` folder and use this file for troubleshooting script errors.

- Create a shard map manager database, `toystore_SMM`.

- Rename the `toystore` database as `toystore_Shard_1_100` (shard1).

- Create a new database, `toystore_Shard_200` (shard2).

- Create shard management objects in the `toystore_SMM` database under the `ShardManagement` schema.

- Create a new range shard map, `toystorerangemap`.

- Add `toystore_Shard_1_100` (shard1) and `toystore_Shard_200` (shard2) to the range shard map.

- Add the key range mappings in `toystore_Shard_1_100` (shard1).

- Add the table schema for `Sales.Customers`, `Sales.Orders`, and `Application.Countries` in the shard map manager database.

You should get the following output after successful execution of the script:

```
Configuring database toystore_SMM as Shard Map Manager
Adding toystore_Shard_1_100 to the Shard Map toystorerangemap Adding
toystore_Shard_200 to the Shard Map toystorerangemap Add range keys to
toystore_Shard_1_100 (Shard1)
Adding schema mappings to the Shard Map Manager database toystore is now
Sharded.
```

Let's now review the shards created by executing the **shard-toystore.ps1** script.

Reviewing the shard configuration

You'll now review the shard configuration the PowerShell script created:

1. Open **SQL Server Management Studio** on your local machine and connect to the **toyfactory** server.

2. Connect to **Object Explorer** (if **Object Explorer** isn't open, press F8 to connect to it). You should see the following databases:

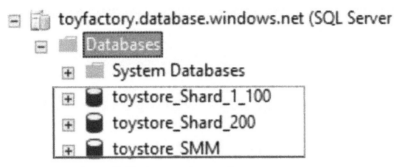

Figure 7.42: Connecting to the toystore server

toystore_Shard_1_100 is the renamed **toystore** database. **toystore_Shard_200** is the new **Shard 2** database. **toystore_SMM** is the shard map manager database.

3. In **Object Explorer**, right-click **toystore_SMM** and select **New Query** from the context menu.

4. Execute the following query in a new query window:

```
SELECT
st.Name As ShardTables
FROM sys.tables st JOIN sys.schemas ss on st.schema_id=ss.schema_id WHERE
ss.Name=' ShardManagement'
```

You should get the following output:

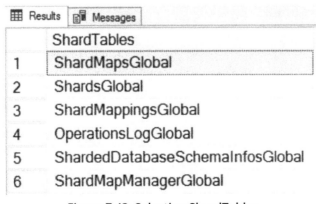

Figure 7.43: Selecting ShardTables

5. Six tables have been added to the **toystore_SMM** database.

6. Execute the following query to view the data for the **ShardMapsGlobal** table:

```
SELECT * FROM ShardManagement.ShardMapsGlobal
```

You should see the following output:

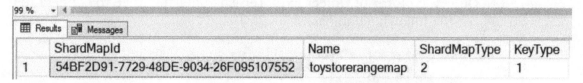

Figure 7.44: ShardMapsGlobal table

The **ShardMapsGlobal** table will have one row for each shard map you created. Notice that it contains **toystorerangemap**, which was created by the **Shard- toystore.ps1** script. Each shard map is assigned a unique **ShardMapId**.

7. Execute the following query to view the data for the **ShardsGlobal** table:

```
SELECT ShardId,ShardMapId,ServerName,databaseName FROM ShardManagement.
ShardsGlobal
```

You should get the following output:

Figure 7.45: ShardsGlobal table

The **ShardsGlobal** table contains one row for each shard in the sharded environment. It has two rows, one for each shard, **toystore_ shard_1_100** and **toystore_Shard_200**.

The **ShardMapId** column is used to map a shard with its corresponding shard map in the **ShardsMapGlobal** table.

The table also stores the **ServerName** for each of the shards (databases). This table is used to route the requests to the correct shard based on the sharding key when a request is received from an application.

Execute the following query to view data for the **ShardMappingsGlobal** table:

```
SELECT MappingId,ShardId,ShardMapId,MinValue,MaxValue FROM
ShardManagement.ShardMappingsGlobal
```

You should get the following output:

Figure 7.46: ShardMappingsGlobal table

ShardMappingsGlobal stores the low and high key-value mappings for each shard in the **ShardsGlobal** table.

The **ShardId** and **ShardMapId** columns map the rows with their corresponding shards and shard map in the **ShardsGlobal** and **ShardMapsGlobal** tables respectively.

8. Execute the following query to view the data for the **ShardeddatabaseSchemaInfosGlobal** table:

```
select * from ShardManagement.ShardeddatabaseSchemaInfosGlobal
```

You should get the following output:

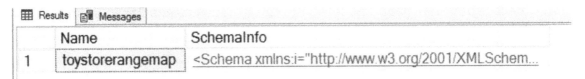

Figure 7.47: ShardeddatabaseSchemaInfosGlobal table

The **ShardeddatabaseSchemaInfosGlobal** table stores the schema info for each shard map defined in the **ShardsMapGlobal** table.

These are the same schema details as were provided in the *Sharding the toystore database* section in the **shard-toystore.ps1** script.

In the results pane in SSMS, click the XML under the `Schemainfo` column. You should see the following XML:

```
<Schema xmlns:i="http://www.w3.org/2001/XMLSchema-instance">
<ReferenceTableSet i:type="ArrayOfReferenceTableInfo">
<ReferenceTableInfo>
<SchemaName>Application</SchemaName>
<TableName>Countries</TableName>
</ReferenceTableInfo>
</ReferenceTableSet>
<ShardedTableSet i:type="ArrayOfShardedTableInfo">
<ShardedTableInfo>
<SchemaName>Sales</SchemaName>
<TableName>Customers</TableName>
<KeyColumnName>Customerid</KeyColumnName>
</ShardedTableInfo>
<ShardedTableInfo>
<SchemaName>Sales</SchemaName>
<TableName>Orders</TableName>
<KeyColumnName>Customerid</KeyColumnName>
</ShardedTableInfo>
```

Observe that it contains the schema, table, and sharding key column values for the **Sales.Customer**, **Sales.Orders**, and **Application.Countries** tables.

9. In **Object Explorer**, expand **toystore_Shard_1_100** and then expand **Tables**:

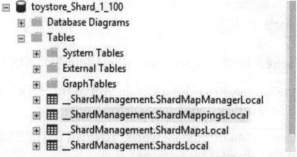

Figure 7.48: Tables in the toystore_Shard_1_100 database

We can see that, since **toystore_SMM** has global shard management tables, **toystore_Shard_1_100** has local shard map management tables. **toystore_shard_200** will also have local shard management tables.

The local shard management tables store shard metadata specific to the particular shard. You can query the tables to review the data if you want to know more. This completes the activity.

Activity: Splitting data between shards

In the previous activity, you created two shards, **toystore_Shard_1_100** and **toystore_Shard_200**. However, all of the data is available in the **toystore_ Shard_1_100** database, and you have been asked to split the data between **toystore_Shard_1_100** and **toystore_Shard_200**. Therefore, you can use the split-merge service to split the data.

In this activity, you'll use the split-merge service to split the data between **toystore_Shard_1_100** and **toystore_Shard_200**.

Deploying the split-merge cloud service

The split-merge tool is an Azure web service deployed to your Azure environment. Once deployed, you can either invoke the web service from the web service URL or from PowerShell.

> **Note**
>
> A web service is any service that is available over the internet or intranet. It has a certain set of functions that can be either invoked from the web service's web interface or using any of the programming languages supporting web service calls.

To deploy the split-merge cloud service in your Azure environment and then call the cloud service function to split the data, first follow these steps to deploy the split-merge cloud service:

1. Open a browser and navigate to the following URL: https://docs.microsoft.com/azure/azure-sql/database/elastic-scale-configure-deploy-split-and-merge.

   Follow the instructions listed at this URL to deploy the split-merge service.

   In addition to the steps mentioned at the URL, make the following additional changes before deploying the web service. In the **ServiceConfiguration.cscfg** file, set the value of the following settings to **false**:

   ```
   <Setting name="SetupWebAppForClientCertificates" value="false" />
   <Setting name="SetupWebserverForClientCertificates" value="false"
   />
   ```

   > **Note**
   >
   > The **ServiceConfiguration.cscfg** location is provided in the URL in *Step 1*.

   Deploy the cloud service in a production environment, not staging, as mentioned at the URL.

2. If you get an error when deploying the web service, refer to the **C:\Code\Chapter07\ Splitting** folder for the sample files:

    - **Serviceconfigurtion.cscfg**:
      C:\Code\Chapter07\Splitting\SplitMergeLibraries\Microsoft.Azure. Sqldatabase.ElasticScale.Service.SplitMerge.1.2.0\content\splitmerge\ service

    - **SplitMergeService.cspkg**:
      C:\Code\Chapter07\Splitting\SplitMergeLibraries\Microsoft.Azure. Sqldatabase.ElasticScale.Service.SplitMerge.1.2.0\content\splitmerge\ service

    - **Self-signed certificates**:
      C:\Code\Chapter07\Splitting\Certificate

    > **Note**
    >
    > Alternatively, you can create your own certificates by following the steps here: https://docs.microsoft.com/powershell/module/pkiclient/new-selfsignedcertificate?view=win10-ps.

Right-click on the **toyfactory.cer** certificate at the location specified by the self-signed certificates and select **Install** to install the certificate on your local machine. Upload the **toyfactory.pfx** file to the Azure cloud as per the instructions at the URL given previously. Make sure you have enabled the **toyfactory** server firewall to allow connections from services within Azure. You can do this by switching the **Allow access to Azure services** toggle button to **ON** in the **Firewall** section of the **toyfactory** server:

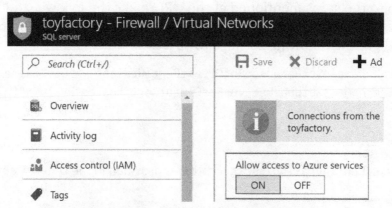

Figure 7.49: The Firewall section of the toyfactory server

Once your web service is deployed, you should see this output in the Azure portal's **Cloud service|Overview** section:

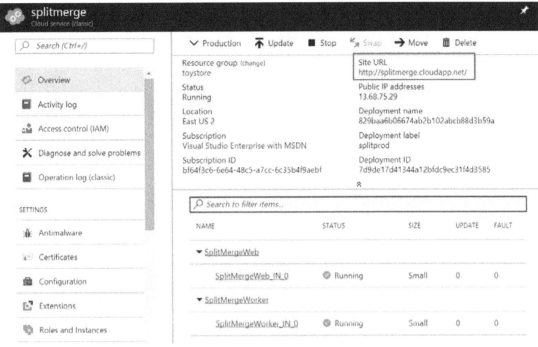

Figure 7.50: Azure portal Cloud service Overview section

3. Copy the web service URL, https://splitmerge.cloudapp.net, change **http** to **https**, and open the URL in a browser. If the web service is deployed successfully, you should see the following page:

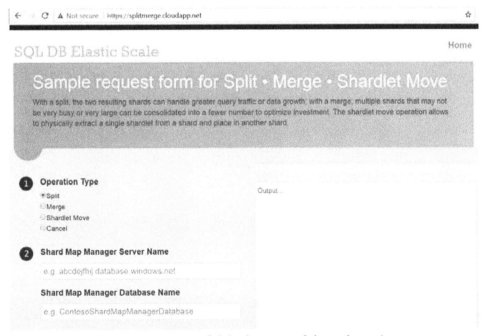

Figure 7.51: Successful deployment of the web service

You can split the data by either filling out the web form or by calling the web service using PowerShell.

Follow these steps to call the split-merge cloud service using PowerShell:

> **Note**
>
> If you are short of time, you can execute the **C:\Code\Chapter07\Splitting\ SplitToyStoreShard.ps1** file, providing appropriate parameters.

A. Press the *Windows* key + R to open the **Run** command window. Type **PowerShell_ISE.exe** in the **Run** command window and hit *Enter*. This will open a new **PowerShell ISE editor** window. This is where you'll write the PowerShell commands:

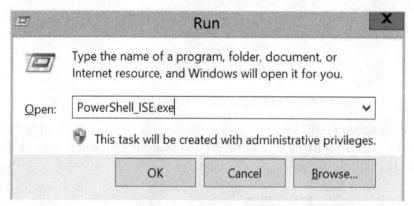

Figure 7.52: Opening a PowerShell editor window

B. In the PowerShell ISE, select **File** from the top menu and click **Save**. Alternatively, you can press *Ctrl* + *S* to save the file. In the **Save As** dialog box, browse to the **C:\Code\Chapter07\Splitting** directory. In the **File name** text box, type **Split-toystore- shard.ps1** and click **Save** to save the file:

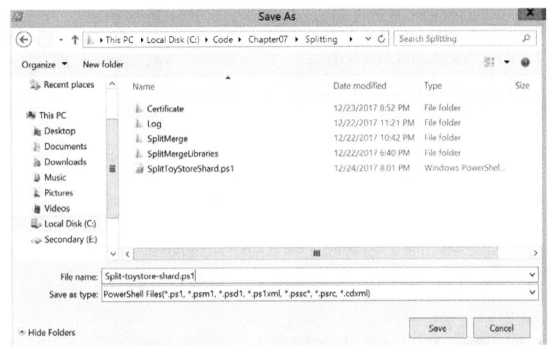

Figure 7.53: Saving the Split-toystore-shard.ps1 file

4. Copy and paste each code snippet in the following steps into the **Split-toystore-shard.ps1** file to implement the split operation. The code explanation, wherever required, is given in the following code snippet and in the comments within the code snippet.

5. Copy and paste the following code to define the parameters:

```
param (
[parameter(Mandatory=$true)] [String] $ResourceGroup,
[parameter(Mandatory=$true)] [String] $SqlServer,
[parameter(Mandatory=$true)] [String] $UserName,
[parameter(Mandatory=$true)] [String] $Password,
[parameter(Mandatory=$true)] [String] $SplitMergeDatabase,
[String] $AzureProfileFilePath,
[parameter(Mandatory=$true)] [String] $SplitMergeServiceEndpoint,
[parameter(Mandatory=$true)]
[String] $ShardMapManagerDatabaseName, [parameter(Mandatory=$true)]
[String] $Shard2, [parameter(Mandatory=$true)] [String]
$ShardMapName, [parameter(Mandatory=$true)] [String] $SplitRangeLow,
[parameter(Mandatory=$true)] [String] $SplitRangeHigh,
[parameter(Mandatory=$true)] [String] $SplitValue,
[bool] $CreateSplitMergeDatabase = $false
)
```

Most of the parameters were described in the previous activity. Here are the descriptions of the additional parameters:

- **SplitMergedatabase**: This is the split-merge database we created as part of the split-merge cloud service deployment.

- **SplitMergeServiceEndpoint**: This is the split-merge cloud service URL copied in the previous section.

- **ShardMapManagerdatabaseName**: This is the shard map manager database we created in the *Activity: Creating alerts* section.

- **Shard2**: This is the **shard2** database (**toystore_Shard_200**) we created in the *Activity: Creating alerts* section.

- **ShardMapName**: This is the name of the shard map (**toystorerangemap**) we created in the *Activity: Creating alerts* section.

- **SplitRangeLow**: This is the lower value for the range mapping. This is **0** in our case.

- **SplitRangeHigh**: This is the higher value for the range mapping. This is **200** in our case.

- **SplitValue**: This is the value at which the split will take place. This is **100** in our case.

- **CreateSplitMergedatabase**: This is a Boolean value that, when set to true, will provision a new database to be used as the split-merge database. You can use this to provision the database if you haven't created it yet.

6. Copy and paste the following code to set the login to the Azure subscription:

```
Start-Transcript -Path "$ScriptPath\Log\SplitToyStoreShard.txt" -Append
$CertificateThumbprint = $null
# Get the parent directory of the script.
$ScriptPath = split-path -parent $MyInvocation.MyCommand.
Definition
# set the AzureProfileFilePath
$AzureProfileFilePath = "..\..\MyAzureProfile.json"
#Login to Azure Account
if((Test-Path -Path $AzureProfileFilePath))
{
$profile = Select-AzProfile -Path $AzureProfileFilePath
$SubscriptionID = $profile.Context.Subscription.SubscriptionId
}
#Set the Azure Context
```

```
Set-AzContext -SubscriptionId $SubscriptionID | Out-Null

# create the split-merge database.
# if you have already deployed the web service this step isn't required.
if($CreateSplitMergeDatabase)
{
#Create a database to store split merge status
$command = "..\..\Chapter01\ProvisionAzureSQLdatabase.ps1
-ResourceGroup $ResourceGroup -SQLServer $SqlServer -UserName
$UserName -Password $Password -SQLdatabase $SplitMergedatabase
-Edition Basic"
Invoke-Expression -Command $command Exit;


}
```

This code calls the **ProvisionAzureSQLdatabase.ps1** PowerShell script to create a new SQL database to store the split-merge cloud service status. The database is created only if **CreateSplitMergedatabase** is set to true.

7. Copy and paste the following code to import the **split-merge PowerShell** module:

```
# Import SplitMerge module
$ScriptDir = Split-Path -parent $MyInvocation.MyCommand.Path Import-Module
$ScriptDir\SplitMerge -Force
```

The **split-merge PowerShell** module has helper functions to call the split-merge cloud service.

8. Copy and paste the following code to submit a split request:

```
Write-Output 'Sending split request'
$splitOperationId = Submit-SplitRequest '
-SplitMergeServiceEndpoint $SplitMergeServiceEndpoint '
-ShardMapManagerServerName "$SqlServer.database.windows.net" '
-ShardMapManagerdatabaseName $ShardMapManagerdatabaseName '
-TargetServerName "$SqlServer.database.windows.net" '
-TargetdatabaseName $Shard2 '
-UserName $UserName '
-Password $Password '
-ShardMapName $ShardMapName '
-ShardKeyType 'Int32' '
-SplitRangeLowKey $SplitRangeLow '
-SplitValue $SplitValue '
-SplitRangeHighKey $SplitRangeHigh '
-CertificateThumbprint $CertificateThumbprint
```

This code calls the **Submit-SplitRequest** function defined in the **SplitMerge** module. The **Submit-SplitRequest** function submits the split request by specifying the different parameter values.

The **SplitMerge** module contains helper functions for merge requests as well. The merge operation refers to merging two range mappings into a single shard.

Submit-SplitRequest returns the operation ID value. The operation ID is assigned to the **$splitOperationId** variable and is used to get the split request status.

9. Copy and paste the following code to wait on the split request until it completes:

    ```
    # Get split request output
    Wait-SplitMergeRequest -SplitMergeServiceEndpoint
    $SplitMergeServiceEndpoint -OperationId $splitOperationId
    -CertificateThumbprint $CertificateThumbprint
    ```

This code calls the **Wait-SplitMergeRequest** helper function defined in the **Split-Merge PowerShell** module. The function checks for the split operation status of **$splitOperationId** and writes the status to the console.

Executing the PowerShell script

Follow these steps to execute the PowerShell script:

1. Press the *Windows* key + R to open the **Run** command window. Type **PowerShell** and hit *Enter* to open a new PowerShell console window.

2. Change directory to the folder that has the **shard-toystore.ps1** script. For example, if the script is in the **C:\Code\Chapter07\Sharding** directory, then run the following command to switch to this directory:

    ```
    cd C:\Code\Chapter07\Splitting
    ```

3. In the following command, change the parameter values as per your environment. You can also copy the command from the **C:\Code\Chapter07\Executions.txt** file:

    ```
    .\Split-toystore-shard.ps1 -ResourceGroup toystore
    -SqlServer toyfactory -UserName sqladmin -Password Packt@pub2
    -SplitMergedatabase toystore_splitmerge -SplitMergeServiceEndpoint
    "https://splitmerge.cloudapp.net/" -ShardMapManagerdatabaseName toystore_
    SMM -Shard2 toystore_Shard_200 -ShardMapName toystorerangemap
    -SplitRangeLow 0 -SplitRangeHigh 200 -SplitValue
    100 -AzureProfileFilePath C:\Code\MyAzureProfile.json
    ```

Once you have changed the parameter values, copy and paste the command in the PowerShell console window opened in *Step 1* and hit *Enter*.

If the script executes successfully, you should get the following output:

```
Sending split request
Polling request status. Press Ctrl-C to end
Progress: 0% | Status: Queued | Details: [Informational] Operation has
been queued.
Progress: 5% | Status: Starting | Details: [Informational] Starting Split-
Merge state machine for request.
Progress: 5% | Status: Starting | Details: [Informational] Performing data
consistency checks on target shards.
Progress: 20% | Status: CopyingReferenceTables | Details: [Informational]
Successfully copied reference table [Application].[Countries].
…

…
Progress: 80% | Status: CopyingShardedTables | Details: [Informational]
Successfully copied key range [190:200) for sharded table [Sales].
[Orders].

Progress: 90% | Status: Completing | Details: [Informational]
Deleting any temp tables that were created while processing the request.
Progress: 100% | Status: Succeeded | Details: [Informational] Successfully
processed request.
```

4. If you get an error in this command and your split-merge service is deployed correctly, then you can troubleshoot it by checking the **RequestStatus** table in the split-merge database.

    The **RequestStatus** table has one row for each split-merge request. The **Details** column contains the XML with the error details if the request fails.

Verifying the split operation

Follow these steps to ensure that the split request has correctly moved the data:

1. Open **SQL Server Management Studio** on your local machine and connect to the **toyfactory** server.

2. In **Object Explorer**, right-click on the **toystore_Shard_1_100** database and select **New Query** from the context menu.

3. In the **New Query** window, execute the following query:

    ```
    SELECT DB_NAME() AS databaseName, COUNT(*) AS TotalRows FROM Sales.
    Customers
    ```

You should get the following output:

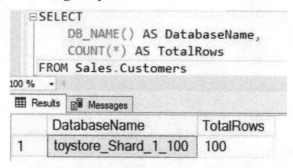

Figure 7.54: Output of the select query

4. In **Object Explorer**, right-click on the **toystore_Shard_200** database and select **New Query** from the context menu.

5. In the **New Query** window, execute the following query:

    ```
    SELECT DB_NAME() AS databaseName, COUNT(*) AS TotalRows FROM Sales.
    Customers
    ```

You should get the following output:

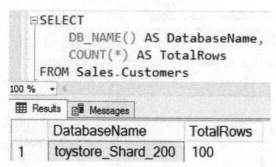

Figure 7.55: Output of the select query

This validates that the split-merge operation has successfully split 200 rows between the two shards, **toystore_Shard_1_100** (100 rows) and **toystore_Shard_200** (100 rows).

6. In **Object Explorer**, right-click on the **toystore_SMM** database and select **New Query** from the context menu. Execute the following query in the new query window:

```
SELECT
sg.databaseName AS ShardName
,sg.ServerName AS ServerName
,smg.Name AS ShardMapName
,smg.KeyType
,CAST(MinValue AS SMALLINT) AS RangeLowKey
,CAST(MaxValue AS SMALLINT) AS RangeHighKey
FROM [ ShardManagement]. [ShardMapsGlobal] smg
JOIN [ ShardManagement].[ShardsGlobal] sg ON sg.ShardMapID = smg.
ShardMapId
JOIN [ ShardManagement].[ShardMappingsGlobal] smng ON smg.
ShardMapID=smng.ShardMapID
AND sg.ShardId=smng.ShardId
```

You should get the following output:

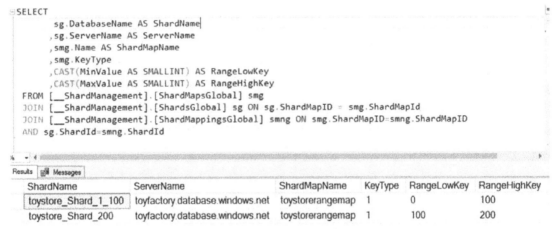

Figure 7.56: Output of the select query

The **MinValue** and **MaxValue** columns are **varbinary** columns and are therefore converted to **SmallInt**.

If you remember the first activity in this chapter, the **ShardMappingsGlobal** table had only one mapping, which was added as part of the sharding configuration.

However, it now has two rows, and the second row for the **toystore_ Shard_200** shard is added as part of the split operation. This completes the activity.

Let's now look at using elastic database queries to run queries against multiple shards created in the preceding activity.

Activity: Using elastic database queries

In this activity, we will use elastic database, or cross-database, queries to query the sharded tables (created in previous activities) across the shards as a single table.

To query multiple shards as a single table using elastic database queries, follow these steps:

1. Open **SQL Server Management Studio** on your local machine and connect to the **toyfactory** server.

2. In **Object Explorer**, right-click on the **Master** database and select **New Query** from the context menu. In the new query window, execute the following query to create the **toystorereporting** database:

    ```
    CREATE DATABASE toystorereporting; GO
    ```

3. Once the database is provisioned, navigate to **Object Explorer**, right-click on the **toystorereporting** database, and select **New Query** from the context menu.

    > **Note**
    >
    > You can also refer to the **C:\Code\Chapter07\ElasticQueries.sql** file for the queries in this activity.

4. Execute the following query to create a master key:

    ```
    CREATE MASTER KEY ENCRYPTION BY PASSWORD = 'Packt@pub2'; GO
    ```

    You may get the following error if a master key already exists in the database:

    ```
    Msg 15578, Level 16, State 1, Line 3
    There is already a master key in the database. Please drop it before
    performing this statement.
    ```

    Ignore the error and proceed to the next step.

5. Execute the following query to create a database-scoped credential:

    ```
    CREATE DATABASE SCOPED CREDENTIAL toystore_creds WITH IDENTITY =
    'sqladmin', SECRET = 'Packt@pub2' GO
    ```

    The identity and secret should be the same as your SQL Server administrator username and password.

6. Execute the following query to create the external data source. The external data source is essentially the connection details or the connection string of the external data source. In our case, the external data source is the shard map manager database:

```
CREATE EXTERNAL DATA SOURCE toystore_dsrc WITH ( TYPE=SHARD_MAP_MANAGER,
LOCATION='toyfactory.database.windows.net', DATABASE_NAME='toystore_SMM',
CREDENTIAL= toystore_creds, SHARD_MAP_NAME='toystorerangemap'
);
```

This query creates an external data source, **toystore_dsrc**, of type **Shard_Map_Manager**, which connects to the shard map manager database **toystore_SMM** using the **toystore_creds** database-scoped credentials created in the previous step.

The shard map name in the external data source will help resolve the individual shards to get the data from.

We didn't specify individual shards as the external data source, **database_Name**, because it'll return the data of individual shards. However, our goal is to get data for the table from all shards.

> **Note**
>
> The external data source type can be Hadoop, RDBMS, or Blob Storage. For more details on external data sources, refer to this link: https://docs.microsoft.com/sql/t-sql/statements/create-external-data-source-transact-sql?view=sql-server-2017&tabs=dedicated.

7. Execute the following query to create the **Customers** table in the **toystorereporting** database. The table is created with the **EXTERNAL** keyword and on the external data source, **toystore_dsrc**, created in *Step 6*:

```
CREATE EXTERNAL TABLE [dbo].[Customers](
[CustomerID] [int] NOT NULL, [CustomerName] [nvarchar](100) NOT NULL,
[BillToCustomerID] [int] NOT NULL, [CustomerCategoryID] [int] NOT NULL,
[BuyingGroupID] [int] NULL, [PrimaryContactPersonID] [int] NOT NULL,
[AlternateContactPersonID] [int] NULL, [DeliveryMethodID] [int] NOT NULL,
[DeliveryCityID] [int] NOT NULL,
[PostalCityID] [int] NOT NULL, [CreditLimit] [decimal](18, 2) NULL,
[AccountOpenedDate] [date] NOT NULL,
[StandardDiscountPercentage] [decimal](18, 3) NOT NULL, [IsStatementSent]
[bit] NOT NULL,
[IsOnCreditHold] [bit] NOT NULL, [PaymentDays] [int] NOT NULL,
[PhoneNumber] [nvarchar](20) NOT NULL, [FaxNumber] [nvarchar](20) NOT
NULL, [DeliveryRun] [nvarchar](5) NULL, [RunPosition] [nvarchar](5) NULL,
[WebsiteURL] [nvarchar](256) NOT NULL,
[DeliveryAddressLine1] [nvarchar](60) NOT NULL, [DeliveryAddressLine2]
[nvarchar](60) NULL, [DeliveryPostalCode] [nvarchar](10) NOT NULL,
[DeliveryLocation] [varchar](1) NOT NULL, [PostalAddressLine1]
[nvarchar](60) NOT NULL, [PostalAddressLine2] [nvarchar](60) NULL,
[PostalPostalCode] [nvarchar](10) NOT NULL, [LastEditedBy] [int] NOT NULL,
[ValidFrom] [datetime2](7) NOT NULL, [ValidTo] [datetime2](7) NOT NULL
) WITH (
DATA_SOURCE = toystore_dsrc, SCHEMA_NAME = 'Sales',
OBJECT_NAME = 'Customers', DISTRIBUTION=SHARDED(customerid)
);
```

dbo.Customers is an external table that gets its data from the **toystore_dsrc** external data source, the **Sales.Customers** table.

The distribution parameter specifies how the data is distributed for this table.

In our case, the table is horizontally partitioned, hence the distribution used is sharded with **customerid** (the sharding key). The other available distributions are as follows:

- **Replicated**: This means that each database has identical copies of the table.

- **Round-robin**: This means that the table is horizontally partitioned, with partition logic specified in the application tier and the sharding method we discussed.

8. Execute the following query to return all the rows from the customer table:

```
SELECT * FROM dbo.Customers
```

You should get all 200 rows.

The database engine uses the information specified in the **toystore_dsrc** external data source to connect to and return data from all the shards.

9. Execute the following queries to get the existing external data source and external tables:

```
-- Get Existing External Data sources SELECT * FROM sys.external_data_
sources;
-- Get Existing External Tables SELECT * FROM sys.external_tables
```

This completes the activity.

In the preceding activities, we have learned how to create shards and split existing data into multiple shards using the split-merge service. We also learned how to use elastic database queries to run queries across multiple shards.

Let's now look at scaling a managed instance.

Scaling a managed instance

SQL Managed Instance gives us the flexibility to dynamically scale up or down instance resources as and when required. You can scale up instance resources whenever there is peak demand and scale down the resources whenever the demand ends. This can help in effectively managing costs for SQL Managed Instance. In previous chapters, we learned about different purchasing options and service tiers for SQL Managed Instance and we also saw how single managed instances are hosted inside a virtual cluster.

SQL Managed Instance provides management operations, and they can be used to deploy a new managed instance, updating existing instance properties and deleting the instance when it's not required. Here, we will be learning about SQL Managed Instance scaling management operations and how they impact the virtual cluster. The duration of these scale-up/down requests depends on virtual cluster operations. Adding additional virtual machines to a virtual cluster can add overhead that needs to be considered before making changes to existing managed instances.

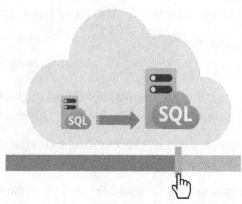

Figure 7.57: Scaling SQL Managed Instance

The duration of scaling management operations depends on internal virtual cluster operations and these operations' duration may vary with respect to scale-up/down activities. Let's take a look at the duration of scaling management operations.

Duration of scale-up/down operations

The duration of management operations may vary according to the SQL Managed Instance service tier, database size, and scaling operation. Microsoft stores all the service-related telemetry data and the following are the estimated times for scaling operations based on telemetry.

- **Virtual cluster resizing operation**: During a scaling operation, the expansion/ shrinking of a virtual cluster may take longer than usual to complete. Based on service telemetry data, 90% of the time this operation finished in 2.5 hours.

- **Database seeding/attach operation**: Attaching database files during storage scaling or Always On seeding may also impact the duration of the scaling operation.

Please refer to *Table 7.3* to see the estimation for each operation.

Activity	Operation	Estimated duration
Scaling up/down General Purpose instance storage	Attaching database files	90% of scaling operations finish in 5 minutes.
Scaling up/down Business Critical instance storage	Virtual cluster resizing	90% of scaling operations finish in 2.5 hours + time to seed all databases (220 GB/hour).
	Always On availability group seeding	
Scaling up/down General Purpose instance vCore	Virtual cluster resizing	90% of scaling operations finish in 2.5 hours.
	Attaching database files	
Scaling up/down Business Critical instance vCore	Virtual cluster resizing	90% of scaling operations finish in 2.5 hours + time to seed all databases (220 GB/hour).
	Always On availability group seeding	
Changing Instance service tier from GP -> BC or BC -> GP	Virtual cluster resizing	90% of scaling operations finish in 2.5 hours + time to seed all databases (220 GB/hour).
	Always On availability group seeding	

Table 7.3: Estimation of each operation

> **Note**
>
> Scaling management operations take longer to complete due to virtual cluster resizing but during these operations, SQL Managed Instance is available for the application workload. At the end of the scaling operation, you may notice a short downtime of 10 seconds during the failover of the instance from one node to another.

Activity: Scaling up SQL Managed Instance using the Azure portal

You can dynamically scale up SQL Managed Instance resources using the Azure portal. In this activity, we are scaling up vCore and storage capacity for General Purpose SQL Managed Instance. You can also scale vCore and instance storage sizes independently. Since these management operations for a single managed instance take longer to complete due to virtual cluster re-sizing operations, SQL Managed Instance also gives the option to cancel these operations in case they're triggered by mistake. In the last part of this activity, we will also see the steps to cancel scaling management operations.

Follow the steps given here to perform a scale-up operation:

1. Go to https://portal.azure.com.

2. Select your managed instance and under **Settings**, select the **Compute + Storage** pane.

3. Choose your desired service tier, vCore, and storage configuration and click **Apply** to save the changes:

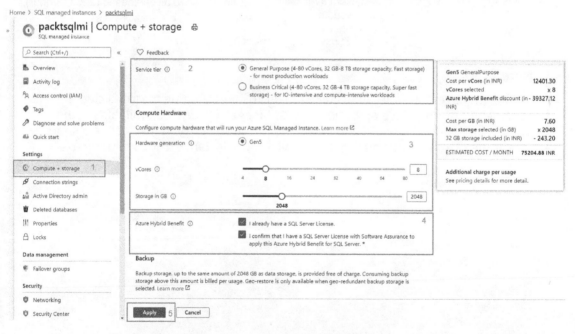

Figure 7.58: Scaling a managed instance using the Azure portal

4. Monitor the notifications to see the progress and wait for the operation to complete; 90% of the time this operation is finished in under 2 hours 30 minutes:

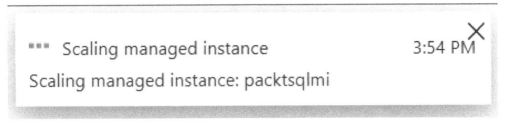

Figure 7.59: Scaling in progress notification

Follow *Steps* 5 and 6 if you need to cancel this ongoing scaling management operation.

5. If this scaling operation needs to be canceled, then go to the **Overview** pane of SQL Managed Instance and under **Notifications**, you will notice an ongoing operation. Click on the **Cancel this operation** button to end the scaling:

Figure 7.60: Canceling the scaling operation

6. After submitting the cancel operation, you will notice a successful submission notification:

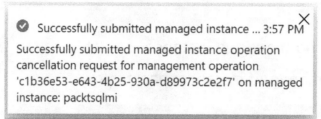

Figure 7.61: Notification for submission of the cancel operation

> **Note**
>
> The cancellation of a General Purpose instance storage scaling up/down operation is not allowed.

In this activity, we have learned how to initiate a scale operation using the Azure portal for a managed instance. We have also seen steps to cancel ongoing scaling operations using the Azure portal. Now let's see the steps to scale up a managed instance using PowerShell commands.

Activity: Scaling a managed instance using the Az.sql PowerShell module

Earlier, we saw the steps needed to perform scaling operations using the Azure portal. In this activity, we will learn how to initiate a scaling management operation using PowerShell commands.

Follow the steps given here to initiate an instance scale-up operation using PowerShell:

1. Open Cloud Shell from the Azure portal by clicking on the **Cloud Shell** icon:

Figure 7.62: Cloud Shell icon

2. Switch to the **PowerShell** terminal to run PowerShell code:

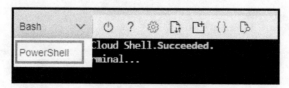

Figure 7.63: Switching to the PowerShell terminal

3. Set the variables according to your environment:

```
#setting up variable as per your environment
$subscription = "6ff855b5-xxxx-4bc2-xxxx-xxxxxxxxx"
$managedInstance = "packtsqlmi"
$resourceGroup = "Packt"
```

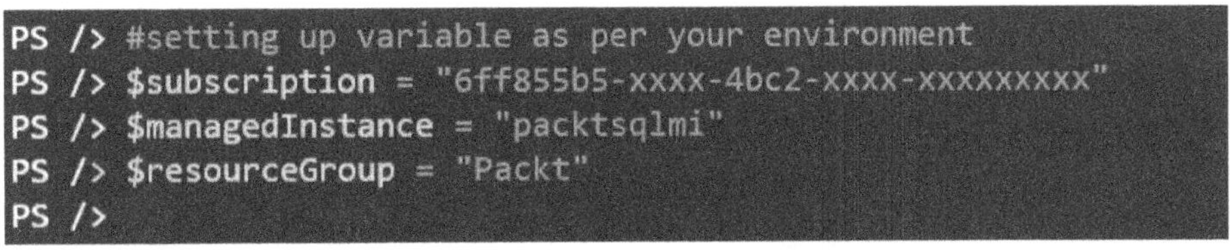

Figure 7.64: Initializing variables

4. Select the managed instance subscription:

```
#Select the managed instance subscription
Select-AzSubscription -SubscriptionId $subscription
```

5. Update the **Instance** properties using this PowerShell command:

```
#Updating license type, storage size and moving instance to business
critical server tier.
Set-AzSqlInstance -Name $manangedInstance -ResourceGroupName
$resourceGroup -LicenseType LicenseIncluded -StorageSizeInGB 1024 -VCore
16 -Edition BusinessCritical
```

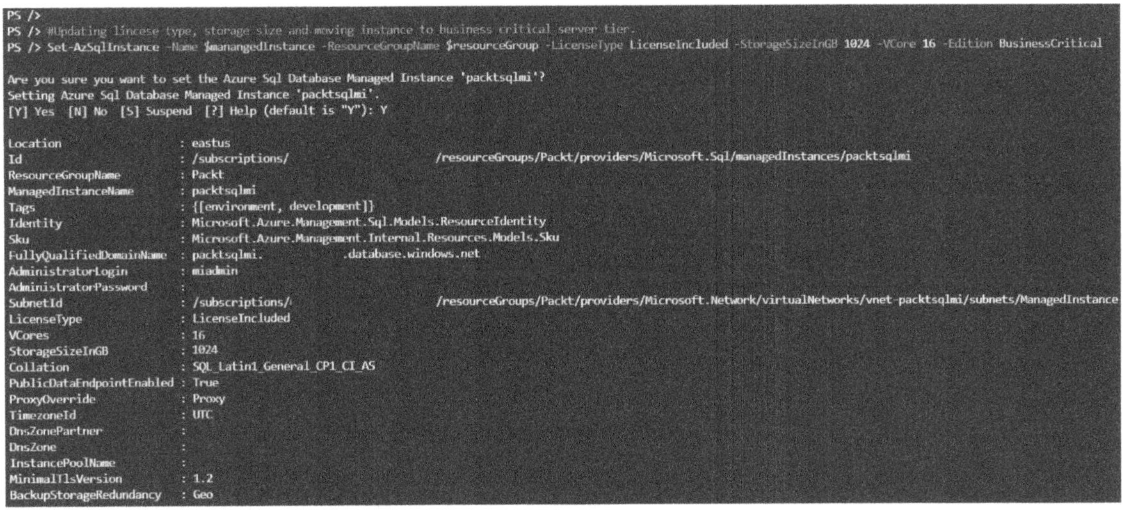

Figure 7.65: Updating the managed instance properties using PowerShell

In this activity, we have learned about scaling SQL Managed Instance using PowerShell commands. We have updated the instance service tier, license type, vCore, and storage size.

Alternate ways of scaling SQL Managed Instance

We have seen the steps for scaling up SQL Managed Instance resources with management operations. Here, we will be learning more about alternate ways to scale a managed instance.

The Business Critical service tier of SQL Managed Instance comes with an in-built read replica and that can be used as a read-only source for your analytics application. An internal read replica in Business Critical SQL Managed Instance runs with the same compute and storage resources similar to its primary node and it can help in off-loading a read-only workload without paying more for extra resources. The internal read-replica server is not visible on the Azure portal and hence needs to be accessed using the `ApplicationIntent=ReadOnly` flag.

The following is the high-level architecture for offloading a read-only workload to the internal read replica in the Business Critical service tier:

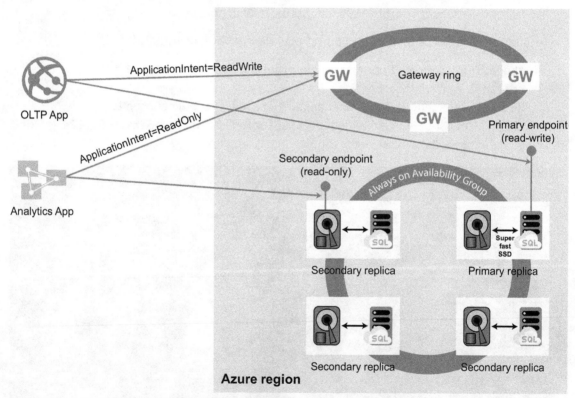

Figure 7.66: Read scale-out architecture for the Business Critical service tier

Note: Read scale-out is also available with the Business Critical and Hyperscale service tiers in SQL Database.

In *Figure* 7.68, **OLTP App** is making a connection to SQL Managed Instance using the `ApplicationIntent=ReadWrite` option in the connection string. The gateway service is redirecting the same connection to the **Primary replica** read-write endpoint. Similarly, **Analytics App** is also connecting to SQL Managed Instance using `ApplicationIntent=ReadOnly` and the gateway service is redirecting the connection to the secondary replica read-only endpoint.

Here, we have seen how **Analytics App** connects to the read replica. You can also connect to the internal read replica using the SSMS application.

Activity: Connecting to the SQL Managed Instance internal read replica using SSMS

In this activity, we will look at the steps needed to connect to the Business Critical SQL Managed Instance internal replica. This can be helpful when you need to troubleshoot any performance or blocking issues while running a read-only workload on an internal replica server, since the internal read-replica server is not visible on the Azure portal and you do not have any direct server name or instance name to connect to the read replica.

You can connect to the internal read replication by specifying the `ApplicationIntent=ReadOnly` flag while connecting from SSMS using the primary managed instance name.

Follow the steps given here to perform this activity:

1. Open SSMS and connect to **Database Engine** and click on **Options**:

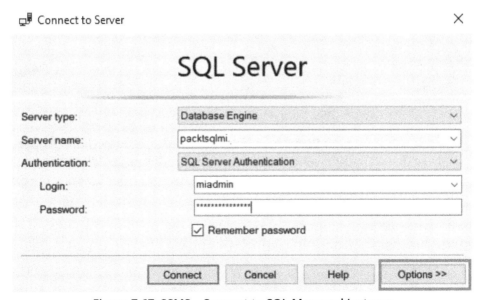

Figure 7.67: SSMS—Connect to SQL Managed Instance

2. Specify the **ApplicationIntent=ReadOnly** flag and connect to the managed instance:

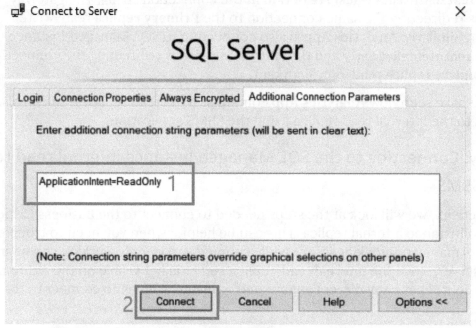

Figure 7.68: SSMS using an additional connection parameter in SSMS

3. Open a new query window and run the following T-SQL command to verify the read-only endpoint connection:

```
SELECT DATABASEPROPERTYEX(DB_NAME(), 'Updateability')
```

Figure 7.69: Verifying the read-only connection

In *Figure 7.71*, we are fetching an **Updateability** database property. This property indicates whether data can be modified for the current database. The **READ_ONLY** output shows that this database supports only read operations and does not support write operations.

In this activity, we have seen steps for connecting to the built-in read replica for a Business Critical managed instance using SSMS, and we also ran a T-SQL query to verify the read-only connection.

Summary

In this chapter, we've seen how easy it is to scale up or scale down an SQL database both automatically and manually. We've looked at both vertical and horizontal scaling. We've also learned how to autoscale SQL databases and shard a database, as well as how to create and maintain SQL database shards.

We have also learned about SQL Managed Instance scaling management operations and durations and we have seen alternate ways of scaling using internal read-replicas for Business Critical SQL Managed Instance. In the next chapter, we will learn how to scale SQL databases using elastic database pools and we will also learn about instance pools in SQL Managed Instance.

Summary

8

Elastic and instance pools

Azure SQL Database has two deployment options, a single database and an elastic pool. A single SQL database is an isolated, standalone database with dedicated resources (DTU or vCore). In all of our previous chapters, we have talked about Azure SQL Database single-database deployments.

An SQL elastic database pool is a group of two or more SQL databases with shared resources (eDTU and vCore) at a specific price.

In a multi-tenant scenario where there's one database for each customer, each database has a varying access pattern with different peak times and low average utilization. We'll see later in the chapter how grouping different customer databases in an SQL Database elastic pool saves costs without affecting performance.

This chapter will teach you how to manage and scale multiple SQL databases by using elastic database pools. You'll also learn how to implement elastic database jobs to manage and maintain databases in an elastic database pool.

We will also look at the new SQL Managed Instance deployment option for instance pools. We will discuss the architecture of instance pools and look at the key differences between instance pools and a single SQL Managed Instance deployment. You will learn how to deploy and manage instance pools using PowerShell commands.

By the end of this chapter, you will be able to:

- Explain the purpose of elastic database pools and identify when to use them.
- Select the size of an elastic database pool.
- Configure elastic database jobs.
- Explain the purpose of instance pools and how they differ from single instances.
- Deploy an SQL Managed Instance pool.

Introducing elastic database pools in SQL Database

The SQL Database elastic pool is a cost-effective solution for managing and scaling a group or a pool of SQL databases, with a utilization pattern characterized by low average utilization and infrequent spikes.

All databases in an elastic database pool:

- Belong to one Azure SQL server.
- Share a set amount of compute resources indexed by **eDTUs (Elastic DTUs)** in the DTU purchasing model and vCores in the vCore purchasing model.
- Share a set amount of elastic database pool storage.
- Have a price based on the amount of elastic database pool resources and not individual databases.
- Can scale up to the given maximum amount of eDTUs or vCores.
- Optionally, have a guaranteed minimum number of eDTUs or vCores.

Let's look at a scenario that highlights when we should think about using an SQL Database elastic pool.

When should you consider elastic database pools?

In *Chapter 7, Scalability,* we worked on sharding the **toystore** database into four individual shards. Each shard had 50 pieces of a customer's/tenant's data. Let's say that each individual database is sized to a Standard S3 service tier—for example, 100 DTUs— and has the DTU utilization levels shown in *Figure 8.1*:

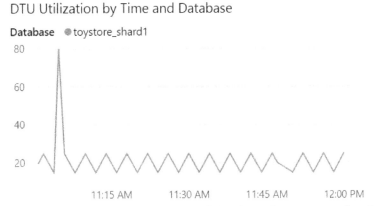

Figure 8.1: DTU utilization by time and database for toystore_shard1

The preceding graph shows the DTU utilization by time for the **toystore_shard1** database. It is evident from the graph that **toystore_shard1** has an average DTU utilization of around **30** DTUs and a spike of **80** DTUs around **11:00 AM**. Let's say that the other three shards have similar graphs; however, they peak at different times, as shown in *Figure 8.2*:

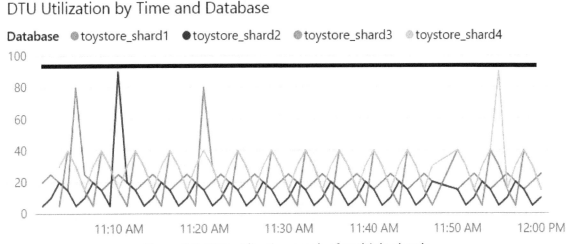

Figure 8.2: DTU utilization graph of multiple shards

The preceding graph shows the four shards in a combined graph. The average utilization is under **40** DTUs and the peak utilization is **90** DTUs. The database peaks at different points in time.

At this point, you might argue that you should use the Standard S2 service tier, which offers 50 DTUs and costs less than S3. This would suffice for most of the database's workload, which is below **50** DTUs. However, this would result in performance degradation for peak hours when the utilization is **90** DTUs, which is much greater than **50** DTUs.

You have two options here:

- Over-provision (Standard S3) to provide optimum performance for peak hours at a higher cost.

- Under-provision (Standard S2) to save costs at the expense of lower performance and bad customer experience during peak hours.

Elastic database pools provide you with a third option, which provides optimum performance at a lower cost.

The four shards are grouped together in an elastic database pool with an eDTU count of 100, as shown in *Figure 8.3*:

Elastic Database Pool
Elastic Database Transaction Unit (eDTU): 100
Max eDTUs Per Database: 100
Max Data Storage Per Database: 750 GB
Free Storage Per Pool: 100 GB

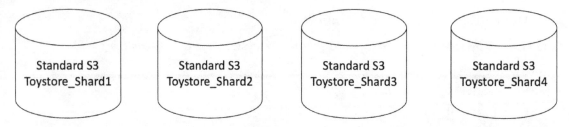

Figure 8.3: Grouping of shards in an elastic database pool

This means that a database:

- In peak hours, can consume a maximum of 100 eDTUs to meet the performance demand.

- In off-peak hours (under light loads), can consume fewer eDTUs.

- Under no load, consumes 0 (zero) eDTUs.

This not only solves the problem of over- and under-provisioning but also saves costs, as you only have to pay for eDTUs and not individual databases' DTUs.

A Standard S3 service tier that has a DTU provision of 100 is priced at $147/month. Four such databases would cost $588/month.

An elastic database pool that has an eDTU provision of 100 is priced at $221/month, which means that you save $367/month (a 62% cost reduction) if you have the database in an elastic database pool.

Let's say that as the number of customers increases, you plan to further shard the databases into eight shards. This means that you would have eight databases in an elastic database pool. This would result in an 85% monthly cost reduction.

This is where elastic database pools are very beneficial.

Sizing an elastic database pool

Elastic database pools have great benefits, but only if they are sized properly. Otherwise, you might end up spending more than expected if they're oversized or risk a poor performance experience if they're undersized.

The ideal utilization pattern of a database to be considered for an elastic database pool should be low average utilization and short, infrequent high utilization. This utilization pattern is best for sharing eDTUs. If a database has high average utilization, then it will take most of the eDTUs. This means that the other databases won't get the required eDTUs and will have lower performance.

To estimate whether or not an elastic database pool would be more cost-effective than having individual databases, these steps can be followed:

1. Find the estimated eDTU provision using the following formula:

   ```
   MAX(<Total number of DBs X Average DTU utilization per DB>, Number of
       concurrently peaking DBs X Peak DTU utilization per DB)
   ```

   > **Note:**
   >
   > For a vCore-based purchasing model instead, the formula is:
   >
   > MAX(<Total number of DBs X average vCore utilization per DB>, <Number of concurrently peaking DBs X Peak vCore utilization per DB>)

2. Find the estimated elastic database pool storage provision by adding the individual database storage. Find the eDTU that provides the estimated necessary storage using this link: https://azure.microsoft.com/pricing/details/sql-database/managed/.

3. Using the link given in *step 2*, find the smallest eDTU that is greater than the largest eDTU from *steps 1 and 2*.

4. Compare the costs of the elastic database pool and the individual databases to evaluate the pricing benefits.

Let's apply the preceding method to our toystore example:

5. Estimated eDTU as per *step* 1:

```
Total Number of DBs= 4
Average DTU utilization per DB = 30
Number of concurrently peaking DBs = 1
Peak utilization per DB = 90
Estimated eDTUs as per Step 1 = MAX (4 * 30,1*90) => MAX (120, 90) =120
```

The estimated eDTU as per *step* 1 is 120.

6. Estimate eDTU as per *step* 2.

Let's say that each shard has a maximum storage of 100 GB. This means that the maximum storage for all four shards would be 4 * 100 = 400 GB.

As per the pricing details link, the 100 eDTUs per elastic database pool satisfies the preceding storage need:

Standard

eDTUs PER POOL	INCLUDED STORAGE PER POOL	MAX STORAGE PER POOL [1,2]	MAX NUMBER DATABASES PER POOL	MAX eDTUs PER DATABASE [3]	PRICE FOR eDTUs AND INCLUDED STORAGE [4]
50	50 GB	500 GB	100	50	~$110.57/month
100	100 GB	750 GB	200	100	~$221.13/month
200	200 GB	1 TB	500	200	~$442.25/month

Figure 8.4: Elastic database pool pricing for the Standard service tier

Therefore, the estimated eDTU as per *step* 2 is 100.

The eDTU as per *step* 1 is 120 and as per *step* 2 is 100. Therefore, we can choose an eDTU of 100 because an eDTU of 120 is closer to an eDTU of 100 than the next available eDTU of 200.

Having four databases in an elastic database pool of 100 eDTU saves 62% on costs compared to having four individual SQL databases.

Creating an elastic database pool and adding toystore shards to the elastic database pool

In this section, we will create an elastic database pool and add **toystore** SQL Database shards to it. Let's go back to our example of ToyStore Ltd. Mike analyzes the report of DTUs and thinks of switching to the Standard service tier 3. Switching all four shards to the Standard service tier S3 will increase the database cost. Therefore, he plans to use an elastic database pool. He must create an elastic database pool and add the **toystore** shards to it by performing the following steps:

1. Open a browser and log in to the Azure portal (https://portal.azure.com/) using your Microsoft Azure credentials.

2. From the left-hand navigation menu, select **All resources**. Under **All Resources**, click the **toyfactory** SQL server to open the **toyfactory Overview** pane.

3. In the **toyfactory Overview** pane, select **New elastic pool** from the top menu:

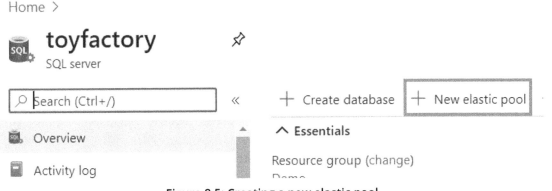

Figure 8.5: Creating a new elastic pool

4. In the **Create SQL Elastic pool** pane, provide the elastic database pool name in the **Elastic pool details** section and set the pricing tier as **Standard**:

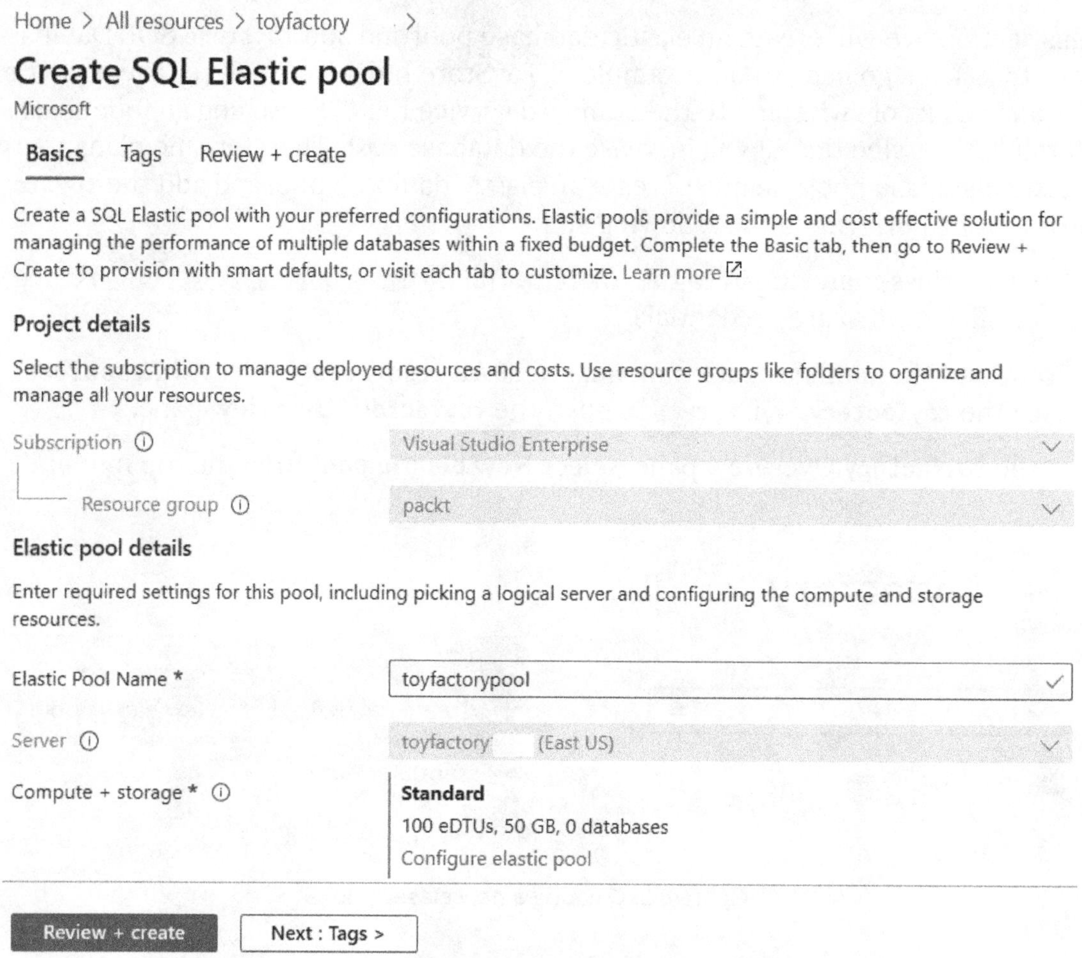

Home > All resources > toyfactory   >

Create SQL Elastic pool
Microsoft

Basics   Tags   Review + create
___

Create a SQL Elastic pool with your preferred configurations. Elastic pools provide a simple and cost effective solution for managing the performance of multiple databases within a fixed budget. Complete the Basic tab, then go to Review + Create to provision with smart defaults, or visit each tab to customize. Learn more ⬈

Project details

Select the subscription to manage deployed resources and costs. Use resource groups like folders to organize and manage all your resources.

Subscription ⓘ   Visual Studio Enterprise   ⌄

    └──── Resource group ⓘ   packt   ⌄

Elastic pool details

Enter required settings for this pool, including picking a logical server and configuring the compute and storage resources.

Elastic Pool Name *   toyfactorypool   ✓

Server ⓘ   toyfactory   (East US)   ⌄

Compute + storage * ⓘ   **Standard**
                                          100 eDTUs, 50 GB, 0 databases
                                          Configure elastic pool

[Review + create]   [Next : Tags >]

Figure 8.6: Providing details for creating the SQL Elastic pool

5. Click **Review + create** and then click **Create** to create the elastic database pool. It'll take 2-5 minutes for the elastic database pool to be provisioned.

   When the elastic database pool is provisioned, navigate to the **All resources** page in the Azure portal and type `toyfactorypool` in the search box. Click `toyfactorypool` to configure it:

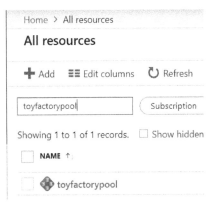

Figure 8.7: Selecting toyfactorypool

6. On the `toyfactorypool` page, select **Configure**:

Figure 8.8: Configuring toyfactorypool

The **Configure pool** page allows you to configure pool settings, add or remove databases, and configure per-database settings.

7. To add databases to **toyfactorypool**, select the **Databases** tab on the **Configure** page.

    On the **Databases** tab, click **Add databases**:

Figure 8.9: Adding databases to toyfactorypool

8. On the **Add databases** page, select `toystore_shard_1_50`, `toystore_50_100`, `toystore_100_150`, and `toystore_150_200`:

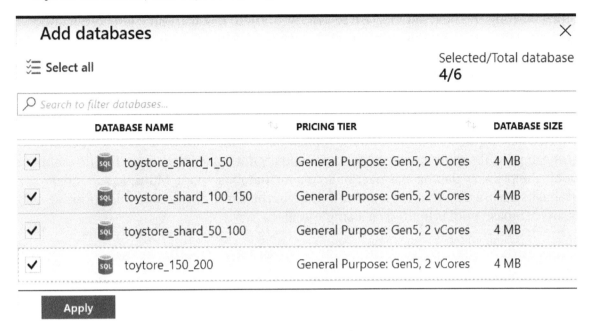

Figure 8.10: Adding databases

Click **Apply** to select the databases and go back to the **Configure** tab.

9. On the **Configure** tab, click **Save** to add the databases:

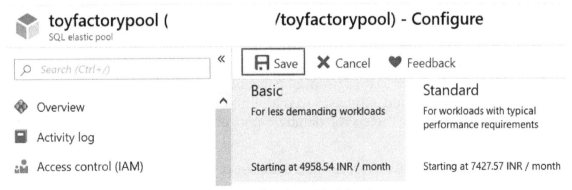

Figure 8.11: Saving the added databases

In this exercise, we created an elastic database pool, **toyfactorypool**, and added SQL databases to the elastic database pool.

Before starting the next activity, we're briefly going to discuss some geo-replication and auto-failover group considerations for elastic database pools. Readers should refer to the next chapter, *Chapter 9, High availability and disaster recovery*, for an in-depth introduction to geo-replication and auto-failover groups.

Geo-replication considerations for elastic database pools

In active geo-replication, a secondary replica may or may not be a part of an elastic database pool. It's not mandatory for a secondary database to be in an elastic database pool if the primary database is part of an elastic database pool. Multiple secondary databases across different regions cannot be in the same elastic database pool, as an elastic database pool is limited to a single region.

Auto-failover group considerations for elastic database pools

In an auto-failover group, unlike geo-replication, the secondary replica inherits the elastic database pool settings from the primary replica. If a primary database is in an elastic database pool, the secondary database is created in an elastic database pool with the same name. We can add all or selected databases from an elastic database pool in the primary replica to an auto-failover group.

Now, let's explore elastic database pools a little further.

Activity: Exploring elastic database pools

Let's go back to our example of ToyStore Ltd. Mike finds out that the **toystore** sharded databases can be put into an elastic database pool to save costs and get the benefits of vertical stability. In order to do a proof of concept, he uses PowerShell to create an elastic database pool and add databases to that elastic database pool. He also writes a PowerShell script to delete the elastic database pool after he is done with the proof of concept.

In this activity, we will create a new elastic database pool, add databases to the elastic database pool, and delete the elastic database pool using PowerShell using the following steps:

> **Note**
>
> If you are short of time, you can execute the `C:\Code\Chapter08\ElasticPool\ Manage-ElasticPool.ps1` file, providing the appropriate parameters.

1. Press *Windows* + R to open the **Run** command window. Type `PowerShell_ISE.exe` in the **Run** command window and hit *Enter*. This will open a new PowerShell ISE editor window. This is where you'll write the PowerShell commands:

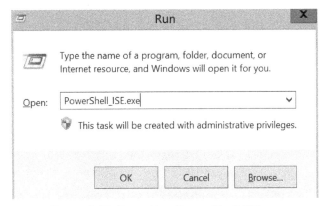

Figure 8.12: Executing PowerShell_ISE.exe

In the PowerShell ISE, select **File** from the top menu and click **Save**. Alternatively, you can press *Ctrl* + S to save the file. In the **Save As** dialog box, browse to the `C:\ Code\Chapter08` directory. In the **File name** textbox, type `Manage-ElasticPool` and click **Save** to save the file:

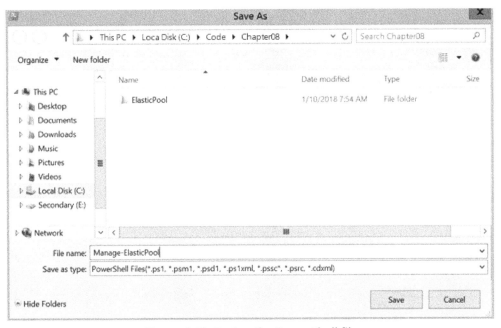

Figure 8.13: Saving the PowerShell file

2. Copy and paste the following code snippets (from *step 2* to *step 6*) into the `Manage-ElasticPool.ps1` file, one after another. The code's explanation, wherever required, is given in the steps and in the comments within the code snippet.

Copy and paste the following code to define the script parameters:

```
param
(
[parameter(Mandatory=$true)] [String] $ResourceGroup,
[parameter(Mandatory=$true)] [String] $SqlServer,
[parameter(Mandatory=$true)] [String] $UserName,
[parameter(Mandatory=$true)] [String] $Password,
[parameter(Mandatory=$true)] [String] $ElasticPoolName,
[parameter(Mandatory=$false)] [String] $ElasticPoolEdition,
[parameter(Mandatory=$false)] [int] $eDTU,
[parameter(Mandatory=$false)] [int] $MaxeDTU,
[parameter(Mandatory=$false)] [int] $MineDTU=0,
[parameter(Mandatory=$false)]
[String] $AzureProfileFilePath,
[parameter(Mandatory=$false)]
# Create/Remove an elastic Pool [String] $Operation = "Create",
# Comma delimited list of databases to be added to the pool
[parameter(Mandatory=$false)]
[String] $DatabasesToAdd
)
```

The parameter descriptions are as follows:

- **ResourceGroup**: The name of the resource group in which the elastic database pool will be created. It should be the same as that of the SQL server.
- **SqlServer**: The SQL server name in which the elastic database pool has to be created.
- **UserName**: The SQL Server database admin username.
- **Password**: The SQL Server database admin password.
- **ElasticPoolName**: The name of the elastic database pool to be created or deleted.
- **eDTU**: The elastic database pool eDTU.
- **MaxeDTU**: The maximum eDTUs available per database in the pool.
- **MineDTU**: The minimum eDTUs available per database in the pool.
- **AzureProfileFilePath**: The full path of the JSON file that has your Azure profile information.
- **Operation**: The operation to be performed. Accepts two values: **Create** and **Remove**.
- **DatabasesToAdd**: A comma-delimited list of the databases to be added to the elastic database pool.

3. Copy and paste the following code to log in to Microsoft Azure and set the Azure context to your subscription:

```
# log the execution of the script
Start-Transcript -Path ".\Log\Manage-ElasticPool.txt" -Append

# Set AzureProfileFilePath relative to the script directory if it's not
provided as parameter

if([string]::IsNullOrEmpty($AzureProfileFilePath))
{
$AzureProfileFilePath="..\..\MyAzureProfile.json"
}

#Login to Azure Account

if((Test-Path -Path $AzureProfileFilePath))
{
$profile - Select-AzProfile -Path $AzureProfileFilePath
$SubscriptionID = $profile.Context.Subscription.SubscriptionId
}
else
{
Write-Host "File Not Found $AzureProfileFilePath"
-ForegroundColor Red
# Provide your Azure Credentials in the login dialog box
$profile = Login-AzAccount
$SubscriptionID =
        $profile.Context.Subscription.SubscriptionId
}

#Set the Azure Context
Set-AzContext -SubscriptionId $SubscriptionID | Out-Null
```

The preceding code starts by logging in to the **Manage-ElasticPool.txt** file created in the **Log** directory within the parent directory of the **Manage-ElasticPool.ps1** script.

It then checks for the profile information in the **json** file provided by the **AzureProfileFilePath** variable. If found, then it sets the PowerShell context to the subscription ID, as specified in the profile file. Otherwise, it asks the user to manually log in to the Azure account to set the context.

4. Create the elastic database pool using the following script, if it doesn't already exist:

```
#Check if the pool exists
Get-AzSqlElasticPool -ElasticPoolName $ElasticPoolName
-ServerName $SqlServer -ResourceGroupName $ResourceGroup
-ErrorVariable notexists -ErrorAction SilentlyContinue

if($Operation -eq "Create")
{
if([string]::IsNullOrEmpty($ElasticPoolEdition))
{
Write-Host "Please provide a valid value for Elastic Pool Edition (Basic/
Standard/Premium)" -ForegroundColor yellow
Write-Host "Exiting...." -ForegroundColor Yellow break;
}


Write-Host "Creating elastic pool $ElasticPoolName "
-ForegroundColor Green
# Create elastic pool if it doesn't exists if($notexists)
{
$CreateElasticPool = @{
ElasticPoolName = $ElasticPoolName; Edition = $ElasticPoolEdition; Dtu =
$eDTU; DatabaseDtuMin = $MineDTU; DatabaseDtuMax = $MaxeDTU; ServerName =
$SqlServer;
ResourceGroupName = $ResourceGroup;
};
New-AzSqlElasticPool @CreateElasticPool;

}
else
{
Write-Host "Elastic pool $ElasticPoolName already exists!!!"
-ForegroundColor Green
}
if([string]::IsNullOrEmpty($DatabasesToAdd) -and $Operation -eq "Create")
{
Write-Host "Please provide a valid value for DatabasesToAdd parameter"
-ForegroundColor yellow
Write-Host "Exiting...." -ForegroundColor Yellow break;
}}
```

The preceding code uses the **Get-AzSqlElasticPool** cmdlet to get the details of the given elastic database pool name. If the elastic database pool with the specified name is found in the given resource group, it succeeds; otherwise, it returns an error: **"Get-AzSqlElasticPool ResourceNotFound: The Resource 'Microsoft.Sql/ servers/ toyfactory/elasticpools/adasdas' under resource group 'toystore' was not found"**.

The error is recorded in the **notexists** variable specified in the **ErrorVariable** parameter.

The code then uses **New-AzSqlElasticPool** to create the elastic database pool if the specified operation is **Create** (the **$operation** parameter) and the **$notexists** variable isn't empty.

5. Copy and paste the following code to add the databases to the elastic database pool:

```
# Add databases to the pool if([string]::IsNullOrEmpty($DatabasesToAdd)
-and $Operation -eq "Create")
{
Write-Host "Please provide a valid value for DatabasesToAdd parameter"
-ForegroundColor yellow
Write-Host "Exiting...." -ForegroundColor Yellow break;
}
$Databases = $DatabasesToAdd.Split(',');
foreach($db in $Databases)
{
Write-Host "Adding database $db to elastic pool $ElasticPoolName "
-ForegroundColor Green
Set-AzSqlDatabase -ResourceGroupName $ResourceGroup
-ServerName $SqlServer -DatabaseName $db -ElasticPoolName
$ElasticPoolName
}
}
```

The preceding code splits the comma-delimited values, as specified in **$DatabasesToAdd**. It adds the separate string values (database names) into an array variable database. It then iterates through each of the databases in the array and sets the elastic database pool using the **Set-AzSqlDatabase** cmdlet.

6. Copy and paste the following code to remove or delete an existing elastic database pool:

```
#remove an elastic pool

if($Operation -eq "Remove")
{
#Get all databases in the elastic pool
$epdbs = Get-AzSqlElasticPoolDatabase -ElasticPoolName
$ElasticPoolName -ServerName $SqlServer -ResourceGroupName
$ResourceGroup

# iterate through the databases and take them out of the pool.
foreach($item in $epdbs)
{
$db = $item.DatabaseName;

#Take database out of pool
Write-Host "Taking database $db out of elastic pool $ElasticPoolName "
-ForegroundColor Green
$RemoveDbsFromPool = @{ ResourceGroupName = $ResourceGroup; ServerName =
$SqlServer; DatabaseName = $db;
Edition = 'Basic'; RequestedServiceObjectiveName = 'Basic';
};
Set-AzSqlDatabase @RemoveDbsFromPool;
}

#Remove elastic pool
Write-Host "Removing Elastic Pool $ElasticPoolName "
-ForegroundColor Green
$RemovePool = @{
ResourceGroupName = $ResourceGroup; ServerName = $SqlServer;
ElasticPoolName = $ElasticPoolName;
};

Remove-AzSqlElasticPool @RemovePool -Force;

}
```

The preceding code only works when the **$operation** parameter is set to **Remove**. An elastic database pool can't be removed or deleted if it has databases assigned to it. First, the code gets all the databases in an elastic database pool using the **Get-AzSqlElasticPoolDatabase** cmdlet.

It then iterates through each database and takes them out of the elastic database pool using **Set-AzSqlDatabase**. It then removes the elastic database pool using the **Remove-AzSqlElasticPool** cmdlet.

This completes the script. Click **Save** from the **File** menu or press *Ctrl* + S to save the script. We'll now look at executing the PowerShell script we've just created:

1. Press the *Windows* + R keys to open the **Run** command window. Type **PowerShell** and hit *Enter* to open a new PowerShell console window.

    Change the directory to the folder that has the **Manage-ElasticPool.ps1** script in it. For example, if the script is in the **C:\Code\Chapter08** directory, then run the following command to switch to this directory:

    ```
    cd C:\Code\Chapter08
    ```

2. To delete an existing elastic database pool, execute the following command. You will have to change the parameter values as per your environment:

    ```
    .\Manage-ElasticPool.ps1 -ResourceGroup toystore
    -SqlServer toyfactory -UserName sqladmin -Password Packt@
    pub2 -ElasticPoolName toyfactorypool -Operation Remove
    -AzureProfileFilePath C:\Code\MyAzureProfile. Json
    ```

    > **Note**
    >
    > If you created **toyfactorypool** earlier in the chapter, then run this command to delete the elastic database pool. If you don't have an existing elastic database pool, then proceed to the next step, which is creating an elastic database pool. If you have an existing pool and you don't want to remove it, then you will have to create an elastic database pool and a separate set of databases for it.

3. To create a new elastic database pool and add databases to it, execute the following command. You will have to change the parameter values as per your environment:

    ```
    .\Manage-ElasticPool.ps1 -ResourceGroup toystore -SqlServer toyfactory
    -UserName sqladmin -Password Packt@pub2
    -ElasticPoolName toyfactorypool -ElasticPoolEdition Standard
    -eDTU 100 -MaxeDTU 100 -MineDTU 10 -AzureProfileFilePath C:\Code\
    MyAzureProfile.json -Operation Create -DatabasesToAdd "toystore_
    Shard_1_50,toystore_Shard_50_100,toystore_Shard_100_150,toystore_
    Shard_150_200"
    ```

The preceding command will create **toyfactoryelasticpool** with **100** eDTUs and the databases specified by the **DatabasesToAdd** parameter.

In this activity, we created and executed a PowerShell script to create an elastic database pool and add databases to the elastic database pool. As an elastic database pool consists of multiple databases, there may be a scenario or a requirement to execute T-SQL scripts across all databases in an elastic database pool. This is done using elastic database jobs. Let's now learn about and implement elastic database jobs in the next section.

Elastic database jobs

Elastic database jobs or Azure-hosted elastic database jobs can be used to schedule a T-SQL task such as index maintenance against an SQL database, a group of SQL Database elastic database pools or an SQL Database shard, all databases in an elastic database pool, a shard map, or a server across different Azure subscriptions.

An elastic database job can span multiple databases in the same subscription or in different subscriptions.

Figure 8.14 illustrates the different components of an elastic database job:

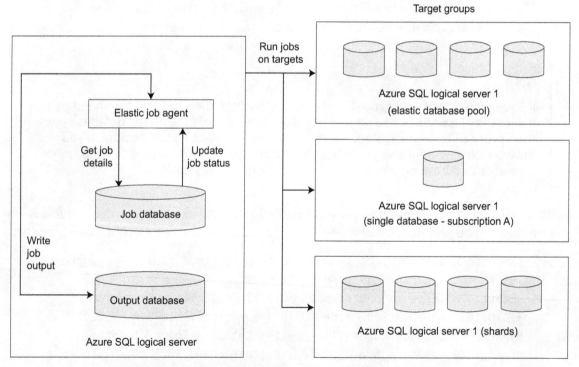

Figure 8.14: Different components of an elastic database job

Let's discuss some of the components in the diagram.

Elastic job agent

An elastic job agent is an Azure resource that's responsible for creating, executing, and managing jobs.

Job database

An existing clean (blank) SQL database of the Standard (S0) or a higher-performance tier is used to store the job definitions, job status, elastic job agent metadata, and stored procedures to create and manage elastic database jobs using T-SQL.

The database job performance tier can be increased based on the number of jobs scheduled and the frequency of the job scheduler; however, a minimum of the General Purpose or S1 pricing tier is recommended.

Target group

A target group defines one or more SQL databases that a job is executed on. A target group can be:

- A single SQL database.

- An Azure SQL logical server. All databases in the server at the time of job creation are considered for job execution.

- An elastic database pool. All databases in an elastic database pool at the time of job creation are considered for job execution.

- A shardmap. All databases in a shardmap.

> **Note**
>
> Particular databases can be included or excluded individually when defining an SQL logical server or an elastic database pool as the target group.

Jobs

A job is a task that can either be scheduled or executed on demand against one or more target groups. A job can have one or more job steps. A job step requires a T-SQL script to be executed and the credentials to connect to the database(s) defined by the target group. The job output can optionally be stored in a specified output database (an SQL Database) in detail.

The job database stores the job execution history in detail. The job history is purged every 45 days by a system clean-up job. The job history can be manually purged using the `sp_purge_history` stored procedure against the job database. The elastic database jobs preview is limited to 100 concurrent jobs at any given time.

Use cases

Elastic database jobs are commonly used for:

- **Database management and maintenance**: Elastic database jobs can be used for deploying schema changes across multiple shards by running database maintenance jobs, such as index rebuilds, collecting database performance data, and updating reference data in a shard set.

- **Reporting**: Elastic database jobs can be used to aggregate data from a shard set and into a single reporting table. The reporting table can then be fed to Power BI, SSRS, or any of the reporting or visualization tools for creating reports.

Normally, you would have to connect to each shard in a shard set to run the report query and insert the data into a single reporting table. Elastic database jobs make it easier to do this, wherein you only have to schedule the T-SQL and it is automatically executed on the shards.

Exercise: Configuring an elastic database job using T-SQL

In this exercise, we'll talk about configuring an elastic database job using T-SQL. An elastic database job can also be configured using PowerShell. When configuring elastic database jobs using T-SQL, the elastic database job agent needs to be provisioned either using PowerShell or the Azure portal.

Follow these steps to create an elastic database job:

1. Provision a blank SQL database to be used as the job database by executing the following script in a PowerShell console window:

    ```
    C:\Code\Chapter01\Provision-AzureSQLDatabase.ps1 -ResourceGroup Packt
    -Location "East US 2" -SQLServer packtdbserver
    -SQLDatabase jobdatabase -Edition Standard -UserName dbadmin -Password
    Awesome@1234 -ServiceObjective S0
    ```

    The preceding command creates a Standard S0 blank SQL database, **jobdatabase**, to be used for the elastic database job.

    You may have to change the database name as you may get an error if **jobdatabase** already exists in Microsoft Azure.

2. We now need to create an Elastic Job agent.

    Log in to the Azure portal and search for **Elastic job agent**:

Figure 8.15: Creating an Elastic Job agent

On the **Elastic Job agents** page, click **Add**:

Figure 8.16: Adding a new Elastic Job agent

In the **Elastic Job agent** window, provide the elastic job agent name, accept the preview terms, and select the `jobdatabase` instance provisioned in *step* 1 as the elastic job agent database.

3. Click the **Create** button to provision the elastic job agent:

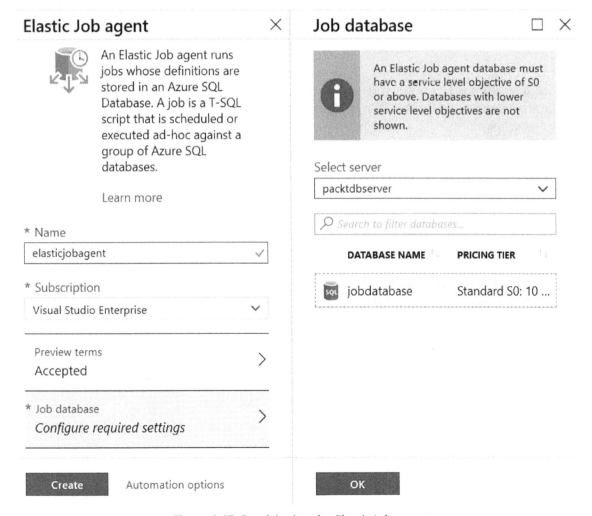

Figure 8.17: Provisioning the Elastic Job agent

4. Once an elastic job agent is provisioned, it'll be listed on the **Elastic Job agents** page:

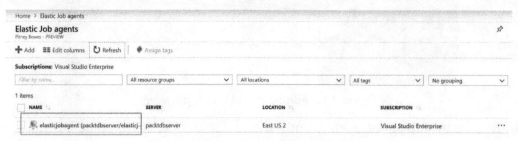

Figure 8.18: The Elastic Job agents page

> **Note**
>
> As the feature is still in preview, you may not see the elastic job agent listed here. For details, please visit https://social.msdn.microsoft.com/Forums/69043053-5de3-40da-8e81-cbfa0ac8363a/elastic-job-agent-exists-but-not-showing-in-azure-portal?forum=ssdsgetstarted.

5. The next step is to create the credentials for the job to connect to the target database and execute the T-SQL queries. To create credentials for the job, follow these steps.

    Create a database-scoped credential in **jobdatabase** to connect to the target master database:

    ```
    CREATE MASTER KEY ENCRYPTION BY PASSWORD = 'Very$trongpass123';
    GO
    CREATE DATABASE SCOPED CREDENTIAL jobmastercred
    WITH IDENTITY = 'masteruser' , SECRET = 'myPassword@123'
    ```

    Create a database-scoped credential for **jobdatabase** to connect to the individual target database in a given target group:

    ```
    CREATE DATABASE SCOPED CREDENTIAL jobusercred
    WITH IDENTITY = 'jobuser', SECRET = 'myPassword@123'
    ```

    Create a login in the target master database with the same identity and password as that of the **jobmastercred** credential in the job database:

    ```
    CREATE LOGIN masteruser WITH PASSWORD='myPassword@123'
    ```

    Create a user in the target master database for the **masteruser** login created previously:

    ```
    CREATE USER masteruser FROM LOGIN masteruser
    ```

Create a login in the target master database with the same identity as the **jobusercred** credentials in the job database:

```
CREATE LOGIN jobuser WITH PASSWORD='myPassword@123'
```

Create a user in the target user database for the **jobcred** login. Grant the user relevant permission to run the T-SQL script, which is to be run as part of the elastic database job:

```
--Execute against toystore (or user) database.
CREATE USER jobuser FROM LOGIN jobuser
GO
GRANT ALTER ON SCHEMA::dbo to jobuser
GO
GRANT CREATE TABLE TO jobuser
```

The preceding scripts create a **jobuser** user for the **jobuser** login and grant the user permission to create tables against the **toystore** database.

6. The next step is to add the target group. To add an SQL logical server as a target group, execute the following scripts in **jobdatabase** (the elastic job agent database).

Add a target group:

```
EXEC jobs.sp_add_target_group 'packtdbserver'
GO
```

Add a server target member:

```
EXEC jobs.sp_add_target_group_member 'packtdbserver'
,@target_type = 'SqlServer'
,@refresh_credential_name = 'jobmastercred'
,@server_name = 'packtdbserver.database.windows.net'
```

referesh_credential_name is the name of the credential created in **jobdatabase** to connect to the target group master database to refresh the list of databases in the target group SQL logical server.

packtdbserver also contains **jobdatabase**. However, we would not like the job to run against **jobdatabase**. To exclude **jobdatabase** from the target group, execute the following:

```
EXEC [jobs].sp_add_target_group_member @target_group_name =
N'packtdbserver'
,@membership_type = N'Exclude'
,@target_type = N'SqlDatabase'
,@server_name = N'packtdbserver.database.windows.net'
,@database_name = N'jobdatabase'
GO
```

The **membership_type** value **Exclude** tells the job that the given database is to be excluded from the job execution.

To see the existing target group and target group members, run the following query:

```
SELECT *
FROM jobs.target_groups
WHERE target_group_name = 'packtdbserver';


SELECT target_group_name,membership_type,target_type,refresh_credential_
name,server_name,database_name
FROM jobs.target_group_members
WHERE target_group_name = 'packtdbserver';
```

You should get an output similar to this:

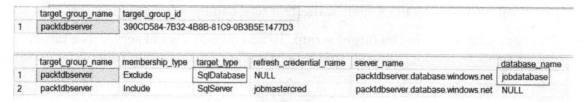

	target_group_name	target_group_id
1	packtdbserver	390CD584-7B32-4B8B-81C9-0B3B5E1477D3

	target_group_name	membership_type	target_type	refresh_credential_name	server_name	database_name
1	packtdbserver	Exclude	SqlDatabase	NULL	packtdbserver.database.windows.net	jobdatabase
2	packtdbserver	Include	SqlServer	jobmastercred	packtdbserver.database.windows.net	NULL

Figure 8.19: Existing target group and target group members

The **jobdatabase** SQL database is excluded from the target group members.

7. The next step is to create an elastic database job that creates a customer table on the target members.

    To create a job, execute the following:

```
EXEC jobs.sp_add_job @job_name = 'CreateCustomerTable'
,@description = 'Create new customer table'
--The query creates a job name, CreateCustomerTable. Let's now add a
---job step to create the customer table.
EXEC jobs.sp_add_jobstep @job_name = 'CreateCustomerTable'
,@step_name = 'CreateTable'
,@command = N'IF OBJECT_ID(''Customer'') IS NULL
CREATE TABLE [dbo].[Customer] (ID int identity(1,1),FirstName
NVARCHAR(100),LastName NVARCHAR(100))'
,@credential_name = 'jobusercred'
,@target_group_name = 'packtdbserver'
```

The query adds a **CreateTable** job step to the **CreateCustomerTable** job. The command parameter specifies the T-SQL to create the customer table. The T-SQL first checks that a customer table exists; if not, it creates a new one. The T-SQL query will therefore not error out if a customer table already exists in any of the user databases in the target group.

Observe that the **jobusercred** credential, mapped to **jobuser**, is used to run the job.

8. The next step is to execute and schedule the job. Run the following query to execute the job on demand:

> **Note**
>
> *Step 8* and *step 9* should be executed as a single code block.

```
DECLARE @jeid UNIQUEIDENTIFIER
,@lifecycle VARCHAR(100) = 'Created'
-- start job execution
EXEC jobs.sp_start_job 'CreateCustomerTable'
,@job_execution_id = @jeid OUTPUT

SELECT @jeid
```

9. Get the job execution status:

```
SELECT *
FROM jobs.job_executions
WHERE job_execution_id = @jeid

/*
Make sure Allow access to Azure services firewall rule is On
*/
WHILE (@lifecycle != 'Succeeded') BEGIN
SELECT *
FROM jobs.job_executions
WHERE job_execution_id = @jeid
-- check job status until it succeeds SELECT @lifecycle = lifecycle
FROM jobs.job_executions
WHERE job_execution_id = @jeid ORDER BY start_time DESC

WAITFOR DELAY '00:00:02'
END
```

The **jobs.sp_start_job** procedure is used to start an ad hoc run of a job. When a job starts, a unique job execution ID is assigned for that particular job run.

The job status is saved in the **jobs.job_execution** table. The **while** loop gets the job status until it succeeds. You should get the following output:

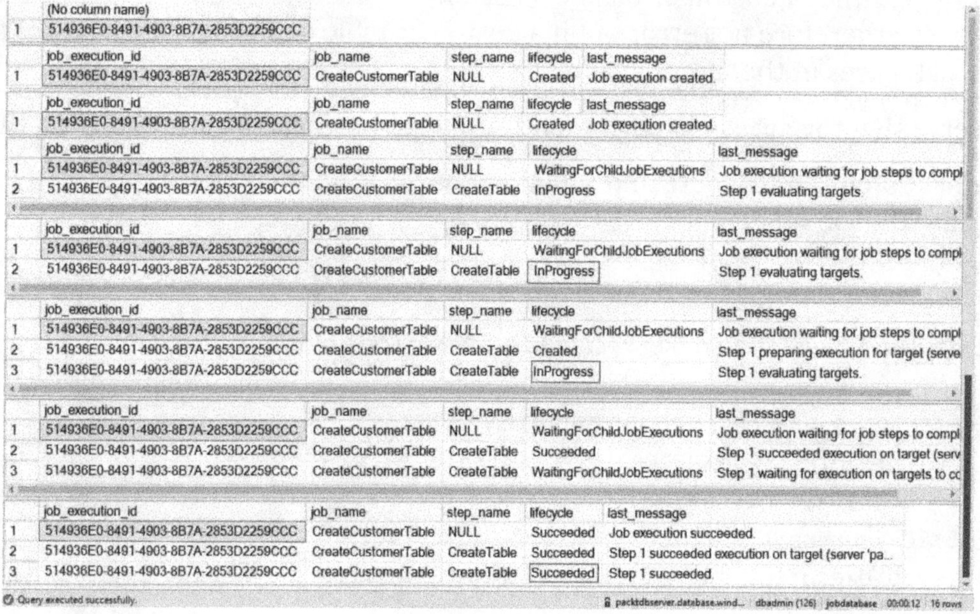

Figure 8.20: Job execution status

Figure 8.20 shows the job status at different stages of the job execution. The next step is to schedule the job.

10. Schedule the job by executing the following query:

```
EXEC jobs.sp_update_job @job_name = 'CreateCustomerTable'
,@enabled = 1
,@schedule_interval_type = 'Minutes'
,@schedule_interval_count = 15
```

11. The query uses the **sp_update_job** stored procedure to schedule the job to run every 15 minutes. To get the job details, execute the following queries.

Get the job and job step details:

```
SELECT job_name,enabled,schedule_interval_type,schedule_interval_count
FROM jobs.jobs
WHERE job_name = 'CreateCustomerTable';
GO
SELECT js.job_name,js.step_name,js.command_type,js.command,js.credential_
name,js.target_group_name FROM jobs.jobsteps js
JOIN jobs.jobs j ON j.job_id = js.job_id
AND j.job_version = js.job_version
GO
```

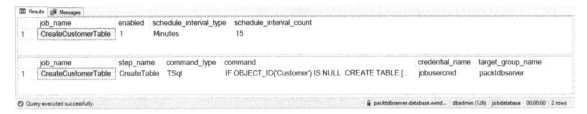

Figure 8.21: Job and job step details

You can also monitor the jobs from the Azure portal. Log in to the portal and open the **elasticjobagent** page:

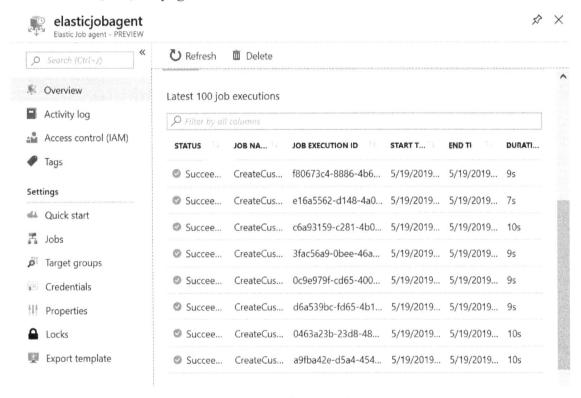

Figure 8.22: Monitoring latest 100 job executions

The **Overview** section lists the last 100 job executions. You can also check the **Credentials**, **Target groups**, and **Jobs** sections. However, the Azure portal doesn't allow the editing of any of the job objects.

Elastic database jobs provide similar functionality for SQL Database as SQL Server Agent does for the on-premises SQL Server.

Elastic database jobs are optimized and designed for SQL databases. Elastic databases, therefore, support the running of T-SQL queries against databases in the specified target group.

The other job types supported by SQL Server Agent, such as PowerShell, WMI, batch file, Integration Services, and Analysis Services, are not supported by elastic database jobs. This goes along with the PaaS model of SQL Database, wherein customers don't manage the underlying infrastructure.

SQL Server Agent, on the other hand, is designed to run on-premises and can therefore be used for job types other than T-SQL. An example is to schedule a PowerShell script to automate database backups of the on-premises databases. This, however, isn't required in SQL Database as the backups are automated.

SQL Server Agent doesn't support a target group. An SQL Server Agent job step can be run against only one database. The T-SQL script scheduled can, however, access other databases in the instance. Elastic database jobs can dynamically enumerate through databases in a server or a pool at runtime and run scripts against them. This particularly helps SaaS customers where databases are added/deleted at various times. Elastic jobs can span databases or pools across servers and subscriptions.

Elastic database jobs make it easy to schedule jobs such as schema deployment or database maintenance. For example, to run index maintenance on two or more databases, schedule an elastic database job with the index maintenance T-SQL script to run against the target group. The elastic database job runs the job asynchronously against the specified target databases. However, when scheduling the index maintenance job with SQL Server Agent, the database iteration logic is to be written as part of the script itself. SQL Server Agent doesn't support the target group concept.

Introducing instance pools in SQL Managed Instance

Instance pools in SQL Managed Instance is a new deployment option and it's currently in the public preview phase. Instance pools allow you to run small compute managed instances in a pre-provisioned compute pool. This is a more cost-effective and convenient way of migrating small SQL Server instances to a managed instance.

Instance pools allow you to provision 2 vCore instances inside a pre-provisioned pool. If you have provisioned an 8 vCore instance pool, you can deploy four 2 vCore SQL managed instances in that pool. Prior to instance pools being available, smaller instance databases needed to be consolidated during migration to the cloud, which required careful capacity planning, resource governance, and security considerations.

Figure 8.23 shows a high-level overview of an instance pool and a managed instance deployed within a virtual network subnet:

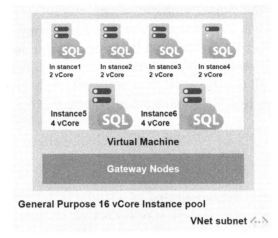

Figure 8.23: High-level overview of an instance pool

Figure 8.23 shows a 16 vCore pre-provisioned instance pool that comprises four 2 vCore instances and two 4 vCore instances that are deployed in the same virtual machine, subnet, and virtual cluster.

Key differences between an instance pool and a single managed instance

Instance pools provide a lot of flexibility in deploying managed instances. Instances can be deployed with independent compute and storage layers.

The following are some of the key differences between an instance pool and a single SQL managed instance:

Instance Pool	Single SQL Managed Instance
Only the General Purpose service tier is supported.	The General Purpose and Business Critical service tiers are supported.
Allows you to create a minimum of 2 vCore SQL managed instances.	A minimum of 4 vCore instances can be deployed.
The initial creation of an instance pool takes longer but SQL Managed Instance management operations are very quick.	Initial deployment and management operations take longer to complete.
The same node is shared to deploy all instances.	Separate nodes for each instance deployment.
Minimal IP address allocation due to sharing of a virtual machine for all instance deployment.	Require additional IP addresses for each instance deployment.
Azure AD authentication is not supported.	Azure AD authentication is supported.

Table 8.1: Differences between an instance pool and a single SQL managed instance

As we saw in *Table 8.1*, all the managed instances are deployed in the same virtual machine node. This node was pre-provisioned with a specified vCore capacity during instance pool creation. After the initial pool deployment, management operations (instance creation and vCore scaling) on instances are much faster than a single SQL managed instance. Since all the instances are deployed in the same virtual machine, an instance pool requires less IP address allocation compared to a single instance.

Architecture differences between an instance pool and a single SQL managed instance

Instance pool architecture is similar to that of a single SQL managed instance. The main difference between the two deployment models is that an instance pool allows you to create multiple instances on the same virtual machine node, which are resources governed by Windows job objects. Job objects allow groups of multiple processes to be managed as a unit, while single managed instances always run in a separate virtual machine node:

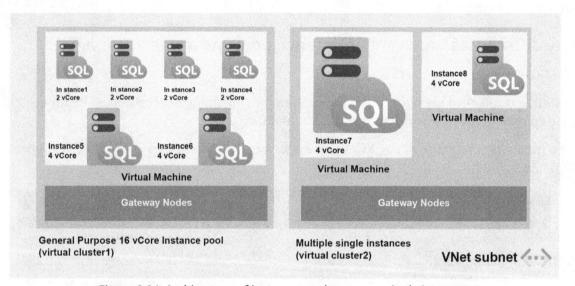

Figure 8.24: Architecture of instance pools versus a single instance

Resource limits

Instance pools have the following resource limitations:

- Instance pools support 8, 16, 24, 32, 40, 64, and 80 vCores.

- Managed instances inside pools support 2, 4, 8, 16, 24, 32, 40, 64, and 80 vCores.

- Managed instances inside pools support storage sizes between 32 GB and 8 TB, except:

- 2 vCore instances support sizes between 32 GB and 640 GB.

- 4 vCore instances support sizes between 32 GB and 2 TB.

- All instances in instance pools follow all the limitations that apply to a single SQL managed instance.

- You can have up to 500 user databases per instance pool. However, this limit depends on the pool vCore value:

- 8 vCore pool supports up to 200 databases

- 16 vCore pool supports up to 400 databases

- 24 vCore pool and larger supports up to 500 databases

- Managed instances inside pools have a limit of up to 100 user databases per instance, except 2 vCore instances, which support up to 50 user databases per instance.

- The total storage for instance pools can be increased to up to 8 TB.

Public preview limitations

Instance pools are a newly added deployment option for SQL Managed Instance in the SQL family and have the following limitations during the preview period:

- Instance pools are only available in the General Purpose service tier.

- You cannot resize instance pools, so be careful when selecting the vCore capacity.

- You cannot move a single managed instance into a pool and you cannot move instances out of a pool.

- Instance pools have limited Azure portal support and most operations are managed by PowerShell commands.

- Azure AD authentication is not supported.

Microsoft might remove some of the limitations once they announce the instance pools offering for General Availability.

Performance and security considerations for instance pools

Managed instances are deployed in the same virtual machine inside an instance pool, and you need to consider the following performance and security considerations:

- Instances are deployed with dedicated vCPU and RAM, but all instances have a shared local disk for the tempdb database and network resources, so there could be a chance of facing a noisy neighbor situation.

- You might have to consider disabling certain features that might have higher security risks such as CLR, native backup/restore, and database mail.

In the event of performance challenges with instance pools, consider deploying the instances to a bigger pool, or move to a single managed instance.

Deploying an instance pool using PowerShell commands

In this activity, we will learn how to deploy an instance pool for ToyStore Ltd. This instance pool deployment is used to manage low-compute managed instances. Since there is no Azure portal support for instance pools during the public preview phase, we will deploy these resources using PowerShell cmdlets.

You will learn how to deploy an instance pool with 8 vCore capacity with a new virtual network and subnet configuration. Follow these steps to perform this activity.

Before deploying an instance pool, first, we need to prepare a virtual network and subnet. If you are deploying an instance pool in an existing SQL Managed Instance subnet, then this step can be skipped:

1. Prepare a virtual network for the instance pool.

    To set up a new virtual network, you might need help from network admins in your organization. Alternatively, you can use an in-built ARM template to create a virtual network resource with all the pre-requisites needed to deploy a managed instance or instance pool. Please visit the following link to read more about ARM template deployment and see the steps to create a virtual network using an ARM template: https://docs.microsoft.com/azure/azure-sql/managed-instance/virtual-network-subnet-create-arm-template.

    Direct Template link: https://portal.azure.com#createMicrosoft. Templateurihttps%3A%2F%2Fraw.githubusercontent.com%2FAzure%2Fazure-quickstart-templates%2Fmaster%2F101-sql-managed-instance-azure-environment%2Fazuredeploy.json

When you visit the preceding link, it will redirect you to the Azure portal and you will see the following template deployment screen:

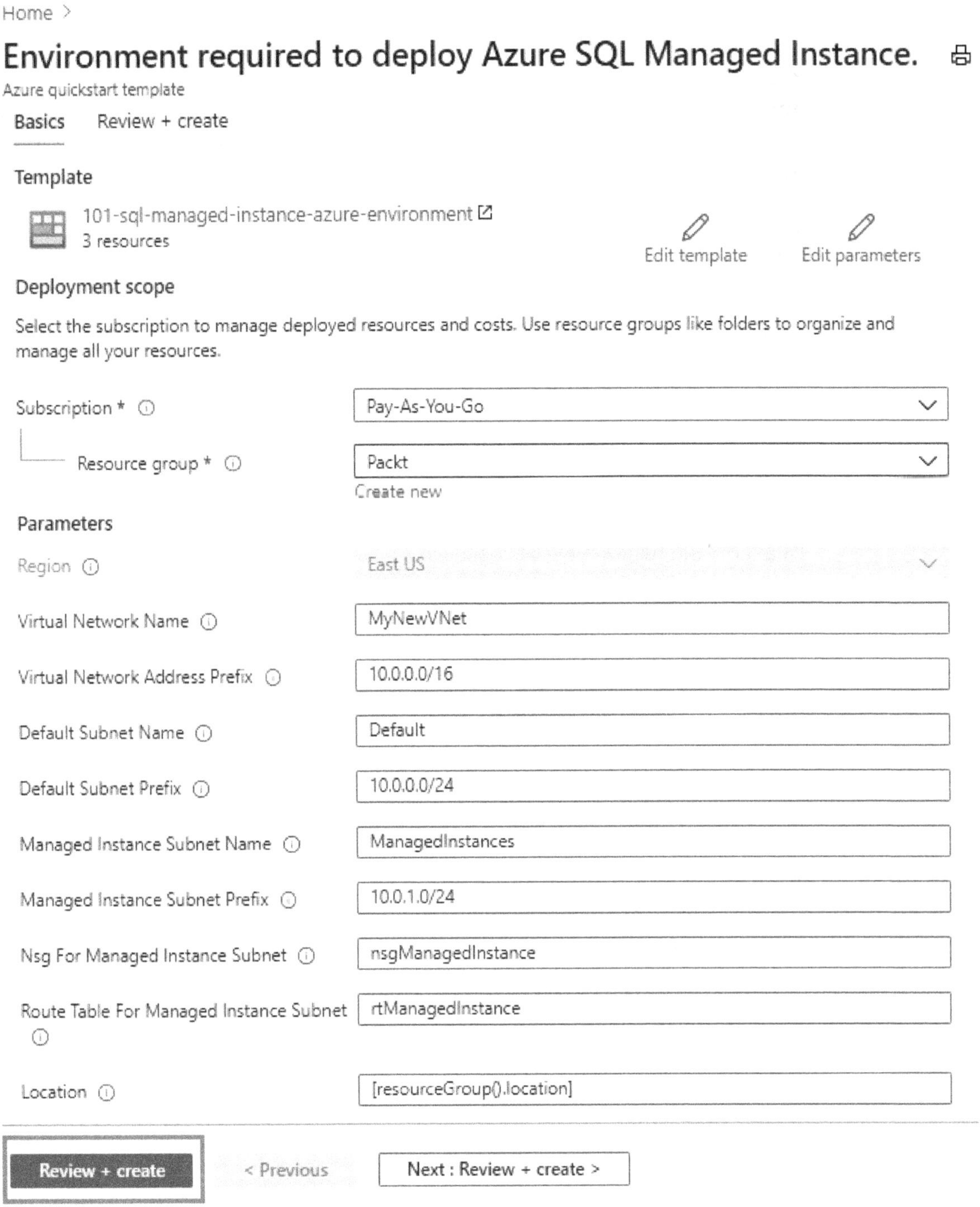

Home >

Environment required to deploy Azure SQL Managed Instance. 🖨

Azure quickstart template

Basics   Review + create

Template

▦ 101-sql-managed-instance-azure-environment ☑
3 resources

✎ Edit template   ✎ Edit parameters

Deployment scope

Select the subscription to manage deployed resources and costs. Use resource groups like folders to organize and manage all your resources.

Subscription * ⓘ

Pay-As-You-Go ⌄

└── Resource group * ⓘ

Packt ⌄
Create new

Parameters

Region ⓘ
East US ⌄

Virtual Network Name ⓘ
MyNewVNet

Virtual Network Address Prefix ⓘ
10.0.0.0/16

Default Subnet Name ⓘ
Default

Default Subnet Prefix ⓘ
10.0.0.0/24

Managed Instance Subnet Name ⓘ
ManagedInstances

Managed Instance Subnet Prefix ⓘ
10.0.1.0/24

Nsg For Managed Instance Subnet ⓘ
nsgManagedInstance

Route Table For Managed Instance Subnet ⓘ
rtManagedInstance

Location ⓘ
[resourceGroup().location]

[Review + create]   < Previous   [Next : Review + create >]

Figure 8.25: Creating a new virtual network using an ARM template

In *Figure 8.25*, most of the details are pre-populated and you need to just select the subscription and enter the resource group name. These details can be modified as per your environment. Click **Review + create** after completing the form.

This ARM template will deploy a virtual network with two subnets. One subnet, called `ManagedInstances`, is reserved for managed instance and instance pool deployment and has a pre-configured route table and network security group. The other subnet, with the name `Default`, is used to deploy other resources (such as a virtual machine).

2. With the virtual network ready, let's deploy the instance pool using PowerShell commands. Open `SQLMI_InstancePoolDeployment.ps1` from the `Chapter08` source code and read through the PowerShell statements.

3. Set up the script parameters by running the following PowerShell commands:

```
##Instance pool deployment script
##Setting up parameters

param(

        [Parameter(Mandatory=$true)]
            [string]$resourceGroup,
        [Parameter(Mandatory=$true)]
            [string]$subscription,
            [Parameter(Mandatory=$true)]
            [string]$instancePoolName,
            [Parameter(Mandatory=$true)]
            [string]$vnetName,
        [Parameter(Mandatory=$true)]
            [string]$subnetName,
        [Parameter(Mandatory=$true)]
            [string]$LicenseType,
        [Parameter(Mandatory=$true)]
            [string]$Edition,
        [Parameter(Mandatory=$true)]
        [string]$ComputeGeneration,
        [Parameter(Mandatory=$true)]
            [string]$Location

)
```

4. Log in to your Azure account:

```
Write-Host "Login to Azure account" -ForegroundColor Green


##Login to Azure
#Set Azure subscription for deployment
Login-AzAccount
Select-AzSubscription -SubscriptionId $subscription
```

5. Get the subnet resource ID for instance pool deployment:

```
Write-Host "Get virtual network and subnet configuration" -ForegroundColor
Green
###Get virtual network and subnet configuration
$virtualNetwork = Get-AzVirtualNetwork -Name $vnetName -ResourceGroupName
$resourceGroup
$subnet = Get-AzVirtualNetworkSubnetConfig -Name $subnetName
-VirtualNetwork $virtualNetwork
```

6. Use the **New-AzSqlInstancePool** cmdlet to deploy the instance pool with the specified **vCore** capacity:

```
Write-Host "Deploying instance pool " $instancePoolName -ForegroundColor
Green
#Creating new instance pool with 8-vCore
$instancePool = New-AzSqlInstancePool -ResourceGroupName $resourceGroup
-Name $instancePoolName -SubnetId $subnet.Id -LicenseType $LicenseType
-VCore 8 -Edition $Edition -ComputeGeneration $ComputeGeneration -Location
$Location
```

7. Run the **SQLMI_InstancePoolDeployment.ps1** file from any client of your choice:

```
.\SQLMI_InstancePoolDeployment.ps1 -resourceGroup Packt -subscription
xxxxxxxx-xxxx-xxxx-xxxx-xxxxxxxxxxxx -instancePoolName mi-toyfactory-
pool -vnetName MyNewVNet -subnetName ManagedInstances -LicenseType
LicenseIncluded -Edition GeneralPurpose -ComputeGeneration Gen5 -Location
eastus
```

Figure 8.26: PowerShell commands output

> **Note**
>
> The creation of an instance pool is a long-running operation and generally needs 4.5 hours.

8. Let's check the Azure portal after deployment. The Azure portal shows the empty instance pool with its used capacity:

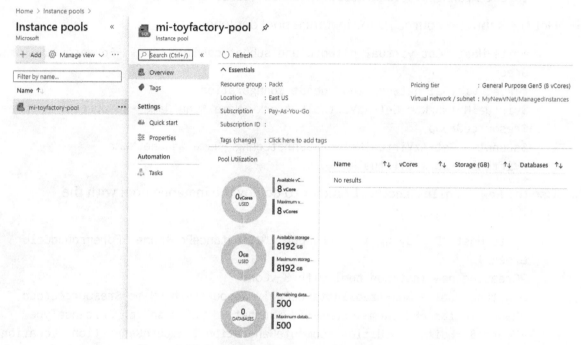

Figure 8.27: An empty instance pool in the Azure portal

In this activity, we created a virtual network using ARM templates to deploy an instance pool. Finally, we checked the pool utilization statistics through the Azure portal.

Activity: Deploying and managing a managed instance in an instance pool

In the previous activity, we deployed an empty instance pool with an 8 vCore capacity. Here, we will see how to provision a managed instance in that pool. We will be deploying a 2 vCore instance and later will scale up to 8 vCores, taking note of how much time it takes to deploy and scale up a new instance in a pre-provisioned pool.

We will be using PowerShell commands since there is no Azure portal support during preview. Let's look at the steps.

Follow these steps to create a managed instance inside an instance pool and scale up instance resources using PowerShell cmdlets:

1. Open Azure Cloud Shell from the Azure portal by clicking the **Cloud Shell** icon:

Figure 8.28: Cloud Shell icon

2. Switch to the PowerShell terminal to run PowerShell code:

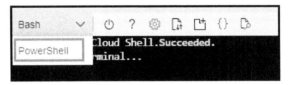

Figure 8.29: Switching to the PowerShell terminal

3. Run the following commands to create a managed instance with a 2 vCore capacity in an instance pool and monitor the deployment time:

```
##Deploying new SQL Managed Instance in pool.
##Get the instance pool properties.
$instancePool = Get-AzSqlInstancePool -ResourceGroupName Packt -Name
mi-toyfactory-pool

#Using measure-command cmdlet to calculate time for new instance
deployment in pool.
Measure-Command {$toystoreInstance = $instancePool | New-AzSqlInstance
-Name mi-toystore-1 -AdministratorCredential (Get-Credential)
-StorageSizeInGB 32 -VCore 2}
```

```
PS /> ##Deploying new SQL Managed Instance in pool.
PS /> ##Get the instance pool properties.
PS /> $instancePool = Get-AzSqlInstancePool -ResourceGroupName Packt -Name mi-toyfactory-pool
PS /> #Using measure-command cmdlet to calculate time for new instance deployment in pool.
PS /> Measure-Command {$toystoreInstance = $instancePool | New-AzSqlInstance -Name mi-toystore-1 -AdministratorCredential (Get-Credential) -StorageSizeInGB 32 -VCore 2}

PowerShell credential request
Enter your credentials.
User: miadmin
Password for user miadmin: *****************


Days             : 0
Hours            : 0
Minutes          : 2
Seconds          : 37
Milliseconds     : 440
Ticks            : 1574402520
TotalDays        : 0.00182222513888889
TotalHours       : 0.0437334033333333
TotalMinutes     : 2.6240042
TotalSeconds     : 157.440252
TotalMilliseconds : 157440.252
```

Figure 8.30: New instance deployment in an instance pool

In *Figure 8.30*, we see that the new instance deployment only took 2 minutes and 37 seconds.

4. Let's look at the Azure portal and see what the new instance pool looks like after the managed instance deployment. Go to the Azure portal, and in the **Overview** tab of the instance pool, click on the managed instance to see its properties:

Figure 8.31: Instance pool-Overview

In *Figure 8.31*, you can see that the `mi-toystore-1` managed instance with a 2 vCore capacity is deployed in the instance pool `mi-toyfactory-pool`.

5. Once you click on the managed instance (`mi-toystore-1`), it will redirect you to the managed instance **Overview** tab, which displays the host, admin account, and instance pool information. Also, you can use the **New database** option to create a managed database using the Azure portal:

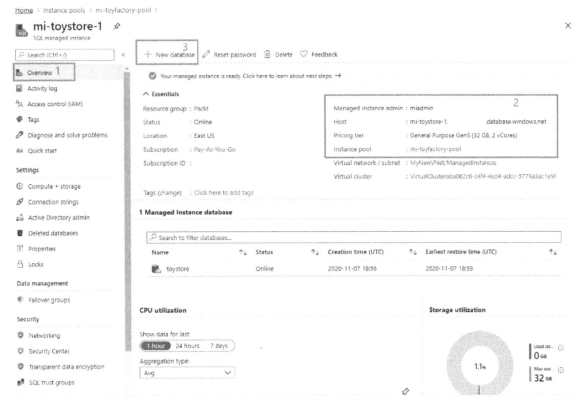

Figure 8.32: Managed instance Overview

6. After adding/migrating multiple databases on the same instance, you might hit the resource limits or face performance challenges. You can scale up instance resources if you have available capacity in the instance pool. Scaling pooled managed instance resources takes only a few minutes.

Run the following command using the same Cloud Shell session:

```
#Scaling SQL Managed Instance resources
Measure-Command {$toystoreInstance | Set-AzSqlInstance -VCore 8
-StorageSizeInGB 512 -InstancePoolName "mi-toyfactory-pool"}
```

```
PS /> Measure-Command {$toystoreInstance | Set-AzSqlInstance -VCore 8 -StorageSizeInGB 512 -InstancePoolName "mi-toyfactory-pool"}

Are you sure you want to set the Azure Sql Database Managed Instance ''?
Setting Azure Sql Database Managed Instance ''.
[Y] Yes  [N] No  [S] Suspend  [?] Help (default is "Y"): Y


Days              : 0
Hours             : 0
Minutes           : 6
Seconds           : 11
Milliseconds      : 942
Ticks             : 3719428322
TotalDays         : 0.0043048938912037
TotalHours        : 0.103317453388889
TotalMinutes      : 6.19904720333333
TotalSeconds      : 371.9428322
TotalMilliseconds : 371942.8322
```

Figure 8.33: Scaling a managed instance in a pool

As we can see, the scaling operation took 6 minutes and 11 seconds to complete. This is much faster than single managed instance scaling, which takes hours.

7. Let's check the instance pool resource usage after the scaling operation using the Azure portal:

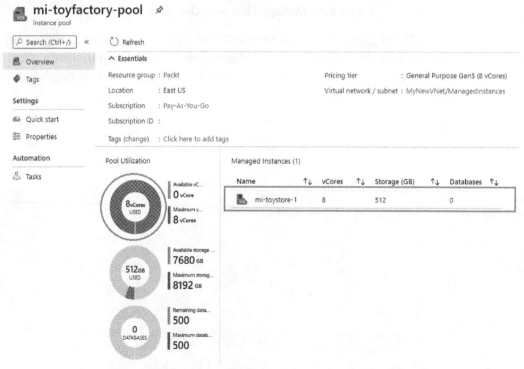

Figure 8.34: Instance pool resource usage after scaling

After the scaling operation, we have exhausted the CPU capacity, but storage and database capacity is still available. If more CPU is required, then the instance needs to be migrated to a bigger instance pool. For the migration of databases from one pooled instance to another pooled instance, the cross-instance point-in-time restore method can be used, which we discussed in *Chapter 5, Restoration*. This method is only supported for the same region and subscription.

In this activity, we learned about the creation of a managed instance in an instance pool. We up-scaled the instance resources within the pool and noted the completion times for deployment and scaling operations in the pre-provisioned pool.

An instance pool gives you the flexibility to manage resources in an easier way, since management operations such as creation and scaling only require a couple of minutes. Scaling a single managed instance takes longer since it must resize the virtual cluster for new capacity, and here, we had already provisioned resources in advance at the time of instance pool creation.

Summary

In this chapter, we learned a simple and cost-effective way of managing multiple SQL databases using an elastic database pool and also learned a convenient way of consolidating low-compute managed instances inside an instance pool. We discussed when and how to use an elastic database pool and an instance pool to be cost-effective without affecting database performance. We also learned how to use elastic database jobs to manage and maintain the databases in an elastic database pool.

In the next chapter, we will be discussing high availability and business continuity solutions for SQL Database and SQL Managed Instance. You will learn how to implement standard geo-replication, active geo-recovery, and failover groups for disaster recovery solutions.

High availability and disaster recovery

High availability and disaster recovery planning is essential to any database service or application deployment. In an on-premises SQL Server, database administrators have multiple options to configure high availability and disaster recovery solutions.

In this chapter, we will talk about high availability and disaster recovery options available for Azure SQL Database and SQL Managed Instance. Azure SQL Database and SQL Managed Instance come with built-in high availability and easily configurable disaster recovery solutions.

By the end of this chapter, you will be able to do the following:

- Describe the built-in high availability features in Azure SQL Database and Azure SQL Managed Instance
- Implement standard and active geo-recovery for **Disaster Recovery (DR)** solutions
- Implement standard and active geo-replication
- Implement the Accelerated Database Recovery feature
- Implement a failover group for Azure SQL Database and SQL Managed Instance

This chapter will teach you about the built-in high availability features in Azure SQL Database and SQL Managed Instance. It'll also teach you how to implement a DR solution using geo-replication and failover groups.

High availability

High availability refers to providing service availability in case of any hardware, software, or network failure. Azure SQL guarantees up to 99.995% availability of service. Although Azure SQL Database and SQL Managed Instance are resilient to transitive infrastructure failures, such events might impact application connectivity. Applications can handle these failures by employing retry logic in code.

Azure SQL Database and SQL Managed Instance can quickly recover in the most critical situations, ensuring that your data is always available.

The availability of SQL Database and SQL Managed Instance depends on the service tier and underlying architecture model. Let's take a look at the high availability architecture models based on service tier configuration.

The basic, standard, and general-purpose service tier locally redundant availability model

This architecture is based on the separation of the compute and storage layers to ensure data availability; it is similar to **failover cluster instances (FCIs)**. The architecture depends on Azure premium storage high availability and reliability.

> **Note**
>
> This is similar to an SQL Server (on-premises or SQL on Azure Virtual Machine) failover cluster installation.

Let's look at the high-level architecture diagram:

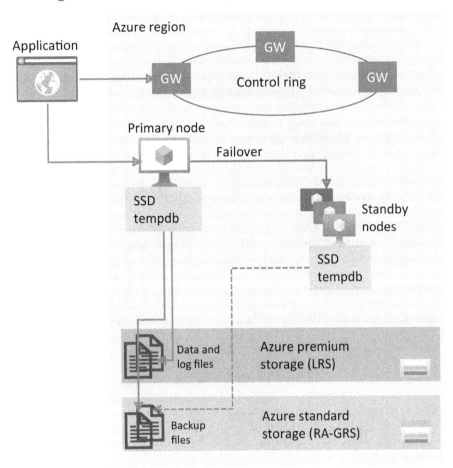

Figure 9.1: High availability architecture for the basic, standard, and general-purpose service tiers

In *Figure 9.1*, there are two layers:

- A stateless compute layer, which runs the **sqlserver.exe** process. Compute nodes have a local SSD that hosts the **tempdb**, a model system database. The primary node can perform failover to another stateless compute node with sufficient free capacity if necessary.

- A stateful data layer with the database files (**.mdf**/**.ldf**); these files are stored in Azure Storage and copied synchronously three times within a single physical location in the Azure region. This guarantees no data loss even when the **sqlserver.exe** process crashes.

This architecture model is applicable to a provisioned and serverless compute tier.

General-purpose service tier zone-redundant configuration

The general-purpose service tier zone-redundant configuration uses Azure Availability Zones to replicate a database across multiple physical locations within the same Azure region. Each Availability Zone in a region is physically separate, and made up of one or more datacenters equipped with independent power, cooling, and networking. This architecture model can tolerate zone-level failures.

This architecture model is like the previous architecture model, with a separation of the compute and data layers. Here, the difference is in the storage layer, where database files (.mdf / .ldf) are now stored in zone-redundant Azure Storage instead of locally redundant storage. Utilizing zone-redundant storage ensure that the data will be copied synchronously three times across three Availability Zones in the same region.

Additionally, nodes with spare capacity are readily available in other Availability Zones for failover. This allows the compute node to automatically failover to another Availability Zone in the case of a zone-level outage.

The zone-redundant configuration is currently not available in SQL Managed Instance.

The zone-redundant architecture model for the general-purpose tier is illustrated in *Figure* 9.2:

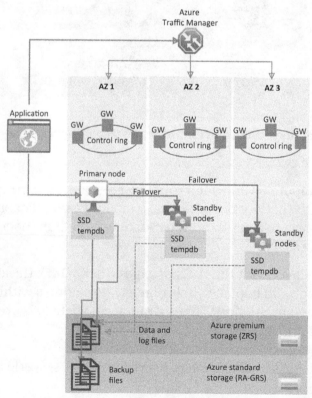

Figure 9.2: Zone-redundant high availability architecture for the general-purpose service tier

The zone-redundant configuration can be enabled for both new and existing general-purpose databases and elastic pools. Once the zone-redundant option is enabled, Azure SQL Database will automatically reconfigure the database or pool. You can configure this setting by using the Azure portal, the Azure CLI, PowerShell, or the ARM API. *Figure* 9.3 illustrates how to use the Azure portal to configure an existing general-purpose elastic pool to be zone redundant:

Figure 9.3: Using the Azure portal to enable zone-redundant high availability architecture for the general-purpose service tier

The premium/business-critical tier locally redundant availability model

This high availability architecture model is dependent on clusters of nodes replicating both compute and storage. The cluster has a primary replica that constantly pushes changes to the secondary nodes and ensures that the data is synchronized to at least one secondary replica before committing each transaction. This guarantees that there is always a quorum of available database nodes for automatic failover. This architecture model relies on the **Always On availability group** setup:

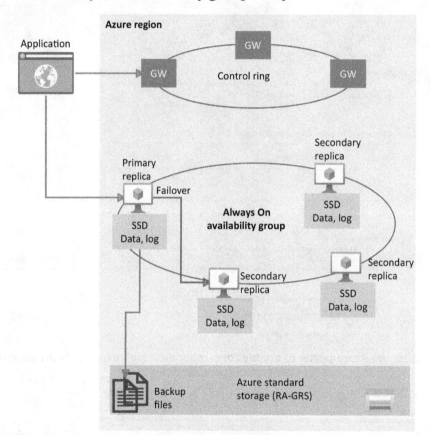

Figure 9.4: High availability architecture for the premium/business-critical service tier

In *Figure 9.4*, there is a cluster of four replicas with high availability implemented using technology similar to SQL Server Always On availability groups. Each replica has a local attached SSD for higher I/O throughput.

This architecture model is designed for mission-critical applications. It also provides access to one internal secondary replica to offload the read workload.

The premium/business critical service tier zone-redundant configuration

This architecture model ensures the highest uptime percentage SLA that Azure SQL offers. The premium/business-critical service tier with zone-redundant configuration offers 99.995% SLA availability:

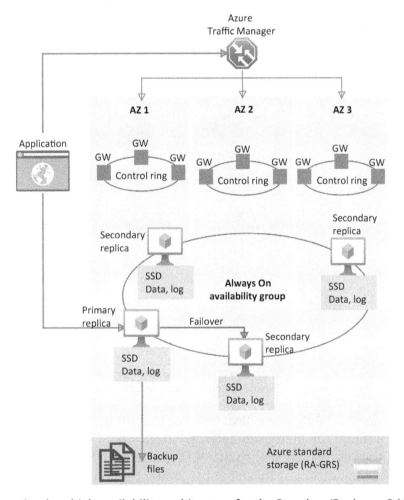

Figure 9.5: Zone-redundant high availability architecture for the Premium/Business-Critical service tier

This architecture model is like the previous architecture model, except the replicas are placed across different Availability Zones within the same region. This allows a replica to automatically fail over to another Availability Zone in the case of a zone-level outage. The zone-redundant configuration can be enabled for both new and existing Business-Critical and Premium databases and elastic pools. Once the zone-redundant option is enabled, Azure SQL Database will automatically reconfigure the database or pool. You can configure this setting by using the Azure portal, the Azure CLI, PowerShell, or the ARM API. The following figure illustrates how to use the Azure portal to configure a new business-critical single database to be zone redundant:

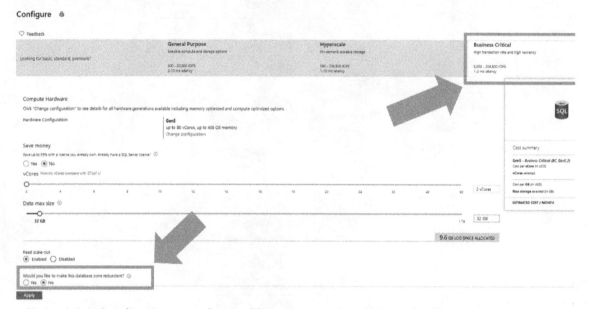

Figure 9.6: Using the Azure portal to enable zone-redundant high availability architecture for the Business-Critical service tier

Because zone-redundant databases have replicas in different datacenters with some distance between them, the increased network latency may increase the commit time and thus impact the performance of some OLTP workloads. You can always return to the single-zone configuration by disabling the zone redundancy setting.

Built-in high availability

Azure SQL Database and SQL Managed Instance have built-in high availability solutions that are deeply integrated with Azure infrastructure. They depend on a service fabric layer for fault detection and recovery and Azure Storage for data protection. Azure Availability Zones can be used for higher fault tolerance (only applies to Azure SQL Database). You would have to configure, manage, and maintain Always On in an on-premises environment. In SQL Database and SQL Managed Instance, it's configured, managed, and maintained by Microsoft.

Up to now, we have discussed multiple built-in high availability options for SQL Database and SQL Managed Instance. In the next section, we will discuss the Accelerated Database Recovery feature, which helps Azure SQL Databases and Managed Instances recover more quickly.

Accelerated database recovery (ADR)

Accelerated database recovery, or **ADR**, is a new database recovery process that greatly increases availability and decreases database recovery time in scenarios such as crash recovery (database recovery in the event of a server/database crash) and long-running transaction rollback (for example, a large bulk insert or an index rebuild rollback).

An SQL database consists of data and a transaction log file. A data file contains the table data. A transaction log file keeps track of all the changes made to the data and the schema; for example, if there is an insert in a table, the transaction log file contains the insert statement and whether the insert statement was committed or not.

The standard database recovery process

To better understand ADR, let's first get an understanding of the standard database recovery process:

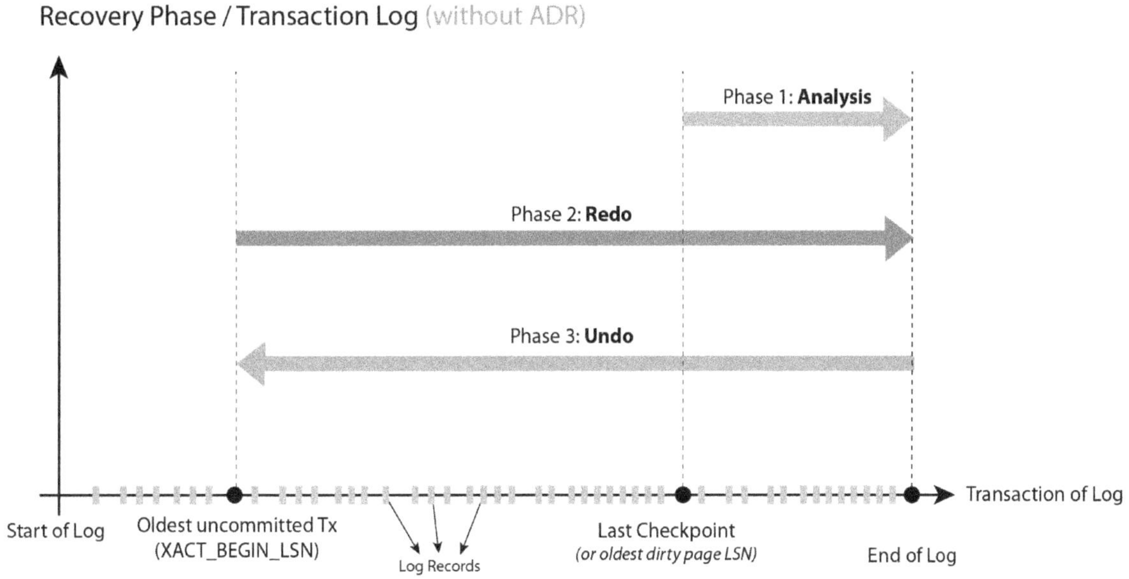

Figure 9.7: The recovery phase without ADR

> **Note**
>
> Image taken from https://docs.microsoft.com/azure/sql-database/sql-database-accelerated-database-recovery.

As shown in the preceding figure, the standard recovery process consists of three phases: **Analysis**, **Redo**, and **Undo**. Let's look at what happens in each of these phases.

Analysis

In the analysis phase, a forward scan of the transaction log is performed from the last checkpoint or the oldest dirty page's **log sequence number** (**LSN**).

> **Note**
>
> A dirty page is a page in memory with data modifications. A checkpoint is the process of writing dirty pages from the memory to the physical disk. A checkpoint is therefore a point at which a database is in a consistent state.
>
> An LSN is a number assigned to each entry made on the transaction log.

The output of the analysis phase is a list of transactions:

- These are written to the log and committed but are not written to the physical database file.

- They are in the log file, but they don't have a commit or rollback, or they are already in the rollback state (active transactions).

> **Note**
>
> The transaction log is scanned from the last successful checkpoint, because all the dirty pages before the checkpoint will have already been written to the physical data file.

Redo

In this phase, the log is read forward from the oldest uncommitted transaction, and the transactions that were committed to the log but not to the database are redone. In other words, you flush or harden all the dirty pages to disk, from the oldest uncommitted transaction to the end of the log, to restore the system to the state it was in at the time of the crash.

Undo

In this phase, the log is read backward from the end of the log to the oldest uncommitted transaction and all the active transactions at the time of the crash are rolled back or undone.

This process is good for recovering a database to a consistent state after a crash; however, it takes a long time and is proportional to the longest-running transaction.

The older the longest uncommitted transaction, the more log records there are to be scanned, thereby increasing the recovery time.

Moreover, the recovery time also depends on the amount of work the longest-running transaction has performed. The more work it performs, the more time it takes to roll back and recover the database.

The ADR process

ADR improves database availability from the standard database recovery process and provides faster database recovery.

ADR has the following new components, which are used to redesign the standard recovery process:

- **Persistent Version Store** (**PVS**): Whenever a data row is modified, the previous version of the row is kept in PVS.

  PVS is similar to the version store used in the Snapshot and Read committed isolation levels; however, PVS is stored in the user database instead of `tempdb`.

- **Logical revert:** Logical revert is an asynchronous process to perform undo/rollback operations using PVS.

  In the standard database recovery process, if a transaction aborts or rolls back, all other transactions have to wait for the first transaction to roll back to access the rows. However, in ADR, logical revert allows the other transactions to access the previous version of the rows from PVS instead of waiting for the first transaction to roll back.

- **sLog:** sLog is a low-volume, in-memory log stream to store log records for non-versioned operations such as lock acquisitions and **Data Definition Language** (**DDL**) commands. In other words, it stores the operations that don't go into PVS.

  sLog is written to disk during the checkpoint operation and is kept low-volume by periodically removing entries for committed transactions.

- **Cleaner:** This is an asynchronous process that cleans obsolete row versions from PVS. The cleaner process runs every minute and can also be run manually using the `sys.sp_persistent_version_cleanup` system stored procedure.

The database recovery process with **ADR** is shown in *Figure 9.8*:

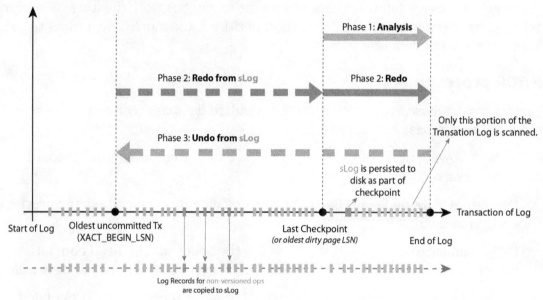

Figure 9.8: The recovery phase with ADR

> **Note**
>
> Image taken from https://docs.microsoft.com/azure/sql-database/sql-database-accelerated-database-recovery.

The ADR process consists of the same three phases as the standard recovery process; however, the work performed by each phase differs from the standard recovery process.

Analysis

The log is read forward from the last checkpoint to the end of the log.

sLog is rebuilt (read from disk into memory) and the log records for non-versioned operations are written into sLog from the transaction log.

Redo

The redo is done in two phases:

- **Phase 1**: The sLog is read from the oldest uncommitted transaction to the last checkpoint and non-versioned log records are redone.

- **Phase 2**: The transaction is redone in the transaction log from the last checkpoint to the end of the log.

Undo

The undo phase consists of the following:

- Undoing all of the non-versioned operations from sLog by reading it backward from the end of the log to the oldest uncommitted transaction

- Using logical revert to perform a row-level, version-based undo, as explained earlier, in the *Logical revert* section

ADR is fast as it doesn't depend on the work or the duration of the oldest active transaction. The transaction log is scanned only from the last checkpoint to the end of the log.

Active transactions at the time of the crash are marked as aborted and the row versions for aborted transactions are ignored during the recovery process.

Other than fast database recovery, with ADR, the transaction log can be truncated aggressively during checkpoint and backup. This is because the log records for the oldest uncommitted transactions are not required for the database recovery.

ADR is enabled by default for Azure SQL Database and SQL Managed Instance. Disabling ADR is not supported for either.

Activity: Evaluating ADR

In this activity, we'll evaluate the ADR performance of a transaction rollback.

It's advised to perform this activity on SQL Server 2019 Developer Edition since ADR was introduced in the SQL Server 2019 release.

> **Note**
>
> If you would like to perform the activity on Azure SQL Database, write an email to **adr@microsoft.com** to disable ADR on Azure SQL Server.

The **toystore_ADR** database used in the activity is similar to **toystore**, but **toystore** has ADR turned off. Perform the following steps to complete the activity:

1. Connect to a database with SSMS and execute the following query to verify that ADR is off:

   ```
   SELECT
   [Name], is_accelerated_database_recovery_on
   FROM sys.databases WHERE [Name]='toystore'
   ```

You should get an output similar to the following:

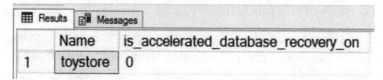

Figure 9.9: The result of the query denoting that ADR is turned off

> **Note**
>
> The database name may differ in your case.

The value **0** for **is_accelerated_database_recovery_on** confirms that ADR is turned off.

2. Execute the following query to simulate a long-running transaction:

```
CREATE TABLE Orders (
OrderId INT IDENTITY,
Quantity INT, Amount MONEY, OrderDate DATETIME2
)
GO
BEGIN TRANSACTION DECLARE @i INT=1

WHILE (@i <= 10000000) BEGIN
INSERT INTO Orders VALUES(@i*2,@i*0.5,DATEADD(MINUTE,@i,getdate())) Set
@i = @i + 1
END
```

The query creates an **Orders** table and inserts sample records into the **Orders** table in an explicit transaction. Observe that **BEGIN TRANSACTION** has no corresponding rollback or commit transaction.

Note the session ID of the query. The session ID of the query is in the bottom-right corner of the query window:

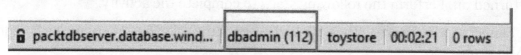

Figure 9.10: The session ID of the query

Let the query run for around five minutes or so.

3. While the query is running, open a new query window and execute the following query to start the query rollback:

```
KILL 112
GO
KILL 112 with statusonly
GO
SELECT session_id,status from sys.dm_exec_requests where session_id=112
```

> **Note**
>
> The session ID will be different in your case.

In the **Results** tab, observe that the query status is **rollback**:

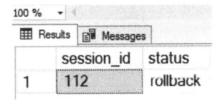

Figure 9.11: The Results tab denoting that the query status is set to rollback

In the **Messages** tab, observe the estimated time remaining to roll back the transaction. In this example, the estimated time was approximately 30 seconds:

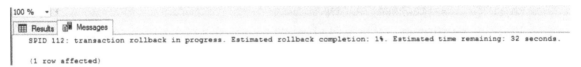

Figure 9.12: The Messages tab denoting the estimated time of the query

> **Note**
>
> The estimated time remaining may be different in your case.

Let's perform the preceding steps against a database with ADR turned on and measure the time taken for transaction rollback.

4. Open a new query window and connect to the **toystore_ADR** database:

> **Note**
>
> If you are performing the activity on SQL Server 2019, you can run the following command to enable ADR on an existing database:
>
> `ALTER DATABASE Toystore_ADR SET ACCELERATED_DATABASE_RECOVERY = ON;`

5. Execute the following query to verify whether ADR is turned on or not:

```
SELECT
[Name], is_accelerated_database_recovery_on
FROM sys.databases
WHERE [Name]='toystore_ADR'
```

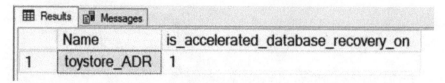

	Name	is_accelerated_database_recovery_on
1	toystore_ADR	1

Figure 9.13: The result of the query denoting that ADR is turned on

The **is_accelerated_database_recovery_on** bit is **1**, which means that ADR is turned on.

6. Execute the following query to simulate a long-running transaction:

```
CREATE TABLE Orders (
OrderId INT IDENTITY,
Quantity INT, Amount MONEY, OrderDate DATETIME2
)
GO
BEGIN TRANSACTION DECLARE @i INT=1

WHILE (@i <= 10000000) BEGIN
INSERT INTO Orders VALUES(@i*2,@i*0.5,DATEADD(MINUTE,@i,getdate())) Set
@i = @i + 1
END
```

The query creates an **Orders** table and inserts sample records into the **Orders** table in an explicit transaction. Observe that **BEGIN TRANSACTION** has no corresponding rollback or commit transaction.

Note the session ID of the query. The session ID of the query is in the bottom-right corner of the query window:

Figure 9.14: The session ID of the query is 131

The query session ID or the SPID is **131**.

Let the query run for around five minutes.

7. While the query is running, open a new query window and execute the following query to start the query rollback:

```
KILL 131
GO
KILL 131 with statusonly
GO
SELECT session_id,status from sys.dm_exec_requests where session_id=131
```

In the **Results** tab, notice that the query status is **rollback**:

Figure 9.15: The Results tab denoting that the query status is set as rollback

In the **Messages** tab, notice that the estimated time remaining to roll back the transaction is 0 seconds:

```
100 %  ▼ ◀
    Results    Messages
    SPID 131: transaction rollback in progress. Estimated rollback completion: 0%. Estimated time remaining: 0 seconds.

(1 row affected)
```

Figure 9.16: The Messages tab denoting the estimated time of the query (0 seconds)

ADR provides an instant **rollback**, compared to non-ADR, where the estimated time remaining to roll back was 30 seconds.

Disaster recovery

Disaster recovery (**DR**) refers to having business continuity during and after events that impact an Azure region, such as a natural disaster or hacking incident that terminates an entire Azure region.

DR for Azure SQL Database can be implemented through active geo-replication. An auto-failover group can be configured for Azure SQL Database and SQL Managed Instance as a business continuity solution. A failover group is designed to ease out the deployment and management of geo-replication databases at scale.

Active geo-replication

Active geo-replication uses Always On technology to asynchronously replicate data to a maximum of four readable secondaries in the same or any other Azure region. Active geo-replication is available across all performance tiers except Hyperscale. A typical active geo-replication environment is shown in *Figure 9.17*:

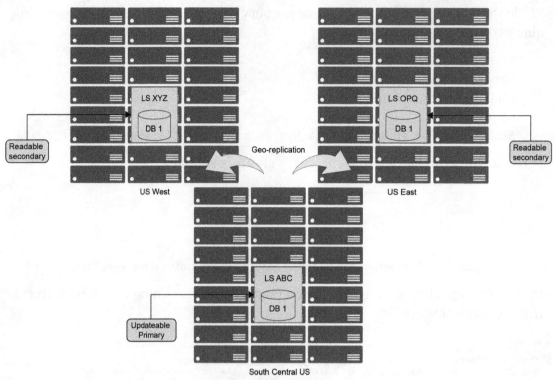

Figure 9.17: A typical active geo-replication environment

The DB 1 database is primarily stored in the South-Central US region, with two readable secondaries in the US West and US East regions.

When you fail over to the secondary database, the endpoint or the connection string is changed and you will have to make changes to the application so that you can connect to the new primary.

Once the failover is complete, all secondary databases will automatically point to the new primary. In addition to manual failover, active geo-replication also supports automatic failover using auto-failover groups.

The default replication type in active geo-replication is asynchronous. However, if the application needs to have synchronous replication, then you can do so by calling **sp_wait_for_database_copy_sync** immediately after committing a transaction. This will block the calling thread until all of the committed transactions have been replicated to the secondary.

The procedure can add significant delay to the calling thread if the size of the transaction log is being replicated is large. It's advised to use this procedure to prevent the loss of critical data only, not all data.

Auto-failover groups represent another high availability and DR option available with Azure SQL Database. Let's take a look at them now.

Auto-failover groups

Auto-failover groups allow you to automatically recover one or more groups of SQL databases or all the databases in an SQL Managed Instance in the event of a region failure. All databases in an auto-failover group should belong to a single server, and they will fail over to a single server as well.

Auto-failover group terms

- **Failover group**: A group of databases or all the instance databases between the primary server and the secondary server that are to be recovered as a unit if there is an outage in the primary region. A failover group in SQL Managed Instance replicates all user databases in the instance and therefore only one failover group can be configured on an SQL Managed Instance.

> Note
>
> The primary server is the one that hosts the primary database. The application can read and write on the primary database. The secondary server is the one that hosts the secondary database. The application can only read from the secondary databases. The data is asynchronously replicated from the primary database to the secondary databases. Primary and secondary servers can't be in the same region.

- **Adding single and elastic databases to a failover group**: When a database within a server or an elastic pool is added to the failover group, a secondary database with a performance level similar to that of the primary database is automatically created on the secondary server (see *Figure 9.18*). If the primary database is in an elastic pool, then an elastic pool with the same name is automatically created on the secondary server.

  When adding a database that already exists in the secondary database server, however, it's not part of the failover group, and so a new secondary database is created in the secondary server.

- **Read-write listener**: This is a DNS CNAME record that points to the primary server URL. It allows the application to transparently connect to the available primary server in the event of a failover. This is similar to an availability group listener in an on-premises Always On configuration. The application doesn't connect to the primary or the secondary server URL. Instead, it connects to the read-write listener. In the event of a failover, the read-write listener will automatically point to the new primary (secondary) server. Therefore, unlike manual failover, the user doesn't have to change the application connection string in the event of a failover.

- **Read-only listener**: This is a DNS CNAME record that points to the secondary server. It allows the application to transparently connect to the secondary server for read-only queries. However, the read workload should be tolerant of a certain staleness of data. This is because the replication is asynchronous, and the secondary database will be some data behind the primary database.

- **Failover group initial seeding**: When the failover group is configured for single, elastic, or instance databases, there is an initial seeding (streaming existing data from the primary database to the secondary database using the failover group endpoint) that takes place before the data replication starts. Initial seeding is the longest and most expensive operation. The seeding speed depends on the size of your database, the number of databases, and the speed of the network link between failover group entities. For SQL Managed Instance, now you can take advantage of a low-latency, high-bandwidth, global virtual network peering setup.

- **DNS zone**: A unique DNS zone ID is automatically created when SQL Managed Instance is deployed. A secondary instance in the failover group should share the same DNS zone ID. A DNS zone is not required for Azure SQL databases.

- **Failover policy**: The default failover policy is set to automatic; however, this can be turned off if the failover process is controlled by the application.

  Manual failover is required if automatic failover is turned off and the failover process isn't controlled by the application.

  Manual failover can also be initiated at any time it is required, independent of the automatic failover policy. An example of manual failover is switching back to the primary region once the region recovers from the outage and is available to host resources.

- **Planned failover**: Users can initiate a planned failover to perform DR drills, moving databases to different regions, or return (fail back) to the primary region after an outage. There is no data loss during a planned failover. A planned failover performs a full synchronization between the primary and secondary databases before switching the roles.

- **Unplanned failover**: Unplanned failover or forced failover needs to be a trigger during an outage when the primary server is not accessible. There is no data synchronization between the primary and secondary servers during the switching of the roles, hence it results in data loss. When the original primary server comes up, it automatically reconnects with the new primary server without synchronization and becomes the secondary server.

- **Manual failover**: You can initiate a manual failover at any point as per your requirements. You can initiate a friendly failover (with full data synchronization) or a forced failover with data loss. Manual failover is required to recover the databases when an auto-failover policy is not configured.

- **Grace period with data loss hours**: This setting controls the duration the system fails for before initiating an automatic failover. For example, if the grace period with data loss hours is set to 2 hours, then in the event of an outage in the primary region, failover will take place after 2 hours. However, if the outage is resolved before the grace period expires, failover isn't performed.

- **Upgrading the primary database service tier**: The service tier and performance level of the primary database can be modified as and when required. The performance level within the same service tier can be modified without disconnecting the secondary database. In other words, you can upgrade the primary database from **Standard S0** to **Standard S1** without disconnecting the corresponding secondary database connection.

However, if you are switching between service tiers, then it's recommended (and enforced) to first upgrade the secondary database and then the primary database to avoid the termination of the secondary database connection.

If the secondary database is part of an auto-failover group, then it's advised not to downgrade the secondary database service tier. This is to avoid performance degradation in the event of a failover.

A high-level overview of an auto-failover group in Azure SQL Database

An auto-failover group must be configured with servers in different regions. You can include all or some of the databases of a server in a failover group.

Figure 9.18 illustrates a typical configuration of a geo-redundant cloud application using multiple databases in an auto-failover group:

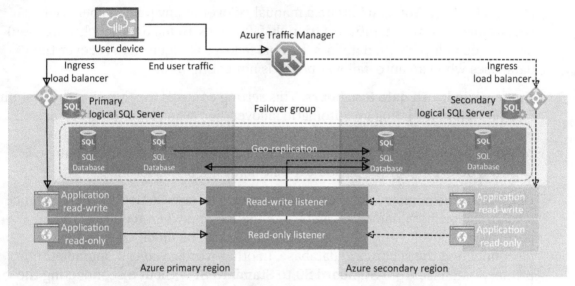

Figure 9.18: Failover group data traffic flow for Azure SQL Database

In *Figure* 9.18, you can see that there are two logical Azure SQL Servers configured in an auto-failover group with a geo-redundant application. This application accesses multiple databases within Azure SQL Server.

A high-level overview of an auto-failover group in Azure SQL Managed Instance

In SQL Managed Instance, a failover group must be configured with a primary instance that connects to a secondary instance in a different Azure region. The failover group replicates all user databases to the secondary instance. *Figure* 9.19 shows a typical overview of failover group data traffic:

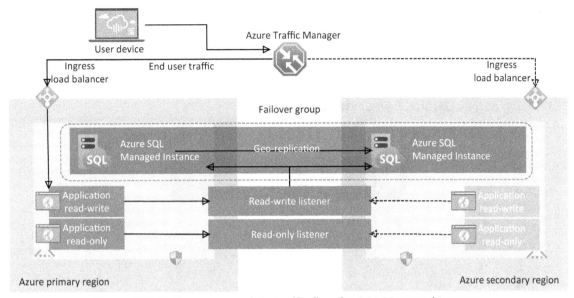

Figure 9.19: Failover group data traffic flow for SQL Managed Instance

In *Figure 9.19*, you can see two SQL managed instances configured in the auto- failover group with the same DNS zone. These instances are accessed by a geo-redundant application. This application uses read-write and read-only listeners to connect to databases.

Activity: Configuring active geo-replication and performing manual failover using the Azure portal

Consider a scenario: Mike needs to ensure that the data of **Toystore Ltd.** is shielded from disaster or the failure of an entire region. To do this, Mike can configure active geo-replication using the Azure portal to recover data and maintain business continuity. He can also take precautions by performing manual failover from the primary server to the secondary server. This activity has the following aims:

- To configure active geo-replication using the Azure portal for the `toyfactory` database

- To perform manual failover from the primary server to the secondary server

Configuring active geo-replication

The following section explains how to configure active geo-replication for a standalone Azure SQL Database:

1. Open the Azure portal in a web browser (https://portal.azure.com) and navigate to the **toyfactory** database **Overview** pane.

2. Under the **SETTINGS** menu, find and select the **Geo-Replication** option:

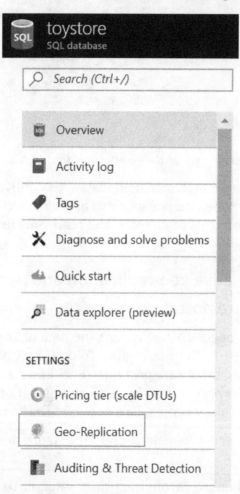

Figure 9.20: The Geo-Replication option in the SETTINGS menu

In the **Geo-Replication** pane, you will see a list of target Azure regions:

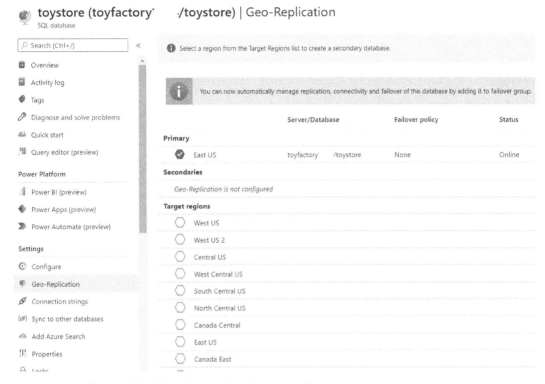

Figure 9.21: The Geo-Replication pane displaying the target regions

The **Primary** regions for the database is **East US** and there aren't any secondary replicas for the database.

3. Select the region name from the target region list to create a secondary replica:

Region: This shows you the region you selected to create the secondary server.

Database name: The name of the database that is to be replicated.

Secondary type: The type of the secondary database—readable or offline.

Elastic database pool: The elastic pool the database is part of. It displays none if the database is not part of an elastic pool.

Pricing tier: The secondary database pricing tier. This is inherited from the primary database.

> **Note**
>
> The lock icon in front of an option indicates that the option is locked and can't be configured.

4. Click the **Target server** option to create a new target server in the secondary region.

    In the **New server** pane, provide **Server name**, **Server admin login**, and **Password** details, as shown in *Figure 9.22*:

    > **Note**
    >
    > The server admin name and password should be the same as those of the primary server. This is to prevent login issues resulting from orphaned users.

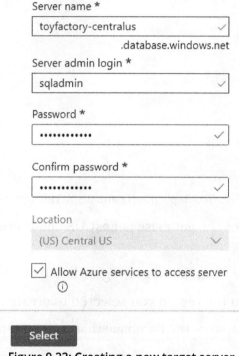

Figure 9.22: Creating a new target server

Click the **Select** button to continue.

5. You'll be taken back to the **Create secondary** pane:

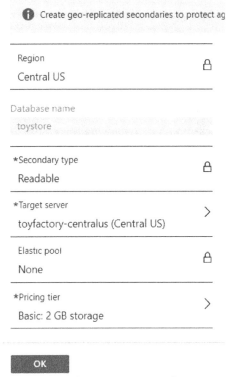

Figure 9.23: The Create secondary pane

Click **OK** to create the secondary server and start the geo-replication.

As the geo-replication is being configured, you'll see the status on the **Geo-Replication** pane:

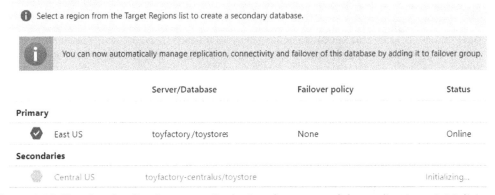

Figure 9.24: The Geo-Replication pane displaying the status of the replication—Initializing...

The **Initializing...** status means that the secondary server is being provisioned and the replication link is being established:

Figure 9.25: The Geo-Replication pane displaying the status of the replication—Seeding

The seeding process copies the existing data to the secondary server and it is the most time-consuming and costly process. The seeding time depends on the size of the database.

When the seeding is done, the data is replicated to the secondary database as and when it arrives at the primary database:

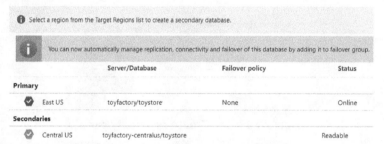

Figure 9.26: The Geo-Replication pane displaying the completion of the replication

6. To verify this, open **SQL Server Management Studio (SSMS)** and sign in to the new secondary server.

> **Note**
>
> When connecting to the secondary server, you'll have to add the firewall rule. It is therefore advised to use the database-level firewall on the primary server.
>
> This makes sure that the firewall rules are also copied to the secondary database during the active geo-replication setup so that you can log in easily.
>
> It's also advised to use contained users so that you don't have to move server logins to the secondary server. *Chapter 6, Security*, covers firewall rules and contained users in detail.

7. In the **Object Explorer** window, expand the server, and then expand **Databases**. You should see the **toystore** database. Expand the **toystore** database. You should see all the objects in the toystore database:

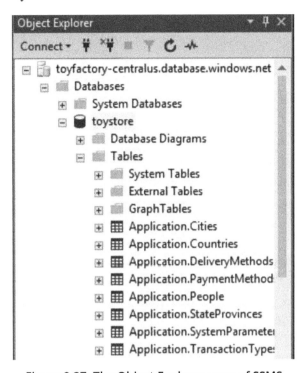

Figure 9.27: The Object Explorer pane of SSMS

8. Press *Ctrl* + N to open a new query window. Execute the following query in the new query window:

```
SELECT COUNT(*) FROM Sales.Customers GO INSERT INTO Warehouse.Colors
VALUES(100,'Light Green',1,getdate(),getdate()+10);
```

The select query will return as a success; however, the insert query will fail with the following error:

Results   Messages

```
(1 row affected)
Msg 3906, Level 16, State 2, Line 3
Failed to update database "toystore" because the database is read-only.
```

Figure 9.28: The error displayed while inserting values

This is because the secondary database is read-only in an active geo-replication configuration. The secondary database is therefore only available for read transactions and now write transactions.

9. In the same SSMS session, connect to the primary server and execute the following query against the **toystore** database in the primary server. Do not close the secondary server query window:

```
INSERT INTO Warehouse.Colors
VALUES(100,'Magenta',1,getdate(),getdate()+10);
```

One row will be inserted into the **Colors** table.

Switch over to the query window with the secondary database connection. Execute the following query to verify whether the newly inserted value has been properly replicated to the secondary database or not:

```
SELECT @@ServerName As SecondaryServerName,* FROM Warehouse.Colors WHERE
ColorName='Magenta'
```

You should get the following output:

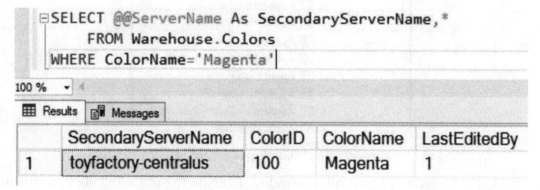

Figure 9.29: Confirming whether the inserted data is replicated in the secondary database

The data has indeed been correctly replicated to the secondary database. Now for the second part of the activity, performing a manual failover.

Performing a manual failover

To perform a manual failover, the following steps need to be taken:

1. In the **toystore Geo-Replication** pane, scroll down and locate the **PRIMARY** and **SECONDARIES** databases:

Figure 9.30: The toystore Geo-Replication pane denoting the primary and the secondary databases

2. Select the three dots (highlighted in the red rectangle) as shown in *Figure 9.30*. In the context menu, select **Forced Failover**:

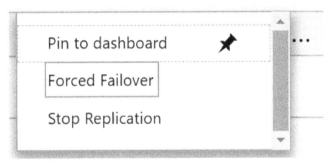

Figure 9.31: The Forced Failover option in the context menu

3. Click **Yes** on the **Failover** message pop-up window to start the failover:

Figure 9.32: The Failover message pop-up window

The failover request will be submitted, and the failover will be initiated.

4. The failover status is displayed as shown in the following figure. The primary status changes to **Pending** and the secondary replica status changes to **Failover...**:

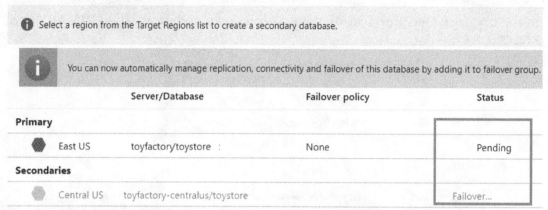

Figure 9.33: The Geo-Replication pane denoting that the failover is in progress

Once the failover is complete, observe that the primary and secondary replica roles have been reversed:

	Server/Database	Failover policy	Status
Primary			
✔ Central US	toyfactory-centralus/toystore	None	Online
Secondaries			
✔ East US	toyfactory/toystore		Readable

Figure 9.34: The Geo-Replication pane denoting that the failover is complete

Observe that the region color has also been reversed. The blue hexagon now denotes that the primary region is the **Central US** region, and the green hexagon denotes that the secondary region is now **East US**.

This completes the activity. In this activity, we configured active geo-replication and performed a manual failover from a primary Azure SQL Server to a secondary Azure SQL Server.

Activity: Configuring an Azure SQL Database auto-failover group using Azure portal

This activity covers the configuration of auto-failover groups for a standalone Azure SQL Database. Consider the following scenario, again involving **ToyStore Ltd.**.

Mike wants to ensure that whenever there is a disaster or an entire region fails, there is no effect on the business of **ToyStore Ltd.**, so he configures auto-failover groups that allow him to automatically recover one or more groups of SQL databases. To configure an auto-failover group for a standalone Azure SQL Database, the following steps need to be taken.

1. Log in to the Azure portal (https://portal.azure.com) and open the **packtdbserver** Azure SQL Server overview page. In the overview page, select **Failover groups** in the **Settings** section and then select **+ Add group**:

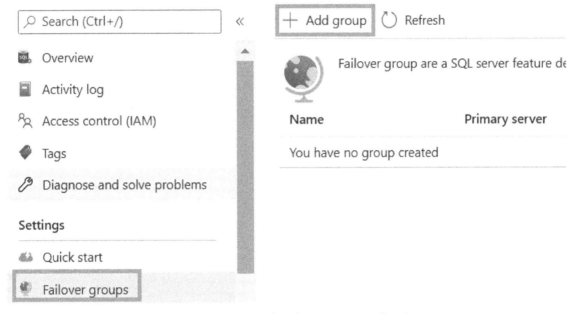

Figure 9.35: The toystore_Shard_1_50 Geo-Replication pane

2. In the **Failover group** pane, configure the following settings:

    Secondary Server: The Azure SQL server on another region that will host the secondary databases. You'll have to create a new server if you don't have one already.

    Failover group name: The name of the failover group.

    Read/Write failover policy: The default value is **Automatic**. Leave it as it is.

    Read/Write grace period (hours): The default value is **1 hours**. Leave it as it is.

    Database within the group: Select the databases to add to the group:

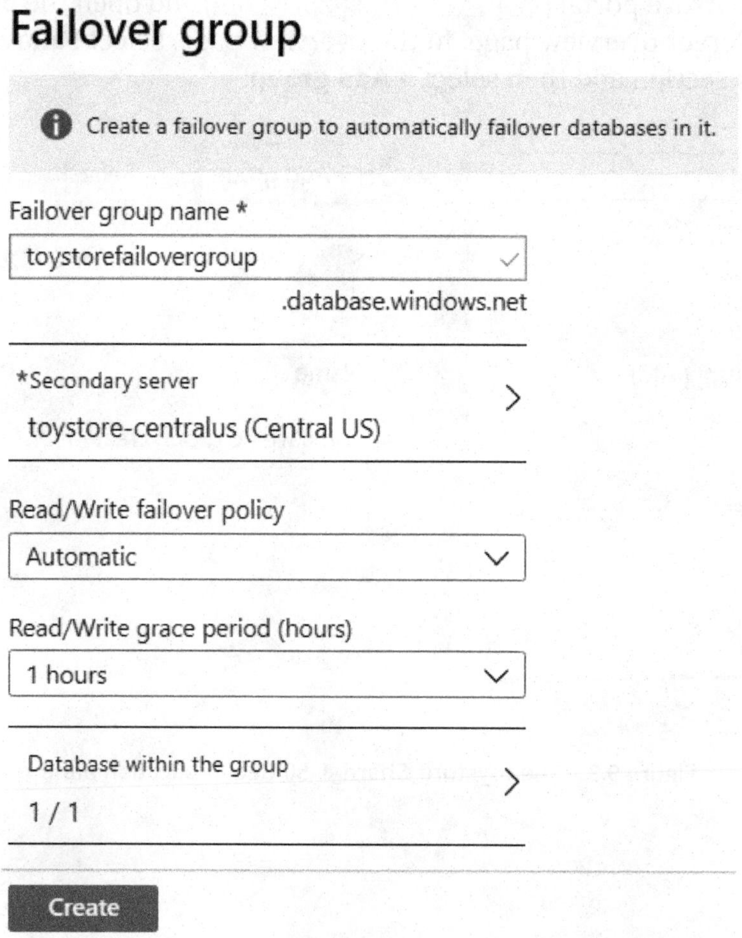

Failover group

ⓘ Create a failover group to automatically failover databases in it.

Failover group name *

| toystorefailovergroup | ✓ |

.database.windows.net

*Secondary server   ❯
toystore-centralus (Central US)

Read/Write failover policy

| Automatic | ∨ |

Read/Write grace period (hours)

| 1 hours | ∨ |

Database within the group   ❯
1 / 1

Create

Figure 9.36: The Failover group pane

To add databases, click on **Database** within the group and then select the databases from the **Databases** page as shown in *Figure* 9.37:

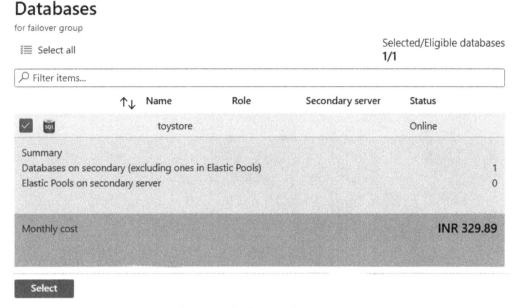

Figure 9.37: The Database page

Click **Select** to choose the selected databases and go back to the **Failover groups** page as shown in *Figure* 9.38.

Click **Create** to provision the secondary server and the failover group. The failover group shows the failover group details as shown in *Figure* 9.38:

Figure 9.38: Failover group page with the failover group name

Click on the failover group name to check the failover group progress:

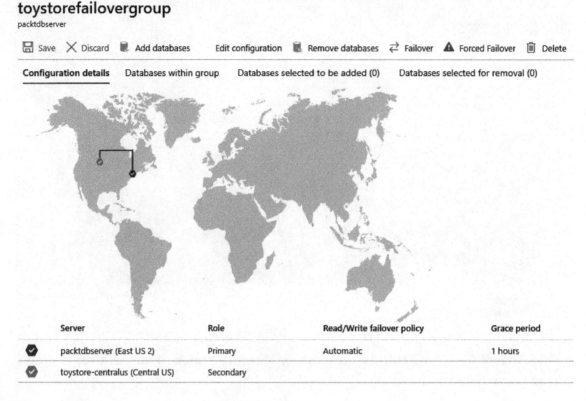

toystorefailovergroup
packtdbserver

💾 Save ✕ Discard 📇 Add databases   Edit configuration 📇 Remove databases ⇄ Failover ⚠ Forced Failover 🗑 Delete

Configuration details   Databases within group   Databases selected to be added (0)   Databases selected for removal (0)

	Server	Role	Read/Write failover policy	Grace period
✅	packtdbserver (East US 2)	Primary	Automatic	1 hours
✅	toystore-centralus (Central US)	Secondary		

Figure 9.39: Failover group detail

Figure 9.39 shows that the failover group has been created. The primary Azure SQL Server **packtdbserver** is in **East US 2** (shown in blue) and the secondary Azure SQL Server **toystore-centralus** is in **Central US**.

The solid line from blue to green means that the failover group is created, and a dotted line means that the failover group is being created.

You can also add/remove Azure SQL Databases, edit/remove failover groups, and perform a forced failover from the failover group detailed view as shown in the preceding figure.

Once created, you can follow the steps from the previous section to fail over and verify the replication.

Creating an auto-failover group is as simple as shown here. The time it takes to provision and replicate the database to a secondary Azure SQL Server depends on the number of databases in the failover group and the size of the databases.

Activity: Configuring active geo-replication for Azure SQL Database using PowerShell

Mike ensures that the data of the **Toystore Ltd.** is shielded from the disaster. In the case of a disaster or an entire region failure, he can recover or maintain his business continuity by configuring the active geo-replication **toystore** database using PowerShell.

> **Note**
>
> If you are short of time, you can execute the `C:\Code\Chapter09\ActiveGeoReplication\Manage-ActiveGeoReplication.ps1` file, providing the appropriate parameters.

To configure active geo-replication for the **toystore** database using PowerShell, perform the following steps:

1. Press the *Windows* + R keys to open the **Run** command window. Type `PowerShell_ISE.exe` in the **Run** command window and hit *Enter*. This will open a new **PowerShell ISE** editor window, where you'll write the PowerShell commands:

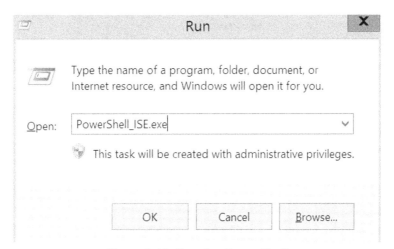

Figure 9.40: Opening PowerShell

2. In the **PowerShell ISE** window, select **File** from the top menu and click **Save**. Alternatively, you can press *Ctrl + S* to save the file. In the **Save As** dialog box, browse to `C:\Code\Chapter09\`. In the **File name** textbox, type `Manage-ActiveGeoReplication` and click **Save** to save the file:

Figure 9.41: Creating the Manage-ActiveGeoReplication.ps1 file

3. Copy and paste the following code into `Manage-ActiveGeoReplication.ps1` to define script parameters:

```
param
(
[parameter(Mandatory=$true)] [String] $ResourceGroup,
[parameter(Mandatory=$true)] [String] $PrimarySqlServer,
[parameter(Mandatory=$true)] [String] $UserName,
[parameter(Mandatory=$true)] [String] $Password,
[parameter(Mandatory=$true)] [String] $SecondarySqlServer,
[parameter(Mandatory=$true)] [String] $SecondaryServerLocation,
[parameter(Mandatory=$false)] [bool] $Failover = $false,
[parameter(Mandatory=$false)] [String] $DatabasesToReplicate,
```

```
[parameter(Mandatory=$false)]

# Add/Remove database to/from secondary server [String] $Operation = "none",
[parameter(Mandatory=$false)]

[String] $AzureProfileFilePath

)
```

The parameter descriptions are as follows:

ResourceGroup: The resource group that hosts the primary Azure SQL server and databases.

PrimarySqlServer: The name of the primary Azure SQL server.

UserName: The primary and secondary Azure SQL server admin username.

Password: The primary and secondary Azure SQL server admin password.

SecondarySqlServer: The secondary Azure SQL server name.

SecondaryServerLocation: The secondary Azure SQL server location.

Failover: A Boolean value set to **false** by default. When **true**, the script does the failover from the primary Azure SQL server to the secondary SQL server.

DatabasesToReplicate: A comma-delimited list of Azure SQL Databases to be replicated.

Operation: Accepts two values: **Add** and **Remove**; it is **none** by default. When set to **Add**, the active geo-replication link is established for the databases. When set to **Remove**, the active geo-replication link is removed for the databases.

AzureProfileFilePath: The full path of the Azure profile JSON file used for logging in to an Azure subscription.

4. Copy and paste the following code to log in to Microsoft Azure, and set the Azure context to your subscription:

```
# log the execution of the script
Start-Transcript -Path ".\Log\Manage-ActiveGeoReplication.txt" -Append

# Set AzureProfileFilePath relative to the script directory if it's not
provided as parameter

if([string]::IsNullOrEmpty($AzureProfileFilePath))
{
$AzureProfileFilePath="..\..\MyAzureProfile.json"
}

#Login to Azure Account

if((Test-Path -Path $AzureProfileFilePath))
{
$profile = Select-AzProfile -Path $AzureProfileFilePath
$SubscriptionID = $profile.Context.Subscription.SubscriptionId
}
else
{
Write-Host "File Not Found $AzureProfileFilePath" -ForegroundColor
Red


# Provide your Azure Credentials in the login dialog box
$profile = Login-AzAccount
$SubscriptionID = $profile.Context.Subscription.SubscriptionId
}

#Set the Azure Context
Set-AzContext -SubscriptionId $SubscriptionID | Out-Null
```

The preceding code starts by logging in to the `Manage-ActiveGeoReplication.txt` file created under the log directory within the parent directory of the `Manage-ActiveGeoReplication.ps1` script.

It then checks for the profile information in the JSON file provided by the `AzureProfileFilePath` variable. If found, it then sets the PowerShell context to the subscription ID, as specified in the profile file; otherwise, it asks the user to annually log in to the Azure account to set the context.

5. Copy and paste the following code to provision the secondary Azure SQL server if it doesn't already exist:

```
if($Operation -eq "Add")
{
# Check if Azure SQL Server Exists
# An error is returned and stored in notexists variable if resource group
exists
Get-AzSqlServer -ServerName $SecondarySqlServer
-ResourceGroupName $ResourceGroup -ErrorVariable notexists
-ErrorAction SilentlyContinue
# provision the secondary server if it doesn't exist
if($notexists)
{
Write-Host "Provisioning Azure SQL Server
$SecondarySqlServer" -ForegroundColor Green
$credentials = New-Object -TypeName System.Management.
Automation.PSCredential -ArgumentList $UserName, $(ConvertTo- SecureString
-String $Password -AsPlainText -Force)
$_SecondarySqlServer = @{ ResourceGroupName = $ResourceGroup; ServerName =
$SecondarySqlServer; Location = $SecondaryServerLocation;
SqlAdministratorCredentials = $credentials; ServerVersion = '12.0';
}
New-AzSqlServer @_SecondarySqlServer;
}

}
else
{
Write-Host $notexists -ForegroundColor Yellow
}
```

The preceding code will provision a new secondary Azure SQL server if the **$Operation** parameter is set to **Add**. The SQL server creation code is similar to what was used in *Chapter 1, Introduction to Azure SQL managed databases*.

6. Copy and paste the following code to configure active geo-replication for the individual databases:

```
# Configure Active Geo-Replication for individual databases
if(![string]::IsNullOrEmpty($DatabasesToReplicate.Replace(',','')) 
-and $Operation -eq "Add")
{
$dbname = $DatabasesToReplicate.Split(',');
foreach($db in $dbname)
{
Write-Host "Replicating database $db to 
$SecondarySqlServer " -ForegroundColor Green
#Get the database object for the given database name
$database = Get-AzSqlDatabase -DatabaseName $db 
-ResourceGroupName $ResourceGroup -ServerName $PrimarySqlServer #pipe the 
database object to New-
AzSqlDatabaseSecondary cmdlet
$database | New-AzSqlDatabaseSecondary 
-PartnerResourceGroupName $ResourceGroup -PartnerServerName 
$SecondarySqlServer -AllowConnections "No"
}
}
```

The preceding code first checks whether the **$DatabaseToReplicate** parameter is empty. If it's not and the **$operation** parameter is set to **Add**, it splits the comma-delimited list of the databases and configures active geo-replication for each one of them using the **New-AzSqlDatabaseSecondary** cmdlet.

New-AzSqlDatabaseSecondary takes three parameters:

-   **PartnerResourceGroupName**: The resource group name that contains the secondary SQL Server. The primary and secondary resource groups are assumed to be the same in this script.

-   **PartnerServerName**: The name of the secondary Azure SQL server.

-   **AllowConnections**: This specifies the read intent of the secondary database. It's set to **No**.

7. Copy and paste the following code to remove active geo-replication for the individual Azure SQL Databases:

```
if($Operation -eq "Remove")
{
$dbname = $DatabasesToReplicate.Split(','); foreach($db in $dbname)
{

Write-Host "Removing replication for database $db "
-ForegroundColor Green
$database = Get-AzSqlDatabase -DatabaseName $db
-ResourceGroupName $ResourceGroup -ServerName $PrimarySqlServer
$database | Remove-AzSqlDatabaseSecondary
-PartnerResourceGroupName $ResourceGroup -ServerName
$PrimarySqlServer -PartnerServerName $SecondarySqlServer
}
}
```

The preceding code runs when **$Operation** is set to **Remove**. It first splits the comma-separated database list in the **$DatabaseToReplicate** parameter. It then removes the replication link for each database using the **Remove- AzSqlDatabaseSecondary** cmdlet.

Remove-AzSqlDatabaseSecondary accepts three parameters:

- **PartnerResourceGroupName**: The resource group of the secondary SQL server. The script assumes that it's the same as the primary SQL server.

- **ServerName**: The primary SQL server's name.

- **PartnerServerName**: The secondary SQL server's name.

This only stops the replication between the primary and the secondary databases; it doesn't delete the secondary databases. The database and server can be removed separately if required.

8. Copy and paste the following code to fail over individual databases to the secondary SQL server:

```
# failover individual databases from primary to secondary
if($Failover -eq
$true)
{
$dbname = $DatabasesToReplicate.Split(','); foreach($db in $dbname)
{
Write-Host "Failover $db to $SecondarySqlServer..."
-ForegroundColor Green
$database = Get-AzSqlDatabase -DatabaseName $db
-ResourceGroupName $ResourceGroup -ServerName $SecondarySqlServer
$database | Set-AzSqlDatabaseSecondary
-PartnerResourceGroupName $ResourceGroup -Failover
}
}
```

The preceding code executes if the **$Failover** parameter is set to **true**. It first splits the comma-delimited list of the databases in **$DatabaseToReplicate** and then performs manual failover from the primary server to the secondary server using **Set-AzSqlDatabaseSecondary**.

Set-AzSqlDatabaseSecondary accepts two parameters:

- **PartnerResourceGroupName**: The resource group of the secondary SQL server. The script assumes that it's the same as the primary SQL server.

- **Failover**: Initiates the failover.

The database to fail over is piped to the **Set-AzSqlDatabaseSecondary** cmdlet. This completes the script. Press *Ctrl* + S to save the file.

Executing the PowerShell script

1. Press *Windows* + R to open the **Run** command window. Type PowerShell and hit *Enter* to open a new PowerShell console window.

2. Change the directory to the folder that has the **Manage-ActiveGeoReplication.ps1** script inside of it. For example, if the script is in the **C:\Code\Chapter09\ ActiveGeoReplication** directory, then run the following command to switch to that directory:

   ```
   cd C:\Code\Chapter09\ActiveGeoReplication
   ```

3. In the PowerShell console, execute the following command to establish active geo-replication for the **toystore_Shard_1_50** and **toystore_ Shard_50_100** databases:

   ```
   .\Manage-ActiveGeoReplication.ps1 -ResourceGroup toystore
   -PrimarySqlServer toyfactory -UserName sqladmin -Password Packt@pub2
   -SecondarySqlServer toyfactory-centralus
   -SecondaryServerLocation "Central US" -DatabasesToReplicate "toystore_
   Shard_1_50,toystore_Shard_50_100" -Operation "Add"
   -AzureProfileFilePath C:\Code\MyAzureProfile.json
   ```

   The preceding command will call **Manage-ActiveGeoReplication.ps1** to start active geo-replication for the **toystore_Shard_1_50** and **toystore_Shard_50_100** databases on the **toyfactory** primary server to the **toyfactory-centralus** secondary Azure SQL server.

4. You will have to modify the command to provide the relevant parameter values. In the PowerShell console window, run the following command to fail over the databases to the secondary SQL server:

   ```
   .\Manage-ActiveGeoReplication.ps1 -ResourceGroup toystore
   -PrimarySqlServer toyfactory -UserName sqladmin -Password Packt@pub2
   -SecondarySqlServer toyfactory-centralus
   -SecondaryServerLocation "Central US" -DatabasesToReplicate "toystore_
   Shard_1_50,toystore_Shard_50_100" -failover $true
   -AzureProfileFilePath C:\Code\MyAzureProfile.json
   ```

   The preceding command will fail over the databases from the primary server to the secondary server. In other words, the primary becomes the secondary and vice versa.

5. In the PowerShell console window, execute the following command to remove active geo-replication:

```
.\Manage-ActiveGeoReplication.ps1 -ResourceGroup toystore
-PrimarySqlServer toyfactory -UserName sqladmin -Password Packt@pub2
-SecondarySqlServer toyfactory-centralus
-SecondaryServerLocation "Central US" -DatabasesToReplicate "toystore_
Shard_1_50,toystore_Shard_50_100" -Operation "Remove"
-AzureProfileFilePath C:\Code\MyAzureProfile.json
```

The preceding command will remove the replication link between the primary and the secondary servers, though please note that the secondary server and the databases will not be removed.

In this activity, we used PowerShell commands to create a secondary Azure SQL Server, create active geo-replication between primary and secondary Azure SQL Servers, add/remove databases to active geo-replication, and remove active geo-replication.

Activity: Configuring auto-failover groups for Azure SQL Database using PowerShell

In this activity, we will configure auto-failover groups using PowerShell for **ToyStore Ltd.**:

> **Note**
>
> If you are short of time, you can execute the **C:\Code\Chapter09\ ActiveGeoReplication\Manage-FailoverGroup.ps1** file, providing the appropriate parameters.

1. Press *Windows* + R to open the **Run** command window. Type **PowerShell_ ISE.exe** in the **Run** command window and hit *Enter*. This will open a new **PowerShell ISE** editor window. This is where you'll write the PowerShell commands:

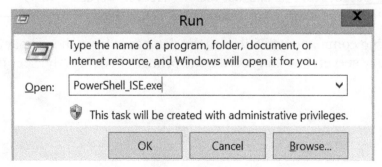

Figure 9.42: Opening PowerShell

In the **PowerShell ISE**, select **File** from the top menu and click **Save**. Alternatively, you can press *Ctrl* + S to save the file. In the **Save as** dialog box, browse to the `C:\Code\Chapter09\` directory. In the **File name** textbox, type `Manage-FailoverGroup.ps1` and click **Save** to save the file:

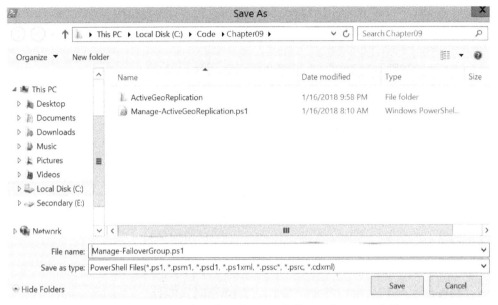

Figure 9.43: Creating the Manage-FailoverGroup.ps1 file

2. In the `Manage-FailoverGroup.ps1` file, copy and paste the following code to define the script parameters:

```
param (
[parameter(Mandatory=$true)] [String] $ResourceGroup,
[parameter(Mandatory=$true)] [String] $PrimarySqlServer,
[parameter(Mandatory=$false)] [String] $UserName,
[parameter(Mandatory=$false)] [String] $Password,
[parameter(Mandatory=$true)] [String] $SecondarySqlServer,
[parameter(Mandatory=$false)]
[String] $SecondaryServerLocation, [parameter(Mandatory=$false)] [bool]
$Failover = $false, [parameter(Mandatory=$false)] [String]
$DatabasesToReplicate, [parameter(Mandatory=$true)] [String]
$FailoverGroupName, [parameter(Mandatory=$false)] [String] $Operation =
"none", [parameter(Mandatory=$false)] [String] $AzureProfileFilePath

)
```

Most of the parameters are similar to what was explained in the previous activity, except `FailoverGroupName`. This is the name of the failover group that is going to be created.

3. Copy and paste the following code to log in to Microsoft Azure and set the Azure context to your subscription:

```
# log the execution of the script
Start-Transcript -Path ".\Log\Manage-FailoverGroup.txt" -Append # Set
AzureProfileFilePath relative to the script directory if it's not provided
as parameter if([string]::IsNullOrEmpty($AzureProfileFilePath))
{
$AzureProfileFilePath="..\..\MyAzureProfile.json"
}

#Login to Azure Account

if((Test-Path -Path $AzureProfileFilePath))
{
$profile = Import-AzContext -Path $AzureProfileFilePath
$SubscriptionID = $profile.Context.Subscription.SubscriptionId
}
else
{
Write-Host "File Not Found $AzureProfileFilePath" -ForegroundColor
Red

# Provide your Azure Credentials in the login dialog box
$profile = Login-AzAccount
$SubscriptionID = $profile.Context.Subscription.SubscriptionId
}

#Set the Azure Context
Set-AzContext -SubscriptionId $SubscriptionID | Out-Null
```

The preceding code starts by logging in to the **Manage-FailoverGroup.txt** file, created in the **log** directory within the parent directory of the **Manage-FailoverGroup.ps1** script.

It then checks for the profile information in the JSON file provided by the **AzureProfileFilePath** variable. If found, it sets the PowerShell context to the subscription ID, as specified in the profile file; otherwise, it asks the user to manually log in to the Azure account to set the context.

4. Copy and paste the following code to provision a new secondary SQL server, if one doesn't already exist:

```
IF($Operation -eq "Create")
{
# An error is returned and stored in notexists variable if resource group
exists
Get-AzSqlServer -ServerName $SecondarySqlServer
-ResourceGroupName $ResourceGroup -ErrorVariable notexists
-ErrorAction SilentlyContinue
# provision the secondary server if it doesn't exist if($notexists)
{
Write-Host "Provisioning Azure SQL Server $SecondarySqlServer"
-ForegroundColor Green
$credentials = New-Object -TypeName System.Management.Automation.
PSCredential -ArgumentList $UserName, $(ConvertTo-SecureString -String
$Password -AsPlainText -Force)
$_SecondarySqlServer - @{ ResourceGroupName = $ResourceGroup; ServerName
= $SecondarySqlServer; Location = $SecondaryServerLocation;
SqlAdministratorCredentials = $credentials; ServerVersion = '12.0';
}
New-AzSqlServer @_SecondarySqlServer;
}


else
{
Write-Host $notexists -ForegroundColor Yellow
}
```

The preceding code is the same as what was explained in *Chapter 1, Introduction to Azure SQL managed databases*, to provision a new SQL server. The new server is provisioned only when **$Operation** is set to **Create**.

5. Copy and paste the following code to create the failover group:

```
# Create the failover group
Write-Host "Creating the failover group $FailoverGroupName "
-ForegroundColor Green
$failovergroup = New-AzSqlDatabaseFailoverGroup '
-ResourceGroupName $ResourceGroup '
-ServerName $PrimarySqlServer '
-PartnerServerName $SecondarySqlServer'
-FailoverGroupName $FailoverGroupName '
-FailoverPolicy Automatic '
-GracePeriodWithDataLossHours 1
}
```

The preceding code creates a new failover group if the **$Operation** parameter is set to **Create**. The **New-AzSqlDatabaseFailoverGroup** cmdlet accepts the following parameters:

- **ResourceGroupName**: The name of the resource group that contains the primary SQL server

- **ServerName**: The primary SQL server name

- **PartnerServerName**: The secondary SQL server name **FailoverGroupName**: The name of the failover group to be created

- **FailoverPolicy**: The failover policy, **Automatic** or **Manual**

- **GracePeriodWithDataLossHours**: The value for the duration the automatic failover should wait after a region outage, in hours

The failover group is created at the primary server location.

6. Copy and paste the following code to add the databases to the failover group:

```
# Add databases to the failover group
if(![string]::IsNullOrEmpty($DatabasesToReplicate.Replace(',',''))
-and $Failover -eq $false -and $Operation -eq "Create")
{
$dbname = $DatabasesToReplicate.Split(','); foreach($db in $dbname)
{
Write-Host "Adding database $db to failover group
$FailoverGroupName " -ForegroundColor Green
$database = Get-AzSqlDatabase -DatabaseName $db
-ResourceGroupName $ResourceGroup -ServerName $PrimarySqlServer
Add-AzSqlDatabaseToFailoverGroup -ResourceGroupName
$ResourceGroup -ServerName $PrimarySqlServer -FailoverGroupName
$FailoverGroupName -Database $database
}

}
```

The preceding code splits the comma-delimited database names in the **$DatabasesToReplicate** parameter and adds them to the group.

The **Add-AzSqlDatabaseToFailoverGroup** cmdlet adds the databases to the group and accepts the following parameter values:

- **ResourceGroupName**: The name of the primary SQL Server resource group.

- **ServerName**: The primary SQL server's name.

- **FailoverGroupName**: The name of the failover group the databases are to be added to.

- **Database**: The database object of the database to be added. This is set by calling the **Get-AzSqlDatabase** cmdlet.

The databases are added to the failover group and replication sync is started.

7. Copy and paste the following code to manually fail over all the failover groups to the secondary server:

```
# failover to secondary
if($Failover)
{
Write-Host "Failover to secondary server $SecondarySqlServer "
-ForegroundColor Green
Switch-AzSqlDatabaseFailoverGroup -ResourceGroupName
$ResourceGroup -ServerName $SecondarySqlServer -FailoverGroupName
$FailoverGroupName
}
```

The **Switch-AzSqlDatabaseFailoverGroup** cmdlet does the manual failover. It accepts the following parameters:

- **ResourceGroupName**: The failover group that includes the SQL Server resource group name

- **ServerName**: The primary SQL server name

- **FailoverGroupName**: The failover group name

8. Copy and paste the following code to remove the failover group and stop active geo-replication between the primary and secondary servers:

```
if($Operation -eq "Remove")
{
Write-Host "Deleting the failover group $FailoverGroupName "
-ForegroundColor Green
Remove-AzSqlDatabaseFailoverGroup -ResourceGroupName
$ResourceGroup -ServerName $PrimarySqlServer -FailoverGroupName
$FailoverGroupName

# remove the replication link
$dbname = $DatabasesToReplicate.Split(','); foreach($db in $dbname)
{
Write-Host "Removing replication for database $db "
-ForegroundColor Green
$database = Get-AzSqlDatabase -DatabaseName $db
-ResourceGroupName $ResourceGroup -ServerName $PrimarySqlServer
$database | Remove-AzSqlDatabaseSecondary
-PartnerResourceGroupName $ResourceGroup -ServerName
$PrimarySqlServer -PartnerServerName $SecondarySqlServer
}
}
```

The preceding code is executed when the **$Operation** parameter is set to **Remove**. Now, **Remove-AzSqlDatabaseFailoverGroup** deletes the failover group. It accepts the following parameters:

- **ResourceGroupName**: The failover group resource group name

- **ServerName**: The primary SQL server name

- **FailoverGroupName**: The name of the failover group that is to be deleted. Removing the failover group doesn't stop replication sync.

The databases are still being replicated and are not part of a failover group. The databases can still fail to the secondary server individually, as shown in the previous activity.

Remove-AzSqlDatabaseSecondary removes or stops the replication, as explained in the previous activity.

This completes the script. Press *Ctrl* + S to save the script.

Executing the PowerShell script

To execute the PowerShell script, perform the following steps:

1. Press *Windows* + R to open the **Run** command window. Type `PowerShell` and hit *Enter* to open a new **PowerShell** console window.

2. Change the directory to the folder that has the `Manage- FailoverGroup.ps1` script in it. For example, if the script is in the **C:\Code\Chapter09** directory, run the following command to switch to that directory:

   ```
   cd C:\Code\Chapter09
   ```

3. In the PowerShell console window, execute the following command to create a new failover group and add databases to it:

   ```
   .\Manage-FailoverGroup.ps1 -ResourceGroup toystore
   -PrimarySqlServer toyfactory -UserName sqladmin -Password Packt@pub2
   -SecondarySqlServer toyfactory-centralus
   -SecondaryServerLocation "Central US" -DatabasesToReplicate "toystore_
   Shard_100_150,toystore_Shard_150_200" -Operation "Create"
   -FailoverGroupName toyfactoryfailovergroup
   -AzureProfileFilePath c:\Code\MyAzureProfile.json
   ```

The preceding command will create a new failover group, **toyfactoryfailovergroup**, and add the **toystore_Shard_100_150** and **toystore_150_200** databases to the newly created failover group.

The failover group name is the new endpoint to be used by the application to connect to the failover group. In other words, the application connects to **toyfactoryfailovergroup.database.windows.net** and not individual primary or secondary database endpoints.

> **Note**
>
> The **toystore_Shard_100_150** and **toystore_150_200** databases were created in *Chapter 7, Scalability*.

This is similar to the availability group listener in an Always On configuration.

The Azure SQL server that the failover group points to is transparent to the user. In the case of a failover, the failover group endpoint points to the new primary.

Therefore, unlike active geo-replication, you don't need to manage the database connection string (endpoint) within the application when the failover occurs.

4. In the PowerShell console window, execute the following code to perform the manual failover:

```
.\Manage-FailoverGroup.ps1 -PrimarySqlServer toyfactory -ResourceGroup
toystore
-SecondarySqlServer toyfactory-centralus -FailoverGroupName
toyfactoryfailovergroup -Failover $true -AzureProfileFilePath c:\Code\
MyAzureProfile.json
```

The preceding command will fail over all the databases in the **toyfactoryfailovergroup** failover group to the secondary server and make it the new primary server.

You can verify this from the Azure portal.

5. Copy and paste the following command to remove the failover group and stop the replication between the primary and secondary servers:

```
# delete failover group and stop the replication
.\Manage-FailoverGroup.ps1 -ResourceGroup toystore
-PrimarySqlServer toyfactory-centralus -UserName sqladmin -Password Packt@
pub2 -SecondarySqlServer toyfactory -SecondaryServerLocation "Central US"
-DatabasesToReplicate "toystore_Shard_100_150,toystore_Shard_150_200"
-Operation "Remove" -FailoverGroupName toyfactoryfailovergroup
-AzureProfileFilePath c:\Code\MyAzureProfile.json
```

The preceding command will remove the **toyfactoryfailovergroup** failover group and break the replication link between the primary and secondary databases.

However, the secondary server and the databases won't be deleted.

Notice that the **PrimarySqlServer** parameter value is **toyfactory-centralus** and that the **SecondarySqlServer** parameter value is **toyfactory**, which is the reverse of what we provided in *Step 2* of *Executing the PowerShell script* when creating the failover group. This is because, when we did a manual failover, the primary and secondary server roles were reversed. As mentioned earlier, the failover group is maintained by the primary database, so, to delete the failover group, the primary is now the secondary and the secondary is the new primary.

Up to now, we have seen steps to configure an auto-failover group for Azure SQL Database. Now let's see the steps for configuring an auto-failover group in SQL Managed Instance.

Activity: Configuring an auto-failover group for SQL Managed Instance

In this activity, we will learn to set up a failover group between SQL managed instances.

We will cover the following:

- Deploying a secondary virtual network
- Deploying secondary SQL managed instances for failover group setup
- Setting up global virtual network peering between a primary and secondary virtual network
- Creating and testing a failover group

You need to have a primary SQL managed instance before deploying the secondary SQL managed instance. We are using the same SQL managed instance as the primary one that we deployed in *Chapter 1, Introduction to Azure SQL managed databases*.

Deploying a secondary virtual network

You need to manually prepare a virtual network before deploying a secondary SQL managed instance using the Azure portal. This step is essential since it is a requirement of having different IP ranges for the SQL Managed Instance subnet.

To verify the primary virtual network subnet IP ranges, follow these steps:

1. Go to the Azure portal and navigate to SQL Managed Instance resource group and select the primary virtual network.

2. Select **Subnets** under **Settings** and keep a note of IP ranges for the SQL Managed Instance subnet:

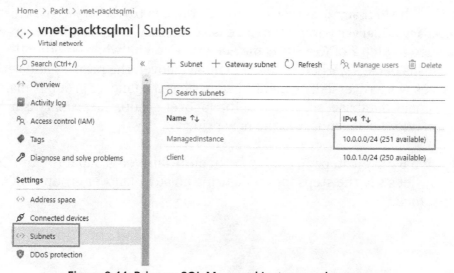

Figure 9.44: Primary SQL Managed Instance subnet range

To create a secondary virtual network, follow these steps:

1. Go to the Azure portal and select **Create a resource**:

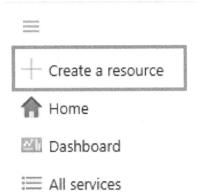

Figure 9.45: Creating a resource

2. Search for `Virtual Network`:

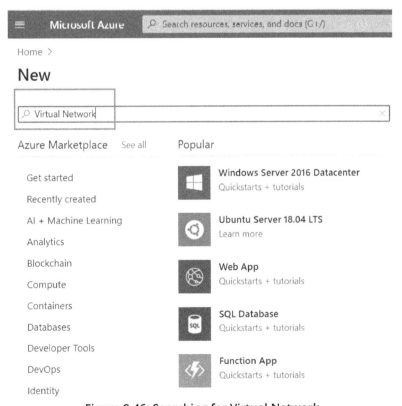

Figure 9.46: Searching for Virtual Network

3. Click on **Create** to deploy the virtual network resource:

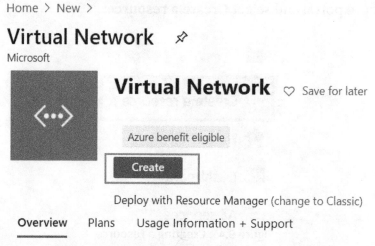

Figure 9.47: Creating a virtual network resource

4. Fill the required details on the form, including the **Subscription**, **Resource group**, **Name**, and **Region** fields, then move to the **IP Addresses** tab:

Create virtual network

Basics   IP Addresses   Security   Tags   Review + create

Azure Virtual Network (VNet) is the fundamental building block for your private network in Azure. VNet enables many types of Azure resources, such as Azure Virtual Machines (VM), to securely communicate with each other, the internet, and on-premises networks. VNet is similar to a traditional network that you'd operate in your own data center, but brings with it additional benefits of Azure's infrastructure such as scale, availability, and isolation. Learn more about virtual network

Project details

Subscription * ⓘ	Pay-As-You-Go
Resource group * ⓘ	(New) SecondaryMI
	Create new

Instance details

| Name * | packtsqlmi2 |
| Region * | (US) West US 2 |

Review + create   < Previous   Next : IP Addresses >   Download a template for automation

Figure 9.48: The Basics tab

5. Make sure that you choose different IP ranges for the SQL Managed Instance subnet than for the primary instance and click on the **Review + create** button to deploy this virtual network. To read more about virtual networks and CIDR, please visit https://devblogs.microsoft.com/premier-developer/understanding-cidr-notation-when-designing-azure-virtual-networks-and-subnets/:

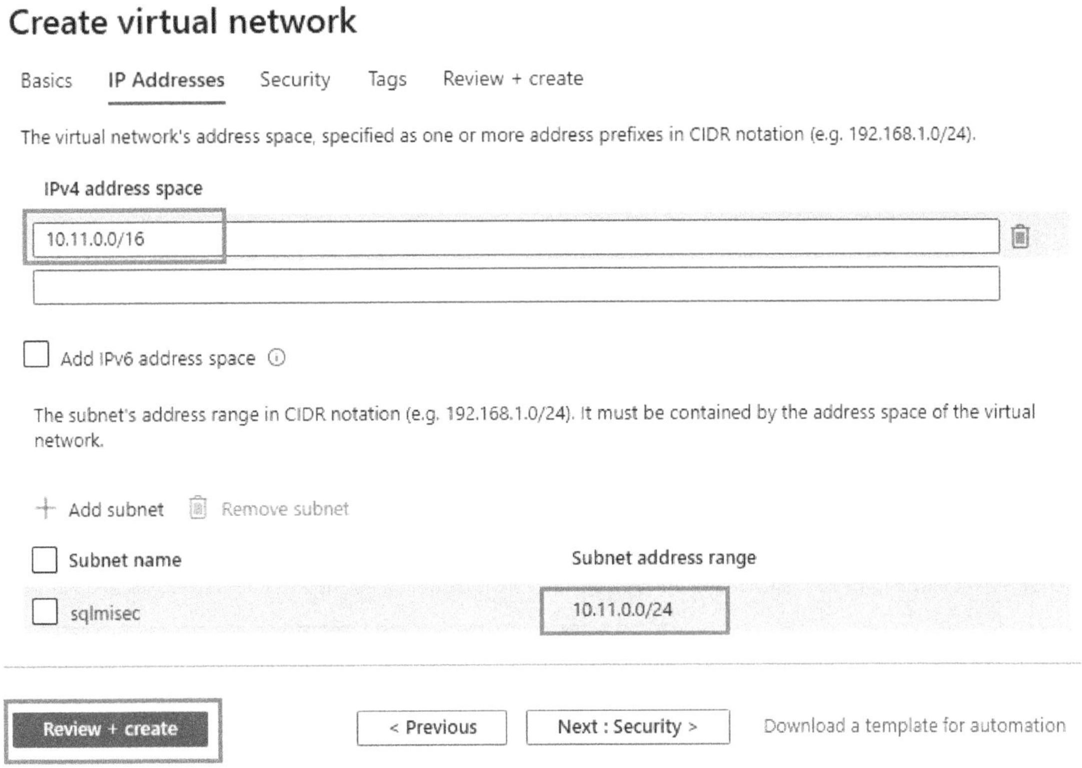

Create virtual network

Basics   **IP Addresses**   Security   Tags   Review + create

The virtual network's address space, specified as one or more address prefixes in CIDR notation (e.g. 192.168.1.0/24).

IPv4 address space

    10.11.0.0/16   🗑

☐ Add IPv6 address space ⓘ

The subnet's address range in CIDR notation (e.g. 192.168.1.0/24). It must be contained by the address space of the virtual network.

＋ Add subnet   🗑 Remove subnet

Subnet name	Subnet address range
☐ sqlmisec	10.11.0.0/24

Review + create   < Previous   Next : Security >   Download a template for automation

Figure 9.49: Virtual network IP Addresses tab

Deploying a secondary SQL managed instance

Deployment steps for secondary SQL managed instance deployment are mostly the same as those we followed in *Chapter 1, Introduction to Azure SQL managed databases*, for deploying an SQL managed instance. We will quickly recap some steps and look at the steps that are essential to set up a secondary instance with a primary instance DNS zone.

Follow these steps to create a secondary SQL managed instance:

1. Go to the Azure portal and select the single SQL Managed Instance deployment option and fill the necessary details in the **Basics** form, then move to the **Networking** tab:

Home > SQL managed instances >

Create Azure SQL Database Managed Instance

Microsoft

Basics   Networking   Additional settings   Tags   Review + create

SQL Managed Instance is a fully managed PaaS database service with extensive on-premises SQL Server compatibility and native virtual network security. Learn more ☑

Project details

Select the subscription to manage deployed resources and costs. Use resource groups like folders to organize and manage all your resources.

Subscription * ⓘ

| Pay-As-You-Go | ⌄ |

Resource group * ⓘ

| SecondaryMI | ⌄ |
Create new

Managed Instance details

Enter required settings for this instance, including picking a location and configuring the compute and storage resources.

Managed Instance name *

| packtsqlmi2 | ✓ |

Region *

| (US) West US 2 | ⌄ |

Not seeing a region?

Compute + storage * ⓘ

General Purpose
Gen5, 4 vCores, 32 GB storage, Geo-redundant backup storage
Configure Managed Instance

Administrator account

Managed Instance admin login *

| miadmin | ✓ |

Password *

| ••••••••••••••• | ✓ |

Confirm password *

| ••••••••••••••• | ✓ |

| Review + create | | < Previous | | Next : Networking > |

Figure 9.50: SQL Managed Instance Basics tab

2. Select the virtual network and subnet that we created in the previous virtual network activity and move to the **Additional settings** tab:

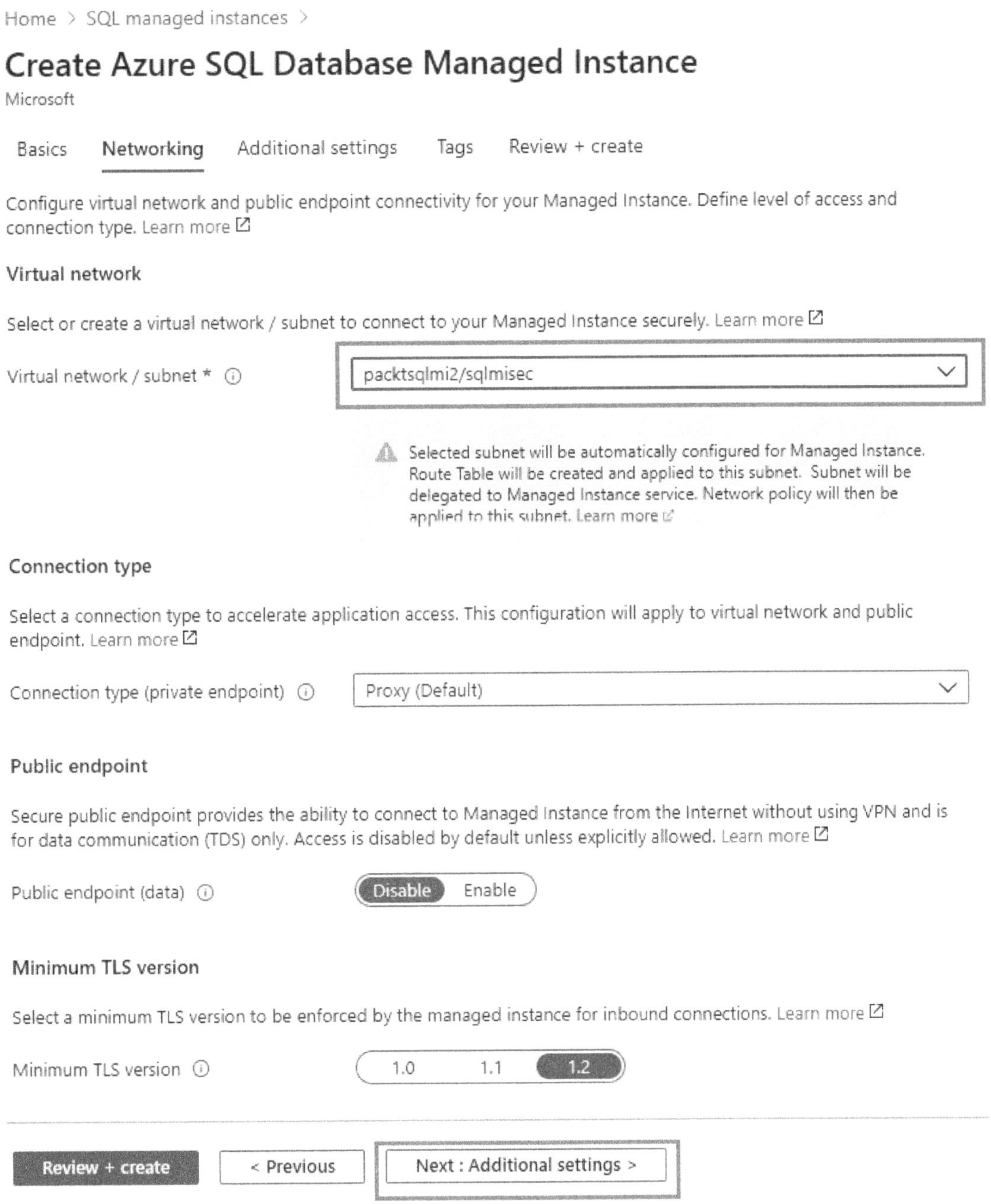

Home > SQL managed instances >

Create Azure SQL Database Managed Instance
Microsoft

| Basics | **Networking** | Additional settings | Tags | Review + create |

Configure virtual network and public endpoint connectivity for your Managed Instance. Define level of access and connection type. Learn more ☑

Virtual network

Select or create a virtual network / subnet to connect to your Managed Instance securely. Learn more ☑

Virtual network / subnet * ⓘ

packtsqlmi2/sqlmisec   ∨

⚠ Selected subnet will be automatically configured for Managed Instance. Route Table will be created and applied to this subnet. Subnet will be delegated to Managed Instance service. Network policy will then be applied to this subnet. Learn more ☑

Connection type

Select a connection type to accelerate application access. This configuration will apply to virtual network and public endpoint. Learn more ☑

Connection type (private endpoint) ⓘ   Proxy (Default)   ∨

Public endpoint

Secure public endpoint provides the ability to connect to Managed Instance from the Internet without using VPN and is for data communication (TDS) only. Access is disabled by default unless explicitly allowed. Learn more ☑

Public endpoint (data) ⓘ   (**Disable**   Enable)

Minimum TLS version

Select a minimum TLS version to be enforced by the managed instance for inbound connections. Learn more ☑

Minimum TLS version ⓘ   (1.0   1.1   **1.2**)

[Review + create]   [< Previous]   [Next : Additional settings >]

Figure 9.51: SQL Managed Instance Networking tab

3. Select the geo-replication settings, such as deploying this instance as a failover secondary and specifying the primary DNS zone, and make sure that the collation and time zone settings match the primary instance. Finally, click on **Review + create** to deploy the secondary SQL managed instance:

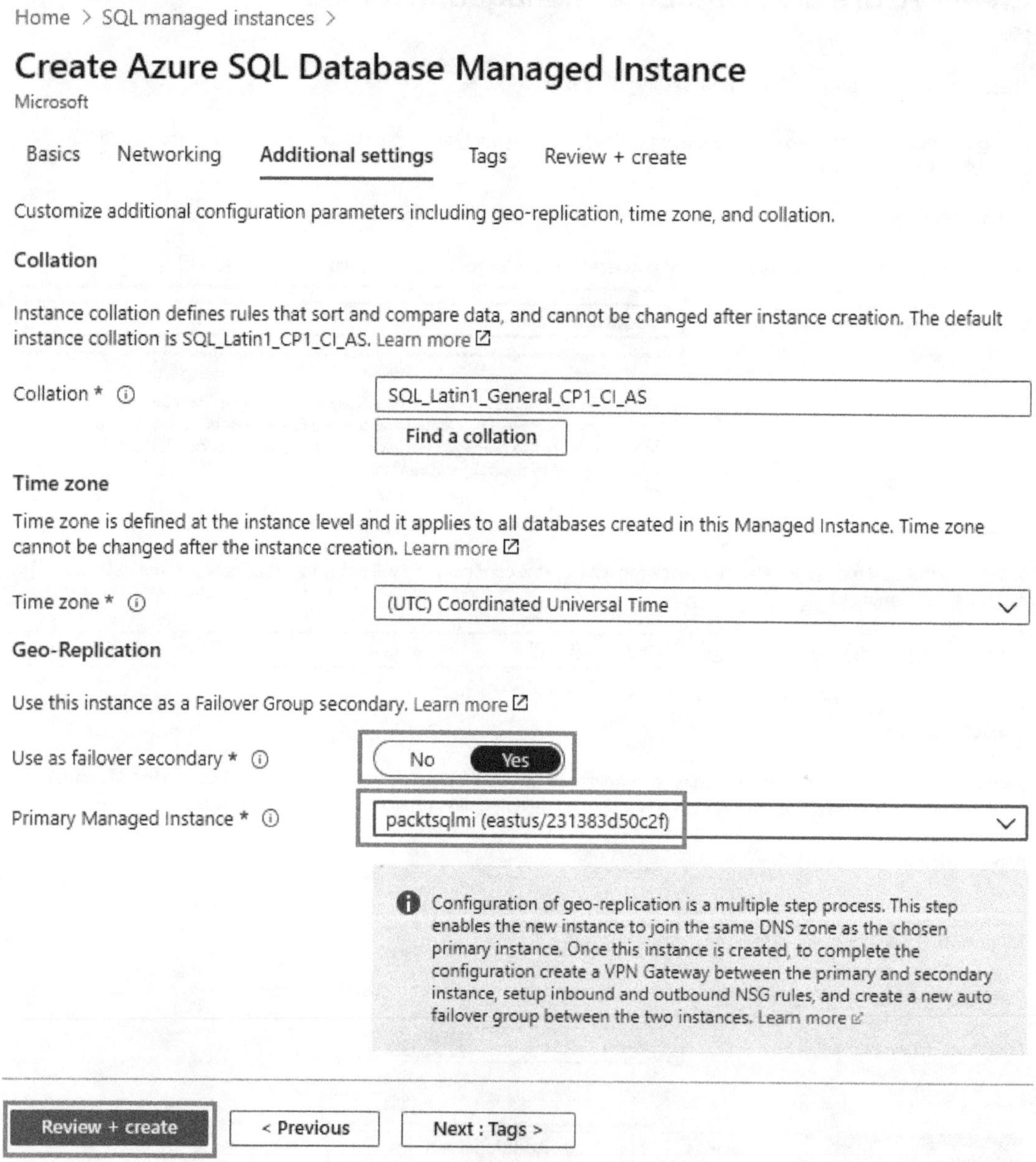

Home > SQL managed instances >

Create Azure SQL Database Managed Instance

Microsoft

| Basics | Networking | **Additional settings** | Tags | Review + create |

Customize additional configuration parameters including geo-replication, time zone, and collation.

Collation

Instance collation defines rules that sort and compare data, and cannot be changed after instance creation. The default instance collation is SQL_Latin1_CP1_CI_AS. Learn more ☑

Collation * ⓘ

```
SQL_Latin1_General_CP1_CI_AS
```

Find a collation

Time zone

Time zone is defined at the instance level and it applies to all databases created in this Managed Instance. Time zone cannot be changed after the instance creation. Learn more ☑

Time zone * ⓘ

```
(UTC) Coordinated Universal Time                                        ⌄
```

Geo-Replication

Use this instance as a Failover Group secondary. Learn more ☑

Use as failover secondary * ⓘ   (No   Yes)

Primary Managed Instance * ⓘ

```
packtsqlmi (eastus/231383d50c2f)                                        ⌄
```

> ⓘ Configuration of geo-replication is a multiple step process. This step enables the new instance to join the same DNS zone as the chosen primary instance. Once this instance is created, to complete the configuration create a VPN Gateway between the primary and secondary instance, setup inbound and outbound NSG rules, and create a new auto failover group between the two instances. Learn more ☑

| Review + create | | < Previous | | Next : Tags > |

Figure 9.52: SQL Managed Instance Additional settings tab

Configuring global virtual network peering between primary and secondary virtual networks

This step is required to allow traffic between two SQL managed instances to transfer data. You can use ExpressRoute or a virtual network–to–virtual network VPN tunnel to set up this traffic, but here we are using an easy, low-latency, high-bandwidth global VNet peering setup.

Please follow these steps to configure global VNet peering between cross-region virtual networks:

1. Go to the Azure portal, navigate to the primary instance resource group, and select the virtual network.

2. Select the **Peerings** option under **Settings** and click on **Add**:

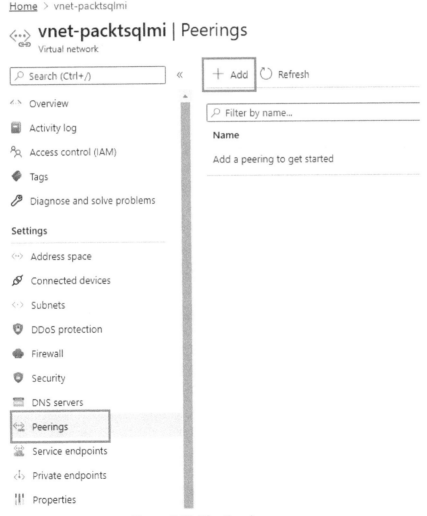

Figure 9.53: The Peerings pane

3. Input the primary and secondary link names, choose the remote virtual network for the secondary server, and click on **Add**:

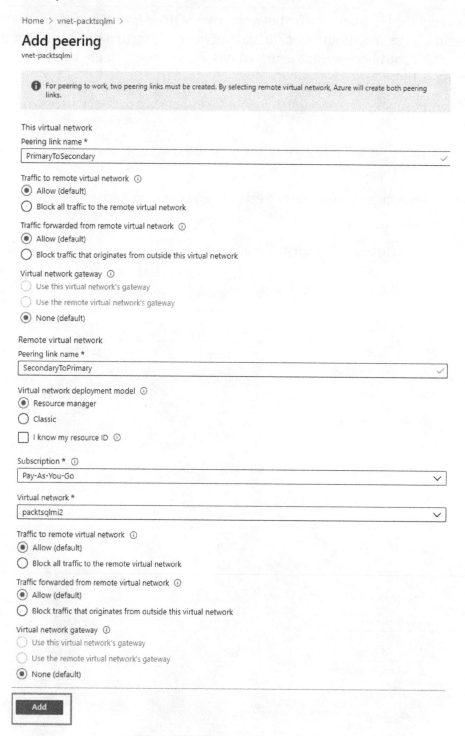

Figure 9.54: The Add peering form

4. You can monitor the notification bell icon for an indication of the successful deployment of peering connections:

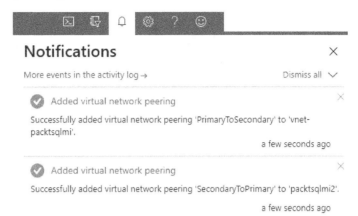

Figure 9.55: Notification for peering connections

Creating and testing the failover group

So far, we have deployed a secondary SQL managed instance and set up the data traffic between the primary and secondary virtual network using global virtual network peering. Now let's create a failover group to start the geo-replication. The secondary instance should be empty before adding it to the failover group.

To create and test the failover group, follow these steps:

1. Go to the Azure portal, navigate to the primary SQL managed instance and select **Failover groups** under **Data management**. Click on **Add group**:

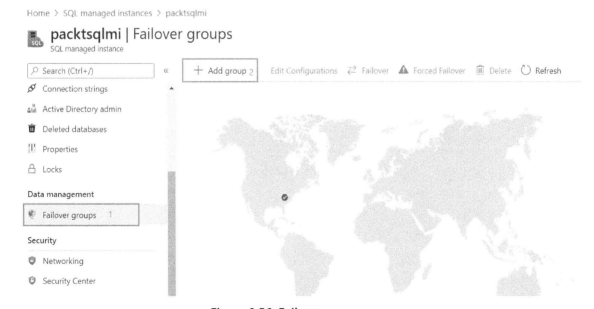

Figure 9.56: Failover groups pane

2. Fill in **Failover group name** and select the secondary SQL managed instance. Click on **Create** to deploy:

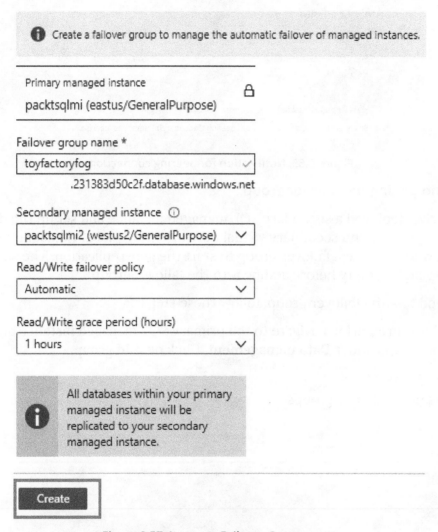

Figure 9.57: Instance Failover Group pane

3. After successful deployment, you will see the status of the failover group using the **Failover groups** pane in SQL Managed Instance:

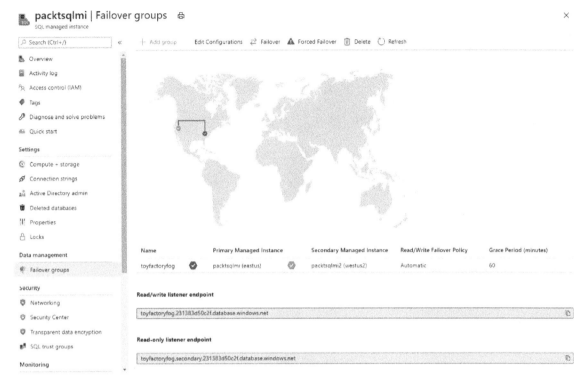

Figure 9.58: Failover groups pane after deployment

Testing the failover

In this step, you will fail your failover group over to the secondary server, and then fail back using the Azure portal:

1. Go to the Azure portal and navigate to your secondary SQL managed instance. Select **Failover groups** under **Data management**.

2. Review which SQL managed instance is the primary, and which instance is the secondary:

Figure 9.59: Secondary SQL Managed Instance failover group

3. Select **Failover** and then select **Yes** on the warning about TDS sessions being disconnected:

Figure 9.60: TDS warning notification

4. Review the failover group state; the two SQL managed instances should have switched roles:

Name	Primary Managed Instance	Secondary Managed Instance	Read/Write Failover Policy	Grace Period (minutes)
toyfactoryfog	packtsqlmi2 (westus2)	packtsqlmi (eastus)	Automatic	60

Figure 9.61: Verifying the role change after failover

5. Go to the new secondary SQL managed instance and select **Failover** once again to failback to the primary instance.

In this activity, we have learned to create a failover group for an SQL Managed Instance for a business continuity solution. We have seen steps to deploy a secondary SQL managed instance and global virtual network peering. At the end of the activity, we created and tested the failover group.

Summary

In this chapter, you learned about the high availability and DR features of Azure SQL Database and SQL Managed Instance. High availability is built into Azure SQL Database and SQL Managed Instance and is managed by Microsoft, whereas DR can be achieved by configuring active geo-replication and failover groups as and when required.

You also learned about ADR, a new feature introduced with Azure SQL Database, SQL Managed Instance, and SQL Server 2019, which provides instant database recovery, transaction rollbacks, and aggressive log truncation.

Furthermore, you saw how zone-redundant configuration provides additional high availability by replicating the database in multiple Availability Zones within the same region.

In the next chapter, you will learn about how to monitor an Azure SQL Database and SQL Managed Instance using the Azure portal, dynamic management views, and extended events to help improve the performance of your application.

10

Monitoring and tuning

This chapter covers different techniques to monitor and tune a SQL database and a managed instance. You will learn how to monitor Azure SQL Databases and managed instances using the Azure portal, **dynamic management views (DMVs)**, and extended events. You will learn how to tune an Azure SQL Database using automatic tuning and Query Performance Insight. You will also learn how to implement in-memory features to improve workload performance.

By the end of this chapter, you will be able to:

- Monitor and tune an Azure SQL Database or SQL Managed Instance from the Azure portal

- Monitor an Azure SQL Database or SQL Managed Instance using DMVs

- Monitor an Azure SQL Database using extended events

- Implement in-memory technologies to improve database performance

- Monitor an Azure SQL Database and SQL Managed Instance using Azure SQL Analytics

- Monitor and tune an Azure SQL Managed Instance using HammerDB and the QPI library

The following section demonstrates how to monitor an Azure SQL Database or SQL Managed Instance through the Azure portal.

Monitoring an Azure SQL Database and SQL Managed Instance using the Azure portal

Firstly, it is easy to monitor Azure SQL Database and SQL Managed Instance storage utilization using the Azure portal. The **Database data storage** option in the Azure SQL Database **Overview** section provides a chart of used space, allocated space, and the maximum storage size:

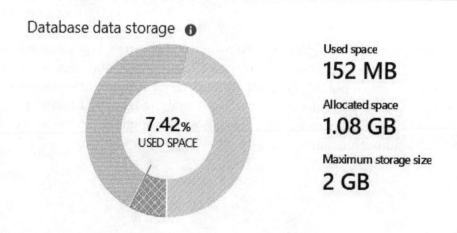

Figure 10.1: Database data storage chart

Similarly, the **Storage utilization** section in the SQL Managed Instance **Overview** tab can give you a quick overview of the used storage and maximum storage of a managed instance:

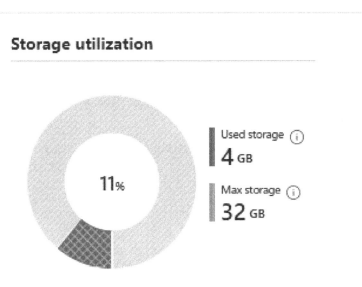

Figure 10.2: Storage utilization overview chart

Beyond storage, the Azure portal provides some other more sophisticated monitoring options, which are available in the **Monitoring** section for Azure SQL Database and SQL Managed Instance.

The **Monitoring** section for Azure SQL Database and SQL Managed Instance in the Azure portal has the following options:

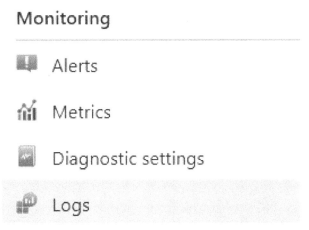

Figure 10.3: The Monitoring section for Azure SQL Database and SQL Managed Instance

There is an additional functionality for Azure SQL Database in the Azure portal called Intelligent Performance, which we will discuss in a later section.

Let's look at each of these options in detail.

Monitoring database metrics

Database metrics such as CPU percentage, DTU percentage, and data I/O can be monitored in the **Overview** section of Azure SQL Database. For SQL Managed Instance, you can monitor the average CPU percentage metric and storage usage for an instance using the **Overview** tab.

The **Overview** section of Azure SQL Database displays the CPU percentage for the past hour, the last 24 hours, or the last 7 days, in the form of a line chart:

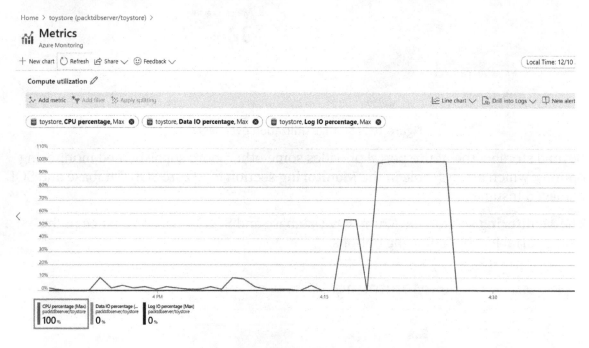

Figure 10.4: Compute utilization metrics

The **Overview** section of SQL Managed Instance displays the average CPU percentage for the past hour, the last 24 hours, or the last 7 days, in the form of a line chart:

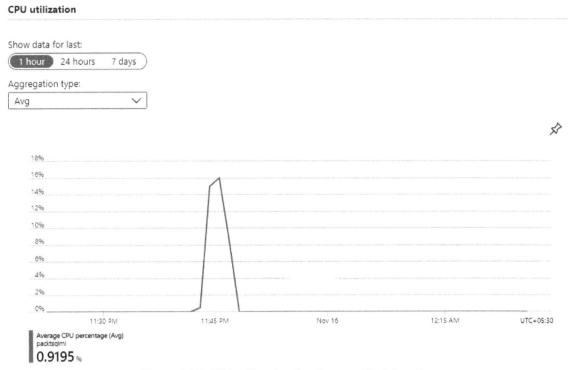

Figure 10.5: CPU utilization for the specified duration

You can even pin the chart to your Azure portal dashboard by clicking on the pin icon in the upper-right corner of the chart.

This way, you can monitor your database DTU percentage or instance CPU usage as and when required.

> **Note**
>
> In order to see the graph working, a workload needs to be running. You can achieve this by executing the **Start-Workload.sql** file in the **C:\Code\Chapter10** folder.

To view the metrics by running the workload, open a new PowerShell session and run the following command:

SQL Database

```
.\Start-Workload.ps1 -sqlserver toyfactory -database toystore -sqluser
sqladmin -sqlpassword Packt@pub2 -workloadsql .\workload.sql
```

SQL Managed Instance

```
.\Start-Workload.ps1 -sqlserver 'packtsqlmi.<dnszone>.database.windows.net'
-database toystore -sqluser miadmin -sqlpassword 'Password' -workloadsql .\
workload.sql
```

The preceding command will use the **ostress.exe** RML utility (in the **Start-Workload.ps1** file) to execute the queries specified in the **workload.sql** file against the **toystore** database in the **toyfactory** Azure SQL server.

For a more detailed analysis and to monitor other metrics, click the line chart and it will redirect you to the **Metrics** section of Azure SQL Database or SQL Managed Instance. The following DTU percentage chart is displayed under the **Metrics** section of a database:

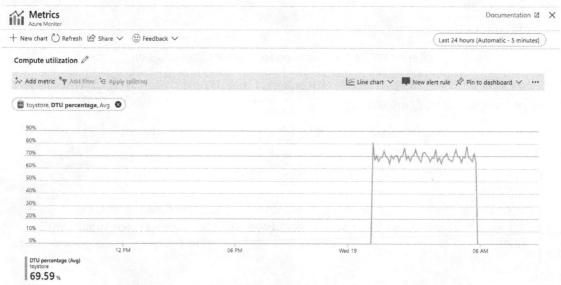

Figure 10.6: Avg DTU utilization for the toystore database

The average CPU percentage chart shown in *Figure* 10.7 is for SQL Managed Instance:

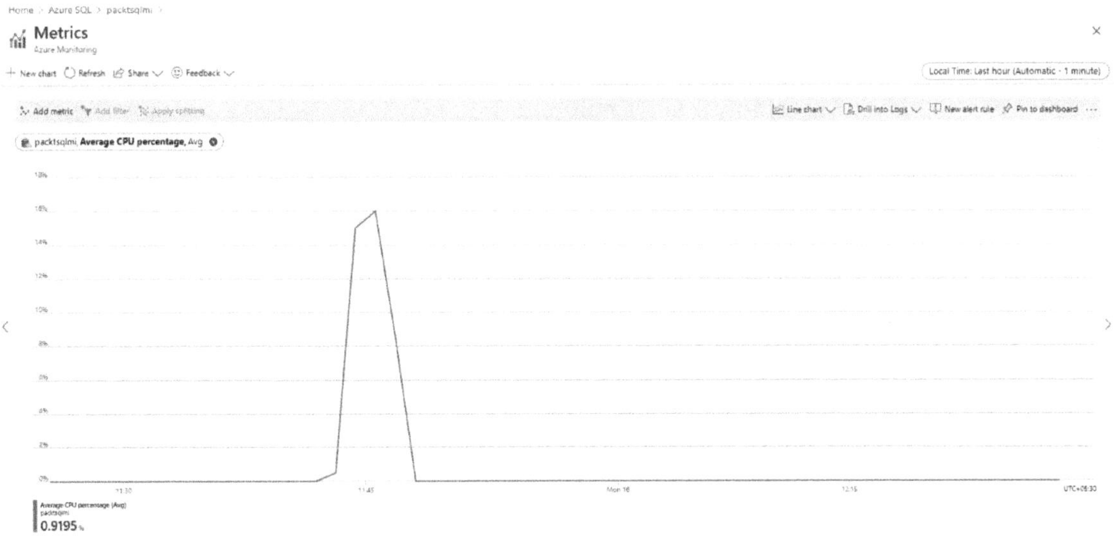

Figure 10.7: Avg DTU utilization for the packtsqlmi managed instance

The **Metrics** pane gives you further insight into the workload by allowing you to monitor other metrics, such as CPU percentage, data I/O percentage, and database size percentage for Azure SQL Database. For SQL Managed Instance, the average CPU percentage, I/O bytes read/written, and storage space reserved/used metrics can be monitored using the **Metrics** pane. Hover the mouse over the line chart, and the metrics at that point in time will be displayed at the bottom.

The **Metrics** pane also allows you to view metrics in multiple ranges, such as the past hour, the past 24 hours, the past week, and even a custom time range.

Select the metrics you want to monitor, name the chart, and pin it to the Azure portal dashboard for future monitoring.

> **Note**
>
> To name the chart, select the pen icon next to **Compute utilization**. The default chart name is **Compute utilization** for Azure SQL Database.

You can select one or more metrics and analyze the type of workload. For example, in the preceding chart for Azure SQL Database, the workload is CPU-intensive because the DTU percentage is equal to the CPU percentage, and because a data I/O percentage hasn't been recorded during the time period for Azure SQL Database.

You can add an alert for the proactive monitoring of a particular metric. For example, you can add an alert to send email notifications whenever the Azure SQL Database DTU percentage or SQL Managed Instance average CPU percentage crosses a threshold, such as 80%, or if the database size gets bigger than a certain threshold. In the next section, we'll talk about setting up alert rules.

You can even take preventative action automatically by using runbooks, similar to what was explained in *Chapter 7, Scalability*.

Alert rules, database size, and diagnostic settings

In this section, we will discuss how to create alerts for Azure SQL Database and SQL Managed Instance using the Azure portal, view the database size, and capture data using diagnostic settings. This section remains the same for Azure SQL Database and SQL Managed Instance, since both offerings use the Azure monitoring service to configure and manage metrics-based alerts.

Alert Rules

As stated earlier, you can create email alerts on the metrics you wish to monitor.

To create an alert using the Azure portal, follow these steps:

1. From the database **Overview** pane, select **Alerts** in the **Monitoring** section.

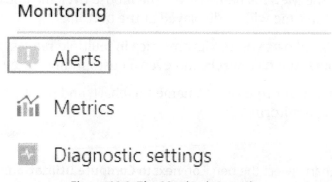

Figure 10.8: The Monitoring section

2. On the **Alerts** page, select **New alert rule** and fill out the alert details to create and set up the alert:

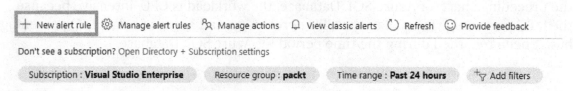

Figure 10.9: Creating a new alert rule

3. On the **Create alert rule** page, you'll have to specify the alert **Condition** (when it is to be triggered) and the alert **Actions** (what is to be done when the alert is triggered):

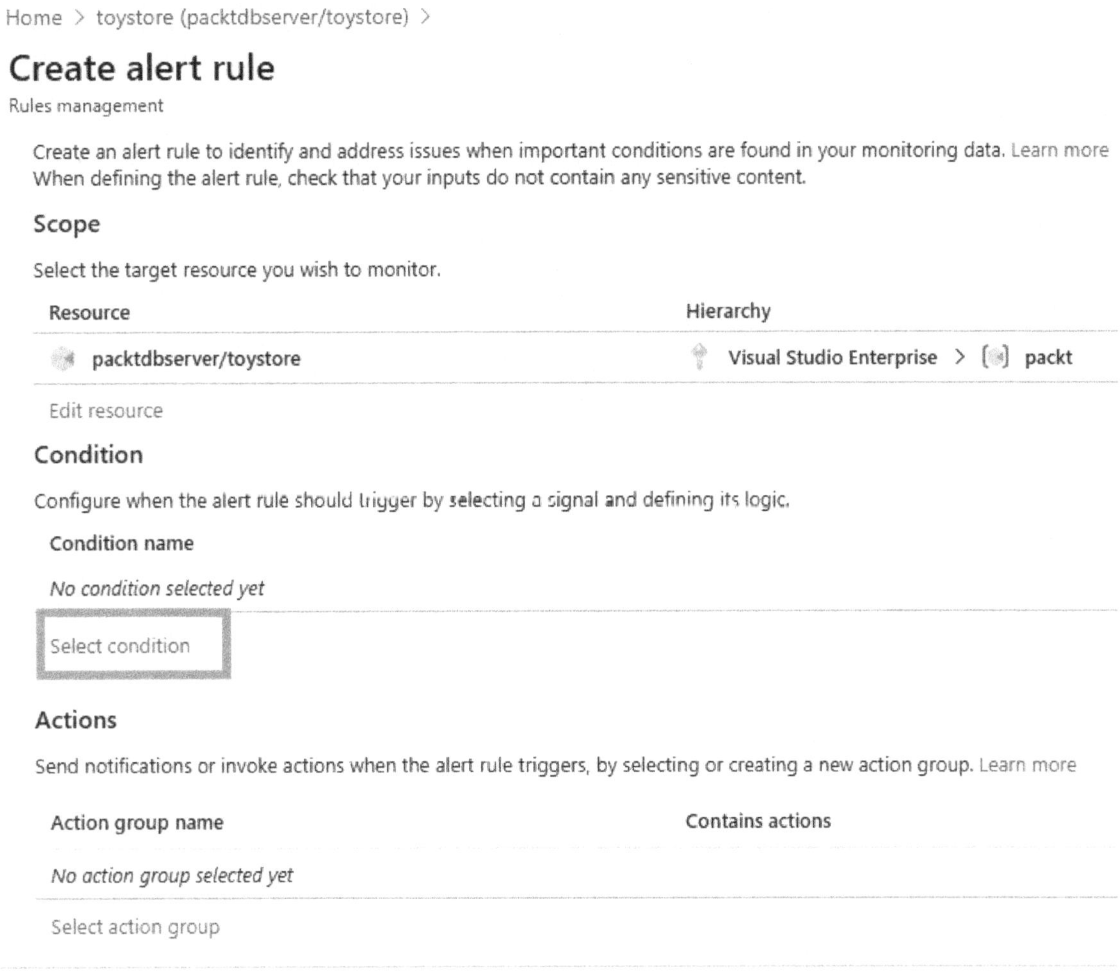

Home > toystore (packtdbserver/toystore) >

Create alert rule
Rules management

Create an alert rule to identify and address issues when important conditions are found in your monitoring data. Learn more
When defining the alert rule, check that your inputs do not contain any sensitive content.

Scope

Select the target resource you wish to monitor.

Resource	Hierarchy
packtdbserver/toystore	Visual Studio Enterprise > [ ] packt

Edit resource

Condition

Configure when the alert rule should trigger by selecting a signal and defining its logic.

Condition name

No condition selected yet

Select condition

Actions

Send notifications or invoke actions when the alert rule triggers, by selecting or creating a new action group. Learn more

Action group name	Contains actions
No action group selected yet	

Select action group

Figure 10.10: Specifying the alert condition

4. To add a condition, click the **Select condition** button under the **Condition** heading. On the **Configure signal logic** page, select **CPU percentage** as the alert condition:

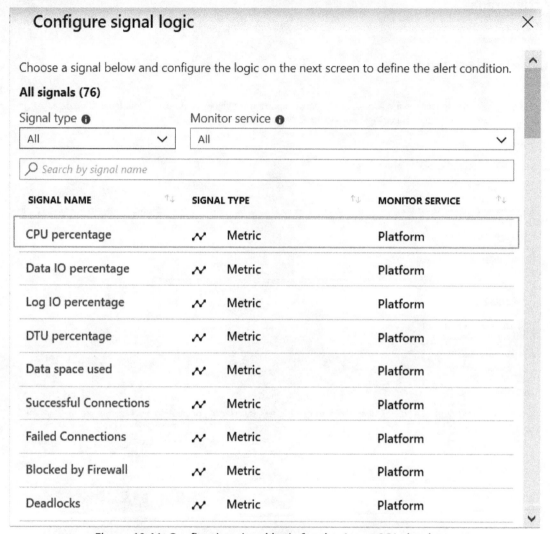

Figure 10.11: Configuring signal logic for the Azure SQL database

Figure 10.12 shows the **Configure signal logic** page for SQL Managed Instance:

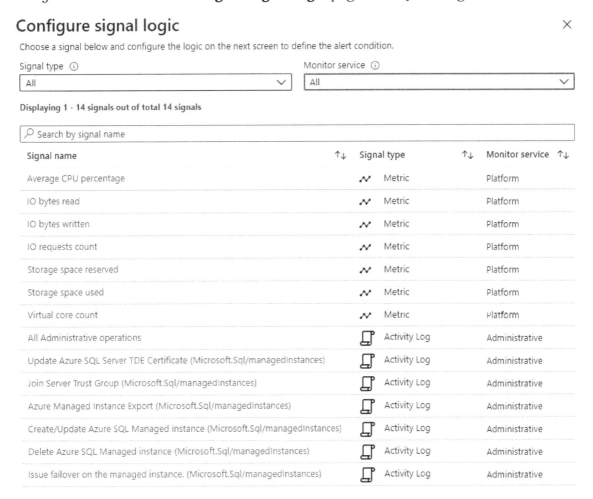

Figure 10.12: Configuring signal logic for the SQL managed instance

The new page displays a line chart for the last hour for the selected signal, CPU percentage. Scroll to the bottom and locate the **Alert logic** section.

The **Alert logic** section defines the threshold. There are two types of threshold, **Static** and **Dynamic**:

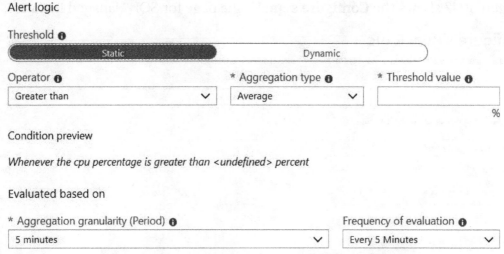

Figure 10.13: Using Static threshold for the alert logic

A **Static** threshold defines a threshold value, say, 70%. Therefore, whenever, the average (as defined by **Aggregation type**) CPU percentage is greater than 70% (as defined by **Operator**), the alert is triggered.

A **Dynamic** threshold uses advanced machine learning to automatically determine the threshold value using the metric's historical values:

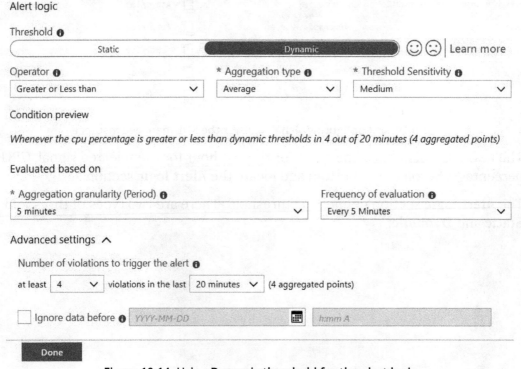

Figure 10.14: Using Dynamic threshold for the alert logic

The **Dynamic** threshold doesn't have a static threshold value. The **Threshold Sensitivity** setting defines the amount of deviation of the metric from the threshold that triggers an alert.

A high **Threshold Sensitivity** setting triggers an alert if there's the slightest deviation from the metric series pattern. A medium **Threshold Sensitivity** setting is less stringent and more balanced than a high threshold. A low **Threshold Sensitivity** setting triggers an alert when there's a large deviation from the metric series pattern. There are no defined values for deviation with high, medium, or low threshold sensitivities.

The **Dynamic** setting also allows us to configure the number of violations required during a certain time period to trigger an alert. This setting is found in the **Advanced** settings. The default is at least 4 violations in the last 20 minutes. This means that if, in the past 20 minutes, the CPU utilization has gone above the threshold of, say, 70% four times, then an alert is triggered.

The **Dynamic** threshold can also ignore data before a given time. When this is specified, the **Dynamic** threshold calculation is done after the date specified in the **Ignore data before** setting.

The **Dynamic** threshold setting helps us to configure alerts for different metrics when there are no defined alert threshold values.

5. Click **Done** to save the settings and return to the **Create alert rule** page. On the **Create alert rule** page, we can see that the **CPU percentage** alert condition has been added.

   The **Actions** section defines the action or the steps to be performed when an alert is triggered. The action could be an email to the concerned person, or automated steps defined by webhooks, runbooks, or functions.

   Scroll down to **Alert rule details** and provide **Alert rule name**, **Description** (optional), and **Severity** values:

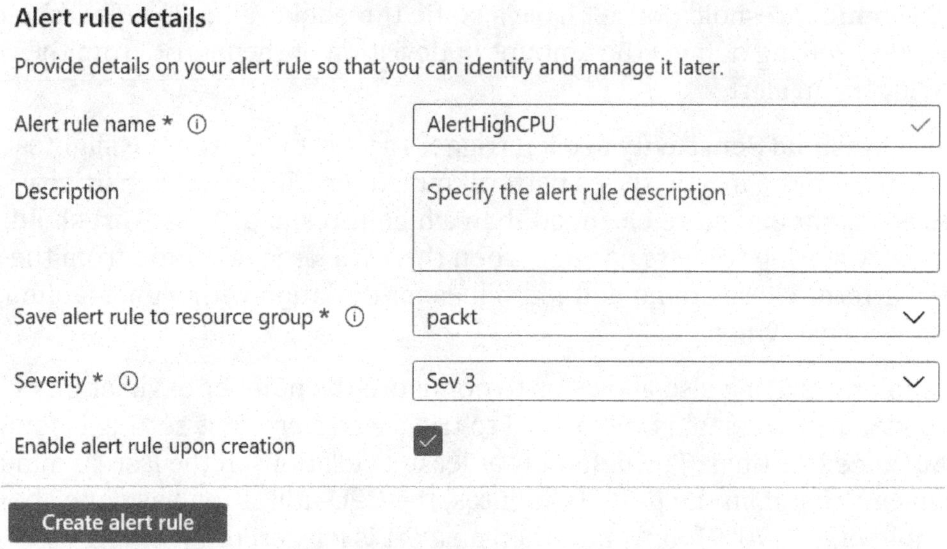

Alert rule details

Provide details on your alert rule so that you can identify and manage it later.

Alert rule name * ⓘ
`AlertHighCPU` ✓

Description
`Specify the alert rule description`

Save alert rule to resource group * ⓘ
`packt` ⌄

Severity * ⓘ
`Sev 3` ⌄

Enable alert rule upon creation ✓

Create alert rule

Figure 10.15: Alert rule details

6. Click **Create alert rule** to create the alert.

   You can also add a webhook to the alert to take preventative action automatically when the alert threshold is reached. For example, let's say you create an alert that sends out an email whenever the database size crosses the 80% threshold.

The administrator sees the email alert and increases the database size so that the customers aren't affected. However, you can automate this in the following ways:

- By creating an Azure Automation job that runs a PowerShell script to increase the database's size

- By creating a webhook for the Azure Automation job

- By specifying the webhook in the alert definition

The next time the database size percentage is greater than 80%, the alert will send out an email notification to the administrator and will trigger the webhook. This will start the Azure Automation job, and the database size will be increased.

Diagnostic settings and logs

Like alerts, this feature is also the same for both Azure SQL Database and SQL Managed Instance, since it's inherited from the Azure Monitor service.

Diagnostic settings allow you to collect data such as database wait statistics, timeouts, errors, and database blocks to troubleshoot performance issues or audit an Azure SQL database.

The following data can be captured using diagnostic settings:

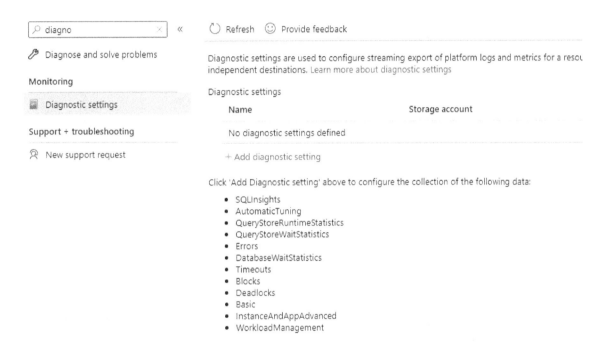

Figure 10.16: Data captured using diagnostic settings for Azure SQL Database

For SQL Managed Instance, using diagnostic settings, you can collect resource usage stats, DevOps operations audit events and SQL security audit events at the instance level, and SQL Intelligent Insights and SQL Server Query Store runtime stats/wait stats at the database level.

The following data can be captured for SQL Managed Instance at the instance level:

Figure 10.17: Adding a diagnostic setting for capturing data at the instance level

The following data can be captured for SQL Managed Instance at the database level:

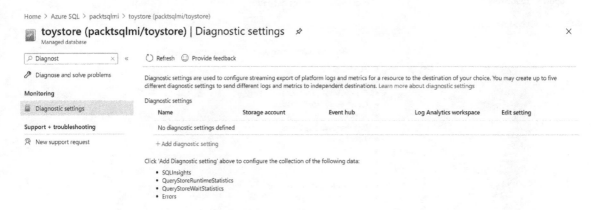

Figure 10.18: Adding a diagnostic setting for capturing data at the database level

The method for enabling the diagnostic logs is the same for both Azure SQL Database and SQL Managed Instance, and the following is an example of enabling diagnostic settings for Azure SQL Database.

To enable diagnostic settings, on the **toystore** database page, search for `diagnostic`, and click to open the **Diagnostic settings** page:

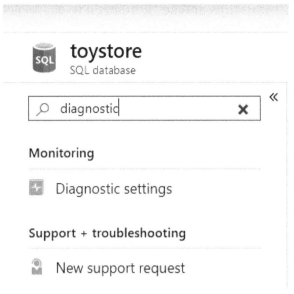

Figure 10.19: Diagnostic settings

On the **Diagnostics settings** pane, follow these steps:

1. Click **Add diagnostic setting** to add a new diagnostic setting.

2. Provide a name for this setting. For example, if you plan to collect wait stats, you can name it `toystore wait stats`.

3. Select **Archive to a storage account** and then select the storage account where the diagnostic data will be saved.

   You can also stream the data to an event hub for real-time monitoring or send it to Log Analytics.

4. Check **DatabaseWaitStatistics** and set **Retention** to 0. The retention only applies to the **Archive to a storage account** option.

    The **Archive to a storage account** option lets you save the diagnostic data to an Azure Storage container. The log files can therefore be used for troubleshooting as and when required:

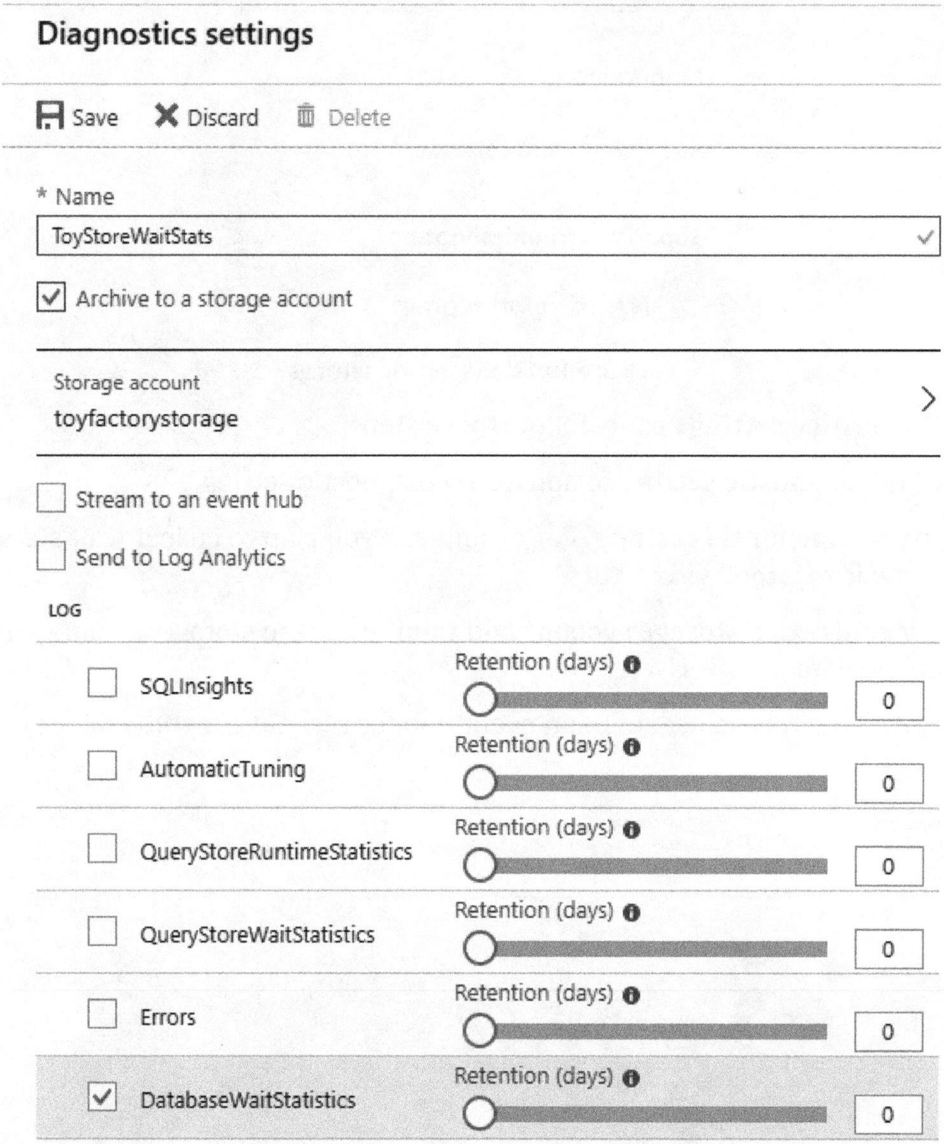

Diagnostics settings

🖫 Save   ✖ Discard   🗑 Delete

* Name

| ToyStoreWaitStats | ✓ |

☑ Archive to a storage account

Storage account
toyfactorystorage   ＞

☐ Stream to an event hub

☐ Send to Log Analytics

LOG

		Retention (days) ❶	
☐	SQLInsights	○────────────	0
☐	AutomaticTuning	○────────────	0
☐	QueryStoreRuntimeStatistics	○────────────	0
☐	QueryStoreWaitStatistics	○────────────	0
☐	Errors	○────────────	0
☑	DatabaseWaitStatistics	○────────────	0

Figure 10.20: The Diagnostics settings pane

5. Click **Save** to start collecting data.

The logs will be captured and archived to the given storage account:

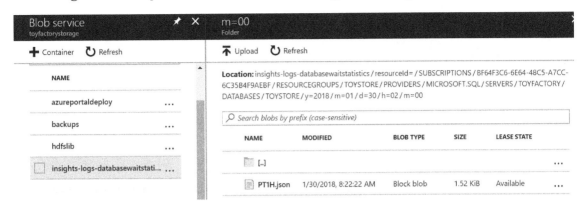

Figure 10.21: Logs captured to the storage account

The logs are saved in **JSON** format as shown in the following code:

```
{
"records": [

{
"LogicalServerName": "toyfactory", "SubscriptionId": "bf64f3c6-6e64-48c5-
a7cc-
6c35b4f9aebf", "ResourceGroup": "toystore",
"time": "2018-01-30T02:42:27.2000000Z", "resourceId": "/SUBSCRIPTIONS/
BF64F3C6-6E64-48C5-
A7CC-6C35B4F9AEBF/RESOURCEGROUPS/TOYSTORE/PROVIDERS/MICROSOFT.SQL/
SERVERS/TOYFACTORY/DATABASES/TOYSTORE",
"category": "DatabaseWaitStatistics", "operationName":
"DatabaseWaitStatistcsEvent", "properties":
{"ElasticPoolName":"","DatabaseName":"toystore","start_utc_date":"2018-01-
30T02:42:27.2000000Z","end_utc_date":"2018-01-30T02:47:27.1530000Z","wait_
type":"SOS_SCHEDULER_
YIELD","delta_max_wait_time_ms":0,"delta_signal_wait_time_
ms":3267,"delta_wait_time_ms":3266,"delta_waiting_tasks_count":51}
...
...
]
}
```

You can analyze the JSON in your favorite JSON editor.

6. To delete a diagnostics setting, navigate to the **Diagnostics settings** pane and click **Edit setting** next to the diagnostics setting you wish to delete:

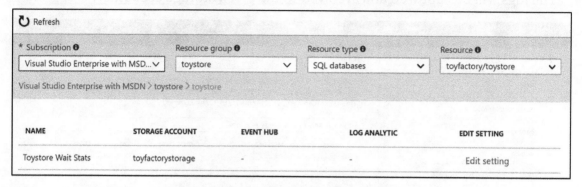

Figure 10.22: Editing a diagnostic setting

On the resulting pane, select **Delete** to delete the setting:

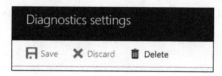

Figure 10.23: Deleting a diagnostic setting

In this section, we talked about configuring database alerts to monitor an Azure SQL Database and enable diagnostic logs for the detailed monitoring of an Azure SQL Database. In the next section, we'll look at some of the built-in monitoring capabilities of Azure SQL Database, such as performance recommendations, Query Performance Insight, and automatic tuning to analyze and tune the database.

Intelligent Performance

The **Intelligent Performance** section for an Azure SQL Database on the Azure portal has the following options:

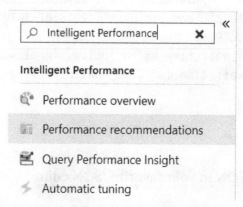

Figure 10.24: Intelligent Performance section options

We will discuss the **Query Performance Insight** option in particular.

Query Performance Insight

Query Performance Insight works on top of the Query Store and requires that Query Store is enabled on the Azure SQL Database.

Query Store, introduced in SQL Server 2016, records queries, plans, and runtime statistics for detailed query performance analysis.

In an on-premises SQL Server instance, as well as in Azure SQL, Query Store provides a graphical interface, which lists queries by time window. This helps with analyzing database usage patterns and query plan changes.

It provides an easy way to identify and force the best query plan out of multiple query plans for the same query.

> **Note**
>
> To read more about Query Store for on-premises SQL servers, visit https://docs. microsoft.com/sql/relational-databases/performance/monitoring-performance-by- using-the-query-store.

Query Performance Insight analyses the data collected in the Query Store and does the following for Azure SQL Database:

- Shows the percentage usage of CPU, data I/O, and log I/O database metrics, which constitute DTUs.

- Lists the top queries by CPU, data I/O, log I/O, duration, and execution count. It also provides further details on individual queries such as execution count, duration, CPU, data I/O, and log I/O percentage utilization.

- Lists performance recommendations for creating an index, dropping an index, fixing schema issues, and parameterized queries.

In this section, we learned how to save diagnostic data using **Diagnostics settings**. The diagnostic logs can be saved to an Azure Storage account, saved to a Log Analytics workspace, or streamed to an event hub. In order to read the diagnostic logs from an Azure Storage account or event hub, you'll have to write a custom solution. However, we can use **the Kusto query language (KQL)** to read and parse diagnostic logs in a Log Analytics workspace. We'll learn how this is done in the next section.

To learn more about KQL, visit https://docs.microsoft.com/azure/data-explorer/ kusto/query/tutorial?pivots=azuremonitor.

Analyzing diagnostic logs using Azure SQL Analytics

Azure SQL Analytics (which is in preview at the time of writing this book) is a cloud monitoring solution that can be used to monitor one or more Azure SQL Databases, SQL Managed Instances, or elastic database pools. This solution shares the same method of configuration for both SQL Database and SQL Managed Instance, so all the activities will be concerned with Azure SQL Database only.

Azure SQL Analytics analyses diagnostics data that was logged by enabling the diagnostic settings (as discussed previously in the *Diagnostic Settings and Logs* section) to provide insights into things such as blocks, resource limits, deadlocks, wait stats, and timeouts. Moreover, custom monitoring rules and alerts can also be set up to enhance existing monitoring capabilities.

Azure SQL Analytics uses diagnostic logs for Azure SQL Database. Therefore, the first step is to enable diagnostic logs to send the logs to the Log Analytics workspace.

The Log Analytics workspace acts as a container for the Azure SQL Database diagnostic logs. The Log Analytics workspace is the input for Azure SQL Analytics.

Creating a Log Analytics workspace

To create a Log Analytics workspace, follow these steps:

1. In the Azure portal search box, type `Log Analytics` and select **Log Analytics workspaces** from the search results:

Figure 10.25: Navigating to Log Analytics workspaces in the Azure portal

2. On the **Log Analytics workspaces** page, click **Add** to create a new Log Analytics workspace:

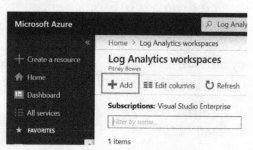

Figure 10.26: Creating a new Log Analytics workspace

3. On the **Create Log Analytics workspace** page, provide the values shown in *Figure 10.27*:

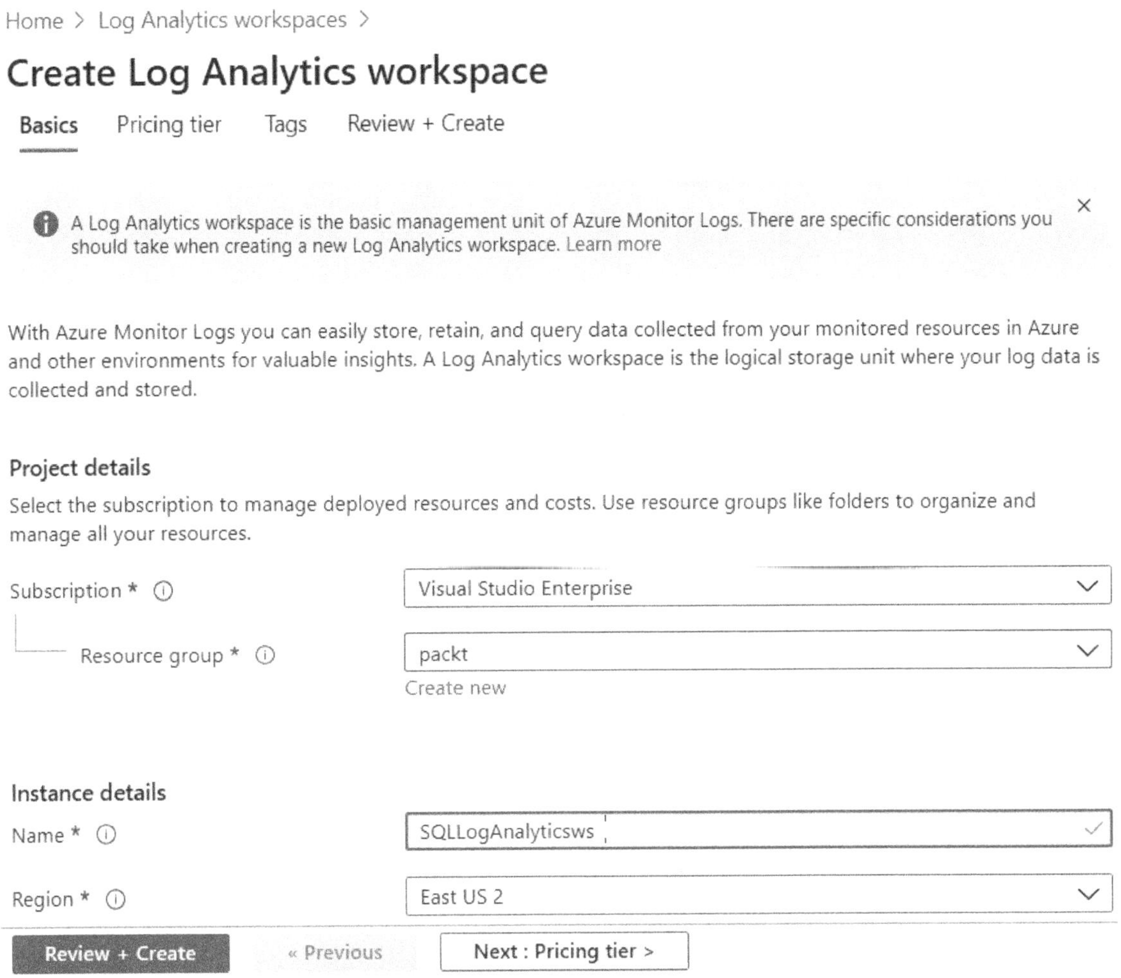

Home > Log Analytics workspaces >

Create Log Analytics workspace

Basics   Pricing tier   Tags   Review + Create

> ⓘ A Log Analytics workspace is the basic management unit of Azure Monitor Logs. There are specific considerations you should take when creating a new Log Analytics workspace. Learn more   ✕

With Azure Monitor Logs you can easily store, retain, and query data collected from your monitored resources in Azure and other environments for valuable insights. A Log Analytics workspace is the logical storage unit where your log data is collected and stored.

Project details

Select the subscription to manage deployed resources and costs. Use resource groups like folders to organize and manage all your resources.

Subscription * ⓘ	Visual Studio Enterprise ⌄
└─ Resource group * ⓘ	packt ⌄
	Create new

Instance details

Name * ⓘ	SQLLogAnalyticsws ✓
Region * ⓘ	East US 2 ⌄

[Review + Create]   « Previous   [Next : Pricing tier >]

Figure 10.27: Log Analytics workspace details

> **Note**
>
> Choose a different name for your Log Analytics workspace.

4. Click **Next: Pricing tier** to continue. There's only one pricing option available at the time of writing this book:

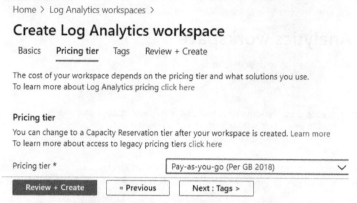

Figure 10.28: Log Analytics workspace - Pricing tier

5. Click **Review + Create** and then **Create** to create the new **Log Analytics workspace**. We can skip the **Tags** tab.

6. The next step is to send the diagnostic data to the Log Analytics workspace created in the previous steps. To do that, navigate to the **toystore** database page.

    In the search box, type `diagnostic`:

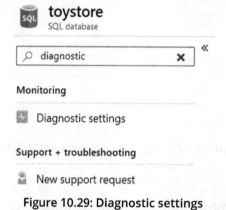

Figure 10.29: Diagnostic settings

> **Note**
>
> You can do this for all of the shards created in *Chapter 7, Scalability*.

7. Select **Diagnostic settings** to open the **Diagnostic settings** page.

    If you already have a diagnostic setting, then click **Edit setting**. Otherwise, select **Add diagnostic setting** to create a new one.

    As we already have an existing diagnostic setting from the previous exercise, we'll edit the existing one:

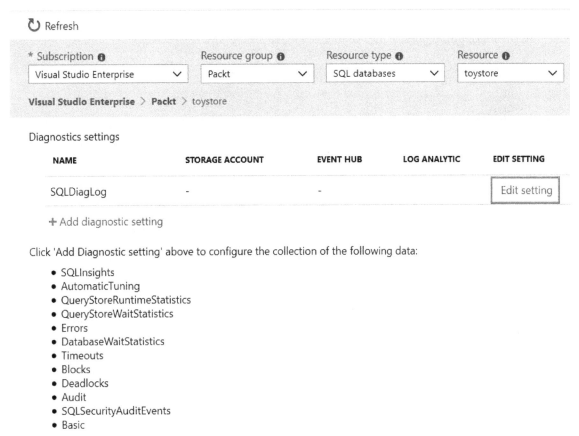

Figure 10.30: Editing an existing diagnostic setting

8. On the **Diagnostics settings** page, check the **Send to Log Analytics** checkbox and then select the Log Analytics workspace created in the last step.

    Under the **Log** section, select all the values.

9. Click **Save** to save the settings:

Figure 10.31: Selecting all Log values

We now have a Log Analytics workspace that's connected to the **toystore** diagnostic settings log. Do this for all the existing **toystore** shards (databases).

We don't need to access the Log Analytics workspace to query the diagnostic logs. We can analyze the logs from the Azure portal's **Monitoring | Logs** section. The **Logs** section provides a UI KQL editor to write KQL queries to analyze logs:

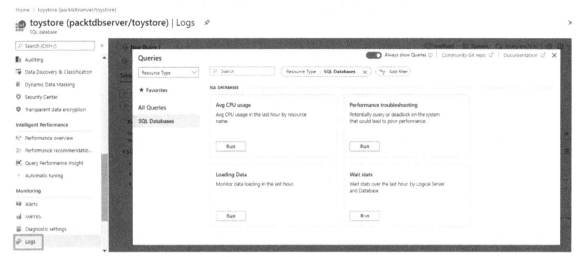

Figure 10.32: Querying for the Avg CPU usage

The preceding figure shows the **Logs** section. When you click on **Logs**, you are presented with ready-to-use queries such as **Avg CPU usage**, **Loading Data**, **Wait stats**, and **Performance troubleshooting**. You can get more KQL queries from the **Community Git repo** link at the top-right corner of the window.

Click on the **Run** button for the Avg CPU usage query. The query is copied to a new query window and is executed as shown here:

Figure 10.33: Analyzing the average CPU statistics

The preceding figure doesn't show any data as there are no logs available. However, if you run this after running the scripts in the **Generating a workload and reviewing insights** section under **Creating an Azure SQL Analytics solution**, you will see the statistics from the preceding query.

As KQL is a new language and it may take time to learn it, we can use Azure SQL Analytics to analyze the diagnostics logs visually using graphs. Let's see how this is done in the next section.

Creating an Azure SQL Analytics solution

The next step is to create an Azure SQL Analytics solution.

1. Type `Azure SQL Analytics` in the search box and select **Azure SQL Analytics (Preview)** from the search results:

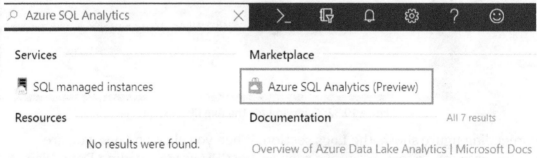

Figure 10.34: Navigating to Azure SQL Analytics (Preview)

2. On the **Azure SQL Analytics** page, select the Log Analytics workspace created in the previous step, and click **Create** to create the Azure SQL Analytics solution:

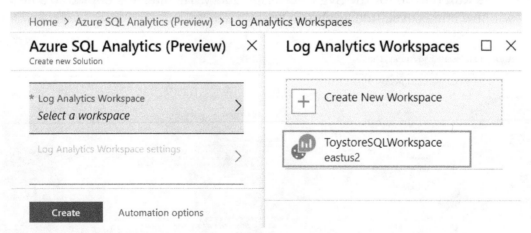

Figure 10.35: The previously created Log Analytics workspace

Once the Azure SQL Analytics solution is provisioned, it'll be available under **All resources** in the Azure portal, as shown here:

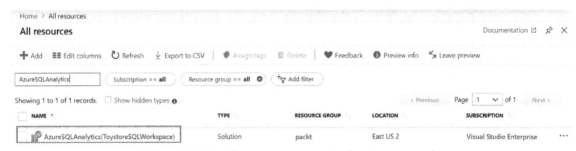

Figure 10.36: All resources page in the Azure portal

As we don't have any workload or activity on the databases, we won't be able to see any analytics as such. Let's generate some activity and then review the insights from the Azure SQL Analytics solution.

Generating a workload and reviewing insights

To generate a workload, execute each of the following PowerShell scripts in its own PowerShell console window. There should be five different PowerShell console windows, one for each of the scripts.

> **Note**
>
> The PowerShell scripts are in the `~\IntelligentInsights\Chapter10` folder in the code bundle.

The **Blocking1.ps1**, **Blocking2.ps1**, and **Blocking3.ps1** scripts simulate a blocking scenario:

```
.\Blocking1.ps1 -server packtdbserver.database.windows.net -database toystore
-user dbadmin -password Awesome@1234
```

```
.\Blocking2.ps1 -server packtdbserver.database.windows.net -database toystore
-user dbadmin -password Awesome@1234
```

```
.\Blocking3.ps1 -server packtdbserver.database.windows.net -database toystore
-user dbadmin -password Awesome@1234
```

The **HighIO_Timeouts.ps1** script simulates a timeout scenario:

```
.\HighIO_Timeouts.ps1 -server packtdbserver.database.windows.net -database
toystore -user dbadmin -password Awesome@1234
```

The **HighIO1.ps1** script simulates a high log I/O scenario:

```
.\HighIO1.ps1 -server packtdbserver.database.windows.net -database toystore
-user dbadmin -password Awesome@1234
```

You will have to change the server, database, user, and password parameter values before you run the scripts.

Let the scripts run for an hour or so, and the analytics should show in another hour or two. We can view the analytics by following these steps:

1. To view the analytics, navigate to the **All resources** page in the Azure portal and locate and open the Azure SQL Analytics solution created in the previous section. If you are unable to locate this, go to **General** and then **Workspace Summary**. In the **Azure SQL Analytics (Preview)** tile, click **View Summary**:

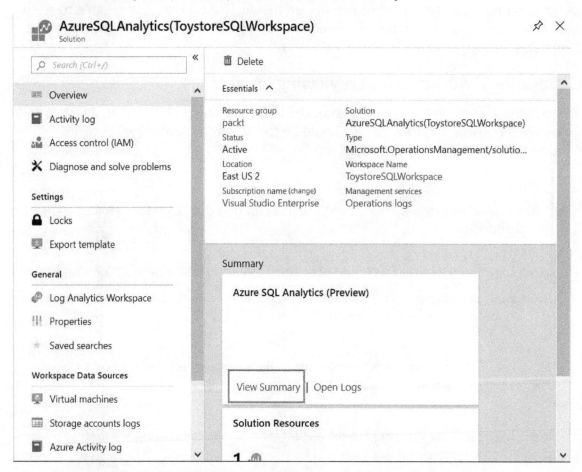

Figure 10.37: Azure SQL Analytics summary

2. The summary shows two Azure SQL databases for which Azure SQL Analytics was enabled. You can, however, monitor managed instances, managed instance databases, and elastic database pools through one single monitoring interface:

Figure 10.38: Azure SQL Analytics—Summary

3. Click **Azure SQL Databases**. There's a lot of information being displayed. Let's look at the graphs one by one:

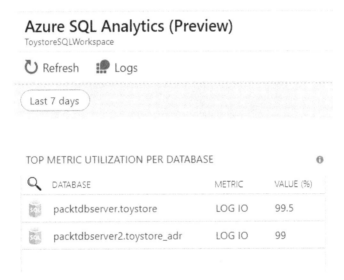

Figure 10.39: The TOP METRIC UTILIZATION PER DATABASE analytic

The **TOP METRIC UTILIZATION PER DATABASE** analytic displays the top basic metrics (CPU/I/O/memory) for each monitored database.

The top metric is **LOG IO**. This is because of the workload we ran in the previous step.

You can browse Azure SQL Analytics for things such as blocks, wait statistics, and resource limits. However, let's see how Intelligent Insights helps to sum up the issues for a database.

4. Click on the **packtdbserver.toystore** database in *Figure 10.39* to open the insights for the database:

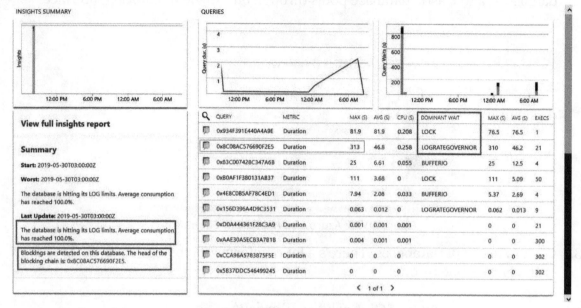

Figure 10.40: The packtdbserver.toystore database insights

We can see the two problems that we simulated with the workload we ran previously. The Intelligent Insights summary highlights the following:

*   The database is hitting its log limits, and the average log consumption has reached 100%.

*   The blocking provides the query hash for the head blocker. Clicking on the lead blocker query hash will give you the lead blocker query.

Moreover, to get into details of the blocks, click on the blocking graph on the Azure SQL Analytics overview page.

The right side of the Intelligent Insights page displays the top queries by duration. To get the details of a query, click the query row. For example, to find out the query text for the longest-running query, sort the query by maximum duration (**MAX (S)**) and click on the top row:

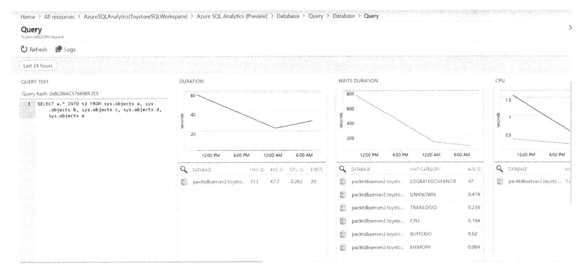

Figure 10.41: The Query page

Along with the query text, duration, waits duration, CPU, data I/O, log I/O, CPU, and the number of query executions with timestamps are also displayed. The preceding snapshot is cropped for the sake of brevity.

Creating alerts

Enabling diagnostic settings to send logs to the Log Analytics workspace allows us to create alerts for incidents such as blocking, resource limits, and deadlocks:

1. To create alerts from the Azure portal, select the Log Analytics workspace created earlier:

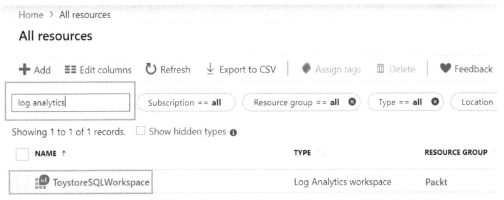

Figure 10.42: The previously created Log Analytics workspace

2. Click on the Log Analytics workspace, named **ToystoreSQLWorkspace** (the name may be different in your case).

3. On the Log Analytics workspace page, search for **Alert** and click to open the **Alerts** page. Click **New alert rule** to define a new alert:

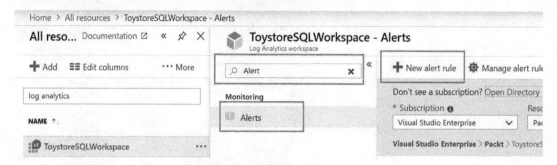

Figure 10.43: Creating a new alert rule

The **Create alert rule** page is where we define the alert condition and the action to be taken (if any) when the alert is raised.

4. Click the **Select condition** button under the **Condition** heading to define the alert condition:

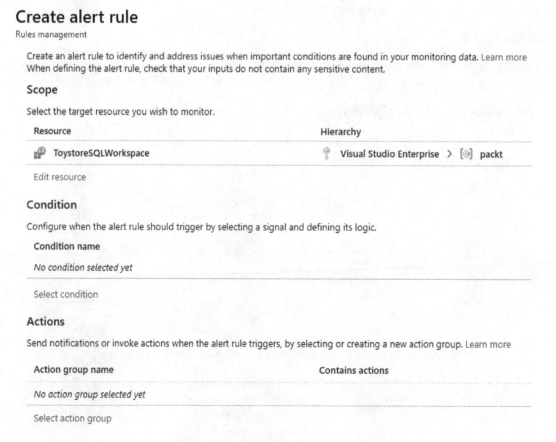

Figure 10.44: Defining the alert condition

5. On the **Configure signal logic** page, click on **Custom log search**. Signals are pre-saved queries that can be used to set up alerts. However, as we are defining a custom alert, we'll choose **Custom log search**:

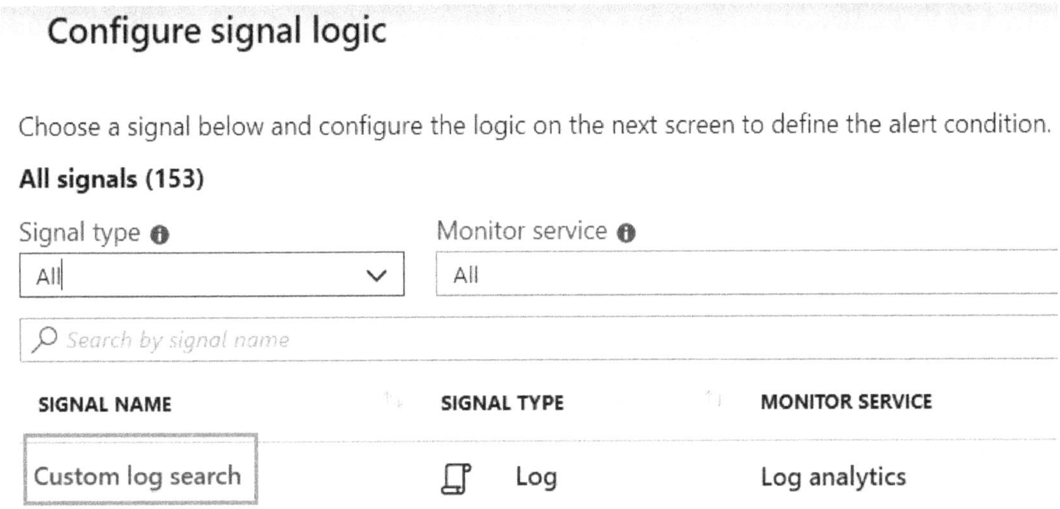

Figure 10.45: The Custom log search logic

6. **Custom log search** sets up the alert on a user-defined log query. On the **Custom log search** page, copy and paste the following query into the **Search query** text box:

```
let time_range = 1h;
let block_threshold = 1; AzureDiagnostics
| where ResourceProvider=="MICROSOFT.SQL"
| where ResourceId contains "/SERVERS/"
| where ResourceId contains "/DATABASES/"
| where (Category == "Blocks")
| summarize block_count = count() by DatabaseName_s, bin(TimeGenerated,
time_range)
| where block_count > block_threshold
```

This query returns the number of blocks grouped by databases in the past hour if the number of blocks is greater than 1.

7. In the **Alert logic** section, in the **Based on** drop-down menu, select **Number of results**, and in the **Operator** drop-down menu, select **Greater than**, and type in 0 as the threshold value.

The alert is raised whenever there have been 1 or more blocking sessions in the past hour.

8. In the **Evaluated based on** section, set **Period** to **30** minutes and **Frequency** to **5** minutes.

    The query will run every 5 minutes on the data collected over the previous 30 minutes. If the blocking count is greater than or equal to 1 in any of the 5-minute runs, the alert will be raised:

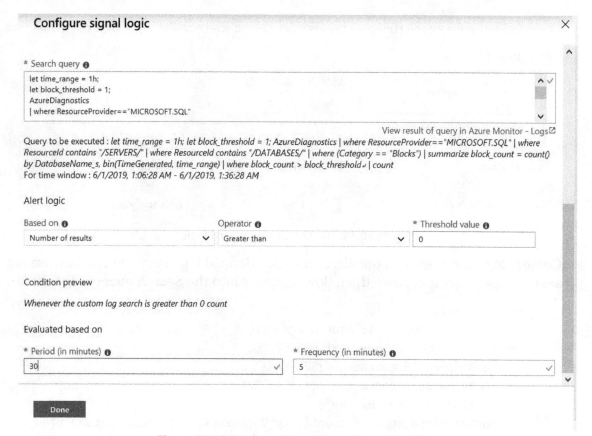

Figure 10.46: Setting a time interval for evaluation

9. Click **Done** to save the alert configuration:

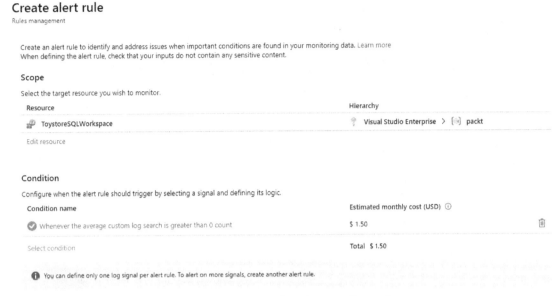

Figure 10.47: Saving the alert configuration

The alert condition has been added and will cost $1.50 per month.

10. Scroll down to set **Alert rule name** and **Severity**, and check **Enable rule upon creation**:

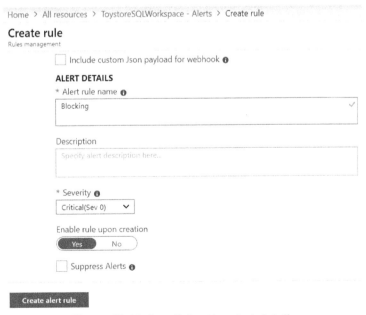

Figure 10.48: Specifying the alert details

11. Click **Create alert rule** to create the new alert rule.

12. To test the alert, create a blocking scenario as explained in the previous steps. Navigate to the Log Analytics workspace page on the Azure portal, and we can see that the alert has been fired:

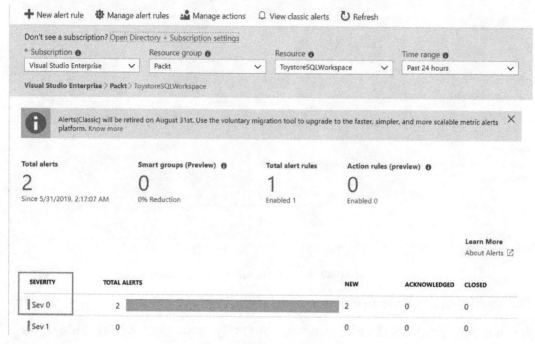

Figure 10.49: Fired alerts

There are two new **Sev0** errors. Click on **Sev0** to view the alert details:

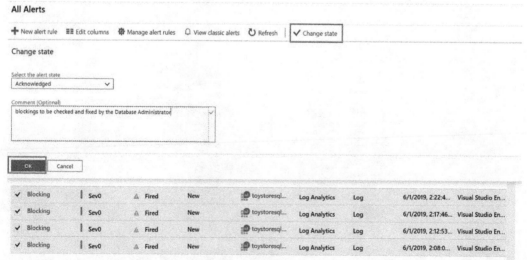

Figure 10.50: Changing the state of the alert to either Acknowledged or Closed

On the **All Alerts** page, we can change the state of the alert to either **Acknowledged** or **Closed**.

Activity: Monitoring Azure SQL Database with Log Analytics and Power BI

In this activity, we'll learn how to import Log Analytics workspace data into Power BI, and we'll create a report in Power BI.

> **Note**
>
> The purpose of the activity is not to create a performance monitoring dashboard. The purpose is to explain how to get Log Analytics workspace data into Power BI, which can then be used to create a dashboard as and when required.

Follow these steps to complete the activity:

1. Log in to the Azure portal. Search for and open the previously created Log Analytics workspace:

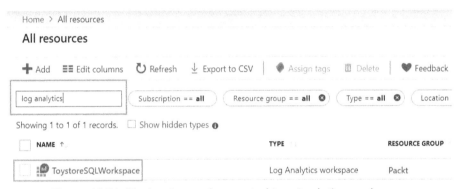

Figure 10.51: Navigating to the created Log Analytics workspace

2. On the Log Analytics workspace page, find and open **Logs**:

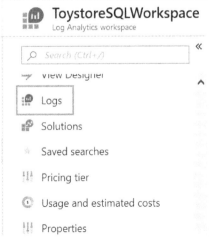

Figure 10.52: The Log Analytics workspace

3. On the **New Query 1** page, copy and paste the following query:

```
AzureMetrics
| where ResourceProvider=="MICROSOFT.SQL" | where ResourceId contains "/
SERVERS/"
| where ResourceId contains "/DATABASES/" and MetricName in ('cpu_
percent', 'physical_data_read_percent', 'log_write_percent', 'workers_
percent', 'sessions_percent')
```

The query gets the details for the **cpu_percent**, **physical_data_read_percent**, **log_write_percent**, **workers_percent**, and **sessions_percent** metrics.

4. Click **Run** to execute the query. From the top-right menu, select **Export** and then select **Export to Power BI (M Query)**:

> **Note**
>
> Power Query Formula language or M Query is used in Power BI during data import to transform and clean up data.

Figure 10.53: Exporting the query to Power BI (M Query)

In the resulting dialog box, choose to open the file with Notepad and click **OK**:

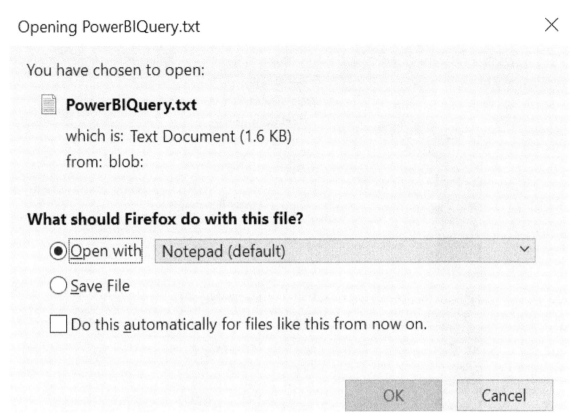

Figure 10.54: Opening the M Query with Notepad (default)

A new **TXT** file with the M Query will open. Save the query.

The next step is to use the M Query to create a Power BI report. To do this, open **Power BI Desktop**.

5. In Power BI Desktop, on the **Home** tab, click **Get Data** and then click **Blank Query**:

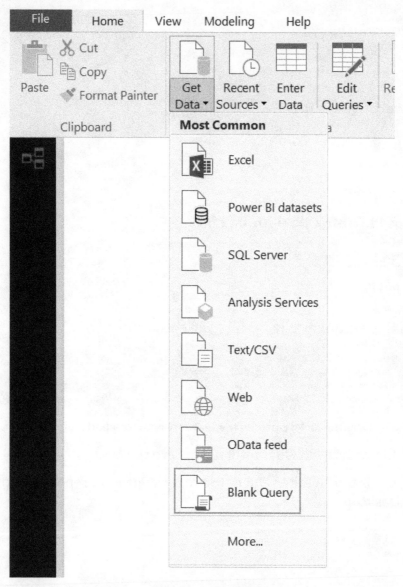

Figure 10.55: Creating a Power BI report

6. In Power Query Editor, right-click on **Query1** and select **Advanced Editor** from the context menu:

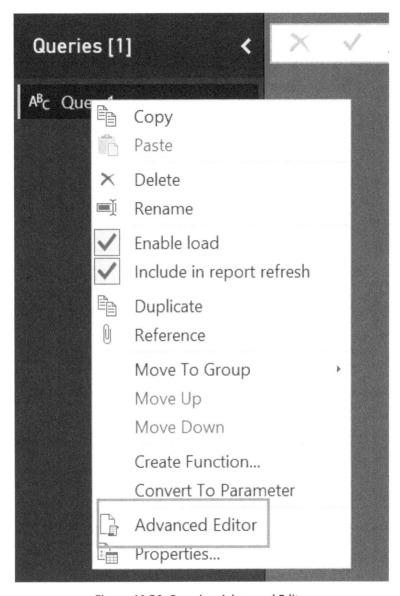

Figure 10.56: Opening Advanced Editor

7. In **Advanced Editor** for **Query1**, copy and paste the M Query from *step* 4 and click **Done**:

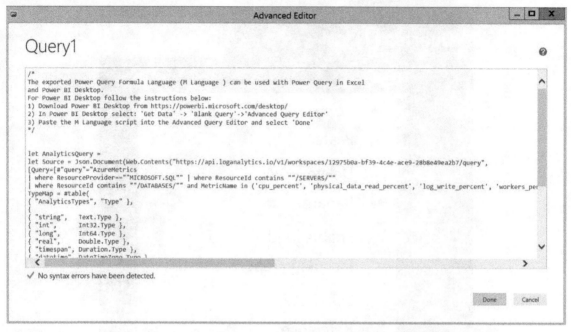

Figure 10.57: Copying and pasting the M Query into Advanced Editor

8. The next step is to provide the credentials to Power BI to connect to the Log Analytics workspace. To do this, click on **Edit Credentials**:

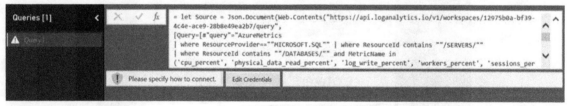

Figure 10.58: Edit Credentials

9. In the **Access Web content** window, select **Organizational account** and provide the username and password you use to log in to the Azure portal:

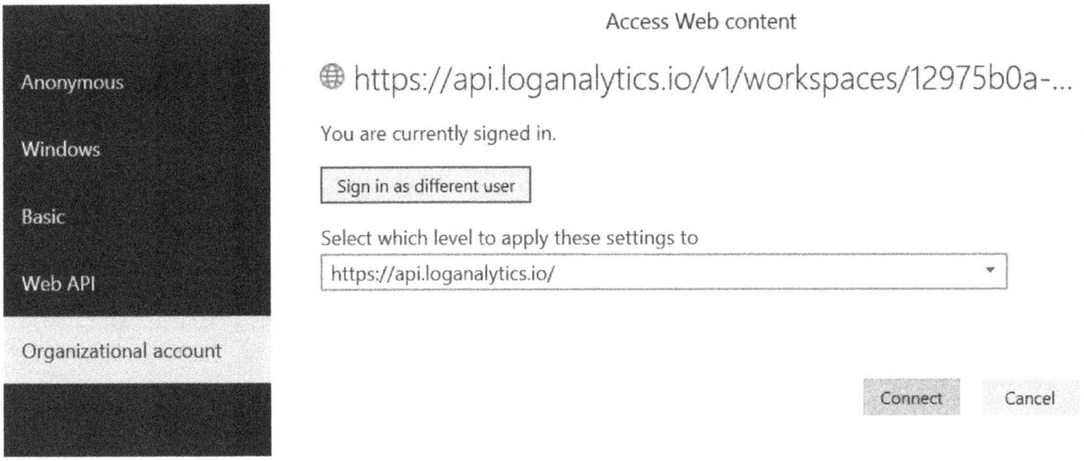

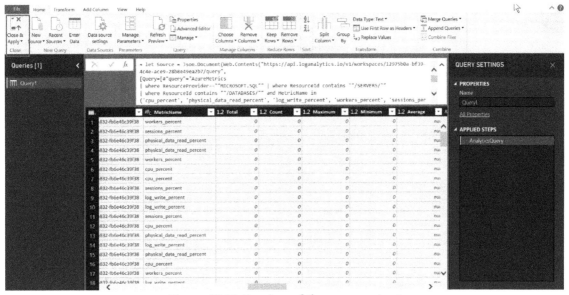

Figure 10.59: The Access Web content window

10. Click the **Connect** button to connect and fetch the query results from the Log Analytics workspace.

Power Query Editor will display a preview of the output from the query:

Figure 10.60: Preview of the query output

11. In the data preview, right-click on the **ResourceId** column, select **Split Column**, and then select **By Delimiter...**:

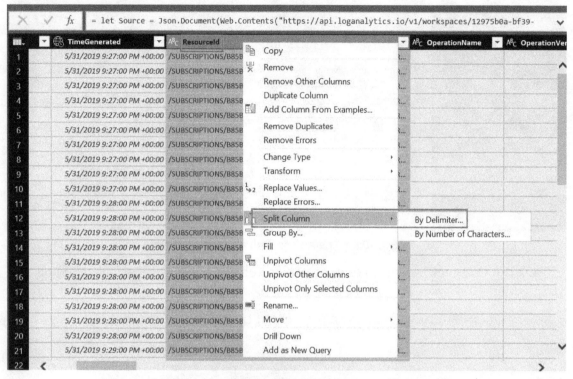

Figure 10.61: Splitting the column with a delimiter

12. In the **Split Column by Delimiter** window, choose **Right-most delimiter** and then click on **OK**:

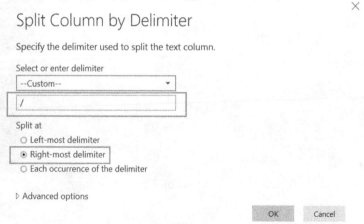

Figure 10.62: Splitting at the right-most delimiter

This will create a new column called **ResourceId.2** with the database name by splitting the **ResourceId** column.

13. Double-click the new column and rename it **Database**:

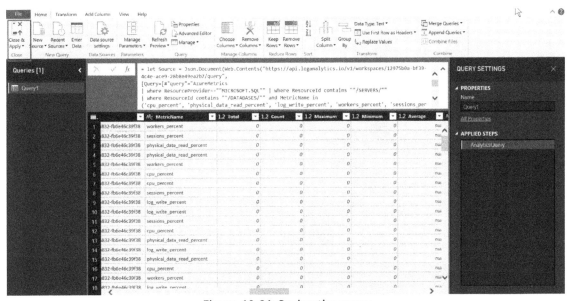

	TimeGenerated	ResourceId.1	Database	OperationName
1	5/31/2019 9:27:00 PM +00:00	/SUBSCRIPTIONS/B85B0984-A391-4F22-A832-FB6E46C39F38/RESOUR...	TOYSTORE	
2	5/31/2019 9:27:00 PM +00:00	/SUBSCRIPTIONS/B85B0984-A391-4F22-A832-FB6E46C39F38/RESOUR...	TOYSTORE	
3	5/31/2019 9:27:00 PM +00:00	/SUBSCRIPTIONS/B85B0984-A391-4F22-A832-FB6E46C39F38/RESOUR...	TOYSTORE	
4	5/31/2019 9:27:00 PM +00:00	/SUBSCRIPTIONS/B85B0984-A391-4F22-A832-FB6E46C39F38/RESOUR...	TOYSTORE_ADR	
5	5/31/2019 9:27:00 PM +00:00	/SUBSCRIPTIONS/B85B0984-A391-4F22-A832-FB6E46C39F38/RESOUR...	TOYSTORE_ADR	
6	5/31/2019 9:27:00 PM +00:00	/SUBSCRIPTIONS/B85B0984-A391-4F22-A832-FB6E46C39F38/RESOUR...	TOYSTORE_ADR	
7	5/31/2019 9:27:00 PM +00:00	/SUBSCRIPTIONS/B85B0984-A391-4F22-A832-FB6E46C39F38/RESOUR...	TOYSTORE	
8	5/31/2019 9:27:00 PM +00:00	/SUBSCRIPTIONS/B85B0984-A391-4F22-A832-FB6E46C39F38/RESOUR...	TOYSTORE_ADR	
9	5/31/2019 9:27:00 PM +00:00	/SUBSCRIPTIONS/B85B0984-A391-4F22-A832-FB6E46C39F38/RESOUR...	TOYSTORE	
10	5/31/2019 9:27:00 PM +00:00	/SUBSCRIPTIONS/B85B0984-A391-4F22-A832-FB6E46C39F38/RESOUR...	TOYSTORE_ADR	
11	5/31/2019 9:28:00 PM +00:00	/SUBSCRIPTIONS/B85B0984-A391-4F22-A832-FB6E46C39F38/RESOUR...	TOYSTORE	
12	5/31/2019 9:28:00 PM +00:00	/SUBSCRIPTIONS/B85B0984-A391-4F22-A832-FB6E46C39F38/RESOUR...	TOYSTORE_ADR	
13	5/31/2019 9:28:00 PM +00:00	/SUBSCRIPTIONS/B85B0984-A391-4F22-A832-FB6E46C39F38/RESOUR...	TOYSTORE_ADR	
14	5/31/2019 9:28:00 PM +00:00	/SUBSCRIPTIONS/B85B0984-A391-4F22-A832-FB6E46C39F38/RESOUR...	TOYSTORE	
15	5/31/2019 9:28:00 PM +00:00	/SUBSCRIPTIONS/B85B0984-A391-4F22-A832-FB6E46C39F38/RESOUR...	TOYSTORE	
16	5/31/2019 9:28:00 PM +00:00	/SUBSCRIPTIONS/B85B0984-A391-4F22-A832-FB6E46C39F38/RESOUR...	TOYSTORE	
17	5/31/2019 9:28:00 PM +00:00	/SUBSCRIPTIONS/B85B0984-A391-4F22-A832-FB6E46C39F38/RESOUR...	TOYSTORE_ADR	
18	5/31/2019 9:28:00 PM +00:00	/SUBSCRIPTIONS/B85B0984-A391-4F22-A832-FB6E46C39F38/RESOUR...	TOYSTORE_ADR	
19	5/31/2019 9:28:00 PM +00:00	/SUBSCRIPTIONS/B85B0984-A391-4F22-A832-FB6E46C39F38/RESOUR...	TOYSTORE_ADR	
20	5/31/2019 9:28:00 PM +00:00	/SUBSCRIPTIONS/B85B0984-A391-4F22-A832-FB6E46C39F38/RESOUR...	TOYSTORE	
21	5/31/2019 9:29:00 PM +00:00	/SUBSCRIPTIONS/B85B0984-A391-4F22-A832-FB6E46C39F38/RESOUR...	TOYSTORE_ADR	
22				

`= Table.RenameColumns(#"Changed Type",{{"ResourceId.2", "Database"}})`

Figure 10.63: The new Database column

We are now ready to save the query and create a visualization for the imported data. To save the query, click on the **Close & Apply** button in the top left:

Figure 10.64: Saving the query

The next step is to create a line chart visualization to display the metrics' trends over time.

14. In the **VISUALIZATIONS** tab, select the line chart visualization:

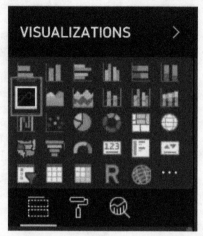

Figure 10.65: The VISUALIZATIONS tab

Click on the line chart to make it active.

15. From the **Fields** list, drag `TimeGenerated` to the **Axis** section of the visualization, **Average** to the **Values** section of the visualization, **MetricName** to the **Legend** section of the visualization, and **Database** to **Visual level filters**, and select the `toystore` database.

The **VISUALIZATIONS** section should be as shown in *Figure 10.66*:

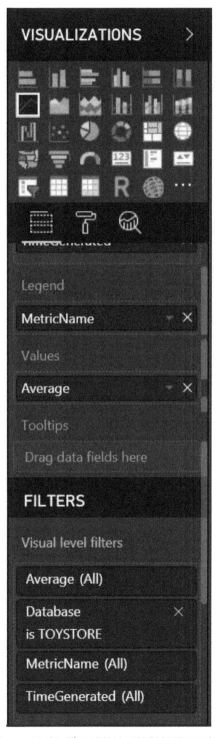

Figure 10.66: The VISUALIZATIONS section

You should now get a line chart, as shown in *Figure* 10.67:

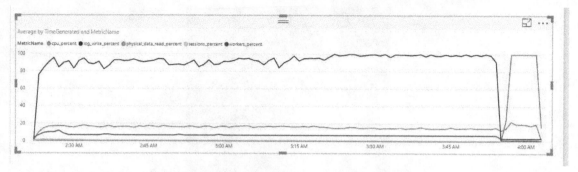

Figure 10.67: Line chart representation of averaged metrics

The line chart plots the different metric values against time for the **toystore** database. Each metric is identified by a different color. This completes the activity.

Monitoring queries using the Query Performance Insight pane

In this section, we will learn how to monitor queries using the **Query Performance Insight** pane for Azure SQL Database. Consider a scenario where Mike plans to keep track of Query Performance Insight and monitor queries of **Toystore Ltd.**. He runs through a workload to generate some database activity and then observes the **Query Performance Insight** pane for the queries. He can follow these steps in order to achieve this:

1. To start the workload, open a new PowerShell console window and execute the following command:

    ```
    powershell.exe "C:\Code\Chapter10\Start-Workload.ps1 -sqlserver toyfactory
    -database toystore -sqluser sqladmin -sqlpassword Packt@pub2 -workloadsql
    "C:\Code\Chapter10\workload.sql"
    -numberofexecutions 10"
    ```

    > **Note**
    >
    > You may get the following warning—ignore it:
    >
    > "WARNING: Could not obtain SQL Server Service information. An attempt to connect to WMI on 'Microsoft.WindowsAzure. Commands.SqlDatabase.Types. ps1xml' failed with the following error: The RPC server is unavailable. (Exception from HRESULT: 0x800706BA)"

The preceding command will execute the queries specified in the **workload.sql** file 10 times, as specified by the **numberofexecutions** variable. This will generate some database activity for you to analyze.

You will have to wait for another 5-10 minutes for the details to show on the Azure portal.

2. Navigate to the **toystore** database on the Azure portal (https://portal.azure. com). On the **Overview** pane, select **Query Performance Insight** in the **Support + Troubleshooting** section. You will then see the following:

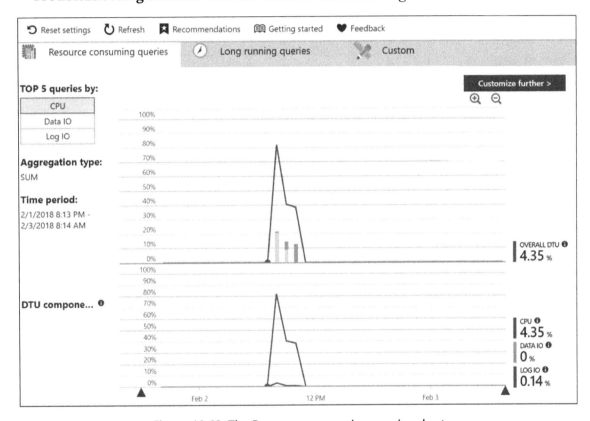

Figure 10.68: The Resource consuming queries chart

Query Performance Insight displays a line chart showing CPU consumption for the past 24 hours by the top queries. CPU consumption is selected by default; however, you can see all five queries by data I/O and log I/O as well. The default aggregation applied is SUM, which is customizable, and the top five queries' details include CPU%, data I/O%, log I/O%, duration, and execution count:

Click on a row below to get the details for the selected query. ⓘ

QUERY ID	CPU[%]	DATA IO[%]	LOG IO[%]	DURATION[HH:MM:SS]	EXECUTIONS COUNT	#
468	0.83	0	0.02	00:44:33.760	12	☑
492	0.47	0	0.01	00:27:01.780	5	☑
472	0.01	0	0	00:00:47.290	13	☑
480	0	0	0	00:00:00.360	262	☑
265	0	0	0	00:00:00.230	442	☑

Figure 10.69: Statistics of the top five queries

3. Click on **ID 472** to get the query's details. The query ID will be different in your case. The **Query details** pane shows the following:

- Query text:

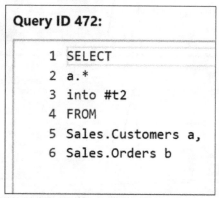

Query ID 472:

```
1  SELECT
2  a.*
3  into #t2
4  FROM
5  Sales.Customers a,
6  Sales.Orders b
```

Figure 10.70: The Query details pane showing the query text

- Overall CPU, data I/O, and log I/O

- CPU, data I/O, log I/O, duration, and execution count for a one-hour interval:

INTERVAL	CPU[%]	DATA IO[%]	LOG IO[%]	DURATION[HH:MM:SS]	EXECUTIONS ...
2/2: 9 AM - 10	0.22	0	0.01	00:00:27.000	8
2/2: 8 AM - 09	0.09	0	0	00:00:12.190	3
2/2: 10 AM - 11	0.06	0	0	00:00:08.100	2

Figure 10.71: Query statistics at hourly intervals

You can select an area on the timeline from the line chart to see insights for that time duration. To do that, click and hold the mouse at the starting point on the line chart and drag it to the time interval you wish to see the insight for:

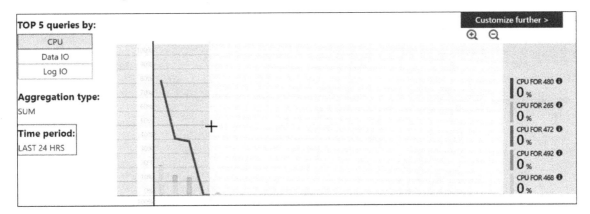

Figure 10.72: Analyzing line chart insights for the required time interval

The second graph shows the insights for the time period from 8:10 AM to 11:34 AM instead of 24 hours, which is shown in *Figure 10.73*:

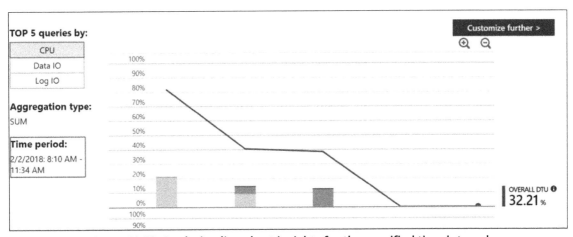

Figure 10.73: Analyzing line chart insights for the specified time interval

You can also click on the zoom-in and zoom-out icons in the upper-right corner of the chart to change the time interval.

4. Close the **Query details** pane to return to the **Query Performance Insight** pane. Select the **Long running queries** tab:

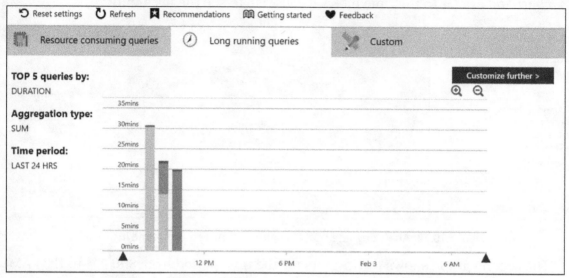

Figure 10.74: Long running queries chart

The **Long running queries** tab displays the top five long-running queries from the past 24 hours:

QUERY ID	CPU[%]	DATA IO[%]	LOG IO[%]	DURATION[HH:MM:SS]	EXECUTIONS COUNT	#
468	1.23	0.01	0.02	00:44:33.760	12	☑
492	0.69	0	0.01	00:27:01.780	5	☑
472	0.02	0	0	00:00:47.290	13	☑
480	0	0	0	00:00:00.360	265	☑
265	0	0	0	00:00:00.240	303	☑

Figure 10.75: The top five long-running queries for the past 24 hours

The interval can be changed by clicking on either the **Custom** tab or the **Customize further** button, as shown in *Figure 10.74*. Click on a **QUERY ID** to get the query details.

5. Select the **Custom** tab on the **Query Performance Insight** pane. The **Custom** tab provides options to further filter the insights on **Time period**, **Number of queries**, **Metric type**, and **Aggregation type**:

Figure 10.76: Customizing the bar chart

6. Change the Metric type to **Duration**, set **Time period** to **Last 6 hrs**, and set **Aggregation type** to **max**. Then click **Go >** to filter the insights:

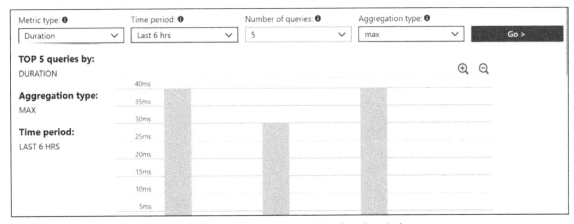

Figure 10.77: The top five queries for the six hours

This filters out the top five queries with a maximum duration of six hours. You can get further query details, as explained earlier in this section. This completes the section.

Monitoring an Azure SQL Database and SQL Managed Instance using DMVs

DMVs return diagnostic data that can be used to monitor a database's health and performance. We'll cover monitoring data metrics, connection statistics, blocking status, and query performance in the following sections.

Monitoring database metrics

The Azure SQL Database metrics available on the Azure portal can also be monitored using the `sys.resource_stats` DMV. This DMV returns the historical analysis for all the databases in an Azure SQL server. For SQL Managed Instance, you can use the `sys.server_resource_stats` DMV to monitor SQL Managed Instance CPU storage usage. The data for this DMV is collected and aggregated every 5 minutes and is retained for 14 days.

The following query returns the resource utilization from the last six hours for the Azure SQL Database:

```
-- Execute in master database

-- Get utilization in last 6 hours for the toystore database

Declare @StartTime DATETIME = DATEADD(HH,-6,GetUTCDate()),

@EndTime DATETIME = GetUTCDate()

SELECT

database_name, start_time, end_time, avg_cpu_percent, avg_data_io_percent,
avg_log_write_percent, (SELECT Max(v) FROM (VALUES (avg_cpu_percent), (avg_
data_io_percent), (avg_log_write_percent)) AS

value(v)) AS [avg_DTU_percent] FROM sys.resource_stats

WHERE database_name = 'toystore' AND start_time BETWEEN @StartTime AND @
EndTime ORDER BY avg_cpu_percent desc
```

> **Note**
>
> You can also copy the queries from the **C:\Code\Chapter10\MonitoringDMVs.sql** file. The file location may change depending on where you have unzipped the code files.

The following query returns the resource utilization from the last six hours for the Azure SQL Managed Instance:

```
-- Get utilization in last 6 hours for the SQL Managed Instance
Declare @StartTime DATETIME = DATEADD(HH,-6,GetUTCDate()), @EndTime DATETIME
= GetUTCDate()
SELECT start_time,resource_name, avg_cpu_percent,storage_space_used_
mb,reserved_storage_mb,io_requests
FROM sys.server_resource_stats
WHERE start_time BETWEEN @StartTime AND @EndTime
ORDER BY start_time desc
```

The following query returns the average CPU utilization across databases for Azure SQL Database. This helps us find the most used databases:

```
-- Execute in master database
SELECT database_name,
AVG(avg_cpu_percent) AS avg_cpu_percent FROM sys.resource_stats GROUP BY
database_name
ORDER BY avg_cpu_percent DESC
```

The following query returns the average CPU utilization for SQL Managed Instance. This helps us find out about CPU overconsumption for an instance:

```
-- Get the CPU usage>80%
select start_time,
    [cpu usage %] = avg_cpu_percent
from sys.server_resource_stats where avg_cpu_percent>80
order by start_time desc
```

You can further modify the preceding query to return databases exceeding a certain threshold value–say, databases with a CPU utilization greater than 80%.

The sys.dm_db_resource_stats DMV records data for individual Azure SQL databases every 15 seconds, and this is retained for an hour. This allows you to drill down for deeper insights into individual database utilization.

The following query returns the average CPU, data I/O, log I/O, and memory utilization for the **toystore** database:

```
-- Get Average CPU, Data IO, Log IO and Memory utilization

-- Execute in toystore database

SELECT AVG(avg_cpu_percent) AS avg_cpu_percent, AVG(avg_data_io_percent) AS
avg_data_io_percent, AVG(avg_log_write_percent) AS avg_log_write_percent,
AVG(avg_memory_usage_percent) AS avg_memory_usage_percent

FROM sys.dm_db_resource_stats;
```

The following query returns the average DTU utilization for the **toystore** database over the past hour. **avg_DTU_percent** only applies to DTU-based service tiers.

```
-- Get the Average DTU utilization for toystore database

-- Execute in toystore database

SELECT end_time, (SELECT Max(v)

FROM (VALUES (avg_cpu_percent), (avg_data_io_percent), (avg_log_write_
percent)) AS

value(v)) AS [avg_DTU_percent] FROM sys.dm_db_resource_stats ORDER BY end_
time DESC
```

Monitoring connections

The DMVs used to monitor connections are the same as the ones used to monitor connections in an SQL Server (on-premises or SQL on Azure VM), which are **sys.dm_exec_connections**, **sys. dm_exec_sessions**, and **sys.dm_exec_requests**.

The following query returns all sessions for the **sqladmin** login:

```
-- Get all sessions for user sqladmin

SELECT session_id, program_name, status, reads, writes, logical_reads from
sys.dm_exec_sessions WHERE login_name='sqladmin'
```

> **Note**
> The login name may be different in your case.

The following query returns all requests for the **sqladmin** login:

```
-- Get all the requests for the login sqladmin
SELECT s.session_id,
s.status AS session_status, r.status AS request_status, r.cpu_time, r.total_
elapsed_time, r.writes,
r.logical_reads,
t.Text AS query_batch_text,
SUBSTRING(t.text, (r.statement_start_offset/2)+1, ((CASE r.statement_end_
offset
WHEN -1 THEN DATALENGTH(t.text)
ELSE r.statement_end_offset
END - r.statement_start_offset)/2) + 1) AS running_query_text FROM sys.dm_
exec_sessions s join sys.dm_exec_requests r
ON r.session_id=s.session_id
CROSS APPLY sys.dm_exec_sql_text(r.sql_handle) AS t WHERE s.login_
name='sqladmin'
```

The **Dynamic Management Functions (DMF)**, **sys.dm_exec_sql_text**, returns the query text for the given **sql_handle**.

The **query_batch_text** column returns all the queries being sent as a request in one batch. If you run the workload as mentioned earlier, you will find that the **query_batch_text** column contains all the queries specified in the **workload.sql** file.

The **running_query_text** column returns the query that is currently being executed. It is calculated using the statement offset start and end values from the **sys.dm_exec_requests** DMV.

Monitoring query performance

The following DMVs can be used to monitor query and procedure performance.

> **Note**
>
> The DMVs mentioned here are not specific to Azure SQL Database. They can be used on on-premises SQL Server as well. These are not the only DMVs used to monitor performance. You can get a complete list of DMVs for Azure SQL Database from https://docs.microsoft.com/sql/relational-databases/system-dynamic-management-views/system-dynamic-management-views?view=sql-server-2017.
>
> You can also visit the following link to find more details about DMV queries to monitor Azure SQL Database and SQL Managed Instance: https://docs.microsoft.com/azure/azure-sql/database/monitoring-with-dmvs.
>
> You can also refer to the following article for troubleshooting performance problems: http://download.microsoft.com/download/D/B/D/DBDE7972-1EB9-470A-BA18-58849DB3EB3B/TShootPerfProbs2008.docx.
>
> This article is for Microsoft SQL Server 2008; however, it also applies to Azure SQL Database and SQL Managed Instance and other later on-premises SQL Server versions.

The `sys.dm_exec_query_stats` DMV returns aggregated statistics such as execution count, reads, writes, and worker time for the cached query plans.

The following query returns the top five most CPU-intensive queries:

```
SELECT TOP 5
(total_worker_time/execution_count)/(1000*1000) AS [Avg CPU Time(Seconds)],
SUBSTRING(st.text, (qs.statement_start_offset/2)+1, ((CASE qs.statement_end_offset
WHEN -1 THEN DATALENGTH(st.text)
ELSE qs.statement_end_offset
END - qs.statement_start_offset)/2) + 1) AS statement_text, qs.execution_count, (qs.total_elapsed_time/execution_count)/(1000*1000) AS [Avg
Duration(Seconds)]
FROM sys.dm_exec_query_stats AS qs
CROSS APPLY sys.dm_exec_sql_text(qs.sql_handle) AS st ORDER BY total_worker_time/execution_count DESC;
```

The following query returns the top five longest-running queries:

```
SELECT TOP 5

(total_worker_time/execution_count)/(1000*1000) AS [Avg CPU Time(Seconds)],

SUBSTRING(st.text, (qs.statement_start_offset/2)+1, ((CASE qs.statement_end_
offset

WHEN -1 THEN DATALENGTH(st.text)

ELSE qs.statement_end_offset

END - qs.statement_start_offset)/2) + 1) AS statement_text, qs.execution_
count, (qs.total_elapsed_time/execution_count)/(1000*1000) AS [Avg

Duration(Seconds)]

FROM sys.dm_exec_query_stats AS qs

CROSS APPLY sys.dm_exec_sql_text(qs.sql_handle) AS st ORDER BY (qs.total_
elapsed_time/execution_count) DESC;
```

You can order by the preceding query on the **total_logical_reads** column to get the top five most extensive read-intensive queries.

Monitoring blocking

Blocking is a scenario where a query is waiting to acquire a lock on a resource that is already locked by another query. Blocking causes major performance problems and can bring a database to a halt.

The following query returns the blocking details:

```
-- Get blocked queries

SELECT w.session_id

,w.wait_duration_ms

,w.wait_type

,w.blocking_session_id

,w.resource_description

,t.text

FROM sys.dm_os_waiting_tasks w INNER JOIN sys.dm_exec_requests r ON
w.session_id = r.session_id

CROSS APPLY sys.dm_exec_sql_text (r.sql_handle) t WHERE w.blocking_session_
id>0

GO
```

In order to see the preceding query results, generate a blocking scenario by following these steps:

1. Open a new query window in SQL Server Management Studio and connect to the **toystore** database. Execute the following query:

```
Begin Tran
INSERT INTO [Warehouse].[Colors] (
ColorID, ColorName, LastEditedBy, ValidFrom, ValidTo
)
VALUES ( 1001,
'Pulpy Orange', 1, getdate(), getdate()
)
-- ROLLBACK
```

The preceding query will open a new transaction to insert a new row in the **Colors** table. However, the transaction is left open and is not closed, as **ROLLBACK** is commented out.

2. Open another query window in SSMS and connect to the **toystore** database. Execute the following query:

```
INSERT INTO [Warehouse].[Colors] (
ColorID, ColorName, LastEditedBy, ValidFrom, ValidTo
)
VALUES ( 1001,
'Pulpy Green', 1, getdate(), getdate()
)
```

The preceding query tries to insert a row in the **Colors** table; however, it is blocked by the query in *step 1*.

3. Run the following query to detect blocking:

```
-- Get blocked queries
SELECT w.session_id
,w.wait_duration_ms
,w.wait_type
,w.blocking_session_id
,w.resource_description
,t.text
FROM sys.dm_os_waiting_tasks w INNER JOIN sys.dm_exec_requests r ON
w.session_id = r.session_id
CROSS APPLY sys.dm_exec_sql_text (r.sql_handle) t WHERE w.blocking_
session_id>0
GO
```

You should get the following output. The **session_id** value may be different in your case:

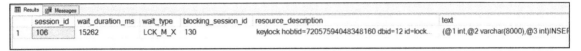

Figure 10.78: Session ID 106 is blocked by session ID 130

Session ID **106** is requesting an exclusive lock on the **Colors** table; however, session ID **130** already has an exclusive lock on the **Colors** table. Therefore, session ID **106** is blocked by session ID **130**.

To remove the block, uncomment and execute the **ROLLBACK** command in the first query provided in *Step 1*.

In this section, we learned how to monitor Azure SQL Database using T-SQL. Let's now look at monitoring Azure SQL Database using extended events.

Extended events

Extended events, introduced in SQL Server 2008, are lightweight methods used to capture diagnostic information in SQL Server.

Extended events are similar to SQL Trace; however, they're more lightweight and scalable than SQL Trace.

The following are the important components of an extended event:

- **Session**: An extended event session, when started, captures the specified data for one or more events.

- **Events**: Events are the activities or actions that the data is to be recorded for. For example, **sql_statement_starting** and **sql_statement_completed** are the events raised whenever an SQL statement is started or completed on the given database.

- **Event Fields**: Every event has a set of event fields or data points that are recorded whenever the event is triggered. For example, the **sql_statement_completed** event has a duration event field.

- **Global Fields**: These are the common data points to be recorded whenever the specified event occurs. Examples of global fields are **session_id**, **sql_text**, **database_name**, and **database_id**.

- **Target**: The target specifies the storage to be used for the data capture. The following targets are allowed in an SQL database:

- **Ring Buffer Target**: The data is stored in memory for a brief interval of time.

- **Event Counter**: Counts all events that occurred during a particular extended event session instead of capturing full event details. It can be used to characterize a workload to be CPU-intensive, I/O-intensive, or memory-intensive.

- **Event File Target**: Writes full event details to an Azure Storage container. This allows you to do historical analysis on the saved data.

Examining queries using extended events

In this section, we'll examine queries made to the **toystore** database using extended events. Imagine we're looking after the Query Performance Insight report of Toystore Ltd.

After generating the report, we plan to look at the extended events to track down the queries that are taking longer than 10 seconds to complete on the **toystore** database. We'll use extended events to capture such queries:

Open a new query window in SQL Server Management Studio and connect to the **toystore** database.

1. Execute the following query to create the extended event session:

```
CREATE EVENT SESSION [LongRunningQueries] ON DATABASE ADD EVENT sqlserver.
sql_statement_completed
( ACTION (
sqlserver.database_name, sqlserver.query_hash, sqlserver.query_plan_hash,
sqlserver.sql_text, sqlserver.username
)
WHERE ([sqlserver].[database_name]=N'toystore' AND duration > 1000)
)
ADD TARGET package0.ring_buffer WITH (STARTUP_STATE=OFF)
GO
```

The preceding query creates an extended event session, **LongRunningQueries**, with the event as **sql_statement_completed**, an action that specifies the global fields to capture, the target as a ring buffer, and **Startup_State** set to **Off**, which means that the session will not automatically start when the SQL Server services are started.

> **Note**
>
> You can copy the code from **C:\Code\Chapter10\CreateExtendedEvent.sql**.
>
> The file location may change depending on where you have unzipped the code files.

2. Execute the following query to start the **LongRunningQueries** session:

```
-- Start the Event Session
ALTER EVENT SESSION [LongRunningQueries] ON DATABASE STATE = START;
```

3. Execute the following PowerShell command to start the workload:

```
powershell.exe "C:\Code\Chapter10\Start-Workload.ps1 -sqlserver toyfactory
-database toystore -sqluser sqladmin -sqlpassword Packt@pub2 -workloadsql
"C:\Code\Chapter10\workload.sql"
-numberofexecutions 10"
```

4. Wait for at least one execution to complete. In *Steps* 4 and 5, we execute queries to get the output from the extended event target. Execute the following query to get the target data into a temporary table:

```
-- Get the target data into temporary table
SELECT
    se.name   AS [XEventSession],
    ev.event_name,
    ac.action_name,
    st.target_name,
    se.session_source,
    st.target_data,
    CAST(st.target_data AS XML)  AS [target_data_XML]
into #XEventData
FROM
                sys.dm_xe_database_session_event_actions  AS ac

    INNER JOIN sys.dm_xe_database_session_events        AS ev  ON
ev.event_name = ac.event_name
        AND CAST(ev.event_session_address AS BINARY(8)) = CAST(ac.event_
session_address AS BINARY(8))

    INNER JOIN sys.dm_xe_database_session_object_columns AS oc
        ON CAST(oc.event_session_address AS BINARY(8)) = CAST(ac.event_
session_address AS BINARY(8))

    INNER JOIN sys.dm_xe_database_session_targets       AS st
        ON CAST(st.event_session_address AS BINARY(8)) = CAST(ac.event_
session_address AS BINARY(8))

    INNER JOIN sys.dm_xe_database_sessions              AS se
        ON CAST(ac.event_session_address AS BINARY(8)) = CAST(se.address
```

```
AS BINARY(8))
WHERE
        oc.column_name = 'occurrence_number'
    AND
        se.name        = 'LongRunningQueries'
    AND
        ac.action_name = 'sql_text'
ORDER BY
    se.name,
    ev.event_name,
    ac.action_name,
    st.target_name,
    se.session_source;
```

5. Then, execute the following query to parse the target XML **xEvent** into a table:

```
-- Parse the target xml xevent into table
SELECT * FROM
( SELECT
xed.event_data.value('(data[@name="statement"]/value)[1]',
'nvarchar(max)') AS sqltext,
xed.event_data.value('(data[@name="cpu_time"]/value)[1]', 'int') AS cpu_t
ime,
xed.event_data.value('(data[@name="duration"]/value)[1]', 'int') AS
duration,
xed.event_data.value('(data[@name="logical_reads"]/value)[1]', 'int') AS
logical_reads
FROM #XEventData
CROSS APPLY target_data_XML.nodes('//RingBufferTarget/event') AS xed
(event_data)
) As xevent
WHERE duration > = 10000000
GO
DROP TABLE #XEventData
```

> **Note**
>
> You can also copy the code from *Steps 4* and *5* from **C:\Code\Chapter10\ReadExtendedEventData.sql**.

The extended event data is stored in XML format. First, the query puts the target XML into a temporary table. The extended event target details are stored in a **sys. dm_xe_database_session_targets** DMV.

A sample target XML is shown in the following code:

```
<event name="sql_statement_completed" package="sqlserver" timestamp="2018-
02-03T16:19:28.708Z">
<data name="duration">
<type name="int64" package="package0"></type>
<value>1</value>
</data>
<data name="cpu_time">
<type name="uint64" package="package0"></type>
<value>0</value>
</data>
<data name="physical_reads">
<type name="uint64" package="package0"></type>
<value>0</value>
</data>
<data name="logical_reads">
<type name="uint64" package="package0"></type>
<value>0</value>
</data>
...
...
</data>
```

Each event has an XML element with event fields as the child elements. This makes it easy to parse the event data.

When parsing data, make sure that the event field data type is the same as what is mentioned in the XML. For example, for the **statement** field, the data type should be **nvarchar**, because in XML, the data type mentioned is the Unicode string.

Once you have at least one execution of the workload completed, you should get an output similar to the following:

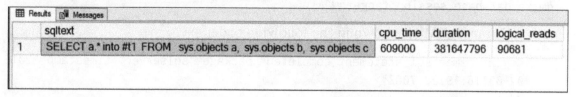

	sqltext	cpu_time	duration	logical_reads
1	SELECT a.* into #t1 FROM sys.objects a, sys.objects b, sys.objects c	609000	381647796	90681

Figure 10.79: The Result of the workload execution

The query returns all of the SQL statements that have durations greater than 10 seconds.

6. Run the following query to stop and drop the extended event session:

```
-- Stop the Event Session
ALTER EVENT SESSION [LongRunningQueries] ON DATABASE STATE = STOP;
GO
-- Drop the Event Target
ALTER EVENT SESSION [LongRunningQueries] ON DATABASE DROP TARGET package0.
ring_buffer;
GO
-- Drop the Event Session
DROP EVENT SESSION [LongRunningQueries] ON DATABASE;
GO
```

This completes the section.

> **Note**
>
> Here's some additional reading for extended events.
>
> More information on extended events DMVs can be found at https://docs.
> microsoft.com/sql/relational-databases/system-dynamic-management-views/
> extended-events-dynamic-management-views?view=sql-server-2017.
>
> More information on extended event lists can be found at https://docs.microsoft.
> com/sql/relational-databases/system-catalog-views/sys-server-event-sessions-
> transact-sql?view=sql-server-2017.

Tuning an Azure SQL database

In this section, we'll look at the out-of-the-box performance tuning features provided by automatic tuning in an Azure SQL database.

Automatic tuning

Azure SQL Database automatic tuning utilizes artificial intelligence to continuously monitor and improve queries executed on an Azure SQL database.

Automatic tuning observes the workload and applies recommendations to speed up performance. The recommendations are applied when database activity is low so that there aren't any performance impacts when applying recommendations.

The following options are available for automatic tuning:

- **Create Index**: Automatically identifies and implements missing indexes to improve workload performance. It also verifies whether the indexes created have improved the performance. The **Create Index** option is disabled by default.

- **Drop Indexes**: Automatically identifies and removes duplicate, redundant, and unused indexes. The **Drop Indexes** option is disabled by default.

- **Force Last Good Plan**: Using the execution plan, it automatically identifies the queries that are slower than the previous good plan and forces the use of the last-known good plan to improve the query's performance. **Force Last Good Plan** is enabled by default.

Automatic tuning has to be manually switched to ON, and is set to OFF by default. Also, it gives you an option to either automatically or manually apply the recommendations.

To enable automatic tuning, follow the following instructions:

1. Open a browser and log in to the Azure portal (https://portal.azure.com) with your Microsoft Azure credentials.

2. Open the `toystore` database and select the **Automatic Tuning** option from the **Intelligent Performance** section on the `toystore` database page.

On the **Automatic tuning** pane, under **Inherit from**, select **Don't inherit**. Under **Configure the automatic tuning options**, toggle **ON** for **FORCE PLAN** and the **CREATE INDEX** and **DROP INDEX** options. Click **Apply** to save the automatic tuning settings:

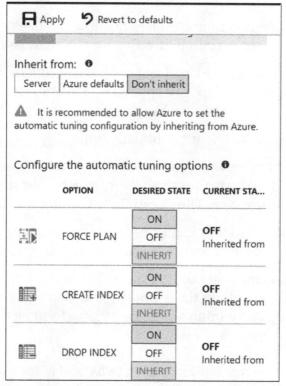

Figure 10.80: Configuring the automatic tuning options

Alternatively, you can also enable automatic tuning by executing the following query in the **toystore** database:

```
ALTER DATABASE current SET AUTOMATIC_TUNING = CUSTOM
ALTER DATABASE current SET AUTOMATIC_TUNING (FORCE_LAST_GOOD_PLAN
= ON, CREATE_INDEX = ON, DROP_INDEX = ON)
```

> **Note**
>
> The **DROP INDEX** feature should be used carefully. There may be an index that is used specifically for a query (say, a report query) which runs once a month but is still important. **DROP INDEX** may drop that index as it's used only once a month.

Existing Azure SQL logical servers with no pre-configured automatic tuning option and new Azure SQL servers are both configured to automatically inherit the Azure defaults.

In-memory technologies

In-memory technologies were first introduced in SQL Server 2012, and are built into the SQL Server Database Engine. They can improve performance significantly for workloads such as data ingestion, data load, and analytical queries.

In Azure SQL Database, in-memory technologies are only available in the Premium and Business Critical service tiers.

Azure SQL Database has the following in-memory technologies: in-memory OLTP and columnstore indexes. Let's talk about them briefly.

In-memory OLTP

As the name suggests, in-memory OLTP improves performance for transaction processing scenarios where a major portion of the workload consists of inserts, updates, and deletes.

In-memory OLTP is achieved by using one of the following objects: memory-optimized tables and natively compiled stored procedures.

Memory-optimized tables

Memory-optimized tables are used to store data in memory. All of the data in a memory-optimized table resides in memory. Memory-optimized tables and disk-based tables can reside within the same database simultaneously.

A table is defined as being a memory-optimized table at the time of its creation. A memory-optimized table creation script is shown in the following code snippet:

```
CREATE TABLE dbo.Orders (
OrderId int not null IDENTITY PRIMARY KEY NONCLUSTERED,
CustomerId int not null, OrderDate datetime not null, Quantity int not null
) WITH
(MEMORY_OPTIMIZED = ON, DURABILITY = SCHEMA_AND_DATA);
```

The `Memory_Optimized` keyword specifies whether the table is a memory-optimized table. The durability refers to retaining only the schema, or the schema and data, for the memory-optimized table. As the table is in memory, the data will go out of memory if the machine is restarted. However, if the durability is set to `SCHEMA_AND_DATA`, SQL Server makes sure that the data isn't lost.

There are two types of indexes allowed on an in-memory table, and these are hash and non-clustered indexes. The indexes don't contain data rows. Instead, they contain memory pointers to the data rows. The indexes are also in memory. Hash indexes are used to optimize point lookups and aren't suitable for range lookups; non-clustered indexes are best suited for range lookups.

Memory-optimized tables can be accessed through the regular **Data Definition Language** (DDL) and **Data Manipulation Language** (DML) commands.

Natively compiled procedures

A regular or `InterOP` stored procedure is compiled and the plan is cached within the SQL server. However, a natively compiled procedure is compiled into DLL and is loaded in memory. This further improves DML command performance on memory-optimized tables.

> **Note:**
> Any query or stored procedure other than a natively compiled stored procedure is referred to as `InterOP`.

The natively compiled procedure syntax is displayed in *Figure 10.81*:

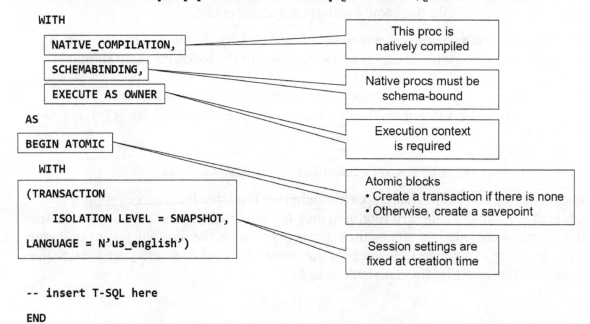

Figure 10.81: Syntax of a natively compiled procedure

A natively compiled procedure contains the regular T-SQL code as the **InterOP** or regular procedures; however, it's defined differently at the time of creation. The term **Native_Compilation** defines that the procedure is a natively compiled procedure and is to be compiled into DLL.

A natively compiled procedure should be schema-bound and should have the execution context. A natively compiled procedure is always executed in a snapshot transaction isolation level. Memory-optimized tables and natively compiled procedures can be used together to speed up an OLTP workload and make it up to 20 times faster.

Columnstore indexes

Columnstore indexes, introduced in SQL Server 2012 (as non-clustered columnstores), use columnar storage instead of regular row-based storage to store data. A row-store has rows with multiple columns arranged sequentially on a page; however, in a column store, the values of a single column (from different rows) are stored contiguously.

> **Note**
>
> Clustered columnstore indexes were added in SQL Server 2014, whereas non-clustered columnstore indexes were introduced in SQL Server 2012.

In a row-store, this is how data is stored on disk:

Data Page – Rowstore		
Name	**Profession**	**State**
Abel	Doctor	WA
Abha	Engineer	UT
Adrian	Doctor	HA

Figure 10.82: Data storage representation in a row-store

However, in a columnstore, the same information is stored as follows:

Data Page – Columnstore
Name
Abel
Abha
Adrian

Data Page – Columnstore
Profession
Doctor
Engineer
Doctor

Data Page – Columnstore
State
WA
UT
HA

Figure 10.83: Data storage representation in columnstore

This allows faster response times and less storage for data warehouse scenarios.

A columnstore has better compression than a row-store, because values of the same data type compress better than values of different data types (a row-store contains columns with different data types, while a columnstore has values from the same type).

This improves query performance, as only those pages that contain the selected column values are scanned or fetched, thereby decreasing the reads.

For example, consider the following query:

```
SELECT Name, profession FROM Employees
```

The preceding query will only touch pages with the **Name** and **Profession** columns if run against a columnstore. However, against a row-store, the query will run through all the pages. This significantly improves the performance in data warehouse scenarios with huge tables.

There are two types of columnstore indexes, clustered and non-clustered:

- **Clustered columnstore index**: Clustered **columnstore** indexes store the entire table data as **columnstores**. They can reduce the storage footprint by up to 10 times its original size. They can be used on fact tables in a data warehouse to speed up queries and fit more data into the available storage.

The syntax for creating a clustered column store index is as follows:

```
CREATE CLUSTERED COLUMNSTORE INDEX CCS_Orders ON [Sales].[Orders]
```

- **Non-clustered columnstore index**: Non-clustered **columnstore** indexes are created on sets of table columns and can co-exist. When introduced in SQL Server 2012, non-clustered column indexes weren't updatable; in other words, if you had a non-clustered column index on a table, you were not allowed to update the data in that table using DML statements.

However, starting from SQL Server 2016, they are now updatable and can be used to gain real-time operational insights into your transactional data. You can query operational data directly instead of spending time doing ETL and loading the data into a data warehouse. You can do all of this without any impact on operations.

The syntax for creating a non-clustered columnstore index is as follows:

```
CREATE NONCLUSTERED COLUMNSTORE INDEX nccsix_CustomerID
ON [Sales].[Orders] (CustomerID,ContactPersonID,OrderDate);
```

The preceding query creates a non-clustered column store index on **customerid**, **contactpersonid**, and **orderdate**. The columnstore structure is stored separately from the table structure.

> **Note**
>
> To learn more about columnstore indexes, refer to https://docs.microsoft.com/sql/t-sql/statements/create-columnstore-index-transact-sql?view=sql-server-2017&viewFallbackFrom=sqlserver-2017.

Columnstore indexes have two types of data compression. The default columnstore compression is **columnstore_archive** compression. A columnstore index is good at compression by design. A page in a columnstore index has data from one column, which is one data type. Therefore, compression is better when compressing data of a similar data type, instead of mixed data types, as is the case with a row-store.

columnstore_archive compression further increases the compression rate. The compression is 37-66% percent higher than the default columnstore compression. Archive compression can be used to compress infrequently used data to save disk space.

To enable **columnstore_archive** on an existing column store index, execute the following query:

```
ALTER INDEX nccsix_CustomerID ON [Sales].[Orders] REBUILD WITH (DATA_
COMPRESSION=COLUMNSTORE_ARCHIVE)
```

To disable **columnstore_archive** compression on an existing columnstore index, execute the following query:

```
ALTER INDEX nccsix_CustomerID ON [Sales].[Orders] REBUILD WITH (DATA_
COMPRESSION=COLUMNSTORE)
```

To create a new **columnstore** index with **columnstore_archive** compression, execute the following query:

```
CREATE NONCLUSTERED COLUMNSTORE INDEX nccsix_CustomerID_AC

ON [Sales].[Orders] (

CustomerID, ContactPersonID, OrderDate

) WITH(DATA_COMPRESSION=COLUMNSTORE_ARCHIVE)
```

> **Note**
>
> Starting from SQL Server 2019, you can use the **sp_estimate_data_compression_savings** DMV to compare the relative data compression benefits of columnstore indexes. However, this DMV isn't supported in Azure SQL Database.

In addition to compression, columnstores also support **batch execution mode**. There are two types of execution modes when reading data from an index: row execution and batch execution. In row execution mode, the data is processed row by row, whereas in batch execution mode, the rows are processed in batches (between 64 and 912 rows) at a time. This significantly benefits aggregation queries, meaning aggregations can be applied to one batch at a time instead of one row at a time.

> **Note**
>
> Batch mode execution is supported in a row-store from SQL Server 2019 onward.

Let's see batch mode in action.

Connect to the **toystore** Azure SQL Database using SSMS. Open a new query window. Copy and paste the following query:

```
select

    stockitemid,

    sum(unitprice) AS totalprice,

    sum(quantity) AS quantity

from sales.orderlines

group by stockitemid
```

Press *Ctrl + M* to enable the actual execution plan and execute the query. You should get an execution plan as shown here:

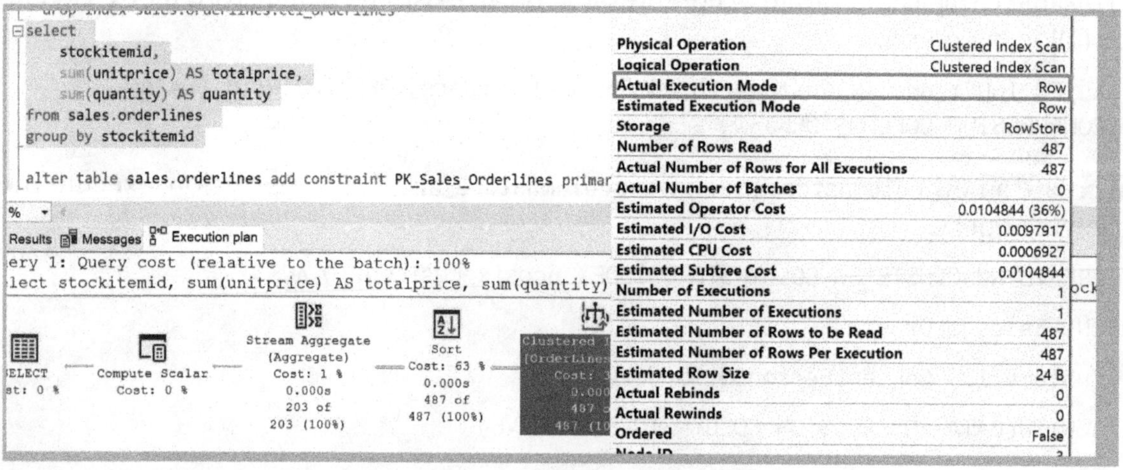

Figure 10.84: Actual execution mode

Observe that the execution mode is **Row**.

Let's execute the following query to create a **nonclustered** columnstore index on the **Sales.orderlines** table:

```
CREATE NONCLUSTERED COLUMNSTORE INDEX CCI_Orderlines ON Sales.
Orderlines(stockitemid,unitprice,quantity)
```

Let's run the following aggregate query again and observe the execution plan:

```
select
    stockitemid,
    sum(unitprice) AS totalprice,
    sum(quantity) AS quantity
from sales.orderlines
group by stockitemid
```

The following is the execution plan of the preceding query:

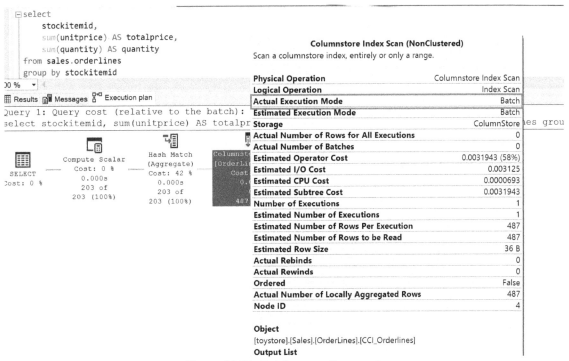

Figure 10.85: Batch execution mode

Observe that the row execution mode is **Batch**. However, there is no guarantee that we will get the batch execution mode for every query that uses columnstore indexes.

Monitoring cost

Managing cost is as important as getting the best performance out of a database. As we work to tune and optimize a database, we can scale down to a lower performance tier, resulting in cost savings without any performance degradation. Cost is another metric that can be used to show management the benefits of database tuning.

We can use the **Cost Management** feature to monitor costs. To do that, in the Azure portal, search for and open **Cost Management + Billing**.

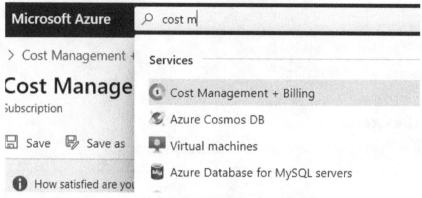

Figure 10.86: Navigating to Cost Management + Billing

On the **Cost Management + Billing** page, select **Cost Management**:

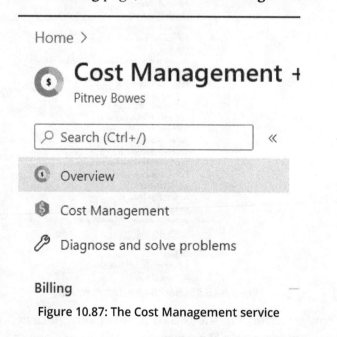

Figure 10.87: The Cost Management service

On the **Cost Management** page, select **Cost analysis**. On the **Cost analysis** page, group costs by resource and then specify the database in the **Filter items** text box:

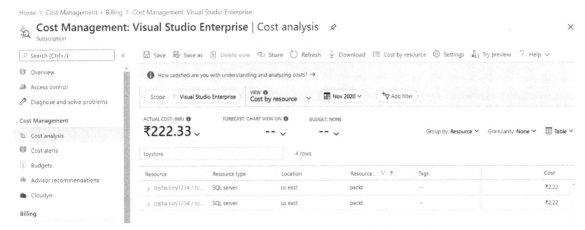

Figure 10.88: Cost analysis by Azure SQL databases

> **Note**
>
> The currency shown is in Indian Rupee (INR). The currency will be different in your case. We can further specify budgets and create alerts whenever the cost reaches the budget.

Activity: Exploring the in-memory OLTP feature

In this activity, we'll compare the performance of a disk-based table with a memory-optimized table for an OLTP workload for our **toystore** database. Let's consider a case where we want to explore the new in-memory OLTP feature using memory-optimized tables. But before we do that, to check whether it is truly profitable, we compare the performance of disk-based tables and memory-optimized tables. This can be done via the following steps:

1. Run the following command in a PowerShell console to change the service tier of the **toystore** database to the Premium tier. The in-memory technologies are only available for the Premium service tier:

```
PowerShell.exe "C:\Code\Chapter02\ScaleUpAzureSQLDB.ps1"
-resourcegroupname toystore -azuresqlservername
toyfactory -databasename toystore -newservicetier Premium
-servicetierperfomancelevel P1 -AzureProfileFilePath "C:\Code\
MyAzureProfile.json"
```

2. Navigate to **C:\Code\Chapter10\InMemoryOLTP** and open the **CreateObjects.sql** file in SQL Server Management Studio. This query creates the following objects:

- **uspInsertOrders**: A traditional disk-based stored procedure that inserts new orders, as specified by the **@numberoforderstoinsert** parameter. If **@numberoforderstoinsert** is set to **10**, then it will insert 10 new orders into the **Sales.Orders** table.

- **Orders_Inmem**: The memory-optimized version of the **Sales.Orders** table. The schema is the same as that of the **Sales.Orders** table; however, it has **Memory_ Optimized** set to **ON**.

- **Customers_Inmem**: The memory-optimized version of the **Sales.Customers** table. The schema is the same as that of the **Sales.Customers** table; however, it has **Memory_ Optimized** set to **ON**. All of the existing customers in the **Sales.Customers** table are inserted into the **Sales.Customers_Inmem** table.

- **uspInsertOrders_Inmem**: This is a natively compiled version of the **uspInsertOrders** procedure. It inserts a number of orders, as specified by the **@numberoforderstoinsert** parameter, into the **Sales.Orders_Inmem** table.

The following query automatically maps all the lower isolation levels to the snapshot isolation level for memory-optimized tables:

```
ALTER DATABASE CURRENT SET MEMORY_OPTIMIZED_ELEVATE_TO_SNAPSHOT = ON
```

This changes the database context to **toystore**. Press F5 to execute the query.

3. Execute the following command in a PowerShell console. This will insert 10,000 orders into the **Sales.Orders** table using the **ostress** utility described at the beginning of the chapter:

```
PowerShell.exe "C:\Code\Chapter10\InMemoryOLTP\Start-Workload.ps1
-sqlserver toyfactory -database toystore -sqluser sqladmin
-sqlpassword Packt@pub2 -ostresspath '"C:\Program Files\Microsoft
Corporation\RMLUtils\ostress.exe"' -workloadtype disk"
```

The **workloadtype** parameter specifies which procedure is executed. If the value is **disk**, the **InterOP** procedure is executed (**uspInsertOrders**), which inserts a value into the **Sales.Orders** (disk-based) table.

Otherwise, if the **workloadtype** parameter is set to **inmem**, the natively compiled procedure is executed (**uspInsertOrders_Inmem**), which inserts a value into the **Sales.Orders_Inmem** (memory-optimized) table.

You should get the following output. The elapsed time might be different in your case:

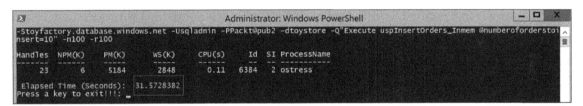

Figure 10.89: The time elapsed for the query execution

As you can see, it took 163 seconds to insert 10,000 orders into the disk-based table. You can execute the following query to count the number of orders that have been inserted:

```
SELECT COUNT(*) FROM sales.orders WHERE orderdate=CONVERT(date, getdate())
Output of inserting orders into the Sales.Orders table
```

4. Execute the following command in a PowerShell console. This will insert 10,000 orders into the **Sales.Orders_Inmem** table using the **ostress** utility described at the beginning of this chapter:

```
PowerShell.exe "C:\Code\Chapter10\InMemoryOLTP\Start-Workload.ps1
-sqlserver toyfactory -database toystore -sqluser sqladmin-sqlpassword
Packt@pub2 -ostresspath '"C:\Program Files\Microsoft Corporation\RMLUtils\
ostress.exe"' -workloadtype inMem"
```

Figure 10.90: Time elapsed for inserting 10,000 orders into the Sales.Orders_Inmem table

It took only 31 seconds to insert 10,000 records into the memory-optimized table using the natively compiled stored procedure.

You can execute the following query to count the number of orders inserted into the **Sales.Orders_Inmem** table:

```
SELECT COUNT(*) FROM sales.orders_Inmem WHERE orderdate=CONVERT(date,
getdate())
```

5. Navigate to **C:\Code\Chapter10\InMemoryOLTP** and open the **Cleanup.sql** file in SQL Server Management Studio:

```
-- Clean up
DROP PROCEDURE IF EXISTS uspInsertOrders_Inmem
GO
DROP PROCEDURE IF EXISTS uspInsertOrders
GO
DROP TABLE IF EXISTS [Sales].Orders_Inmem
GO
DROP TABLE IF EXISTS [Sales].Customers_Inmem
GO
-- delete inserted data from the orders table.
DELETE FROM sales.orders WHERE orderdate=CONVERT(date, getdate())
GO
-- Change the database edition to basic ALTER DATABASE toystore MODIFY
(EDITION = 'basic');
```

The script drops the memory-optimized objects, deletes the rows inserted into the **Sales.Order** table as part of the activity, and changes the database edition to Basic from Premium. This completes the activity.

Monitoring and tuning an Azure SQL Managed Instance

In this section, we will be using HammerDB, the most popular open-source load testing software, to simulate a real-time workload. We are running the workload against a 4 vCore General Purpose SQL Managed Instance. We are using 50 HammerDB virtual users to measure the performance of the workload on a TPCC database with 50 warehouses.

Requirements:

- Client machine from which to run this workload

- SQL Server client tools, such as SQL Server Management Studio

- HammerDB to generate the workload

- The Query Performance Insight library to monitor real-time workload performance

Choose the client within the same Azure region to avoid network latency issues.

> **Note**
>
> To download the HammerDB tool and install the Query Performance Insight library for SQL Managed Instance, please visit the following links:
>
> The Query Performance Insight library: https://github.com/JocaPC/qpi
>
> HammerDB: https://hammerdb.com/download.html

General Purpose instance I/O characteristics

Let's recap the I/O characteristics of a General Purpose SQL Managed Instance. This was discussed in *Chapter 2, Service tiers*:

File size	>=0 and <=128 GiB	>128 and <= 512 GiB	>0.5 and <=1 TiB	>1 and <=2 TiB	>2 and <=4 TiB	>4 and <=8 TiB
IOPS per file	500	2300	5000	7500	7500	12,500
Throughput per file	100 MiB/s	150 MiB/s	200 MiB/s	250 MiB/s	250 MiB/s	480 MiB/s

Figure 10.91: I/O characteristics for a General Purpose SQL Managed Instance

In this section we will generate a load test data and run a workload with 50 virtual users using the HammerDB tool. Follow these steps to complete this task:

1. Open the **HammerDB** tool and click on **SQL Server**, then select the **TPROC-C** option:

Figure 10.92: HammerDB SQLServer TPC workload

2. In this step, we will see options to prepare the schema for a load test. Double-click on **Options** under the **Schema Build** tree and fill in the details as per your environment. In this step, we are using SQL Managed Instance and an existing database:

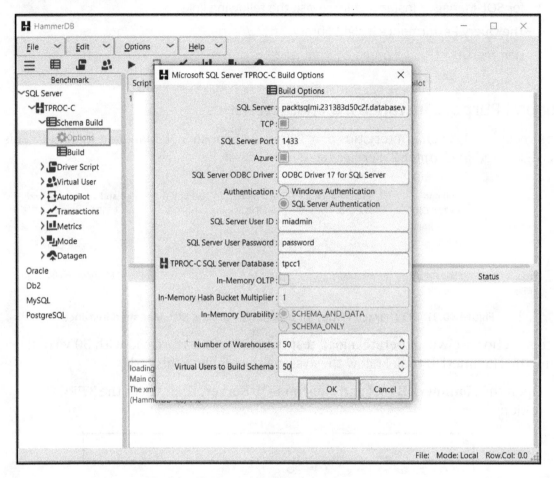

Figure 10.93: HammerDB Schema Build tree options

3. Expand the **Schema Build** option and double-click on **Build** to start generating the schema creation scripts. This step will take a while since it's building the schema and populating the workload data:

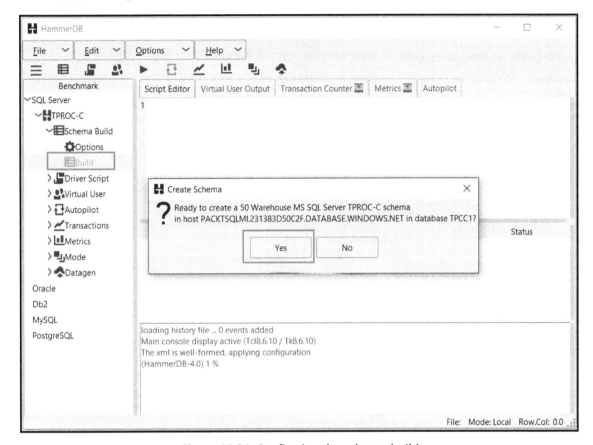

Figure 10.94: Confirming the schema build

4.   The preceding steps may run for quite a while, depending on your instance resources; once the **Schema Build** step is completed, we need to prepare the load script to run the workload. To generate the load script, double-click on **Options** under **Driver Script**. Enter the SQL Managed Instance details, such as the hostname, port, and ODBC driver version, and click **OK**.

To find the correct ODBC driver version on your client machine, please follow the steps here: https://docs.microsoft.com/sql/database-engine/configure-windows/check-the-odbc-sql-server-driver-version-windows?view=sql-server-ver15:

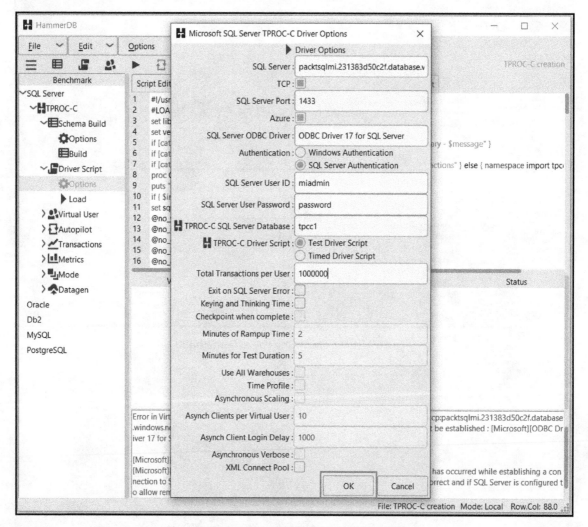

Figure 10.95: HammerDB driver script options

5.   When we are ready with the load script, it's time to deploy virtual users to simulate a real-time workload. Double-click on **Options** under the **Virtual User** tree and fill in the **Virtual Users** and **Iterations** values:

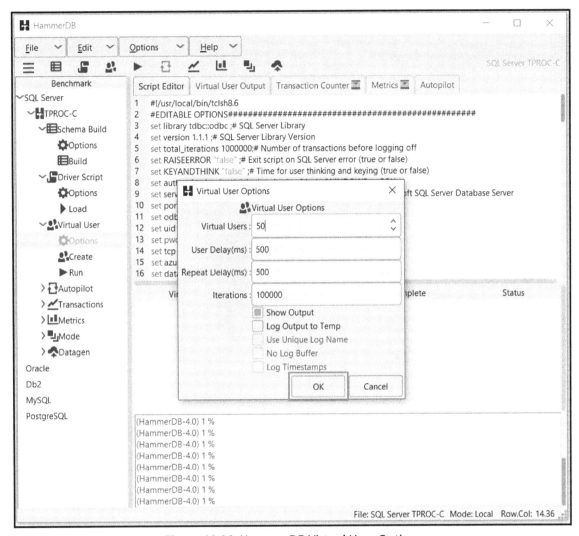

Figure 10.96: HammerDB Virtual User Options

6. Here we are almost ready to start the workload. Click on **Create** to deploy virtual users, and after that, click on **Run** to start the load test:

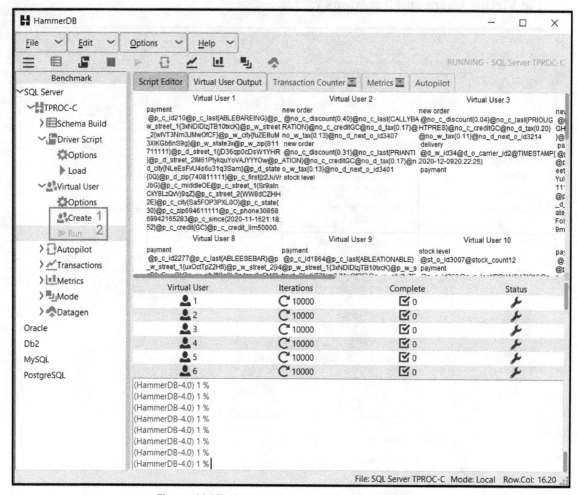

Figure 10.97: HammerDB—running the load test

7. To monitor the transaction counter, click on the **Start Transaction Counter** button in the toolbar:

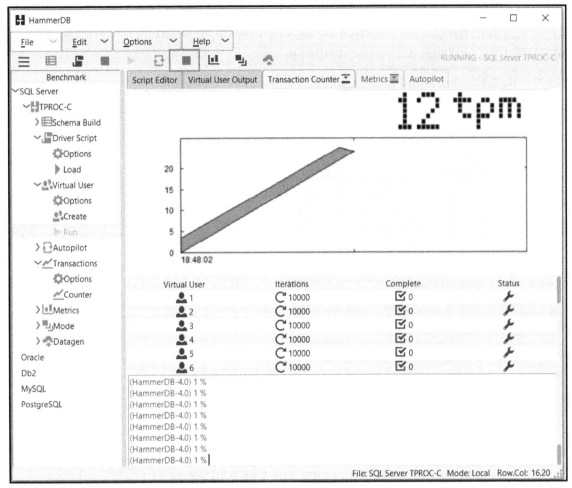

Figure 10.98: Monitoring the tpm counter

So far, we have seen steps for generating load test data and running a workload with 50 virtual users using the HammerDB tool. In the next section, we will see scripts for workload monitoring and **transaction per minute (tpm)** counter performance.

Monitoring the first run with the default file configuration of the TPC-C database

Now the load test is running with the default file configuration for the TPC-C database, and we can see that the transaction per minute counter is fluctuating between 6,000 and 8,500 tpm, and that it's stable at this point.

Let's monitor the workload using Query Performance Insight library queries:

1. Run the following statements to set the baseline for the file and wait statistics. You can run these queries in the database where you have deployed the Query Performance Insight script:

   ```
   --Take the file snapshot stats baseline
   exec qpi.snapshot_file_stats;
   -- Take the wait statistics baseline
   exec qpi.snapshot_wait_stats;
   ```

2. Run the following statement to get the current file snapshot:

   ```
   --Get the current file stats.
   --Enter the database name used by HammerDB.
   select * from qpi.file_stats where db_name='tpcc1';
   ```

	db_name	file_name	size_gb	throughput_mbps	read_mbps	write_mbps	iops	read_iops	write_iops	latency_ms	read_latency_ms	write_latency_ms	read_io_latency_ms	write_io_latency_ms
1	tpcc1	data_0	5.15625000000	12.48	6.75	5.73	490	108	382	1726.0	254.2	2142.9	6.00	4.00
2	tpcc1	log	2.08593750000	2.63	1.34	1.29	40	0	40	5.2	40.8	4.9	40.00	4.00

Figure 10.99: Query Performance Insight file statistics

The preceding figure shows that the **data_0** file for the **tpcc1** database is struggling, with IOPS throughput at 490, since the file size is in the 0>=to <=128 GB range and **latency_ms** is higher (around 1,700 ms). Generally, I/O latency for the General Purpose tier should be around 4-5 ms.

3. Let's also monitor the instance wait statistics at the same time using the Query Performance Insight library. Run the following SQL query to get the top instance wait types:

   ```
   -- Get the wait stats
   select * from qpi.wait_stats order by wait_time_s desc;
   ```

Here is the output of the preceding wait statistics query:

	category	wait_type	waiting_tasks_count	wait_time_s	wait_per_task_ms	max_wait_time_ms	signal_wait_time_s	category_id	info
1	Buffer IO	PAGEIOLATCH_SH	12874	4330.6	336	8954	4	6	www.sqlskills.com/help/waits/PAGEIOLATCH_SH
2	Buffer IO	PAGEIOLATCH_EX	6739	2341.5	347	9336	3	6	www.sqlskills.com/help/waits/PAGEIOLATCH_EX
3	Lock	LCK_M_X	1123	664.7	591	23911	0	3	www.sqlskills.com/help/waits/LCK_M_X
4	Tran Log IO	WRITELOG	14504	119.0	8	256	9	14	www.sqlskills.com/help/waits/WRITELOG
5	Buffer Latch	PAGELATCH_SH	534	78.9	147	5039	0	5	www.sqlskills.com/help/waits/PAGELATCH_SH
6	Buffer Latch	PAGELATCH_EX	364	43.5	119	7344	0	5	www.sqlskills.com/help/waits/PAGELATCH_EX
7	Buffer IO	PAGEIOLATCH_UP	64	21.3	332	4414	0	6	www.sqlskills.com/help/waits/PAGEIOLATCH_UP
8	Lock	LCK_M_U	26	12.7	488	2977	0	3	www.sqlskills.com/help/waits/LCK_M_U
9	Other Disk IO	BACKUPIO	2449	12.7	5	245	0	21	www.sqlskills.com/help/waits/BACKUPIO
10	Lock	LCK_M_S	34	10.3	301	3101	0	3	www.sqlskills.com/help/waits/LCK_M_S
11	Buffer Latch	PAGELATCH_UP	29	5.7	196	3882	0	5	www.sqlskills.com/help/waits/PAGELATCH_UP
12	Preemptive	PREEMPTIVE_HTTP_EVENT_WAIT	309	3.4	10	50	0	12	www.sqlskills.com/help/waits/PREEMPTIVE_HTTP_EVE...
13	Memory	CMEMTHREAD	470	1.6	3	6	0	17	www.sqlskills.com/help/waits/CMEMTHREAD
14	CPU	SOS_SCHEDULER_YIELD	2069	1.3	0	61	1	1	www.sqlskills.com/help/waits/SOS_SCHEDULER_YIELD
15	Tran Log IO	LOGBUFFER	77	1.2	15	46	0	14	www.sqlskills.com/help/waits/LOGBUFFER

Figure 10.100: Query Performance Insight wait statistics

The preceding figure shows the top wait types, and here we can see that the **PAGEIOLATCH_SH** and **PAGEIOLATCH_EX** wait types are dominating the instance wait statistics.

At the same time, the HammerDB transaction counter is moving up and down between 6,000 and 8,500 transactions per minute:

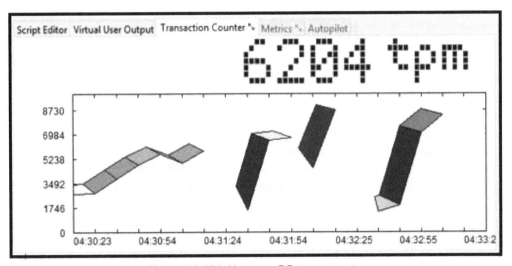

Figure 10.101: HammerDB tpm counter

4. Let's increase the **tpcc1** database data file size and see the impact on the load test. Run the following T-SQL query to increase the **tpcc1** database data file size to 250 GB and it will fall under the >128 to <=512 GB and 2,300 IOPS limits:

```
ALTER DATABASE [tpcc1] MODIFY FILE ( NAME = N'data_0', SIZE =  250GB)
```

5. After the file size increment, you will start observing an improvement in the tpm counter and file statistics for the instance. Run the following to see a current snapshot of the file statistics:

```
select * from qpi.file_stats where db_name='tpcc1';
```

	db_name	file_name	size_gb	throughput_mbps	read_mbps	write_mbps	iops	read_iops	write_iops	latency_ms	read_latency_ms	write_latency_ms	read_io_latency_ms	write_io_latency_ms
1	tpcc1	data_0	250.00000000000	34.82	7.33	27.49	1834	117	1716	34.2	18.1	35.3	6.00	11.00
2	tpcc1	log	2.08593750000	7.06	0.00	7.06	224	0	224	7.0	NULL	7.0	NULL	7.00

Figure 10.102: Query Performance Insight file statistics snapshot

The previous figure shows increased IOPS throughput and better read and write latency for the data file on the **tpcc1** database.

At the same time, you can see the jump in the tpm counter for the load test:

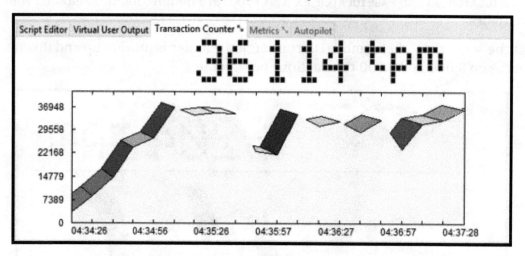

Figure 10.103: HammerDB tpm counter

Here, we can observe 36,000 transactions per minute executing on the managed instance with the same vCore capacity and an increased file size.

In this section, we have seen quick steps to take to run and monitor load testing on managed instances using open-source tools such as HammerDB and the Query Performance Insight library.

The purpose of this section is only to show you how easily you can simulate a near real-time workload and benchmark the performance of your workload for a General Purpose managed instance. These tpm counter numbers may be different in your environment, based on the current workload or client configuration.

Summary

In this chapter, we covered different ways of monitoring and tuning Azure SQL Databases and SQL Managed Instances. We learned how to use Azure SQL Database performance metrics and Query Performance Insight to monitor database metrics and queries from the Azure portal.

The chapter talked about using Azure SQL Analytics to monitor Azure SQL Database and SQL Managed Instance. Intelligent Insights, provided by Azure SQL Analytics, can be used to set up alerts on different metrics such as CPU, log I/O, blocks, and deadlocks for Azure SQL Database. Intelligent Insights can also be used to fine-tune long-running and CPU- or I/O-intensive queries to further optimize an Azure SQL database.

We also learned how to set up alerts on database metrics, and proactively acted as and when alerts were raised. We learned about important DMVs and how to set up extended events to monitor a SQL database or a managed instance.

Following this, we set up automatic tuning for an Azure SQL database, and we used in-memory OLTP to improve the performance of an OLTP workload. We also looked at the steps to monitor and benchmark SQL Managed Instance using open-source tools such as HammerDB and Query Performance Insight queries. Performance tuning is a vast topic, and this book doesn't cover every aspect of it; however, it does give you an insight into the available options. You can explore these options in detail to optimize your environment.

In the next chapter, we will look at improving performance using in-memory technologies, online and resumable DDL operations, SQL Graph queries, Azure Machine Learning, and other improvements that you can make.

11

Database features

In the previous chapter, we learned various ways of monitoring and performance tuning options for Azure SQL Database and SQL Managed Instance. This chapter talks about the important database features available in Azure SQL Database and Azure SQL Managed Instance.

We will learn about **SQL Data Sync**, which is used to sync data between two or more Azure SQL databases or on-premises SQL servers, and we'll look at the SQL Graph capabilities and enhancements in Azure SQL Database. We will also explore newly added features, such as the Azure Machine Learning service and distributed transaction support by creating SQL trust groups in Azure SQL Managed Instance.

By the end of this chapter, you will be able to:

- Implement SQL Data Sync to sync an Azure SQL database with an on-premises database.

- Use SQL Graph queries to create and query graph tables.

- Implement SQL Graph enhancements.

- Create a model to predict future sales using the Azure Machine Learning service in Azure SQL Managed Instance.

- Run distributed transactions and create Server Trust Groups in Azure SQL Managed Instance.

This chapter talks about improving performance using in-memory technologies, online and resumable **Data Definition Language** (**DDL**) operations, and also SQL Graph queries and improvements.

This chapter also covers the machine learning features for executing in-database R and Python scripts.

Azure SQL Data Sync

As the name suggests, Azure SQL Data Sync allows bi-directional data syncing between one or more Azure SQL databases and on-premises databases. The Azure SQL Data Sync service is free; however, there are charges for data movement into and out of an Azure SQL database.

> **Note**
>
> Azure SQL Sync doesn't support SQL Managed Instance at the time of writing.

Figure 11.1 shows how data is typically synced between an Azure SQL database and an on-premises database:

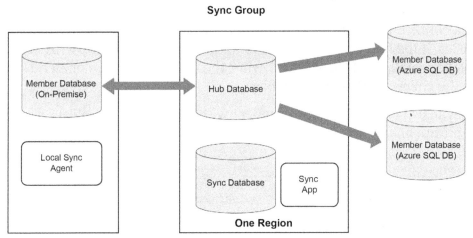

Figure 11.1: Syncing between an Azure SQL database and on-premises database

Azure SQL Data Sync is based around the idea of sync groups. A sync group has a hub database and one or more member databases. The Data Sync is always from hub to member, or from member to hub. There's no data sync between two member databases.

A sync group has the following components:

- **Hub database**: This should be an Azure SQL database. The Data Sync happens to or from the hub database.

- **Member database**: A member database is an Azure SQL database, an on-premises database, or SQL Server running on an Azure VM.

- **Sync database**: This should be an Azure SQL database in the same region as the hub database. The sync database has the Data Sync metadata and log.

- **Sync schema**: This specifies the table and columns to be synced (not included in the diagram).

- **Sync direction**: The Data Sync direction can be from hub database to member database, from member database to hub database, or bi-directional.

- **Sync interval**: The frequency at which the Data Sync occurs.

- **Local sync agent**: The local sync agent or gateway is required for data sync from an on-premises database. The agent is installed on-premises and connects to the Azure SQL database for the Data Sync. To find out more about local sync agents, please visit https://docs.microsoft.com/azure/azure-sql/database/sql-data-sync-agent-overview.

Azure SQL Data Sync works by tracking data changes using insert, update, and delete triggers in a separate table in the user database. The sync app then takes care of merging the tracked data to the member database.

If there is a conflict, there are two potential solutions: either the hub wins, or the member wins. If the hub wins, the changes to the hub database overwrite the changes in the member database. If the member wins, the changes to the member database overwrite the changes to the hub database.

SQL Data Sync can be configured to connect with member and hub databases securely using the private link, which is in public preview at the time of writing. For more details, refer to https://docs.microsoft.com/azure/azure-sql/database/sql-data-sync-data-sql-server-sql-database#private-link-for-data-sync-preview.

Data Sync can be used for the following scenarios:

- Synchronizing on-premises data to Azure SQL Database when moving to the cloud. Consider a scenario where there is a database for multiple applications and the applications are to be moved to the cloud. Data for particular applications can be synced from on-premises to Azure SQL Database.

- Separating the reporting workload from the transactional workload. The member database can be used for reporting, thereby offloading read workloads from the transactional database. The Data Sync is not real time, or as spontaneous as Always On or transactional replication. This should be considered when using Data Sync for such scenarios.

- Applications nowadays have users across the globe. Therefore, having a database closer to users speeds up the application's performance by reducing network latency. Data Sync can be used to synchronize data between the databases in different regions.

Data Sync is not a recommended solution for disaster recovery, read-scale, and when migrating from an on-premises computer running SQL Server to an Azure SQL database. However, Data Sync is helpful for post-migration, to keep the source and target databases in sync.

Data Sync has the following limitations:

- Data Sync doesn't have transactional consistency; rather, it has eventual consistency. Data Sync guarantees that all changes will be synced eventually and that there will be no data loss. This implies that there can be a delay for the data to be synced between the target and source databases. Therefore, SQL Data Sync can't be used for real-time reporting.

- Data Sync has a performance impact on the database as it uses triggers to track changes. It's therefore advised to assess data sync requirements before using it.

- Data Sync doesn't support Azure Active Directory authentication.

- A table participating in Data Sync can't have an identity column that's not the primary key.

- Data Sync doesn't support tables with the same name but different schema; for example, tables such as `Finance.Person` and `Sales.Person` aren't supported.

- Schema changes are not automatically synced. Workarounds are available. Refer to the following link to automate the replication of the schema changes in SQL Data Sync: https://docs.microsoft.com/azure/azure-sql/database/sql-data-sync-update-sync-schema.

- When using Always Encrypted, only the tables and columns that aren't encrypted can be synced.

- With encrypted columns, only columns up to 24 MB in size can be synced.

Let's look at configuring data sync between two Azure SQL databases using PowerShell.

Activity: Configuring Data Sync between two Azure SQL databases using PowerShell

In this activity, we'll configure Data Sync between two Azure SQL databases using PowerShell. We'll configure Data Sync from the `toystore` database to the `toystore_rpt` database. The `toystore_rpt` database is a copy of the `toystore` database. We'll use the PowerShell script provided by Microsoft with a few modifications.

Before we configure the Data Sync, we'll restore a copy of the `toystore` database as the `toystore_rpt` database. The `toystore_rpt` database will be the Data Sync member, and the `toystore` database will be the Data Sync hub.

To restore a copy of **toystore** as **toystore_rpt**, follow these steps:

1. Open a new PowerShell console window and change the directory to **Chapter05**.

2. Execute the following command to restore **toystore** as **toystore_rpt**:

```
PS E:\Professional-Azure-SQL-Database-Administration-Second-Edition\
Chapter05> .\PITRAzureSQLDB.ps1 -sqlserver toyfactorytem -database
toystore
-sqluser test -sqlpassword SuperSecret! -resourcegroupname toystore
-newdatabasename toystore_rpt
```

> **Note**
>
> You may have to change the file location, database user, and password.

3. You'll be prompted to provide the point in time to which to restore the database. Use the one mentioned in the prompt shown in *Figure 11.2*:

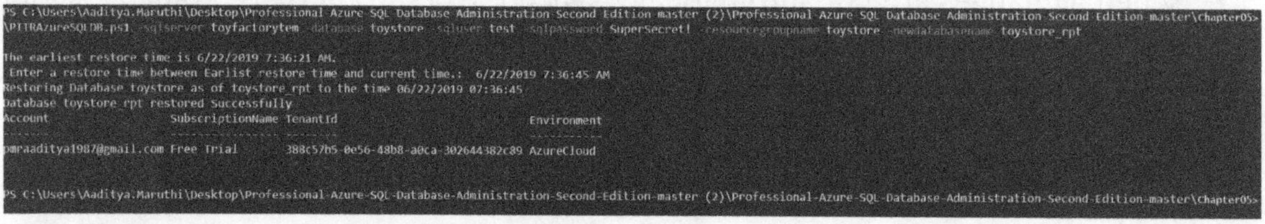

Figure 11.2: Specifying the point in time for restoration of the database

> **Note**
>
> The time highlighted in *Figure 11.2* will be different in your case.

When the restore command completes successfully, the database will be created and will be available for use.

The next step is to configure Data Sync. The Data Sync PowerShell script is taken from the documentation (with some modifications), available at https://docs.microsoft.com/azure/azure-sql/database/scripts/sql-data-sync-sync-data-between-sql-databases.

The new version of the script is in the **Chapter11** directory in the code base for the book.

The script is explained with relevant comments, and it's recommended you go through the script before executing it. The script:

- Creates the Data Sync metadata database and the Data Sync group, and adds the member database to the Data Sync group.

- Updates the database schema from the hub database in the Data Sync metadata database.

- Adds the specified tables and columns to be synced in the Data Sync metadata database.

- Triggers a manual sync, verifies whether Data Sync is working properly, and updates the Data Sync schedule in order to run as specified by the **IntervalInSeconds** parameter.

The script expects the following parameters:

- **SubscriptionID**: The subscription ID of the Azure subscription under which the objects will be created.

- **ResourceGroupName**: The hub database server resource group name. As the Data Sync metadata is created under the same logical server as the hub database, the resource group for the hub and Data Sync metadata is the same.

- **ServerName**: The Azure logical SQL Server name of the hub database.

- **DatabaseName**: The hub database name.

- **SyncDatabaseResourceGroupName**: The resource group of the sync database. This should be the same as the **ResourceGroupName** parameter value.

- **SyncDatabaseServerName**: The Azure logical SQL Server name for the Data Sync metadata database. This is the same as the logical server name for the hub database. This is not a prerequisite. The logical server name for the Data Sync metadata database can be different; however, the location of the server should be the same as that of the hub server.

- **SyncDatabaseName**: The Data Sync metadata database name.

- **SyncGroupName**: The Data Sync group name.

- **ConflictResolutionPolicy**: The Data Sync group conflict resolution policy.

- **IntervalInSeconds**: The Data Sync frequency.

- **SyncMemberName**: The name of the Data Sync member.

- **MemberServerName**: The logical SQL server name of the member database.

- **MemberDatabaseName**: The member database name.

- **MemberDatabaseType**: The member database type; either Azure SQL Database or an on-premises database.

- **SyncDirection**: The Data Sync direction.

- **TablesColumnsToSync**: A comma-separated list of the tables and columns to be synced.

- **Hubdbuser**: The SQL user for the hub database. The script assumes that the user is the same for the hub database, Data Sync, and the member database.

- **Hubdbpassword**: The password for the SQL user. The script assumes that the password is the same for the hub database, Data Sync, and the member database.

Now let's run the script and take a look at the result:

1. To execute the script, open a new PowerShell console window and change the directory to **Chapter11**.

2. Copy and paste the following command. You may have to change the parameter values to suit your environment:

```
.\ConfigureDataSync.ps1 -SubscriptionId "b85b0680-m764-9I88-x7893-
fb6e89c39f38" -ResourceGroupName Packt -ServerName packtdbserver
-DatabaseName toystore -SyncDatabaseResourceGroupName Packt
-SyncDatabaseServerName packtdbserver -SyncDatabaseName syncdb
-SyncGroupName toystoresyncdb -ConflictResolutionPolicy "HubWin"
-IntervalInSeconds 300 -SyncMemberName member1 -MemberServerName
packtdbserver -MemberDatabaseName toystore_rpt -MemberDatabaseType
"AzureSQLDatabase" -SyncDirection "Bidirectional" -TablesColumnsToSync
'[Sales].[Orders].[CustomerID]' -hubdbuser dbadmin -hubdbpassword
Awesome@1234
```

3. When the script completes successfully, navigate to the Azure portal to verify that the objects have been created.

4. In the Azure portal, open the **toystore** database (the hub database) and select **Sync to other databases**:

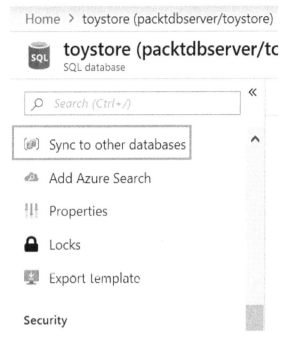

Figure 11.3: The database on the Azure portal

5. Observe that the sync group, **toystoresyncdb**, is created as part of the execution of the preceding script:

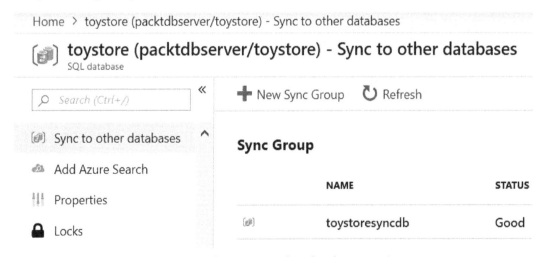

Figure 11.4: The Sync to other databases option

6. Click the sync group name to open the **Database Sync Group** page:

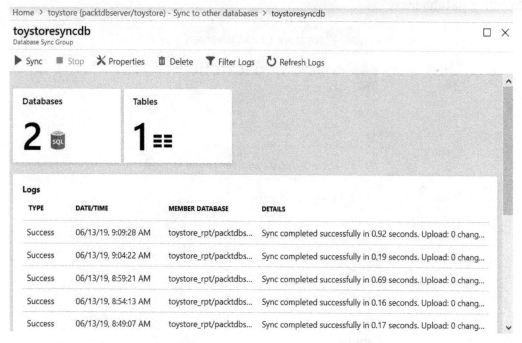

Figure 11.5: The Database Sync Group page

The **Database Sync Group** page lets you add or remove a data sync member and add tables and columns to sync.

7. Click the **Databases** tile to add/remove a data sync member:

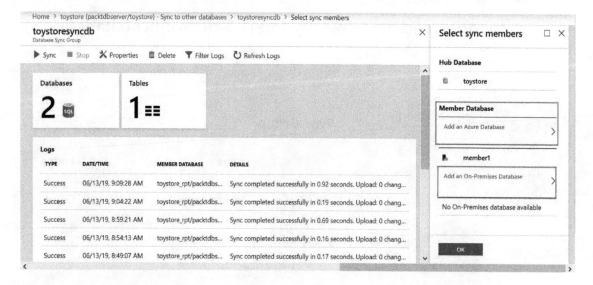

Figure 11.6: The Select sync members pane

8. Click the **Tables** tile to add/remove tables or columns to sync:

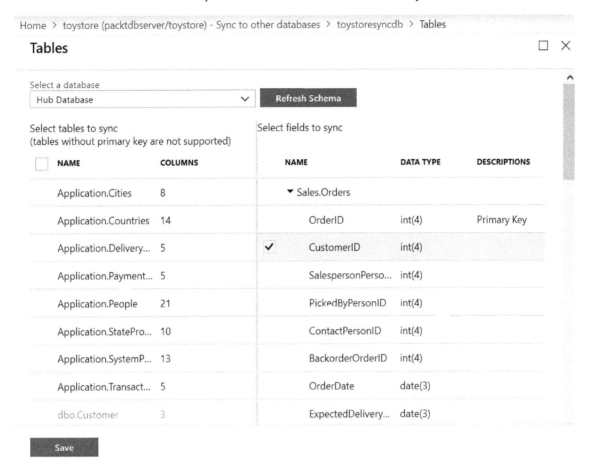

Home > toystore (packtdbserver/toystore) - Sync to other databases > toystoresyncdb > Tables

Tables

Select a database

Hub Database   Refresh Schema

Select tables to sync
(tables without primary key are not supported)

Select fields to sync

	NAME	COLUMNS		NAME	DATA TYPE	DESCRIPTIONS
	Application.Cities	8		▾ Sales.Orders		
	Application.Countries	14		OrderID	int(4)	Primary Key
	Application.Delivery...	5	✓	CustomerID	int(4)	
	Application.Payment...	5		SalespersonPerso...	int(4)	
	Application.People	21		PickedByPersonID	int(4)	
	Application.StatePro...	10		ContactPersonID	int(4)	
	Application.SystemP...	13		BackorderOrderID	int(4)	
	Application.Transact...	5		OrderDate	date(3)	
	dbo.Customer	3		ExpectedDelivery...	date(3)	

Save

Figure 11.7: The tables pane

The existing tables or columns that are being synced are marked with a checkmark. To add tables and columns, check the one you want to add and click **Save**.

Let's now see Data Sync in action.

9. Connect to the `toystore` database in SSMS and execute the following query to update the `CustomerID` column for a given `orderid`:

```
UPDATE Sales.Orders SET CustomerID=30 WHERE orderid=73096;
```

10. Switch to the Azure portal **Database Sync Group** window and click **Sync** to start the Data Sync:

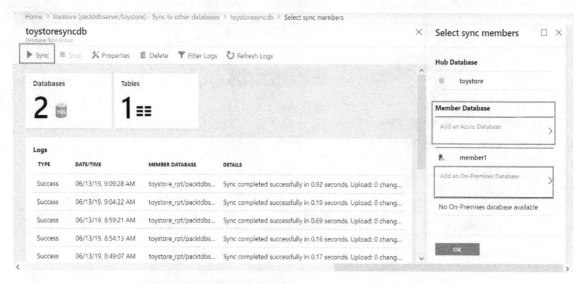

Figure 11.8: The Sync option on the database pane

11. In a new query window in SSMS, execute the following query against `toystore_rpt` (the member database) to verify whether or not it has the updated `CustomerID` from `toystore` (the hub database):

```
SELECT * FROM Sales.Orders WHERE orderid=73096
```

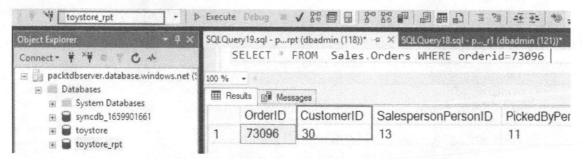

Figure 11.9: Query output on the member database

The sync was successful, and the `CustomerID` column in both the hub and the member database has the same value for the `OrderID 73096`.

12. Once you are done, click **Delete** on the Data Sync group page to delete the sync group and the associated configuration:

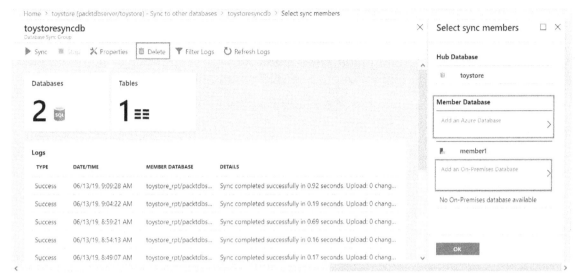

Figure 11.10: Deleting the sync group

This completes the activity. In this activity, we learned how to set up SQL Data Sync between two Azure SQL databases using PowerShell.

Online and resumable DDL operations

The online `CREATE INDEX` and `REBUILD INDEX` operations can be paused and resumed as and when required, or when killed/failed.

The operation is marked as resumable by specifying `RESUMABLE=ON`. For example, the following `CREATE INDEX` operation is a resumable operation:

```
CREATE INDEX IX_Orders_CustomerID_Includes ON Sales.
Orders(CustomerID,Comments)

INCLUDE(DeliveryInstructions,InternalComments)

WITH(ONLINE=ON,MAXDOP=1,RESUMABLE=ON)

GO
```

To pause an ongoing online resumable **CREATE INDEX** operation, either kill the session or execute the **PAUSE** statement, as shown here:

```
ALTER INDEX IX_Orders_CustomerID_Includes on Sales.Orders PAUSE
GO
```

To resume a paused online resumable **CREATE INDEX** operation, either execute the **CREATE INDEX** query mentioned earlier or execute the following query:

```
ALTER INDEX IX_Orders_CustomerID_Includes on Sales.Orders RESUME
GO
```

You can also specify **MAX_DURATION** in minutes that the resumable operation should run before it's paused. For example, the following query runs for 1 minute. If the index isn't created in 1 minute, the operation is paused and can be resumed by using any of the methods specified earlier:

```
CREATE INDEX IX_Orders_CustomerID_Includes ON Sales.Orders(CustomerID)
INCLUDE(Comments,DeliveryInstructions,InternalComments)
WITH(ONLINE=ON,MAXDOP=1,RESUMABLE=ON,MAX_DURATION=1)
GO
```

The values for **MAX_DURATION** must be between 1 and 10,080 minutes.

The following query returns all the ongoing resumable operations:

```
SELECT

Object_Name(Object_id) AS TableName, [name] as IndexName,

sql_text, last_max_dop_used, state_desc, percent_complete

FROM sys.index_resumable_operations;
```

Here's an example output from the preceding query when a resumable **CREATE INDEX** operation is running:

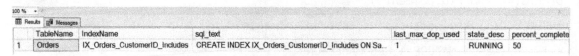

Figure 11.11: Output for the CREATE INDEX operation

The resumable operation has the following limitations:

- **SORT_IN_TEMPDB=ON** isn't supported.

- The resumable **CREATE INDEX/REBUILD INDEX** command can't be executed within an explicit transaction.

- Filtered Index isn't supported with the resumable option.

- The LOB, Computed, and Timestamp columns can't be included.

SQL Graph queries and improvements

A graph database consists of nodes and edges. The nodes represent entities in your graph, such as people or organizations, and edges represent the relationship between two entities. The graph databases are optimized for implementing hierarchies and many-to-many relationships, and for analyzing interconnected data and relationships. This is difficult to implement in a relational database.

Let's look at modeling a very popular use case for a graph database: a social media application. A social media application allows users to follow, like, post, comment, and tag other users. Let's look at a simple model in *Figure 11.12* that allows users to do this:

> **Note**
>
> To find out more about graphs, refer to https://docs.microsoft.com/sql/relational-databases/graphs/sql-graph-overview?view=sql-server-ver15.

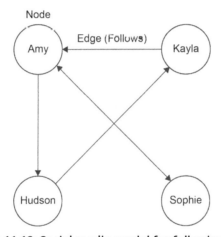

Figure 11.12: Social media model for following users

In *Figure 11.12*, the circles represent nodes and the lines represent edges or relationships. The relationship is **follows**. The graph tells us that Amy follows Hudson, Hudson follows Kayla, Kayla follows Amy, Amy follows Sophie, and Sophie follows Amy.

In Azure SQL Database, nodes and edges are stored as tables. Therefore, to model this example, we'll need two tables: a **Person** node table, and a **follows** edge table.

The following query creates a node table called **Person**:

```
CREATE TABLE [Person] (

Id int identity, FullName varchar(100), PhoneNumber varchar(25),

EmailAddress varchar(100)

) AS NODE;
```

A node can have properties such as phone number and email address in the **Person** table. All indexes and data types are supported. That is, you can define any type of index on a node property, including columnstore indexes.

Let's insert some sample records in the **Person** table:

```
Insert into Person Values ('Kayla Woodcock','(415) 555-0102','kaylaw@
widexworldimporters.com'),
('Hudson Onslow','(415) 555-0102','Hudson@widexworldimporters.com'),
('Sophia Hinton','(415) 555-0102','Sophia@widexworldimporters.com'), ('Amy
Trefl','(415) 555-0102','Amy@widexworldimporters.com');
```

The preceding query inserts people's details.

A **Select** query executed on the **Person** table gives the following output:

	$node_id_237716FDB2954B32847FA1EEAEF0069D	Id	FullName	PhoneNumber	EmailAddress
1	{"type":"node","schema":"dbo","table":"Person","id":0}	1	Kayla Woodcock	(415) 555-0102	kaylaw@widexworldimporters.com
2	{"type":"node","schema":"dbo","table":"Person","id":1}	2	Hudson Onslow	(415) 555-0102	Hudson@widexworldimporters.com
3	{"type":"node","schema":"dbo","table":"Person","id":2}	3	Sophia Hinton	(415) 555-0102	Sophia@widexworldimporters.com
4	{"type":"node","schema":"dbo","table":"Person","id":3}	4	Amy Trefl	(415) 555-0102	Amy@widexworldimporters.com

Figure 11.13: The Person table output

Take a look at the **$node_id** column in the output. **$node_id** is a pseudo-column that uniquely identifies each node in the database.

Let's now create an edge table, as follows:

```
create table follows AS EDGE
GO
```

An edge table may or may not have user-defined properties in it. In this example, we did not define any properties. Like the node tables, all data types and indexes are supported on edge table properties.

A **Select** query on the **follows** table gives the following output:

Figure 11.14: Select operation on the follows table

There are no records in the edge table yet. Take a look at the different columns in the edge table. **$edge_id** is a pseudo-column that uniquely identifies an edge in the database.

$from_id contains the **$node_id** of the node from where the edge originates.

The **$to_id** column contains the **$node_id** of the node at which the edge terminates. Let's insert values into the **follows** table as per the following relationship:

"Amy follows Hudson | Hudson follows Kayla | Kayla follows Amy | Amy follows Sophie | Sophie follows Amy"

When inserting data into an edge table, along with the user-defined properties that you might have in the edge table, you must insert values for the **$from_id** and **$to_id** columns. **$from_id** and **$to_id** must hold the **$node_id** of the nodes that you are trying to connect using the given edge in the graph:

```
insert into follows values

((select $node_id from Person where FullName='Kayla Woodcock'),(select

$node_id from Person where FullName='Amy Trefl')),

((select $node_id from Person where FullName='Amy Trefl'),(select $node_id
from Person where FullName='Sophia Hinton')),

((select $node_id from Person where FullName='Sophia Hinton'),(select $node_
id from Person where FullName='Amy Trefl')),

((select $node_id from Person where FullName='Amy Trefl'),(select $node_id
from Person where FullName='Hudson Onslow')),

((select $node_id from Person where FullName='Hudson Onslow'),(select $node_
id from Person where FullName='Kayla Woodcock'))

GO
```

A select query on the **follows** table gives the following result:

Figure 11.15: Output of the select query

The **follows** table correctly defines the relationship between each of the node IDs.

To query the relationships, a new **match** built-in operator is used. **match** is used in a **WHERE** clause. The following query lists all the people that Amy follows:

```
SELECT person1.Fullname ,person2.fullname

FROM person AS person1, person AS person2, follows WHERE match(person1
-(follows)-> person2)

AND person1.fullname = 'Amy Trefl'
```

Here's the output from the preceding query:

	Fullname	fullname
1	Amy Trefl	Sophia Hinton
2	Amy Trefl	Hudson Onslow

Figure 11.16: Output of the SELECT query

The syntax for the `match` operator is defined as `(person1-(follows)->person2)`. Anything that appears at the two ends of the arrow are nodes, and edges appear inside the parenthesis. When using `match`, you always go from one node to another via an edge. This was a simple example of how a graph schema can be implemented in Azure SQL Database.

Graph database integrity using edge constraints

Edge constraints can help enforce a specific semantic between nodes. To explain this, let's extend the preceding example with a new node that contains a list of the people with deactivated, or inactive, accounts. A deactivated account cannot follow any other person. Therefore, an active person (in the `Person` node) can follow an inactive person (in the `Blocked` node); however, an inactive person (in the `Blocked` node) can't follow an active person (in the `Person` node).

Execute the following query to create a `Blocked` node and mark `Hudson Onslow` as blocked or deactivated:

```
CREATE TABLE [Blocked] (

Id int identity, FullName varchar(100), PhoneNumber varchar(25),

EmailAddress varchar(100)

) AS NODE;

GO

Insert into Blocked Values ('Hudson Onslow','(415) 555-0102','Hudson@
widewworldimporters.com');
```

Let's create the "follows" (edge) table with an edge constraint:

```
CREATE TABLE follows (

CONSTRAINT ec_blocked Connection (Person To Blocked,Person To Person)

)

As Edge
```

The preceding query creates an edge table called **follows**, with an edge constraint called **ec_blocked**. The edge constraint only allows connections from the **Person** node to the **Blocked** node, and from the **Person** node to itself.

Execute the following query to insert relationships in the edge table. This is allowed as per the constraint definition:

```
insert into follows values

((select $node_id from Person where FullName='Kayla Woodcock'),(select

$node_id from Person where FullName='Amy Trefl')),

((select $node_id from Person where FullName='Amy Trefl'),(select $node_id
from Person where FullName='Sophia Hinton')),

((select $node_id from Person where FullName='Sophia Hinton'),(select $node_
id from Person where FullName='Amy Trefl')),

((select $node_id from Person where FullName='Amy Trefl'),(select $node_id
from Blocked where FullName='Hudson Onslow'));

GO
```

Let's now insert a connection from a **Blocked** node to a **Person** node, which isn't allowed as per the constraint's definition:

```
insert into follows values

((select $node_id from Blocked where FullName='Hudson Onslow'),(select

$node_id from Person where FullName='Kayla Woodcock'));

GO
```

The preceding query terminates with the following error:

```
Msg 547, Level 16, State 0, Line 58
```

```
The INSERT statement conflicted with the EDGE constraint "ec_blocked". The
conflict occurred in database "GraphDB", table "dbo.follows".
```

The statement has been terminated.

You can also define cascading actions on an edge constraint. Cascading actions on an edge constraint let users define the actions that the database engine takes when a user deletes the node(s), which the given edge connects. The following referential actions can be defined:

- **NO ACTION:** The database engine raises an error when you try to delete a node that has connecting edge(s).

- **CASCADE:** When a node is deleted from the database, connecting edge(s) are deleted.

The following example creates the **follow** edge with an **ON DELETE CASCADE** action. That is, when a **Person** node is deleted from the **Person** node table, all connecting edges (incoming or outgoing) to that node will be automatically deleted. If cascading delete actions are not defined on the edge constraint, it will be the user's responsibility, after deleting a node, to delete all the connecting edges. If they do not do so, there will be dangling edges in the graph:

```
CREATE TABLE follows (

CONSTRAINT ec_blocked Connection (Person To Blocked,Person To Person) ON
DELETE CASCADE

)

As Edge
```

To learn more about implementing **ON DELETE CASCADE**, refer to the following link: https://docs.microsoft.com/sql/relational-databases/tables/graph-edge-constraints?view=sql-server-ver15#defining-referential-actions-on-a-new-edge-table.

Using derived tables or views in match

Graph queries on Azure SQL Database support using views and derived table aliases in a match query. To use these aliases in **match**, the views and derived tables must be created either on node or edge tables, which may or may not have some filters on them, or a set of node or edge tables combined using the **UNION ALL** operator. The ability to use derived table and view aliases in **MATCH** queries could be very useful in scenarios where you are looking to query heterogeneous entities or heterogeneous connections between two or more entities in your graph.

Match in merge DML

The **match** operator is supported with the **MERGE DML** statement. The **MERGE DML** statement allows you to run **insert**, **update**, and **delete** statements on a target table based on the values matched from the source table. You can read more about this at https://docs.microsoft.com/sql/relational-databases/graphs/sql-graph-overview?view=sql-server-ver15&viewFallbackFrom=sql-serverver15.

One of the most important features of a SQL Graph database is the **SHORTEST_PATH** function. You can read more about it at https://docs.microsoft.com/sql/relational-databases/graphs/sql-graph-shortest-path?view=sql-server-ver15.

In this section, we have discussed SQL Graph queries features for Azure SQL Database. Next, let's look at the Machine Learning Services feature in Azure SQL Managed Instance.

Machine Learning Services

Machine Learning Services was first introduced in SQL Server 2016 (on-premises) as R Services. Machine learning is now available in Azure SQL Managed Instance. It's in preview at the time of writing.

Machine Learning Services provides machine learning capabilities for Azure SQL Managed Instance and allows in-database R and Python scripts to be run for high-performance predictive analytics. Running in-database R and Python scripts uses the data in the managed instance instead of pulling the data over the network from a different source. In the absence of Machine Learning Services, you would have to set up R and Python and get the data from a remote data source for the analysis.

Machine Learning Services makes it possible to run R and Python scripts in stored procedures or T-SQL statements.

R is a programming language that's extensively used for data analysis, machine learning, and predictive analytics. R packages provide out-of-the-box methods to implement statistical and machine learning algorithms such as linear and non-linear regression, classification, and decision tree classification.

Python is one of the most popular programming languages. Using Python, you can do all sorts of tasks, such as web development and data analysis, and it's emerged as a great language for implementing machine learning.

Common R and Python packages are included in Machine Learning Services. You can use **RevoScaleR**, **MicrosoftML**, **olapR**, and **sqlrutils** for R. For Python, in addition to Microsoft packages such as **revoscalepy** and **microsoftml**, you can also use and install open-source packages and framework such as **PyTorch**, **TensorFlow**, and **scikit-learn**.

Differences between Machine Learning Services in SQL Server and Azure SQL Managed Instance

The SQL Managed Instance and SQL Server Machine Learning Services are quite similar; however, there are some important differences:

Machine Learning Services	
Azure SQL Managed Instance	**SQL Server**
R (v3.5.2) and Python (v3.7.1) are supported.	R (v3.3.3) and Python (v3.5.2) are supported.
No additional configuration required after sign-up.	**external scripts enabled** needs to be configured using **sp_configure**.
No support packages that depend on external runtimes such as Java or the OS API.	Packages can use external runtimes.
Packages can make outbound calls using NSG rules.	Packages can make network calls.
Not possible to limit R resources using **Resource Governor**. In preview, R resources can use a maximum 20% of Azure SQL Managed Instance resources.	Yes, **Resource Governor** can be used to limit R resources.

Table 11.1: Azure SQL Managed Instance Vs. SQL Server - Machine Learning Services

The Machine Learning Services public preview for SQL Managed Instance has the following limitations:

- Only Python and R packages are supported, and external languages such as Java cannot be used.

- Loopback connections are not supported.

- It's available in the US, Asia, Europe, and Australia regions only.

- **Message Passing Interface (MPI)** scenarios are not supported.

If you change the pricing tier of your Azure SQL Managed Instance, then a support request needs to be raised to re-enable the dedicated resource limits for R/Python.

> **Note**
>
> Machine Learning Services in SQL Managed Instance is in public preview. To sign up, please visit https://docs.microsoft.com/azure/azure-sql/managed-instance/machine-learning-services-overview#signup.

Activity: Run basic Python scripts

In this activity, you will learn to write basic scripts to run a simple Python program, check the Python version, and check the installed Python packages from an SSMS query window.

Perform the following steps to complete the activity:

1. Open a new query window in SSMS and run the following script to run a simple **Hello, World!** program:

    ```
    EXECUTE sp_execute_external_script @language = N'Python',
    @script = N'print("Hello, World!")';
    GO
    ```

    If you get an error instead of the following output, then Machine Learning Services isn't enabled on the Azure SQL Managed Instance, and you should refer to the earlier note to enable it:

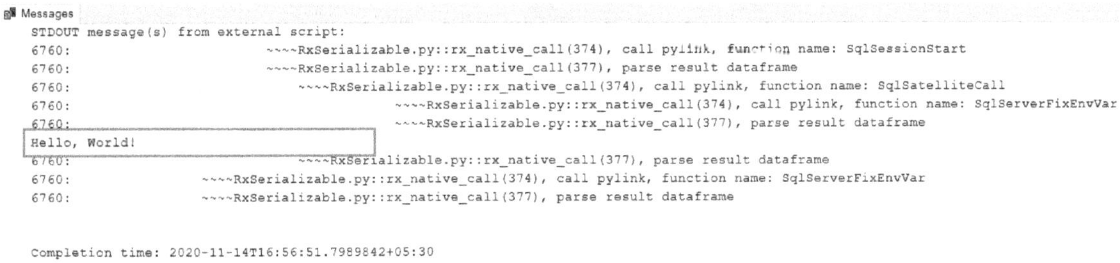

Figure 11.17: Output for Hello, World! using Python

2. Run the following script to check the Python version:

    ```
    EXECUTE sp_execute_external_script @language = N'Python'
        , @script = N'
    import sys
    print(sys.version)
    '
    ```

    The preceding script will display output such as the following:

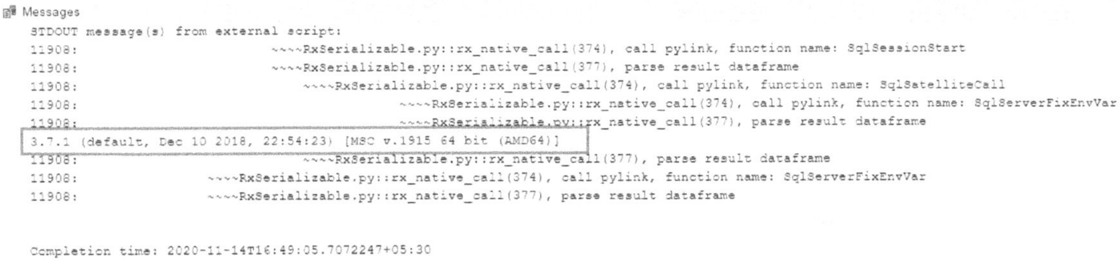

Figure 11.18: Output for Python version

3. Run the following script to check installed Python packages:

```
EXECUTE sp_execute_external_script @language = N'Python'
    , @script = N'
import pkg_resources
import pandas
dists = [str(d) for d in pkg_resources.working_set]
OutputDataSet = pandas.DataFrame(dists)
'
WITH RESULT SETS(([Package] NVARCHAR(max)))
GO
```

You will see output like this:

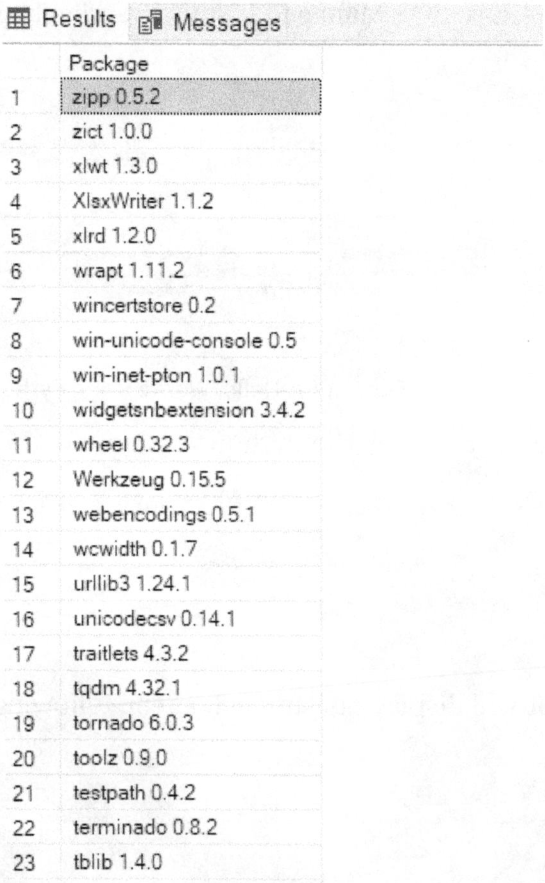

	Package
1	zipp 0.5.2
2	zict 1.0.0
3	xlwt 1.3.0
4	XlsxWriter 1.1.2
5	xlrd 1.2.0
6	wrapt 1.11.2
7	wincertstore 0.2
8	win-unicode-console 0.5
9	win-inet-pton 1.0.1
10	widgetsnbextension 3.4.2
11	wheel 0.32.3
12	Werkzeug 0.15.5
13	webencodings 0.5.1
14	wcwidth 0.1.7
15	urllib3 1.24.1
16	unicodecsv 0.14.1
17	traitlets 4.3.2
18	tqdm 4.32.1
19	tornado 6.0.3
20	toolz 0.9.0
21	testpath 0.4.2
22	terminado 0.8.2
23	tblib 1.4.0

Figure 11.19: Output for Python packages

In this activity, we learned to run some basic scripts using Python. We have also verified the installed Python version and Python packages that are pre-installed by Microsoft in Machine Learning Services.

Activity: Using Machine Learning Services in Azure SQL Managed Instance to forecast monthly sales for the toystore database

In this activity, you'll use linear regression on the monthly sales data in the **toystore** Azure SQL Managed Instance database to forecast the sales for the coming months. You'll run R scripts in Azure SQL Managed Instance to train and save a model in a database table. You'll then use the saved model to forecast sales in upcoming months.

> **Note**
>
> The Machine Learning Services public preview should be enabled in Azure SQL Managed Instance in order to perform the steps in the activity.

All the steps in this activity are on the **toystoreml** managed database with the Machine Learning Services public preview enabled. You can use an existing or a new managed database; however, the Machine Learning Services public preview should be enabled in Azure SQL Managed Instance.

Follow these steps to complete the activity:

> **Note**
>
> The queries used in the activity can also be copied from the ~/**Chapter11/ ActivityMachineLearning.sql** file in the code bundle.

1. We'll import the monthly sales data into the **MonthlySales** table in the **toystoreml** database. The **MonthlySales** table will be used to train the machine learning model. Execute the following query to create the **MonthlySales** table:

    ```
    CREATE TABLE [dbo].[MonthlySales]( [year] [smallint] NULL, [month]
    [tinyint] NULL, [Amount] [money] NULL
    )
    ```

    Execute the following **bcp** command in a command-line console window. The **bcp** command inserts the data in the ~/**Chapter11/MonthlySales.dat** file into the **MonthlySales** table:

    ```
    bcp MonthlySales in "E:\Professional-Azure-SQL-Database-Administration-
    Second-Edition\Chapter11\MachineLearning\monthlysales.dat" -c -t -S
    packtsqlmi.<dnszone>.database.windows.net -d toystoreml -U dbadmin -P
    xxxxxxx
    ```

    You'll have to change the managed instance name, the database name, the user, and the password for your environment.

You should get the following output from the **bcp** command:

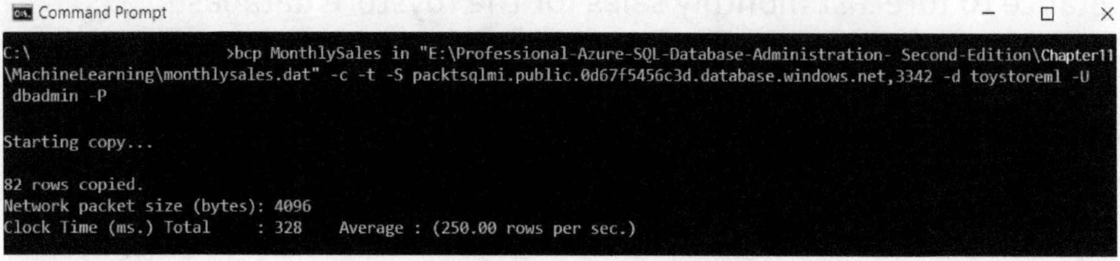

Figure 11.20: Output of the bcp command

Open a new query window in SSMS, connect to the **toystoreml** database, and query the **MonthlySales** table:

```
SELECT * FROM MonthlySales
```

You should get an output similar to *Figure 11.21*:

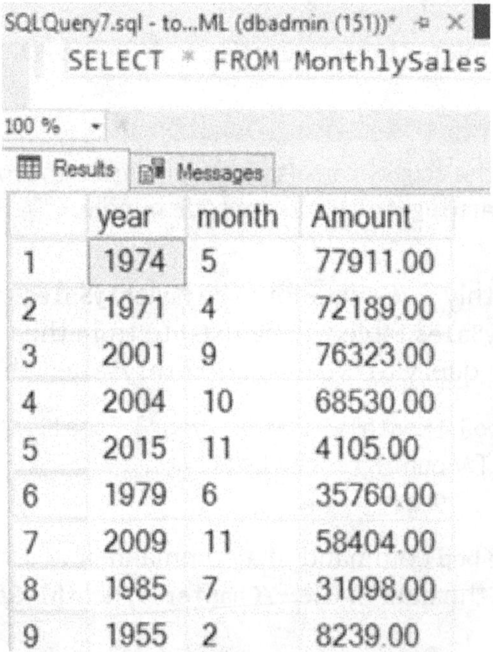

Figure 11.21: The MonthlySales table data

The **MonthlySales** table contains the monthly sales amount for each year. We'll use this data to predict the sales amount for the upcoming months.

2. Before we start creating the model, execute the following query in SSMS to verify whether the Machine Learning Services public preview is enabled on the database:

    ```
    EXECUTE sp_execute_external_script @language =N'R', @script=N'print("Hello
    World")';
    ```

    If you get an error instead of the following output, then Machine Learning Services isn't enabled on the managed instance:

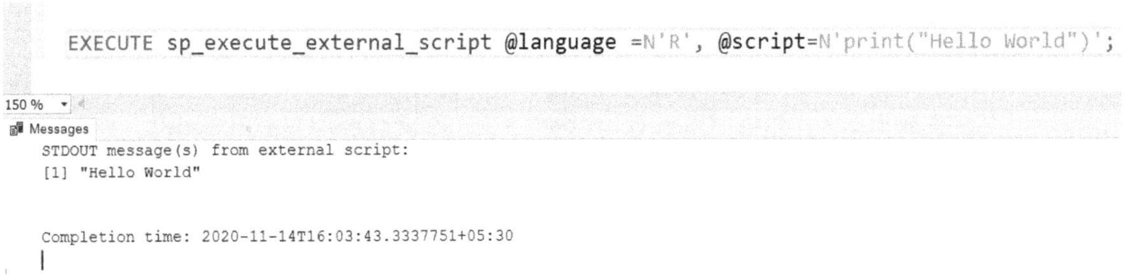

    ```
    EXECUTE sp_execute_external_script @language =N'R', @script=N'print("Hello World")';
    ```

    150 %
    Messages
    STDOUT message(s) from external script:
    [1] "Hello World"

    Completion time: 2020-11-14T16:03:43.3337751+05:30

    Figure 11.22: Output for Hello World using R

    The **sp_execute_external_script** stored procedure executes a given R script on a given dataset. The dataset is a valid input database query.

3. The **MonthlySales** table has three columns: **year**, **month**, and **amount**. The **amount** column contains the sales amounts for the given year and month.

    The linear regression model will describe the relationship between the sales amount (the **dependent** variable) and the year and month (**independent** variables).

    A linear regression algorithm requires a formula to describe the relationship between the dependent variable (**amount**) and the independent variables (**year** and **month**), as well as input data, to train the model.

    The linear regression formula is defined in an R script, and the input data is provided from the **MonthlySales** table.

Execute the following query to create a **generate_linear_model** procedure to create a linear regression model:

```
DROP PROCEDURE IF EXISTS generate_linear_model;
GO
CREATE PROCEDURE generate_linear_model
AS
BEGIN
EXECUTE sp_execute_external_script @language = N'R',
@script = N'
lrmodel <- rxLinMod(formula = amount ~ (year+month), data = MonthlySales);
trained_model <- data.frame(payload = as.raw(serialize(lrmodel,
connection=NULL)));
' ,
@input_data_1 = N'SELECT
year,month,amount FROM MonthlySales',
@input_data_1_name =
N'MonthlySales',
@output_data_1_name = N'trained_model'
WITH RESULT SETS
(
(
model VARBINARY(MAX)
)
);
END;
```

sp_execute_external_script executes the R script against the data from the **MonthlySales** table.

The **@script** variable has an R script that uses the **rxLinMod** function. The first argument to **rxLinMod** is the formula that defines the amount as dependent on the year and month. The second variable defines the dataset.

@input_data_1 is the SQL query that sets the training data to train the model.

@input_data_1_name is the name given to the data return by the query in **@ input_data_1**. The dataset's name is used as the second argument to the **rxLinMod** function.

@output_data_1_name is the name of the output dataset. The procedure returns a model in the **varbinary data type**.

4. The next step is to execute the **generate_linear_model** procedure and store the data model in a table.

    Execute the following queries to create a table and then execute the **generate_linear_model** procedure to store the model in the table:

```
DROP TABLE IF EXISTS dbo.monthly_sales_models
GO
CREATE TABLE dbo.monthly_sales_model
(
model_name VARCHAR(30) NOT NULL
DEFAULT ('default model') PRIMARY KEY, model VARBINARY(MAX) NOT NULL
);
GO
INSERT INTO dbo.monthly_sales_models
(
model
)
EXECUTE generate_linear_model;
GO
Query the monthly_sales_models table to verify the row inserted.
SELECT * FROM monthly_sales_models
```

    You should get output as shown in *Figure 11.23*:

Figure 11.23: Output for the generate_linear_model function

5. The next step is to insert the year and month in the **MonthlySales** table for which we need to predict the sales amount.

    Execute the following query to insert the values:

```
INSERT INTO dbo.MonthlySales
(
year, month
)
VALUES
        (2019, 7),
        (2019, 8),
        (2019, 9),
        (2019, 10),
        (2019, 11),
GO
```

6. The next step is to predict the sales amount for the years and months inserted in *step* 5. These year and month values were not in the `MonthlySales` table and the sales amount is not available for them.

    Execute the following query to predict the sales amount:

    ```
    DECLARE @salesmodel VARBINARY(MAX) = (
    SELECT model FROM dbo.monthly_sales_models
    WHERE model_name = 'default
    model'
    );
    EXECUTE sp_execute_external_script @language = N'R',
    @script = N'
    current_model <- unserialize(as.raw(salesmodel));
    new <- data.frame(NewMonthlySalesData);
    predicted.amount <- rxPredict(current_model, new);
    OutputDataSet <- cbind(new, ceiling(predicted.amount));
    ',
    @input_data_1 = N'SELECT [year],[month]
    FROM [dbo].[MonthlySales] where amount is null',
    @input_data_1_name =
    N'NewMonthlySalesData',
    @params = N'@salesmodel
    varbinary(max)',
    @salesmodel = @salesmodel
    WITH RESULT SETS
    (
    (
    [year] INT,
    [month] INT,
    predicted_sales INT
    )
    );
    ```

    The query passes the new year and month values and the saved model to the **rxPredict** function to generate the predictions for the sales amount. The **@ salesmodel** variable contains the model created in *step* 4.

    The **@script** parameter is the R script that generates predictions. The **rxPredict** function takes two arguments, the model and the new data. The first argument, **current_model**, is the **unserialized** form of the **@salesmodel**. The second argument, **new**, is the data from the T-SQL query as specified in the **@input_data_1** parameter.

    The **@input_data_1** parameter specifies the data for the prediction. The query selects the year and month from the **MonthlySales** table where the amount is not available.

@output_data_1_name is the name given to the dataset returned by the query specified by the **@input_data_1_parameter** parameter.

@params defines the **@salesmodel** input parameter. **@salesmodel** contains the model created in *step* 4.

You should get the output shown in *Figure 11.24*:

	year	month	predicted_sales
1	2019	7	53489
2	2019	8	54848
3	2019	9	56207
4	2019	10	57566
5	2019	11	58925

Figure 11.24: Output for the predicted monthly sales data

Note that this is not a business-ready solution to forecast sales. It only illustrates the use and benefits of Machine Learning Services for analyzing the data in Azure SQL Managed Instance by running in-database R scripts.

This concludes Machine Learning Services in Azure SQL Managed Instance. Let's also look at the newly added distributed transaction feature in SQL Managed Instance.

Distributed transactions in Azure SQL Managed Instance

A distributed transaction is a database transaction in which there are two or more database servers involved. In an on-premises computer running SQL Server, this is managed by the **Microsoft Distributed Transaction Coordinator (MSDTC)** process. Microsoft recently announced support for distributed transactions in SQL Managed Instance, and this feature is available in preview. Since the MSDTC service is not available for Platform-as-a-Service in Azure, this feature is directly integrated with Azure SQL Managed Instance.

Before you run a transaction across multiple instances, first you need to add all the instances into a mutual security and communication relationship. This can be done by creating a **Server Trust Group** between all the instances using the Azure portal. If the instances are not part of the same virtual network, then **Virtual Network Peering** (discussed in *Chapter 9, High availability and disaster recovery*) is required to have a communication link between instances. Also, you need to configure network security group inbound and outbound security rules for port **5024** and **11000-12000** on all participating virtual networks.

Server Trust Group

By using a Server Trust Group, you can manage the trust between managed instances. Once you create a Server Trust Group, a certificate-based trust is established between its participants. Creation and deletion of the Server Trust Group are only allowed using the Azure portal during the preview period and there is no support for PowerShell or the Azure CLI.

Figure 11.25 shows multiple managed instances in a Server Trust Group that can execute distributed transactions using T-SQL:

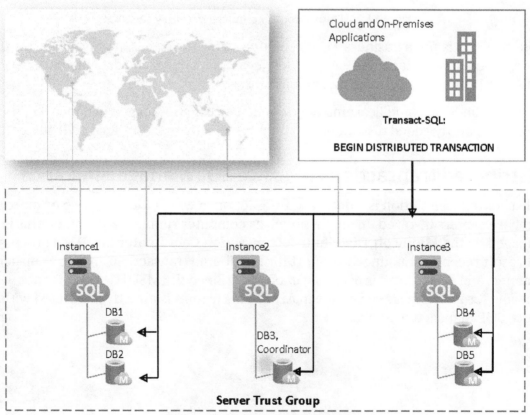

Figure 11.25: Server Trust Group

Figure 11.25 shows a quick overview of running a distributed transaction using the T-SQL command line from cloud or on-premises applications. All the managed instances are part of a **Server Trust Group**, and **Instance2** is coordinating a distributed transaction across multiple databases hosted on managed instances.

Activity: Creating a Server Trust Group using the Azure portal

In this activity, we will be creating a Server Trust Group between two SQL Managed Instances running in different regions. We have already set up Global VNet peering between two VNets. You can refer to *Chapter 9, High availability and disaster recovery,* in *Activity: Configuring an auto-failover group for SQL Managed Instance.*

Follow these steps to create a **Server Trust Group**:

1. Go to the Azure portal by using https://portal.azure.com.

2. Navigate to **SQL Managed Instance** where you want to add the **Server Test Group**.

3. Under **Security**, select the **SQL trust groups** blade and click on the **New Group** button:

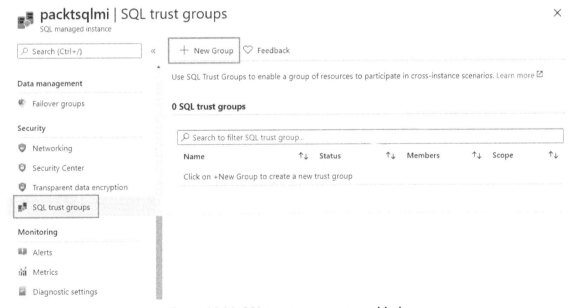

Figure 11.26: SQL trust groups server blade

4. Enter a **Group name**, select the secondary managed instance, and click on **Save** to create the SQL trust group:

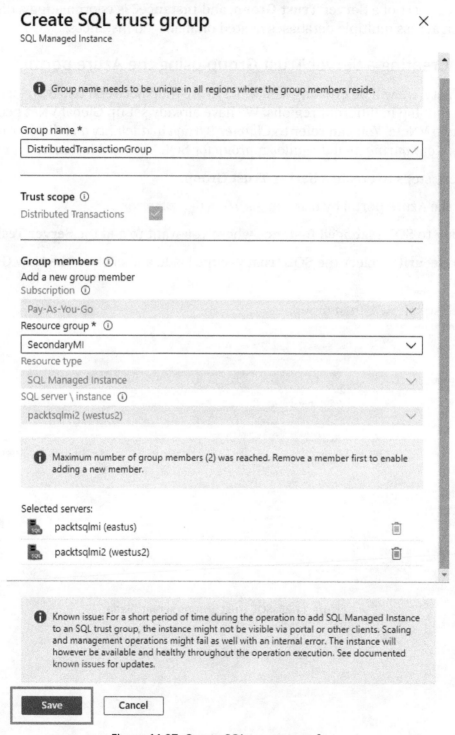

Figure 11.27: Create SQL trust group form

5. After deployment, the SQL trust groups page looks like the following:

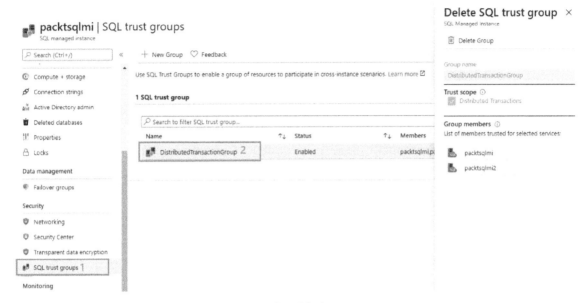

Figure 11.28: Newly added SQL trust group

In this activity, you have learned to create SQL trust groups using the Azure portal. We have added two managed instances running in different regions from the same subscription. If you want to edit group members then you have to delete and re-create the Server Trust Group.

In preview, you are only allowed to add two managed instances in a group. If you wish to run distributed transaction for more than two managed instances, then you need to create a Server Trust Group for each pair of managed instances.

Activity: Running distributed transactions using T-SQL

T-SQL support for running distributed transactions is only available in SQL Managed Instance. You can only run distributed transactions on managed instances that belong to the same Server Trust Group. Using T-SQL, you can run distributed transactions using SQL Managed Instance public and private endpoints.

In this activity, managed instances refer to each other using a **linked server**.

Follow these steps to run a distributed transaction on SQL Managed Instance:

1. Add a linked server for a remote managed instance:

```
-- Configure the Linked Server
-- Add second Azure SQL Managed Instance as Linked Server
EXEC sp_addlinkedserver
    @server='RemoteSQLMI', -- Linked server name
    @srvproduct='',
    @provider='sqlncli', -- SQL Server Native Client
    @datasrc='packtsqlmi2.231383d50c2f.database.windows.net' - SQL
Managed Instance endpoint

-- Add credentials and options to this Linked Server
EXEC sp_addlinkedsrvlogin
    @rmtsrvname = 'RemoteSQLMI', -- Linked server name
    @useself = 'false',
    @rmtuser = 'miadmin',           -- login
    @rmtpassword = '<Enter your password here>' -- password
```

This T-SQL query adds a linked server called **RemoteSQLMI** for the **packsqlmi2** managed instance. We are using the SQL Server native client as a provider to connect the remote instance. We are also specifying the login credentials for remote managed instance authentication. In this exercise, we have used **miadmin** account, but you can also use any account that has the required privileges.

2. Run a distributed transaction using T-SQL:

```
USE toystore;
GO
--Stopping execution and rolling it back for any error
SET XACT_ABORT ON;
GO
--Start of distributed transaction
BEGIN DISTRIBUTED TRANSACTION;


--Select order before deletion on local instance
Select * FROM [toystore].[Sales].[Orders] WHERE OrderID = 73499;
Delete Order from local instance.
DELETE FROM [toystore].[Sales].[Orders] WHERE OrderID = 73499;
--Select Order After deletion on local instance
Select * FROM [toystore].[Sales].[Orders] WHERE OrderID = 73499;


--Select order before deletion on remote instance
Select * FROM [RemoteSQLMI].[toystore].[Sales].[Orders] WHERE OrderID =
73499;
Delete candidate from remote instance.
DELETE FROM [RemoteSQLMI].[toystore].[Sales].[Orders] WHERE OrderID =
73499;
--Select order after deletion on remote instance
Select * FROM [RemoteSQLMI].[toystore].[Sales].[Orders] WHERE OrderID =
73499;


--Commit
COMMIT TRANSACTION;
GO
```

These T-SQL statements run a distributed transaction between two SQL Managed Instance parts of an SQL trust group. These are simple SQL statements for deleting a record and verifying the execution by running a **SELECT** statement. Here, we are using a linked server (**RemoteSQLMI**) to run queries against the secondary managed instance.

You will see output similar to *Figure 11.29*:

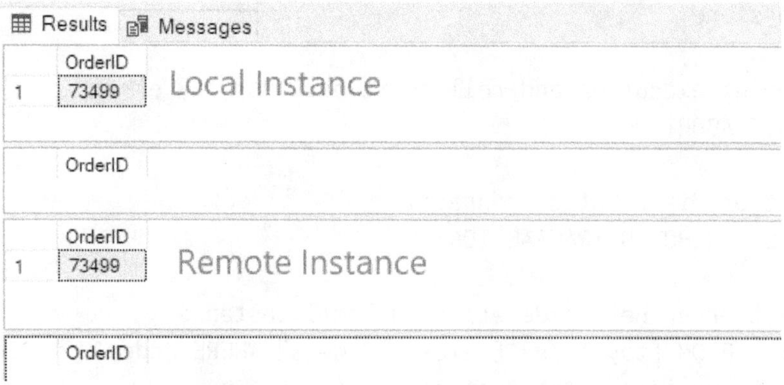

Figure 11.29: Output window for the distributed transaction

In this activity, we have learned how to run a distributed transaction on SQL Managed Instance. We created a linked server to establish communication between members of a SQL trust group. We also ran a distributed transaction to delete an order based on the **OrderID** field from **toystore** database hosted on the managed instances. Distributed transactions are only limited to Server Trust Group members.

In this exercise, we talked about running distributed transactions using T-SQL. For a .NET development experience, please visit https://docs.microsoft.com/azure/azure-sql/database/elastic-transactions-overview#net-development-experience.

Summary

In this chapter, we learned about database features, Azure SQL Data Sync, online and resumable DDL operations, and SQL Graph database. We also explored Machine Learning Services and distributed transaction features for Azure SQL Managed Instance.

Azure SQL Data Sync is an easy-to-set-up process of syncing data between two or more Azure SQL databases, or an Azure SQL database and an on-premises computer running SQL Server. Data Sync can be used to support cloud migration or to offload reporting workloads.

Resumable DDL operations allow **CREATE INDEX** and **REBUILD INDEX** tasks to be paused or resumed as and when required. This helps when we need to recover from problems wherein a long-running **CREATE INDEX** or **REBUILD INDEX** statement causes blocking and slows system performance.

SQL Graph capabilities provide a flexible and easy way to implement many-to-many relationships or hierarchies.

Machine Learning Services allows you to run R and Python scripts on Azure SQL Managed Instance. Server Trust Groups in Azure SQL Managed Instance allow you to run distributed transactions.

In the next chapter, we'll learn about modernizing applications using Azure SQL Managed Instance, Azure SQL Database serverless compute, and the Hyperscale performance tier.

12

App modernization

Application modernization is the process of upgrading an application to a better infrastructure or architecture using new platforms or technologies so as to improve overall application performance, deployment quality and frequency, business continuity, and scalability with limited cost and management.

Public cloud computing platforms, such as Microsoft Azure, Amazon Web Services, and Google Cloud Platform, provide modern infrastructure to host and run applications. Application modernization today mostly refers to running an application (and databases) on a public cloud platform.

Microsoft Azure provides multiple database deployment options to migrate to or to host new databases. These are SQL Server on Azure Virtual Machines (IaaS), Azure SQL Database, and Azure SQL Managed Instance (PaaS):

Azure SQL Family

SQL Server on Azure Virtual Machine	Azure SQL Managed Instance	Azure SQL Database
Best for lift & shift cloud migrations and apps requiring OS level access	Best for modernizing existing apps	Best for modern and cloud apps
Full administrative rights to build highly customized systems	Nearly 100% compatible with on-premises SQL Server and fully managed by Microsoft	Pre-provisioned and serverless compute and hyperscale storage to meet specific workload requirements.
Automated manageability features		
Infrastructure-as-a-Service (IaaS)	Platform-as-a-Service (PaaS)	

Figure 12.1: The Azure SQL family

Azure's managed SQL database offerings (SQL Database and SQL Managed Instance) allow you to concentrate on application development and optimization by providing managed services such as backup, business continuity, security, infrastructure management, OS management, SQL Server installation, and scaling.

Azure's managed SQL database offerings allow the use of an existing SQL Server license and enable you to save licensing costs under Azure Hybrid Benefit, with multiple service tiers for running different application workloads. This makes them a good option when running SQL Server on Azure.

SQL Database provides similar PaaS features to SQL Managed Instance, with Serverless and Hyperscale service tiers, giving customers multiple options to choose a suitable pricing tier as per their workloads.

> **Note**
>
> We can also migrate databases other than SQL Server on SQL Managed Instance or SQL Database by migrating the data and schema using Azure Data Migration Services.

In this chapter, we'll discuss managed SQL database features that facilitate easy cloud adoption with very little cost and effort.

By the end of this chapter, you will be able to understand:

- Migration to Azure's managed SQL databases
- Backup and restore
- Scaling and business continuity features
- The SQL Database serverless compute tier
- Scaling to the Hyperscale service tier

Let's get started with migrating an SQL Server workload to SQL Managed Instance.

Migrating an SQL Server workload to SQL Managed Instance

SQL Managed Instance is nearly 100% compatible with SQL Server (on-premises or on Azure Virtual Machines) and provides easy lift and shift when migrating databases from an on-premises environment.

You get the following benefits when migrating to SQL Managed Instance:

- Easy migration with minimal application changes
- Saved costs by using existing SQL Server licenses under Azure Hybrid Benefit
- Managed service benefit, wherein you can concentrate on database development and optimization, while backup, restore, business continuity, security, and scaling are provided out of the box

You can attain SQL Server database compatibility using Data Migration Assistant and then migrate the schema and the data using any of the migration methods discussed in *Chapter 4, Backups,* such as backup and restore, transactional replication, or Azure Data Migration Services.

SQL Managed Instance works well with single-instance, multiple-database applications.

You can also choose to do an offline or an online migration. An offline migration is one in which there's downtime, and an online migration is one that has near-zero downtime. Offline migration can be done using native backup and restore, whereas Azure Data Migration Services and transactional replication can be used for online migration.

After a successful migration, you can focus on improving application performance, while regular database administration is managed by Microsoft. Let's now look at the managed services you get with SQL Managed Instance.

Backup and restore

One of the most important tasks for DBAs is configuring backup and restore in SQL Server (on-premises or SQL on Azure Virtual Machines). Although there are multiple native and third-party tools and scripts available to configure backups, it is still necessary to define a recovery strategy, configure the backup, set up alerts for backup failures, verify backups by restoring them on another instance, and automate point-in-time restore.

Backups are natively available with SQL Managed Instance as described in *Chapter 5, Restoration*. Moreover, a database can easily be restored to a point in time from the Azure portal with a few clicks or a simple PowerShell command. This takes away the time and complexity of setting up backups when migrating to SQL Managed Instance.

SQL installation and patches

SQL Managed Instance comes with the latest SQL Server version installed. We have seen in *Chapter 1, Introduction to Azure SQL managed databases*, that provisioning a managed instance can be easily done through the Azure portal and PowerShell. It takes around 3–4 hours for the managed instance to be available; however, it will be available to use without any further installation.

Installing SQL Server manually is easy, and there are certain best practices to consider that are already taken care of in SQL Managed Instance.

Zero-downtime SQL Server patching is another important task that is to be performed manually for an on-premises or SQL Server on Azure Virtual Machines. Zero-downtime patching requires either a failover cluster installation or an Always On implementation. The patch is first installed on the passive or the secondary SQL Server Instance. After a successful patch installation, a manual failover is performed to the secondary/passive instance. The patch is then installed on the new secondary instance. All of the steps are to be properly documented and discussed prior to patch installation.

SQL Managed Instance takes care of zero-downtime patching natively. This saves a lot of time that would be spent on doing it manually, which can instead be utilized to improve the application.

> **Note**
>
> Refer to the following link to upgrade replicas in an Always On availability group: https://docs.microsoft.com/sql/database-engine/availability-groups/windows/upgrading-always-on-availability-group-replica-instances?view=sql-server-ver15.

Scaling

There are two types of scaling options available with SQL Managed Instance:

- Scaling up/down by changing the number of vCores
- Scaling out by offloading reads to read-only replicas

Scaling up and down by increasing or decreasing the number of vCores is done transparently by setting up a new managed instance (handled by the service, not manually), and there's no downtime. When the target instance is up and running, the connections are switched to it. This affects in-process transactions, which can be mitigated by implementing a retry logic. It may take 2–4 hours to scale a managed instance up or down. The scaling up and down example is covered in detail in *Chapter 3, Migration.*

Scaling not only improves performance but can also save costs when you scale down to a lower performance tier. For example, imagine you have optimized database performance so your database can now work with fewer resources. You can scale down to a lower performance tier to save SQL licensing as well as performance tier costs. This is possible in an on-premises environment; however, it requires a lot of work and time to set up an infrastructure with reduced resources.

Scaling out refers to offloading reads to secondary read-only replicas. SQL Database and SQL Managed Instance provide read-only replicas, which can be used to redirect read queries. The inserts are done at the primary replica phase, whereas the reads are done during the read-only secondary replicas. This removes the load from the primary replica, thereby providing increased throughput for write queries.

High availability and disaster recovery

SQL Managed Instance guarantees 99.99% uptime. You can visit the following link for details about SLAs on different service tiers: https://azure.microsoft.com/support/legal/sla/sql-database/.

The General Purpose service tier uses SQL Server in a **failover cluster instance** (active/passive virtual machine) with shared storage to provide high availability. The shared storage used is Azure premium storage, which has built-in high availability and redundancy. If the primary (active) virtual machine fails, an automatic failover is performed on the passive node to provide high availability.

The Business Critical service tier uses an Always On availability group to provide high availability. Configuring a failover cluster instance and Always On requires knowledge and expertise in Windows Server Failover Cluster and Always On. Moreover, it takes a considerable amount of time. These are available natively in SQL Managed Instance.

Refer to the following link for details on configuring failover cluster instances: https://docs.microsoft.com/en-gb/azure/azure-sql/virtual-machines/windows/failover-cluster-instance-overview.

Let's now look at the newly introduced features in SQL Managed Instance.

Newly introduced features

In this section, we will look at the newly added features of the SQL Managed Instance offering, such as support for SQL Server Reporting Services databases, distributed transactions, Azure Machine Learning, improved database backup retention, and support for global virtual network peering.

Support for hosting SSRS catalog databases

If your **SQL Server Reporting Services (SSRS)** reports pull data from databases hosted on SQL Managed Instance, then you can also host the reporting services catalog databases on SQL Managed Instance to reduce the database engine footprint.

With SSRS 2019, now you can point to SQL Managed Instance during the SSRS configuration or re-point the existing reporting databases to SQL Managed Instance using SSRS Configuration Manager. You can also migrate the databases using backup and restore methods from an on-premises SQL Server to a managed instance:

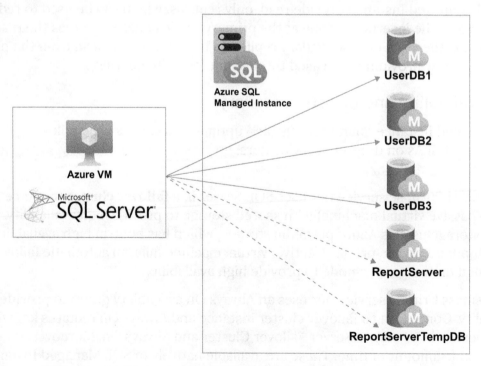

Figure 12.2: SSRS database configuration with SQL Managed Instance

Figure 12.2 is an illustration of how reporting services are typically configured with SQL Managed Instance. Here, we are running SSRS on Azure Virtual Machines and hosting the report server databases (**ReportServer** and **ReportServerTempDB**) on SQL Managed Instance.

If you have SSRS 2016 or 2017 in your environment, then you can still host the reporting databases on SQL Managed Instance. You just need to configure the instance before installing the reporting services on Azure Virtual Machines, and you need to enable the **suppress recovery model errors** configuration on SQL Managed Instance prior to SSRS configuration. For more information on the **suppress recovery model errors** configuration, please visit https://docs.microsoft.com/sql/database-engine/configure-windows/suppress-recovery-model-errors-server-configuration-option?view=sql-server-ver15.

Azure Machine Learning

Azure Machine Learning provides machine learning capabilities for SQL Managed Instance and allows in-database R and Python scripts to be run for high-performance predictive analytics. Running in-database R and Python scripts uses the data in the managed database instead of pulling the data over the network from a different source. In the absence of Azure Machine Learning, you would have to set up R and Python and get the data from a remote data source for the analysis:

Figure 12.3: R and Python support SQL Managed Instance

Azure Machine Learning makes it possible to run R and Python scripts in stored procedures or T-SQL statements. You can refer to a detailed discussion of this topic in *Chapter 11, Database features.*

Distributed transaction support

Distributed transactions have been available in the SQL Server world for a very long time with the help of **Microsoft Distributed Transaction Coordinator** (popularly known as **MSDTC**). Microsoft recently announced support for distributed transactions on SQL Managed Instance. This allows you to run distributed transactions in a cloud environment just like you would with on-premises SQL Server. Now you can run transactions across instances deployed in different Azure regions and virtual networks.

This feature is useful for scenarios, for example, where a modern application has separate database instances for hosting **Sales** and **Warehouse** databases. When users update records in the **Sales** databases, the associated records are updated in the **Warehouse** database.

This cross-instance collaboration is secured with the help of the **Server Trust Group** entity.

During the preview phase, managed instances are only supported as transaction participants with **.NET** and **T-SQL** client application layers.

For more detailed information, please refer to the distributed transactions information in *Chapter 11, Database features*.

Global virtual network peering support

SQL Managed Instance runs in a secure isolated virtual network. With global virtual network peering available, you can enable connectivity across all Azure public regions without additional bandwidth restrictions and, as always, keep all your traffic on the Microsoft backbone. This configuration simplifies the auto failover group deployment for SQL Managed Instance. Prior to global virtual network peering, you needed to rely on a VPN or ExpressRoute setup.

A cost-effective way of managing backups

SQL Managed Instance now allows you to manage your backups in a more cost-effective way by providing improved compressed backups, short-term retention, and multiple options to choose backup storage redundancy.

Microsoft has improved the backup compression by up to 30% for database backups. This can cut your backup storage costs by reducing the database backup size. There is no additional configuration required for this improvement.

You can now configure the backup retention for active databases from anywhere between 1 and 35 days (reduced from 7-35 days). You can also configure the deleted database backup retention to 0-35 days (reduced from 7-35 days). Setting backup retention to 0 means there will be no backup stored for the selected database. This can be helpful in reducing backup costs for large deleted databases.

With this, Microsoft also allows you to choose less expensive backup storage redundancy options during managed instance creation. You can now choose between RA-GRS, ZRS, and LRS. For more information on backup retention and backup storage redundancy options, please refer to *Chapter 4, Backups*.

These were some of the new features that were introduced for SQL Managed Instance recently. You can visit https://azure.microsoft.com/updates/?category=databases for more recent announcements related to SQL Database and SQL Managed Instance.

PaaS capabilities and nearly 100% compatibility with on-premises/Virtual Machines SQL Server makes SQL Managed Instance the most suitable deployment option for modernizing your applications. This allows you to focus on major application development while Microsoft manages all the instance availability, backups, patching, and other management activities.

Now, let's look at the SQL Database serverless pricing tier and understand how it's a good fit for application modernization.

SQL Database serverless

SQL Database serverless automatically scales compute based on workload demand and bills for the amount of compute used per second. Serverless databases can also be configured to automatically pause during inactive periods when only storage is billed and automatically resume when database activity returns.

Serverless is available for single database deployments in the General Purpose tier of the vCore purchasing model at the time of writing this book.

Serverless use cases

Auto-scaling and auto-pausing and resuming in serverless often provide an optimal balance between performance and compute cost trade-offs for both production or development databases.

Serverless databases are well suited to the following scenarios:

- Databases with intermittent, unpredictable usage patterns interspersed with periods of inactivity and lower average compute utilization over time.

- New databases without usage history or SQL Server migrations where compute sizing is difficult or not possible to estimate prior to deployment in SQL Database.

- Applications that require the database to be frequently rescaled can benefit from the serverless auto-scaling feature.

Creating a serverless database

Let's start by looking at how to provision a serverless database using the Azure portal:

1. Open the Azure portal, https://portal.azure.com. In the search box, type **sql database** and then select **SQL databases** from the search drop-down list:

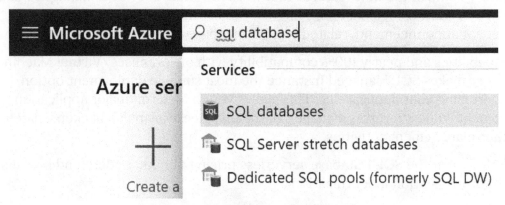

Figure 12.4: Searching for SQL databases

On the **SQL databases** page, click **Add** to add a new SQL database:

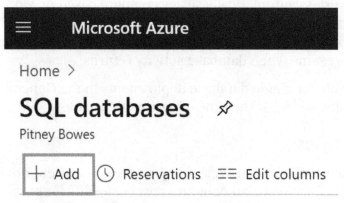

Figure 12.5: Creating a new SQL database

2. On the **Create SQL Database** page, provide information for **Subscription**, **Resource Group**, **Database name**, and **Server**. If you don't have an existing server, you can create a new **Azure SQL Logical Server** by clicking **Create new** and following the instructions:

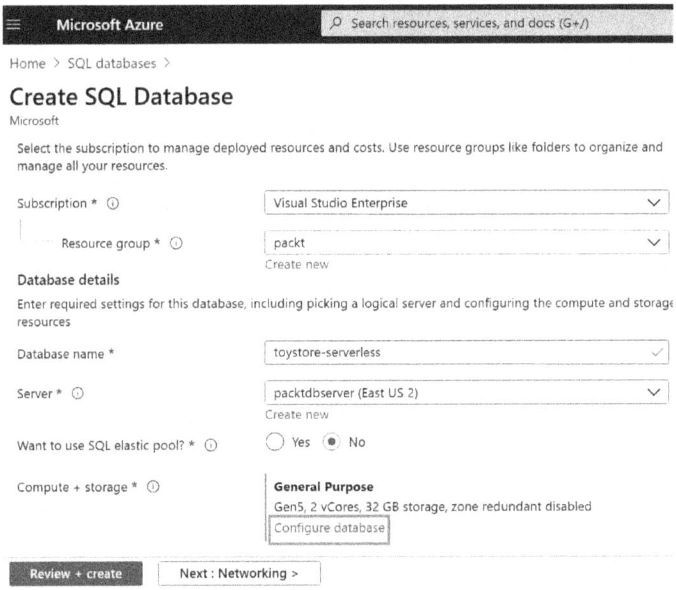

Figure 12.6: The Create SQL Database pane

Click on the **Configure database** link to configure the database properties.

3. On the **Configure** page, under the **General-Purpose** tab (vCore pricing model), select **Compute tier** as **Serverless**.

Set **Min vCores** to **1** and **Max vCores** to **8**:

> **Note**
>
> The amount of memory available depends on the minimum and maximum vCore numbers. As you increase/decrease the minimum and maximum vCores, the minimum and maximum memory change accordingly.

Figure 12.7: Configuring the number of minimum and maximum vCores

The default auto-pause delay is set to 1 hour, which is the minimum auto-pause limit available at the time of writing.

4. Set **Data max size** to **10 GB**:

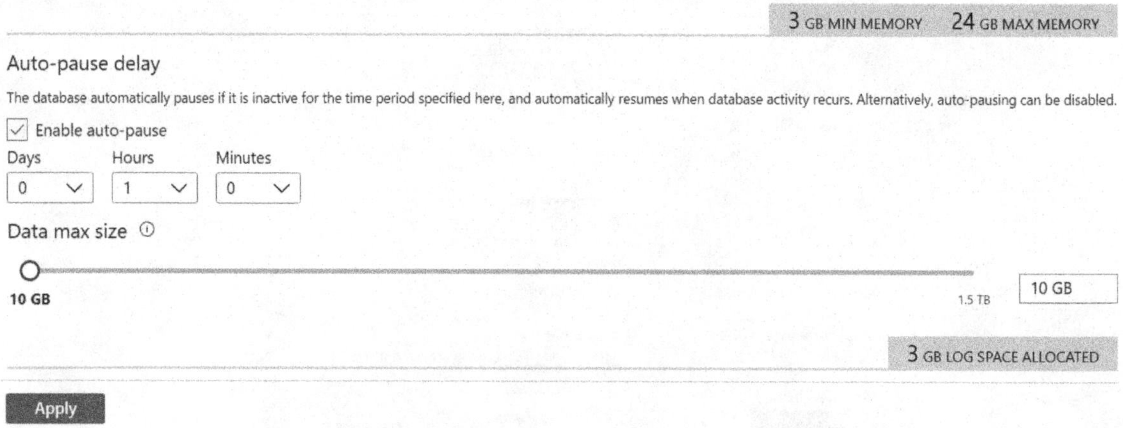

Figure 12.8: Configuring the Auto-pause delay and Data max size

The maximum storage limit for the serverless tier is 4 TB. The transaction log size allocated is **~30%** of the data max size. The log space allocated in this case is 3 GB, as shown in *Figure 12.8*.

The **Configure** page also provides a cost summary as per the selected configuration options. The compute and storage are billed separately in serverless. The billing is covered in detail under the *SQL Database serverless billing* section later in the chapter.

5. Click **Apply** to save the selected configuration and return to the **Create SQL Database** page.

6. On the **Create SQL Database** page, click **Review + create** to get a summary of the selected configuration:

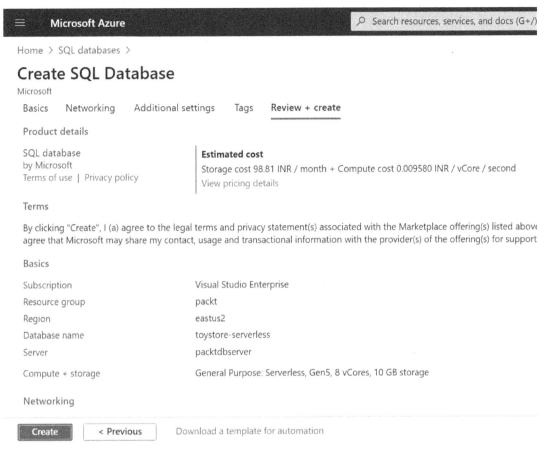

Figure 12.9: The Review + create page

7. Click **Create** to provision the database. It usually takes 1–5 minutes to provision SQL Database with this particular configuration.

Auto-scaling in serverless

The compute for a serverless database is automatically scaled based on workload demand between the minimum and maximum vCores configured and a corresponding range in memory. In general, serverless databases are run on a machine with sufficient capacity to provide resources with near instantaneous responsiveness and without interruption for any amount of compute requested within limits set by the max vCores configured. Occasionally, load balancing occurs to provide additional capacity if the underlying host machine is unable to satisfy workload demand. In this case, the scaling latency can take up to several minutes and the database remains online during the load balancing operation except when connections are briefly dropped when switching to the new host machine.

Cache Reclamation

Memory for serverless databases is reclaimed more frequently than for provisioned compute databases which is important to control costs, but can impact performance. Unlike provisioned compute databases, memory from the SQL cache is reclaimed from a serverless database when CPU or active cache utilization is low. Active cache utilization is considered low when the total size of the most recently used cached entries is below threshold for a period of time. When reclamation occurs, the cache size is reduced incrementally to a fraction of its previous size and this iteration only continues if usage remains low. However, the cache size is never reduced below the minimum memory limit as defined by the minimum vCores. When demand for more memory returns, the cache is allowed to grow unconstrained up to the max memory limit.

Auto-pausing in serverless

A serverless database auto-pauses whenever the idle time of the workload exceeds the elapsed time specified by the auto-pause delay. The auto-pause delay can be set between 1 hour and 7 days.

The idle time is described by the following conditions:

- If the number of user sessions is zero
- If CPU usage of the user workload is zero

Auto-pausing can be disabled altogether if the performance impact outweighs the cost savings. Moreover, there is no option to manually pause and resume a serverless database.

Additionally, certain features are not supported if auto-pause is enabled. For details on features that require disabling auto-pause refer to https://docs.microsoft.com/azure/azure-sql/database/serverless-tier-overview#autopausing.

Note that if auto-pause is disabled, the serverless database can still benefit from compute auto-scaling and billing based on the amount of compute used per second.

Auto-resuming in serverless

A serverless database automatically resumes when database activity occurs. A common auto-resume trigger is a database login, but there are a variety of conditions that can trigger auto-resume. For details on auto-resume triggers refer to https://docs.microsoft.com/azure/azure-sql/database/serverless-tier-overview#autoresuming. Once auto-resume is triggered, the latency before the database is back online is typically around one minute or less.

When the database auto-resumes it takes time for the SQL cache to warm-up and the queries may have slower response times for the warm-up duration. The applications running on Azure SQL Database serverless should be able to cope with this delay in compute warm-up. Alternatively, if the performance impact of compute warm-up due to auto-resuming cannot be tolerated, then auto-pausing can be disabled while still enjoying the serverless benefits of auto-scaling and compute billing based on usage.

We discussed the auto-scaling capabilities in serverless a few pages ago. It is important to note that auto-scaling is independent of auto-pausing and resuming, and can function either alone or in conjunction with auto-pausing and resuming.

SQL Database serverless billing

The compute (CPU and memory) cost is calculated as the maximum CPU (vCore) and memory used per second. There's no compute cost for the duration when serverless is paused. The minimum compute bill when serverless isn't paused and isn't used (CPU and memory utilization is less than the minimum vCore/memory provisioned) is calculated on the basis of minimum vCores provisioned.

The following formula is used to calculate the compute cost:

Compute cost = vCore unit price * max (min vCores, vCores used, min memory * 1.3, memory GB used * 1/3)

The vCore unit price is the cost per vCore per second. To get the updated price, refer to https://azure.microsoft.com/pricing/details/sql-database/single/.

For example, consider the following scenario. Imagine that a serverless database, configured with 8 max vCores, 1 min vCore, and 1-hour auto-pause delay runs for 4 hours, consuming 4 vCores and 8 GB memory (for the 4-hour duration). It's then idle for the next hour and is auto-paused as per the auto-pause configuration.

Let's now apply the preceding compute cost formula and list the variable values:

- *vCore unit price = $0.0001450/sec (East US Region)*
- *min vCores = 1*
- *vCores used = 4*
- *min memory = 3 GB*
- *memory used = 8 GB*

> **Note**
>
> The vCore unit price varies from one Azure region to another. You can get the vCore unit price from here: https://azure.microsoft.com/pricing/calculator/?service=sql-database.

Applying the preceding values to the formula, we get:

Compute cost per second = $0.0001450 * max(1,4,(3*1.3),(8*1/3))

$$= \$0.0001450 * max(1,4,3.9,2.7)$$

$$= \$0.0001450 * 4 = \$0.00058/sec$$

The amount `$0.00058` is for 1 second. As per our example scenario, the database was used for 4 hours, so the hourly cost will be `$0.00058 * 60 * 60 * 4 = $8.352`.

In addition to this, the database was running idle for the next hour before getting paused. The database is billed for the minimum cost for this duration and is calculated as:

*vCore unit price * max(min vCores, min memory GB * 1/3)*

Substituting values into the preceding formula, we get:

Compute cost per second (idle) = $0.0001450 * max(1,3*1/3)

$$= \$0.0001450 * max(1,1)$$

$$= \$0.0001450 * 1 = \$0.0001450/sec$$

The per-second cost for the time that the database was idle turns out to be `$0.0001450`, which is equivalent to the cost of 1 vCore. The hourly cost will be `$0.0001450 * 60 * 60 = $0.522`.

Therefore, the total cost for the database will be `$8.352 + $0.522 = $8.874`.

We can also use **Azure Pricing Calculator** to calculate the pricing for the given scenario. To do that, go to https://azure.microsoft.com/pricing/calculator and add SQL Database from the list of productions.

To use the calculator, set the region as **East US** (you can change it as per your environment), **TYPE** as **Single Database**, **PURCHASE MODEL** as **vCore**, **SERVICE TIER** as **General Purpose**, and **COMPUTE TIER** as **Serverless**.

Under **Billed vCores**, set **Maximum vCores** to **8** and **Minimum vCores** to **1**.

Set **CPU Used (vCores)** to **4**, **Memory used (GB)** to **8**, and **Duration (in seconds)** to **14400** (4 hours):

Azure SQL Database

REGION:		TYPE:		BACKUP STORAGE TIER:		PURCHASE MODEL:	
East US	⌄	Single Database	⌄	RA-GRS	⌄	vCore	⌄

SERVICE TIER:		COMPUTE TIER:		HARDWARE TYPE:	
General Purpose	⌄	Serverless	⌄	Gen 5	⌄

Billed vCores

Maximum vCores:		Minimum vCores:	
8	⌄	1	⌄

4	8	14400
CPU Used (vCores)	Memory used (GB)	Duration (in seconds, max 2,678,400 seconds (744 hours))

Minimum memory	3 GB
Maximum memory	24 GB

Billed vCores ⓘ	4	=	$8.35

Figure 12.10: Using Azure Pricing Calculator to calculate SQL Database serverless pricing

As shown in Figure 12.10, the total amount for our example is $8.35, which is similar to the amount we calculated manually using the formula.

Demonstration of auto-scaling and compute billing in serverless

To see auto-scaling in action, we'll run a workload against a serverless database and observe the CPU percentage and **app_cpu_billed** counter. The **toystore** serverless database is configured with 4 max vCores and 0.5 min vCores, 20 GB storage, and a 1-hour auto-pause delay.

The CPU percentage counter shows the percentage of vCores used by the workload relative to the maximum vCores. The **app_cpu_billed** counter shows the amount of compute billed during the reporting period. The **app_cpu_billed** metric is calculated by aggregating the amount of vCores and memory used per second. The serverless database cost is the product of the vCore unit price and this metric.

To demonstrate this, follow these steps:

1. Execute the following query against the **toystore** serverless database to create the **orders** table:

```
CREATE TABLE orders (
    id int IDENTITY,
    productid INT,
    quantity INT,
    MONEY,
    orderdate DATETIME DEFAULT getdate()
)
```

2. Execute the following query against the **toystore** serverless database to create the **InsertOrders** procedure:

```
CREATE OR ALTER PROCEDURE InsertOrders
AS
SET NOCOUNT ON
DECLARE @i INT = 1
WHILE(@i<=10000)
BEGIN
INSERT INTO orders(productid,quantity,unitprice) VALUES(@i*2,@i,@i*2.3)
SET @i=@i+1
END
```

This query inserts **10000** records in the orders table created in the previous step.

3. Execute the following code in the Replay Markup Language (RML) command prompt:

```
ostress.exe -Spacktdbserver.database.windows.net -Uaosama -PAwesome@1234
-dtoystore -Q"Execute InsertOrders" -n100 -r100
```

The code creates 100 threads to run the **InsertOrders** stored procedure against the **toystore** serverless database. Each thread is executed **100** times.

As the workload is executing, switch over to the Azure portal and open the **toystore** serverless database overview page:

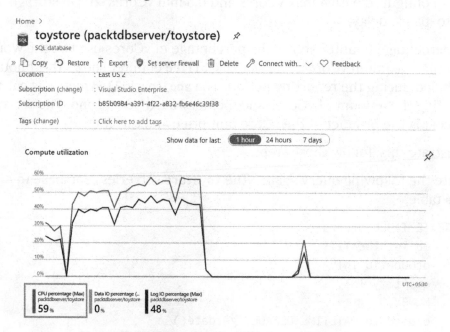

Figure 12.11: Examining the CPU percentage metric

Figure 12.11 shows the increase in the CPU percentage as the workload progresses.

The database auto-scales to use the vCores as required by the workload. A CPU percentage of 59% refers to 59% of 4 (maximum vCores configured), which is equivalent to 2.36 vCores.

Let's now look at the **app_cpu_billed** metric for the same duration:

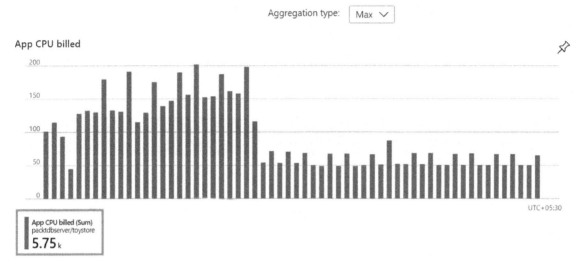

Figure 12.12: App CPU billed metric

Figure 12.12 shows the **App CPU billed** metric for the duration of the workload. The total CPU billed is 5,750 vCore seconds (~1.5 hours). The cost for the workload is therefore **5750 * $0.0001450 = $0.83**. $0.0001450 is the vCore unit price for the **East US** region.

The total amount billed will be $0.83 plus the minimum cost for an hour before the **toystore** database is paused.

If this workload runs, say, four times a day, then the total hours charged will be **4*1.5 = 6 hours** and the total cost will be around **4*0.83 = $3.32** (plus the minimum amount for 4 hours) for 1 day.

If we compare this with a General Purpose provisioned compute with a maximum of 4 vCores, the cost will be $24.21 for a day. The storage cost is the same for both serverless and provisioned compute.

> **Note**
>
> The preceding cost is from the Azure pricing calculator (https://azure.microsoft.com/pricing/calculator) for a General Purpose Gen5, 4 vCore provisioned compute in the East US 2 region, running one instance for 24 hours.

As we can see, there's a significant cost saving with SQL Database serverless for intermittent, unpredictable workloads with periods of inactivity. A serverless database is therefore the recommended option for such workloads.

Let's compare the provisioned compute and serverless compute tiers in the next section.

Serverless vs. provisioned compute

The provisioned compute tier allows us to choose a fixed number of vCores which are billed hourly. The number of vCores can be scaled up or down manually as and when required. Let's look at the differences between the provisioned and serverless compute tiers.

Feature	Serverless compute	Provisioned compute
Performance management	Automatic scaling and sizing	Manual scaling and sizing
Scaling speed	Fastest	Slower
Compute responsiveness	Lower after inactive usage periods	Immediate for a fixed amount of compute
Auto-pause	Supported	Not supported
Billing granularity	Per second	Per hour
Hardware Generation	Only supported with Gen5	Supports Gen5, M-series, and Fsv2-series
Service tier	Only supported in General Purpose	Supported in General Purpose, Hyperscale, and Business Critical
Database usage pattern	Intermittent, unpredictable usage with lower average compute utilization over time.	Regular usage patterns with higher average compute utilization over time or multiple databases using elastic pools

Table 12.1: Serverless vs. provisioned compute

SQL Database provides different compute tiers for different application workloads. Choosing an appropriate compute tier provides better performance with optimum cost savings.

Scaling to the Hyperscale service tier

SQL Database introduced the Hyperscale service tier in May 2019 for General Availability; since then, it's been a popular choice for users who seek high performance and high scalability. The Azure SQL Hyperscale service tier solves most of the **very large database (VLDB)** problems, such as backup, restore, and scaling.

Considering moving to the Hyperscale service tier

The Hyperscale service tier should be considered as the first choice for a typical workload. Here are some example scenarios:

- If you have a large on-premises SQL Server database and want to modernize applications while moving to the cloud.

- If you are hitting max storage limits in the existing service tier of an Azure SQL database. Hyperscale supports a max storage amount of up to 100 TB.

- If you require fast database backups/restore operations irrespective of database size.

- If you need higher log throughput irrespective of database size and vCore count.

- If you need fast scale-up/down operations.

- If you need to scale out a read-only workload by provisioning one or more read replicas.

These are some of the qualities that make the Hyperscale service tier an ideal choice for any database. The Hyperscale service tier is designed to run a broad range of SQL Server workloads, but it's primarily optimized for **online transaction processing (OLTP)** and **hybrid transaction and analytical processing (HTAP)** workloads.

> **Note**
>
> Please refer to the FAQs here to learn more about the Hyperscale service tier: https://docs.microsoft.com/azure/azure-sql/database/service-tier-hyperscale-frequently-asked-questions-faq.

Now, we will go through an activity that demonstrates how to move an existing SQL database to the Hyperscale service tier.

Activity: Updating an existing SQL database to the Hyperscale service tier using the Azure portal

You can move your existing SQL database to the Hyperscale service tier. At this point, moving to the Hyperscale service tier is a one-way operation; you can't move databases from Hyperscale to another service tier other than by exporting and importing data. Microsoft recommends trying out the Hyperscale service tier by making a copy of production databases and then moving the copy to the Hyperscale service tier.

In this activity, we will learn how to move an existing SQL database to the Hyperscale service tier using the Azure portal.

Follow these steps to complete the activity:

1. Go to the Azure portal and navigate to the SQL database that you are moving to the Hyperscale service tier.

2. Under **Settings**, select **Configure** and choose the **Hyperscale** option:

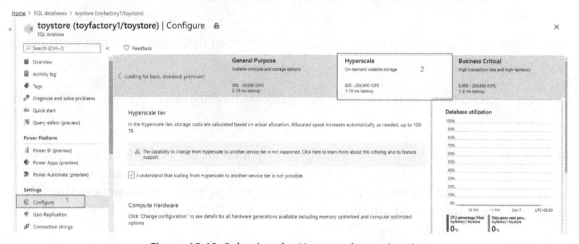

Figure 12.13: Selecting the Hyperscale service tier

3. Remember that scaling from Hyperscale to another service tier is not possible and set the **Azure Hybrid** option and **vCores** and **Secondary Replicas** counts. Once finished, click on **Apply** to start the migration:

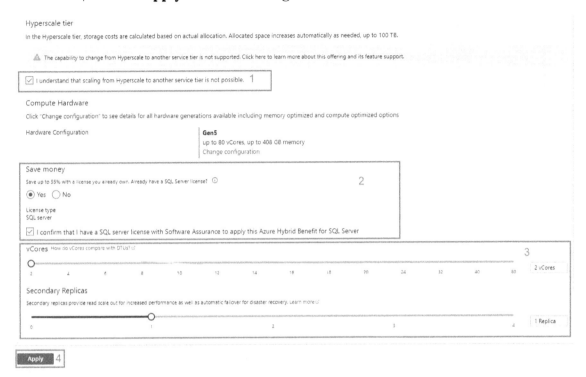

Figure 12.14: Hyperscale service tier options

4. Monitor the **Notifications** tab for deployment progress:

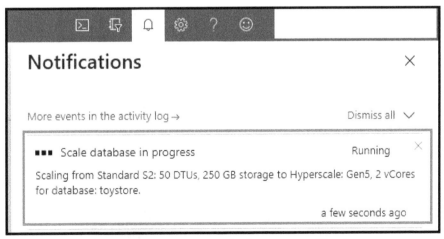

Figure 12.15: Hyperscale deployment notification

Success notification

This may take some time depending on the data size; you will receive a notification that looks like this:

Figure 12.16: Hyperscale deployment success notification

In this activity, we have scaled an existing **toystore** DTU-based SQL database to the Hyperscale service tier with 2 vCore compute and one secondary replica configuration. Now let's look at how to move an existing SQL database to the Hyperscale service tier using PowerShell commands.

Activity: Updating an existing SQL database to the Hyperscale service tier using PowerShell commands

In the previous activity, we have seen quick steps to move an existing SQL database to the Hyperscale service tier using the Azure portal. Here we will perform the same activity using PowerShell commands.

Follow these steps to complete this activity:

1. Open **Cloud Shell** from the Azure portal by clicking on the **Cloud Shell** icon:

Figure 12.17: Navigating to Cloud Shell

2. Switch to the PowerShell terminal to run PowerShell code:

Figure 12.18: Switching to the PowerShell terminal

3. Set the variables according to your environment:

```
#setting up variable as per your environment
$subscription = "xxxxxxx-xxxx-xxxx-xxxx-xxxxxxxxx"
$resourceGroup = "SQLServer"
$serverName = "toyfactory1"
$databaseName = "toystore1"
$edition = "Hyperscale"
$sku = "HS_Gen5_2"
$replicaCount =1
```

4. Select the SQL Database subscription:

```
#Select the Azure SQL Database subscription
Select-AzSubscription -SubscriptionId $subscription
```

5. Update the database properties using the following PowerShell command:

```
#Updating existing Azure SQL Database to Hyperscale service tier.
Set-AzSqlDatabase -ResourceGroupName $resourceGroup -DatabaseName
$databaseName -ServerName $serverName -Edition $edition
-RequestedServiceObjectiveName $sku -ReadReplicaCount $replicaCount
```

```
ResourceGroupName              : SQLServer
ServerName                     : toyfactory1
DatabaseName                   : toystore1
Location                       : westus2
DatabaseId                     : 0d8786f4-084a-4c24-ad05-627a0d81eade
Edition                        : Hyperscale
CollationName                  : SQL_Latin1_General_CP1_CI_AS
CatalogCollation               :
MaxSizeBytes                   : -1
Status                         : Online
CreationDate                   : 12/6/2020 8:14:40 PM
CurrentServiceObjectiveId      : 00000000-0000-0000-0000-000000000000
CurrentServiceObjectiveName    : HS_Gen5_2
RequestedServiceObjectiveName  : HS_Gen5_2
RequestedServiceObjectiveId    :
ElasticPoolName                :
EarliestRestoreDate            : 12/6/2020 8:14:40 PM
Tags                           : {}
ResourceId                     : /subscriptions/    /resourceGroups/SQLServer/providers/Microsoft.Sql/servers/toyfactory1/databases/toystore1
CreateMode                     :
ReadScale                      : Enabled
ZoneRedundant                  :
Capacity                       : 2
Family                         : Gen5
SkuName                        : HS_Gen5
LicenseType                    : LicenseIncluded
AutoPauseDelayInMinutes        :
MinimumCapacity                :
ReadReplicaCount               : 1
BackupStorageRedundancy        : Geo
```

Figure 12.19: Set-AzSqlDatabase PowerShell command output

Note that the **Edition** setting is **Hyperscale**, which confirms that the database has been upgraded to the Hyperscale tier.

In this activity, we have used **Az.sql** PowerShell module commands to scale an existing DTU-based SQL database to the Hyperscale service tier.

Read scale-out an SQL Hyperscale database

A Hyperscale database also provides an option to read scale-out by offloading read-only workloads to secondary read replicas. This is a similar option to the Premium/Business Critical service tiers, where you can offload the read-only workload by adding the `ApplicationIntent=ReadOnly` flag to the application connection string. Hyperscale uses a different architecture to the Premium/Business Critical service tiers to provide the read scale-out feature. Please refer to *Chapter 2, Service tiers*, to learn more about the Hyperscale service tier architecture.

Hyperscale secondary replicas share the same page servers as the primary database. If you have more than one replica, then the workload will be distributed across the available replicas. All the data changes are updated independently on replicas, so you will see a different data latency between replicas. In addition to read scale-out, these replicas also serve as hot-standbys in case of a failover from the primary replica.

Summary

In this chapter, we discussed different deployment options for the Azure SQL family, such as SQL Managed Instance, SQL Database serverless, and the Hyperscale service tier. We also learned how managed databases help in application modernization by leveraging PaaS capabilities, such as backups, patching, availability, and easy scaling options. This allows developers to focus on their key application development and leave most of the database management operations to Microsoft.

With this, we have learned how to successfully set up SQL Database and SQL Managed Instance, migrate our data from an on-premises database to provisioned cloud databases and instances, how to scale these databases and instances as per our requirements, and how to manage our costs optimally. We've also looked at how to secure these databases and instances and the built-in high-availability features of SQL Database and SQL Managed Instance, and we discussed some of their more advanced functions. We will now be able to work on applications that are built on SQL Database and SQL Managed Instance with ease.

Index

About

All major keywords used in this book are captured alphabetically in this section. Each one is accompanied by the page number of where they appear.

A

aborts: 469

access: 5, 17-18, 20, 31-32, 53, 129, 134, 140, 182, 185-187, 217, 239-240, 244, 249, 254-255, 260-264, 268-274, 277-278, 280, 285, 294-299, 304-305, 309, 311, 315-317, 322, 325, 335, 390, 415, 441, 444, 464, 469, 555, 573

account: 44, 46, 51, 71-72, 129-130, 134-135, 147-148, 161, 168, 173, 177, 179-183, 185-186, 205, 219, 222, 241, 260-262, 264, 268, 286-288, 293-294, 297, 302, 307, 311, 343-345, 372, 376-377, 394, 429, 451, 454, 498, 506, 545-547, 549, 573, 640, 658

activity: 21, 42, 46, 73, 77, 91, 95, 105-106, 112, 116-117, 125, 138-139, 141-142, 144-145, 148-149, 152, 156, 162, 167-168, 172, 179, 185, 188, 191, 205-206, 217, 221, 224, 227, 235-236, 285, 298, 302, 304-305, 308-309, 315-317, 322, 325-326, 330, 342-343, 360, 363, 371-372, 381, 388-389, 394, 399-400, 403, 406, 408-409, 411-412, 426, 434, 448, 452, 457, 471, 473, 481, 488, 490-491, 495, 504-505, 511, 514, 519, 527, 557, 567, 578-579, 597, 607, 610, 627, 635, 645-647, 655, 657, 660, 671, 676, 683-684, 686-687

address: 17, 27, 49-50, 114, 241-251, 254, 264, 279, 283, 289, 302, 316, 326, 335, 446, 593, 638

alerts: 302, 304, 325-326, 331-334, 343, 353, 361-362, 394, 536, 541, 543, 548, 550, 561-563, 566, 607, 621, 666

algorithm: 649

analytics: 286-288, 410-411, 530, 545, 549-553, 555-562, 566-567, 572-573, 621, 643, 669

artificial: 597

asymmetric: 302

attacks: 5-6, 325, 330

auditing: 31, 285-290, 293-294, 303

azure-sql: 28, 30, 38, 56, 64, 72-73, 91, 165, 185, 302, 389, 448, 588, 625-628, 644, 660, 668, 676, 683

B

back-end: 148

backup: 1, 3, 24-25, 29, 38, 71-72, 95, 117, 122, 138-141, 147-150, 155-163, 165, 167-174, 183-185, 187-189, 191-193, 202-203, 205-206, 211, 215-216, 225-226, 231, 236-237, 240, 298-300, 302, 448, 471, 664-666, 668, 670-671, 683

bacpac: 29, 77-78, 92-93, 120, 122, 173-175, 177-178, 181-183, 191-192, 201, 217, 219-220, 237, 383

balancer: 27

benchmark: 60, 620-621

binary: 593-594

blocking: 364, 411, 557, 560-561, 563-564, 566, 584, 589-590, 660

boolean: 394, 497

buffer: 65, 70, 591-592, 596

C

cached: 70-71, 249, 367, 369, 588, 600, 676

calculator: 677-679, 681

cascading: 641-642

catalog: 74, 668

checkpoint: 468-471

cleanup: 301, 469, 610

client: 5, 17-18, 27, 40, 243-244, 251, 254, 292, 297, 300, 305, 316, 335, 368, 372, 451, 610-611, 614, 620, 658, 670

cluster: 25-28, 65, 403-406, 445, 457, 460, 464, 666-668

cmdlet: 47-49, 181-182, 215, 226, 377-379, 431-433, 451, 453, 500-502, 508-510

Printed in the USA
CPSIA information can be obtained
at www.ICGtesting.com
BVHW020010100823
668387BV00002B/3

9 781801 076524